Classical Arabic Lite

Library of Arabic Literature
Editorial Board

General Editor
Philip F. Kennedy, New York University

Executive Editors
James E. Montgomery, University of Cambridge
Shawkat M. Toorawa, Cornell University

Editors
Julia Bray, University of Oxford
Michael Cooperson, University of California, Los Angeles
Joseph E. Lowry, University of Pennsylvania
Tahera Qutbuddin, University of Chicago
Devin J. Stewart, Emory University

Managing Editor
Chip Rossetti

Volume Editor
Philip F. Kennedy

Letter from the General Editor

The Library of Arabic Literature is a new series offering Arabic editions and English translations of key works of classical and premodern Arabic literature, as well as anthologies and thematic readers. Books in the series are edited and translated by distinguished scholars of Arabic and Islamic studies, and are published in parallel-text format with Arabic and English on facing pages. The Library of Arabic Literature includes texts from the pre-Islamic era to the cusp of the modern period, and will encompass a wide range of genres, including poetry, poetics, fiction, religion, philosophy, law, science, history, and historiography.

Supported by a grant from the New York University Abu Dhabi Institute, and established in partnership with NYU Press, the Library of Arabic Literature produces authoritative Arabic editions and modern, lucid English translations, with the goal of introducing the Arabic literary heritage to scholars and students, as well as to a general audience of readers.

Philip F. Kennedy
General Editor, Library of Arabic Literature

المنظوم والمنثور

Classical Arabic Literature

A Library of Arabic Literature Anthology

selected and translated by

GEERT JAN VAN GELDER

NEW YORK UNIVERSITY PRESS

New York and London

NEW YORK UNIVERSITY PRESS
New York and London

Copyright © 2013 by New York University
All rights reserved

Library of Congress Cataloging-in-Publication Data

Classical Arabic literature : a library of Arabic literature anthology /
selected and translated by Geert Jan van Gelder.
p. cm. — (Library of Arabic Literature)
Includes bibliographical references and index.
ISBN 978-0-8147-7027-6 (cl : alk. paper) — ISBN 978-0-8147-3826-9 (pb : alk. paper)
— ISBN 978-0-8147-4511-3 (e-book) — ISBN 978-0-8147-7120-4 (e-book)
1. Arabic literature—Translations into English. I. Gelder, G. J. H. van
PJ7694.E1C53 2012
892.7'08—dc23
2012030086
CIP

New York University Press books are printed on acid-free paper,
and their binding materials are chosen for strength and durability.

Series design by Titus Nemeth.

Typeset in Tasmeem, using DecoType Naskh and Emiri.

Typesetting and digitization by Stuart Brown.

Manufactured in the United States of America
c 10 9 8 7 6 5 4 3 2 1
p 10 9 8 7 6 5 4 3 2 1

Table of Contents

Acknowledgements

I am greatly indebted to the editors of the Library of Arabic Literature for accepting this anthology in the series, as a kind of hors d'œuvre or meze (for it is not a regular volume consisting of the edition and translation of one particular work). That only one name appears on the title page is misleading: in a real sense this anthology is a collective effort. The translations were made over a number of years, in the course of which I must have consulted many colleagues and students about particular points, and I apologize to them if I have forgotten the details. In the later stages I received very many useful suggestions and corrections from various sides, notably from an anonymous non-Arabist reader and the three LAL editors, Philip Kennedy, James Montgomery, and Shawkat Toorawa. The last-mentioned, especially, made heroic efforts to polish my English. I have accepted, with deep gratitude, the great majority of all their suggestions, while stubbornly sticking to my own versions, or making new ones, when I believed them to be more faithful to the Arabic original, or when I rejected a suggestion for metrical reasons (like the Arabs, I prefer poetry that has some kind of meter).

Oxford, March 2012

Abbreviations

ABL	Julia Ashtiany et al., ed. *ʿAbbasid Belles Lettres* The Cambridge History of Arabic Literature. Cambridge, New York: Cambridge University Press, 1990.
ALUP	A. F. L. Beeston et al., ed. *Arabic Literature to the End of the Umayyad Period* The Cambridge History of Arabic Literature. Cambridge, New York: Cambridge University Press, 1983.
b.	born; (in names) *ibn* "son (of)"
bt.	(in names) *ibnat* or *bint* "daughter (of)"
ca.	*circa*
d.	died
EAL	Julie Scott Meisami and Paul Starkey, ed. *Encyclopedia of Arabic Literature*. London: Routledge, 1998.
EI2	*The Encyclopaedia of Islam, New[= Second] Edition* (11 vols. with Supplement vol. and Index vol.). Leiden: Brill, 1960–2009.
fl.	*floruit*
H	(in dates) Hijrī, Muslim calendar
PCP	Roger Allen and D. S. Richards, ed. *Arabic Literature in the Post-Classical Period*. Cambridge History of Arabic Literature, Cambridge. New York: Cambridge University Press, 2006.
r.	ruled
Q	Qur'an

Introduction

Many ancient Arabic Bedouin or quasi-Bedouin poems begin with the exclamation *khalīlayya*, "My two friends!" According to a literary convention, never fully explained,[1] the poet, who is supposed to be traveling in the desert when he spots a place that reminds him of past pleasures, asks two companions to sympathize with his feelings of loss, or at least to wait for him until he has poured out his elegiac verse. The poet, or rather his persona, does not keep his private feelings to himself, silently or soliloquizing: he must have an audience. Whether the feelings are real or imagined, whether the two companions are real or fictional (their names are never given), all this does not matter. The poem must be heard, and its emotions understood and recognized, not only by the anonymous friends but by everyone. The past love affair is the theme of the beginning of the poem only, which moves on to other things, present or future: the description of the poet's trusty camel, the desert, tribal matters, feuds and loyalties, patrons or enemies, or anything else that is on the poet's mind.

In this anthology there is, as it happens, no poem that begins with *khalīlayya*, but the motif occurs several times. The desert poem is only one of the many forms and genres found in the long history of Arabic literature. Arabic poetry and prose: just as the desert poems they must be heard, or read, preferably in their original language; but in a time when the growing interest in the Arab world is matched only by ignorance of its literary heritage, translations can be informative, entertaining, and perhaps even enjoyable not only as curiosities but as examples of genuine works of literary art. In the western world the two Arabic books that are best known are, inevitably, the *Thousand and One Nights* and the Qur'an; but neither is typical or representative of Arabic literature, the one being partly a product of European literature, at least in the form that has become world literature, and the other a unique text in more ways than one (and one that should not be read by the uninitiated without some guidance). This book aims at filling some of the large gaps.

"Literature" is difficult to define even in modern Western culture. In a premodern Arabic context the problem is no less daunting. For the purposes of the present anthology it is taken not in the general sense of everything written but in the narrower sense of texts, whether oral or written, that do more, and are intended to do more, than instruct and inform, by being "literary," being cast in wording and style that are meant to please, entertain, or evoke admiration. A key term and concept is *adab*, which means "literature" as well as "good manners" in modern Arabic and which in the pre-modern period also meant "erudition" and "knowledge of the Arabic language and the important works composed in it." The term *adab* is often applied to literary output that is entertaining and edifying at the same time, based on the notion that ethics and aesthetics should go together—though not all classical literature is edifying by any means. Another key concept is *balāghah*, "eloquence": if its language and style are eloquent, a text may be said to be literary. Much of Arabic poetry—most, in fact—was produced for a special occasion, when the poet responded to a specific event or to the needs of a particular person. The poems were preserved, however, by later generations, who enjoyed them for qualities that could be called "literary," being worthy of admiration and emulation.

This anthology grew from a much smaller selection made for Oxford undergraduates studying Arabic, to acquaint them with a wider range of genres than the "set texts" allow. There is something very unsatisfactory about being expected (as in Oxford) to write essays and answer examination questions about the history of Arabic literature basing oneself almost exclusively on secondary sources, because reading the original texts is so time-consuming and, often, difficult. This book, with its translations and notes, is intended to serve as a kind of introduction to classical Arabic literature by showing rather than telling.

It is my hope, however, that this anthology will also be used and appreciated by a general readership interested in a relatively unknown literature, and part of the annotation is written with them in mind; no knowledge of the Arabic language or of the history of the Arabs is required. The anthology offers some examples of the main genres of classical Arabic literature that can be said to be literary, above all poetry, but it includes prose forms, whether or not they employ *saj'* ("rhymed prose").

"Classical" is a confusing word with many senses. Here it means "pre-modern;" the language of the selected texts is almost always "Classical Arabic," i.e. the standard form as it was codified in the course of the eighth century on the basis, mostly, of pre-Islamic and early Islamic poetry; but in some cases (as in the *zajal*) the vernacular language was used in forms that acquired "literary" status.[2] The vernaculars never reached the degree of emancipation that was seen in medieval Europe and even today they are written only in a limited number of contexts. The lack of an Arabic Dante or Chaucer may be deplored for various reasons but it has the undeniable advantage of keeping the Arab world united in a literary sense and keeping the literary heritage (*al-turāth*, as the Arabs now call it) accessible to a degree wholly unknown in the western world since Latin fell into disuse as the language of scholarship and literature.

The texts in this anthology range from the early sixth to the first half of the eighteenth century, i.e. from the pre-Islamic period or Jāhiliyyah[3] until well into the period sometimes (and rather misleadingly) called "post-Classical." Some of my colleagues strongly object to the term "medieval" when applied to Arabic literature, arguing that it conveys negative connotations, that it misuses a term from European history for a very different culture, and that it implies, wrongly for Arabic, a stretch of time between an older, "classical" period and a newer one. They are right, but I do not think "pre-modern" is a very felicitous designation either. It is convenient to have a word for a period that more or less coincides with the European Middle Ages, and I have not shunned it altogether.

Periodization within this long stretch, after the Jāhiliyyah and the early Islamic period following the Hijra (AD 622), is traditionally accomplished using dynastic labels: Umayyad (660–750), Abbasid (750–1258), Mamluk (1258–1517), followed by Ottoman, until the "Renaissance" or "Revival" (*Nahḍah*, literally "rise") in the course of the nineteenth century and the beginnings of modern Arabic literature. In addition, a topographic label ("al-Andalus," or "Arabic Spain") is often somewhat uncomfortably inserted into the scheme. These labels have a limited use; the terms "Mamluk" and "Ottoman" work for Syria and Egypt but not, for instance, for Morocco or Spain. They also suggest that these periods are more distinct and internally uniform than they are. Thus Arabic literature in the Mamluk period resembles that of the Ottoman period far more closely than early Abbasid literature resembles that of the late Abbasid period. I have elected not to chop up the history of Arabic literature with these somewhat arbitrary labels.

In each of the two main sections, verse (*shiʿr*) and prose (*nathr*),[4] the arrangement is roughly chronological. Poetry in *rajaz*, however, the most prose-like and presumably the oldest of all meters, is placed at the end of the Verse section. The Arabs traditionally kept it separate from the other meters; in heaven, as imagined by Abū l-ʿAlāʾ al-Maʿarrī, the *rajaz* poets occupy a special, somewhat less luxurious, place.[5] The strict segregation of verse and prose is traditional; it is true that the two may freely mix, prose may be "poetical" and verse "prosaic," yet they can never be confused, for verse is metrical and prose is not. Rhyme, always used in verse, is not restricted to it, for rhymed prose (*saj'*) has been a favored medium for literary texts throughout the pre-modern period.

The restriction to literary texts, vague though the criterion may be and based more on present-day standards than on those contemporary with those who produced and consumed the texts, has meant the exclusion of genres such as religious law and jurisprudence (*fiqh*), strictly theological texts (*kalām*), "Prophetic Tradition" (*ḥadīth*), and purely scholarly works for specialists (e.g. medical, linguistic, philosophical). The present anthology does not exhaust all the genres that have literary characteristics. Historiography lies on the borderline; much of it can be read as belles lettres and some of it has been incorporated. Among the important "literary" kinds that are not included here are prosopography (short biographies of famous people, composed of facts, anecdotes, and characterisations); tales about the prophets who preceded Muḥammad (*qiṣaṣ al-anbiyā'*); sermons and orations (*khuṭab*, sg. *khuṭbah*); ornate chancery or private epistles (*inshā'* or *rasā'il*, sg. *risālah*); "shadow plays" (*khayāl al-ẓill*); travelogues; geographical works; the exceedingly long popular romances and epics (*siyar*, sg. *sīrah*) in verse, prose, or a mixture; or the semi-popular *Thousand and One Nights* (*Alf laylah wa-laylah*), also known as the *Arabian Nights,* the importance of which is rather distorted by its fame in western languages.[6] The Qur'an, which among many other things is also a literary text, is likewise not included, though quotations often appear in some of the prose texts;[7] it is sufficiently accessible in a variety of translations, old and recent.[8]

From an anthology of classical Arabic literature the reader may expect both a fairytale and an erotic tale in the style of the *Nights*. A fairytale is included from a collection similar to the *Nights*; sex and eroticism are also represented, not by the *Nights* but in various poems, anecdotes, and a more or less pornographic tale. Undoubtedly the small number of bawdy and obscene passages will be disproportionately represented in the reviews this anthology may receive, as I have experienced with my Dutch anthology of classical Arabic poetry,[9] but I am resigned to this. The selection in this anthology is a personal one, even though I could not include every poet or writer who should be included. I have neglected some important genres: religious, pious, and gnomic poetry get short shrift, such as praise of the Prophet,[10] laments on the Shī'ite martyrs, and moralistic epigrams. The effusions in poetic prose by the mystic al-Niffarī undoubtedly have literary qualities, but, unwilling to translate texts that are impenetrable to me, I have not included them (they are available in translations by R. A. Nicholson and Michael Sells).

The selected texts are a mixture of the familiar and the unfamiliar. Thus one finds a famous Bacchic poem by Abū Nuwās, a celebrated panegyric ode by al-Mutanabbī, a well-known *muwashshaḥah* by the so-called "Blind (Poet) of Tudela"; but not once again the *Muʿallaqah* by Imruʾ al-Qays or that of Labīd, or al-Shanfarā's *Lāmiyyat al-ʿArab*: these splendid poems are readily available in numerous translations and interpretations. Instead, I have selected three shorter, and perhaps more representative, pieces to illustrate the pre-Islamic *qaṣīdah* or longer poem. Generally, short and relatively accessible poems are somewhat over-represented at the expense of the high-status but rather more daunting panegyric or congratulatory odes, in spite of their importance.

Only complete poems have been included, with a few exceptions, as indicated. Since the form (meter and rhyme) is of prime importance in defining "literariness," two lines of each poem, or a strophe of a formal poem, have been given in the original Arabic, in Arabic script and transliteration, for those who do not read Arabic. Although some Arabists and Arabs dislike transliteration, in my experience there are readers who like to have at least an idea of how a poem sounds, even if they do not know the language. When reading Japanese haikus, a transcription in Latin script may be informative: it is the same with Arabic. Ideally, this entire anthology would be bilingual and the poetic texts presented in Arabic script as well as transliteration; this is not possible for practical reasons.

Though annotation and further references have been kept to a minimum, the former is essential: it is naïve to think that literary texts from a different culture, period, and language can be properly understood and appreciated without adequate notes. It would have been possible to select only poems, fragments, and prose passages that are so general and universal in their meanings that no, or hardly any, annotation and explanation would be necessary. It is also possible to replace all exotic and obscure passages with accessible and familiar English near-counterparts. Such anthologies have been made; they cannot, of course, present a true picture of Arabic literature. It is only in the combination of the accessible with the strange, the universal with the particular, and the familiar with the puzzling, that a foreign culture can be understood, appreciated, and studied.

It should be mentioned that pre-modern Arabic poems, unlike prose works or modern poems, do not usually have titles. In the list of contents they have been indicated by their opening words, which is a traditional way of referring to them; another way is referring to the collection of which they formed a part, such as "the *Muʿallaqah* of Imruʾ al-Qays," because it was one of seven or ten famous poems called "the suspended ones" for reasons not wholly clear. Or else one spoke, for instance, of "a *mīmiyyah*" of al-Buḥturī, meaning a poem with rhyme-consonant *m* (*mīm*); he wrote many poems that could be so designated. Modern editors often add titles: the poem by al-Akhṭal in this anthology is entitled, after its most famous line, "They Tell Their Mother: Piss on the Fire" in an edition of 1994; its reply by Jarīr, in another edition, is called "My Quraysh and My Helpers," after its nineteenth line. This imposes an unauthentic element and provides unnecessary emphasis; it has not been followed by me. The long, quasi-didactic poem by Ibn Makānis, however, has a title, probably given by the author himself.

The section on poetry is shorter than that on prose: a natural result of the nature of Arabic verse, which favors conciseness. Unlike, for instance, ancient Greek, Latin, Persian, Italian, or English literature, with their Homer, Virgil, Firdawsī, Dante, and Chaucer or Milton, Arabic literary history has no famous long narrative poems by poets of the highest rank. The discrepancy between the lengths of the two sections would seem to belie the dominance of poetry as the literary form par excellence; but it will be seen that the prose section contains numerous shorter poems and single lines, which makes up for the seeming imbalance; this also shows how poems do not exist in isolation but usually need a context in which they are composed or recited.

All translations are by me, apart from a number of short quotations, e.g. of the Qur'an or where I mention alternative, published versions for the sake of comparison; in a few cases felicitous expressions or phrases in existing and published translations by others (mentioned in the annotation) have been adopted. I will not offer the tired caveat about poetry being untranslatable or about translators being traitors: if I believed that, this anthology would not have been made. Rather than providing prosaic cribs without any pretension to being literary, in most of the translations of verse offered here I have made some attempts at making "poetry," or at least verse, with iambic or other rhythmic structures with lines of variable length, or with a sprinkling of alliteration, to make up to some extent for the impossibility of imitating the very strict, quantitative Arabic meters (the soul of poetic form) and the rhyme. However, I have stayed as close to the original Arabic as possible and the translations are not meant to be "poetic recreations" that turn the poems into modern English poetry and thus betray the original.[11] Contrary to what is often thought, the task of the literary translator is not to transport the original author to the English-speaking world of today, rather, one must transport the reader to the place and time of the author as much as possible and as much as is tolerable. It is fashionable among translators these days to break up the Arabic *bayt* (verse or line) into four or even more short lines, thus making each *bayt* a little stanza. This, too, is a distortion; I have usually divided the two hemistichs of a *bayt* over two lines, the length of the average *bayt* making the translation too long to appear on one line. A slightly archaic diction is not always a bad thing, but I believe I have moved away from Nicholson and Arberry's poetic renderings. If the translations still seem stilted on occasion, this may be partly because of my not being a native speaker of English, partly because of the exigencies of the form, and in some cases because the Arabic original cannot be called anything but stilted. I have not shunned four-letter words if the original has Arabic equivalents and I have therefore not translated *ayr* as *membrum virile*.

All classical Arabic poetry rhymes, normally in "monorhyme" (*aaaa...*); the nature of Arabic morphology together with the enormously rich vocabulary makes this possible even for relatively long poems. For obvious reasons it is virtually impossible to adopt this in English, although this has not stopped earlier translators, such as Richard Burton when rendering poems of the *Arabian Nights* in his inimitable English. My translations use rhyme only for a number of epigrams and a few longer poems of "light" verse,[12] where rhyme cannot be missed. The peculiarity of *sajʿ*, rhymed prose, has been imitated in several pieces, at the risk of sounding rather quaint in English: it is an acquired taste.[13] It is far easier to rhyme in Arabic than in English; consequently some liberties have been taken in the rhymed translations, but the more serious ones are explained in the notes. Similarly, untranslatable wordplay, at times replaced by an attempt at an English pun, has been elucidated in the annotation. I should add that the reader should set aside the idea that wordplay or punning is frivolous and trivial, worthy of a groan even if witty, and to be condemned when found in serious contexts. Paronomasia and double entendre (to avoid the negative connotations of "wordplay" and "pun") are very common in most periods of pre-modern Arabic literature and one should not be shocked to see them in a heart-felt elegy. In order to appreciate Arabic literature and judge it not only subjectively but also on its own terms, one ought to be aware of Arabic literary criticism; sections of two eleventh-century works on poetry have been included here; as for the various kinds of wordplay and figures of speech (collectively called *badīʿ*), an excellent introduction is provided by Pierre Cachia's abbreviated translation of an eighteenth-century work.[14]

Unlike the pre-modern Arabs, we live in a literary culture in which silent reading is vastly dominant over reciting and reading aloud, but I hope that readers, if they do not actually pronounce the poetry translations, will at least make them sound mentally. For the prose translations I have also kept close to the original, translating, for instance, the direct speech in dialogues as direct speech, instead of occasionally reverting to indirect speech, as is normal in English.[15] Medieval Arabic narrative texts have a habit of letting the reader guess to whom the pronouns (the countless hes, hims, and its, notably) refer, to an extent that would be unacceptable in modern English. Wherever it seemed desirable I have silently supplied a clarification, such as "his father said to him" instead of "he said to him."

Most of my translations have been newly made for this anthology; a few have been published before. Several texts I have read with undergraduate and graduate students in Oxford over the years, who have often helped me by finding a better phrase or a plausible interpretation, for which I thank them. Instead of presenting whole poems it would have been perfectly legitimate to pick selected passages, since medieval Arabic anthologists did so all the time. The decision to include complete poems as much as possible is prompted by the consideration that the readers should be allowed to decide for themselves about reading whole poems or picking out the plums. The same decision puts pressure on the translator, who cannot simply omit the lines he or she does not understand, as one would normally do—I have done it myself in the past. There are few classical Arabic poems that do not present at least some difficulties; as a result the present anthology contains a few confessions of aporia and, worse, is bound to have several instances where the translator is himself ignorant of his ignorance. I have never seen books or articles with substantial amounts of translated classical literary Arabic that were devoid of at least some howlers, and I have no illusions about this anthology either. I am eager to hear from readers about any possible improvements, corrections, or clarifications.

Transliteration and Pronunciation

Many publishers seem to think that the general reader is put off by diacritical dots and other special signs in foreign language terms and names. I have never met such a general reader. Lately some otherwise respectable publishing houses have even abandoned full transliteration in specialist monographs and collections. This deplorable tendency should be resisted.[16] A full scholarly transliteration has been used here, one that is common in English-language publications. Non-specialists can ignore, if they wish, the diacritics, such as the subscript dots that distinguish some consonants, to be pronounced with a somewhat duller, darker sound (*ḍ*, *ṣ*, *ṭ*, *ẓ*), from their "lighter" counterparts (*d*, *s*, *t*, *z*), or *ḥ* (a more throaty version) from *h*. Likewise, the glottal stop (ʾ) is distinguished from the sound that is so characteristic of Arabic, the *ʿayn* (ʿ), a voiced pharyngeal fricative not found in English. Long vowels are distinguished from short ones by macrons (*ā*, *ī*, *ū*). Vowels have "continental" values; their realization varies depending on the context, so that, for instance, *ā* in the vicinity of the *ḍ*, *ṣ*, *ṭ*, *ẓ*, *q*, and *r* usually sounds much "darker" than elsewhere. There are only two diphthongs, *ay* and *aw* (approximately as in "eye" and "now," respectively, but shorter). *Dh* and *th* are pronounced as in "this" and "thin," respectively. *Kh* is like in Scottish "loch" or German "Bach;" *gh* is its voiced counterpart, somewhat like a Parisian *r* but not rolled; *q* is like *k* but pronounced farther back, never with a following *w* sound as in "quick." Consonants can be lengthened (as for instance in Italian), indicated in transliteration by doubling.

The transliteration used in the text samples themselves differs slightly from the one used elsewhere, in order to clarify the actual sounds and the prosody: initial *hamzah* (glottal stop) is indicated (e.g. *ʾilā*) and the assimilation of the article is represented (*al-rīḥu* and *al-shamsu* becoming *ar-rīḥu* and *ash-shamsu*). Long vowels in rhyme position are always rendered as long even if they are not written in the Arabic; however, vowels written as long but pronounced short because they are followed by two consonants (as in *fī l-bayt*, pronounced *filbayt*) have been kept long in the transliteration. I have not indicated optional further assimilations (thus in the first line of the poem by al-Khansāʾ included here, *li-ṣakhrin bi-damʿin minki* may be read as *li-ṣakhrim-bi-damʿim-minki*). The very common ending *-ah*, a marker of feminine nouns, is often transliterated *-a* because the *h* is not always sounded; but here I have preferred *-ah*, true to the principle in Arabic prosody that demands that a "pausal" form (as e.g. in rhyme position) ends in either a consonant or a long vowel, never in a short vowel.

Stress falls on the last syllable only when it ends in a long vowel plus consonant as in Baghdādˊ, *hijāʾˊ*, or a short vowel plus two consonants, as in Ḥusaynˊ, Dimashqˊ (Damascus); note that a digraph such as *sh* or *kh* counts as one consonant only, and that *y* and *w* in the diphthongs *ay* and *aw* count as consonants. Otherwise, in words of two syllables the first syllable is stressed (*ghaˊzal*, Aˊbū, Ḥaˊsan, Layˊlā). In words of more syllables the stress is on the penultimate if it is long (i.e. contains a long vowel or ends in a consonant): *qaṣīˊdah*, Jāhiliyˊyah, al-Mutanabˊbī. Otherwise it usually moves to the antepenultimate (al-Ṭaˊbarī,

Muʿāʹwiyah, *madʹrasah*), but there are regional variations in stress patterns (Egyptians will say *madraʹsah*).

Names and Dates

Arab names can be lengthy. A full name may consist of a personal name (*ism*), often preceded by a *kunyah* or teknonym[17] (Abū "Father of," or Umm "Mother of," followed by a son's name) and followed by a genealogy (*nasab*) in the male line, which may go back several generations. Note that *ibn* "son (of)" is sometimes shortened to "b." but should never be written or pronounced *bin* in pre-modern Arabic (even though this bad habit seems to be spreading). The female equivalent, *bint* or *ibnat* "daughter (of)" may be shortened to "bt." Names beginning with *ibn* have often developed into family names; Ibn Sīnā (Avicenna) was not the son of someone called Sīnā, just as someone called Johnson is not necessarily the son of a John. Non-specialists should be aware that Ibn, Bint, Abū, Umm, ʿAbd, and similar elements are inseparable from what follows and should never be omitted as if they were first names.

A name often includes one or more *nisbah*s, adjectives that end in *-ī* (for women *-iyyah*) and which refer to a tribe, a place of birth, or residence. Many people have, and are known by, a *laqab* or nickname (al-Jāḥiẓ means "Pop-eye," al-Mutanabbī means "the would-be prophet"), which may take the form of a *kunyah* (Abū Nuwās, "He with the dangling forelock"). Honorific names are common especially from the Abbasid period onward, for rulers (al-Rashīd, "the Rightly Guided One," Sayf al-Dawlah, "Sword of the Dynasty") and others. Many names are regularly given short tags by way of respect: Allāh, "God" may be followed by *taʿālā*, "Exalted is He" or *ʿazza wa-jalla*, "Mighty and Lofty is He"; when the Prophet Muḥammad is named or referred to, one very often finds *ṣallā llāhu ʿalayhi wa-sallam* "God bless him and give him peace" (it is often, somewhat inaccurately, translated "Peace be upon him" and abbreviated as "p.b.u.h."). Names of "Companions" of the Prophet, the early Muslims, may be followed by "God be pleased with him." Non-Muslim translators sometimes omit these pious phrases; I have generally kept them. Some people think that "Allah" is preferable to "God" in Muslim contexts, arguing that the god of Islam is different from the Christian god. It is true that Muslims and Christians attribute somewhat different characteristics to this imagined being, but Allāh means "God" and Arab Christians also use it. Therefore "God" is the obvious form to use.

Dates are normally given according to the Muslim and the Christian calendar, e.g. as 656/1258. A Muslim year (lunar, and some eleven days shorter than the solar year) normally straddles two Christian years; if a precise date (month, day) is not known, as happens often, the given AD date may therefore be one year short or too many. In bibliographical references only AD dates are given, unless an Arabic publication only mentions the Muslim year, indicated here as H (Hijrī).

Arabic Prosody

Classical Arabic poetry (*shiʿr*), much like ancient Greek, Latin, and Sanskrit, has a quantitative prosody, based on the contrast between long and short syllables, rather than stressed and unstressed ones as in English.[18] The rather intricate system is found already in the earliest recorded poems. In bygone days some Western scholars, noticing the resemblance of the Arabic meters to those of other classical languages, decided that the illiterate Arab Bedouins were far too uncouth and uncivilized to have developed such a sophisticated prosody and must therefore have taken it from others, the Greeks for instance. It seems certain, however, that Arabic prosody was an internal development.[19] It was first described and systematized, as *ʿilm al-ʿarūḍ* ("the science of prosody"), by the great grammarian and lexicographer al-Khalīl ibn Aḥmad (d. 160/776 or 175/791).

A meter (*wazn* or *baḥr*) is one of a series of recognized patterns of long, short, and neutral positions (which may be either long or short); all lines of a poem must have the same meter. I have indicated the meter of each poem in the verse section, using *L* for a long syllable, *S* for a short syllable, and *X* for a neutral position, where the poet is at liberty to use either a long or a short syllable. Short syllables consist of a consonant and a short vowel (*ba*, *bi*, *bu*), long syllables end in a consonant or a long vowel (*bal*, *bā*). In all meters except *rajaz* a line or verse (*bayt*) consists of two hemistichs that are metrically equivalent, apart from a possible difference in the last foot; a caesura (syntactic or semantic break) often but by no means always coincides with the division between the hemistichs. A *bayt* is usually longer than the average English verse: it can have up to thirty syllables. There are some fifteen classical meters, each with its variants; some are very rare. The most frequently used meter, called *al-ṭawīl* ("the long one"), may be represented as follows, in its most common form: SLX SLLL SLX SLSL / SLX SLLL SLX SLSL, as in the famous opening of Imru' al-Qays's pre-Islamic ode (sixth century): *qifā nabki min dhikrā ḥabībin wa-manzilī / bi-siqṭi l-liwā bayna d-dakhūli fa-ḥawmalī*

("Stop, you two, let us weep for the remembrance of a loved one and a dwelling place, / where sand dunes twist between Dakhūl and Ḥawmal").[20] The Arabs did not use the concept of the syllable for metrical analysis; instead they used (and still use) "dummy" words of different patterns, derived from the root *F-ʿ-L* (of the verb "to do"); a *ṭawīl* hemistich would be represented as *faʿūlun mafāʿīlun faʿūlun mafāʿilun*. Another meter is *al-wāfir* ("the ample one"): SLSSL SLSSL SLL / SLSSL SLSSL SLL (in which SS may be freely replaced by L), as in a line from a poem by al-Mutanabbī (d. 354/965): *wa-lammā ṣāra wuddu n-nāsi khibban / jazaytu ʿalā btisāmin bi-btisāmī* ("And since people's affection has turned into deceit, / I reward a smile with a smile"). Some meters are much shorter, such as *al-hazaj*: SLLX SLLX / SLLX SLLL, used by the second/eighth-century poet Ḥammād ʿAjrad in a lampoon on the blind poet Bashshār: *wa-yā ʾaqbaḥu min qirdin / ʾidhā mā ʿamiya l-qirdū* ("O you uglier one than a monkey /—if the monkey is blind").[21] The language of poetry differs from that of prose in some minor matters of grammar; the word order is somewhat freer in poetry. By far the most important differences are those of style and theme. Although the style of some prose genres tends to encroach on that of poetry and vice versa, there are many kinds of discourse for which poetry is the preferred medium, such as professing one's love, the description of wine and wine drinking, praising a patron, or lampooning an enemy.

As I noted above, all classical Arabic poetry rhymes: blank verse was introduced only in the modern period. Not only the meter but also the rhyme (*qāfiyah*) is constant in a given poem ("monorhyme"), except in the strophic forms (*muwashshaḥ* and *zajal*) and in lengthy, often didactic or narrative poems that use paired rhyme (*aabbccdd*...). The hemistichs of the opening line of a poem often rhyme too, although this is not obligatory (the line by Imruʾ al-Qays quoted above is an example). The basis of the rhyme is a consonant (*l* in Imruʾ al-Qays's poem, *m* in al-Mutanabbī's). If a long vowel precedes (as does *ā* in al-Mutanabbī's line) this must be maintained in every rhyme-word (although *ī* and *ū* may be used interchangeably), as must anything that follows the rhyme-consonant (here -*ī* in both poems). This "tail" may be more than one syllable, as in a poem by al-ʿAbbās ibn al-Aḥnaf included here, where the rhyme is -*ābihā* (-*hā* being a pronominal suffix, "her"). As pointed out above, rhyming is much easier in Arabic than in English; some poets, in need of a challenge, imposed on themselves further restrictions, such as "rich rhyme," based on two consonants rather than one (see Abū l-Maʿarrī's epigrams, included here). Rhyme is often used in prose of the more flowery and ornate kind; this is called *saj*ʿ and does not count as verse because it has no meter, although it may be rhythmical.

As a result of the length of the average *bayt* and the presence of the rhyme at its end, each line of a poem tends to be a more or less complete unit, in terms of syntax and sense. The running on of lines (enjambment), so common in Homer or Milton, is generally avoided: the ideal *bayt* can stand alone, by itself. This does not mean, however, that the lines in a poem are regularly independent or could be exchanged indiscriminately, the order being arbitrary: Arabic poets were able to build complex syntactic and semantic structures and long periods in verse.[22]

Notes to the Introduction

1 See Lyons, "The Two Companions Convention"; Abu-Haidar, "*Qifā nabki*: The Dual Form of Address in Arabic Poetry in a New Light."

2 The Arabs call the standard form *al-lughah al-ʿarabiyyah al-fuṣḥā* ("the pure Arabic language"), or *fuṣḥā* for short; the vernacular forms are called *ʿāmmiyyah* ("common," from *al-ʿāmmah*, "the common people"). There is some controversy whether or not the standard language differed from everyday speech from the outset; in the course of the centuries the two diverged considerably. For an introduction to Arabic, its structure and history, see Versteegh, *The Arabic Language*; useful, too, is Holes, *Modern Arabic: Structure, Functions, and Variations*, Ch. 1, "A Brief History of Arabic," pp. 9–36.

3 In spite of its negative sense, "(the time of) Ignorance," or "Brutishness," the word *al-Jāhiliyyah* also has positive connotations for the Arabs: a time that formed the classical Arabic language and its many desert-derived idioms, a period of unsurpassed heroic poetry and virtues deemed essential to the Arab identity, such as hospitality and natural eloquence. The Islamic era is traditionally said to begin with the emigration or *hijra* of the Prophet Muḥammad from Mecca to Medina in 622.

4 The term *naẓm* ("verse, versification," literally "arrangement, stringing") is often used for poetry when it is distinguished from *nathr* ("prose," literally "scattering"). Stringing and scattering pearls are images found countless times in literary texts.

5 See below, p. 93

6 For more than a century English readers have had to make do with Richard Burton's idiosyncratic translation and since 1990 the much better but incomplete one by Husain Haddawy; readers now have the reliable and complete version by Malcolm C. Lyons, *The Arabian Nights: Tales of 1001 Nights*.

7 To mark its special status in Islam and in Arabic literature alike I have used angle brackets (« ») for Qur'anic quotations. I have mostly but not exclusively used the translation by A. J. Arberry, *The Koran Interpreted*, as acknowledged in relevant notes; where no translator is mentioned the translation is my own. The verse numbering is that of the Egyptian standard edition (but note that the numbering in Arberry's translation often differs from this).

8 It is ironic that the dogma according to which Muslims (including, one must assume, the Prophet Muḥammad himself) have traditionally believed that the Qur'an is God's literal speech has denied Muḥammad a place among the world's most gifted and original authors.

9 G. J. van Gelder, *Een Arabische tuin: klassieke Arabische poëzie.*

10 I have not made an English version of my translation, in Dutch rhymed couplets, of the long and extremely famous ode on the Prophet, al-Burdah by al-Būṣīrī (d. ca. 694/1296); for unrhymed English translations, see the one by Stefan Sperl, in Sperl and Shackle (eds), *Qasida Poetry in Islamic Asia and Africa*, II:388–411 (reproduced in Irwin, *Night and Horses and the Desert*, 334–45), and by Suzanne Stetkevych, *The Mantle Odes*, 70–150.

11 An example among several is the slim anthology by G. B. H. Wightman and A. Y. al-Udhari, *Birds Through a Ceiling of Alabaster: Three Abbasid Poets. Arab Poetry of the Abbasid Period, translated with an Introduction*, in which poems by al-ʿAbbās ibn al-Aḥnaf, Ibn al-Muʿtazz, and Abū l-ʿAlāʾ al-Maʿarrī have been subjected to amputation, reinterpretation, and rewriting (while the complete lack of bibliographical references makes it difficult even for specialists to consult the originals). The result, it must be admitted, is often far from unpleasing; to paraphrase Richard Bentley (who commented on Alexander Pope's version of Homer's *Iliad*), they are pretty poems, but they must not call it "Arab poetry," as the translators did.

12 I have used monorhyme for a poem by Qays ibn Dharīḥ of twelve lines.

13 Recent examples in English translations from the Arabic may be found in Paul M. Cobb's translation of *al-Iʿtibār*, the memoirs of Usama ibn Munqidh (d. 584/1188), as *The Book of Contemplation*, and in Humphrey Davies's translation of a seventeenth-century work, *Yūsuf al-Shirbīnī's Brains Confounded by the Ode of Abū Shādūf Expounded.*

14 Cachia, *The Arch Rhetorician, or The Schemer's Skimmer*. For a short survey, see "rhetorical figures" by W. P. Heinrichs in *EAL*, 656–62.

15 I have, however, often omitted the ubiquitous *qāla* "he said," because punctuation and layout are a sufficient equivalent.

16 It is sometimes claimed that diacritics are superfluous to the specialist, who will usually know the correct form. This is, however, often untrue: when confronted with names such as "Salim" or "Husayn," one cannot tell whether it is Sālim or Salīm, Ḥusayn or Ḥuṣayn; the word "sahara" could be "he melted" (*ṣahara*), "he became a brother-in-law" (*ṣāhara*), "he bewitched" (*saḥara*), "he was wakeful together with someone" (*sāhara*), "(the milk) boiled" (*ṣaḥara*), and "deserts" (*ṣaḥārā*). Specialists and general readers alike deserve better.

17 Often wrongly called "patronymic" (as in the entry "Kunya" in *EI2*).

18 There are several helpful introductions to Arabic meter and rhyme; a short and handy survey is the entry "prosody" by W. Stoetzer in *EAL*, 619–22.

19 For more on Arabic metrics, see especially Stoetzer, *Theory and Practice in Arabic Metrics* and Frolov, *Classical Arabic Verse: History and Theory of ʿArūḍ*.

20 Part of its fame is due to the fact that the first hemistich compactly offers five key concepts of the introduction (*nasīb*) to the classical ode (*qaṣīdah*): lingering, lamenting, memory, love, and location, together with the "two companions" motif in the dual imperative *qifā*.

21 Those who know Arabic will notice that the verse ends with *qirdū*, whereas in prose one would find *qirdu*, with a short vowel. This is because a verse must end in a consonant or a long vowel, the latter being far more common. Another rule specifies that the nominal ending *-n*, indicating indefiniteness, is dropped in rhyme, which accounts for *manzilī* and *(i)btisāmī* in the lines by Imru' al-Qays and al-Mutanabbī, instead of the prose forms *manzilin* and *(i)btisāmin*.

22 Much has been written in recent decades on the structure of classical Arabic poems. See, for example, my *Beyond the Line*; Julie Scott Meisami, *Structure and Meaning in Medieval Arabic and Persian Poetry: Orient Pearls*; and the many studies by Suzanne Pinckney Stetkevych, including *The Mute Immortals Speak: Pre-Islamic Poetry and the Poetics of Ritual*, *Abū Tammām and the Poetics of the ʿAbbāsid Age*, and *The Poetics of Islamic Legitimacy: Myth, Gender, and Ceremony in the Classical Arabic Ode*.

شعر

Verse

A *Qaṣīdah* by ʿAbīd ibn al-Abraṣ

يا دار هند عفاها كل هطّال | بالجوّ مثل سحيق اليمنة البالي
جرت عليها رياح الصيف فاطّردت | والريح فيها تعفّيها بأذيال

yā dāra hindin ʿafāhā kullu haṭṭālī | *bil-jawwi mithla saḥīqi l-yumnati l-bālī*
jarat ʿalayhā riyāḥu ṣ-ṣayfi fa-ṭṭaradat | *war-rīḥu fīhā tuʿaffīhā bi-ʾadhyālī*[1]

Meter (*al-basīṭ*): XXSL XSL LLSL SSL / XXSL XSL LLSL LL. Note the internal rhyme in line 1, which makes the meter of the hemistichs identical. Such internal rhyme is very common at the beginning of a poem but not mandatory.

ʿAbīd ibn al-Abraṣ, of the Asad tribe, is one of the earliest known pre-Islamic Arabic poets. The word *qaṣīdah* is used for any poem of some length (according to some critics as few as ten), but especially for formal polythematic odes, that open with a lyrical, elegiac passage and followed by one or more sections, often abruptly without transition and without obvious connections to the opening passage. The thematic structure of this *qaṣīdah* is as follows: lines 1–4: the *aṭlāl* (the deserted campsite; often introducing the *nasīb*, the description of a past love affair or of a girl, here reduced to a mere name, but cf. 15–16); line 5: a return to the present; the poet is old and can only reminisce and boast of his past, a mixture of hardship and pleasure; lines 6–8: the linking motif ("consolation"), a brief camel description (*waṣf al-nāqah*), with an implied journey (*raḥīl*); lines 9–12: the boast (*fakhr*) of martial prowess; lines 13–14: boast of drinking wine provided by an unidentified liberal host (often the poet himself is the generous giver and perhaps he is referring to himself here); lines 15–16: boast of amorous adventures; lines 17–18: back to the present and to the mode of the poem's opening.

O home of Hind,[2] effaced by all the heavy rains
in Jaww:[3] like cloth from Yemen,[4] worn!

The summer winds have blown above it, one behind another,
and still the wind, trailing its skirts, obliterates the traces.
There I detained my friends, interrogating the abode,
the collar of my cloak soaking with tears,
In yearning for the tribe, the days the clans were gathered there.
—but how can those like me be moved[5] and yearn?
For grayness has now come over my locks; the fair
bade me farewell, forever, in disgust.
Yet often have I soothed[6] my cares, when they appeared to me,
with a she-camel, sturdy, like a blacksmith's anvil, swift,
A strong one, strutting with the saddle frames,
traversing through the midday heat, trotting or ambling;
Her flanks are covered with firm flesh;
she's like a lonely oryx bull in Jaww, trailing its tail.
—Enough of this! Many's the war I joined,
fanning its fire to a fierce blaze,
With under me a mare with mighty limbs, short haired and muscular,
fast like an arrow by the hand of a far-aiming bowman sent.
Many's the warrior who bared his teeth, the chief of a packed throng,
their armor gleaming, clad in coats of mail, men of mettle,
Whose chest I pierced with a lance tip, so that he reeled
as bends a broken bough of a lithe jujube tree.
And many a wine, fragrant as musk when crushed, that long
dwelt in its cask, year after year,
Have I drunk in the early morning, before dawn appeared,
in a man's tent, whose hands with bounty overflowed.
With many a girl, plump, soft like a gazelle of Jaww,
saliva tasting as if mixed with water sweet,[7]
Have I spent half the night; I play with her and she with me,
and then I leave her while she is still on my mind—
Now youth is gone and has sworn never to return to us;
grayness has settled firmly on my hair.
Gray hair: an ugly shame to him in whose courtyard it dwells;
O God, how wonderful were those black locks, now gone!

A *Qaṣīdah* by ʿAlqamah ibn ʿAbadah

طحا بك قلبٌ في الحِسان طَروبُ   بُعيد الشباب عصرَ حانَ مَشيبُ
يكلّفني ليلى وقد شطّ وليُها   وعادت عوادٍ بيننا وخطوبُ

ṭaḥā bika qalbun fī l-ḥisāni ṭarūbū   *buʿayda sh-shabābi ʿaṣra ḥāna mashībū*
yukallifunī laylā wa-qad shaṭṭa walyuhā   *wa-ʿādat ʿawādin baynanā wa-khuṭūbū*[8]

Meter (*al-ṭawīl*): SLX SLLL SLX SLSL / SLX SLLL SLS SLL; the second/sixth foot is occasionally SLSL (e.g. in line 1b), which only occurs in older poetry. *Ṭawīl* is the most common meter in all periods of classical Arabic verse. The rhyme is *-ī/ūbū* (in rhyme, *ī* and *ū* are interchangeable immediately before the rhyme consonant, but not following it).

This and the next two poems from the mid-sixth century are taken from an ancient and highly valued anthology of 126 pre-Islamic and early Islamic poems, called *al-Mufaḍḍaliyyāt* after the compiler, the philologist al-Mufaḍḍal al-Ḍabbī of Kufa (d. after 163/780). It is said that the anthology was composed at the request of the Abbasid caliph al-Manṣūr, the founder of Baghdad, for his son, the future caliph al-Mahdī. ʿAlqamah's famous poem was composed on the occasion of the Battle of ʿAyn Ubāgh which took place in AD 554 pitting the Ghassānid king, al-Ḥārith al-Aʿraj, against the Lakhmid king, al-Mundhir ibn Māʾ al-Samāʾ of al-Ḥīrah.

The poem opens with *nasīb*, or amatory introduction (1–10). Whatever the real origins of the *nasīb*, Arab critics explained that its function in an ode addressed to a patron was to put him in a favorable mood. As Shakespeare writes, in *Love's Labour Lost* (IV, iii): "Never durst poet touch a pen to write / Until his ink were tempered with Love's sighs; / O! then his lines would ravish savage ears, / And plant in tyrants mild humility."[9]

Then the poem turns to a description of the camel (11–21) that brings the poet to the court of al-Ḥārith; this is followed by a depiction of the battle (24–35), and closes with an appeal to al-Ḥārith to free the poet's brother, taken prisoner at the battle (36–38). The petition was successful.

A heart by pretty girls enraptured carries you away;
long gone, though, is your youth; gray hairs appear.[10]
Laylā is on my mind, though she be far from me,
and obstacles, grave matters, are between us two.
She lives a life of luxury; one cannot speak to her:
a guard stands at the door to bar all visitors.
Her spouse's secrets she does not divulge, when he's away;
she makes his homecoming a pleasure for her spouse.
Do not equate me then, girl, with a callow youth—
may rain-filled clouds pour down their loads on you!
May southern, towering, low-lying clouds rain down
for you, borne by an evening south wind!
—But why should you be thinking of her, that Rabīʿah girl,
for whom a well is being dug in Tharmadā'?[11]
You ask me about women? I'm a specialist,
an expert, knowing women's ailments all![12]
When a man's hair turns gray, or when his wealth is scarce,
he has no share of tenderness from them.
What women want is wealth, wherever they know it is;
to them the bloom of youth is wonderful.
So leave her, and dispel your worries with a sturdy mount,[13]
like your desires and aims, which with two riders[14] trots apace.
Toward al-Ḥārith the Munificent I made
my camel walk; her chest and end-ribs throbbing.
She's fast; her flanks' and shoulders' flesh has been
consumed by midday heat and tireless pressing on.
I brought her to a well of brackish water, with
the taste of henna and *ṣabīb*.[15]
At dawn, after the nighttime journey, she looks like
a strong, young oryx with striped legs, fearing the hunter's pack;[16]
(Amidst the *arṭā* trees men lurked, lying in wait for her;[17]
she dodged their arrows, and their dogs)

That she might take me to a man's abode who once was far,
but now my nearing brought me near to your munificence.[18]
To you—may you be safe from curses[19]—was her course,
through frightful, fearsome lands that looked alike.
The lodestars[20] led me, and a pathway plain to see,
with stones as marks upon the rocky ground.
There, corpses lie, abandoned beasts, their bones
bleached, and their hides dried hard.
She's left to drink the cisterns' dung-fouled dregs;
loathe it she may, but pasture fresh is a distant ride away.
Do not withhold favor from me, a foreigner:
I am a man who is a stranger in pavilions like yours.
You are a man in whom I put my trust.
Before you, lords have lorded over me and I was lost.
The Banū Kaʿb ibn ʿAwf brought home their lord;
another lord was left amidst his legions there.
By God! But for that knight of theirs on the black horse
they would have reached their homes—sweet home!—in shame.[21]
You drive him on until his fetlocks' white turns red with blood;
you smite the helmets of the chainmailed men;
Wearing two hauberks over one another, carrying
two noble swords, "Clean Cutter," "Sinker-in."[22]
You fought them till they sought protection by their champion;
the sun was ready then to set.
The chainmail on their bodies rustled like
the rustling of dry cornfields when the wind is southerly.
Ghassān's defenders battled there,
while Hinb and Qās stood firm, together with Shabīb.[23]
The man of Aws, and those that had been mustered by
ʿAtīb and Jall, stood ready at his horse's breast.
The camel calf above them in the sky roared loud.[24]
Some, dying, twitched their legs, still armored; some were stripped.
It was as if a cloud had hit them with its thunderbolts,
that made the birds crawl on the ground.
No one escaped, except a tall mare with its bridle, or
a lively stallion, a thoroughbred, slim like a lance,

Or else a warrior who guards his own, dyed red
    by what had dripped from his sword's edge.
You are the one who left his mark upon his foe,
    the scars of a bad beating but of bounty too.
On every tribe you have conferred a benefit:
    so Shaʾs, too, is entitled to a bucketful of boon.
Al-Ḥārith has no peer among the people, none comes near,
    except his prisoner; not even a kinsman comes as close.

A *Qaṣīdah* by al-Muthaqqib al-ʿAbdī

أفاطمَ قبل بينك متّعيني   ومنعُك ما سألتُ كأن تَبيني
فلا تَعِدي مواعدَ كاذباتٍ   تمرّ بها رياحُ الصيف دوني

ʾa-fāṭima qabla bayniki mattiʿīnī   *wa-manʿuki mā saʾaltu ka-ʾan tabīnī*
fa-lā taʿidī mawāʿida kādhibātin   *tamurru bihā riyāḥu ṣ-ṣayfi dūnī*[25]

Meter (*al-wāfir*): SLSSL SLSSL SLL (SS may be replaced by L); rhyme: -*ī/ūnī*. Note the internal rhyme in line 1 (also in ll. 4 and 36).

The pre-Islamic poet ʿĀʾidh ibn Miḥṣan ibn Thaʿlabah, nicknamed al-Muthaqqib (or al-Muthaqqab), of the ʿAbd al-Qays tribe, came from al-Baḥrayn (larger than the modern state and covering the eastern part of the Peninsula) and visited al-Ḥīrah in the time of the Lakhmid kings ʿAmr ibn Hind and al-Nuʿmān Abū Qābūs. His nickname ("the piercer") derives from line 11 of the following poem. It opens with a *nasīb* (1–18), first on the poet's beloved, and then describing her companions when they part; this is followed by a relatively long camel description (*waṣf al-nāqah*, 19–39). The poem concludes with five lines (40–45) addressed to a certain ʿAmr, possibly the king of al-Ḥīrah. The concluding part of a *qaṣīdah* is often mistakenly called its *gharaḍ* or "purpose"; in fact, each of its constituent sections is a *gharaḍ* in its own right, at least for the pre-modern Arab critics. By dint of the final section this poem might be called a eulogy or panegyric (*madīḥ*), but the bulk of the poem is not about the patron but about the poet himself. *Fakhr*, as this vaunting, boasting, or self-glorification is called, dominates here, as it often does.

O Fāṭimah, before you go, give me some pleasure! You
    deny me what I ask as if you have already gone!
And do not make false promises
    that summer winds will sweep out of my reach.[26]

If my left hand were as contrary as you are to me,
I would not let it join my right,
But I would cut it off and say, "Begone!"
Thus I dislike those who dislike me too.
Who are these women, going up in litters from Ḍubayb,[27]
so slowly they've not left the wadi yet?
They passed along Sharāf and then Dhāt Rijl,
while keeping al-Dharāniḥ on their right.
And thus they were when crossing Falj;
their litters looked like cargo loaded on ships' decks:
Resembling ships, though Bactrian camels instead,[28]
broad in the back and in the sutures of their skulls.
The women sit, nested in shaking howdahs, unconcerned,
those killers of brave men made meek.
They're like gazelles that lingered at a lote tree bush,
and nibble at the nearest twigs.
They're visible through the thin drapes and have let down a cloth[29]
in which they pierced[30] some peepholes for their eyes.
For all their cruelty they are much sought,
those ladies long of tresses and of locks.
Some of their charms they show, others they hide
—their necks, their well-protected skins;
Gold glittering on their chests,
colored like ivory, no wrinkles there.
When on a day they leave a man behind, and carry off
a pledge he values most, it will not come again.[31]
Thus, jesting about her, I'm feathering my arrow shafts;[32]
she who excels all of the herd's gazelles that stand and gaze.
A hillock they ascended, and into a hollow they went down,
they hardly halted for the midday rest.
I said to one of them, my saddle fastened for
a fiery noontide against which I set my face,
"Though you may cut the bond between us, I
remain the master of myself!"
Therefore, dispel your[33] sorrow with a camel strong
and sturdy, like the hammer of a blacksmith, hard,

True in her steady, rapid pace, as if a cat
were racing with her, clawing at her girth;[34]
Topped with a towering hump with matted hair,
fed with crushed date-stones, fodder from the fertile land.
Her strap upon her breast I fasten when it slackens,
loosened by the slackness of her girth.[35]
Five marks are left upon the earth when she lies down, small as the spots
that black-backed sandgrouse leave, drinking at dawn.[36]
She fills her chest, takes a deep breath, and snaps
the strands of plaited untanned leather thongs.
She strikes, when coursing fast, the two great veins between her thighs
with cast-up pebbles, that resound with a dull thud.
Her forelegs throw up stones like those a hired camelherd
would pelt at a strange camel, driving it away.
She blocks with ever-moving bushy tail a womb's
mouth that has never given birth; nor has she milk.
Your hear the flies that buzz and hum,
singing like doves above their nests.
I cast the reins to her, dismounting, and she slept
as she was wont, when dawn appeared.
Her resting place upon the stony, rugged ground
was like the place one throws one's bridle down.[37]
Her saddle and her leather thongs seem fixed
upon a long-keeled, well-greased ship that sails the sea,
Its prow cleaving the water, climbing
towering billows, on their highest crests.
She has become long-necked and her sciatic vein sticks out between
the muscles of her thighs, thick at the back-vein and aorta.[38]
When I get up at night to saddle her
she moans the moaning of a melancholy man,
And says, when I unfurl her girth strap:[39]
"Is this to be his custom then, and mine, forever?
Always untying, saddling; staying, traveling on?
Will he not spare me and save me then?"
My jesting and her earnestness have left of her
a body like a clay-daubed doorman's hut.[40]

I wound her reins around my hand, I placed
the saddle and a cushion propping my right hand,
Then I went off with her at night, along a track
that stretched out over ridges and flat plains,
To ʿAmr—and it was from ʿAmr she had come to me—
the man of sober wisdom and of valiant deeds.[41]
So either be my brother then in truth,
that I may know from you my lean and fat,
Or cast me off and take me as an enemy—
I will beware of you and you beware of me!
I do not know, when I set out to do things for the best,
which of the two will be my share:
Either the good I seek,
or else the evil that seeks me.

An Elegy (*Marthiyah*) by al-Khansā'

يا عينُ جودي بدمعٍ منك مغزارِ　　وابكي لصخرٍ بدمع منك مدرارِ
إني أرقت فبتُّ الليل ساهرةً　　كأنما كُحلت عيني بعُوّارِ

yā ʿaynu jūdī bi-damʿin minki mighzārī　　*wa-bkī li-ṣakhrin bi-damʿin minki midrārī*
ʾinnī ʾariqtu fa-bittu l-layla sāhiratan　　*ka-ʾannamā kuḥilat ʿaynī bi-ʿuwwārī*[42]

Meter (*al-basīṭ*): XXSL XSL LLSL SSL / XXSL XSL LLSL LL.

Tumāḍir bint ʿAmr, known as al-Khansā' ("Snub-nose"), is the most famous Arabic female poet. She composed numerous elegies on her two brothers, Ṣakhr and Muʿāwiyah, who died in the pre-Islamic period as a result of injuries sustained in tribal battle. Al-Khansā' is said to have converted to Islam and to have died ca. 24/644. An elegy is called *marthiyah* (pl. *marāthī*) and the genre is called *rithā'*. The *marthiyah* may include a range of elements, such as lament, praise of the deceased, and call for vengeance. For reasons of custom and decorum it was difficult for women to excel in other genres—indeed, in any genre, after the early Islamic period, though there are exceptions and several medieval authors compiled books that are devoted to poetry by women; but these compilations tend to be rather slim.

Be generous, my eyes,[43] with shedding copious tears
　and weep a stream of tears for Ṣakhr!
I could not sleep and was awake all night;
　it was as if my eyes were rubbed with grit.
I watched the stars, though it was not my task to watch;
　at times I wrapped myself in my remaining rags.
I heard someone who told a story, and it did
　not make me glad; and he repeated it:

He said that Ṣakhr lay there, in a grave,
slain, near his tomb, covered with stones.
Be gone! May God not keep you far from us—a man
who always righted wrongs and sought revenge.
You used to bear a heart unhumbled, set
in a proud ancestry, and far from weak.
Keen as a spear, his image casting light at night,
of bitter resolve, noble, son of noble men.
Thus I shall weep for you as long as ringdoves wail,[44]
as long as night stars shine for travelers.
I'll not make peace with people that you fought,
until black pitch turns white.
Inform Khufāf and ʿAwf,[45] leave nothing out,
bring them a message that reveals the secrets all.
The war now rides a bad and mangy mount
that settled on a patch with naked sharp-edged rocks.[46]
Tuck up your loincloths, that you may fight easily,
turn up your sleeves: these are the days to turn up sleeves!
And weep for him, man of the tribe, whom Death has reached,
a day of dire events and destinies.
It was as if, the day they went for him,
they all went for a lion, strong and fierce,
And when the warriors dispersed they left a man
mangled by swords, but one who never strayed.
Blood gushed and foamed upon his breast,
uninterrupted, from his heart-straps welling forth.
The fighters' spears from all sides covered him,
now in the charge of Death, sought for revenge.
He was your cousin, one of yours, a guest
of yours, someone you never turned away.
If one of yours were among us he'd not be harmed
until events with consequences would occur.[47]
I mean those people that he dwelled with: Do
you know the claims of guest and protégé?
No sleep for me until the horses, somber-faced, return,
having discarded colts and fillies newly born,[48]

Or else until you stab, while death is prowling near
their tents, Ḥuṣayn and Ibn Sayyār,[49]
And thus wash off the shame that covers you,
like menstruating women wash during that time of month.
He would protect his comrade in a fight, a match
for those who fight with weapons, tooth, or claw,
Amidst a troupe of horses straining at their bridles eagerly,
like lions that arrive in pastures lush.[50]

Polemics in Verse: An Invective *Qaṣīdah* by al-Akhṭal and a Reply by Jarīr

The lives and works of three of the four great poets of the Umayyad period were intimately intertwined. All three were esteemed as eulogists of leading persons. Moreover, for several decades al-Farazdaq (ca. 20/640–ca. 110/728) and Jarīr (ca. 33/653–111/729) attacked each other in vicious poems of invective and satire (*hijāʾ*), and a similar but less extensive series was produced between Jarīr and al-Akhṭal (ca. 20/640–ca. 92/710). (On the fourth of these, Dhū l-Rummah, see immediately below). Their invective verse (usually combined with *fakhr*) is an odd mixture of the personal and collective; all three had Bedouin backgrounds and their poetry is strongly tribal, full of names and allusions to genealogies and tribal feuds and battles, often going back to pre-Islamic times. These may not fascinate modern readers with literary interests, and I have accordingly kept the annotation to a minimum; but contemporaries, urban as well as Bedouin, took a lively interest in all this. Such exchanges were part of state politics, and the three poets were highly esteemed by governors and caliphs. Al-Akhṭal was a Christian, which was exceptional for a leading poet in Islamic times; this was exploited by his opponents but did not prevent him from functioning as a kind of court poet. It was customary, when replying to a poem, to use the same meter and rhyme; such a reply poem was called *naqīḍah* and the plural *naqāʾiḍ* is used for the whole series. The reply poem, while not necessarily a blow-by-blow refutation, normally alludes to and echoes the earlier poem, as the following example will show.

I. al-Akhṭal, "Among us, thoroughbreds are always marked"

ما زال فينا رباطُ الخيل مُعَلِمة　　　وفي تميمٍ رباطُ الذلّ والعاري
النازلين بدار الذلّ إن نزلوا　　　وتستبيح كُليبٌ مَحَرَم الجارِ

mā zāla fīnā ribāṭu l-khayli muʿlimatan *wa-fī tamīmin ribāṭu dh-dhulli wal-ʿārī*
an-nāzilīna bi-dāri dh-dhulli ʾin nazalū *wa-tastabīḥu kulaybun maḥrama l-jārī*[51]

Meter (*al-basīṭ*): XXSL XSL LLSL SSL / XXSL XSL LLSL LL.

Among us, thoroughbreds are always marked with honor; but
among Tamīm they're bred in lowliness and shame.[52]
They dwell in lowliness wherever they dwell;
Kulayb will seize their neighbor's land unlawfully.[53]
They move from one place to another at their women's whims;
they have no ancient glory (but their donkeys do!).
Is it with Muʿriḍ or Muʿayd, or with the sons of Khaṭafā
that he, Jarīr, thinks he can vie with me and my prestige?[54]
Sit down, Jarīr, you've found a height too arduous for you
to climb, you've met a turbulent and overflowing sea!
When guests make their dog bark these people urge
their mother, "Quick, piss on the fire!"[55]
But she is stingy and holds back her stream of piss
and urinates for them only in dribs and drabs.
They don't avenge the blood of kinsmen killed,
they never rally when they have been routed once.
They're always busy sitting in their tents,
some are depressed, some cowards want to flee.
Did you perhaps assist Maʿadd in a fierce fight
like we stood by Maʿadd, during the battle of Dhū Qār?[56]
There Kisrā's squadrons came, the horses marked, but they
eradicated them, killed every tyrant foe.[57]
Did you perhaps stop Shuraḥbīl from being killed
when rabble from Tamīm surrounded him?[58]
It was the battle of Kulāb; your womenfolk were led
away like cattle to be sold, women and maids,
As pillion-riders taken, spoils gained by our spears,
while crying for Riyāḥ and crying for Marrār.[59]
There Abū Ḥanash stabbed him, giving him
a gaping, wide-mouthed wound too deep for probes.[60]

Al-Ward with ʿUṣum in pursuit chased those of yours who fled,
    as if he were a polo player, a mallet at the ready,
Calling the riders of Lahāzim, armed, no cowards they,
    gray haired, not lacking in experience,[61]
Who in the horror of war's morning keep bad things at bay,
    when the advancing and retreating men are mixed,
Who dole out food when a cold north wind blows
    that drives rain-emptied clouds: fat camel's hump,
While you lived in Marrūt and chose to stay aloof,
    son of the Willing Wallower, the She-ass, pregnant one![62]
She, prematurely, after seven months gave birth to him,
    from yawning depths, a pit as black as pitch:
Vile mother of a foal of a foul stallion;
    she spawned him for a vile and snorting male.

II. Jarīr, "Greet this abode"

حيّوا المقامَ وحيّوا ساكنَ الدارِ   ما كِدتَ تعرف إلا بعد إنكارِ
إذا تقادمَ عهدُ الحيّ هيّجني   خيالُ طيّبةِ الأردانِ مِعطارِ

ḥayyū l-muqāma wa-ḥayyū sākina d-dārī   *mā kidta taʿrifu ʾillā baʿda ʾinkārī*
ʾidhā taqādama ʿahdu l-ḥayyi hayyajanī   *khayālu ṭayyibati l-ʾardāni miʿṭārī*[63]

Meter (*al-basīṭ*): XXSL XSL LLSL SSL / XXSL XSL LLSL LL.

The poem opens with a traditional greeting of abandoned abodes and an *aṭlāl*-cum-*nasīb* passage (1–13) mixed with a few hints of self-praise; this is followed rather abruptly by tribal vaunting (14–34) and the poem concludes with fierce invective, tribal and personal, obviously intended to surpass the model.

Greet this abode and greet who dwelt here once—
    you hardly recognize it, first so unfamiliar.
Not having seen the tribe for ages, I am stirred
    by a nocturnal phantom, fragrance wafting from its sleeves.[64]

A man of strength is never safe, his force will be destroyed:
I find that Time destroys as well as builds.
I've always striven for the furthest aim, attaining it:
I'm not a frequent visitor of nearest neighbor girls,
Except with brimful bowls of shining *shīzā* wood,
topped with "fat camel's hump."[65]
Now, when I say "I give up folly," I am stirred
by traces in Dhū l-Bayḍ or traces in Duwwār,[66]
Where winds are wailing like she-camels, calf-bereft,
that sniff at dummies, straw-stuffed camel hides.[67]
Is there still someone at the pool of al-Naqīʿah, at
the lotus trees, the meadows of Aʿyār where wormwood grows?
If I were not ashamed my yearning would be stirred
by ashes, gray as pigeons, lying at the hearth.
May you be watered by a pouring rain,
and every drenching deluge sent by the two lucky stars.[68]
That day the tribe's departure bore me down, I could not be
consoled; I nearly gave away my secret thoughts.
She looked at me at first with a gazelle's eye; then,
robbing all sense from me, struck with ferocious falcon's eye.
She fills the eye with beauty, then her voice
delights me, so melodious, no loud lowing noise!
My tribe: Tamīm! They are the men
who from their heartlands drive the Taghlib tribe,[69]
Who, settled in protected pastures never grazed before,
defend it, needing neither neighbor nor confederate.
By "horses marked with honor"[70] you were driven from
the highlands; now you dwell, not of your choice, alone.
When Khindif rises you cannot resist hard rock
of mountains, or the billows of a foaming sea.[71]
Khuzaymah strikes those whom I strike; the sons of Murr,
sons of a mother who bears males, are wroth on my behalf.[72]
Men chosen for their glory and for honor: these
are my "Quraysh," my "Helpers" are those helping me.[73]
The real tribe is Qays, highest in glory, who derive
nobility from stocks like fire sticks giving fire.[74]

They are my tribe,[75] their stem's my stem, their branch
my branch; their bonds my bonds, my strength.
I am a Muḍar man by roots;
you cannot "vie with me and my prestige."[76]
From us the horsemen at Dhū Bahdā came and at
Dhū Najab, marked, the morning of Dhū Qār,[77]
Led at the front in the first ranks by Jaz'
and Qaʿnab, and by warriors "not lacking in experience."[78]
Our horsemen bound Bisṭām in bonds,
earning the gratitude of Ḥajjār's men.[79]
Bring me the likes of Banū Badr, or
men like the kinsmen of Manẓūr, son of Sayyār,[80]
Or like Ṭufayl's son, ʿĀmir, of noble descent,
or Ḥārith, when "Hey Ḥāri!" hails the tribe,[81]
Or like Zuhayr's clan, when the lances break,
and horsemen ride through whirling clouds of dust,[82]
Or like Ḥuṣayn, attacking on his strong-flanked steed,
when he protects his neighbor's undefended spot,[83]
Or Hāshim, on the day he led the horses, marked,
amidst a host advancing like the black of night:
He slew the leaders with a slashing, slicing Indian sword,
and now they lie around him, slaughtered.
Or like the clan of Shamkh—but you'll not find their likes
for those who ask a boon or seek revenge.[84]
We test our swords—and they are no newfangled ones—
on every tyrant king who wears a crown.
I am always the first to reach and gain the goal
when I've long set my mind to it.
You pig-eyed[85] folk of Taghlib! I have branded you
upon your noses with a mark that lasts.
Don't boast, for God has fashioned you,
pig-eyed Taghlib, to dwell "in lowliness and shame"![86]
With you there is no man whose judgment counts
among the Muslims, nor a martyr for Islam.
You're people who would gather for their hajj and then
put money in their purse: no pious pilgrims they!

I have been told you had entrenched yourself
at the Khābūr and then broke loose.[87]
You surely could have got a flame from someone else than me!
You've put Taghlib to shame and kindled from my fire.
That little Akhṭal's mother bears no noble sons:
she spawned for one that snorts with tusks of varied size.[88]
The hair that hangs down from her naked holes
resembles two crows' shadows coupled in a cave.
Her mandibles when she is drunk I would compare
to ass's bollocks, strung up by a vet.
Your mother didn't know what judgment she had given:
she was too drunk with what was in her bleeding jug.[89]
The piglets and broad beans that she has eaten bubble in
the bowels of that shitting female, one that farts at night.

Love in the Desert: A *Qaṣīdah* by Dhū l-Rummah, "To Mayyah's Two Abodes, a Greeting!"

أمنزلتيّ ميّ سلامٌ عليكما على النأي والنائي يودّ وينصحُ

ولا زال من نوء السماك عليكما ونوء الثريا وابلٌ متبطحُ

'a-manzilatay mayyin salāmun ʿalaykumā ʿalā n-na'yi wal-nā'ī yawaddu wa-yanṣaḥū
wa-lā zāla min naw'i s-simāki ʿalaykumā wa-naw'i th-thurayyā wābilun mutabaṭṭiḥū[90]

Meter (*al-ṭawīl*): SLX SLLL SLX SLSL / SLX SLLL SLX SLSL.

Abū l-Ḥārith Ghaylān ibn ʿUqbah, commonly known as Dhū l-Rummah ("the one with the frayed rope") was the last of the great desert poets. Two themes dominate his poetry: love for a woman called Mayyah, and the desert. His verse was a goldmine for early Arabic philologists and lexicographers.

The poem is a somewhat longer than average *qaṣīdah*. It opens with a greeting to the *aṭlāl*, the abandoned abodes (lines 1–5). Why there are two is not clear: perhaps they are the place where she once was and the place where she is now. An extended *nasīb* follows, in which the poet reminisces about and describes his beloved. After the *nasīb* section older poets often mention that they turn away from the folly of love, and then describe their camel and turn to other matters. Dhū l-Rummah, however, says that in spite of his advanced age (thirty!) he still loves Mayyah (line 6): perhaps the sign of a new sensibility? Only at line 44, mentioning Mayyah one last time (though there is an implicit mention in line 50), does he begin with a description of the desert that separates him from Mayyah, and of his camel, which he compares to a wild ass (a standard comparison). In all likelihood the poem originally ended with line 64; indeed, such abrupt endings are very common in pre-Islamic and early Islamic Arabic poetry. Michael Sells prefers an ending with line 66a, which again mentions Mayyah; like many modern literary critics he is eager to find the kind of coherence that he expects from a poem.

(See Sells's fine poetic translation in *Desert Tracings*, pp. 67–76, which includes a short introduction and analysis. My translation I offer as a friendly *muʿāraḍah* or emulation).

Although Dhū l-Rummah is not the only character in the poem—there are many references to other persons, implicitly and explicitly, especially traveling companions (see lines 5, 15, 18, 48–51, 55, 57, 66)—his tribe does not figure prominently here.

The poem seems to have been inspired by another poem by the earlier poet, Tamīm ibn Muqbil, who died at some time in the second half of the seventh century (see Ibn Maymūn, *Muntahā l-ṭalab*, I:66–68); it has the same meter and rhyme and there are a number of clear parallels. Dhū l-Rummah and Mayyah remained among the famous loving couples in Arabic lore; compare the poem by al-Shushtarī, below, p. 83.

To Mayyah's two abodes, a greeting to you both;
    though far, a far-off friend wishes you well.
Arcturus and the Pleiades may send upon
    you both a downpour and a spreading steady rain,[91]
Even though you have aroused, again, the passion
    of a yearning one, whose eyes are ever shedding
Yes! Tears, that nearly would have killed, if not released,
    when recognizing an abode as Mayyah's .[92]
And this when I was nearing thirty, all my friends
    turned sober, sense outweighing, nearly, stupid folly.
If distance changes lovers, I at least have not,
    at Mayyah's mention, found that love has lost its touch.
And nearness brings no boredom to my longing,
    nor does the love for her leave me when she has left.
The hearts of all who love, would they be sore
    just as my heart is sore at Mayyah's memory?[93]
When Mayyah's memory springs up
    it almost wounds your heart.[94]
Hearts' longings tend to change their course; I think
    your share in my heart won't be granted to another.
Ah, Mayyah, don't you know, while now between us
    there are wastelands where the eye may roam,

I scan the desert with my eye: perhaps
I'll see you, while my eyes are shedding tears of love.
Moaning and grieving for her all day long,
while what the night brings is more painful yet.
I see that love may be effaced, by absence swept away:
your love for Mayyah is renewed and thrives.
I thought of you when a gazelle, a doe with fawn,
neck stretched, passed by before our camels, from the right,[95]
Used to the sands, light brown, a noble beast,
the morning sunbeams gleaming on her back.
She leaves in the soft grassy sands, the sands of Mushrif,[96]
a fawn, her eyes around it glancing.
She glimpsed us, as if heading for it where she left it;
now nearing, now backing away.
She is like her, in limbs and neck and eyes,
yet Mayyah is more beautiful than she, and prettier.
Slow moving; fragrant from her perfume is her tent
right after slumber too; adorning it at morningtime.
Her anklets and bone wristlets seem to twist
round *ʿushar* twigs that block the wadi's torrent.[97]
Her rump is like a dune that towers, where
the sprinkling rains have shaped firm hillocks.[98]
Her locks hang loose and low over her back,
over a willow tree, in curls and combed with combs.
Smooth where her tears flow down and where
she wears a shawl, donned loosely as a sash.[99]
You see, along her bare white neck, her earrings, high
as if they dangle over an abyss in a ravine.[100]
Using a twig of the *arāk* tree, in the morning, as if scented
with Indian ambergris and musk, she polishes
The tops of chamomile cooled by the night, ascended by
the dew that rises in the evening from Ráma,[101]
The meadow's earth from every side enveloped by 27a
a breeze as if a musk-pod had been opened.[102]
Her front teeth being shining white: if she would show
them, smiling to a deaf-mute, he would speak out loud and clear.[103]

She is my cure and sickness, and her memory my care;
but for the painful distance, passion dies.
30 But she is far away, her tribe beyond
strong, evil winds that scar the stony plains,[104]
And crows that croak of parting, like
bereaved, lamenting, high-born Nubian women,[105]
Confirming what I feared: that Mayyah's plans
were changed, the rod of parting struck with rot.[106]
Mayy's husband wept, because young camels were kneeled down
at Mayyah's tent, exhausted, in the deep of night.[107]
So die of grief, you, Mayyah's spouse! Those hearts
are Mayyah's that are free of blame, well meaning.
35 If they had left the choice to her, she would have chosen well;
the likes of you aren't suitable for one like Mayyah.
Mayyah is near! I say—but then dust-colored deserts loom
between us two, as far as eyes can stare.
Mayy has been carried off, and here is her abode:
left to limping black crows and ringnecked doves.
When I complained to Mayyah of my love, that she might give
me love's reward, she said, "You jest!"
Keeping aloof, leading me on, when she had seen
my hidden passion almost make my body disappear.
40 I spend the night as if sleeping on needles, while
her husband sleeps and sprawls as if upon a sandy hillock.
Toward many a blazing noonday, fiery hot, the pebbles
almost cracking from the heat,
I've set my face, together with Aṭlāl, the shadows shrunk,
the solitary white-striped bull back in its hideaway.[108]
If, as its seems to me, my world is only torments
on account of Mayyah, death will be more restful.
On many a hot midday, with Mayyah far away, my camel did
not halt to take a nap, while black and white locusts hop,[109]
45 In wasteland where the way is lost, which seems to stir
with the mirage at morn and afternoon, blinding one's gaze,
The hillocks' tops as if enwrapped with pure white silk,
now torn away from them, and then patched up,

When the chameleon, struck by the heat,
begins to twist its head and reel.
From many a man in drunken stupor by long drowsiness,
just as a two-roped bucket in a well sways to and fro,
I have dispelled his slumber when his head
swayed like a reeling drunkard who has swilled his last.
If he hung lifeless in his saddle, I revived his spirit
mentioning your name, while nimble ruddy camels pace along.
When tips of whips are split, and frames of mounts
are sickles thin like crescent moons, still Ṣaydaḥ[110] sets a bracing pace.
Her ears are narrow, long and smooth her nape,
her cheeks are burnished like a foreign woman's looking glass;[111]
Eyes of a black-horned solitary bull, and lips
like soft Yemeni leather. Impetuous is she when buoyant.
Legs like the shadow of a wolf, the foreleg, twisted by
the shin bone, swinging sideward out,
At a quick pace when night's dark veils are rent
by morning's well-known shining shape, thus showing up the riders.
When I cry *Aij!* or sing, she lifts a tail like secondaries of
an eagle's wing, in calf or with a phantom pregnancy.
You see her, after I've imposed upon her every hardship,
leaving fast dromedaries, trampling, far behind.
Her forelegs move like waves, lungeing her bulk,
wary of threat, the head pulled upward by the reins.
A tawny, sturdy animal: as if, saddle and all, I cruise
the steppe upon a thick-set, bite-scarred onager,[112]
Who drives and turns his cows, all similar, their backs
like bare, smooth boulders where the barley-grass may grow,
Cows that have grazed the wasteland ground until they are
as lean as lances, brown and straight, from Khaṭṭ,[113]
Until there came a day so blazing hot
that pearly ostrich eggs in shallow nests would almost crack:
Then he would coax them ceaselessly, and they would stand,
parched, as if flocking birds were perched upon their heads,[114]
Upon a vantage point, the time when dust flies up
and locusts flee from the fierce heat.

65 There where she goes at night you see the wind
playing between her and the place she reaches in the morn.[115]
Our mounts, in every barren wasteland, are like boats
that float upon the Tigris in the desert sands.
66a My heart can only think of Mayyah—she with many guises,
who torments it, now in earnest, now in jest.[116]

An Umayyad *Ghazal* Poem, Used as an Abbasid Song Text

ألا يا حماماتِ اللوى عُدْنَ عودةً   فإني إلى أصواتكنّ حزينُ
فعُدْنَ فلما عدن كِدْنَ يُمِتْنَني   وكدت بأسراري لهنّ أُبينُ

ʾalā yā ḥamāmāti l-liwā ʿudna ʿawdatan   *fa-ʾinnī ʾilā ʾaṣwātikunna ḥazīnū*
fa-ʿudna fa-lammā ʿudna kidna yumitnanī   *wa-kidtu bi-ʾasrārī lahunna ʾubīnū*[117]

Meter (*al-ṭawīl*): SLX SLLL SLX SLSL / SLX SLLL SLS SLL; rhyme: *-ī/ūnū*.

The poet is unknown, but versions or lines of the poem are attributed to the semi-legendary Majnūn Laylā (see below), to Jamīl (d. 82/701), and to Ibn al-Dumaynah (second/eighth century).

These lines served as a song text (indicated by the heading *ṣawt*, literally "voice") for at least two famous early Abbasid singers, and may be considered an independent poem even though these lines can be found as part of longer pieces too. About the music we know virtually nothing (Muḥammad ibn al-Ḥārith sang these lyrics in *khafīf al-ramal* rhythm, a kind of triple measure, "with the middle finger," referring to a particular scale or mode on the lute). The general term for "love poetry" is *ghazal*; in later times, in Persian, it comes to mean "short love poem." It is distinguished (but not always too clearly) from the elegiac *nasīb* that serves as introduction to *qaṣīdahs*.

The large work from which this song text is taken, *Kitāb al-Aghānī* (*The Book of Songs*) is an extremely important source for our knowledge of Arabic poetry, poets, and singers. Its author, Abū l-Faraj al-Iṣfahānī (d. ca. 363/972), took as his starting point a collection of famous song lyrics. They are almost always very short, a handful of lines: it is sometimes incorrectly assumed that long poems were regularly sung.[118]

Like countless other Arabic poems, this piece is about lost love and memory and clearly part of the ʿUdhrite tradition (after the tribe of ʿUdhrah, who had a reputation for their chaste and self-effacing love for an unattainable woman; see the story of Qays and Lubnā in this volume, translated from *al-Aghānī*). Al-Liwā is either a place name or a description of a place ("the twisted sand dune") where the poet-lover presumably once met his absent beloved. Doves, in Arabic poetry and lore, are supposed to be perpetually lamenting the loss of a young pigeon who was killed after leaving Noah's ark (this dove chick was called al-Hadīl; *hadīl*, mentioned in a variant, also means the cooing sound of pigeons). When the poet says in the last line that he cries for them, he means that he cries for their loss as well as his own. The basic structure: line 1: apostrophe (the quotation marks in the translation are the equivalent of the implicit "I said:"; lines 2–4: "narrative" sequence describing the result of the apostrophe, with line 4 serving as general statement by way of conclusion, which seems to look back on the events described in 2–3. There are therefore three temporal levels implied in this otherwise not very remarkable poem—but note the level of sounds, such as the repetition of *n* and *m*: a suitable text for singing.

"O doves of al-Liwā, turn back again!
  I sadly long to hear your voices."
So they turned back, but when they did I nearly died
  and I almost revealed my hidden feelings.
They called, repeating their sounds as if
  they had been given wine to drink, or were possessed.
Whenever my eyes saw doves like them,
  crying, these eyes would shed tears for them.

ʿUdhrī *Ghazal*: a poem attributed to Majnūn Laylā

أصوّر صورةً في التُّرب منها   وأبكي إنّ قلبي في عَذابِ
وأشكو هجرها منها إليها   شكايةَ مُدْنفٍ عظِم المُصابِ

ʾuṣawwiru ṣūratan fī t-turbi minhā   *wa-ʾabkī ʾinna qalbī fī ʿadhābī*
wa-ʾashkū hajrahā minhā ʾilayhā   *shikāyata mudnafin ʿaẓimi l-muṣābī*[119]

Meter (*al-wāfir*): SLSSL SLSSL SLL / SLSSL SLSSL SLL (SS may be replaced by L).

Qays ibn al-Mulawwaḥ, nicknamed Majnūn Laylā ("Laylā's Madman"), or al-Majnūn for short, is said to have lived in the Umayyad period. He is very likely legendary or semi-legendary; there is little point in worrying about the authenticity of this or other poems attributed to him (any poem of uncertain provenance mentioning a Laylā could be ascribed to him). The story of al-Majnūn's unhappy love for Laylā is the most famous one among several similar stories (such as the story of Qays ibn Dharīḥ and Lubnā translated below). Although al-Majnūn was not of the tribe of ʿUdhrah, his verse is characteristic of what is known as ʿUdhrite *ghazal*. The central motif of the poem, picturing the beloved in the dust, is also found in a poem by Bashshār ibn Burd (d. ca. 167/784), and the present poem may well be based on his, rather than the reverse.

I draw a picture of her in the dust
    and cry, my heart in torment.
I complain to her about her: for she left me,
    love-sick, badly stricken.
I complain of all the passion I have
    suffered, with a plaint toward the dust.[120]
Love makes me want to turn to Laylā's land,
    complaining of my passion and the flames in me.

I make rain fall upon the dust from my eyes' clouds;
my heart is in distress and grief.
I complain of my great passion
while my tears are flowing, streaming.
I'm talking to her picture in the dust:
as if the dust were listening to me,
As if I were near her, complaining to her
of my plight, while talking to the dust.
No one returns an answer to my words,
not even the reproacher answers me.
So I turn back, hope dashed, tears pouring
down as if from showering clouds,
Truly, madly possessed by her,[121]
my heart in torment for the love of her.

Umayyad *Ghazal*: A Poem by ʿUmar ibn Abī Rabīʿah

يا من لقلب متيَّمٍ كَلِفِ
تمشي الهُوَينا إذا مشت فُضُلاً

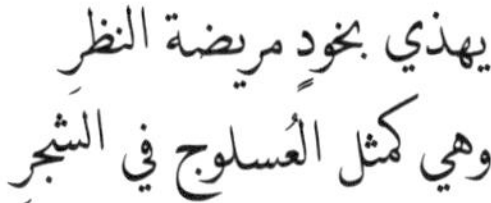

yā man li-qalbin mutayyamin kalifin *yahdhī bi-khawdin marīḍati n-naẓarī*
tamshī l-huwaynā ʾidhā mashat fuḍulan *wa-hya ka-mithli l-ʿuslūji fī sh-shajarī*[122]

Meter (*al-munsariḥ*): XXSL LXLS LSSL / XXSL LXLS LSSL.

ʿUmar Ibn Abī Rabīʿah (d. 93/712 or 103/720) lived in Mecca and many of his somewhat frivolous love lyrics are about affairs with women who visit the town as pilgrims. His *ghazal* is often contrasted with the more serious, self-sacrificing *ghazal* called ʿUdhrite. The poem begins as if the poet were yet another hopeless lover, but it soon becomes obvious that he is boasting of his success with women.

Who'll help my heart, enslaved, doting?
It raves about a pretty girl with languid looks,
Who walks so slowly when she walks, dressed in her shift;
she's like a newly sprouted twig upon a tree.
I don't know where to look when she is looking—
and then one night we met; it was our Destiny.
I spied her and her womenfolk; they walked
between the Station and the Stone:[123]
White-skinned, attractive virgins, sauntering,
they walked with an easy gait, the gait of oryx cows,
Possessing beauty and attractiveness alike,
possessing gentle coquetry with bashfulness.
They listened to her as she spoke, one day,
(they thought she was the best thing in the world);

She said, in jest, to one of her companions:
"We'll spoil our circumambulation on account of 'Umar![124]
Come on girl, show yourself to him, let him see us,
and signal to him, girl, but coyly!"[125]
The girl told her: "I signaled to him. He said No!"
And then she hurried off and followed me!
Whoever drinks, when she awakes, the water of
her mouth, drinks musk and cool, refreshing water
Her eyes are large and black, she's plump and lovable,
and, flirtingly, she tosses stones with her left hand.[126]

A Love Poem by Umm Khālid

ألا من لعينٍ دمعُها يتحضّرُ وقلبٍ معنًّى بالصبابة مُسعَرُ
ونفسٍ بها غُلٌّ بعيدٌ شفاؤها ولستُ عليه آخر الدهر أقدرُ

ʾalā man li-ʿaynin damʿuhā yataḥaḍḍarū *wa-qalbin muʿannan biṣ-ṣabābati musʿarū*
wa-nafsin bihā ghullun baʿīdun shifāʾuhū *wa-lastu ʿalayhi ʾākhira d-dahri ʾaqdirū*[127]

Meter (*al-ṭawīl*): SLX SLLL SLX SLSL / SLX SLLL SLX SLSL.

When women speak in classical Arabic literature it is usually in poems and prose composed by men, which hardly counts as authentic speech by women. It is only in the genre of the early elegy (*marthiyah*) that one finds a few famous female names such as al-Khansāʾ (translated above). However, in spite of the male dominance, love poetry by women is not wholly absent.

Nothing is known about Umm Khālid or about the object of her feelings. She probably lived in the early Islamic period, judging by the material quoted in the source, *Balāghat al-nisāʾ* by Ibn Abī Ṭāhir (d. 280/893), a work devoted to women distinguished by their eloquence. These lines contain the motif "I wish I were her/his...," also found in poems by al-ʿAbbās ibn al-Aḥnaf (see p. 2); compare its analog in Greek poetry (εἴθε γενοιμεν).

O who will help my eyes, from which the tears[128] flow down,
  my captive heart, distressed, ablaze with love,
My soul, with burning thirst so hard to slake,
  I can no longer bear it, after all this time!
[My love][129] is truly visible, although I never spoke a word
  to anyone whenever his name was dropped.
I say, while tears from my sore eyes are streaming like
  a brook in which the water gushes forth:
I wish I were the baby daughter of al-Ḥājibī's,[130]
  I wish I were his shadow or his shade,[131] whenever he appears,
I wish I were his coat when he protects himself against
  the cold east wind, or else his shoes for his cold feet.[132]

Anti-Arab, Pro-Iranian Lampoon (*Hijā'*), by Bashshār ibn Burd

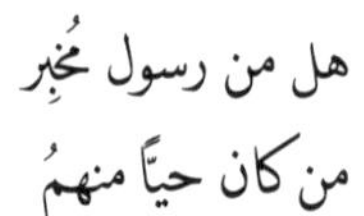

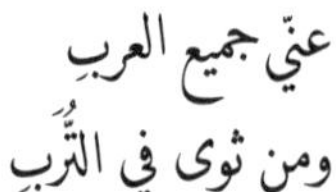

hal min rasūlin mukhbirin	*'annī jamī'a l-'arabī*
man kāna ḥayyan minhumū	*wa-man thawā fī t-turabī*[133]

Meter (*al-rajaz*): XXSL XXSL / XXSL XXSL.

Shorter meters such as this one and those of the following two poems became more frequent among the "Moderns," even though the longer meters remained popular.

In this poem Bashshār ibn Burd (ca. 95/715–ca. 167/784), the first great poet of the "Moderns" (*al-Muḥdathūn*) and the first important non-Arab Arabic poet, mocks the uncouth Bedouin ancestors of the Arabs and boasts of his noble Persian ancestry and of the fact that Iranian troops were instrumental in bringing the Abbasid dynasty to power during his lifetime. The poem is thus a mixture of *hijā'* (lampoon, invective) and *fakhr* (boasting).

Who'll be my messenger and tell
  all Arabs who I am,
Those still alive and those
  who are lying in the earth:
That I'm of noble lineage,
  high above all others!
My grandfather is Chosroes,
  my father is Sasan,
Caesar's my mother's brother, if
  I reckon my descent.[134]

I have so many an ancestor,
a crown upon his head.
With proud disdain he sits in court;
all knees are bent for him.
Each morning to his court he comes,
arrayed with blazing gems.
Only in ermine dressed, he stands
screened from the common gaze.
Attendants, hurriedly, bring him
the vessels made of gold.
He did not drink diluted milk
from goatskin poured in mugs.
My father never urged
a scabby camel with a song;
He never, forced by famine, pierced
a bitter colocynth;
He never hit acacia trees
with sticks, to get the fruits.
We never roasted monitors
that flick their quivering tails.
I never dug for, never ate
a lizard from the rocks.
My father never warmed himself,
astraddle, at a fire,[135]
No, and my father never rode
a camel's pack saddle.
But we are kings and always were,
for ages in the past.
It's us who brought the cavalry
from Balkh—and that's no lie—
And let them, safe from foe, drink from
Aleppo's rivers two.[136]
Then, after Syria was subdued,
of Christian crosses full,
We marched with them to Egypt, in
an army large and loud,

And seized its realm, instead of ours
that had been seized from us.
The horses took us past Tangier,[137]
a place so marvellous.
Then we restored the power to
the Arab Prophet's kin.[138]
Who will oppose the Guidance and
the Faith, and is not seized?
And who, who will resist it, and
will be from plunder free?
Our wrath is a most worthy wrath,
for God and for Islam.
I, son of double Persian stock,
defend it zealously.
We bear our crowns and own our strong,
disdainful sovereignty.

A *Muḥdath* ("Modern") *Ghazal* Epigram by Abū Nuwās

يا قمرًا أبصرتُ في مأتمٍ يندُبُ شَجْوًا بين أترابِ

يبكي فيذري الدُّرَّ من نرجسٍ فيلطِمُ الورْدَ بعُنّابِ

yā qamaran 'abṣartu fī ma'tamin *yandubu shajwan bayna 'atrābī*
yabkī fa-yadhrī d-durra min narjisin *fa-yalṭimu l-warda bi-'unnābī*[139]

Meter (*al-sarī'*): XXSL LXXL LSL / XXSL LXXL LL.

Al-Ḥasan ibn Hāni', known as Abū Nuwās (ca. 140/755–ca. 198/813), whose mother was Persian and whose father's lineage, possibly Arab, is uncertain, lived in Kufa, Basra, and the new city of Baghdad.[140] He is reckoned among the greatest and most versatile of Arabic poets.

The poem is about a girlfriend of the poet who himself was fonder of boys than girls. It is an exercise in metaphor (*isti'ārah*), not of the "old" kind (genitive metaphor, as "the reins of the morning are held by the hand of the north wind") but a word standing for another: moon for pretty girl, pearls for tears, daffodils for eyes, roses for cheeks, jujube fruits for fingers dyed with henna. The poet poses as a lover dying from love but he is not serious, as shown by the cynical and paradoxical wish in the "punch line": a true lover would not wish the loved ones of his beloved to die; and if he were not loved by the girl, he would wish death upon himself.

A full moon at a funeral I saw
    lamenting grievously among its friends.
It wept and scattered pearls from daffodils
    while slapping roses with the jujube fruits.
I said, "Don't weep for someone dead and gone,
    weep, rather, for a slain one at your door!"
The funeral exposed it, grudgingly,
    to me, despite porter and chamberlains.
Ah, may its loved ones always die,
    that I could always see it too!

A *Ghazal* by Abū Nuwās: On a Boy Called ʿAlī

يا لاعبًا بحياتي　　　وهاجرًا ما يؤاتي
وزاهدًا في وِصالي　　　ومشمِتًا بي عِداتي

yā lāʿiban bi-ḥayātī　　　*wa-hājiran mā yuʾātī*
wa-zāhidan fī wiṣālī　　　*wa-mushmitan bī ʿidātī*[141]

Meter (*al-mujtathth*): XLSL XSLL / XLSL XSLL.

Abū Nuwās was the first great Arabic poet to cultivate the genre of *ghazal mudhakkar*, love poetry about boys, although he also produced *ghazal muʾannath*, about women. Arabic homoerotic poetry is not known before the Abbasid period and references to homosexuality, although not absent, are rare; consequently, Arabs both ancient and modern have ascribed its introduction to the Persians.[142]

You who play with my life,
　who shun me and play hard-to-get,
You who are stingy with your trysts
　and make my enemies gloat,
Taking my heart away from me,
　planted on a lance tip,
And who unjustly has confined
　my passion to my soul, unable to speak it:
This is a letter meant for you,
　my tears its ink,
Its contents my heart's yearning
　for you, myself laid open.
If only you would hear my excuse
　or accept my innocence

My sleepless eyes would not
observe the rising stars.
You peerless novelty,
beyond description!
Your face is the full moon,
Your eyes those of desert gazelles,
Uniquely blessed
among those gazelles that[143]
Explore meadows
in winter or summer pastures.
Frail of frame, near-falling,
slender-necked,
You have the body of a boy,
though you flirt like a girl.
Male in your appearance,
female in private;
Locks like a pretty girl,
with curls in ringlets
Above smooth cheeks
lighting the dark,
And a moustache starting
to sprout:
That is the one I shall not name,
for I respect my friends.
But when I can take it no more,
I mention him by spelling out his name:
An A, an L, an I:
such a sweet sound they make!

Two Wine Poems by Abū Nuwās

I. “Don’t cry for Laylā”

لا تبكِ ليلى ولا تطربْ إلى هندِ	واشربْ على الورد حمراءَ كالوردِ
كأسا إذا انحدرت في حلق شاربها	أحذته حمرتها في العين والخدِّ

lā tabki Laylā wa-lā taṭrab ʾilā Hindī	*wa-shrab ʿalā l-wardi ḥamrāʾa kal-wardī*
kaʾsan ʾidhā nḥadarat fī ḥalqi shāribihā	*ʾaḥdhatʾhu ḥumratahā fī l-ʿayni wal-khaddī*[144]

Meter (*al-basīṭ*): XXSL XSL LLSL SSL / XXSL XSL LLSL LL.

Abū Nuwās may not be the first Bacchic poet in Arabic but he is certainly the greatest; more than four hundred wine poems (*khamriyyāt*) are ascribed to him. Laylā and Hind, mentioned here, are traditional girls’ names, often used in Bedouin love poetry, which Abū Nuwās often mocks in his poems.[145]

Don’t cry for Laylā, don’t rave about Hind!
    But drink among roses a rose-red wine,
A draught that descends in the drinker’s throat,
    bestowing its redness on eyes and cheeks.
The wine is a ruby, the glass is a pearl,
    served by the hand of a slim-figured girl,
Who serves you the wine from her hand, and wine
    from her mouth—doubly drunk, for sure, will you be.
Thus I am drunk twice, my friends only once:
    a favor special, for me alone!

II. “Come on, pour me some wine”

ألا فاسقِني خمرًا وقل لي هي الخمرُ　　ولا تسقني سرًّا إذا أمكن الجهرُ

ولا تسقِيَنْ منها المُرائين قطرةً　　لأنّ رياء الناس عندي هو الهُجرُ

ʾalā fa-sqinī khamran wa-qul lī hiya l-khamrū　*wa-lā tasqinī sirran ʾidhā ʾamkana l-jahrū*

wa-lā tasqiyan minhā l-murāʾīna qaṭratan　*li-ʾanna riyāʾa n-nāsi ʿindī huwa l-hujrū*[146]

Meter (*al-ṭawīl*): SLX SLLL SLX SLSL / SLX SLLL SLX SLLL.

This is a combination of a Bacchic and homoerotic love poem (*ghazal mudhakkar*), included in the *khamriyyāt* (wine poetry) section of Abū Nuwās’s *Dīwān*.

Come on, pour me some wine and tell me it is wine:
　Don’t pour it secretly when one can do it openly.
Don’t pour a single drop of it for hypocrites:
　hypocrisy to me is mere obscenity.[147]
A good life for a man is being drunk and drunk again:
　when that goes on and on, time seems to shrink for him.
To see me sober: I would be a fraud, for sure;
　to totter in a stupor: that is my neat gain.
So speak your lover’s name; no more allusions:
　there is no good in pleasures that are veiled,
No good in being outrageous without impudence,
　nor in licentiousness not followed up with unbelief,
Together with a brother-friend in revelry, his brow
　a crescent moon surrounded by bright stars.
There was this woman selling wine I roused at night,
　Orion being on the rise, when Aquila had plunged.
She said, “Who’s knocking there so late?” We said, “A band
　with lightweight water skins,[148] who need some wine.
They also must have whores.” “Now what about,” she said,
　“a bright-eyed boy instead, like a gold coin, with languid looks,

A joy to those who whore, a pleasure to the pederast:
  two things combined in one?"
We said, "Yes, bring him here: someone like that,
  dear lady, we can't bear to be without."
She brought him: like a twig, shaking his bum:
  you'd think it magic, but no magic there!
The likeness of the moon at night when it is full,
  with slender waist and saw-edged pretty teeth.
To him each one of us applied himself in turn,
  breaking our fast with him, after long abstinence.
We spent the night while God saw us, a wicked band,
  trailing the trains of sin. No idle boast!

A Lampooning Epigram (*Hijā'*) by Abū Nuwās

من ينأ عنه مَصادُه فمصاد زنبورٍ ثيابُهْ
تكفيه فيها نظرةٌ فتعُلّ من عَلَقٍ حِرابُهْ

man yan'a 'anhu maṣāduhū *fa-maṣādu Zunbūrin thiyābuh*
takfīhi fīhā naẓratun *fa-ta'ullu min 'alaqin ḥirābuh*[149]

Meter (*al-kāmil*, shortened): SSLSL SSLSL / SSLSL SSLSL L (SS may be replaced by L).

This mocking poem on a "lousy" person called Zunbūr ("Wasp") ibn Abī Ḥammād is relatively innocent. *Hijā'* can be extraordinarily coarse and obscene, such as other lines by Abū Nuwās on the same person.[150]

Other people's hunting grounds may be far away,
 but Zunbūr's hunting grounds are his clothes.
One glance at them will suffice: his lance
 drinks blood of lice (not once but twice).
Ah, many a creature lurking in the seams' folds,
 flanked by its nits,
Spreading its mischief without being seen
 when it creeps along—
Ah, many a jumping-jack was not saved
 by his jumping!
He was killed by the sharp sword-edges
 sheathed in his finger.
Bravo, you hunter whose hounds
 are his nails!

A *Ghazal* Poem by al-ʿAbbās Ibn al-Aḥnaf

بخلتْ عليّ أميرتي بكتابِها   وتبذلت بصدودها وحجابِها
فالنفس في كُرَب الهوى مغمورة   والعين ما تنفكّ من تَسكابِها

bakhilat ʿalayya ʾamīratī bi-kitābihā   *wa-tabadhdhalat bi-ṣudūdihā wa-ḥijābihā*
fa-n-nafsu fī kurabi l-hawā maghmūratun   *wal-ʿaynu mā tanfakku min taskābihā*[151]

Meter (*al-kāmil*): SSLSL SSLSL SSLSL / SSLSL SSLSL SSLSL (SS may be replaced by L).

Al-ʿAbbās ibn al-Aḥnaf, (d. ca. 188/804), who lived in Baghdad, composed only love poetry of a kind sometimes called "courtly," most of it for a high-born, inaccessible lady whose identity is unknown and whom he calls Fawz ("Victoria") and sometimes Ẓalūm ("Unjust"). Suʿād is Fawz's servant girl. The motif of "I wish I were...," at the end, he also employs in other poems; in one he puts into the mouth of Fawz these words: "ʿAbbās, I wish you were my trousers on my body, or / I wish I were the trousers of ʿAbbās! // I wish he were the wine and I the water from / a cloud, forever mixed together in a glass!"[152]

My princess, stingy with her letters, spends
  a lot on spurning me, hiding from sight.
Thus is my soul submerged in passion's pangs;
  my eyes shed streams of tears incessantly.
For how much longer will her anger last?
  I've melted from her anger and reproach.
She seizes someone's heart, all of it; then
  she turns away, leaving him mindless, mad.
5 So much have I endured from Love: woe Love!
  If Love had hands, it would cast out my soul.

Suʿād came, gloating, with a message: "Fawz
  forbids you to come walking past her door!"
What can one, passion's slave, say in reply?
  One is made speechless and cannot respond.
Woe to me, if I try to get in touch,
  and woe to me if I won't try the same.
Suʿād, I beg you, fetch me from her house
  a handful of its dust for me to smell!
Then it will be as if I sip her sweet
  saliva, touch her hennaed fingers fine.
I wish I were her toothbrush, in her hand,[153]
  that I could smell the sweetness of her teeth;
Or that I were her shift, enjoying all
  the softness of her skin and of her clothes,
So that I would not leave her for one hour,
  beneath her clothes, close neighbor to her belt!

Three Love Epigrams by ʿUlayyah bint al-Mahdī

Among the very few free women whose love poems have been preserved is a princess, ʿUlayyah (160/777–210/825), daughter of the caliph al-Mahdī and half-sister of the famous Hārūn al-Rashīd.[154] She was a gifted singer, composer, and poet, and said to have been pious.[155] She composed many short love poems on a few palace servants—one can assume they were eunuchs. One of them was called Rasha' ("Fawn"); in order to conceal not only his identity but also his sex, she referred to him in her verse by a girl's name, Zaynab. Another was called Ṭall ("Dew"), whose name she hid in her verse by adding one dot, changing Ṭall into *ẓill*, meaning "shade" or "shadow". In the first poem it is as if she describes a pretty girl, even though she speaks of a male gazelle. In a strange reversal of gender roles ʿUlayyah thus seems to pose as a man speaking of a girl; the fact that the men were probably eunuchs makes it odder still. In the second piece, in spite of her love for two men, she claims to love only one (at a time?). The third is on the ubiquitous theme of being unable to mention the name of the beloved. ʿUlayyah set all three poems to music and sang them herself.

I. "Greetings to that gazelle"

سلّمْ على ذكرِ الغزا ‍ ‍ ‍ لِ الأغْيدِ المُسْبي الدلالِ
سلّمْ عليه وقلْ له ‍ ‍ ‍ يا غُلَّ ألبابِ الرجالِ

sallim ʿalā dhikri l-ghazā- *li l-ʾaghyadi l-musbī d-dalālī*
sallim ʿalayhi wa-qul lahū *yā ghulla ʾalbābi r-rijālī*[156]

Meter: (*al-kāmil*, shortened form): SSLSL SSLSL / SSLSL SSLSLL (SS may be replaced by L).

Greetings to that gazelle,
so graceful and so tempting!
Greetings to him, and say to him:
O You who keep men's hearts enchained,
You left my body scorching in the sun
while you live in the *shade* of women's quarters.
You've brought me to my wits' end, where
I don't know what to do.

II. "Whoever loves two persons"

حقّ الذي يعشق نفسيْن أن   يُصْلَبَ أو يُنْشرَ بمنشارِ
وعاشقُ الواحد مثلُ الذي   أخلص دِينَ الواحد الباري

ḥaqqu lladhī yaʿshaqu nafsayni ʾan *yuṣlaba ʾaw yunshar*[157] *bi-minshārī*
wa-ʿāshiqu l-wāḥidi mithlu lladhī *ʾakhlaṣa dīna l-wāḥidi l-bārī*[158]

Meter (*al-sarīʿ*): XLSL LXSL LSL / XLSL LXSL LL.

Whoever loves two persons should
be crucified or sawn in twain.
But loving only one is like believing with
one's whole heart in the One Creator.
I have endured it until sickness conquered me:
Can halfa grass[159] withstand the fire?
If I can't hope for his, my master's, sympathy
I will remain as if I sat between two stools.[160]

III. "I have hidden the name of my love"

كتمتُ اسم الحبيب من العباد وردّدتُ الصبابة في فؤادي
فواشوقي إلى بلدٍ خليّ لعلّي باسْم من أهوى أنادي

katamtu sma l-ḥabībi mina l-ʿibādī *wa-raddadtu ṣ-ṣabābata fī fuʾādī*
fa-wā-shawqī ʾilā baladin khaliyyin *laʿallī bi-smi man ʾahwā ʾunādī*[161]

Meter (*al-wāfir*): SLSSL SLSSL SLL / SLSSL SLSSL SLL (SS may be replaced by L). Note that the rhyming hemistichs in the first line give the poem the rhyme scheme (though not the meter) of the *rubāʿiyyah* or quatrain (*aaba*), a later, Persian form adopted by Arab poets too.

I have hidden the name of my love from the crowd:
for my passion my heart is the only safe space.
How I long for an empty and desolate place
in order to call my love's name out aloud.

A *Zuhdiyyah* (“Poem of Asceticism”) by Abū l-ʿAtāhiyah

أهلَ القبورِ عليكُمُ منّي السلامُ إنّي أكلّمكم وليس بكم كلامُ
لا تحسبوا أنّ الأحبّةَ لم يسُغْ من بعدكم لهمُ الشرابُ ولا الطعامُ

ʾahla l-qubūri ʿalaykumū minnī s-salāmū *ʾinnī ʾukallimukum wa-laysa bikum kalāmū*
lā taḥsabū ʾanna l-ʾaḥibbata lam yasugh *min baʿdikum lahumu sh-sharābu wa-lā ṭ-ṭaʿāmū*[162]

Meter (*al-kāmil*): SSLS SSLS SSLSL / SSLS SSLS SSLSL L[163] (SS may be replaced by L).

Most of the output of Abū l-ʿAtāhiyah (131/748–211/826) is devoted to the gloomy theme of *zuhd*: abstemiousness, renunciation of worldly pleasures, asceticism. To some extent one might consider it religious poetry; but Abū l-ʿAtāhiyah is more concerned with death and decay than with resurrection and the Afterlife. In this poem the poet alludes to several motifs found in the opening of traditional *qaṣīdah*s: the abode abandoned by those who have departed, the “interrogation” of the remains, and the addressing of two friends. The diction is relatively simple, as in most of his poetry. (For a small fragment of his sententious “Poem of Proverbs,” see below, p. 95, in the section on *rajaz*.)

You who dwell in graves: from me, a greeting!
 I speak to you but there’s no speech in you.
Don’t think that those you loved cannot enjoy,
 now that you’re dead, their food and drink!
O no! They have dismissed you and made others take
 your place, and death has separated you.
All people are like that: no one who’s dead
 has claims on those who live.
I asked the tombs of kings: they told me they
 contained but limbs and skulls:

Nothing remains of bodies fed on finest food
and lives of luxury but bones.
Fine fellows they, now decked with dust,
such noble men, when people spoke of noble men!
Fine fellows they, now decked with dust,
whose protégés were safe and unabused!
All brought to nought by him who brings great kings to nought:
mankind is made for nothingness and for decay.
O my two friends! I have forgotten my lasting Abode;
I have inhabited a house that will not stay,
A house whose dwellers Fate will want to move,
while they appear to be asleep to what its wants from them.
Whatever pleasure I derived from it, Time's course
refused to make it last.

Ibn al-Rūmī: On His Poetry

قولا لمن عاب شِعر مادح　　أما ترى كيف رُكّب الشجرُ

رُكّب فيه اللحاءُ والخشب　　اليابس والشوك بينه الثمرُ

qūlā li-man ʿāba shiʿra mādiḥihī　　*ʾa-mā tarā kayfa rukkiba sh-shajarū*

rukkiba fīhi l-liḥāʾu wal-khashabu　　*l-yābisu wash-shawku baynahu th-thamarū*[164]

Meter (*al-munsariḥ*): XXSL LSLS LSSL / XXSL LSLS LSSL.

ʿAlī ibn al-ʿAbbās ibn Jurayj, called Ibn al-Rūmī (221/836–283/896), was the son of a Byzantine convert. He lived in Baghdad as a professional poet, excelling not only in panegyrical odes (some of them very long) but also in epigrams. He produced a large number of extremely vile lampoons, both short and lengthy. His style is often argumentative, almost prosaic. He is known for his exhaustive treatment of themes and motifs, as if milking them dry, and for his wayward, unconventional opinions, such as preferring black to white, as in the next poem, or the narcissus to the rose, as in the passage quoted by ʿAbd al-Qāhir al-Jurjānī (see below, p. 282).[165]

Say, you two,[166] to the man who finds fault with his eulogist:
　　Do you not see how a tree is composed?
It's composed of bark and dry wood
　　and of thorns, with fruits in between.
One might expect a good finish in things that the Lord
　　of Lords has created, rather than man;
But there isn't! Or rather, there is the opposite,
　　for reasons ordained by divine decree.
And God knows better than we about the decrees in His
　　providence: everything is for the best.
So let people forgive him who falters and him
　　who falls short in his verse: he is human!

8 And let them consider that minds are exhausted
and thoughts worked to death for its sake!
7 In his quest he resembles a diver who dives in the depths
of the sea, seeking pearls at his peril;
9 There, choices are made when one picks up the precious
and leaves what remains.
10 He who dives deep cannot help coming up
with choice pearls and with trash.

A *Qaṣīdah* by Ibn al-Rūmī: A Party at ʿAbd al-Malik ibn Ṣāliḥ al-Hāshimī's

تبارك الله خالق الكرم البارع من حمَأة ومن علَقِ
ماذا رعيناه في جناب فتًى كا لبدر يجلو غواشيَ الغسَقِ

tabāraka llāhu khāliqu l-karami l- *bāriʿu min ḥamʾatin wa-min ʿalaqī*
mādhā raʿaynāhu fī janābi fatan kal- *badri yajlū ghawāshiya l-ghasaqī*[167]

Meter (*al-munsariḥ*): XXSL LSLS LSSL / XXSL LSLS LSSL.

The poem begins as a eulogy (with some twenty rather unremarkable lines), on the patron, Abū l-Faḍl ʿAbd al-Malik ibn Ṣāliḥ, a rather obscure member of the ruling Abbasid dynasty.[168] More interesting is the description of a drinking party in ʿAbd al-Malik's house, which serves as an excuse for singing the praises of a black slave girl belonging to him, in highly erotic, even pornographic style. The section on the black girl is often quoted in medieval anthologies. The anthologist al-Ḥuṣrī (*Zahr al-ādāb*, pp. 274–277) praises the poem because of its original and unconventional argument in favor of the color black.[169] Perhaps because of the presence of the erotic passage in the course of the poem the poet has dispensed with a *nasīb* ("amatory introduction.")

Blessed be God, creator of munificence, who made
mankind from mud and clotted blood!
Such things we saw in the protection of a man
like the full moon, dispelling twilight's gloom!
All times are, through his bounties, like
the springtime in its loveliness.
More famous for his bounty among men
than Piebald Palace, for all its colors;[170]
A valiant man who thinks that glory is impaired
by being glorified, a box without a lid.

He dearly pays for praise, even though it robs him
of everything except the barest needs.[171]
You'll find in him, if you desire, a pasture lush
or else a flowing well;
Thus one may graze there, without fear of surfeit, or
one drinks there without fear of being choked.
His name is Abū l-Faḍl, "Favor's Father,"
favor's refuge—I speak not out of flattery.
The best of names for men to have are those
not arrogated falsely, names not stolen.
He, ʿAbd al-Malik has adorned himself with necklaces
of splendid favors[172] as of old.
He uses money, when he has it, as protection
like coats of mail or shields.[173]
His kin are the Abbasids, noble folk,
leaders, at the forefront from the start.
He is a sea of seas: you stay with him and you'll
be buffeted by waves of his munificence.
His bucket overflows with boons
for those who ask for them.
His hands give freely and his tongue
speaks freely when approached for gifts:
A gift of goods and one of wisdom, in one man
most perfectly combined.
He strives for any aim that is extreme,
never yet sought, never achieved,
Like an unstumbling noble steed, without
knock-knees that might impair his speed.
A witness testifying to his noble stock
is his pure character, unstained.
His excellence makes him the meeting-place
of every creed or sect or tendency.
We fell on fertile ground with him,
a pasture ground, or rain-soaked land.
A singer like a bird sang at his place for us,
a first-class singer, and no mere supporting act.[174]

He sang, and he revived our happiness,
even when he found it on the point of death.
He whose good fortune makes him drink with him
at dawn will still be drinking in the evening.
He pours the wine for them: they drink
like Pharaoh when he drowned.[175]
His old and modern songs both give delight;
the new and threadbare, both sound new with him.[176]
His only fault is that he is a man
who calls upon wise people to be frivolous.
The good things that he brings upset a sober man
but soothe someone who is upset.
His nickname: "Piece of Well-Being and Peace":
peace be upon those pieces![177]
It's Abū Sulaymān, the master of what's right
and beautiful, the son of princes, not the common crowd.
How beautiful that singing, in duet
with the sad cooing of the doves,
From one with many-colored, finely-woven clothes,
from gloom of night to snowy white,
While we are given wine to drink, poured in
profusion, praised by pleasant company.
He lets all those who ask it drink their fill;
he's never angry when he pours his fellow drinker's cup.
His butler takes good care of all his guests,
his hand dispenses fearlessly
From ample amphoras like corpses of
the bulky-bodied tribe of ʿĀd.[178]
There came a thing that, if a fly came near it, then
the fly would soon be near its death.[179]
It comes to you as delicate as wine itself, with scent
of lavender and yellowness of evening glow.
In its appearance it appears to be forbidden, but
its drinkers would commit no sin.[180]
Contained in it is a pure drink, like gold,
spumante, with the frothy bubbles like split pearls.

It prances proudly, its apparel
 stolen from the old full-bodied wine.
It is passed round by a dark girl who with her charms
 burns with a blaze where white girls merely give a spark,
A black girl, not one of those leprous white,
 the spotty freckled, or albino pale,
Not one of those with as-if-dirty hands,
 or with split lower lip, or reeking sweat,
But a sweet princess, one who with her charms
 would resurrect a moribund libido,
Sleek like a sable marten favored by
 the furrier, smooth like a first-rate weasel pelt,
She will remind you of sweet scents: musk, *ghāliyah*,
 and *sukk*, with all their smells and fragrances.[181]
A slender girl, adorned with a slim waist that may be hugged,
 above which swelling breasts may be embraced;
A branch of ebony, composed of parts
 wrapped in a skirt, encircled by a belt,
That trembles with its swelling fruits
 and the dark foliage above.
Dyed with the dye of a man's heart of heart
 and of the pupils of his eyes, she has earned love.[182]
Thus minds and eyes are turned
 toward her, galloping at breakneck speed.
Smiling, that blackness shows her
 bright, white teeth, like well-strung pearls.
When laughing at a joke, she's like a night
 the gloom of which is ripped apart by dawn.
A deep-black girl, dark like a flawless filly that
 outruns the clouds of dust that it kicks up,
It runs, its rival running next to her,
 a racing couple at full speed hurtling along.
She has a cunt[183] the blaze of which is borrowed from
 a lover's heart, a furious breast;
Its heat, to him who tries it, seems to be
 the burning flames she kindled in his heart.

When in the act, its tightness steadily
    increases, like the slipping knot of a lasso.
When a strong long-necked thing will interfere with it,
    it grips it, as a strangling noose throttles a throat.
He who imagines this in his own mind
    says, "Blessèd be the key that will unlock this lock!"
How she deserves to stand up from a penis like
    a sword that pierces double coats of mail!
Sword sheaths are mostly black:
    this is a fact that's true and not made up.
Accept this poem, Abū l-Faḍl, as a cloth made
    from the silk[184] of eulogies and not of rags.
I have described in it what I had wished in my
    imagination, without testing her or tasting her,
But only from what you have told me, of that sweet
    gazelle of sandy, rocky tracts.[185]
Far be it that a black-skinned woman living in your house
    should have a reputation anything but spotless white!
One of the reasons for preferring black
    (truth may be reached with ladders or dark tunnels underground)
Is that pitch-black is never blamed, while white
    is sometimes blamed when livid, pale and wan.[186]
Ah, what a robe of honor that emaciates a spiteful man
    but which will not reveal the fires underneath![187]
Here, of its own accord, its poet's love has come to you,
    and not unwillingly, driven by force,
Though you deny your friends such robes that shield
    from harm of cold or harm of a damp day,
Preferring to clothe others with them, not
    producing any milk when it is due:[188]
Give them what is their due, don't set yourself
    in blame's way or you'll find yourself in a bad spot!
My need, if you will send it to me in Iskāf or in
    the Monastery, will have a friendly face.[189]
Or else, the door of an apology is still unbarred,
    for sure, nor is the door of livelihood.

A Panegyric *Qaṣīdah* by al-Buḥturī

أكان الصِّبا إلا خيالا مسلّما أقام كرجع الطرْف ثمّ تصرّما
أرى أقصرَ الأيام أحمدَ في الصبا وأطْولها ما كان فيه مذمّما

ʾa-kāna ṣ-ṣibā ʾillā khayālan musallimā ʾaqāma ka-rajʿi ṭ-ṭarfi thumma taṣarramā
ʾarā ʾaqṣara l-ʾayyāmi ʾaḥmada fī ṣ-ṣibā wa-ʾaṭwalahā mā kāna fīhi mudhammamā[190]

Meter (*al-ṭawīl*): SLX SLLL SLX SLSL / SLX SLLL SLX SLSL.

Abū ʿUbādah al-Walīd ibn ʿUbayd al-Buḥturī (206/821–284/897) has often been compared and contrasted with his older colleague, Abū Tammām; both came from Syria (belonging to the tribe of Ṭayyiʾ) and specialized in odes composed for a range of patrons, although both excelled in other genres too. Whereas Abū Tammām was considered the prototype of the "difficult" poet, with his artful and often rather contrived style, al-Buḥturī, less original but smoother, was deemed the more naturally gifted poet. The present ode, dedicated in 255/869 to a general called Abū l-Qāsim al-Haytham ibn ʿUthmān al-Ghanawī, is praised especially for its nature description: the patron is compared with springtime. It opens in traditional style, with a *nasīb*, containing a departure scene. The transition to the eulogy (lines 10–11) is rather abrupt.

What else was youth if not a phantom:[191] it arrived
to greet us, stayed the twinkling of an eye, and passed.
The shortest day, in youth, I found the best;
even the longest, then, could not be spurned.[192]
I lingered long in blameful, youthful folly, cared
for nothing else—a fool, would he accept rebuke?
On many a day of meeting before parting I
held back my tears—my eyes shed blood instead.[193]

We found the tribe all set, that morning, for
departure to their own protected pasture grounds.
I said, Good morrow[194] to you all!—but I,
in what I said, meant only her, that sweet gazelle.
Only a man in love lives in the folds
of freely giving favors, after separation.
I lived a life of luxury, alongside beauties who
led me along, until youth's bloom had gone, even beyond.
I used to disobey reproachful women, heedless of
the first white hairs appearing on my head.
I say to the torrential evening rain cloud that
has packed its downpours for a deluge all-pervading:
Let loose a little or a lot, you'll never reach
a level to be noted, until you are Haytham's like!
He's Death, beware of him and his sword's edge:
to meet this warrior in battle's dust cloud is your death.
A hero[195] with whose virtues Fate[196] has clothed itself,
illuminating the horizon that was dark before;
A man well-tried in war, which straightened strong resolve:
a Khaṭṭī lance will not be true until made straight.
He came; Nizār and Yaʿrub came to pray for him
that he may live forever safely in their midst.[197]
He humbly owns their glory and nobility:
high-minded men hate haughtiness.
In every tribe there is a branch of his beneficence;
among them, one is special when he names his tribe.
So far went his munificence to them: they swore
his generosity is the twin brother of the sea.[198]
So copious, Abū l-Qāsim, are your merits that
they fill all roads on earth for good or ill.[199]
Those trying to keep up with you in glory fall
behind as much as you're ahead.[200]
Salaam!—if this word is a greeting, then your face
alone suffices as an answer to the greeter.
Look! the Euphrates swells as if it were
the mountains of Sharawrā, swimming in the flood,[201]

Which it was not its wont to do: it saw
its neighbor's nature, and it learned from him.
Nor is it Syria's garden blossoming:
a hero in the east has smiled, and so it smiled.
Bright Spring has come to you, so proudly strutting,
laughing in its beauty, that it almost speaks.
New Year[202] has woken, in the dark before the dawn,
the early roses that, last night, were still asleep.
The coolness of the dew has opened them: as if
to let them hear some news, suppressed until today.
Many a tree, its clothes restored by spring
as one unfolds embroidered, multicolored cloth,
Has donned its proper dress, appearing joyously,
eyesore no longer, as it was in pilgrim's gear.
So softly blows the gentle breeze you'd think
it brings the tender breaths of those you love.
So what is holding back the wine, whose friend you are,
and what forbids the strings to sing?[203]
For you remain a sun for drunken boon companions, when
they have become full moons, urging on stars.[204]
But you were generous to them before the cups;
those could not make you more so than you are!

A Victory Ode by al-Mutanabbī: The *Qaṣīdah* on Sayf al-Dawlah's Recapture of the Fortress of al-Ḥadath in 343/954

على قدرِ أهل العزم تأتي العزائمُ وتأتي على قدر الكرام المكارمُ
وتعظُم في عين الصغير صغارُها وتصغُر في عين العظيم العظائمُ

ʿalā qadri ʾahli l-ʿazmi taʾtī l-ʿazāʾimū *wa-taʾtī ʿalā qadri l-kirāmi l-makārimū*
wa-taʿẓumu fī ʿayni ṣ-ṣaghīri ṣighāruhā *wa-taṣghuru fī ʿayni l-ʿaẓīmi l-ʿaẓāʾimū*[205]

Meter (*al-ṭawīl*): SLX SLLL SLX SLSL / SLX SLLL SLX SLSL.

Abū l-Ṭayyib Aḥmad ibn al-Ḥusayn (ca. 303/915–354/365), nicknamed al-Mutanabbī ("the would-be prophet") for a youthful escapade, is generally considered (especially by Arabs) as the greatest Arabic poet in Islamic times. He excelled in panegyric odes, such as the famous *Sayfiyyāt* dedicated to the Ḥamdānid ruler Sayf al-Dawlah who regularly campaigned against the Byzantines. Although *qaṣīdah*s normally begin with a *nasīb* or some kind of lyrical introduction, it was customary to omit this in congratulatory poems and victory odes such as the following.[206]

Firm resolutions happen in proportion to the resolute,
  and noble deeds come in proportion to the noble.
Small deeds are great in small men's eyes,
  great deeds, in great men's eyes, are small.
Sayf al-Dawlah charges the army with the burden of his zeal,
  which large hosts are not strong enough to bear,
And he demands of men what only he can do—
  even lions do not claim as much.
The longest-living birds, the desert vultures, young and old,
  offer themselves as ransom for his arms.[207]

It would not harm them had they been created without claws:
his swords have been created and their hilts.
Does "Red" al-Ḥadath know its color, does it know
which of the two wine-pourers was the clouds?[208]
White clouds have watered it before he came,
and then, when he drew near, the skulls drenched it again.
He built it, raised it high, while shaft beat against shaft,
and waves of Doom clashed all around.
Possessed by some demonic madness, it was decked
with corpses of the slain, as charms and amulets.
Driven off by Fate it was: but you restored it to the Faith,
with Khaṭṭī lances, in spite of Fate.[209]
You force the Nights[210] to give up all you seize
and if they seize from you they must repay.
If what you plan is an imperfect verb it is
past tense before preventing prefixes can be attached.[211]
How can the Byzantines and Russians[212] hope to raze the place
when it is propped by lance thrusts as its pillars and its base?
To court they took it, with the Fates as judges, but
the wronged ones did not die, nor any wrong-doer live.
They came to you, trailing their steel, as though
they rode by night on horses without feet.
Brightly they shone; their white swords could not be distinguished from
their clothing and their head gear, all alike of steel;
An army crawling forth from east and west,
its din, cacaphonous, reaching Orion's ears;
Each tongue, each nation gathered there:
only interpreters could make the speakers understood.
Ah, what a time! Its fire melted the counterfeit as dross
and only left sharp swords and warriors like lions.
A sword that could not cut a mail-coat or a spear was cut itself,
a warrior who would not fight his foe would flee.
You stood your ground when standing firm seemed certain death,
as though you were in Death's eye, Death being asleep.
The warriors passed by you, wounded, routed, but
your face shone brightly, your mouth smiled.

You passed beyond the bounds of courage and of intellect:
they said that you had knowledge of the supernatural.
You pressed their wings upon the heart, so that
the coverts[213] and the primaries were dying under it,
With blows that struck the skulls when victory was distant,
and then struck breasts, as victory advanced.
Despising the Rudaynī spears,[214] you flung them far away:
it was as if the sword reviled the spear.
Whoever wishes to unlock a glorious victory,
its keys are light, bright, cutting swords.[215]
You scattered them all over al-Uḥaydib,[216] just
like dirhams strewn over a bride.
Your horses trampled birds' nests on the hilltops, but
plenty of food was left there round the nests!
The eaglets thought that you had brought their mothers back:
they were in fact your noble sturdy steeds.
Whenever horses slipped you made them walk upon
their bellies, just as speckled snakes crawl on the earth.
Will this "Domesticus" advance upon you every day,
his neck blaming his face for his advance?[217]
Does he not know the lion's scent before he gets a taste of it?
Dumb beasts know well the lion's scent!
The brutal onslaughts of our leader hit him hard:
his son, his brother-in-law and his son, all killed.
He left, thanking his troops for his escape from the sharp swords,
that were too busy dealing with their heads and limbs.
He understood the speech of swords from Mashraf[218] to his troops,
even though they speak a foreign speech.
He was so glad with what he gave to you, not out of ignorance,
but by escaping with such losses, gaining life as spoils of war.[219]
And you are not a king who routs his rival: you
are Monotheist Faith that routs Polytheism,
In whom not just Rabīʿah are ennobled but all Arabs of ʿAdnān,[220]
in whom not just the frontier towns but all the world takes pride.
Yours is the praise due for these pearls that I am uttering:
you are their giver, I am merely stringing them.[221]

Your gifts gallop with me into the din of war;[222]
I earn no blame and you have no regrets
Of giving any horse that flies into the fray, yet on its feet,
as soon as it can hear the battle cries.
O Sword never to be sheathed, in whom there is no doubt,
from whom no one can ever be protected:
Let there be joy to smiting heads, to glory, and high deeds,
to all who hope Islam and you are safe!
Why should the Merciful not guard your cutting edges as before,
so that through you He will forever cleave the heads of foes!

Nature Poetry: Two Epigrams by Ibn Khafājah

Ibn Khafājah (450/1058–533/1139), who lived in the province of Valencia in al-Andalus, was famous for his nature poetry, in which he often personifies or humanizes nature.

I. Hail

يا ربّ قطرٍ جامد حلّى به   نحرِ الثرى بَرَدٌ تحدّر صائبُ
حَصَب الأباطحَ منه ماءٌ جامد   غشى البلادَ به عذابٌ ذائبُ

yā rubba qaṭrin jāmidin ḥallā bihī   *naḥra th-tharā baradun taḥaddara ṣā'ibū*
ḥaṣaba l-abāṭiḥa minhu mā'un jāmidun   *ghashā l-bilāda bihī 'adhābun dhā'ibū*[223]

Meter (*al-kāmil*): SSLSL SSLSL SSLSL / SSLSL SSLSL SSLSL (SS may be replaced by L).

With solid drops[224] the hail that showered down
has oft adorned the neck of Mother Earth.
The frozen water pelts the plains with pebbles and
the land is covered by a melting punishment.
The earth is laughing, flaunting necklaces of stars,
but strewn, unstrung; the sky is sullen, glowering:
As if the earth, beneath, were an adulteress
and pelting clouds were busy stoning it.

II. A River

لله نهرٌ سال في بطحاءِ أشهى ورودا من لمى الحسناءِ
متعطف مثل السوار كأنه والزهرُ يكنفه مجرُّ سماءِ

lillāhi nahrun sāla fī baṭḥā'ī *'ashhā wurūdan min lamā l-ḥasnā'ī*
muta'aṭṭifun mithla s-siwāri ka-'annahū *waz-zahru yaknufuhū majarru samā'ī*[225]

Meter (*al-kāmil*): SSLSL SSLSL SSLSL / SSLSL SSLSL LLSL (SS may be replaced by L).

Ah God, what a river! It flows in the valley,
 a watering place lovelier than a girl's crimson lips,
As it bends like a bracelet; flanked by flowers
 it resembles the Milky Way.
So delicate that one would think it a ribbon[226] of silver,
 set in a mantle of green.
It is bordered by branches
 like eyelashes round a blue eye.
So oft have I drunk there a yellowish wine
 that would dye drinkers' hands[227]
As the wind plays with twigs, and the afternoon's gold
 moves along on the silvery water.

Strophic Poem: A *Muwashshaḥah* by al-Aʿmā al-Tuṭīlī

دمعٌ صَفوحٌ وضُلوعٌ حرارْ   ماءٌ ونارْ   ما التقيا إلا لأمرٍ كُبارْ
بئس لعمري ما أراد العَذولْ   عمرٌ قصيرٌ وعناءٌ طويلْ
يا زفراتٍ نطقتْ عن غليلْ   ويا دموعًا قد أصابت مسيلْ

damʿun safūḥun wa-ḍulūʿun ḥirār
māʾun wa-nār
mā ltaqayā ʾillā li-ʾamrin kubār
biʾsa la-ʿamrī mā ʾarāda l-ʿadhūl
ʿumrun qaṣīrun wa-ʿanāʾun ṭawīl
yā zafarātin naṭaqat ʿan ghalīl
wa-yā dumūʿan qad ʾaṣābat masīl[228]

In order to show the structure of this and a few other strophic poems, a complete strophe is given in transliteration.

Structure: RRR aaaa RRR bbbb RRR cccc RRR dddd RRR eeee RRR; strophes indicated with capitals are *asmāṭ*, sg. *simṭ*, those with lower case are *aghṣān*, sg. *ghuṣn*. The opening *simṭ* is sometimes called *maṭlaʿ* and the last *simṭ* is called *kharjah*, which often employs a form of colloquial Arabic and sometimes, as here, Romance or proto-Spanish. The *kharjah* is often put into the mouth of a girl who sings (but here a masculine form is found). The reading and interpretation of this *kharjah* are controversial.[229] Strophic poetry, which originated in Spain, spread to the East. The poems, mostly lyrical, are usually meant to be sung.

Meter: not all *muwashshaḥāt* can be scanned according to the classical meters, but this one is clearly based on the *sarīʿ*: XXSL XXSL LSL, with an extra foot (XLSL) inserted in the *simṭ*.

The poet Aḥmad ibn ʿAbd Allāh (d. 525/1130), known as al-Aʿmā al-Tuṭīlī ("the blind man from Tudela") was active mostly in Seville.

tears poured out and hot ribs
water and fire
do not come together but for a grave matter
  bad, surely, what the censor wants
  a short life, long misery
  o sighs that speak of ardent love
  o tears that have made a stream
being together is impossible, visiting is remote
where can one find rest
I would fly but have found no place to fly
  o kaaba to which hearts go on pilgrimage
  between passion that calls and yearning that answers
  everyone, moaning, turns to it
  here I am, here I am![230] say to the spy
take me on pilgrimage to her, the greater and the lesser
no excuse
my heart the sacrifice, my tears the pebbles[231]
  welcome though he expose me to death
  one with swaying body and languid eyelids
  o harshness which the lover thinks is softness
  you have taught me how to mistrust
since he holds back from these short nights
my sleep is just a wink
as if a sword's blade lay between my lids
  I have made a master rule whose judgment is unjust
  I allude to him not saying his name outright
  marvel at my fairness against his iniquity
  and ask him about my state and his cutting-off
he took away my share of good fortune, willfully and by choice
obeying his shyness
every human company after him may be chosen freely (?)[232]
  I cannot be without him wherever and wherever
  a master who accuses, is harsh, is arrogant
  he left me a hostage to grief and madness
  then he sang between soberness and seduction:[233]
mon darling est infirme de mon amour
... (?)
... (?)

An Anonymous *Muwashshaḥah* from Spain

من أودع الأجفانْ صوارمَ الهندِ
وأنبت الريحانْ في صفحة الخدّ
قضى على الهيمانْ بالدمع والسُّهدِ
أنّ وللكتمانْ
للهائم المُغرمْ بدمعٍ نمّ إذا يسجمْ بما يكتمْ
من السرّ في عاطلٍ حالي غريرٍ ساطي عليّ بالدُّعج

*man 'awda'a l-'ajfān * ṣawārima l-hindī*
*wa-'anbata r-rayḥan * fī ṣafḥati l-khaddī*
*qaḍā 'alā l-haymān * bid-dam'i was-suhdī*
'annā wa-lil-kitmān
*lil-hā'imi l-mughram * bi-dam'in namm * 'idhā yasjum * bimā yaktum*
*mina s-sirrī * fī 'āṭilin ḥālī * gharīrin sāṭī * 'alayya bid-du'jī*[234]

Structure: abababa RRRR STUV cdcdcdc RRRR STUV efefefe RRRR STUV ghghghg RRRR STUV ijijiji RRRR STUV; meter (non-classical): XXSL LL (8 times) SLLL (4 times) XLSL LL SLLLL XXSL LL.

This poem has been chosen partly because of the complex nature of its prosodic structure. Its *kharjah* is in vernacular Arabic. *Dār al-ṭirāz* (*The House of Embroidery*)[235] is a work by the Egyptian poet Ibn Sanā' al-Mulk (d. 608/1211) in which he discusses the *muwashshaḥ* genre, especially its formal aspects, and illustrates it by incorporating a number of Andalusian examples, from among which this one is taken, followed by his own compositions. The editor thinks the poet may be Ibn al-Labbānah (d. 507/1113),[236] because his poetry shows some parallels in diction and, like in the present poem, a certain Aḥmad is mentioned in his poetry.

He who loads his eyes
    with cutting Indian swords
and grows sweet basil on
    the surface of his cheeks[237]
condemns the one who loves him madly
    to tears and sleeplessness.
How could he hide it,

the witless lover?
His tears reveal
when they flow
what he hides
    in his breast
        for a pretty one not in need of ornaments,
            inexperienced, yet overpowering
                me with his black eyes.

How dear to me, this big-eyed boy,
    like a full moon on the fullest night,
revealing pearls
    sweet to kiss,
while his radiant cheek
    bleeds from mere fancy:[238]
how can I be excused,

now that a speckled snake has crept
over the brazilwood[239]
so that it can't be kissed,
and he has empowered
    with his magic,
        to kill heroes,
            with the Nabataeans,
                an army of Negroes.[240]

I prostrate myself before the fire
    like the Man of Mount Sinai.[241]
He's like a full moon in the dark
    with his body like a reed,
he's like a rod of crystal
    set on a hillock of camphor.[242]
With the soul of an abandoned one[243]

I ransom him though he makes me an orphan
In the sealed place
of the teeth of his mouth,
a string
    of pearls,
        is my wine and my fresh water;
            teeth in rows
                with fragrant gaps.

Beauty inalienably
    is yours, Aḥmad,
command is turned over to you,
    slender one,
your slave madly in love
    with you, enslaved.
Will you rebuke me,

or will you pity me,
stop the wasting away
of a lover
when he ails?
    Woe unto me! Imprisoned in
        my sea of fears
            with far-off shore
                I cling to waves.

A pretty girl appears,
    just like a rising moon,
swaying with the weight of her breasts[244]
    on a laurel branch,
its leaves a mantle
    flowering with roses.
At night she sings:

Sweet love, make up your mind!
Come on, attack!
And kiss my mouth
and come and press yourself
    against my breast
        and raise my anklets
            to my earrings.[245]
                My husband is at work!

"There Descended to You": A Philosophical Allegory by Ibn Sīnā

هبطتْ إليك من المحلّ الأرفعِ　　ورقاءُ ذاتُ تعزّزٍ وتمنّعِ
محجوبةٌ عن كل مُقلةِ عارفٍ　　وهي التي سفرتْ ولم تتبرقعِ

habaṭat ʾilayka mina l-maḥalli l-ʾarfaʿī　　*warqāʾu dhātu taʿazzuzin wa-tamannuʿī*
maḥjūbatun ʿan kulli muqlati ʿārifin　　*wa-hya llatī safarat wa-lam tatabarqaʿī*[246]

Meter (*al-kāmil*): SSLSL SSLSL SSLSL / SSLSL SSLSL SSLSL (SS may be replaced by L).

Ibn Sīnā or Avicenna (d. 428/1037) was a scholar of Persian descent who wrote most of his extremely influential medical and philosophical works in Arabic prose. Unlike most other philosophers writing in Arabic he had distinctly literary gifts. He wrote several allegorical tales on esoteric matters. His most famous poem is the following, an interpretation of the old Platonic idea of the human soul: it exists before birth, descends into a body, first longing back for the higher world but eventually returning reluctantly. It should be mentioned that one scholar, al-Sharīshī (d. 619/1222) believed that Ibn Sīnā could not have composed the poem, on the grounds that he did not believe in the existence of the individual soul before birth.[247]

There descended to you from the highest place
　an ash-colored dove, inapproachable, proud,
One veiled from even every Knower's eye,[248]
　yet herself without burka or veil.
She came to you with reluctance; she may well part
　from you reluctantly too, dismayed.
Disdainful at first, ill at ease; but, going along,
　getting used to living so close to desolate wasteland,

Forgetting, I think, her old haunts: sacred meadows
and dwellings, unhappy to have been left behind.
When joined to the *D* of Descent from the *S*
of her Station in Dhāt al-Ajraʿ,
She adhered to the *H* of Heavy and came to stay
among waymarks and humble vestigial abodes.[249]
Now she cries, when she thinks of the homes of
her meadows, her eyes full of tears unstinting,
Cooing continuously on the dung-strewn remains,
effaced by the four recurrent winds.
The thick, coarse net has trapped her, a cage prevents her
from reaching the highest regions, spacious and lush.
But when it is nearly time to go to those grounds
and departure is nigh, to that widest expanse,
And she parts from all things left as allies of earth
that are not to accompany her,
She slumbers; the covers are raised; and she sees
what will never be seen by slumbering eyes.
And she starts to sing on the top of a lofty mount
—and knowledge will raise all those not raised—.
So why was she made to descend from that high,
lofty place to the depth of the lowest abyss?
If God in His wisdom has made her descend,
that wisdom is hidden from even the cleverest mind.
For if the descent had to be, so that
she could hear what she had not yet heard,
And return with the knowledge of both worlds' secrets,
the rents in her dress will never be mended.
For Time has crossed her path, cut her off:
her sun has set, never to rise again.
She was like the lightning that flashed in the meadow,
then vanished, as if it had never flared.

Five Epigrams on Death and Belief, by Abū l-ʿAlāʾ al-Maʿarrī

Abū l-ʿAlāʾ al-Maʿarrī (363/973–449/1057) was born in Maʿarrat al-Nuʿmān in Syria. Blind from early childhood, he was an important poet and prose writer, and also an eccentric, controversial for his allegedly heretical ideas (including being a vegan). Of his two substantial collections of verse the later one is called *Luzūm mā lā yalzam* (*The Necessity of What is Not Necessary*), or *al-Luzūmiyyāt*, after the self-imposed "rich rhyme" (the rhyme of each poem is based on two consonants rather than one) and some further voluntary restrictions. Instead of the conventional mixture of genres this large collection consists only of gnomic poetry, mostly short and epigrammatic. The poet pours his scorn on the world; he hates all men, and women even more. At times he seems to reject the conventional dogmas and rites of Islam, even though in most other poems he is, or poses as, a pious Muslim. A splendid selection of more than three hundred fragments in English translation, often rendered as poetry, is contained in Nicholson, *Studies in Islamic Poetry*, pp. 43–289 ("The Meditations of Maʿarrí"). In the prose section of this anthology a lengthy passage from his most famous prose work is offered.

I. "We laughed"

ضحكنا وكان الضحكُ منا سفاهةً وحُق لسُكّان البسيطة أن يبكوا
يحطّمنا رَيبُ الزمان كأننا زُجاج ولكن لا يُعاد له سَبْكُ

ḍaḥiknā wa-kāna ḍ-ḍiḥku minnā safāhatan wa-ḥuqqa li-sukkāni l-basīṭati ʾan yabkū
yuḥaṭṭimunā raybu z-zamāni ka-ʾannanā zujājun wa-lākin lā yuʿādu lahū sabkū[250]

Meter (*al-ṭawīl*): SLX SLLL SLX SLSL / SLX SLLL SLS LLL.

We laughed, and O how foolish was our laughter!
Dwellers on earth should cry and never cease.
Time's vagaries crush us like glass; thereafter
We'll never be remolded as one piece.

II. "If after death"

لوكان جسمك متروكًا بهيئته	بعد التلاف طمعنا في تلافيهِ
كالدَّنّ عُطّل من راحٍ تكون به	ولم يحطَّم فعادت مرةً فيهِ

law kāna jismuka matrūkan bi-hay'atihī	*ba'da t-talāfi ṭami'nā fī talāfīhī*
ka-d-danni 'uṭṭila min rāḥin takūnu bihī	*wa-lam yuḥaṭṭam fa-'ādat marratan fīhī*[251]

Meter (*al-basīṭ*): XLSL XSL LLSL SSL / XLSL XSL LLSL LL.

If after death your body kept its shape,
We might hope it will be revived again,
Just as a jug, emptied of wine, could be
Refilled, as long as it remains unbroken.
But all its parts have come undone and turned
To particles of dust swept by the winds.

III. "I wish my death would happen in a desert land"

وددتُ وفاتِيَ في مَهْمَهٍ	به لامعٌ ليس بالمَعْلِم
أموت به واحدًا مُفردًا	وأُدفن في الأرض لم تُظلَمِ

wadidtu wafātiya fī mahmahin	*bihī lāmi'un laysa bil-ma'lamī*
'amūtu bihī wāḥidan mufradan	*wa-'udfanu fī l-'arḍi lam tuẓlamī*[252]

Meter (*al-mutaqārib*): SLX SLX SLX SL(S) / SLX SLX SLX SL.

I wish my death would happen in a desert land
Where shimmering mirages mark no roads.
There would I die, all on my own, alone,
Be buried in unsullied, virgin soil,

Far from a man who says, "No peace on you!"
  Or one who says, "Be greeted, earth!"
I fear you'll make my resting place
  Next to a traitor unbeliever or a Muslim.
"You're pushing!" he will say; I shall reply,
  "It's they who did us wrong; I did not know."

IV. "For holy fear"

يحرّق نفسَه الهنديُّ خوفاً   ويقصر دون ما صنع الجهادُ
وما فعلتْه عُبّاد النصارى   ولا شرعيّة صبأوا وهادوا

yuḥarriqu nafsahu l-hindiyyu khawfan   *wa-yaqṣuru dūna mā ṣanaʿa l-jihādū*
wa-mā faʿalatʾhu ʿubbādu n-naṣārā   *wa-lā sharʿiyyatun ṣabaʾū wa-hādū*[253]

Meter (*al-wāfir*): SLSSL SLSSL SLL / SLSSL SLSSL SLL.

For holy fear the Hindu burns himself
  (Muslim Jihad has never done as much,
Neither did Christian worshipers, nor those
  Who followed Sabian[254] or Jewish creed.)
He takes his body freely to the fire,
  By his religion driven and his zeal.
Man's death is but a very lengthy sleep
  And all his lifetime but insomnia.
We're bid farewell with prayer and despair
  And left alone, unmoving, in the dust.
Should I be scared of earth, of Mother Earth?
  Your mother's lap: a splendid resting place.
When I am parted from my subtle soul,
  Let no spring rains pour on the rotting bones!

V. "Your mouths proclaim"

إن هللتْ أفواهُكم وقلوبكم ونفوسكم دون الحقوق مهلّلهْ
آليتُ ما توراتُكم بمُنيرة إن أُلفيتْ فيها الكُميتُ محلّلهْ

ʾin hallalat ʾafwāhukum fa-qulūbukum *wa-nufūsukum dūna l-ḥuqūqi muhallalah*
ʾālaytu mā tawrātukum bi-munīratin *ʾin ʾulfiyat fīhā l-kumaytu muḥallalah*[255]

Meter (*al-kāmil*): SSLSL SSLSL SSLSL / SSLSL SSLSL SSLSL (SS may be replaced by L).

Your mouths proclaim "There is no god but God,"
Your hearts and souls are scared of being just.
I swear, your Torah brings no light if there
One finds that wine may lawfully be drunk.
Beware the lightning flashes in the clouds:
They are drawn swords of Fate, ready to strike.
A true reflection on Time's incidents
Will ease the fears one finds most difficult.[256]
True Faith[257] has stumbled, Christians are lost,
Jews erring, Zoroastrians astray.
People on earth are two: one bright without
religion[258], one religious without wit.

Mystical *Ghazal*: A Poem by Ibn al-Fāriḍ

ما بين معترَك الأحداق والمُهَج — أنا القتيلُ بلا إثمٍ ولا حَرَج
ودّعتُ قبل الهوى روحي لما نظرتْ — عيناي من حُسْنِ ذاك المنظر البَهِج

mā bayna muʿtaraki l-ʾaḥdāqi wal-muhajī *ʾana l-qatīlu bi-lā ʾithmin wa-lā ḥarajī*
waddaʿtu qabla l-hawā rūḥī li-mā naẓarat *ʿaynāya min ḥusni dhāka l-manẓari l-bahijī*[259]

Particularly euphonious are lines 29–34:

tarāhu ʾin ghāba ʿannī kullu jāriḥatin *fī kulli maʿnan laṭīfin rāʾiqin bahijī*
fī naghmati l-ʿūdi wan-nāyi r-rakhīmi ʾidhā *taʾallafā bayna ʾalḥānin mina l-hazajī*
wa-fī masāriḥi ghizlāni l-khamāʾili fī *bardi l-ʾaṣāʾili wal-ʾiṣbāḥi fī l-balajī*
wa-fī masāqiṭi ʾandāʾi l-ghamāmi ʿalā *bisāṭi nawrin mina l-ʾazhāri muntasijī*
wa-fī masāḥibi ʾadhyāli n-nasīmi ʾidhā *ʾahdā ʾilayya suḥayran ʾaṭyaba l-ʾarajī*
wa-fī ltithāmiya thaghra l-kaʾsi murtashifan *rīqa l-mudāmati fī muntazahin farijī*

Meter (*al-basīṭ*): XXSL XSL LLSL SSL / XXSL XSL LLSL SSL.

The Egyptian ʿUmar Ibn al-Fāriḍ (576/1181–632/1235) is one of the greatest mystical (*Ṣūfī*) poets in Arabic. He uses profane themes and imagery, taken from love poetry (as here) or Bacchic verse. The ultimate aim of the mystic is Union with God, through annihilation of the self. In their endless attempts to express the inexpressible, the mystic poets find many suitable motifs in secular love poetry, especially of the ʿUdhrite type, where the beloved is remote and the lover relishes his suffering. The following poem elaborates this theme in several paradoxes.

Amidst the battleground of eyes and souls
I'm slain, but without sin or guilt.[260]

I bade my soul farewell before I fell in love,[261]
after my eyes beheld that radiant sight.
O eyelids, justly sleepless on account of you,
in yearning, and a heart anguished with love,
And ribs wasted with love, their crookedness
straightened, almost, by the hot passion of my heart,
And streaming tears, in which I nearly drowned,
had I not sighed hot breaths from passion's fire!
Welcome to sicknesses because of you, that hid me from
myself:[262] my proofs that in love's court stand up.
Morning and evening I am sad because of you,
yet do not cry in anguish: "Misery, be gone!"
I long for every loving heart preoccupied with love,
for every tongue that speaks of love,
For every ear that to the slanderer[263] is deaf,
and every eyelid that is not inclined to sleep:
Love's passion cannot be if eyes are dry,
nor any ardor if one's yearnings are not stirred.
Torment me any way you wish except with being far from you,
and you'll find me the truest lover, glad with all that pleases you.
Take what remains of what you've left of my last breath:
there is no good in love that spares one's life.
Who'll help me to destroy my spirit for the love
of a gazelle, sweet-natured, mingled with the souls?
Whoever dies in him for love will live, raised up
among the Lovers, in the highest rank.[264]
He's veiled; were he to walk in darkness like his locks,
his dazzling, beaming face would serve him for a lamp;
And if I wandered in the black night of his hair,
the bright dawn of his face would show me the right path.
Were he to breathe, musk would confess to those who know
its fragrance: "All my perfume spreads from him."[265]
The years he turns toward me are like days, so short;
but if he turns away one day it is like years in length.
If he goes far away, then O my soul, depart!
If he is near and visits me, then O my eye, rejoice![266]

Say to the one who blames me and reproaches me:
Leave me alone and spare me your ill-judged advice!
For blame is baseness: none has ever been extolled for it;
and did you ever see a lover for his love lampooned?
My friend, I'm being kind, compassionate;[267] I give
you freely my advice: don't stop to turn to yonder tribe![268]
O you with tranquil heart: don't look at my soul's comfort, but
keep safe your heart, beware of those bewitching eyes!
For him I've thrown off all restraint, cast off
all my acknowledged piety, all my accepted pilgrimage.
My passion's face has whitened, loving him; the face
of my rebuke on his account has blackened with clear proofs.
Blessed be God! How sweet his nature, which
has slain and then revived so many souls!
My ear loves those who keep reproaching me,
because I hear his name, but not the blame.
I've pity on the lightning when at night it claims to be
kin to his mouth, since it is shamed by his white teeth.[269]
When he is absent all my limbs see him
in every subtle, splendid, radiant thing:
In tones of lute and the melodious flute,
when they combine to make their thrilling tunes;
In thickets where gazelles roam freely, in
cool afternoons and when the morning dawns;
In places where the dew drops from the clouds
on carpets made of blossom woven with flowers;
In places where the soft breeze drags its skirts,
and brings me, at daybreak, the sweetest scent;
And when I kiss the wine cup's mouth and sip
the wine-saliva, in a pleasure ground.
I don't know what it is to be a stranger far from home
when he's with me; I'm undisturbed wherever we may be.
That home is my home where my love is present, and
where he appears, the turning of the sandy dune is where I turn.[270]
Happy the riders traveling by night and you among them, when
they travel in a dawn that breaks from you!

And let them do whatever they want: they are the men
of Badr: they shall have no fear of any guilt.[271]
I beg, by my defiance of my slanderer, and my
obedience to the blaze that burns between my ribs:
Look at a heart that, for the love of you, has melted down,
and at a bloodshot eye, submerged in tears!
Have mercy on my hopes that falter, my reverting to
my self-deceiving wishes for a promise of relief!
Have pity on my humble craving for a "Will it be?" or a "Perhaps";
grant me relief in my constricted breast!
Welcome to that event that I do not deserve: the words
of him who brings glad tidings of relief after despair:
"Good news for you! Take off what you are wearing,[272] for
you have been mentioned There,[273] despite your crookedness."

A Mystical *Zajal* by al-Shushtarī

سافرْ ولا تجزعْ واسكنْ إليّ   ومتْ وعشْ واسمعْ   كي تبقى حيّ
يا سائلا مني   كيف الوصولْ   إن كان تصدّقني   فما نقولْ   ادنو وخذْ منّي   بعض الاصولْ

sāfar wa-lā tajzaʿ wa-skun ʾilayy
wa-mut wa-ʿish wa-smaʿ kay tabqa ḥayy
yā sāʾilan minnī kayf al-wuṣūl
ʾin kān tiṣaddaqnī fimā naqūl
ʾadnū wa-khudh minnī baʿḍ al-ʾuṣūl[274]

Meter (non-classical): XLSLLL XLSL. Structure: *RR ababab RR cdcdcd RR efefef RR ghggh RR*; some *asmāṭ* have internal rhyme (*QRQR*).

The mystic and poet al-Shushtarī (ca. 610/1212–668/1269) was born in Shushtar (a village near Guadix, in Spain) and later moved to Egypt and Syria. His verse comprises poems in classical form, *muwashshaḥāt*, and *zajal*s. A *zajal* is a strophic poem in the vernacular, or a mixture of vernacular and classical Arabic. It is usually simpler in structure than a *muwashshaḥah*, but often longer. It is probably older than the *muwashshaḥah* but surfaces later in written sources, no doubt because of its language. Like the *muwashshaḥah* it originated in Spain, where Ibn Quzmān (d. 555/1160) is the great master of the genre; like the *muwashshaḥah* it spread to the East. Al-Shushtarī was the first to make mystical *zajal*s. For a secular *zajal*, see the poem by al-Ghayṭī, below, p. 89.

Travel and fear not; stay, dwell with me!
Die, live, and hear, that you may stay alive.
O you who ask me, "How does one arrive?"
If you believe what I shall say,
Come near and learn some rules from me.

You will find happiness by joining me;
Thereafter I'll give you sweet medicine to drink.
    Look into your mirror and behold a miracle;
    Transcend your temporal conditions, banish doubts,
    For nothing will be veiled from your own self.
And when your life turns pure, untroubled, a short while,
You'll see Existence, all spread out and folded up.
    Say to the censor he has suffered quite enough!
    If he would listen to his own advice
    He would take heed; but he has gone astray
Swimming in seas of error, without knowing where:
Such is he who sets sail with the sweet breeze of whims.[275]
    Where is the one who'll perish in his love for us
    And understands the meaning, from amongst our tribe?[276]
    He'll tell the one who sings to chant for us:
"Naked I want to walk, the greatest thing,
Just as, before, Ghaylān and Mayy once walked."[277]

Two Elegies on the Death of his Concubine, by Ibn Nubātah al-Miṣrī

Jamāl al-Dīn Muḥammad ibn Nubātah (686/1287–768/1366), a leading poet of the Mamluk era, is often called Ibn Nubātah al-Miṣrī to distinguish him from one of his forebears, the famous Aleppan preacher and stylist Ibn Nubātah al-Saʿdī al-Khaṭīb. The scholar and poet Salma Jayyusi does not think much of him: "In Ibn Nubāta's verse one senses little depth or philosophy of life." In the printed *Dīwān* this poem is said to be an elegy on the poet's wife. Jayyusi finds it interesting that the poet dwells on his wife's physical beauty, admittedly a rare occurrence.[278] She finds "a greater intensity" in the elegy on one of his concubines, also translated here. Elegy (*rithā'*) on one's wife is relatively rare and usually shorter and less rhetorical than the many grand and formal laments for leading personages. Adam Talib, who has studied the extant manuscripts, has discovered that this poem and the following were in fact composed on the death of the same person, a concubine.[279] In the first short elegy the poet expresses the not uncommon paradoxical motif of saying, in verse, that he has forsaken verse.

I. "I have renounced"

هجرتُ بديع القول هجرُ المباينِ   فلا بالمعالي لا ولا بالمعاينِ
وكيف أعاني سجعة أو قرينة   وقد فُقدت مني أجلُّ القرائنِ

hajartu badīʿa l-qawli hajra l-mubāyinī   *fa-lā bil-maʿālī lā wa-lā bi-maʿāyinī*
wa-kayfa ʾuʿānī sajʿatan ʾaw qarīnatan   *wa-qad fuqidat minnī ʾajallu l-qarāʾinī*[280]

Meter (*al-ṭawīl*): SLX SLLL SLX SLSL / SLX SLLL SLX SLSL.

I have renounced and given up all speech sublime,
 no glorious deeds, no more seductive charms![281]

How can I bear to pair fair words in rhyme
when I have lost the one with whom I was a pair?
She, pure as gold, rests deep down in the earth;
I know now that the earth, too, is a precious mineral.
I don't know if it is for her sweet ways
that I am crying, or for her sweet looks.
I've buried you, the form of my beloved: if
you saw me, you would say you've buried me,
Each of us crying for the days gone by;
although the keenest pain is hidden in the heart.
My grievance is with God; till Judgment Day
the day I lost you is a Day of Fraud.[282]
I used to be afraid of leaving before you
and now I'm inconsolable for a departed one.
It is as if you hastened your departure, fearing that
I'd be enamored of your beauty overmuch.
My dear one—who will grant me of your radiance
a glance? And who can take her place?
Will I ever forget a frame thus fine, straight as
a lance, not to be stabbed with finding faults?
Her face, which every moonlit night would favor?
Her eyes, the talk of every fawn of a gazelle?
Woe is me!—until the earth will be my pillow, and
my death will bring me near to my departed one.
I wish I knew if I might see, on Resurrection Day,
her beauties in those other habitats:
Her graceful figure[283] on the Path to Paradise,
her cheeks, bright as gold coins, between the Scales.[284]
May morning rainclouds drench your grave;
I thirst for earth, obeying stubborn Time.
My plaint is against Time the traitor, the
aggressor who spreads malice, with my loved ones gone.
—But then again, were Time and life both good to me,
I'd turn on my departed love a traitor's face.

II. "Observe the rites of grief"

أقيموا فروضَ الحزن فالوقتُ وقتُها   لشمسِ ضُحًى عند الزوال ندبتُها
ولا تبخلا عنّي بإنفاق أدمعٍ   ملوّنة أُكوى بها إن كنزتُها

ʾaqīmā furūḍa l-ḥuzni fa-l-waqtu waqtuhā   li-shamsi ḍuḥan ʿinda z-zawāli nadabtuhā
wa-lā tabkhalā ʿannī bi-ʾinfāqi ʾadmuʿin   mulawwanatin ʾukwā bihā ʾin kanaztuhā[285]

Meter (*al-ṭawīl*): SLX SLLL SLX SLSL / SLX SLLL SLX SLSL.

Observe the rites of grief, you two:[286] the time is now!
  I mourn a morning sun that set at noon.
Do not be stingy with your blood-stained tears,
  that, if I horded them, would scald me deep within;
For one who left, though in my heart she is still there,
  as if I had moved her from my eyes into my heart.
They say, how long will you go crying for a mere girl?
  But they don't know the bliss that I have lost.
My love in all its six directions you possessed:
  One could correctly say that you directed me.
Alas! She went to God, that sun of charms—if she
  was not the shining sun, its sister then was she.
I knew her far too briefly; she left me
  a lasting grief: I wish I'd never known that girl!
They say: in tears there is relief!
  Such a relief, upon my life, I do refuse!
What else are tears but eyes that I've dissolved
  for you, or else a soul I've washed away!
Since you went far away I've turned my eyes to gloom;
  I've turned away from tales in slumber told.
Take here, said Time to me, after your bliss,
  the brimming cups of grief and sorrow!—Here!, I said.
I cry for you for all the charms I saw in you,
  the promising and shining traits I knew in you.

Her grave: a garden where her branch-like figure lies;
upon my life, how fine it was, how fine it grew!
She has departed to a rough and rugged desert; but
gazelles dwell in the desert and its barren land.
Our bodies both are down, decayed: if she but knew,
she, in the earth, would mourn for me who mourns for her.
I'd give my life for her whose grave I visit and from whom
I hide my grief, lest I would not be true to her;
Her charms were hidden, in which I delighted so—
although unwillingly I buried her in earth.
A young, sweet woman: conjugated with me once,
she now remains declined to me.[287]
I call the earth in which her beauty rests, the dust
between us; and its silence hurts the ardent love-slave's ear.[288]
It's sad enough that no one helps me grieve,
now that I've sent her down into the dark.
I speak fine, polished words for you, as if I thread
the prose of scattered tears on to a string of verse.
I'm done for; after you there's no more joy in life
and no more wishes to attain, even if I live on:
Farewell, world, which I sought and wanted only for
the sake of she who has moved on.

A *Zajal*: An Elegy on the Elephant Marzūq

تعا اسمعوا بالله يا ناس اللي جَرَهْ
الفيل وقع يوم الاثنين في القنطَرَهْ
لما افلسوا غلمان الفيلْ   راموا الحرافْ
خدوه وراحوا صوب بولاقْ   يجبوا المطافْ
رأوا شويخ من أهل اللهْ   ما فيه خلافْ

taʿā smaʿū billāh yā nās   ʾillī garah
ʾil-fīl waqaʿ yōm il-ʾithnēn   fī l-qanṭarah
lammā -flasū ghilmān il-fīl   rāmū l-ḥirāf
khadūh wa-rāḥū ṣōb Būlāq   yagbū l-maṭāf
raʾū shuwēkh min ʾahl Allāh   mā fīh khilāf

Structure: RR aaa RR bbb RR ccc RR ddd RR eee RR fff RR ggg RR hhh RR iii RRR (imitated in the translation).[289]

Meter: XLSL LLLL XLSL (not corresponding to any classical meter). "Over-long" syllables containing long vowels (e.g. *lāh*, *-nēn*) count as long. The transliteration is an attempt at making a compromise between classical (*fuṣḥā*) Arabic and vernacular (*ʿāmmiyyah*) Arabic; the *jīm*, for instance, has been given its modern Cairene rendering as *g*.[290] The translation, too, is uncertain in some places.

This *zajal* (strophic poem in the vernacular) is an amusing (but moving) elegy on the elephant Marzūq, donated by Tīmūr (Tamerlane) to the Mamluk sultan al-Malik al-Nāṣir, which died in the Nāṣirī Canal in Cairo in 804/1401. The poem is introduced by the historian Ibn Iyās (d. ca. 930/1524) as follows:

> *On Monday, the 2nd of Shaʿbān, the men looking after the big elephant went out to walk it, going toward Būlāq, on the road that leads to the River Gate Aqueduct. At the head of a bend in the road leading to the*

Nāṣirī Canal there was a conduit.[291] *The elephant stepped into that conduit and sank so that its leg disappeared in it up to its thigh. Nobody could free it. Thus it remained for some time and then it died. When the news spread in Cairo people came in droves to look at the spectacle. That day all markets and shops were closed because everyone left to have a look at the elephant. Poets composed many elegies on it, of which I know only the following zajal by some zajal poet.*[292]

O people come to me and listen to what I will tell:
On Monday, at the Aqueduct, the Elephant—he fell!

When his mahouts were broke they thought they had to act:
They took him to Bulaq,[293] for money to extract.
They saw a pious little greybeard; that's a fact.

They took his skullcap[294] from him, just for fun and "What the Hell!"
He cursed the elephant and at the Aqueduct he fell!

They said, "Stuck in the conduit! There it lies, it's crying!"
I said, I'll have a look, to see if they're not lying.
I come there, see the elephant, cast down and dying!

People were climbing on its back with utmost care, pell-mell,
When, Monday, at the Aqueduct, the elephant—he fell.

The gentlemen of Cairo all around him flocked,
To marvel at the elephant and see him docked,
They saw his tears fall down like rain and they felt shocked.

He bellowed loudly and it made the people think: "Well. Well!"
When, at the Aqueduct on Monday it befell he fell.

I said to him, "Marzuq, black elephant, hey mate,
Where is your dignity, you are in quite a state!
You were a Sultan, ornament of beasts, of late!

Strutting so proudly in a pageant; you looked really swell,
But now you are laid low since at the Aqueduct you fell."

It was as if he spoke to all those who had come:
"How often did I march, on top of me a drum,
A howdah on my back! And everybody's chum!

Shown to the public just as, at her wedding, is a belle!
And now my last walk was here at the Aqueduct: I fell!"

And then his wife cried out: "Ah, who can give relief?
An arrow struck my heart, ye of Muslim belief,
I'm foreign, Indian, and my heart is full of grief.

This elephant here was my spouse, it is no shame to tell;
And now he's breathed his last when at the Aqueduct he fell."

She wept and made her neighbor friends weep too, those dears;
She wailed and cried so much that they all shed their tears.
From burning grief she slapped her cheeks with floppy ears.

Even the giraffe came, to express her sorrow for the el
-ephant that passed away when at the Aqueduct he fell.

When this occurred (it was the month Shaʿban) the sky
Showed to us all a star that trailed a tail on high.
And all of us said, "Sure, there is a reason why!

This star, what does it signify and what does it foretell?
It's that dead elephant, when at the Aqueduct he fell."

Nāṣir al-Dīn am I;[295] I get on well with folk;
They say that I'm all right, a decent sort of bloke.
Now when that elephant Marzuq was dead I spoke:

"O people come to me and listen to what I will tell:
On Monday, at the Aqueduct, the Elephant—he fell!"

Rajaz

Rajaz is the simplest Arabic meter (a basic foot of XXSL, not unlike an ancient Greek iambic metron;[296] lines are normally short and not divided into two hemistichs) and generally believed to be the oldest. There are some early pieces that are irregular and difficult to distinguish from early *saj*ʿ. Poetry in *rajaz* was never accepted as being on a par with poetry in other meters (collectively called *qarīḍ*, sometimes *qaṣīd*), which is one reason why I have banished it to the end of the poetry section (compare Abū l-ʿAlāʾ al-Maʿarrī's description of the *rajaz* poets on the outskirts of heaven, below). It was used for short, improvized utterances, for instance at the beginning of a battle, such as the lines attributed to Hind bint ʿUtbah given below. In early Islamic times *rajaz* was also used for longer poems, notably by some specialists who were very popular with lexicographers because of their extravagantly large and exotic vocabulary.[297] Abū Nuwās and others employed it especially in poems describing hunting animals such as dogs, falcons, or cheetahs. *Rajaz* was also used for longer narrative poetry (see the comic poem by Abū l-Ḥakam al-Maghribī translated below) and didactic verse (as in the fragments by Abū l-ʿAtāhiyah and Ibn Mālik, below), in which monorhyme was normally abandoned in favor of paired rhyme (*aabbccdd*...), which allowed for poems of indefinite length. Such versified knowledge has no literary pretensions; it is different from the "educational" but entertaining verse illustrated below by Ibn Makānis's poem.

I. Early *Rajaz*

نحن بناتُ طارق ٭ نمشي على النمارق ٭ والدُّرّ في المَخانق ٭ والمِسْك في المَفارق ٭ إن تُقبلوا نُعامق ٭ أو تُدبروا نُفارق ٭ فِراقَ غير وامق

naḥnu banātu ṭāriqī
namshī ʿalā n-namāriqī
wad-durru fī l-makhāniqī
wal-misku fī l-mafāriqī
ʾin tuqbilū nuʿāmiqī
ʾaw tudbirū nufāriqī
firāqa ghayri wāmiqī[298]

Meter (*al-rajaz*): XXSL XLSL.

Incitement of the warriors by Hind bint ʿUtbah (wife of Abū Sufyān, leading Meccan opponent of Muḥammad; mother of Muʿāwiyah, who became the first Umayyad caliph) before the Battle of Uḥud, a place not far from Medina, where in the year 3 or 4 of the Hijrah the early Muslim community experienced a setback:

We are those Ṭāriq[299] girls
We walk on carpets fair
Our necks are hung with pearls
And musk is on our hair
If you advance we'll hug you
Or if you flee we'll shun you
And we'll no longer love you

II. A Few Lines from Abū l-ʿAtāhiyah's *Poem of Proverbs*

ما انتفع المرء بمثل عقلِه   وخير ذُخر المرء حُسن فعلِهِ
إنّ الفساد ضدُّه الصلاحُ   وربّ جِدّ جرّه المزاحُ

mā ntafaʿa l-marʾu bi-mithli ʿaqlihī   *wa-khayru dhukhri l-marʾi ḥusnu fiʿlihī*
ʾinna l-fasāda ḍidduhu ṣ-ṣalāḥū   *wa-rubba jiddin jarrahu l-muzāḥū*[300]

Abū l-ʿAtāhiyah (d. 211/826) was among the first to use the *muzdawij* (rhyming couplets) form. For one of his many sententious poems of *zuhd* (asceticism, renunciation) in traditional style, see above, p. 49. A pedestrian and archaic kind of English seems appropriate here.

'Tis not his *Reason* that a Man most needs:
'Tis what he may have stored of his good *Deeds*.
Corruption is opposed to what is Best;
A serious thing is often caused by *Jest*.
Believing *Slander* leads one to Perdition;
Who tells you Ill, your Ill is his Ambition.
Here are three baneful things: *Youth*, *Riches*, *Leisure*,
That have corrupted People without Measure.

III. A Few Lines from *The Thousand-liner* by Ibn Mālik

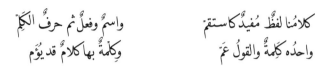

kalāmunā lafẓun mufīdun ka-"staqim"	*wa-smun wa-fiʿlun thumma ḥarfuni l-kalim*
wāḥiduhū kalimatun wal-qawlu ʿamm	*wa-kilmatun bihā kalāmun qad yuʾamm*[301]

Jamāl al-Dīn Ibn Mālik (ca. 600/1203–672/1274) was a grammarian famous especially for his versification of Arabic syntax, in about one thousand (*alf*) lines. The poem was meant to be memorized, often before understanding it: that could come later with the help of teachers and commentaries, of which there are a great number. The fragment given here presents ll. 8–10, the beginning of the discussion of syntax. In the last couplet, *al* is the Arabic definite article; "nunation" is the Arabo-Latin technical term (Arabic: *tanwīn*) for the ending *n*, a mark of indefiniteness. Again, a rhyming archaic diction has been used. "Teach" is used for the sake of the rhyme; the meaning of -*staqim* is "be upright!"

Meaningful Utterance is *Speech*, like "Teach!"
And *Noun*, *Verb*, *Particle*: the *Parts of Speech*.
The Unit: *Word*; *Discourse*: the whole Extent,
Although at times with "Word" a *Speech* is meant.
A *Noun* is known by *al* or by *Nunation*,
Vocative, *Genitive*, or *Predication*.

IV. Light Verse: *A Domestic Disaster*, by Abū l-Ḥakam al-Maghribī

مَعرّةُ البيت على الإنسانِ تترى بلا شكّ من الإخوانِ
فاصْغ إلى قول أخي تجريبِ يأتيك بالشرح على الترتيبِ

maʿarratu l-bayti ʿalā l-ʾinsānī *tatrā bi-lā shakkin mina l-ʾikhwānī*
fa-ṣgha ʾilā qawli ʾakhī tajrībī *yaʾtīka bish-sharḥi ʿalā t-tartībī*[302]

Meter: *al-rajaz* (XXSL XXSL XLL); paired rhyme throughout (*aabbccdd*...). The numbering below is of couplets, not lines.

Ibn Abī Uṣaybiʿah's work is a biographical encyclopedia of physicians, including many philosophers and scientists (starting with the ancient Greeks). ʿUbayd Allāh Ibn al-Muẓaffar, also known as Abū l-Ḥakam al-Maghribī, probably came from Spain (although some say he was born in Yemen) and was active mainly in Baghdad and Damascus. He was also a poet of mostly satirical and "light" verse, the author of a collection called *Nahj al-waḍāʿah li-ulī l-khalāʿah* (*The Lowly Route for the Dissolute*).

Any domestic scandal tends
To happen through one's own best friends.
Now listen to a well-tried man:
He'll tell you how it all began:
All that may come from invitations
And all their diverse tribulations.
Provide the food, provide the fun:
Then suffer all the damage done.
Disliked by all, the Awful Bore
Comes first. Then: spongers at the door!
Whatever food may be provided,
The host will be severely chided.
Creep up his mother's cunt he may,
From censure he can't hide away.
"Not enough spices!" says one guest,
"It's rather burnt!" declare the rest.

Another says, "Too little salt!
—I am just helping, finding fault."
He grabs the food from far and near,
Then drinks some water, fresh and clear,
Since "wholesome water has no peer."
The next thing he demands is beer,
With ice in summer. When it's cold:
"A fire, if I may be so bold!"
Who needs a tooth pick? Take a straw:
The mats lie ready on the floor.
And after this there comes the wine,
Delicious, choice; it tastes divine.
One person says, "It's vinegár!"
Another says, "Defective jar!"[303]
And someone else is now complaining:
He wants a filter, for the straining.
Some large carafes are brought in there,
In which the wine is mixed with care.
Someone cries out, "But that's still pure!"
And pours more water, to be sure.
"He's got an ulcer," mocks another,
"O, don't add water! Please, don't bother!"
Fruits, nuts, with any fragrant smell,
Go down, it seems, extremely well.
Some fussy person's fancy's tickled
Only by basil and things pickled,
While yet another man supposes
Wine goes with apples and with roses.
The singers' fee may cause some tension,
The taxman causes apprehension;
A fix you should be quick to handle:
Spread round your cash,[304] for fear of scandal.
Sometimes they fall into a swoon:
Fear not! They'll have their breakfast soon.
If you invite them in December,
Make sure of stove and burning ember!

From which there flies up many a spark
That on your carpet leaves its mark:
Your once new carpet now is peppered
With dots like any spotted leopard.
And don't forget the meat: kebab
Or sliced, for everyone to grab.
And when the cold is over, pep
Them up with fans and cool julep.[305]
Your drinking friends come in all sorts:
The wine reveals their favorite sports.
There's one whose forte and whose strength
Is telling stories at great length,
While he is busy masticating.
—Nobody heeds what he's relating.
Forgets himself, speaks out of turn;
They slink away in unconcern.
Another weighs his words with care
And gives himself a haughty air.
Another acts the fool. He's after
A cheap but all embracing laughter.
Someone becomes morose when stewed;
Instead of leaving he gets rude.
Someone as sober as a judge
Arrives, and bears all drunks a grudge.
There's one light fingered Jim'll fix it
Sees something rather nice: he nicks it.
A knife, a flask, a handkerchief,
A dicing bowl fit for a thief.
Now someone pulls (abracadabra!)
A chain right off the candelabra,
"Extinguishing" (he says) "a wick."
It is, of course, a little trick.
Don't mind their winks whenever any
Should leave the room "to spend a penny":
It's slaves and slave girls they will seek,
To squeeze a tit or bite a cheek.

45 One's hospitality's abused
Yet worse: one's wife is being seduced,
One's sister, daughter, or one's son
(Especially a pretty one).
In this one ought to be forgiving,
For, after all, your friends are living;
A man is made of flesh and blood;
He is no piece of stone, no dud.
And if among them is a glutton(?)[306]
Your banquet isn't worth a button.
50 He eats as much as he is able,
And has no manners at the table.
"You'll drink with us?" "I must decline."
(He says he doesn't care for wine).
He buggers sleeping drunks at night,
Consumes their sweets in broad daylight.[307]
Your friends will start an ugly brawl,
But *you* will suffer, that is all.
They break the cups and bottles each
And every vessel within reach.
55 The row spreads to your neighbors, too,
Who falsely will belabor you.
Police are called, and jurisdiction
Completes the extent of your affliction.
57 Thus may a man gain loss of face;
And if the party did take place
On Friday eve: there's worse disgrace.
58 If in the fighting blood is shed,
The host may just as well be dead.
If someone tumbles and gets killed,
One merely pays some light wergild;
60 For drinking in an upstairs room
Brings people closer to their Doom.
Such heavy drinking! What comes from it?
The mats are soiled with bits of vomit.

Yet someone asks for more to eat,
His drinking bout not yet complete.
When you wake up—you've hardly slept—
And now the floor has to be swept,
You will be henpecked by your wife,
In bed, awake, always at strife,
Who in great detail will remind you
Of last night's trials, now behind you.
—That is, if they have gone. If not
(They stayed, toped on, slept on the spot),
For you no rescue any more
When they're found lying on the floor.
Offer your friends your choicest wine,
And cakes, and heads of sheep and kine;
Pawn chairs and stools, pull out all stops,
Pledge them at the off-license shops.
But if a guest misses one sandal,
You'll be involved in one more scandal;
So tell your boy to guard them well,
Lest your kind fellows give you hell.
Don't mind your losses in this fix.
Provide your lamps with numerous wicks.
Someone at last wants to strike camp:
He leaves and robs you of your lamp;
With in his hand a full wineskin
To please his friends and next of kin.
If oil runs out, give it no thought:
Amidst this ruin, it is naught.
All costs must by the Host be paid
When in the Balance he is weighed.[308]
Latter Day prophets who go dry
Deserve a good punch in the eye.[309]
His heavy debts—a pretty sum—
Prove him a very stupid bum.
He would be spared all this forever
Were he but wise, astute, and clever.

A scandal, quite without a match:
He whom it strikes, strikes a bad patch!
At others' houses to be drinking
Is better, in my way of thinking.
Well, then. Repentance of one's vices
Is always best when there's a crisis.

V. "Didactic" Verse: From a Poem on How to Behave in Society, by Ibn Makānis

هل من فتى ظريفِ　　مُعاشرٍ لطيفِ
يسمع من مَقالي　　ما يُرخص اللآلي

hal min fatan ẓarīfī　　*muʿāshirin laṭīfī*
yasmaʿu min maqālī　　*mā yurkhiṣu l-laʾālī*[310]

Meter: *rajaz* (XXSL XXSL, with variations SLL and LLL in last foot); paired rhyme.

The poem is in fact a versified *adab al-nadīm*, "rules of conduct of the drinking companion," and the poet describes the "good manners" not without some irony and satire, and at times with plain nonsense, in true doggerel style. It is obvious that "didactic" should be taken with a pinch of salt, hence the inverted commas. The Egyptian Fakhr al-Dīn ʿAbd al-Raḥmān ibn ʿAbd al-Razzāq Ibn Makānīs (745/1345–794/1392) was famous as a poet and a prose writer; he served as vizier of Damascus under the Mamluk Sultan Barqūq. On his way to take up the post of vizier of Egypt he died in 794/1392, poisoned, it is said.

Is there a man full of esprit,
Adept at keeping company,
Who'll listen to my sound advice?
Higher than pearls should be its price!
To him my counsel I'll confide:
By night it travels far and wide;

In darknesses it shines and gleams
Just as a lamp that casts its beams.
Great joy it brings and spreads around;
With noble news it does resound.
It's wanton, even impudent,
But natural[311] and eloquent.
Its words are elegant and smart:
With ease one learns them all by heart.
By my great innate talent driven,
This friendly counsel's hereby given:
Advice to your best interest;
I'm serious and yet in jest.
With people I shed gravity,
Behaving with depravity,[312]
Bringing Abū Nuwās's time
To life again, that golden prime!
If you want honor and respect,
And suffer no bad side effect,
Always to people show good breeding,
And you'll see marvels all-exceeding.
Soften your words to them: 't will save you
If you are on your best behavior,
And what you're seeking you will find
By thus bewitching every mind.
Put on the dress of non-restraint,
Take off patched rags of Sufi saint!
Don't brag of wealth and property,
Don't boast of ancient ancestry.
Life's but a day: one lives in it
With the best ornament: one's wit.
Managing people much less tough is
For people holding a high office.
You'll find a hoped-for patron high:
Don't ever use the pronoun "I."
If you are wanted, don't say "Nay,"
If you are trusted, don't betray.

Be strong and be reliable;
And smart: be shrewd and pliable.
The middle course: the door to blessing;
Folly is fatal and distressing.
Your close companion, do not hurt him,
Your closest friend, do not desert him.
Do not befriend inferiors;
Don't anger your superiors.
And do not always blame your friend,
Lest he detests you in the end,
For an abundance of reproof
Makes one be shunned and kept aloof.
When you receive an invitation
From leading persons in the nation,
Everyone's favor you must crave,
And act as everybody's slave.
With kind and civil words you'll flatter;
Beware of odious, foolish chatter.
Don't lie, whatever things you say.
Take note of those with whom you play;
For with one's buddies, of necess-
ity, one plays backgammon, chess.
Whenever you ask, concision seek,
And brevity whenever you speak.
Don't quarrel, do not misbehave,
Don't be a loathsome, odious knave.
When joined with comrades in a session,
Display to them no bold aggression.
Their cups and glasses do not take:
You'll spoil the fun, a grave mistake.
Snub not the waiters when you dine;
Do not monopolize[313] the wine.
Don't pilfer wine, or snacks, or food:
At parties that is very rude,
And not condoned by any gent
Who isn't poor or indigent.

Speak only words that go with wine:
Poems sublime and stories fine.
Shun words that come from lowly folk,
Or any trite and vulgar joke.
Some shrewd advice: it comes to pass
That wine is spilt from upset glass:
Act promptly then, and in a jiff
Be ready with your handkerchief;
A proper gentleman will lunge
And use his cloak as a wine sponge.
You'll stay the night: don't misbehave
By chatting up your host's own slave.
You may escape discovery once,
But don't do it again, you dunce.
Caught for a second time, my friend,
You're done for: it will be the End.[314]
Don't get yourself into a scrape:
Do not commit nocturnal rape.[315]
It is a major sin, a shame,
An ugly evil, much to blame.
Its perpetrator counts for nought,
He's shown no mercy when he's caught.[316]
So many a nocturnal creep
Lies in the earth some six feet deep!
So many of them who reached their goal
Were pierced themselves in their own hole!
They paid them back[317] in their own kind:
They were to lasting shame consigned
And no one in the population
Would give them any consolation.
Such infamy! That should suffice
As a deterrent to this vice.
Beware of being a parasite;
Avoid this blight with all your might!
It is a terrible disgrace,
It is demeaning, it is base.

Don't be a nagging sycophant:[318]
You'll be a mighty irritant.
And don't be vulgar to the core,
And never be a crushing bore.
When friends send you an invitation
To join them in a wine-potation,
Don't be a fool in what you do:[319]
Don't bring along your son with you,
A neighbor, or a stranger too
Or any friend you've bumped into,
But spare your host and do not tax him
By quoting to your friends this maxim:
"It's an ignoble host indeed
Whose guests come unaccompanied."
Stale proverb! Just an empty word,
Like most of them wholly absurd,
Made current by the Bedouin,
Those starving beggars and their kin.
They coined them as a form of wit
To mock[320] the people, sons of shit.
Now, if it ever comes to pass
You're drinking with the illiterate class,
Don't drink too much: better stay dry
When you are mixing with *canaille*.
Don't pester them, don't be provoking,
Refrain from jesting and from joking.
…[321]
It is a fact: the common masses[322]
Are merely beasts, like mules and asses.
Prepare yourself, meeting a Turk,
For being beaten: just a quirk
Of his, when friendly and not rough:
When he is angry it's more tough.
For then he moves around the place
Shaking his sword, or else his mace.

A day of woe! You will be thrilled
To know that people will be killed.
He goes for you—you want to live:
Get up, take the initiative,
And cut his neck from throat to nape[323]
And don't come back if you escape.
Be his procurer, be his pimp,
Or lose your balls and die, you wimp!
Here's my advice. Rely on it
And use it to your benefit.[324]
Don't contradict, for you'll be sorry;
Don't joke:[325] it brings no end of worry.
'Tis ill luck to recriminate;
A gent does not dissimulate.
These words of wisdom I direct
At people who have self-respect.
With it, I mostly have in mind
Myself, my friends, and my own kind.
Into a camel saddle never hop,
And never scale a mountaintop.
With ghouls be not on marriage terms.
On no account should you kill worms.
With lions you should spend no time.
On fortresses[326] you should not climb.
Don't go to sea in boats or ships,
Don't go to deserts or to steppes.
No visits to the countryside,
But with choice wine always abide.
Don't stupidly lament the traces
Left at your love's deserted places.
Don't roam in valley or in dell,
Make always sure that you eat well.
From eating lizards be averse;
Lone wastelands you should not traverse.
A diet such as that is best
Left to the Bedouins and the West,[327]

Those hedgehog-eaters,[328] in those fara-
way wastelands or in the Sahara.
Rather, to pleasant gardens lush
You ought to hasten and to rush.
Look at the spring: its blossoms blush!
105 Who does not follow where I lead
Will never in his life succeed.
Have you then never heard my name,
You don't know how I play the game?
Ask my companions then, feel free!
Or, if you wish, you can ask me.
I am experienced, astute,
I am adept, of good repute,
I am the Father of Good Wine,
The Brother of all Fellows Fine.
110 In fact I'm rather like the Devil,
A magnet of all sport and revel.
...[329]
162 This world has chances to be taken:
Leave them, and you'll be badly shaken.
So here is my recommendation,
Together with a salutation.
Through noble friends to you I send
My greetings and this verse. THE END.

Prose

Examples of Early Rhymed Prose (*Sajʿ*)

Not everything that rhymes is verse: only metrical, rhymed speech is considered poetry according to traditional Arabic opinion. Non-metrical, rhymed prose is called *sajʿ*. In pre-Islamic and early Islamic times it was used for special occasions and genres: pithy sayings, maxims, proverbs, speeches of heightened emotion or for solemn occasions, and for the oracular, often enigmatic, mantic utterances of soothsayers and diviners (*kuhhān*, sg. *kāhin*). The early suras of the Qur'an also use rhyme or assonance that resembles the soothsayers' *sajʿ*, and the Prophet took pains to make it understood that he was neither a poet (*shāʿir*) nor a soothsayer (*kāhin*). In the course of the Abbasid period polished and artful kinds of *sajʿ* were used by epistolographers, chancery scribes, and increasingly in other prose genres, notably the *maqāmah*; it is also widely used in book titles.

In Arabic editions rhyming segments are often separated by full stops, even when the sentence runs on. This does not work in English, so I have used asterisks instead to mark these divisions in the pieces below where the *sajʿ* is imitated in translation.

The mother of the pre-Islamic poet-brigand Ta'abbaṭa Sharrā, lamenting her son:[330]

وابناه وابن الليل ☆ ليس بزُمّيل ☆ شَروب للقيل ☆ رَقود بالليل ☆ وواد ذي هوْل ☆ أجزْت بالليل ☆ تضرب بالذيل برجل كالثوْل ☆

*wā-bnāh wa-bna l-layl * laysa bi-zummayl * sharūbun lil-qayl * raqūdun bil-layl * wa-wādin dhī hawl * 'ajazta bil-layl * taḍribu bidh-dhayl * bi-rajlin ka-th-thawl*

O son, son of the night * he is no coward taking flight * who drinks at noon bright * or sleeps at night * many a wadi full of fright * you crossed at night * shaking your coat's hem (?)[331] * with men like bees in a swarm.

Quss Ibn Sāʿidah (legendary pre-Islamic orator), preaching, and apparently foretelling the coming of Islam:[332]

أيها الناس ☆ اسمعوا ☆ وعوا ☆ من عاش مات ☆ ومن مات فات ☆ وكل ما هو آت آت …

*ʾayyuhā n-nāsu smaʿū * wa-ʿū * man ʿāsha māt * wa-man māta fāt * wa-kullu mā huwa ʾātin ʾāt *…*

O people, hear * and be aware! * Whoever lives will die * whoever dies will disappear * and everything that will come to pass will come near! * A dark night * Constellations in the sky * Seas that rise * Stars that shine * Light and darkness * Piety and sins * Eating and drinking * Clothing and mounts for riding * How is it that I see people pass away * and not return? * Are they pleased to stay so they stayed away? * Or have they been abandoned so they went to sleep? * By the God of Quss ibn Sāʿidah: there is on the face of the earth no religion better than a religion the time of which has come, with its shade to protect you * and its moment has reached you * Blessed he who reaches it and follows it * Woe to him who opposes it *

A prophecy about the ruler of Kindah (Central Arabia), Ḥujr ibn al-Ḥārith (father of the poet Imru' al-Qays) by ʿAwf ibn Rabīʿah, a pre-Islamic *kāhin* (soothsayer; first half of the sixth century):[333]

من الملك الأصهب ☆ الغلاّب غير المغلّب ☆ في الإبل كأنها الربرب ☆ لا يعلق رأسه الصخب
☆ هذا دمه ينثعب ☆ وهذا غداً أول من يسلب ☆

*mani l-maliku l-ʾaṣhab * al-ghallābu ghayru l-mughallab * fī l-ʾibili ka-ʾannahā r-rabrab * lā yaʿlaqu raʾsahu ṣ-ṣakhab * hādhā damuhū yanthaʿib * wa-hādhā ghadan ʾawwalu man yuslab **

Who is the fair-haired king * unvanquished, vanquishing * amidst camels like a herd advancing * his head unaffected by the clamoring * this one's blood will be gushing * and this one will tomorrow be the first for plundering.

Two fragments attributed to Musaylimah, the "false prophet" in the time of Muḥammad, who was active in Eastern Arabia and was defeated shortly after Muḥammad's death (the texts sound like a parody of the Qur'an):

ضفدع بنت ضفدعيْن ☆ نِقّي ما تنقّين ☆ أعلاكِ في الماء وأسفلك في الطين ☆ لا الماء تكدّرين ☆ ولا الشارب تمنعين ☆

*ḍifdaʿu bintu ḍifdaʿayn * niqqī mā taniqqīn * ʾaʿlāki fī l-māʾi wa-ʾasfaluki fī ṭ-ṭīn * lā l-māʾa tukaddirīn * wa-lā sh-shāriba tamnaʿīn* *[334]

Frog, daughter of two frogs! * Croak! What are you croaking? * Your top half in the water soaking, * your lower half in the mud poking! * The drinker you rile not, * the water you soil not. * We have half the earth and Quraysh[335] the other half, but Quraysh are a hostile lot.

والمبدياتِ زرعا ☆ والحاصداتِ حصدا ☆ والذاريات قمحا ☆ والطاحنات طحنا ☆ والخابزات خبزا ☆ والثاردات ثردا ☆ واللاقمات لقما ☆ إهالةً وسمنا ☆

*wal-mubdiyāti zarʿā * wal-ḥāṣidāti ḥaṣdā * wadh-dhāriyāti qamḥā * waṭ-ṭāḥināti ṭaḥnā * wal-khābizāti khubzā *wath-thāridāti thardā * wal-lāqimāti laqmā * ʾihālatan wa-samnā* *[336]

By the seed-sowing women * and the crop-reaping women * and the wheat- winnowing women * and the flour-milling women * and the bread-baking women * and the bread-broth-sopping women * and the women gobbling morsels * of fat and butter: * You are better than the dwellers in tents of hair. * Nor do the village dwellers take precedence over you. * Your cultivated fields, defend them! * He who addresses you humbly, harbor him! * And the oppressor, oppose him!

Someone about to be beheaded is asked, “Are you scared (*a-tajza*ʿ)?” He replies:[337]

إن أجزع فقد أرى كفنًا منشورا ☆ وسيفًا مشهورا ☆ وقبرًا محفورا

*ʾin ʾajzaʿ fa-qad ʾarā kafanan manshūrā * wa-sayfan mashhūrā * wa-qabran maḥfūrā!*

Wouldn’t I be scared seeing a shroud spread and aired, a sword bared, and a grave prepared!

A Pre-Islamic Tale: The Princess on the Myrtle Leaf (Three Versions)

Three different versions of the same tale are given; there are many more in Arabic.[338]

I. al-Bayhaqī (early fourth/tenth century).[339]

They say that al-Ḍayzan al-Ghassānī,[340] the king of al-Ḥīrah, was attacked by Sābūr Dhū l-Aktāf.[341] Al-Ḍayzan fortified himself and was besieged for a month. They say that Mulaykah,[342] the daughter of al-Ḍayzan, looked at Sābūr from the city wall[343] and fell in love with him. She sent a note[344] to him, saying, "I have fallen in love with you and I shall point out to you how to conquer this town." He replied, "Do that and I will be yours, and at your command!"

Then she got the guardians of the wall drunk and opened the gates.[345] Sābūr entered the town, killed those he could lay his hands on, and took her father prisoner. The following morning Sābūr ordered that al-Ḍayzan be brought before him, while he sat on a golden throne with the girl at his side. When al-Ḍayzan saw her, he wrung his hands, stamped his feet, and fainted. When he came to his senses he said to her, "Why have you done this? May God blacken your face as you have blackened mine, and may He give him power over you!"

On the orders of Sābūr, he was beheaded. Sābūr and his followers captured many spoils and returned to his royal residence. He had a special apartment built for the girl and made her live there. He was much pleased with her and she stayed with him for a year. Then, one night, he called for her and she spent the night with him on a bed filled with feathers. But she was very restless, so he asked her, "What is the matter with you, my darling?"

"There is something rough in the bed that has made me feel uncomfortable."

He searched the bed and found beneath the feathers a myrtle leaf, and see! This had left a mark on her side of precisely the size of the leaf, because her body was so soft[346] and her skin so tender. He said to her, "What did your father give you to eat?"

"Marrow[347] and bread of the finest wheat flour—meaning white bread[348]—with sugar candy."[349]

The king said, "By God, I shall give you what you deserve!"

He gave orders for her plaits to be fastened to the tails of two horses. They were made to gallop and she was torn to pieces.[350]

II. Ibn Qutaybah (213/828–276/889).[351]

I have read in the *Histories of the Persians*,[352] that Ardashīr[353] marched against al-Ḥaḍr (Hatra). The king of Babylonia[354] had fortified himself there; he was one of the most powerful of the Successor Kings.[355] So Ardashīr besieged him there for some time, unable to find a way to take the town. Then, one day, the daughter of the king of Mesopotamia climbed on the town wall and saw Ardashīr. She fell in love with him, went down, took an arrow and wrote on it: "If you promise to marry me I will show you a place from where you may conquer this town with the least effort and cost." Then she shot the arrow toward Ardashīr, who wrote his reply on the arrow: "I promise to do what you have asked." Then he cast it toward her. She wrote to him, pointing out the place. Ardashīr sent his men there, they breached the town, and he entered with his troops while the townspeople remained unaware. They killed the king and most of the garrison, and Ardashīr married her.

One night, while she was lying on his bed, she felt so uncomfortable that she was sleepless all night long. They searched the bed and found beneath the mattress a myrtle leaf which had left a mark on her body. Thereupon Ardashīr asked her on what food her father had raised her. She said, "My food was mostly honey, cream, and marrow."

Ardashīr said, "Nobody has been as excessively generous and obliging to you as your father. Since his reward from you has been so evil, despite his great kindness, while being so closely related and deserving great respect, I cannot be sure that you will be not the source of something similar befalling me."

Then he gave orders for her hair to be fastened to the tail of a very restive, untamable horse, and for it to be run. This was done, and she was torn limb from limb.

III. al-Akhfash al-Aṣghar (ca. 235/849–315/927).[356]

Al-Ḥaḍr was a town in al-Jazīrah.[357] In the old days a king ruled there called Sāṭirūn. His rule was mild, and he was kind toward his subjects. He adhered to a religion in which he was very pious, even though it was wrong. He deemed it permissible to marry one's own daughters and sisters.[358] He had a daughter who was one of the most beautiful people on earth. He was old, having lived a long time. Then, during the rule of Sābūr Dhū l-Aktāf, an army from Persia attacked him. One of their generals called Sharwīn was the commander of that army. He had with him a servant called Ḥurayn.[359] Sābūr ordered him not to leave the town until he had conquered it, promising to give him anything he wished. He advanced with his army up to the bank of the Euphrates and camped there, with the town lying a short distance from the riverbank.[360] There was a stone building leading from the town to the Euphrates.[361] Sharwīn remained there until those around the town had all fled. They would go to the town in the morning, camping nearby, and fight hard; then he would withdraw. He did this for some time.

Then the wife of Sāṭirūn, who was his daughter, employed a ruse to send a message to Sharwīn, in which she pointed out how to enter the town, on condition he would promise to marry her. She said, "At night only my father's servants guard the town; I shall deal with them on such-and-such a day."

When that night arrived she sent a message to her father's servants who guarded the town and to those with them, saying: "By God, I had no idea of the hardship you must endure, fighting during the day and having to stay awake at night. If I had known I would have sent you food and drink, enough for all of you."

She ordered her servant woman to prepare for them what she used to prepare and give them an excess of it and to put henbane in their drink. That was on the night she had agreed upon with Sharwīn. The men collapsed, intoxicated by the henbane. Sharwīn advanced toward the town and entered it through the entrance that she had promised he would find. He killed her father and the inhabitants of the town. He took the woman and found her to be shapelier and more beautiful than he had ever seen in a woman. He said to himself: *I do not know of a human who is more evil than this woman. I have seen how her father has treated her, honoring her greatly, but she could not be happy until her evil nature moved her to have him and all her brothers killed. It is not fitting for anybody to let her enter his room, nor should one trust her.*

So he ordered her throat to be cut, destroyed the town, and departed.

How the Queen of Sheba Became Queen[362]

Zuhayr ibn ʿAbd Shams, of the Banū Ṣayfī ibn Saba' al-Aṣghar: he was killed by Bilqīs, daughter of Ṣayfī.[363] The cause of this was that he was a king who ruled despotically and overbearingly; he used to deflower women before their husbands, just as ʿImlīq had done.[364] But when Bilqīs reached adulthood, she said to her father, "This man has dishonored your women! Go to him and say, 'I've got a daughter who has become nubile. There is nobody among the people like her in beauty and attractiveness!' Then, if he says to you, 'Send her to me!' you must say, 'The virginity of the daughter of a nobleman like myself is not taken except in his own house!'"

The father went to him and said all this to him. When Zuhayr said, "Send her to me!" he said what his daughter had told him. Zuhayr replied, "What about entertainment for me and the followers I am bringing along?"

He replied, "I am very capable of entertaining the king and very pleased to do so; it will be an honor for me and a favor from the king toward me!"

Zuhayr agreed to come to him, something he had done for nobody else. The father went home and decorated his house; he decorated three rooms in the most ornate fashion of his day, and he made everything ready for the king's entertainment. Then he went to Zuhayr and told him that everything was ready. Zuhayr mounted and rode to him. Bilqīs had hidden a number of her kinsmen, with their weapons. When Zuhayr entered the first room he was amazed by what he saw. Then he entered the second room, which was even more beautiful. Then he entered the third room, where Bilqīs was, all decked out in her jewels and robes, in all her beauty. When he lay down on the bed, having sent his guard and his soldiers outside, and having ordered the door to be locked (he had some vassal princes with him), she said to her own men, "Come out!"

They came out and killed him. Then she sent for one of his vassals and courtiers, calling all of them one after the other, upon which they would kill them; whoever was summoned thought that it was the king who called him. This went on until she had them all killed. Then she called for her father and his people. She left the room and came to them, saying, "This evil man had dishonored your women and made you infamous among the people: God has relieved you of him! Now choose yourself a king, anyone you wish."

They all said, "No one is more worthy of this than you!"

So they made her their queen and she ruled over them, until the matter of the hoopoe and Solomon (peace be upon him).[365]

Two Stories from al-Mas'ūdī's *Meadows of Gold*[366]

Murūj al-dhahab (*Meadows of Gold*), by Abū l-Ḥasan 'Alī ibn al-Ḥusayn al-Mas'ūdī (ca. 282/896–345/956), one of the most entertaining works in Arabic, is a combination of geography and history. A large part of the work is devoted to people other than the Arabs; the historical part begins at the creation of the world and runs to al-Mas'ūdī's own time. It is enlivened by many anecdotes and stories.

I. The origin of drinking wine[367]

Azūr and Khalinjās[368] became kings [of the Syrians]; it is said that they were brothers. Their conduct was excellent and they mutually supported each other in reigning. One of these two kings was sitting one day, it is said, when suddenly he saw on the highest part of his palace a bird with a nest and young birds in it; it was beating its wings and screeching. The king looked more closely and saw a snake creeping up toward the nest, in order to eat the chicks. The king called for a bow and shot the snake, killing it, and the young birds were saved. After a short while, the bird came, flapping its wings, with one seed in its beak and two more seeds in its claws. It stood before the king and cast down what it had in its beak and claws, while the king looked on. The seeds fell in front of the king. He looked at them and said, "The bird must have thrown down these things for some reason. Surely it wants to reward us for what we did."

He picked up the seeds and began to look at them closely, but they were not of a kind known in his country. A wise man from his entourage, who saw the king's perplexity regarding the seeds, said to him, "Sire, this plant ought to be entrusted to the womb of the earth; only then will it show its true nature, will its utility be found out, and the purpose of its stored treasure and hidden nature be fulfilled."

So the king called for some ploughmen and ordered them to sow the seeds and to observe what became of them. They were sown and began to grow, twisting themselves round trees, then producing unripe grapes, then ripe grapes, while the men watched them and the king, too, observed them. Finally they were fully grown. The men did not dare taste them, fearing they might be lethal. The king ordered to have the fruits pressed, the juice put in a container and the seeds separated from it, while leaving some of it intact. When it reached the container as pressed juice, it began to bubble and produce foam, as fragrant odors wafted from it. The king said, "Fetch me an old decrepit man!"[369]

A man was brought and was given some of the substance in a vessel. What he saw was a ruby color, a luminous radiance, and a wonderful and perfect sight. They made him drink it and he had not had three glasses before he became aggressive, partly loosened his loincloth, clapped his hands, moved his head, stamped his feet on the ground, became elated, raised his voice, and began to sing. Thereupon the king said, "This is a drink that takes away one's reason. As likely as not it will be lethal. See how that old man has reverted to his childhood, when sanguinity reigns with the force of growth and youth!"

Then the king ordered that he be given yet more; the old man got drunk and fell asleep. The king said, "He has died!"

But then the old man awoke and asked for more, saying, "When I had drunk it all distress was dispelled; it removed all my sorrows and worries. The bird wanted only to reward you with this noble drink."

Then the king exclaimed, "This is the noblest drink for men!"

This was because he saw that the man had a healthy color and was relaxed and elated in a situation that would normally be dominated by sorrow and by phlegm. His digestion was good; he slept and a joyful feeling overcame him. Then the king ordered the planting of many vines, and many vines were planted. He gave orders for it to be forbidden to the masses, saying: "This is the drink of kings. I was the cause of its coming into being, so let nobody else drink it!"

The king used it for the rest of his life. Then it got into the hands of the people, who used it too. It is also said that Noah (peace be upon him) was the first to sow it. The story of how the Devil stole it when Noah came out of the ark and the ark had settled on Mount Jūdī[370] can be found in my book *The Beginning* and in other books too.

II. The Story of Cleopatra

Then, after Ptolemy (Baṭlīmūs), reigned his daughter Cleopatra (Qilābaṭrah), ruling for twenty-two years. She was a wise woman, a philosopher, who favored scholars and honored sages. She wrote books on medicine and magic and other topics relating to wisdom,[371] which bore her name, were attributed to her, and were well known among physicians. This queen was the last of the Greek monarchs, who reigned until their rule ended; their days fell into oblivion, their traces were obliterated, and their sciences disappeared, apart from what remained in the hands of their sages.

There is a curious story about this queen and how she died, killing herself. She had a spouse called Anthony (Anṭūniyūs), who shared with her the rule of Macedonia, i.e. the land of Egypt including Alexandria and other parts.[372] Then the second king of Rome, Augustus (Aghusṭus), came to her; he was the first to be called Caesar (Qayṣar), and all the subsequent Caesars are traced to him. We shall mention his story in the chapter on the kings of Rome, below.[373] He fought wars in Syria and Egypt with Cleopatra and her husband Anthony, until he killed him and Cleopatra was no longer able to prevent Augustus, the king of Rome, from taking over the rule of Egypt. Augustus intended to capture her by means of a ruse, because he knew about her knowledge and wanted to learn from her, since she was the only remaining sage of the Greeks. His plan was then to torture her and kill her. So he wrote her a letter, but she knew what his intentions were regarding her and the wrong he had done her by killing her husband and her soldiers.

She asked for a snake found in the Hijaz, Egypt, and Syria, a kind of snake that watches a human being closely until, when it is able to reach a part of his body, it leaps up several cubits' distance, swift as the wind, not missing this very part of the body, spitting poison on it and thereby killing him. The cause would not be known because the person would turn into a lifeless corpse on the spot, so that people would imagine that he had died suddenly of a natural cause. I have seen a similar kind of snake in the water, in Khūzistān, in the regions of al-Ahwāz, which one reaches when traveling to Persia from Basra. It is a place known as Khān Mardawayh, between Dawraq and the land of al-Bāsiyān and al-Fandam. The snakes are a span in circumference, and are called *fitriyyah* there.[374] They have two heads and live in the sand or in the earth. When they detect a human being or an animal they leap up many cubits from their place and strike any part of the body of that animal with one of their heads, so that it is overtaken instantaneously and immediately by lifelessness and demise.[375]

This queen, Cleopatra, sent for a snake as described above and which is found in the Hijaz. On the day that she knew Augustus would enter her royal palace, she ordered one of her servants to touch it in its vessel; she wanted her to die before herself so that she would not be subjected to torture after her own death. The woman fell instantaneously lifeless. The queen then sat on her royal throne, placed her crown on her head, and put on her regal clothes and jewels. She had all kinds of aromatic plants, flowers, fruits, and scents spread out in the room where she sat and before her throne were all the combined marvelous aromatic herbs and plants of Egypt such as we have mentioned. She attended to all her affairs as much as was necessary and dismissed the servants around her; they looked after themselves rather than their queen after the enemy arrived and entered the royal palace. She brought her hand near the glass vessel that contained the snake, putting her hand close to its opening. The snake spat on it and it withered on the spot. The snake slid out of the vessel and, not finding a hole or a passage to leave through, since the rooms were built solidly of marble and various paints, hid amidst these plants.

Augustus entered and finally came to that room. He looked at her where she was sitting, with her crown upon her head, and did not doubt but that she would speak. But when he came near her he saw that she was dead. He wondered about the plants, reaching out his hand to each kind, feeling and smelling, and expressing his admiration to those of his retinue that accompanied him, but without knowing the cause of her death and regretting what now escaped him regarding her. While he was thus occupied in picking up and smelling these aromatic plants, suddenly the snake leapt on him and struck him with its poison. The right half of his body withered immediately, he lost sight in his right eye and hearing in his right ear. He was amazed at what she had done, that she had killed herself, preferring death to a life of humiliation, and at her ruse of placing the snake among the plants. He composed a poem on this in Latin, mentioning what had happened to him and also her story. He remained, after what had happened to him as we have recounted, for one day and then died. If the snake had not used some of its poison on the servant girl and subsequently on Queen Cleopatra, Augustus would have died immediately, rather than after this interval. His poem is extremely well known among the Romans, who recite it in their laments and elegize their kings and their dead with it. Sometimes they quote it in their songs; it is very well known and renowned among them.

Lives of The Poets: al-Farazdaq Tells the Story of Imru' al-Qays and the Girls at the Pond[376]

Al-Farazdaq (d. ca. 110/728), one of the greatest poets of the Umayyad period, here figures as a storyteller, relating in prose his adventure with some bathing girls, an encounter which reminded him of a similar story (but erotic rather than burlesque) connected with the most famous poem in Arabic, the *Muʿallaqah* by the pre-Islamic Imru' al-Qays (first half of sixth century AD). Several verses from the poem may be found in the passages from Abū l-ʿAlā' al-Maʿarrī's *Risālat al-ghufrān,* below. For Abū l-Faraj al-Iṣfahānī and his *Book of Songs,* from which this and the following story have been taken, see the introduction to the "Umayyad Ghazal Poem, used as an Abbasid song text," above, p. 27.

ʿAbd Allāh ibn Mālik related to us: Muḥammad ibn Mūsā related to me: al-Qaḥdhamī related to me: one of our friends related to me, on the authority of ʿAbd Allāh ibn Zālān[377] al-Tamīmī, the *rāwī*[378] of al-Farazdaq, that al-Farazdaq said:

One night a heavy rain fell in Basra. The following morning I found some tracks of riding animals that had set out toward the desert. I thought that they must have been left by people who have gone on an outing. *They're sure,* I thought, *to have some food and drink with them!* So I followed their traces, until I came upon some mules, still fully laden, stationed near a pond. I hastened to the pond, where I saw some women bathing in the water. I said, "I have never seen anything like today, not even the day of Dārat Juljul."[379]

I turned away from them, modestly, but they called out to me: "Hey you, you with the mule, come back, we want to ask you something!"

So I turned back, while they were still up to their necks in the water.

"Come on," they said, "you must tell us the story of Dārat Juljul!"

So I said, "Imru' al-Qays was in love with one of his cousins, called ʿUnayzah.[380] He tried to get in touch with her for some time, but in vain. He tried to visit her without her family knowing about it, but it was not to be, until the day at the pond, that is the day of Dārat Juljul. As it happened, the clan had moved on, the men in front, and the women following behind with the servants and the luggage. When

Imru' al-Qays saw this, he lagged behind after he had traveled with his tribesmen, for a distance of a bowshot. Then he hid in a hollow, until the women came by. The girls turned up; 'Unayzah was among them. When they arrived at the pond, they said, 'Why don't we stop here and rest a bit!' So they got down from their camels, told the slaves to move away some distance and then stripped and plunged into the pond, just as you are doing now! Then Imru' al-Qays sneaked upon them, just as I approached you, unawares. He took their clothes and made a pile of them..."

(At this point al-Farazdaq jumped off his mule, grabbed some of the clothes and clutched them to his chest.)

"... and said to them, just as I say to you: 'By God, I shall not give any of you girls your clothes, even if you stay in the pond all day, until you come out naked.'"

Al-Farazdaq continued, "One of them , the sauciest, said, 'That man was in love with his cousin; are you in love with one of us then?'

"'No, by God! I am not in love with any of you, but I do find you attractive.'

"Then they shouted and clapped their hands, and said, 'Go on with your story, since you won't leave before you've got what you want!'"

So al-Farazdaq continued the story of Imru' al-Qays:

"They resisted his request until the sun was high in the sky. Then they became afraid that they would not reach the camp site they intended to reach. So one of them came out, and he placed her clothes to one side. She took them and put them on. Then, one by one, the others followed, until only 'Unayzah was left. She implored him by God to throw her her clothes, but he said, 'Shut up, for I swear a holy oath that you'll have to come and get your clothes yourself!'

"So she came out and he had a good look at her, front and back. Then he put down her clothes and she picked them up. Then they all turned on him, blaming and rebuking him: 'You have seen us naked, you have kept us here all whole time, and you have made us hungry!'

"'What if I slaughter my camel for you, will you eat it?'

'Yes.'

"So he drew his sword, hamstrung his camel, cut its throat, and skinned it. He called for the servants, to collect firewood, and he lit a big fire. Then he began slicing it for them, pieces of hump, the delicacies and the liver, and threw them on the embers. The girls ate and he joined them. He drank from a small wineskin that he carried with him, and sang to them, throwing some pieces of meat to the slaves and the servants, until the girls had eaten their fill and had had lots of fun. When he wanted to move on, one of them said, 'I'll carry the saddle cushion!'

"Another said, 'I'll carry the saddle.'

"Another, 'And I'll carry the saddle pad and the girth straps.'

"In this way they divided his camel's equipment between them. Only 'Unayzah had not been given anything to carry. Imru' al-Qays said, 'Noble lady, you must carry me with you on your camel, for walking is beneath me, it is not my custom!'

"So she carried him on the withers of her camel. He would put his head into her howdah and give her a kiss. But when she resisted, the howdah tilted, at which she said, 'Imru' al-Qays, you've hocked my camel, get off!'

"That is in fact what he says in his verse:

She says, when the howdah tilted with us both, together,
'You've hocked my camel, Imru' al-Qays, get off!'"

When al-Farazdaq had finished his story, the saucy girl said, "Well, well, that was a damn good story, very nice indeed! Who are you, mister?"

I said, "From Muḍar."

"Which tribe?"

"Tamīm."

"Which clan?"

"I won't say another word!"

"I bet you are al-Farazdaq!"

I said, "Al-Farazdaq is a poet, I am only a transmitter."

"Enough of this mystification about your lineage! I'm asking you seriously: are you him?"

"Yes, indeed, I am."

"If you are he, then I think you won't part with our clothes unless you've had your way."

"That's right."

"Turn away for a second!"

She whispered something that I could not understand to her young friends. They dived in the water and hid. Then they showed their heads and came out, their hands filled with mud. They approached me, menacingly. They smeared my face with mud and slime, filling my eyes and covering my clothes. I fell on my face and while I was distracted by the dirt in my eyes they grabbed their clothes and absconded with them. The saucy one sat on my mule and left me flat on my face, in the worst possible state, covered in shame: "That bloke thought he could fuck us!"

I left but not before I had washed my face and clothes and dried them. I returned home on foot as darkness was falling. They had returned my mule and left a message: "Tell him: Your sisters say to you: 'You tried to get something from us that we would not give, but we hereby give you back your wife; now fuck her all night! Here are a few pennies for the public bath in the morning!'"

Whenever he told this story, he would say, "I have never again met their like."

Bedouin Romance: The Unhappy Love Story of Qays and Lubnā[381]

Qays and Lubnā are a famous couple known for their sad love affair (though Abū l-Faraj al-Iṣfahānī, the compiler of the *Book of Songs*, also gives an alternative, happy ending). Their story is told in simple prose, but not in a straightforward manner: it is somewhat rambling and repetitive, with a number of digressions. One could leave out all the chains of authorities and digressions, to make the text more unified and "literary," as has been done for example by Max Weisweiler in his German translation (*Arabesken der Liebe*, pp. 78–90), and long before him by Ibn Wāṣil al-Ḥamawī (d. 697/1298) in his *Tajrīd* or "Abstract" of *al-Aghānī*. But this would distort the character of the original text, which is an illustration of how belles lettres and scholarship often go hand in hand. Here the chapter is translated almost in full, omitting only some lines of long poems and some technical details on the songs and the musicians. The longer chains of authorities have been printed in a smaller font size, to distinguish them from the story.

Qays ibn Dharīḥ (ca. 4/626–70/689), of the tribe of Kinānah, foster-brother of al-Ḥusayn ibn ʿAlī ibn Abī Ṭālib (grandson of the Prophet and the most famous martyr of the Shīʿites), is famous as a poet of *ghazal* of the ʿUdhrī kind.

Qays ibn Dharīḥ, his genealogy and the reports about him

As is mentioned by al-Kalbī, al-Qaḥdhamī, and others, he is Qays ibn Dharīḥ ibn Sunnah ibn Ḥudhāqah ibn Ṭarīf ibn ʿUtwārah ibn ʿĀmir ibn Layth ibn Bakr ibn ʿAbd Manāh, who is ʿAlī ibn Kinānah ibn Khuzaymah ibn Mudrikah ibn Ilyās ibn Muḍar ibn Nizār. Abū Shurāʿah al-Qaysī says that he is Qays ibn Dharīḥ ibn al-Ḥubāb ibn Sunnah; the rest of the lineage is identical. He argues this on the basis of Qays's verse:

If my doting on Lubnā is misguided,
then, Dharīḥ ibn al-Ḥubāb, I am indeed misguided.

Al-Qaḥdhamī says that his mother was the daughter of Sunnah ibn al-Dhāhil ibn ʿĀmir al-Khuzāʿī, which is correct; and that a brother of his mother was called ʿAmr ibn Sunnah, who was a poet. He was the one who said,

They hit the elephant at al-Mughammas, till
 it crept along as if it had a fever.[382]

Of him, Qays said,

My uncle, I am told, is owner of a camel herd
 with smooth heads flat like stone slabs, near the holy place.[383]
In days gone by, when you lived near us as our protégé,
 you had no camel mare to tend, nor stallion.
It would not harm you, Uncle ʿAmr, if they drank
 from other cisterns, while the well is overflowing.[384]

Al-Ḥasan ibn ʿAlī informed me: Muḥammad ibn Mūsā ibn Ḥammād related to me: Aḥmad ibn al-Qāsim ibn Yūsuf related to me: Jazʾ ibn Qaṭan related to me: Jassās ibn Muḥammad ibn ʿAmr, one of the Banū l-Ḥārith ibn Kaʿb, related to us, on the authority of Muḥammad ibn Abī l-Sarī, on the authority of Hishām ibn al-Kalbī, who said:

A number of tribesmen from Kinānah told me that Qays ibn Dharīḥ was a foster brother of al-Ḥusayn ibn ʿAlī ibn Abī Ṭālib (may God be pleased with them), who was suckled by Qays's mother.

Several of our teachers informed me about Qays and Lubnā, his wife, in stories both connected and disconnected, in reports either scattered or properly arranged. I have put them all together to make a coherent text, except those isolated reports that could not be incorporated in the ordered narration, so I have mentioned them separately.

Among those who informed me about Qays is Aḥmad ibn ʿAbd al-ʿAzīz al-Jawharī, who said: ʿUmar ibn Shabbah related to us (giving no link to further informants); and Ibrāhīm ibn Muḥammad ibn Ayyūb, on the authority of Ibn Qutaybah; and al-Ḥasan ibn ʿAlī, on the authority of Muḥammad ibn Mūsā ibn Ḥammād al-Barbarī, on the authority of Aḥmad ibn al-Qāsim ibn Yūsuf, on the authority of Jazʾ ibn Qaṭan, on the authority of Jassās ibn Muḥammad, on the authority of Muḥammad ibn Abī l-Sarī, on the authority of

Hishām al-Kalbī, whose version is the most reliable. I have also quoted some things from the connected reports about Qays that are mentioned by al-Qaḥdhamī, on the authority of his sources, by Khālid ibn Kulthūm, on his authority and of those from whom he is transmitting, and by Khālid ibn Jamal; and some details related by al-Yūsufī, the author of the *Epistles*, on the authority of his father, on the authority of Aḥmad ibn Ḥammād, on the authority of Jamīl, on the authority of Ibn Abī Janāḥ al-Kaʿbī. I have quoted everything that is generally agreed upon in a continuous narrative, and every divergent motif wherever it fits in, duly attributed to its sources.

They all say that his people lived in the region outside Medina; he and his father were from the settled population of Medina. Khālid ibn Kulthūm says that they lived in Sarif, on the evidence of Qays's verse:

God be praised! She's a neighbor of those
in ʿAqīq, while in Sarif are we.[385]

They say that Qays, while on some business of his, came past the tents of the Banū Kaʿb ibn Khuzāʿah. He stopped at one of the tents when the tribesmen were absent. It was the tent of Lubnā bint al-Ḥubāb al-Kaʿbiyyah. He asked her for some water; she gave him some, coming out of the tent and bringing it to him. She was a tall woman, with dark, bluish-black eyes, sweet of face and speech. The moment he saw her he fell in love with her. He drank the water; then she said to him, "Will you stay and cool yourself a while with us?"

"Yes."

He stayed with them. Her father came and slaughtered an animal for him and treated him hospitably. Qays left, in his heart an inextinguishable, ardent passion for Lubnā. He began to compose poetry on her which became well known and was recited widely. He came to her another day, being enamored of her. He greeted her and she emerged, answering his greeting and receiving him kindly. He told her how much he suffered from the passion for her and the love he felt; she told him at length that she, too, suffered from the same thing. They both discoverd what they felt for each other. Then he went to his father and told him about his situation, asking him to marry him to her. But his father refused, saying, "Dear son, you must marry one of your cousins, for they are more entitled to marry you."

Dharīḥ was very wealthy and did not want to let his son marry a stranger. Qays left, very unhappy with what his father had said. He went to his mother and complained, asking for her support against his father. But she did not give him what he wanted. Then he went to al-Ḥusayn ibn ʿAlī ibn Abī Ṭālib and Ibn Abī ʿAtīq[386] and complained to them, sharing his feelings and how his father had reacted. Al-Ḥusayn said, "I will help you."

He went with him to Lubnā's father. When the latter saw him he honored him, hastening toward him, saying, "Grandson of the Messenger of God! Why have you come? Why didn't you send for me so that I would have come to you?"

"The very reason that made it necessary for me to come to you, for I have come to ask for the hand of your daughter in marriage on behalf of Qays ibn Dharīḥ."

"Grandson of the Messenger of God, we would not disobey your command, nor do we dislike this young man. But we would prefer it if Dharīḥ's father asked us to marry her to his son, and that the matter came from him; for we are afraid that if his father does not support this it will be a matter of shame and disgrace for us."

Then al-Ḥusayn (God be pleased with him) went to Dharīḥ and his people while they were together. They stood up and honored him and said the same as the Khuzāʿīs had said.[387] He said to Dharīḥ, "I beseech you, ask for Lubnā's hand for your son Qays!"

"I hear and obey!"

He went with him, together with the leading persons of his clan. When they came to Lubnā, Dharīḥ asked her father for her hand in marriage on behalf of his son, and her father married her to him. Subsequently she was led to him and she stayed with him for a while during which they found nothing to dislike about each other!

He used to be much devoted to his mother; but now Lubnā and his obsession with her distracted him somewhat from this. His mother was upset by this and said, "This woman has distracted my son from his devotion to me."

But she did not find an opportunity to speak out, until one day Qays fell gravely ill. When he had recovered from his illness his mother said to his father, "I was afraid that Qays would die without leaving offspring, since this woman has not had any children. You are wealthy and your possessions would go to distant relations. Marry him to someone else, perhaps God will then grant him children!"

She kept on insisting. He gave it some time, but when his clan was together he called for Qays and said, "Qays, you had this illness and I feared for you. You have no children and I have no one but you. This is not a woman who will have children. Marry one of your cousins, perhaps God will give you a son in whom you and we will rejoice."

But Qays answered, "I will never marry anyone else, I swear by God."

His father said, "I am wealthy; take slavegirls as concubines!"

"By God, I will never hurt her with anything like that."

"I beseech you, divorce her!"

"By God, I would rather die! But I shall make you choose one of three things."

"What are these things?"

"Either you yourself marry again and perhaps God will grant you another son..."

"I am too old for that."

"... or let me leave you with my wife. Then do what you must do, even if I die of this illness..."

"Not that either."

"... or call for Lubnā and let her stay with you, and I'll leave: perhaps I will get over her, as I do not want her to be in my imagination after I had had it so good."

"I do not want that unless you divorce her."

And he swore an oath that no roof would ever shelter him until Qays had divorced Lubnā. He went outside and stood in the blazing sun. Qays would come and stand beside him, giving him shade with his cloak, himself being scorched by the hot sun; only when the shadows became longer would he leave. He would go in to Lubnā, each in the other's embrace, both of them crying and she saying, "Qays, do not obey your father or else you will perish and cause me to perish too."

Then he would say, "I could never obey anybody regarding you."

It is said that this lasted one year. Khālid ibn Kulthūm said: Ibn ʿĀʾishah mentioned that Qays resisted for forty days and then divorced her; but that is incorrect.

Muḥammad ibn Khalaf Wakīʿ informed me: Aḥmad ibn Zuhayr related to me: Yaḥyā ibn Maʿīn related to me: ʿAbd al-Razzāq related to us: Ibn Jurayḥ informed us: ʿUmar ibn Abī Sufyān informed me, about Layth ibn ʿAmr, who had heard Qays ibn Dharīḥ say to Zayd ibn Sulaymān:

"Because of Lubnā my parents avoided me for ten years. I would ask to see them but they would refuse, until in the end I divorced her."

Ibn Jurayḥ said, "I was told that ʿAbd Allāh, the son of Ṣafwān the tall one, met Dharīḥ, Qays's father, and said to him, 'What induced you to separate them?

Don't you know that 'Umar ibn al-Khaṭṭāb[388] said, "It would not make much difference if I separated a couple or killed them with a sword!"'[389]

"They say that when Lubnā was parted from him, after he had divorced her and nothing more could be said, it was not long before his mind gave way and he became like someone possessed. He thought of Lubnā and the time she was still with him, and he grieved, crying and sobbing bitterly. She heard about this and asked her father to take her away. Others say that she stayed until her waiting period[390] was over, during which Qays used to visit her. Her father came with a howdah on a she-camel, and other camels to carry her belongings. When Qays saw this he turned to her servant girl and said, 'Woe is me! What are they doing to me?'

"She replied, 'Don't ask me, ask Lubnā!'

"He went toward her tent to ask her, but her people stopped him. A woman from his own people turned to him and said, 'Come on, why would you ask her? Are you stupid or just pretending to be stupid?! Lubnā is going away, tonight or tomorrow morning.'

"He fainted and fell down unconscious. When he came to he said,

I have exhausted all my tears with crying,
  in dread of what has been and what will be.
They say: tomorrow, or the day after tomorrow
  I will be separated from my love, parting at last.
I never feared my fate: to die
  at your hands. Now the time has come.

"A song was made on these verses; the events are mentioned in the story of al-Majnūn.[391] Qays also said,

'Lubnā,' they said, 'is trouble! You were fine before
  you knew her. Don't be sorry for her and divorce her!'
So I obeyed my enemies and disobeyed who wished me well;
  I gladdened my false gloating rivals' eyes.
I wish, by God! that I had disobeyed them all,
  mortal sins merely to please her,
Plunging into a heaving sea of trouble,
  Biding in the midst of the submersing waves.

I see all loving people, now that she is gone, as if
they are the bitter juice of colocynths;
My eyes reject all pleasant sights,
my ears dislike all speech, since she is gone.

"A crow alighted near him and started to croak repeatedly. He took this as a bad omen and said,

The crow announced Lubnā's departure:
my heart flew up, fearing this crow.
It said, 'Tomorrow Lubnā's dwelling will be far
and distant after all your love and nearness.'
I said, 'Be damned, you wretched crow,
you've been forever bent on ruining.'

"He also said, after his people had forbidden him to visit her:

Song[392]

You crow of separation, woe to you! But tell
me truly about Lubnā; you have knowledge.
If you don't tell me what you know,
may you not fly unless with broken wing,
And may you wander among foes, your love amongst them,
just as you see me wandering with mine.

"Sulaymān, Ḥajabah's brother, made this into song in *ramal* mode, on the middle string.

"They say that, when they had made her enter the camel litter and she had departed, crying, as he followed her, he also said:

Song

You crow of separation, will you tell me of
good things, like you have told of parting and bad things?

You said, 'Fate is like this: forever grievous.'
You spoke the truth. Can anything, with Fate, endure forever?"

Ibn Jāmi' set these two lines to music, in the second heavy mode, with the fourth finger, following al-Hishāmī. Ḥabash mentioned that Qafā, the carpenter, made a song on them in the first heavy mode, with the middle finger.

When she and her people departed he followed her for some time; but then he realized that her father would not allow him to travel with her, so he stopped, watching them and crying, until they were no longer visible. Then he returned. He looked at the traces made by the hooves of her camel, bending over them and kissing them. When he got back he kissed the place where she used to sit, and her footprints. His people scolded him for kissing the dust. He replied,

I do not love your earth: I kiss
the trace of her who trod the dust.
My love for Lubnā has afflicted me,
I cannot swallow any drink.
When someone cries out Lubnā's name
I'm dumb, unable to reply.

He said, looking at her traces:

Song

Lubnā's abode, what do you say?
Tell me today, what have they done who dwelt here once?
If dwelling places answered lovers,
I'd get an answer from a place they left one year ago.
If I were able, on the morning when she said,
"You have betrayed me!", while her eyes were full of tears,
I would have killed myself, hearing her saying this,
—the least thing I could do for her.
I would have cured my burning passion by my act,
I would not have remained, mindlessly roaming.

Ḥusayn ibn Muḥriz sang this in the second heavy mode, in the versions of Badhl and Qurayṣ.[393] The remaining verses are:

Distraught since Lubnā left, I'm like
  a mother of her only child bereft.
Woe unto you, my heart, be hard and strong,
  for she is gone, the ambling camels took her hence.
You can't bring Lubnā back, since she is gone,
  whether or not you cry a lot.
You've lived so long so near to her!
  But separation was the way it had to be.
So bear it patiently! One day the life of
  every loving couple will come to an end.

When night fell and he was alone, he went to bed. But he could not settle, tossing and turning like someone bitten by a snake. He jumped up, went to where her tent had been and wallowed in the sand, crying, and saying:

Song

I spent the night, Lubnā, with sorrow as my bedfellow.
  My tears have poured from me since you have gone away.
I've sighed whenever I thought of you, until
  my ribs have parted with my heart.[394]
I shall pretend I have forgotten you, so that my heart
  will also swerve, and I'll be mad with love.
O Lubnā—may my life and loved ones be your ransom!—
  past times we spent: could they return?

Muḥammad ibn Khalaf informed me: al-Zubayr ibn Bakkār said: ʿAbd al-Jabbār ibn Saʿīd al-Musāḥiqī related to me on the authority of Muḥammad ibn Maʿn al-Ghifārī, who had it from his father, on the authority of an old woman of his tribe called Ḥammādah, daughter of Abū Musāfir. She said:

I was living next to the family of Dharīḥ, with a herd of camels—some of them looking after calves that were not their own, others with a dummy calf,[395] others without any calves, and some followed by their own young. Dharīḥ's son, Qays, climbed on top of a hill, to see how the camels were doing and to admire them. Shortly afterward his father spoke harshly to him, telling him to divorce Lubnā. Qays nearly died. Then his father swore that if she stayed he would not live with Qays. She then left and Qays said,

O my heart that, broken, flies up from my body,
  O my grief, what is it that pierces my heart?
I swear: half-blind old she-camels that care
  for their dummies or tend their calves,
Sniffing at them—if they could only suck them up!—
  and when they smell them their misery increases,
Old camels will never be chased from them,
  they stay with them in dry, unfertile land:
Such camels do not love more strongly than I, the day she
  was carried away, the first riders reaching the mountain path.
All of Time's blows I found easy to bear,
  but the departure of loved ones.

My uncle informed me: al-Kurānī related me: I heard Ibn ʿĀʾishah say: Isḥāq ibn al-Faḍl al-Hāshimī said: Nobody has ever said anything on this motif as good as did Qays ibn Dharīḥ:

All of Time's disasters I found easy to bear
  but the departure of loved ones.

Ibn al-Naṭṭāḥ said: Abū Diʿāmah said:

Qays went off with some of the young men of his people, telling his father that he was going hunting; but he traveled instead to Lubnā's country, expecting he would see her or someone who could be his messenger to her. The men were busy hunting. When they had hunted enough they returned to where he was still standing, and said to him, "We know why you wanted us to come with you. You don't want to hunt, you only want to meet Lubnā. But you can't; now come back!"

But Qays said,[396]

Wild oryxes that circle day and night
around a waterhole, drawn by the reeds,[397]
Seeking the water, never turning from it, yet
not coming any closer to the full, cool cisterns,
Seeing the water ripple, yet between them and
the water lies their death—they hear the voices of the men:
These do not yearn with hotter yearning
than I for you! But I am wronged by enemies.
My two good friends! Either I die or I shall talk
with Lubnā, and in private. Therefore go, leave me alone,
So I can have my wish, alone. I've often had my way,
in spite of fear and terror for my life.
You should not keep away from me, of all people, the one
who if she wished could cure me, and
Who leads me to my death, so sweet to sip,
when she will make me drink a deadly poisoned potion.

But they stayed with him until he met her. She said, "You are making an exhibition of yourself and making a scandal of me!"

He replied,

You've split his heart and strewn in it the love of you.
They censured him; the crack was mended.
The passion penetrated places reached
by neither drink nor grief nor joy.

Al-Qaḥdhamī said: Abū l-Wardān related to me: My father related to me: I recited Qays's verse to al-Sā'ib al-Makhzūmī:

You've split his heart and strewn in it the love of you.
They censured him; the crack was mended.

Then he called a Sindī slavegirl of his called Zubdah,[398] shouting, "Hey Zubdah, come here quickly!" "I am kneading dough," she replied. "Never mind, come here and leave the dough!" So she came. Al-Sā'ib said to me, "Recite these two lines by Qays!" I repeated them. Then he said to her, "Zubdah, these are fine verses by Qays! If I am mistaken I'll make you a free woman! Now go back to your dough, don't let it get cold!"

Qays began to blame himself for obeying his father by divorcing Lubnā. He said to himself, "Why didn't I take her to some place away from him, where I cannot see what he is doing and he cannot see me? Then if he had really missed me, he would not have done what he did, and if I had missed him I would not have given up. What difference would it have made, if I had left him and stayed with her tribe, or with some other Bedouins, or if I had refused to obey him? The crime would be mine only, and nobody else would have been to blame. But now what I have done will be my death! Who will give me my life back? Can I go back to Lubnā after the divorce?"

Whenever he punished and upbraided himself with these and similar thoughts he would cry bitterly, pressing his cheek to her traces on the ground. Then he said,

Song

Woe unto me! What can I do, now that she's gone from me,
after I held her in my hands!
My heart said to my eye, reproaching it:
Here's your reward! Now bite hard stones!
I told you not to deal with her. If only you had listened!
Endure it patiently: but don't expect reward for patience.

They say that he also said,

Sweet Lubnā is gone and your heart is distraught;
your mind, once so firm, is demented.
I commend her to God's care now that she is gone,
in spite of my wishes: her old man's command is the law.
And yet I can see myself happy with Lubnā,
reunited, together, the bonds tied again.

Khālid ibn Kulthūm said: He also said,

Would that Lubnā came to visit me in a lone place;
I could complain of my distress, then she would go.
All sensible and all infatuated men will sober up:
my heart will suffer for the sake of Lubnā all my life.
O, who will help my heart that won't recover from its love,
and who will help my eyes, tearful with ardent love?

They say that he also said, that night,

I said to my heart: no more Lubnā! Concede it!
Make an end of the matter and quit!
I used to swear oaths that I would not desert her—
All these words that were said, all the oaths that were sworn!
I am surrounded by slanderers, she has been taken away.
Never ever feel safe from the falsehood of those who surround you!
No more hope, no more hope! She's a neighbor
of those in ʿAqīq, while in Sarif are we ...[399]

Sarif is six miles from Mecca; al-ʿAqīq is a wadi in al-Yamāmah.[400]

... In a Yemeni tribe, while our dwelling is in al-Baṭḥāʾ:
by your life, we will never be together again!

They say that the morning after she left he went in the direction she had gone, trying to inhale her smell. A gazelle came on his path; he headed for it but it fled, and he said,

Lubnā's lookalike, be not afraid!
Don't flee and scale the rocky mountaintops!

This is part of a long poem, in which he says,

O heart! I have turned pale and sick.
　Lubnā's departure was a kind of fraud.
The slanderers surround and pester me:
　O for a slanderer who would obey me!
Today I blame myself
　for something that is not within my power,
Like someone duped who bites his fingers,
　the fraud apparent when the sale is done.
Lubnā has left you living in a place of loss;
　thus death is led to those who suffered loss.
We lived a life of pleasure for a while:
　if only Time could summon human beings again!
But all must part eventually,
　and death in all its forms will call.

My paternal uncle related to me on the authority of al-Kurānī, on the authority of al-ʿUtbī, on the authority of his father, who said:

The mother of Qays ibn Dharīḥ sent some girls of his people to him, who were charged with finding fault with Lubnā, with blaming him for being so upset and for crying, and with trying to make him fall in love with one of them. They gathered round him and began to jest with him, saying bad things about Lubnā and upbraiding him for his actions. When they had done this for some time, he turned to them and said,

Song

Her nearness cools my eye and those
　who blame her only make my fondness grow,
So many people said: Turn back! I disobeyed:
　That is a turning I shall never take.
Bear it, my soul! By God, you know you aren't
　the first soul that has lost its love.

The girls went back to his mother and convinced her that there was no hope Qays could be consoled.

All other transmitters I have mentioned relate that the women sat with him for a long time, talking to him, while he payed no attention to them. Then he cried, "O Lubnā!" They asked him, "Hey, what's the matter?"

"My leg has gone to sleep. They say that if your leg has gone to sleep this will disappear if you call the name of the one you love the most. So I called her name."[401]

Then they left him. Qays said,

Whenever my leg is numb I think of her who is the cause:
I cry out Lubnā's name and call,
Call her whom, if my soul obeyed me, I would leave
and would have done with loving her.
Lubnā trimmed an arrow for the hunt and feathered it,
I feathered one like it and trimmed it.
Then when she shot at me she hit me with her arrow; but
I missed her with my arrow when I shot.
I have left Lubnā, she is gone: I feel as if
I was together with the highest star, then fell to earth.
Would that I'd died before she left;
Could she come back, undo the thing? Would that... !

[a few lines have been omitted]

Khālid ibn Kulthūm says:

Qays fell ill. His father asked the girls to visit him at his sickbed and to talk to him, so that he might be consoled or become attached to one of them. They did this; a physician accompanied the girls, in order to treat him. When they all sat together they started talking to him and questioning him at length about the reason for his illness. He answered,

Song

Qays is visited again by love for Lubnā:
Lubnā is an illness, love is a bad malady.
The day that women visit me my eye
says: I don't see the one I want.

If only Lubnā came to visit me, and I could die!
But she is not among the ones that visit me.
Woe unto Qays, who caught from her
love-madness; love-sick is his heart.

The doctor asked him, "How long have you had this illness? And how long have you had this passion for that woman?"

Qays replied,

Song

My soul was tied to hers before we were created,
and after we were drops of seed, and in the cradle too.
The attachment grew like we ourselves did, ever stronger,
and will not be cut off, not even when we die;
It will remain whatever happens; it will come
and visit us in the dark gloom of grave and tomb.[402]

The doctor said to him, "Thinking of any of her bad qualities and blemishes, and all the kinds of filth that are loathed by humans, will help you to forget her. That is how one gets over one's feelings."

But Qays said,

If I find fault with her I liken her unto the moon
when full and rising—that is blame enough.
Lubnā surpasses everyone, just as the Night of Power
is better than a thousand months.[403]

Song

When she walks on the earth one span
she trembles, out of breath, unable to proceed.
Her buttocks quiver when she walks; her back
is like a willow branch, her waist is slim.

His father entered while Qays was saying this to the physician. He reproached him and blamed him, saying, "O God, my son! Beware, for if you persist like this you will die!"

Qays said,

I follow, if I die, the example of the ʿUdhrite, ʿUrwah,
and ʿAmr, ʿAjlān's son, who was killed by Hind.[404]
I have the same as what they died of; but
my time has not yet come.

Song

What else is love but tears that follow sighs,
a heated heart that can't be cooled?
A stream of tears that gushes forth when I
hear something from your country that I did not know.

Al-Ḥaramī ibn Abī l-ʿAlāʾ related to me: al-Zubayr related to me—and al-Yazīdī related to us, on the authority of Thaʿlab, on the authority of al-Zubayr: Ismāʿīl ibn Abī Uways related to me:

I was sitting with Abū l-Sāʾib in the arrowmakers' market. He recited to me the verses by Qays ibn Dharīḥ:

Qays was visited again by love of Lubnā: Lubnā
is Qays's illness. Love: a bad disease.
If only she would visit me and I would die:
thereafter she would never have to visit me again.

And then I recited to him Qays's verses:[405]

My soul was tied to hers before we were created,
and after we were drops of seed, and in the cradle too.
The attachment grew like we ourselves did, ever stronger,
and will not be destroyed, not even when we die;

It will remain whatever happens; it will come
and visit us in the dark gloom of grave and tomb.

Then Abū l-Sā'ib swore he would not rest before he memorized them. He entered Arrowmakers' Alley, while I repeated the verses to him, and he stood up and sat down again, until he had committed them to memory.

To return to the story: Khālid ibn Jamal said: When Qays had been suffering for a long time his fellow tribesmen intimated to his father that he should marry him to a pretty woman, so that he might get over his love for Lubnā. The father proposed this to him, but he refused, saying,

Since she has left I fear my soul will be content
with nothing in this world, whatever it offers.
I keep myself aloof from her,[406] since she is barred from me;
my soul will merely watch and wait for her.

His father told his relatives what Qays had said. They replied, "Tell him to travel to various Arab tribes and stay with them; perhaps his eye will fall on a woman who will please him."

The father entreated him to do this; so he left. He came upon a clan of the Fazārah tribe, where he saw a pretty girl who had removed the veil from her face: she looked like the moon when it is at its fullest. He asked, "What's your name, girl?"

She answered, "Lubnā."

He fainted and fell. She sprinkled some water on his face, shocked at what had befallen him. Then she said, "This must be Qays ibn Dharīḥ! He is possessed!"

When he came to, she asked who he was and he told her. She said, "I knew you were Qays! But I implore you by God, and for the sake of Lubnā, take some food from us!"

She brought something to eat and he scooped a bit of it with one finger. Then he mounted his camel and left. A brother of hers who had been away, arrived and spotted his tracks; he saw the traces where his camel had rested. He asked about him and they told him who he was. Thereupon this brother went after Qays and brought him back to his dwelling, adjuring him that he should stay with them for a month. Qays said, "You have already put yourself to a lot of trouble for me, but I will do as you wish."

The Fazārī became more and more impressed with Qays's words, his intelligence, and his erudition.[407] Finally he proposed that Qays become his brother-in-law. But Qays replied, "My friend, you may wish that, but I am preoccupied with something else. There's no point in this."

The man kept coming back to the proposal, until his fellow tribesmen criticized him, saying, "We are afraid that what you are doing will bring shame on us!"

He answered, "Let me go on with it, for someone like this young man is a desirable partner for noble people!"

He persisted until finally Qays gave in, allowing himself to be betrothed to Lubnā, the man's sister. The brother said to him, "I shall pay the bride-price for you."

But Qays replied, "Brother, I am, by God, the richest man of my tribe; why should you have to take this upon yourself? I'll go to my people and I will bring the bride-price to her."

This he did, informing his father what had happened. The father was pleased and paid the bride-price for him. Qays returned to the Fazārīs and his bride was brought to him. But they never saw him smile at her, or approach her and speak even one word to her, or give her the merest glance. He stayed with them for many days in this way; then he told them that he wanted to visit his own people for a few days. They allowed him to go, whereupon he went straight to Medina, where a friend of his, one of the Anṣār, lived.[408] He went to see him and the Anṣārī told him that the news of his marriage had already reached Lubnā, who was saddened by it, saying, "He is faithless! I have resisted the pressure of my people to get married, but now I shall do as they say!"

Her father had complained to Muʿāwiyah[409] and told him that Qays had been harassing her after the divorce. Muʿāwiyah wrote to Marwān ibn al-Ḥakam,[410] with the decree that Qays's blood could be shed with impunity if he harassed her, and ordering her father to marry her to a man called Khālid ibn Ḥillizah, of the tribe of ʿAbd Allāh ibn Ghaṭafān (others say, rather, that he ordered her to be married to a man of the family of Kathīr ibn al-Ṣalt al-Kindī, the ally of Quraysh). Then her father married her to him. On the evening that she was taken to her husband the women of the tribe recited:

Darling Lubnā's husband
has no one who excels him.
He's privileged above all others
by what she nightly tells him.
But Qays is dead while yet alive,
he's slain, midst women wailing, crying.
May God not keep him far from us;
Away with those who say he's dying!

Qays was greatly shocked; he sobbed and cried hot tears. Instantly he rode to where his people lived. The women called out to him, "What are you doing here now? Lubnā is already with her husband!"

The men confronted him with similar words, but he did not answer until he reached the place where her tent had been. He dismounted and started to wallow in the dust, rubbing his cheek on the earth and crying bitterly. Then he said,

Song

I complain to God about the loss of Lubnā, as complains
an orphan child to God, bereft of both his parents,
An orphan harshly treated by his nearest kin;
his body lean, his parents distant memory.
Their home weeps for their absence and my tears
stream forth. Whom of the two who grieve could I condemn:
The one who shed his tears of love and passion, or
the other one, who madly cries from grief?

Ibn Jāmiʿ has a song based on the two first lines, in the first heavy mode, following al-Hishāmī; ʿArīb has one in the second heavy mode. On the third and fourth lines there is one by Mayyāsah, in the light *ramal* mode, with the fourth finger, following ʿAmr, Ḥabash, and al-Hishāmī. The remaining lines of the poem, on which no songs are based, are these:

The love of Lubnā leaves me broken—
in all its forms love is a terrifying thing.

A man whose heart hangs on the love of Lubnā dies
  or lives a wounded man as long as he's alive.
Although I have resolved to bear your absence,
  I'll be always faithful to what was between us two.
A time in which our enemies have scattered what
  was once united is an evil time indeed.
Can it be right, then, that your heart is free
  and sound, and my heart sick with love?

Others say that these verses are not by Qays, but came to be mixed with his poetry; but in this particular report they are attributed to him.

He also said, on Lubnā's departure from her homeland when she was taken to her husband in Medina, while Qays was staying among her tribe:

Song

Sweet Lubnā's gone—my heart is what has gone.[411]
  All that she promised was a putting-off, equivocation.
She failed to keep her promises you hoped for; now
  my heart, since she is gone, is stunned.
God knows, if no one else, how I
  am babbling when I think of you.
You most perfect of people, from your top to toe,
  the prettiest of people, clothed or naked!
Sweet bedfellow when shortly after waking up
  one draws a plump one to oneself, still sleeping or awake!

The poem ends as follows:

May God not bless those who believe that you
  weren't true to me, until events took a bad turn,
Till, finally, I woke, when she was married off:
  my heart was as if stunned.
Her apparition came to me at night and kept me from my sleep;
  I spent the night in yearning, shedding tears in streams.

Whether you cut the bond or merely part with me,
  Fate comes to man in various shapes.
I've never seen someone like you among mankind,
  though I have seen some tribes and womenfolk!

Ibn Qutaybah says, in his version on the authority of al-Haytham ibn ʿAdī, which is also transmitted by ʿUmar ibn Shabbah, that Lubnā's father went to Muʿāwiyah to complain about Qays and his harassment of his daughter after the divorce. Muʿāwiyah wrote to Marwān, or possibly Saʿīd ibn al-ʿĀṣ,[412] decreeing that Qays's blood could be shed with impunity if he visited her. Then Marwān (or Saʿīd) wrote a strongly worded letter to that effect to the owner of the watering place where Lubnā's father lived. Lubnā sent a messenger to Qays to tell him what had happened and to warn him. His father found out and reproached him angrily, saying, "Now you've got yourself declared an outlaw by the authorities!"

Qays replied,

Song

They may bar me from her, they may slander to keep
  me from her, a commander may issue a threat:
But they won't stop my eyes from crying forever,
  and they cannot remove what I keep in my mind.
I complain unto God of the passion I suffer,
  of the burning and sighing that visit me regularly,
And the fire of my loving that burns in my breast,
  and long nights full of grief that is never cut short.
I shall cry for myself with my eyes full of tears
  like a sorrowing captive in fetters.
Yet, before people knew of our love,
  we together enjoyed the most blissful of times;
But as soon as the slanderers had done their worst,
  our loving each other was turned upside down.
You were all my soul needed: if only our union could last!
  But the world and its joys are illusory all.

In the report this poem is attributed to Qays ibn Dharīḥ; but al-Zubayr ibn Bakkar says that it is by his grandfather, ʿAbd Allāh ibn Muṣʿab.[413]—Ibn al-Kalbī, in his version, says that Qays said about Muʿāwiyah's allowing his blood to be shed if he visited her:

A bar may've been placed between Lubnā and me,
unsurmountable, not to be crossed,
Yet the breeze blows the air that we breathe, she and I,
and we both see the beams of the sun when it sets,
And our souls meet at night in our tribe,
and we know, when at daytime siesta we rest,
Terra firma supports both of us, and above,
we can both see the stars that revolve in the sky,
Until Time will at last bring us peace, and the feuds
that it seeks from me now and the hatred will cease.

The following is found in a book by Ibn al-Naṭṭāḥ:[414] Al-ʿUtbī said: My father told me: Qays ibn Dharīḥ went on pilgrimage; as it happened, Lubnā also went on pilgrimage that year. He saw her when a woman of her people was with her. He was perplexed and stood immobile, as she went her way. Then she sent the woman to him with a greeting and inquired about him. The woman found him sitting alone, reciting poetry and crying:

That day in Minā[415] when you turned away from me,
when I spoke not of what my soul would say to Lubnā...
My sickly soul finds consolation in despair
when it desires a goal that cannot be obtained.

She entered his tent and began to speak to him about Lubnā, and he talked about himself for a while. She did not tell him that Lubnā had sent her. He asked her to greet her from him, but she refused. He began to recite again:

When the sun rises, say "Be greeted!" For its rise
serves as my sign for greeting you,

A tenfold greeting when the sun is rising, and
another ten when its grows red,[416] about to set.
Would that a friend could bring to her my greeting! She
would cry in anguish and her tears would drip.
The passion that she keeps a secret in her breast would show,
if she could hear a tale about me that would frighten her.

The pilgrims completed their pilgrimage and left. Qays fell very ill on the way home and nearly died. Lubnā's messenger did not visit him, because her people had seen him and knew about him. Qays said,

O Lubnā, my plight will be grievous to you,
the morning when what I'm expecting will happen!
You are keeping me wishing, denying to me what I wish,
while my soul every day with its longing is cut into pieces,
And your heart never softens although it can see.
Woe to me, for so long have I humbly beseeched you!
I blame you for what you are doing to me; you blame *me*!
You are harsher and more aloof to your lover.
You'll be told I have died of my grief
and your eyes, unmoved, will not shed any tears.
By my life, I cried only for you, even though
all my illness came only from you.
The morning the women who visit the sick
came to me: all the women were shocked.
"He had died," said one woman, "before we arrived!"
And another said, "No, when we left he was breathing his last!"

Here, al-Qaḥdhamī transmits the following:

But no tears on account of this came to your eyes,
while my eyes dripped with tears, for the memory of you.
If you will not cry when a loved one has died,
then don't cry when tomorrow I'm raised on my bier.

The verses reached Lubnā, who was greatly shocked, and she cried a lot. She went out one evening, having arranged a meeting. She apologized and said, "I am only making sure that you stay alive, for I am afraid that you will be killed. That is why I am shunning you. If it weren't for that we would not have parted."

She said farewell and left. Khālid ibn Kulthūm said that her family said to her: "He is ill and he will die on his journey."

She replied, to avoid suspicion, "I think he is a liar in what he claims. He is merely pretending and not really ill."

Qays heard about this, and said,

God's earth, broad as it is, is now almost,
  Umm Maʿmar, too confined for me:
For Lubnā disbelieves my love! If only she
  were burdened with an equal love for me, she'd have a taste.
—If you knew all that's hidden, you would know for certain that
  I am sincere, I swear by all the sacrifices marked for slaughter.
For you my soul is yearning, but I hold it back,
  ashamed—someone like me deserves to be ashamed.
I chase away my roaming soul from you:
  to no one else but you will be its path.
For I, though you may cut our bond and flee from me,
  am anxious for you, fearing fateful incidents.

[Nineteen more lines of the poem have been omitted. Apparently he recovers from his illness.]

He went to his people, took some of his camels, and told his father that he wanted to sell them and donate the proceeds to his family. His father knew very well that he wanted to see Lubnā. He reproached Qays and told him not to go, but Qays persisted. He took his camels and went to Medina. While he was offering them for sale, Lubnā's husband negotiated with him about a she-camel; they did not know each other. Qays sold it to him, and the other one said, "Come and see me tomorrow in the house of Kathīr ibn al-Ṣalt and you'll get your money."

Qays agreed. Lubnā's husband went home and said to her, "I've bought a she-camel from a Bedouin. He'll come tomorrow to fetch his money, so prepare some food for him."

The following morning Qays arrived and said to the servant girl, "Tell your master that the man with the she-camel is at the door."

Lubnā recognized his voice, but did not say anything. Her husband said to the servant, "Tell him to enter."

Qays entered and sat down. Lubnā said to the servant, "Ask him, 'Young man, why are you so disheveled and covered with dust?'"

The servant asked and Qays sighed and said to her, "This is what happens to someone who parts from those he loves and chooses to die rather than to live."

He began to cry. Then Lubnā said to the servant, "Ask him, 'Tell us your story.'"

When Qays began to tell his story, Lubnā removed the curtain and said, "Enough! We know your story."

Then she drew the curtain again. Qays was stupefied for a moment; he could not speak. Then he burst out crying, got up, and left. Her husband called out to him, "I say, what's your story? Come back and take the money for your camel! We'll give you more if you want."

But Qays did not answer; he went outside, jumped into the saddle, and rode away. Lubnā said to her husband, "Man, that was Qays ibn Dharīḥ! Why did you do this?"

"I didn't know it was him!"

Qays cried all the way home, bewailing and blaming himself for what he had done. Then he said,

Song

You are crying for Lubnā after you left her?
  In the open country you had more chances to have her.[417]
Lubnā may move to and fro in the world;
  the world has its ups and its downs.[418]
In her was a place one could trust,
  one's hand could explore her, one's eye could feast,
Her saliva would quench a parched man,
  a wine that inebriates him who is merry and proud.

In her presence I feel like a swing between ropes:
  when my heart hears her name it rocks.

*

Al-Ḥaramī ibn Abī l-ʿAlāʾ informed me: al-Zubayr ibn Bakkār related to me: ʿAbd al-Malik ibn ʿAbd al-ʿAzīz related to me:

A man from Medina called Abū Durrah married a woman who had been married before to another man from Medina called Abū Buṭaynah. The former husband met him and struck him, as a result of which his hand was crippled. Abū l-Sāʾib al-Makhzūmī met him and said to him, "Abū Durrah! Has Abū Buṭaynah struck you because of his wife?"

"Yes."

"Well, I can testify that your wife is not like what Qays ibn Dharīḥ said about his wife Lubnā: 'In her one could trust, one's hand could explore her, one's eye could feast, / Her saliva would quench a parched man, a wine that inebriates him who is merry and proud.'"

This wife of Abū Durrah was in fact black as a dung beetle.

*

He returned to his people, having seen her. He was angry with himself and sorry, and he was in a terrible state. His people were wondering what the matter was and they asked him, but he told them nothing. He fell ill so badly that he was on the point of dying. His father and his kinsmen came to see him and spoke to him. They reproached him, imploring him to forget her. But he said, "Do you really think I am making myself ill? Or that I have consoled myself now that I have lost all hope of having her, and that I willingly choose grief and misery? Would that be of my own doing? All this is what my parents have chosen for me and they have killed me in doing so."

His father began to cry, praying for relief and solace for his son. Qays said,

You have tormented me, O Lubnā's love;
  now strike with either death or life.
For dying is more restful now than living
  at a distance, separate, forever.
My nearest say: console yourself, forget
  her! Yes, I said, I will, the hour I die.

After he had left Lubnā, she sent a messenger, saying to him, "Ask him to recite poetry. If he asks who you are, say you are from the tribe of Khuzāʿah. After he has recited poetry to you, ask him: 'Why did you marry again after the divorce, leading Lubnā to consent to being married too?' Remember what he says so that you can repeat it to me."

The messenger went to Qays, greeted him and said he was a Khuzāʿī. He told him that he had come from Syria to hear him recite poetry. Qays recited his poem that begins with

I swear: half-blind old she-camels that care
for their dummies or tend their calves...

(these verses were quoted above). Then the man asked him, "Why did you get married again after divorcing her?"

Qays told him, swearing that he had never looked at the woman he had married, that he would not even recognize her if he saw her together with other women, that he had never touched her, or talked to her, or removed any of her clothes. The man said, "I am a neighbor of Lubnā's, and she is so badly in love with you that her husband would like you to be near her, so that she will improve. Say anything you wish to her so that I can convey it to her."

Qays replied, "Come back to me when you are about to leave."

[When the man is about to leave, Qays recites to him a poem of twenty lines, which, as the author says, shows some confusion with verses of the same meter and rhyme by Qays ibn al-Mulawwaḥ, known as Majnūn Laylā.]

Al-Madā'inī related to me, on the authority of ʿAwānah, who heard it from Yaḥyā ibn ʿAlī al-Kinānī, who said:

The affair of Qays became widely known in Medina. Al-Gharīḍ, Maʿbad, Mālik[419] and others sang his poems and there was nobody, high or low, who was not greatly moved when they heard it, feeling sorry for Qays's suffering. Lubnā's husband rebuked and reproached her, saying, "You have caused a scandal for me, being mentioned in this way."

But she replied, angrily, "Man, I swear by God I did not marry you because I wanted you or your possessions! And you were not deceived about me. You knew that I was married to him before, and that he was forced to divorce me. By God, I only agreed to remarry when they threatened to make him an outlaw if he visited our tribe. I was afraid that his passion would move him to risk his life and be killed; so I married you. Now it is up to you: divorce me; I don't need you."

The husband did not reply. He began to come to her with girls of Medina, who would sing Qays's poems to her, hoping to be reconciled to her. But she only became more estranged from him. She would cry inconsolably whenever she heard any of these songs.

Back to the story now: al-Ḥirmāzī and Khālid ibn Jamal say that there was a woman called Buraykah, one of the clients of the tribe of Zuhrah—a very well-bred and noble woman. She had a husband from Quraysh and this man had a house for guests. When Qays had been ill for a long time, his father said to him, "I know that you can be cured by being near Lubnā. Go to Medina!"

Qays traveled to Medina and arrived at the guesthouse that belonged to Buraykah's husband, whose servants were about to take down Qays's saddle, but he said, "Don't, for I am not staying here, unless I can see Buraykah, for I want something from her. If she can receive me I will stay or else I'll move on."

They went to her and told her. She came to him, greeting and welcoming him, and said, "It will be done, whatever it is! Stay!"

He dismounted, approached her, and said, "Shall I tell you what I want?"

"If you like."

"I am Qays ibn Dharīḥ."

"May God keep you alive and favor you! Your name sounds new to us every time!"[420]

"I should like to see Lubnā for one moment, any way you want."

"Leave it to me."

He stayed with them and she kept it a secret. He handed her many presents and said, "Be nice to her and her husband, until you are all good friends."

She did so and visited her several times. Then she said to Lubnā's husband, "Tell me about yourself, are you better than my own husband?"

"No."

"And is Lubnā better than me?"

"No."

"So why am I always visiting her and yet she doesn't visit me?"

"It is up to her."

She went to Lubnā and asked her to visit her, and she told her that Qays was staying with her. Lubnā readily responded and came to her. When he saw her and she saw him they both cried until they nearly died. She asked him how he was and about his illness. He told her and asked her about herself and she told him. Then she said, "Recite to me what you composed when you were ill."

He recited:

My soul holds on to remnants of my life;
    while women visit, each a sick man's guest.
When Lubnā's name is mentioned I will smile
    just like a baby at a milky breast.
I calmly speak of Lubnā when addressed,
    but my recurrent sighs are manifest.
She can revive my spirit; and if you
    could see me, I would give my life with zest.

From the same poem:

Song

Would that the days gone by came back again:
    If they returned one day I would be blessed.
May clouds that thunder with their downpours rain
    on Lubnā's home wherever she may rest.

The remaining lines of the poem are:

No matter whether she is near or far:
    the nearer she, the harder I am pressed.
Despair's no comfort, nearness no avail,
    Lubnā's aloof and grants not my request.
I am like someone bitten by a snake,
    by men's hands held; I writhe and find no rest.

Dear Lubnā shot her arrow at my heart
  and darling Lubnā's arrow hit my chest.
My heart loves Lubnā, life-long, though relief
  has come to every man by grief oppressed.
A woman said, He's dead, or dying soon!—
  My soul expects to issue from my breast.
My soul holds on to remnants of my life;
  while women visit, each a sick man's guest.

Al-Ḥirmāzī adds in his version:

She reproached him for getting married; then he swore that he would never look straight at his wife nor ever come near her. She believed him. Then he said,

Song

I wanted to give you up and bear it—I couldn't,
  for the old attachment to love still clings fast to my heart.
It remains in spite of all that took place over time;
  in spite of your harshness, it is still precious to me.
You have broken with him, you are sound, and he in his sickness:
  So far apart are they, the sound and the sick!
For a time you deceived him; he replied with forbearance:
  he who loves is forbearing toward his loved one.

They say that they were together all day, while he talked to her and complained to her, most chastely and nobly, until the evening. Then she left, promising to return the following day. But she did not come back and did not send a messenger. Then he wrote the following verses on a piece of papyrus, gave it to Buraykah, and asked her to convey it to her. Then he traveled on to Muʿāwiyah. The verses were these:

Song

How dear to me, the one who's always in my heart,
  the one who turns her hardened heart away!

The one for whom my love grows stronger all the time,
whose love for me is now a ruin in decay.

So then he traveled to Muʿāwiyah. He called upon Yazīd,[421] complaining about his plight and eulogizing him. Yazīd pitied him and said, "Ask what you will. If you want me to write to her husband and force him to divorce her, I will do so."

But Qays said, "I don't want that; but I want to stay where she lives and find out about her as much as I like without risking to be declared an outlaw."

"Even if you had asked me this without traveling to us, you could not have been refused it. Stay wherever you want."

He got a document from his father stating that Qays could stay wherever he wished and that nobody should oppose him, revoking the earlier decree about shedding his blood with impunity. Then Qays went to his own country. The Fazārīs heard about him and his visits to Lubnā; they wrote to him, reproaching him. Qays said to the messenger, "Say to the man (meaning the brother of the girl he had married): 'Brother, I have not deceived you about myself. I told you that I was wholly preoccupied with someone else. I leave the matter of your sister to you: do what you think fit.'"

However, the man could not bring himself to make the couple separate. So she remained attached to him for a while, until she died.

Al-Ḥaramī ibn Abī l-ʿAlāʾ related to me: al-Zubayr ibn Bakkār transmitted to us: Sulaymān ibn ʿAyyāsh al-Saʿdī transmitted to us, on the authority of his father, who said:

One day I came from al-Ghābah[422] and when I arrived at al-Madhād there was a campsite newly inhabited. A man was sitting on one side, slumped, crying and talking to himself. I greeted him but he did not return the greeting. I said to myself, this man is deranged! So I turned away. But a moment later he called out to me, "Greetings to you, too! Come, come to me, man who greets me!"

I went back to him and he said, "In truth, I heard your greeting but I am a man whose mind is preoccupied: it wanders from me at times and then comes back to me."

I asked, "Who are you?"

"Qays ibn Dharīḥ al-Laythī."

"Lubnā's lover?!"

"Yes, Lubnā's lover, upon my life, and her victim!"

His eyes shed tears like two waterskins. I will never forget his poem:

Has Lubnā left, before we either were a pair
 or else cut off by her so that one can despair?
During the day with love-madness I am affected,
 while all the night I feel by my own bed rejected.
Before today I was still free of love and pain;
 in many diverse ways the dying may be slain.[423]
My heart is throbbing, after Lubnā said goodbye,
 each throb is like a lightning flash that splits the sky.
Mad lovers will not find their sense: God has not willed.
 Whatever has been decreed on them must be fulfilled.
Two things torment me with incessant wailing:
 my heart, my eye, its eyelids shedding tears unfailing.

Al-Ḥasan ibn ʿAlī informed me: Aḥmad ibn Saʿīd related to us: al-Zubayr related to us, as did Wakīʿ on the authority of Abū Ayyūb al-Madīnī: Ẓabyah related to me:

I heard ʿAbd Allāh ibn Muslim ibn Jundab recite to my husband the verses of Qays ibn Dharīḥ:

When Lubnā is mentioned he groans and complains
 like a feverish man in distress who is ailing.
Night and day under shadow of death he's barely
 alive, while the tribesmen and women are wailing.
Loving Lubnā has broken the heart in his breast;
 distracted with love are all lovers, obsessed.

My husband shouted, "Oh! Alas! Poor man!" Then he turned to Ibn Jundab and said, "Do you recite it like this?!" Ibn Jundab said, "How should I recite it then?" My husband said, "Why don't you groan like he groans and complain like he complains!"

Al-Qaḥdhamī said: One day, Ibn Abī ʿAtīq said to Qays, "Recite to me the most passionate verses you have said on Lubnā!"

Then Qays recited:

I love to sleep even though it isn't time
for sleep: perhaps I'll meet her in my dream.
My dreams tell me that I will see you:
Would that dreams came true!
I testify I'll never swerve from loving you
and that—I hope you know—I'll never give you up
And that my heart will never yield to love
for anyone but you, although they say it will.

Ibn Abī ʿAtīq said to him, "You seem content with rather little on her part!"

"That is what the destitute have to bear."

Aḥmad ibn Jaʿfar Jaḥẓah said: Aḥmad ibn Yaḥyā Thaʿlab[424] recited to me these verses by Qays, which he found beautiful:

May rain fall on the remnants of the dwelling where
you were, a downpour, rain in summer and in spring!
A time went by when people asked for me to intercede;
tomorrow, who will plead on my behalf with Lubnā?
I'll cut the bond, Lubnā, with you once and for all,
though cutting bonds with you is frightening.
I shall console myself and think no more of you
just as a man in foreign lands forgets his far-off home.

[seven verses have been omitted]

Song

If the departed tribe did not perturb my mind,
gray doves did so, alighting where they dwelt:
They called to one another and made lovers cry
when they lamented, though they shed no tears.

Song

When women, censuring, told me to give her up
my broken heart rejected what they said,

For how could I obey these censors when the thought
of her keeps me awake while censors sleep?

Al-Ḥaramī informed me: al-Zubayr ibn Bakkār related to us: ʿAbd al-Malik ibn ʿAbd al-ʿAzīz related to me:

I recited to Abū l-Sāʾib al-Makhzūmī these verses by Qays ibn Dharīḥ:

I love you with all kinds of love, the like of which
I've never found described by anyone.
One kind is love for the beloved, sympathy
for what I know of what she's burdened with.
Another is that thoughts of her will never leave
my heart, until my soul is near to death.
And love that in my body and complexion shows;
and love, more subtle than my spirit, in my soul.

Abū l-Sāʾib said, "Truly, I'll be his devoted friend, I will be angry at what makes him angry and I will be pleased by what pleases him!"

Al-Ḥaramī informed me: al-Zubayr related to us: ʿAbd al-Malik ibn ʿAbd al-ʿAzīz related to us, on the authority of Abū l-Sāʾib al-Makhzūmī, that the latter related to him:

I was in the company of ʿAbd al-Raḥmān ibn ʿAbd Allāh ibn Kathīr in the roofed gallery in the house of Kathīr, when a funeral procession went by. Abd al-Raḥmān said to me, "Abū l-Sāʾib, it's your neighbor Ibn Kaladah! Come, let us pray for his soul!"

"Yes, by God, an excellent idea!"

We stood up and went, but when we passed by the house of Uways I mentioned that Ibn Kaladah's grandfather had married Lubnā and lived with her in Medina. So I went back and sat myself down in the roofed gallery again, saying, "God will not see me praying for that man!"

Later, ʿAbd al-Raḥmān returned and asked me, "Were you prevented from praying because of a ritual impurity?"[425]

"No, by God!"

"What was the matter then?"

"I remembered that his grandfather had married Lubnā and thus separated her from Qays when he took her to his country. So I am not going to pray for his soul!"

Muḥammad ibn al-ʿAbbās al-Yazīdī informed me: Aḥmad ibn Yaḥyā related to us: ʿAbd Allāh ibn Shabīb related to us: Hārūn ibn Mūsā al-Farawī related to me: al-Khalīl ibn Saʿīd related to me, saying:

I passed by the bird-market, where I saw a crowd of people packed together. I looked to see what they were about, and there I found Abū l-Sā'ib al-Makhzūmī struggling with a crow that had got hold of the end of his robe, saying to the crow, "Qays ibn Dharīḥ says to you:

O crow that tells of parting, you have flown away
with Lubnā, just as I feared; now, won't you alight?

"So why don't you alight?"

He beat it with his robe while the crow was cawing. Someone said to him, "But Abū l-Sā'ib, God bless you, this isn't the same crow!"

"I know, but I begin with the innocent, until the culprit will 'alight'."

Al-Ḥirmāzī says in his version: When Lubnā heard Qays's verse "O crow that tells of parting, you have flown away / with Lubnā, as I feared; now, won't you alight?", she swore an oath that whenever she would see a crow she would kill it. So whenever she or a servant or a neighbor of his saw one, she would purchase it from its owner and cut its throat.

This verse is from one of Qays's beautiful poems, the best lines of which are the following:[426]

Are you crying for Lubnā after you left her,
like someone willingly going towards his doom?
O heart, be firm and resign yourself to the facts,
and O my love for her, alight where you will!
And O heart, tell me, when Lubnā is far
away from you, what will you do?
Will you endure the pain and the parting,
or will you forget about shame and break down?

You are like a green one, you never saw people
before her, you haven't been tested by Time.
O crow that tells of parting, you have flown away
with Lubnā, just as I feared; now, won't you alight?
Whenever a lover is constant to his beloved
and loyal, Time will afflict him,
The lands on God's earth where she is not,
though people be there, are but desolate wastelands.
You'll never sleep peacefully when sweet Lubnā is far,
although all sleepers are welcomed by beds.

Song

I spend my day in talking and wishing
while at night I am joined by worry.
My daytime is like other people's daytime; but
when darkness comes at night my bed shakes me to you.
My love for you is firmly fixed in my heart
like fingers are fixed to their hands.
Distress attacks me from all sides,
lasting disasters that will never leave.
Ah, I cry for what has happened,
but what's the use of fretting about what may be?
I used to cry when parting was certain,
knowing what being apart would do to us.
I fled from you like someone loathed, while love
for you made cutting wounds in my heart.[427]
I go toward a land I do not want, so that
perhaps one day events will bring me back.
I fear your being far away; and dreadful was
our being parted when united for a while.
You will not get all you wish when free of cares,
you cannot follow passion's course until the end.
Upon my life, the bed of him whose bedfellow
is Lubnā will be preferred above all other beds.
Such is sweet Lubnā; to visit her is out of reach.
And such is parting: absence unrelenting.

What God wants to unite no-one will sever,
 and what He separates nobody can unite.
So do not cry from regret now that Lubnā has gone
 and events have torn her away from your hands.

It is said that the three verses beginning "I spend my day in talking and wishing" are by Ibn al-Dumaynah al-Khathʿamī,[428] which is in fact correct; but people have included them because of their resemblance to the rest.

There are different versions of how the story of Qays and Lubnā ended. Most of the transmitters say that they both died while they were separated. Some say that he died before her and that when she heard this she died from grief. Others say, rather, that she died before him and that he died afterward of grief. This is mentioned by al-Yūsufī, on the authority of ʿAlī ibn Ṣāliḥ, who said: Abū ʿAmr al-Madanī said to me:

When Lubnā died, Qays went out with a number of his relatives and stopped at her grave, saying:

Lubnā is dead: her death is my death too.
 How can my sorrow help? My joy has been denied.
Now I will cry like someone grieving,
 who dies from love for someone who has died.

Then he bent over the grave and cried until he fainted. His people carried him away while he was unconscious. He remained ill, not regaining consciousness and not responding to anyone who talked to him and three days later he died. He was buried next to her.[429]

[In another version,] al-Qaḥdhamī, Ibn ʿĀʾishah, and Khālid ibn Jamal say that Ibn Abī ʿAtīq went to al-Ḥasan and al-Ḥusayn, the sons of ʿAlī ibn Abī Ṭālib, to ʿAbd Allāh ibn Jaʿfar (may God be pleased with them), and to some other people of Quraysh, and said to them, "I want something from a man, but I am afraid that he will refuse. I'd like to use your high position and great wealth, to carry weight with him!"

"We will grant you this."

They met on a day they had arranged, and he took them to Lubnā's husband. When the latter saw them, he was greatly taken aback by their coming to him. They said, "We have come to you, all of us, because Ibn Abī ʿAtīq wants something from you."

"Consider it done, whatever it may be!"

Ibn Abī ʿAtīq said, "You mean consider it done whatever it is, in matters of possessions, money, or family?"

"Yes."

"Then will you give Lubnā, your wife, to them and to me, and divorce her?"

"I testify to you that she is hereby divorced!"

The others were embarrassed; they apologized and said, "We swear by God that we had no idea what he wanted. If we had known what it was we would not have asked you to give us Lubnā."

Ibn ʿĀ'ishah says that al-Ḥasan gave the man one hundred thousand dirhams by way of compensation. Ibn Abī ʿAtīq took Lubnā to him.[430] She stayed with him until her waiting period was over. Then they asked her father, who married her to Qays; they stayed together until they died. Qays eulogized Ibn Abī ʿAtīq in a poem.

The Merciful reward you with the best reward
  for your benevolence towards a friend!
I've tried and tested all my friends
  but I have found nobody like Ibn Abī ʿAtīq.
For he took pains to give me union after severance,
  and put me on the path from which I strayed,
Extinguishing the torment in my heart
  that choked me with its heat.

Ibn Abī ʿAtīq said to him, "Dear friend, please refrain from eulogizing me like this: if people hear it they will think I am a pimp."

A Parable: The Human Condition, or The Man in the Pit[431]

The Persian convert ʿAbd Allāh Ibn al-Muqaffaʿ, one of the pioneers of Arabic literary prose, translated *Kalīlah wa-Dimnah* (a collection of animal fables enframed in a story about two jackals called Kalīlah and Dimnah) from Pahlavi into Arabic. The story is also found in the *Mahābhārata*, bk. 11, ch. 5–6, but not in the *Pañcatantra*, the Sanskrit original of *Kalīlah wa-Dimnah.*

When I[432] thought about the world and its affairs and considered that a human being is the noblest and most excellent part of creation, but only led from one evil and worry to the next, I was amazed. I realized that there could be no human being with understanding who, knowing this, would not seek to save himself and find an escape. Anyone falling short in this respect is, in my opinion, weak and lacking in insight and ambition regarding his situation.

Then I looked about and saw that all people fall short and are oblivious of their situation. I was amazed at this and tried to excuse them. I looked and saw that the only thing that kept people from trying to save themselves was the small and paltry pleasure derived from seeing, hearing, smelling, tasting, and touching: a pleasure of which they may perhaps gain a little and obtain a trifle. It was this that preoccupied them and prevented them from caring for themselves and from seeking an escape.

The parable of the man who has fled from an elephant

Then I sought a parable for Man. And see, his parable is that of a man who, in fear of an enraged elephant,[433] has escaped[434] into a pit, into which he has let himself down, hanging down and holding on to two branches at its edge.[435] His feet have landed on something hidden in the pit: four snakes, their heads sticking out from their holes. He looks down and there is a dragon,[436] its mouth open, waiting for him to fall so that it can devour him. Then he raises his eyes to the two branches and sees two rats at their root, a black one and a white one, that are gnawing at the two branches untiringly and without flagging.

While considering his situation and worrying about his fate, he notices near him a beehive containing honey. He tastes the honey, and its sweetness preoccupies him and the delight of it distracts him from thinking about his plight, or from seeking a means to escape. He no longer remembers that his feet are resting on four snakes and is no longer aware that he has landed on them. He does not remember that the two rats are steadily cutting through the two branches, so that when they are cut through he will fall on the dragon. Thus he remains diverted, unaware, preoccupied with that sweetness, until he falls into the mouth of the dragon and perishes.

*

With the pit I gave a likeness of the world, which is filled with plagues, evils, fears, and maladies. With the four snakes I gave a likeness of the four humors[437] found in the body: whenever they or any one of them are stirred it is like the fang of vipers and lethal poison. With the two branches I gave a likeness of the span of life that will last until a certain moment, after which it must perish and be cut off. With the two rats, the black one and the white one, I gave a likeness of night and day, which are steadily annihilating the lifespan. With the dragon I gave a likeness of the destiny from which one cannot escape. With the honey I gave a likeness of the scant sweetness that Man obtains, by seeing, tasting, hearing, smelling, and touching, by which he is preoccupied and diverted from thinking about himself, so that he forgets to consider the hereafter and is turned away from the path he intended to take.[438]

Mirror for Princes (and Others): Passages from Ibn al-Muqaffaʿ's *Right Conduct*[439]

Al-Adab al-kabīr (*The Large [treatise] on Good Conduct*) by Ibn al-Muqaffaʿ, is, like *Kalīlah wa-Dimnah*, a work of practical rather than religious or ethical wisdom, not addressed to "princes" or rulers only. The sections following the present selection, for example, are about how one ought to behave toward one's superiors and one's equals. The present selection is a translation of the Introduction and the first section: a "mirror for princes."

ʿAbd Allāh Ibn al-Muqaffaʿ says: We have found that people before us had larger bodies. In addition to this they had greater understanding, were stronger, were more expert in their affairs and, by their greater strength, lived longer, and, through their long lives, were more experienced in everything. Their men of religion reached a higher degree of religiosity, both in terms of knowledge and practice, than do the men of religion in our own time; and their men of the world too reached similar levels of eloquence and virtue. We have found that they were not content merely with the merits they acquired for themselves, but also wanted to have us share with them the knowledge they had attained of this world and the next. They therefore wrote books that last, they coined apposite proverbs, and spared us the effort involved in experience and insight. They were very preoccupied with this, to the extent that, whenever one of them was in an uninhabited region and a door of knowledge opened to him, or he hit upon a word of wisdom, he would write it on some rocks before death overtook him, since he was unwilling to let it be lost to those that came after him. In this they acted just as an affectionate, compassionate, and devoted father acts toward his children, amassing wealth and property for them because he wants to save them the trouble of having to seek it for themselves, and because he fears that they will be unable to do so if they seek it.

In our time, the utmost a scholar can know is by drawing on their knowledge, the most beneficent deeds that a benefactor may do is by emulating their conduct, and the best speech that a speaker among us can find is by looking in their writings, so that he appears to be conversing with them and listening to them.

However, what we find in their books are merely a selection of their views and their choice sayings. We discover that they have left nothing for an eloquent speaker who wants to describe something, which they have not said first—neither in the glorification of God Almighty and in making people desirous of His favor, nor in belittling this world and making them renounce it; neither in documenting the various branches of knowledge, their classification and subdivision of their parts, the clarification of their methods, and the exposition of various topics, nor in describing the several types of proper conduct[440] and different kinds of ethics. There is nothing, after them, left to be said on any lofty subject. All that remains are a few things: insignificant[441] matters that might suggest themes for lesser intellects, things deriving from the great instances of wisdom and sayings of the ancients. This is part of what I intend to write in this treatise of mine, on the various types of proper conduct of which people are in need.

Chapter describing the principles of proper conduct in religion and other things

You who seek after proper conduct: learn the principles, then learn the details. Many people look for the details while ignoring the principles, and so achieve nothing. He who secures the principles has no need, consequently, of the details. If, later, he hits upon a detail, having secured the principle, all the better.

In the matter of religion, the principle is that you hold fast to a correct belief, avoid major sins, and fulfill the religious obligations. Hold fast to this, as something indispensable at every moment, like someone who knows he will perish if he is deprived of it. If, after that, you are able to go beyond this by deepening your knowledge of religion and of worship, then all the better.

In the matter of preserving one's physical wellbeing, the principle is not to burden the body with too much food, drink, and sexual intercourse. If, after that, you are able to learn about everything that is beneficial or harmful to the body, and how to make use of this, then all the better.

In matters of courage, the principle is not to tell yourself to retreat when your companions are advancing on the enemy. If, after that, you are able to be the first to attack and the last to turn back, without forsaking due caution, then all the better.

In matters of generosity, the principle is not to withhold from people their rights. If, after that, you are able to give them more than they are entitled to, and to be generous to those who have no right at all, it is all the better.

In matters of speaking, the principle is to avoid errors by being reticent. If, after that, you are able to arrive at a correct expression, then all the better.

In matters of livelihood, the principle is not to be lax in seeking what is licit and to estimate correctly both revenues and expenses. Do not let the comfortable circumstances in which you find yourself delude you: the people of greatest importance in this world are also in greatest need of the ability to estimate correctly. Rulers have greater need of it than the common people, because the latter can subsist without wealth, but rulers cannot function without it. If, after that, you are able to be kind and gentle in seeking wealth, and if you know where it may be found, then all the better.

I shall now advise you concerning some subtle ethical matters, things that are not so obvious, and which, even if you had not been told them, you ought to know if you are an experienced, worldly wise man. But first I would like to offer you some words so that you may train your soul in its good qualities, before it gets accustomed to its bad ones. For it is in youth that a man's bad qualities will break out and may gain the upper hand over him when they do.

On caution when assuming power, and certain other matters

If you are tested by assuming power, seek refuge with scholars. Know that, strangely,[442] when a man is tested by power he wants to reduce the hours he devotes to toil and work and to increase the hours he devotes to rest and pleasure. The correct course and his duty is to take time from all his other occupations and devote them to the work at hand; on his meals, drinking, sleep, conversation, amusements, and his wives, he should only spend as much time as is needed to make his body fit and strong for the completion of his task. Rest should come only after he has completed his work.[443]

When you have assumed power in some form, be one of two men: either the man who relishes it and guards it lest it is taken away from him, or the man who dislikes it, for such a person will work under duress, whether for rulers, if they have granted him power, or, if he has no superiors, then for God. And you know that rulers destroy those who fall short in serving them, so do not give death power over you and a way toward you!

If you are a ruler, beware, of becoming enamored of being praised and commended, and of people learning of this, or it will be a breach through which they will assail you, a door they will open to get at you, and an occasion for them to slander and ridicule you. Know that the recipient of praise is like someone who praises himself. It is proper for a man that his very love of praise move him to reject it; for he who rejects praise is praised and he who accepts it is blamed.

In ruling, you should seek three qualities: the approval of your Lord, the approval of the authority above you, if there is one, and the approval of the virtuous people over whom you rule. It does not matter if you are not concerned about acquiring wealth or fame, for you will come to enjoy enough of both in due course. However, you should never dispense with the three qualities mentioned above, whereas wealth and fame you can treat as dispensable.

Get to know the religious and virtuous people in every town, village, or tribe, so that they will be your friends, your assistants, your inner circle, and your trusted confidants.

On counsel

Do not make yourself believe that if you ask for people's advice you will appear to be someone who needs other people's opinions. After all, you do not want an opinion in order to boast about it: you want one in order to benefit from it. If, at the same time, you are thinking of your reputation, then the better of the two kinds of reputation, according to the virtuous, is that one says of someone: "He does not form opinions on his own: he consults those with sound views."

On seeking people's pleasure

If you seek to please everyone then you seek what cannot be achieved. How could the views of people holding different opinions ever be in agreement? Why should you need to please those whose pleasure lies in injustice, or to approve of those who approve of error and brutal ignorance? You should seek the pleasure of good and intelligent people, and when you have obtained it you will not need to trouble yourself with anything else.

Do not allow people who have behaved well toward you to be humiliated and do not empower others to be insolent to them and to denounce them. Let your subjects be familiarized with the special doors through which you may be approached for your favors, as well as those doors which make them fear you. Be very eager about being well informed about the affairs of your governors, for a bad governor will fear your knowledge before (he does evil and before) your punishment strikes him, and a good one will be glad of your knowledge before your favor reaches him. Let people be aware, regarding what they know of your character, that you are hasty neither in rewarding nor in punishing; for this will prolong both the fear of those who have something to fear and the hope of those who have something to hope for.

General exhortation

Accustom yourself to enduring those sincere counsellors who disagree with you, and to swallowing the bitterness of their words and their censure. Do not, however, smooth this path except to intelligent, mature, and virtuous people, or else, once it becomes widely known, some foolish person might boldly take advantage of it or some spiteful person might think light of doing so.

Do not fail to address directly any matter of grave importance, lest your prestige diminish; and do not deal directly with a small matter, lest a big matter be lost.

Know that your mind cannot encompass everything, so free it up for what is important. Your wealth does not suffice for all people, so direct it specifically to those entitled to it. Your liberality cannot extend to the common people, so single out virtuous people. Your night and day will not be enough for your needs no matter how hard you work; you will not find a way to do your work without giving your body its due share of rest, so divide your time fairly between rest and work.

Know that whatever time you spend thinking about unimportant things is to the detriment of what is important; that whatever money you spend on trivial things you can no longer use for things of true value you may want to do; that whatever generosity you divert to unworthy people will harm you by making you fall short toward virtuous people; and that whatever time of your night and day you devote to unnecessary things will make a mockery of necessities.

Know that there are many people whose anger, if they are angry, reaches such a degree that it will make them scowl and frown at people who have not been the cause of their anger; or to speak harshly to those who have done no wrong; or to punish those they did not intend to punish, or to punish severely, physically or verbally, people they intended to treat less harshly. Subsequently, when such a person is placated, his delight reaches such a degree that he voluntarily offers considerable gifts to those whose status, in relation to him, does not warrant it, or he gives to those he does not intend to give anything, or honors those who do not deserve it and for whom he has no affection.

Beware of this, therefore, for none are in a worse situation than those who have power and who, with their power, exceed the proper bounds in their anger or their pleasure. If someone punishes in his anger those who have not angered him, or favors in his pleasure those who have not been the cause of his pleasure, one can surely describe him as someone whose reason has been affected and who has been touched by madness.[444]

On the different kinds of rulers[445]

Know that there are three kinds of rulers: one of religion, one of judiciousness, and one of personal inclination.[446] As for the ruler who is religious, if he upholds the religion of his people, and if their religion is such that he gives them their due and metes out to them what they deserve, they will be pleased with him and he will turn the discontented among them into people who will gladly conform and submit. The reign of a ruler who is judicious is stable; he will not be free of criticism and discontent, but the criticism of a lowly person will not be harmful if the judicious ruler is strong. As for a ruler of arbitrariness, his reign is one hour of play and an eternity of ruin.

On caution when the dynasty is new and lacks judiciousness

If you acquire authority when the dynasty is young and you see something that looks right without being based on a sound view, or (when you see) servants who function without obtaining anything (in reward),[447] or work that is successful without resulting from judiciousness, then do not be deluded by this and do not be lulled into complacency. For a new thing is respected by some people and attractive to others; thus some people will give their support in person or with their possessions. Thereby the situation may stay stable for a short while; but subsequently matters will revert to their true state and their basic principles. Anything that is not built on reliable cornerstones and a firm pillar will soon collapse and crumble.

Be neither too taciturn in speaking and greeting nor excessively jolly and cheerful, for the former is a kind of haughtiness and the latter a kind of foolishness.

On keeping from untrustworthy companions

If you are not in firm control, and you attack your enemy with the help of people whose opinions you cannot depend on and whose intentions you cannot trust, then nothing will do you any good until you change them, if you are able, into people of sound opinion and refined manners such as can be trusted, or until you replace them, if you cannot change them to your liking. Do not be deluded by the power you exert over others through them, for in this situation you are merely like someone riding a lion: he is feared by whoever sees him, but is himself more fearful of his mount.

A ruler must not get angry, because his need is backed by his power.

He must not lie, because nobody can compel him to do what he does not want to do.

He must not be stingy, because he of all people has the least excuse to fear poverty.

He must not be spiteful, because his status is too grand to requite all people for what they have done.

He should be careful not to swear oaths often, for of all people rulers have most cause to be wary of oaths. A man is moved to swear an oath only by one of the following dispositions: by an abasement and a humbleness that he finds in himself and a need to make people believe him; or by an inarticulateness in his speech, so that he uses oaths as expletives or as connectives; or because he has realized that people do not trust his words, so that he puts himself in the position of someone whose words will only be believed after he takes the trouble to swear an oath; or because of speaking pointlessly and letting loose one's tongue without thought or consideration.

When scrutinizing people's affairs everybody is justified in suspecting his eyes of looking with misgivings, and his heart of feeling hatred.[448] For the eyes and the heart embellish injustice, induce to falsehood, and make the ugly seem beautiful and the beautiful seem ugly. Of all people, the one most obliged to be suspicious of a mistrusting eye and a hateful heart is a ruler, for whatever occurs to his heart will grow, especially when his associates and viziers are bound to embellish it.

Of all people, the one most obliged to force himself to be just, in thought, word, and deed, is a ruler, for it is through his justice that those under him will act justly, and whatever he says or does will be a command to be carried out unopposed.

It does not detract from a ruler when, in his daily life of luxury, he deals personally only with important matters and delegates less important issues to qualified, competent people.

The ruler should know that people describe rulers as being untrue to their pledges and forgetful of their friendships. So he should struggle to refute what they say and to disprove, for himself and all rulers, the bad character with which they are imputed.

The ruler must examine the less important concerns[449] of his subjects, in addition to weighty matters, for a small thing may be the occasion for something useful, whereas a weighty matter cannot be dispensed with.

When examining the affairs of his subjects, the ruler must attend to the needs of the free, noble ones among them; he should make an effort to meet their needs and to quash the oppression they experience from the lower classes. He should feel distressed by a noble man who is hungry and an ignoble man who is sated, for a noble man will be aggressive only when he is hungry, and an ignoble man only when he is sated.

The ruler should not be envious of those under him: this is less excusable for him than when the common people are envious of those who are above them, though neither has an excuse.

The ruler should not blame someone for an error—if he cannot be suspected of anything but trying to obtain the ruler's pleasure—except by means of instruction and correction; and he should not equate just anyone with someone who strives to obtain his pleasure and who shows discernment. For when such traits are found together in a vizier or in a companion, the ruler can sleep and rest easy; his needs will be fulfilled for him even though he is not actively attending to them, and his concerns will be acted upon even though he is not paying attention.

The ruler should not be given to thinking the worst of what people say: he should give over a large part of his mind to favorable opinions. These will reassure him and will allow him to act accordingly.

The ruler should never fail to be firm when speaking, when giving, or when undertaking something, for it is better to go back on one's silence than on one's words. A gift after a rebuff is more decent than rebuff after giving, and proceeding to action after tardiness is better than holding back after having proceeded. All people need to be firm, but none more so than their rulers, whose words and actions cannot be opposed and who have no one to impell them.

The ruler should know that the people will concur with him, except some to whom he need pay no mind. Therefore kindness and virtue should be commodities in great supply to him, and there will consequently be little demand for injustice and baseness in all corners of the land.

In sum, what the ruler requires in worldly matters are two attitudes: one that will strengthen his authority and one that will make his rule appear benevolent to his people. The former attitude, based on power, is the more appropriate at the beginning and the preferable one; the other view, based on propaganda, is more pleasant and produces more allies. It is true that power depends on propaganda, and propaganda on power—but things tend to be ascribed to whatever is more formidable.

Al-Jāḥiẓ on Flies and Other Things[450]

Abū ʿUthmān ʿAmr ibn Baḥr, known as al-Jāḥiẓ ("Pop-eye"), who died well into his nineties in 255/868–69, was one of the most versatile writers in Arabic. He wrote in a personal style, characterized by digressions, a mixture of seriousness and jesting, and by long, cumulative sentences, on an astounding range of subjects. His major work, *al-Ḥayawān* (*Living Beings*) deals, among many other things, with zoology, popular lore, poetry, language, and theology. One of the aims of the book is to show how God's providence may be discerned in everything, including insignificant or abhorrent creatures. He belonged to the "rationalist," Muʿtazilite movement in Islamic theology. The following passages are taken from a very long section on flies, which contains the usual digressions, some of which have been included. The omission of some parts is indicated by an asterisk.

On the Various Kinds of Flies

In the name of God and by God, praise to God! There is neither might nor power except through God. God bless and preserve our Master, the unlettered[451] prophet Muḥammad, his family, his companions, and his pious, goodly, and excellent descendants. I enjoin you, perceptive reader and attentive listener, not to despise anything on account of the smallness of its body, nor to think little of it because of its trifling value. Know that a mountain is not better evidence of God's power than a pebble, that this celestial sphere that contains our world is no better proof of God than a human body, and that small and delicate matters are like those big and sublime. Things do not differ in their true natures: it is those only among us who ponder matters who differ, those who fail to speculate, who ignore the points of difference and the defining distinctions. They differ inasmuch they desist from speculation and abandon it, or they investigate it from the wrong point of view, or they apply the wrong premises, whereas others begin their speculation from the right point of view and complete it with well-ordered premises.

*

If you see any animal that is of no use (to mankind), apparently ignorant of how it avails,[452] or so harmful that one should be extremely wary of it, such as animals with fangs, like snakes and wolves, or those with claws, such as lions and leopards, or those with stings, such as scorpions and hornets: know then that their usefulness lies in the tests and tribulations that God Almighty has prepared for the steadfast, those who understand this and who know that free choice and learning from experience cannot exist in a world that is wholly bad or purely good, that there must be a mixture of what is disagreeable and what is desirable, of what is painful and what is pleasurable, despicable and revered, what can be trusted and what must be feared. If the supreme reward results from free choice and experience, by which one attains the nearness of God Almighty and His eternal magnanimity, and if this can only be in an abode that is a mixture of good and bad, one that partakes in and is composed of usefulness and harm, a blend of easiness and difficulty, you should know therefore wherein lies the usefulness of the creation of the scorpion or the artfulness of the creation of the snake, and one should not despise gnats, moths, ants, or flies.

*

As for the creation of the mosquito, the ant,[453] the moth, fly, dung beetle, drone, and locust: you should take care not to treat these hosts with contempt, nor to belittle the power of these created beings. Many a people has been driven from its lands by large ants, moved from their birthplaces by small ants, destroyed by mice, stripped of vegetation by locusts, tormented by mosquitoes, or had their lives corrupted by flies. They are a host that God Almighty sends when He wants to destroy a people after they have become tyrannical, despotic, and arrogant, so that they know, or that it be known through them, that their great might cannot withstand even a small part of God's command. In this is a lesson for those who contemplate it, an admonition to those who reflect, a salvation for those with insight, a tribulation and a test, a torment and retribution, a true proof, a clear sign, something that leads to steadfastness and reflection, two things that bring about all that is good in matters of knowledge and clear perception, in matters of reward and recompense. We shall now mention a number of things about flies and then say something of what we know about crows and dung beetles.

In a vituperative and invective sense, one says, "They are nothing but moths that fly into the fire, or greedy flies"; one says "as heedless as a moth" and "as proud as a fly."[454] A poet has said,

The Banū Dhuwaybah, Salmā's clan are moths
 that warm themselves around the fire's glow;
They circle round its heat, fall into it:
 how to protect themselves they do not know.

Moths, bees, wasps, and hornets are all called "flies" by the Bedouin Arabs. They say "as proud as a fly" because a fly will settle on the nose of a despotic king, or on the corner of his eye in order to eat it; he then tries to drive it away but it will not be driven away.

*

One speaks of a "fly-ridden camel" when it suffers from something that attracts flies. Rinderpest is recognized when it has spread and afflicted a camel by the fact that flies have settled on it. This is artfully exploited by the camel drivers when the authorities want to take his camels against his will, or when he possesses a particularly valuable camel stallion or a noble camel mare. He will take some pitch, pour some date syrup on it, and smear it on that camel. When the flies smell the syrup they fall on it; then the man claims it is suffering from rinderpest, producing the flies found on it as witness to the authorities. Through such ruses they very often manage to keep their wealth from the hands of the authorities. The authorities think that the man might as well sell a hundred camels for a dirham if he wished.[455] Rinderpest, they know, is contagious, and it is in the nature of camels to be very susceptible to contagious diseases. The camel driver then says to the authorities, "I would not mind, were it not that I am afraid the diseased camel will infect the others! I fear for the contagion of the disease and the harm to my herd as a whole." He keeps pleading and scheming thus, until they let him go.

It is said that flies will not come near a kettle that contains mushrooms, just as a gecko will not enter a room containing saffron.

*

The Bedouin Arabs call the buzzing of flies and mosquitoes "singing." Al-Akhṭal said, describing an oryx bull:

Standing alone, while the flies of the meadow are singing to him,
 As seductive singers who sing with harps to a Persian warlord.[456]

Ḥaḍramī ibn ʿĀmir[457] said on the buzzing of flies:

Exchanging malice is their habit still,
And to revile their friends, lampoon and vilify.[458]
Your reputation among people is no greater now,
in any gathering, than the buzzing of a fly.

One says, "what I am saying is just like the buzzing of flies to you."

During their short lives there is a special time in which flies are driven to copulate. It is said in the hadith: "The life of a fly lasts forty days."[459] There is also a time when they are incited to feed on humans, to bite them and to drink their blood. They come into houses only when their end is near, and perish soon after. Flies are the bane of camels and other cattle at any time. Flies and mosquitoes have a proboscis, which is why their bite is strong enough to pierce thick skins. A *rajaz* poet says, describing a mosquito:

Like a thorn, and always buzzing,
Its proboscis mounted with a knife.

*

When they want to describe something as little and trifling they use expressions involving flies. A poet says,[460]

I saw you hold bread so dear it seemed
to me your bread was high up in the skies.
You did not use the fan to keep the flies away from us:
you only feared the damage done by flies.

Another says:[461]

When I saw that the door of the palace was closed,
and the fortune of Hamdān's tribe was high,
I was sure that of Ibn Muḍārib's rule was left
no more than the prick of a fly.

*

There are two good qualities in the fly. One of them is the ease whereby their harm may be repelled and their nuisance driven away. If one wants the room to have the same amount of light and shade as before, after having driven them away, and to be safe from harm by the flies, one only has to close the door, for they quickly leave, trying to outstrip one another in search of light, fleeing from the darkness. Then if the curtain is let down and the door opened the light will return and the people will be safe from the nuisance of the flies. But if there is a crack in the door, or a gap between the two panels of a closed door that are not aligned perfectly, they will get through. Sometimes they come through the gap between the door and the threshold. It is an easy trick to drive them out and be safe from their harm. It is not so with mosquitoes, for they are very harmful and powerful. They are particularly keen when it is dark, just as the power of flies is strong in the light. People cannot simply make light enter their houses to prevent the mosquitoes from being active, because that can only be done by letting the sun in, and since mosquitoes only come in summer, the sun is then too strong to be endured. All light on earth, besides that of the sun, also has its share of heat. Though heat, in some places, comes without light, light is never separated from heat in any place. Thus using tricks is easy with flies and difficult with mosquitoes. The other good quality is that if flies did not eat mosquitoes, by pursuing them and seeking them on the walls of houses and in nooks and crannies, people could not stay in their homes.

I was told by reliable sources that Muḥammad ibn al-Jahm[462] asked them one day, "Do you know the wisdom we have derived from the fly?" "No," they replied. He said, "They eat mosquitoes, hunt them, snap them up, and destroy them. Once I wanted to have a siesta. I gave orders, some time in advance, that the flies should be driven out of the room, the curtain let down and the door closed. When the flies went out the mosquitoes entered the room, with all their might and power. I went to sleep and the mosquitoes bit me terribly. Another day I went inside at siesta time. The room was open, as it happened, and the curtain was raised; the servants had neglected their duty that day. When I lay down to sleep I did not suffer at all from mosquitoes. I was very angry with the servants, but I slept peacefully. The following day they closed the door and drove out the flies. When I entered in order to take my siesta there were many mosquitoes. Then, another day, they again forgot to close the door.

"When I saw it open I scolded them, but lying down to sleep I did not find a single mosquito. Then I said to myself, I find that I can sleep when they are neglectful and cannot sleep the days they take good care. Why don't I try to leave the door open today? Then, if I sleep for three days running without suffering from mosquitoes with the door open, I will know that it is best to let in the flies and the mosquitoes together, for the flies destroy them. Our well-being will come from doing what we used to avoid. And so I did, and thus it turned out. So whenever we want to drive out the flies we do this with the greatest ease, and when we want to destroy the mosquitoes we do so by means of the flies with the greatest ease."—These are two good qualities in flies.

*

Ibn al-Jahm said, "There are some people in al-Sufālah[463] who eat flies. They do not suffer from ophthalmia. It is not for that reason that they eat them; they are like the people of Khurasan who eat the grubs of wasps, a wasp being a kind of fly. Those who eat fresh cheese take a piece that is infested with maggots; one of them knocks on it so that all the maggots fall into the palm of his hand. Then he swallows them, as one eats the grains from *sawīq*."[464] Al-Farazdaq used to say, "I wish they gave me my share of flies to eat, all in one go, on condition that if I eat them I be spared them forever!" They say he found flies extremely dirty and abhorred them greatly.

*

Al-Makkī told me once, "Flies live for forty days." I answered, "So it is said in the Hadith." That day we were in Wāsiṭ,[465] when the army was camped there. Apart from India there is no place that has more flies than Wāsiṭ. Sometimes you see a wall that looks as if a deep-black rug is hanging on it, so numerous are the flies. I said to al-Makkī, "I reckon flies die after forty days, or more if you like, or less. Now as you see we are actually trampling them with our feet. We have stayed here for more than forty days, months in fact, without ever having seen a dead fly. If it were true, we would have seen dead ones just as we see the live ones!" Al-Makkī replied, "When a fly wants to die it goes to some deserted ruin." I said, "But we have been in every ruin in the world yet we have never seen a dead fly there!"

*

A sage has said that there cannot be anything on earth that stinks worse than excrement. Similarly, there is nothing filthier than flies and lice. As for excrement, if it were not true, then humans, with their long familiarity with it, seeing and smelling it from themselves every day, morning and evening, would necessarily lose their loathing in the course of time: it would disappear or at least diminish; whereas it remains stable, smelling equally bad, during sixty years, give or take. We have found some people who found the same after a hundred years. Yet we have seen the effect on human nature of habits and customs, how they make easy what is hard, and make what seemed much seem little. If excrement did not exceed everything in its stench its perception would not be found to be stable and it would go the way of other bad smells. Moreover, if one smells something that comes out of someone else's body and not from one's own body, it is the same. Now if the bad smell stays in one's nose to that extent even if it is from oneself rather than from someone else, to the extent that one finds it smells worse than the excrement of other species, then this can only be because it is singularly loathsome.

It is the same with lice, which are created from a human being's sweat, from his smells, the dirt of his skin, and the vapors of his body; and similarly the flies that are in contact with them all the time and involved with them more than any other kind of insect, vermin, bird, herbivore, or carnivore: they are more closely associated with them than anything and nearer than anything, to the extent that no part of the human body is barred to them, or of his clothes, his food, his drink: nothing clings closer to him. When he travels far from fertile lands, crossing steppes and deserts without any vegetation in or near them, nor water, nor animals, and when he then seeks a place to relieve himself in the desert, away from his companions, far away and in a bare desert, when he then defecates and his eye falls upon his excrement, he sees flies pouncing on it, whereas before that he had not seen any. If a fly is something that is created there and then, this is more amazing than what he has seen and what we meant and more than we said. Or if that fly can land on a smooth rock and bare patches on a scorching day in the midday heat which roasts everything, and wait for it to come, then this is more amazing than what we said. Or if the fly has followed him from town, either flying with him or having landed on him, and then presents itself when the man has done his business, then this proves what we said about the fly's close association with humans. For sparrows, swallows, starlings, cats, and dogs are all close to humans, but flies will stay with a human, even if he travels, like someone seeking desolate places and settling in deserts. All kinds of domestic animals that are familiar to people will stay where they are as they are wont; they will not follow them from their homes to desolate places, except for flies.

*

We noticed that sometimes people are annoyed by the crackling of a burning wick, the sound it makes when it is about to be extinguished or when it comes into contact with some water. The noise is not loud, but the annoyance and the displeasure are equal to that caused by the loudest noises. A similar irritation affects people on account of the snoring of a sleeping person: the irritation is not caused by the loudness and strength, but by the form and quantity, if not because of the kind of noise (?). It is the same with the noise made by rubbing new bricks against each other, or the rustling of treetops on river banks: the soul dislikes it just as it dislikes the sound of a thunderclap. If one was certain that he was safe from being burnt, one would not mind about the lightning so much.

*

They claim that when a predator hunts with another predator that is a better hunter, it learns from it and imitates it. I have not verified this. But what I do not doubt is that a bird with a good singing voice, when it is with other singing and warbling birds and when one near it of its own kind is better and more skilled than it, it will answer it and imitate it: it learns from it, or engages in something that serves as learning. A packhorse is trained and understands what is demanded from it, and then is useful to men by itself. Sometimes they hire a man to teach birds. I have seen this with nightingales: I saw a man who was summoned to expose them to the kind of sounds they make. There are some birds that invent sounds and tunes that have never been heard from a human composer. A bird may compose a tune that singers have never heard yet. This is most often found in turtledoves and starlings, and also in falcons, which eat flies in large quantities.

It is said that persistence is found in three species of animals: the black beetle,[466] the fly, and the red caterpillar.[467] The last-mentioned tries to climb to the ceiling, crawling up a smooth wall bit by bit; then it falls but returns, advancing a bit and then falling again, persevering until it has reached the ceiling. Sometimes it falls when there is only one inch left, and it tries again. A black beetle will advance toward a human, who then pushes it away. It lands at some distance after this setback, then returns, only to be met with a ruder rebuff, yet it returns again, to the point of causing anger, which may cause it to be killed. People and black beetles have always done this. As a result poor people have come to believe that black beetles bring luck and that their approach is the sign of a windfall in livelihood, in the form of a donation, prize, profit, or a gift. Thus, if a black beetle gets into their clothes and creeps into their trousers they do not utter a sound; at most, these days, they will gently remove them. Some people think that if it is pushed away, comes back, is pushed away, comes back, is pushed away, comes back—that the more often this is done, the more hoped-for riches he will gain!

Now consider how well protected it is, how well preserved and well guarded, what a safe place has been made for it because of this belief! How fortunate for them that people give credence to such things! It is greed that has stirred up this belief from its hiding place, and it is poverty that has brought about this greed. But woe to them if the beetles persist in approaching a rich and learned man, especially if he is not only rich and learned but also short-tempered and impetuous!

People used to kill large flies that buzz loudly and persistently, those that cause a din, the kind the common people call "the prince of the flies." When disturbed by its buzzing, droning, and humming they had various tricks to drive such a fly away, to chase it, and to kill it, for it never slackens. But when they happen to believe that it brings good tidings, such as the return of an absent traveler, or the cure of a sick person, then nobody disturbs it when it enters their house and heaps its evil on them.

Whenever God Almighty wants to give respite to any particular animal, He arranges a cause for that. Likewise, when He wants its life to be short and its day to come to an end, He arranges a cause for it. God is greatly exalted!—We now return to the persistence of flies.

We had a cadi in Basra called ʿAbd Allāh ibn Sawwār.[468] People had never seen a judge as grave, as imperturbable, as dignified, or as mild-tempered as he, or anyone as self-controlled and in command of his every movement as he was. He used to perform the morning prayer in his house (he lived near his mosque). Then he would come and hold session, sitting with his robe wrapped around his drawn-up knees[469] and without leaning against anything. He always sat upright, without moving a limb, not turning, not untying his knee wrap, keeping his feet together, and not supporting himself on either side, so that he looked like a building made of stone, or erect like a rock. He would remain like this, until he would get up to perform the noon prayer. Then he would return to his seat and stay there until he would get up to perform the afternoon prayer. Then he would go back and sit down, remaining like that until he would get up for the sunset prayer. He would sometimes return to his place, but it often happened that he still had something to read such as deeds, contracts, or documents. He would then perform the last evening prayer and go home. Truth be told: during the entire time that he was thus engaged he did not once get up to perform his ablutions, nor had he any need to do so.[470] Nor did he drink water or any other drink. This was his routine, whether the days were long or short, in summer and winter. In addition to this he never so much as moved his hand or gestured by moving his head. He only spoke, and concisely at that, conveying much with few words.

One day, when he was sitting in this way, with his assessors and the public seated around him and in two rows in front of him, a fly landed on his nose and lingered there a long while. Then it moved toward the inside corner of his eye. He wanted to endure when it got into the corner of his eye and bit it with its piercing proboscis, just as he had endured it when it landed on his nose, without twitching the tip of his nose or wrinkling his face or whisking it away with his finger. When the fly had troubled him for some time, hurting him and stinging him, and intending to move on to a spot where it could no longer be ignored, the cadi brought his eyelids together, closing his eye. But it did not move. This induced him to continue closing and opening his eye, but the fly would merely move aside until his eyelid had stopped moving, and then applied itself again to the corner of the eye with a vengeance, worse than before, plunging its proboscis in the same spot where it had injured him before. This time the cadi was even less able to bear and endure it than before. He blinked his eyelids, opening his eyes with ever increasing force, alternately opening and shutting them. The fly would move aside until the movement stopped and would then return to its place, pestering him until it had exhausted his endurance and had done its utmost. At that point the cadi could not refrain from whisking it away with his hand, which he did with the eyes of the people on him, though they pretended not to see him. The fly moved away until he had lowered his hand and had stopped moving, then returned to its place. This caused the cadi to fall back on driving it away with the hem of his sleeve, and to do so repeatedly. He was aware that his every movement was being witnessed by his assessors and the others who were present. As they looked at him he said, "I swear that flies are more persistent than a black beetle and more conceited than a crow! May God forgive me! So many have been pleased with themselves whereupon God, the Mighty and Sublime, wished to make them aware of their own weakness that was hidden from them! I knew that I had a reputation as one of the gravest of people, but now God's feeblest creature has got the better of me and has shamed me."

Then he recited God's word: «And if a fly should rob them of anything, they would never rescue that from it. Feeble indeed are the seeker and the sought!»[471] He was a man of clear speech who did not waste words, respected by his fellows, someone above being criticized himself and above making insinuations about others for the sake of material gain.

I myself have suffered from flies. I was out walking along the Mubārak River[472] once, heading for the monastery of al-Rabīʿ. I had not been able to hire an animal to ride. I passed some fields thick with vegetation and flies. One of these flies settled on my nose; I waved it away, but it moved to my eye. I whisked it away but it came back to the corner of my eye. I began to move my hands rapidly; it moved for as long as I moved and kept it from my eye—flies in fields, woods, and meadows behave differently from others. It came back and I waved it away, it came back and I tried harder. When it returned I used my sleeve and whisked it away from my face. But it came back. All the while I was walking fast, hoping to get rid of it by my speed. When it came back I took off my hood[473] from my shoulders and whisked it away with that instead of my sleeve. When it renewed its attack and I could not think of anything else I began to run, going for some distance, something I had not done since I was a young boy. Al-Andalusī[474] invited me into his place, saying, "What's happened to you, Abū ʿUthmān? Have you had an accident?" "Yes," I replied, "A bad one: I wanted to get away from a place where the flies got the better of me." He laughed and sat down. But the fly was gone! Though I only believed it had gone when it was far away.

*

Some people say that flies are created from putrid matter, vapors, and exhalations, that they disappear when these disappear.[475] They maintain that they know this by their abundance in southern parts and their scarcity in northern parts. They say, "Sometimes we have put a stopper on the mouth of a bottle containing a drink, and when we removed it we found little flies." Dhū l-Rummah said,[476]

They know the shallow water of the pool has now
turned into moths, the plants are dry and withered.

A man from Thaqīf, a maker of *nabīdh*,[477] told me that sometimes when they split a quince, when it is ready to be carried away and eaten, they do not find any small flies in it. But they never fail to see small flies appear where the quince has been cut; they sometimes keep watch on them and find that they get bigger and grow into large ones in the space of an hour.

Flies have one strange and amazing characteristic in common with dung beetles. If one had not seen it with one's own eyes one would be justified in rejecting the truth of the matter. When a dung beetle is buried among roses it appears to die: all its movements cease, it turns rigid and stiff. To an observer it looks no different from a dead beetle. But when it is returned to dung it comes back to life and begins to move immediately. I have tried this with black beetles and found it to be very like the dung beetle in this respect. This must be because the black beetle and the dung beetle are so closely related.

One day I visited Ibn Abī Karīmah.[478] He had just put out a tub containing water that had been used for washing dirty clothes. Many flies had fallen into it overnight and died, or at least so it appeared to the eye. They remained thus during the evening and the night. At noon, the following day, they were swollen, putrid, and flaccid. Then Ibn Abī Karīmah baked some bricks and bits of brick. He took five or six of the flies, put them on the bricks and poured some dust made of ground brick over them, covering them completely. In no time we saw them move, walk, then fly, though they flew rather feebly.

Once Ibn Abī Karīmah said, "By God, I will never bury a dead person until the body stinks!" I asked him why. He said, "Nuṣayr, this servant of mine, had died. I delayed his burial for some reason. That night his brother arrived. He said, 'I think that my brother is not dead!' He then took two large wicks, soaked them in oil and lit them. Then he extinguished them and held them near his brother's nostrils. In no time he began to move. And look, there he is!"

I told him that physicians and the people who wash the corpses of those are killed in battle know about indications and signs of death. Never be tempted to cover and bury a single dead body until it stinks! The Zoroastrians bring a dead body near the nose of a dog, to find out about him. I realized that what we had seen with the flies had strengthened his belief in this.

*

Of all God's hosts flies are a particularly harmful one. At times they cause more damage than hornets. They may destroy a whole caravan, covering the camels, making them throw themselves to the ground in the desert. When they fall, the people of the caravan perish, because they can only travel in the desert on their camels. This is why camelherds and camel drivers turn their camels away from such regions; no one with an animal will go there. They say to one another, "Be quick before the flies are on the move, before the meadow-flies are moving!"

Wasps hardly draw blood when they sting with their tails. But a fly sinks its proboscis right into the flesh of animals, piercing thick skins until it can suck the blood. In addition to its bite it has poison. The mosquito also has poison. If it had a bigger body and a more biting sting—the size of a yellow scorpion (which is the smallest scorpion)—nothing could withstand it and it would be many times more dangerous than the yellow scorpion of Naṣībīn.[479]

*

The common people maintain that flies shit as they like; they say, "We see them shit white on black, and black on white." For flies one uses the verb *wanama*, in the sense of "defecate," for birds *ʿarra*, for ostriches *ṣāma*, for pigeons *dharaqa*. A poet has said,[480]

The flies had shat on it: you'd think
their shit was specks of spattered ink.

A camel stallion mounting a mare, or a boar mounting a sow does not take longer than male flies riding the backs of the females and copulating.

Flies are among those creatures that sometimes originate from copulation and procreation and sometimes from putrefying bodies and the rotting that takes place in them. Broad beans, when growing somewhat old in storehouses, are wholly transformed into flies. Sometimes the beans are left in these storehouses unattended; when the people return to the storehouses the flies fly from the skylights and the cracks, and they find nothing but the pods in the storehouses. The flies that are created from broad beans are formed as maggots and then turn into flies. When God has created the flies from them and has made them fly away, you often see that the beans have been pierced, with something like a powder inside. It also happens often that you find the flies inside, fully formed; if the wings were ready, they would fly.

*

One of our friends, someone from al-Khuraybah,[481] told us:

I used to like broad beans. Once I wanted to go to Basra, or Baghdad—I forget which—so I traveled in a barge that was loaded with broad beans. By God, I said to myself, this is really a stroke of luck! Anyone who has the same thing happening to him as happened to me must be having a good time! I can sit in this barge among these broad beans and eat them raw, boiled, or baked; I can crush them, grind them, and make them into a broth or a condiment. It is a nutritious and healthy food, it is fattening, and it is an aphrodisiac too! I began doing what I had been planning. We pushed off , but I didn't like the many flies. The following day so many of them appeared that I was unable to eat or drink. I was so busy whisking them away that I could not take a midday nap or talk. But they would not be driven away by being chased. There were more of them than I could handle: whenever I chased one hundred away, another hundred took their place. At first when they crept out of the beans it seemed as if they had some kind of illness, but when their flying around became worse, things became worse for me! I said to the bargeman, "Damn you, what are you carrying that these flies follow you everywhere? By God, they have had their fill!"

"You really don't know why, do you?"

"No, I do not!"

"Well, they come from these broad beans. If it wasn't for this plague we would have as many passengers as all the other barge skippers get. I thought you[482] must be someone willing to put up with them because of the reasonable fare and wishing to be alone in the barge."

I asked him to let me off at a boat landing so that I could hire (another barge) there to take me where I was going. He said, "Would you like me to give you some beans?"

"I never again want to cross paths with broad beans!"

*

One day I was sitting in the mosque with some of the young men that hang around it,[483] near the gates of the Banū Sālim. I was young myself, at the time. Abū Sayf the madman approached. He would not hurt a soul; he was witty and he was from a good family. He stopped where we sat and we saw that his face was serious. Then he said, emphatically, "I swear by God—and there is no god but He—that shit is sweet! And, by God—and there is no god but He—shit is sweet! Again, by God—and there is no god but He—shit is sweet! This is a binding oath, may God ask me about it at the Resurrection!"

I said to him, "I am sure you would never eat it or taste it, so how do you know? If you know something we don't, teach us what God has taught you!"

"I have seen that flies alight on sweet fruit wine but not on sour wine, that they alight on honey but not on vinegar, and I see they fall on shit more than on dates. What clearer proof than that can you want?"

I said, "Abū Sayf, by this and similar things one comes to know the superiority of an old man to a young one!"

Now let us return to the matter of the creation of flies from broad beans. Some of the common people or those like them deny that such creation is possible without a male and a female. This shows they are ignorant of the world and of the various kinds of living beings. They think that to affirm this view is harmful to one's religion; but things are not as they say. Every view that is belied by looking with one's eyes is a serious error, a foolish opinion, and a sign of either great stubbornness or excessive gullibility. If someone believes that he can reason on the analogy of outward appearances without deciding in favor of hidden truthful causes, and applies it to everything, then he says something that is also refuted by simple observation, while he also rejects religion. We know that a human being eats food and drinks liquids that do not contain any snakes or maggots, and that from it various kinds of snakes and maggots are created inside his belly, without a male and a female. This kind of procreation and conception is necessarily the result of the copulation of natural elements, the union of things that by their natures resemble wombs with things that by their natures resemble the matters that are made to conceive in the wombs.

*

For the creation caused by God Almighty without a male or a female, it is necessary that two things come together that take the place of male and female, or the place of earth and rain; for natural elements may be related to each other, even though they do not change in every sense, like sperm and blood, or milk and blood. The author of the *Logic*[484] says: "I say in general that all living beings must have blood or something that resembles blood."[485] We see that maggots are created from cadavers and likewise from excrement. That is why when a Zoroastrian defecates he sprinkles some earth over it, so that no maggots are created from it. A Zoroastrian will not defecate in wells or drains because, he claims, the belly of the earth is too noble for that; he holds that the earth is one of the basic elements from which the five worlds are built, so they claim.

*

Moreover, we may take the stopper off the mouths of bottles containing some drink and find there some moths that did not come from a male and a female. Rather, this is the result of the transformation of some particles of air and of that drink when they are conjoined in that vessel. This is as Dhū l-Rummah says, and is the explanation of his verse:

They know the shallow water of the pool has now
  turned into moths, the plants are dry and withered.

The same is true of everything that is created from the pith of a palm tree, which contains various living beings and flying creatures, animals that resemble woodlice, and what in Persian is called *fādhū*,[486] or worms, or canker worms, or woodworms, or woodlice that are created from beams, in wood and in latrines. We may discover that the ice kept in subterranean vaults in Khurasan, is wholly turned into frogs. And the frog is not a better proof of God's power than the moth. The ice changes when an opening is made in it, the size of an ox's nostril, so that wind can enter it, which acts as a fertilizer, like God Almighty said: «We have sent winds, fertilizing»,[487] making them "fertilizing", not "fertilized".

*

Everyone who suffers from bad breath is nicknamed Abū Dhibbān ("Father of Flies"). It was the nickname, they say, of ʿAbd al-Malik ibn Marwān.[488] They recite these verses by Abū Ḥuzābah:[489]

Now the Father of Flies has been stripped of his halter
Like a full-grown horse is stripped of its bridle:
Our allegiance is pledged now in full to the son of al-Ḥasan.[490]

A man said, lampooning Hilāl ibn ʿAbd al-Malik al-Hunāʾī:[491]

Who will buy Hilāl from me,
  his love and friendship, for one penny?
I'm not responsible, to him who buys him from me,
  for five of his peculiarities:

His swollen uvula, his branding marks,
his scars, his rotten teeth,
And picking flies up with two fingers,
straight from a heap of excrement.

It is said: God Almighty has made a parable of man's weakness, saying, «O ye people! A likeness has been struck, so listen to it! Those on whom you call, other than God, will never create a fly, even if they worked together. And if a fly should rob them of anything, they would never rescue that from it. Feeble indeed are the seeker and the sought!»[492] As some people say, He made flies and humans equally weak. They also say that people breed moths and other creatures from putrefaction, which is a kind of "creation" in the sense of God's word,[493] «When you created from mud something like a bird», and of God's word, «The best of creators»,[494] or the words of the poet:[495]

I see you that you cut down what you've created,
while some create but cannot cut.

To those people one should say: God's "creation" means "invention," human "creation" means "shaping."

*

People differ in their interpretation of the Prophet's saying: "The flies are in hell."[496] Some say: flies are created for hell, just as God the Exalted has created many people for hell and has created children for hell. These people are out of their depth. When one of them says that this is God's justice, he could not be more wrong. He thinks that when he attributes the torment of children to God he is praising Him. If he could find a way of saying that it is injustice, he would say that too; and if he could find a way of claiming that God the Exalted informs us of something that is the case while it is not, and then saying that it is the truth, he would say that, too. But he is too afraid of the sword to say the latter, while he is not too unafraid of the sword to say the former, even though it is a greater lie.

Some people maintain that God Almighty torments the children of the polytheists only in order to distress their parents. Those among them who pretend to be clever say: "Rather, He torments them because He wills it thus, and He can do that." I wonder if he believes he will earn God's favor by praising Him with these words!

*

Abū Isḥāq[497] has said that if their acts of obedience are equal, people are rewarded equally and that if their acts of disobedience are equal they well be punished equally. If they neither obey nor disobey, they receive God's grace in equal measure. He holds that the various kinds of living beings, everything that has sense perception and can feel pain, all receive God's grace equally. He says that the children of polytheists and Muslims alike will be in heaven, and that there is no difference between children, beasts, or madmen, nor between carnivores and herbivores. He said, "The bodies of carnivores and herbivores will not enter heaven, but God Almighty will move these spirits, free from defects, and put them into any forms that He likes." Abū Kaladah, Muʿammar, Abū l-Hudhayl, and Ṣaḥṣaḥ[498] disliked this position, and said, "According to us, both our leading scholars and ordinary people, there is no difference between saying 'the souls of our dogs go to heaven' and 'our dogs go to heaven.' Whenever we speak thus of dogs, in whichever way, people will think that we have claimed that there are dogs in heaven! We hold that everything created by God, carnivores, herbivores, insects, vermin, is either ugly and harmful or beautiful and pleasing. Animals such as horses, gazelles, peacocks, and pheasants will be in heaven and by their appearance give pleasure to the friends of God Almighty. Whatever is ugly in this world and harmful God will turn into a torment to His enemies in hell. Thus if it is said in the Hadith that flies and other creatures are in hell, it is this what is intended."

Some say that they are in hell but actually enjoy it, just as the guardians of Gehenna and those angels entrusted with tormenting enjoy their place in hell. Some claim that God the Exalted has stamped their nature with a liking for hell and living in it, just as He has conditioned maggots that live in ice or vinegar to live in these environments. Yet others say that God Almighty has given their bodies some kind of immunity from fire.

*

Al-Ḥasan ibn Ibrāhīm al-ʿAlawī told me: Once, when I met my maternal uncle, he was alone and laughing. I thought it odd that he should be laughing, for I could see that he was alone. I also found it odd because he was a serious, dignified person who rarely laughed. So I asked him about it, and he said, "So-and-so (meaning an old man from Medina) came to me, terrified, so I asked him, 'What's happened to you?'

"He replied, 'I am fleeing my home, by God!'

"'Why?'

"'There's a bluebottle in my house! Whenever I enter, it goes straight for my face, flies around me, and buzzes near my ear. When it sees I am not paying attention it never misses the corner of my eye. This, I swear by God, is what it has been doing to me for ages!'

"I said to him, 'But one fly is like another just as a crow is like any other crow! The one that pestered you today may well be different from the one that hurt you yesterday, and the one yesterday was perhaps not the same as the one from the day before.'

"He said, 'May all my slaves be freed if I didn't know it, after these fifteen years!'

"That is why I was laughing."

Al-Khalīl ibn Yaḥyā said, "I have seen how a boar mounts his sow the whole day long, and I have seen how a camel stallion mounts a she-camel for an hour. Before that I used to envy starlings and hooded crows,[499] for even though the male quickly leaves the female's back, by coming back very quickly and doing it frequently it is in the same category as the boar or the camel. But then I saw flies and came to know their ways: a male fly will mount a female fly for a whole day!" Then Muḥammad ibn ʿUmar al-Bakrāwī said to him, "That is not copulation." Al-Khalīl replied, "What the eye has seen must be the correct judgement. If you want to please yourself by denying the pleasures that you know God Almighty has distributed among His creatures, then do as you please!"

Essayistic Prose: Al-Tawḥīdī on the Superiority of the Arabs[500]

Abū Ḥayyān al-Tawḥīdī's *al-Imtāʿ wal-muʾānasah* (*Enjoyment and Geniality*) presents discussions conducted in Baghdad at the court of the vizier Ibn Saʿdān al-ʿĀriḍ, who was executed in 374/984 after a short period in office. They are wide ranging, dealing with philosophy, religion, poetry, language, and various other topics. The following text illustrates the debates and polemics regarding the movement called Shuʿūbiyyah, which claimed cultural equality or superiority for the Persians over the Arabs.[501] It is unknown whether al-Tawḥīdī (who died at an advanced age after 400/1010, perhaps as late as 414/1023) was himself ethnically an Arab or a Persian, but culturally he was thoroughly Arabic. His polished prose mostly avoids *sajʿ* and, with its balanced phrases, its long series of near-synonyms, and often long periods—the result of cumulative addition rather than intricate syntax—emulates al-Jāḥiẓ. Normally a translation into English would omit many such near-synonymous words and phrases, but in order to give a taste of the style most of it has been kept. The present translation omits a number of passages, as indicated.

I was in his presence on another night, when he opened the session by asking, "Do you think the Arabs are superior to the non-Arabs, or vice versa?"[502] "Scholars recognize four (civilized) nations," I answered, "the Byzantines, the Arabs, the Persians, and the Indians. Three of these are non-Arab. It is difficult to say that the Arabs, on their own, are better than all these three, what with all they have in common and in what ways they differ." The vizier said, "I meant the Persians only." "Before giving my own judgement," I said, "I shall relate the words of Ibn al-Muqaffaʿ;[503] he was a full-blood Persian, with a wholly non-Arab ancestry, highly esteemed by people of merit. He is the author of *al-Yatīmah*; and he said: 'With this book I leave the writers of epistles in the shallows!'" The vizier said, "Let us hear it, with God's blessing and assistance!" So I explained:

"Shabīb ibn Shaybah[504] said: We were standing in the middle of al-Mirbad,[505] a place where nobles and ordinary people often meet; a number of leading personages were present. Then Ibn al-Muqaffaʿ arrived. We all smiled at him and wanted to ask him things: we were pleased to see him. He said, 'Why are you sitting on your animals here in this place? By God, if the caliph were to send people all over the earth to find men like you he would find nobody but you! How about going to Ibn Burthun's house?[506] It has "shade stretching,"[507] it is protected from the sun, it faces the north, and it will refresh the animals and the servants. We will make the earth our cradle,[508] which is the best and most comfortable carpet, and we will listen to one another. That is a better way of sitting together and we will have a better conversation.'

"We readily agreed. We dismounted at Ibn Burthun's place and were breathing in the north wind when Ibn al-Muqaffaʿ turned to us and asked, 'Which is the most intelligent people?'

"We thought he must mean the Persians, so, wanting to seek his favor and to flatter him, we said, 'The Persians are the most intelligent people!'

"But he said, 'No, they do not deserve to be called thus because they aren't. They are people who have been taught and who have learned; they have been given examples which they copied and imitated. Others started things for them and they followed them; but they did not originate or invent anything.'

"So we said, 'The Byzantines!'

"But he replied, 'Not them either. They have strong bodies, they are good at building and at geometry but know nothing besides these two things and are good at nothing else.'

"We said, 'The Chinese then!'

"He said, 'They are good at handicraft and making artefacts; they have no deep thought or reflection.'

"We said, 'Well then, the Turks!'

"He said, 'They are wild animals that can be made to fight.'

"We said, 'The Indians?'

"He said, 'People of delusion, humbug, and conjurer's tricks.'

"We said, 'The Africans!'[509]

"He said, 'Dumb beasts to be left alone.'

"Then we left the matter to him, and he said, 'The Arabs!'

"We glanced at one another, whispering. This made him angry and his face changed color. Then he said, 'I suppose you think that I am ingratiating myself to you. By God, I wish it were otherwise and that you did not deserve it; but, even though the truth is not to my liking, I hate to be wrong. I will not let you leave before I have explained to you why I said this, as I do not wish to be accused of sycophancy or be suspected of toadying. The Arabs had neither a model to follow, nor a book to instruct them. They inhabited a desert and desolate country, everyone on his own and forced to rely on his own thought, his own eyes, and his own reason. They understood that their life depended on the earth's vegetation, so they set about describing and categorizing everything, discovering the beneficial qualities of every variety, whether fresh or dried, its optimal seasons and times, and determining what was wholesome to sheep and camels. They thought about the times and how they differed, so they divided them into spring, early summer, late summer, and winter.[510] Then they realized that their drink came from the sky, so they established a system of "rain stars" for that purpose.[511] They realized how time changes, so they apportioned its stages in the course of the year. They needed to move about on the earth, so they made the stars indicators of the various locations and regions and used them when traveling through the various lands. They laid down rules between them so as to refrain from bad deeds and encourage good deeds, to shun wickedness and to spur on to noble acts. Thus you may meet any one of them on some mountain road, who will extol noble deeds, omitting nothing, and condemn foul deeds at great length. Whenever they speak they exhort one another to do good, to protect neighbors, to spend their wealth, and to adopt praiseworthy qualities. Every one of them has hit upon all this with his reason and discovered this using his insight and his thought, since none have been taught or educated: rather, they have well-educated instincts and knowing intellects. It is therefore that I said to you that they are the most intelligent nation: because of their sound natural disposition, their balanced constitution, and their sharp understanding.'

"This is the end of the story."

*

The vizier said, "Well said by Ibn al-Muqaffaʿ, and well told by you! Now share with me what you yourself can tell me, either something you have heard or something you have thought of yourself."

I said, "If this man, who excels with his erudition and his towering intellect, has said enough about it, then to say more would be superfluous and to add more of the same would serve no purpose."

"But," the vizier replied, "one may have different, diverging opinions about what one believes to be either correct or incorrect bases for attributing fine or ugly qualities. This question—I mean which people is superior to another—is one of the main topics about which people dispute and argue; since they started discussing it they have never reached a sound reconciliation or a clear agreement."

"I believe it could not be otherwise", I said, "for the natural disposition, habits, and upbringing of a Persian will not allow him to acknowledge the superiority of an Arab, nor will the nature and the custom of an Arab allow him to admit the superiority of a Persian. It is the same with the Indians, the Byzantines, the Turks, and the Daylamites.[512] What is more, considerations of superiority and nobility depend on two things. One of them is that each nation, at the time of its origin, has made its own specific choices between good and bad, between what is sound and unsound, and in speculating about first and last things. Seen in this light each nation has both good and bad qualities, each people has its virtues and vices, each group of people is both perfect and falling short in their doing and undoing. This means that good qualities and virtues, as well as bad qualities and shortcomings, are distributed among all people and scattered among them all.

"Thus, the Persians have statecraft, good manners, rules, and protocols; the Byzantines have science and philosophy;[513] the Indians have thought, reflection, sprightliness, magic, and circumspection; the Turks have courage and intrepidness; the Africans have stamina, capacity for labor, and merriment; and the Arabs have bravery, hospitality, loyalty, heroism, generosity, a sense of honor, oratory, and eloquence. These positive qualities in these well-known peoples do not occur in all individuals but they are widely distributed among them. There are some who are devoid of them altogether and characterized by their opposites. This means that there are some Persians who are ignorant of statecraft, wholly without good manners, and to be classified as rabble or savages. Similarly, there are Arabs who are cowardly, brutish, frivolous, stingy, and inarticulate. It is the same with the Indians, the Byzantines, and the others (...)

"Another important aspect that cannot remain unmentioned, is that every nation has its heyday in the course of history. This becomes evident when you consider the empire of the Greeks and Alexander the Great, when he conquered, ruled, reigned, led, governed, did and undid, decreed, directed, commanded, prompted, restrained, deleted, wrote, acted, and informed. Likewise, if you turn to the story of Kisrā Anūsharwān[514] you will find the same things, even though the circumstances and situations were different. That is why Abū Muslim, who brought the Abbasid dynasty to power, when asked which people are most courageous, answered, 'All people are brave when their rule is in the ascendant.' He was right. On this principle every nation, at the onset of its good fortune, is superior, braver, more courageous, more glorious, more generous, more eloquent, more articulate, more judicious, and more truthful. This consideration can be applied in a general sense to all nations, to something that encompasses every single nation, to something involving every single human group, to something that dominates every single tribe, to something that is normal to every single family, and to something that is specific to every single person and human being.

"This transfer of fortune from one nation to another is an indication of God's abundant grace to all His creation, in accordance with their responsiveness and their disposition to acquire this favor from Him, throughout the lengthy course of the ages. Whoever has ascended this height with clear vision will without a doubt have seen the truth of this (...)

"When al-ʿAbbās ibn Mirdās,[515] of the tribe of Sulaym, returned from Mecca he said, 'O Sulaym, I have seen something that will lead to good things: I have seen the sons of ʿAbd al-Muṭṭalib,[516] whose statures were tall like Rudayni lances,[517] whose faces were bright like full moons in the dark, their turbans like banners above them, and their speech like abundant rain on parched earth. When God wants fruit he plants a tree: these people are God's orchard. You may expect its fruits, look forward to abundant rain, anticipate its shade, and welcome God's blessing through it!' With these words al-ʿAbbās made a correct prediction about what was to come; he surmised what was still hidden; he was aware of the unknown; his reason apprehended what was veiled; and with his subtle inner thought he was guided to occurrences that were destined to happen and events that were to take place. This is something that is common among the Arabs, because of their protracted solitariness, their pure thought, their fine build, their balanced constitution, their sound innate character, their untroubled mind, their brightly burning nature, the richness of their language with its various nouns, verbs and particles, its wide variety of morphological derivations, its capacities for original metaphors, its wonderful possibilities for brevity, its subtle allusions as against its explicit statements, its abundance of expressions for one's intentions, and the marvelous harmony of its sounds: all this, and much more, is recognized as belonging to them and is well known, as is their courage, bravery, honor, hospitality, acumen, oratory, zeal, pride, commitment, loyalty, liberality, generosity, extremes in love of praise, and a strong abhorrence of being blamed and reviled—and more, all the things that characterized them in the time of pre-Islamic ignorance, things that cannot possibly be denied, rebutted, declared false, or contested.

"We have heard the many languages of all kinds of people (even though we have by no means exhausted them all), such as the language of our Persian friends, of the Byzantines, the Indians, the Turks, the Khwārazmians,[518] the Slavs, the Andalusians, and the East Africans. But never in any of these languages have we heard the splendor of Arabic: I mean the clear intervals of its words, the space we find between its consonants, and the distance between the places of articulation,[519] the balance we experience in its patterns, and the undeniable regularity of its structures. If you wish to know whether what I say is true and whether my judgement is correct, then consider all other languages, from the most complicated, convoluted, intricate, and difficult, to those that are smoother in sound, softer in pronunciation, lighter in its words, subtler in its patterns, sweeter in its articulation, clearer in its method, more balanced, more distinct in its segmentation,[520] more sound in its connections. If you go from one language to another and finally come to Arabic, you will decide that the difficulty and obscurity that we mentioned gradually disappears, until you reach Arabic, with its pure clarity and lucidity. This is something that anyone with a sound constitution, who is free of defects, devoid of bias and partisanship, is a lover of fairness in debate, strives after truth in judgment, is not enslaved by uncritical acceptance of the views of others, is not deceived by familiarity, and who is not subdued by habit, will find to be true.

"I am often greatly surprised when someone with great merit, vast knowledge, sound intellect, and broad erudition refuses to acknowledge what I have described and denies what I have mentioned. I am even more surprised by what al-Jayhānī writes in the book in which he reviles the Arabs, attacking their reputation and denigrating their worth.[521] He says, 'They eat jerboas,[522] lizards, rats, and snakes. They raid[523] and attack each other; they use obscenities to lampoon one another. It is as if they have been stripped of human virtues and have donned the hides of swine.' He also says, 'This is why Kisrā called the king of the Arabs *sagān-shāh*,' i.e. king of dogs. He continues: 'This is because they strongly resemble dogs and young whelps, or wolves and their brood.' He writes more of this stuff, which I deem beneath a man of his stature, even though he lowers himself by what he says. Surely he ought to know that if anyone found himself in that desert on the Arabian Peninsula, that desolate place, those wastelands and steppes—be he Kisrā of the Persians, Caesar of the Byzantines, Balhawar of the Indians, Faghfūr of the Khurasanians, Khāqān of the Turks, Ikhshād of Farghānah, or Ṣabahbudh of Askanān and Ardawān[524]—he would do precisely these things. In order to stay alive and to survive, fearing death and avoiding perdition, he who is hungry eats whatever he finds, consumes whatever he can get hold of, and drinks whatever he can seize. Surely, if Anūsharwān ended up in the wastelands of the tribe of Asad, in the land of Wabār, the plateaus of Ṭībah, on the sands of Yabrīn, or in the plain of Habīr, he would be hungry, thirsty, and naked: wouldn't he eat jerboas and rats then? Wouldn't he drink camel's urine and well water, stinking, brackish liquid from pools in the hollows? Wouldn't he wear coarse woolen clothes, rags and tatters, or less, or worse? By God, he would! And he would eat vermin and mountain herbs, things sour, bitter, filthy, and indigestible.

"Such accusations are ignorant and whoever makes them is unjust. As it happens, the Arabs live the best of lives when the skies are generous, when the rain stars are true to their promise, when the earth adorns itself: then fruit hangs from its boughs, the river beds flow continuously, and there is an abundance of milk, curds, cheese, meat, dates, and flour. Markets are held; there is fine and fertile pasturage everywhere. Young animals are being born. Food is continually available. Tribes move to their intended destinations and meet one another at watering places; they talk, invite one another, make pacts and covenants, visit one another, recite poetry, make alliances, speak words of wisdom, regale nightly visitors, give to the needy, feed travelers, guide those who have lost their way, pay indemnities, ransom captives, send invitations either to a select group or to everyone in general, vie in virtuous deeds: they did all this in their native lands, in the midst of their hills and sands, where their fathers and grandfathers grew up, where their wives and children were born, in spite of living in the first and second period of Ignorance.[525]

"You have seen what happened when a favorable wind blew for them, how the call to Islam caused their realm to rise like the sun, how, when this call spread with the community of believers, the community gained power through prophethood, how the prophethood gained supremacy through the revealed law, how the law was consolidated through the caliphate, and how sound religious and secular governance made the caliphate flourish. You have seen how all the good qualities of nations accrued to them, how the virtues of peoples through the ages came to be theirs without their having to seek them, or labor to acquire them, or toil to obtain them. Rather, these outstanding traits, these glorious feats, and these rare achievements came to them spontaneously and came to dwell between the guy ropes of their tents of their own accord. Everything that God undertakes comes to pass, He who gives people success and aids them, who privileges those who are deserving by choosing them. Nobody can overcome God's command and no one can change God's decision. As God says,[526] «Say: O God, Master of the Kingdom, Thou givest the Kingdom to whom Thou wilt, and seizest the Kingdom from whom Thou wilt. Thou exaltest whom Thou wilt, and Thou abasest whom Thou wilt; in Thy hand is the good; Thou art powerful over everything.» (...)[527]

"Al-Jayhānī also says, 'That we, the Persians, are noble, preeminent, glorious and exalted is shown by the blessings that God has given us in abundance and has amply allotted to us. He has made us dwell in gardens and fertile lands and has given us luxury and opulence. He did not do the same for the Arabs; rather, He gave them a wretched existence of torment, anguish, and deprivation. He gathered them in a confined peninsula, a mere patch. He gave them turbid, sun-warmed water to drink. What one understands from this is that those who have been favored with blessings and honored are superior to those that have been singled out for humiliation.'

"He goes on like this at length, thinking that he has found an unanswerable and irrefutable argument. If things were as he says, however, it would be clear to others that the Arabs were later given many things, to the lasting sorrow and angry, useless spite of those who missed out on them. His words indicate that he is ignorant of God's blessings and of the wisdom hidden in them. He seems to believe that an ignorant person, when he wears fine clothes, eats white bread, rides a horse, turns himself on cushions, drinks wine, and makes love with a pretty girl, is nobler than a learned man who is dressed in rags, eats herbs, drinks plain water, has the earth as his pillow, is content with little, a frugal existence, not hankering for any luxuries. This is a wrong view, a judgment to be rejected by God and by all virtuous and intelligent people. By his reasoning, too, someone who can see would be nobler than a blind man, and a rich man superior to a pauper (...)

"Al-Jayhānī also says, 'The Arabs have neither the book of Euclid, nor the *Almagest*,[528] nor the *Music*, nor books on agriculture, medicine, therapeutics, or anything dealing with the health of the body or the properties of the soul.' But he ought to know that the Arabs knew all this by divine rather than human inspiration, just as other nations learned it by human instead of divine means. By 'divine' and 'human' I mean 'natural' and 'artificial', even though the divine inspiration of the Arabs is mixed with the human inspiration of the others, and vice versa. In any case, if this slanderer knew his facts he would know that the *Almagest* and the other works he mentioned do not belong to the Persians either. It seems to me that he is boasting and is claiming these works for his people. He may say: they belong to the ancient Greeks, and they are non-Arabs, as are the Persians, so I merely transfer this merit from one group of non-Arabs to another. But this is a false argument that may be used against him. For if he were to boast to the Greeks he would be unable to claim this for the Persians and he could not say 'We are also non-Arabs and your merit on account of these books and crafts also accrues to us!' If he said this, he would be faced with an unpleasant and damaging rejoinder: 'Shut up!' they would say to him, like they say to a stupid person, if not 'Down!', as is said to a dog. If I ignore him, however, I wrong myself; he who shows good will toward his adversary will be overcome."

Abū Ḥāmid al-Marwarrūdhī, the cadi, said:[529] "Suppose that all virtues, like pearls strung as a necklace or unstrung, were combined in the Persians, hanging round their necks, dangling from their ears, or showing on their foreheads, it would still be more befitting to them not to mention these and to keep silent about all virtues, small and great, what with their fucking their mothers, sisters, and daughters! For this is something that is naturally abhorred, loathsome[530] to hear about, and is rejected by everyone of a sound innate disposition, and found repugnant by everyone with a well-balanced nature. To make their insolence and gross perversion complete, they claim that this happens with God's permission, and through a Law coming from God! God has forbidden the eating of abhorrent food; so how could He have allowed abhorrent marriages?

"These people have lied: Zoroaster[531] was no prophet. If he had been a prophet, God would have mentioned him among the prophets He mentions by name, and mentions repeatedly, in His Book. This is why the Prophet—God bless him and give him peace—said, 'Deal with them as with the People of the Book,'[532] for they do not have a book from God and revealed to a messenger. It is nothing more than a fable, by which Zoroaster has deceived them, through the power of the king who accepted this from him and who made the people act in this way, willingly or unwillingly, either enticing them or intimidating them. How could God ever have sent a prophet who would preach belief in two gods? This is rationally absurd, and God has created reason solely so that it can testify to the truth when someone speaks the truth, and to falsehood when someone speaks a falsehood. If this practice were revealed law, it would be widely known among the people of the Two Books, I mean the Jews and the Christians, and similarly among the Sabians,[533] for of all people they were the most interested in religions and in the study of religion, to arrive at the knowledge of the truths of them, so that they could have faith in their own religion. So how is it possible that the Christians know Jesus, and the Jews know Moses, and that Muḥammad—God bless him and give him peace—mentions both of them as well as others, such as David, Solomon, John the Baptist, and Zacharias, but does not mention Zoroaster as a prophet, or say that he brought a true and truthful message from God, as Moses and Jesus did (and Muḥammad, who said,)[534] 'I have been sent to abrogate every revealed law, and to renew a revealed law by which God has singled me out among the Arabs'?

"This is a helpful exposé of their lies. But 'they found a little tear and made a large rip,'[535] they found something reason forbids and declared it lawful, a practice deemed offensive by nature in which they engaged, a foul custom which they approved. We have found in animals that a stallion, if incited to mount his mother, is unwilling; if he is forced by means of deception and then becomes aware of the truth he becomes angry with his owners and either runs away or is vicious to them. What, therefore, can you say about a practice that even a beast rejects because it goes against its nature, and which is scorned by its feelings, however weakly developed, its lust cooling after having flared—while these people, who are so proud of their intelligence and conceited about themselves, accept it gladly?

"Even if Zoroaster had shown them all kinds of miracles and proofs in support of this base conduct, this ugly practice, if he had scattered on them the stars of the sky or made the sun rise in the west for them, or had made the mountains crumble, or had dried up the oceans, or shown them Orion walking in the streets on earth and testifying to the truth of what he said, then it would still have been their duty, on the basis of reason, honor,[536] zeal, disdain, loathing and self-respect, to reject his command, to doubt every miracle he showed them, to kill him, and make an example of him (...)[537]

"If the Bedouin Arabs had this ugly character and had practiced this base deed, considering the fact that their libido and excitability are greater than those of others, and that they are more capable of coition and more inclined to copulate with women, as is demonstrated in their love poetry and their passionate love, expressed in verse and prose, in their leisure[538] and in their lust, they would have a better excuse to do so. In spite of all these urges and drives, you will find that they neither approve of this deed nor practice it. If someone were to force them, if someone urged them to do it, they would not obey. This is why no one among them has ever tried to trick them into this: if there had been someone like that, he would have been the first to have his head bashed in with a cudgel or his belly ripped by a dagger. It is their noble souls that restrain them (from incestuous relationships), their balanced nature, strong pride, disdainful spirit, agreeable habits, and good natural disposition. To them burying girls was a better way to avoid shame or ward off evil than what Zoroaster approved and what the Persians adopted from him,[539] in spite of their claim to wisdom, knowledge, prudence and firm resolution. But by virtue of their boundless ignorance or being overcome by their lust, they remained unaware of what God might have made permissible or forbidden to them, either giving them a free rein or restraining them, making things licit or taboo. No, they wouldn't! But God only imposes a religion and a search for truth on people endowed with intelligence in order to ennoble them in this world and to hold them accountable for it in the next. «The good outcome is to the godfearing.»[540]"

Abū l-Ḥasan al-Anṣārī,[541] who was also present, said: "The Indians would have a better excuse in this matter, for they practice it as a pious act in their temples, thus attaining their desire by means of this (self-)deceit; at least they do not ascribe any of it to God, they do not consider it permissible to utter lies about Him, nor do they attribute it to some prophet who got it from God. Rather, they believe that it is the right thing to do by common consensus, and by force of habit and custom they have come to approve it. In any event, they are mentally disturbed, few among them are intelligent, they are inclined toward lying, delusion, and magic, all things in which they are proficient."

Abū l-Ḥasan continued: "Consider Zoroaster's ignorance in this matter, and the feeble minds of the Persians who adopted this practice from him! Now compare this with the intelligence of the Arabs, who said, 'Marry strangers and you will not produce stunted offspring.' This was a common saying among them, to the extent that the Lawgiver[542]—God bless him and give him peace—was heard to say it too. The reason is that stuntedness is abhorred. The Arabs knew this intuitively, by their pure instincts and bright minds, their noble nature, their high-born lineages, and their sound customs. They realized that the degeneration that affects the body will spread to the mind. The Persians, on the other hand, remained unaware of this truth. Only brilliant and sagacious minds will grasp this and similar facts. Al-Aṣmaʿī quotes a line by an unknown Arab, praising a patron:

A young man not born from a close cousin, father's brother's daughter,
and thus not stunted (the issue of close relatives is often stunted).[543]

"The Arabs also use the expression 'to stunt someone's right,' meaning 'to impair someone's rights.' Another man said to his son, 'By God, I have protected you from stuntedness and have chosen (your mother) from among my maternal uncles' family.'[544] The Arabs also say, 'No one is more stunted than a child from close relatives, nobody gives birth to better children than strange women.' A poet has said,

I warn everyone with far-reaching ambition:
  Do not let children marry their paternal cousins,
For one will not escape stuntedness and sickliness;
  If you feed them they will not grow.

"A man from the tribe of Asad boasted:

I am no runt whose bones are shaky,[545]
  from a line of Khālid after Khālid born,[546]
Repeatedly, until his paternal uncle is his mother's maternal uncle,
  in one line of kinship closer than a single span.[547]

"By this the Arabs actually intend the debility of mind and intelligence, for if they meant physical defects, they would be mistaken, since they mean plumpness of body, together with being sound and firm.[548] It is the same with the nature of soil. This is why, it is said, the earth becomes fertile when it is much overturned by strong winds, because when it is exposed to winds from various sides they move the soil of the earth from one place to another. Now if 'strange' soil affects other soil, all the more so will humans influence other humans by mingling with strangers, for man is made of soil."

Abū Ḥāmid said,

"What do you say about people who are ignorant both of the effects of nature and the secrets of revealed law! It is not for nothing that God has humbled them, and He was not being unjust when He robbed them of their rule. He only struck them with ignominy and degradation as a punishment for their wicked behavior and their insolent and arrogant lying about God. God does not wrong His servants."[549]

When the discussion had reached this point, the vizier said, "That was a long and rich talk! I really needed a conversation like this. You should find some time to write it all down so that I can peruse it, enjoy its sweetness, and extract its original thoughts. When you hear something the words fly up into the sky; but if you see them with your eyes by reading a book they land on earth again. What flies up is hard to grasp; what has landed is available to the eye. If you cannot fully memorize words that are heard you will 'remember' some things only with your fancy, without certainty, helped by your imagination, without being able to check."

I replied, "I will certainly obey and do that, if God wills."

History as Literature: Al-Amīn and al-Maʾmūn, the Sons of Hārūn al-Rashīd[550]

Abū Ḥanīfah al-Dīnawarī's (d. 282/895) history, called *The Long Stories*, unlike that of his great successor al-Ṭabarī (d. 311/923), does not present individual reports each with their *isnād* (chain of transmitters) but gives a series of longer, continuous narratives, making the work more accessible to modern readers. The conflict between the two brothers presented here is a kind of moral tale in terms of the clear contrast it makes between the bad Muḥammad al-Amīn (who succeeded his father Hārūn al-Rashīd as caliph in 193/809) and the good ʿAbd Allāh al-Maʾmūn (who, after a bloody civil war, reigned from 198/813 until 218/833). The "literary" character is enhanced by the many instances of direct speech, reporting what they are imagined to have uttered; these are also found in other accounts but often with many variants, suggesting that the general drift of what was said was regarded as more important than the exact wording.

In that year[551] al-Rashīd went on the Hajj with the people, together with his two sons, Muḥammad and ʿAbd Allāh. He drafted a document between the two, in which Muḥammad was designated heir apparent, and ʿAbd Allāh his successor as next-in-line. He hung up this document inside the Kaaba. He then returned to Baghdad and appointed al-Ghiṭrīf ibn ʿAṭāʾ[552] governor over Khurasan.

*

ʿAlī ibn Ḥamzah al-Kisāʾī[553] says, "Al-Rashīd charged me with the education of Muḥammad and ʿAbd Allāh. I used to take this very seriously and was very strict with both of them, especially with Muḥammad. One day Khāliṣah, the servant of Umm Jaʿfar[554] came to me, saying: 'Kisāʾī, my Mistress greets you and says she desires something from you: "Please be kind to my son Muḥammad, for he is the solace of my heart, the apple of my eye; I have a very soft spot for him!"'

"I said to Khāliṣah, 'Muḥammad is destined to be caliph after his father; we cannot be remiss in his education.'

"Khāliṣah answered, 'My Mistress has tender feelings for a reason I will tell you. The night she gave birth to him she had a dream[555] in which she saw four women approach him and stand round him, on the right, the left, in front, and behind. The one in front of him said, "A king short of life, of anguished breast, of great pride, of weak command, much burdened, full of treachery." The one standing behind him said, "A king much given to revelry, who will squander much and ruin much, of little fairness and much excess." The one on his right said, "A great king with little self-control, sinning much and severing family bonds." The one on his left said, "A king who will betray much, stumble much, and destroy quickly."'

"Thereupon Khāliṣah wept and said, 'O Kisā'ī, what is the use of caution!'"

*

It is related that al-Aṣma'ī said,[556] "Once I entered the presence of al-Rashīd after I had been away in Basra for two years. He gestured that I should sit down close to him. I sat down briefly and then stood up again. But he gestured to me: Sit down! So I sat down until most people had left. Then he said to me, 'Aṣma'ī, wouldn't you like to see Muḥammad and 'Abd Allāh?'

"'Yes, Commander of the Faithful! I should certainly like that. The reason I stood up was so that I could go to them and greet them.'

"'There's no need!'

"Then he said, 'Have Muḥammad and 'Abd Allāh come to me!'

"A messenger left and said to them, 'The Commander of the Faithful wishes to see you.'

"They came, looking like two moons on the horizon, with short steps, their eyes cast down demurely, and stood before their father. They greeted him as caliph and he gestured to them to come closer. He made Muḥammad sit on his right and 'Abd Allāh on his left. Then he told me to question them; and whatever question in the various fields of erudition I asked them they answered correctly. He said, 'What do you think of their erudition and behavior?'

"I replied, 'Commander of the Faithful, I have never seen the like of them, in their intelligence and their sound understanding. May God let them live long and bless the community of believers with their kindness and compassion!'

"He pressed them to his breast and cried until the tears dripped down. Then he let them go, and when they had stood up and left, he said, 'Ah! What will happen to all of you when their mutual enmity becomes apparent, their hatred of each other shows itself and evil things happen between them, so that blood will be shed and many who are alive will wish they were dead?'

"I said, 'Commander of the Faithful, is this something that astrologers determined at their births, or something that scholars have transmitted about them?'

"'Yes, it is something scholars have transmitted about them on the authority of the true heirs,[557] on the authority of the prophets.'"

It is said that al-Ma'mūn, when he was caliph, used to say that al-Rashīd had heard about what was going to happen between the two of them from Mūsā ibn Ja'far ibn Muḥammad;[558] this is why he spoke as he did.[559]

Al-Aṣmaʿī said, "al-Rashīd was fond of evening conversation and loved to hear stories about people. He would send for me whenever he was in the mood for this, when darkness would fall. Then I would converse with him. One night I came to him when there was no one else with him. We spoke for a while; he lowered his head and became pensive. Then he said, 'Boy, bring al-ʿAbbāsī! (meaning al-Faḍl ibn al-Rabīʿ).'[560]

"When al-Faḍl arrived the caliph asked him to be seated and said to him, ''Abbāsī, I have a mind to arrange the succession and to appoint Muḥammad and ʿAbd Allāh as my successors. Now I know that if I appoint Muḥammad, with all his willful, irresponsible behavior and his addiction to pleasure and sensual delights, he will lead the subjects astray and he will make the wrong decisions, so that the most extreme of iniquitous people will set their hopes on him; and (I know) that if I give the succession to ʿAbd Allāh, he is certain to walk the right course with them and to keep the realm in good order, for he possesses the prudence of al-Manṣūr and the courage of al-Mahdī. What are your thoughts?'

"Al-Faḍl said, 'This is a weighty matter, Commander of the Believers, in which a mistake made cannot be rectified later. It ought to be discussed somewhere else.'

"I realized that the two wished to have a talk in private, so I stood up and sat down somewhere else, in a corner of the courtyard, while they continued discussing the matter until the morning, at which time they agreed to appoint Muḥammad heir apparent and ʿAbd Allāh after him, to divide money and troops between them, to let Muḥammad reside in the caliphal palace (in Baghdad) and to appoint ʿAbd Allāh governor of Khurasan. That morning the caliph gave orders that the army commanders be brought together; they came and he called upon them to take the oath of allegiance to Muḥammad and to ʿAbd Allāh after him; they obeyed and pledged their allegiance."

*

[Hārūn dies, in the course of a campaign, in Ṭūs, in Iran in 193/809.]

Muḥammad al-Amīn became caliph in Baghdad on Thursday, in the middle of the month of Jumādā II. He announced the news of his father's death to the people on Friday; he called upon them to renew their pledge of allegiance, which they did. The news of Hārūn's death reached al-Ma'mūn when he was in the city of Marw[561] on Friday, eight days before the end of that month. Then he rode to the great mosque. A proclamation was made to the army and the notables, who all gathered. Al-Ma'mūn ascended the pulpit, praised God, blessed the Prophet and his family, and said, "People! May God give us and you suitable consolation concerning the last caliph, God bless his soul, and may He bless us and you with your new caliph; may He extend his lifetime!"

Then he was overcome by tears. He wiped his eyes with his black clothes;[562] then he continued, "People of Khurāsān, renew your pledge of allegiance to your leader, al-Amīn!"

All pledged their allegiance to him. When al-Amīn had become caliph and the people had sworn their allegiance, poets entered his presence. Among them was al-Ḥasan ibn Hāni'.[563] They all recited poetry. Al-Ḥasan was the last to stand. He recited these verses:[564]

Cajole the wine with water, and thus soften it!
  You will not honor a red wine unless you humble it.
Before the mixing red, and after it rosé;
  It is like sunbeams when you take it up,
Surrounded by what seems like solid rubies and
  black cats that roll their eyes.[565]
Now God has honored all His nation of believers with
  a caliph rightly called "Trustworthy": al-Amīn!
May you protect its sacred land with cavalry and lances,
  may you increase its worldly and religious goods!
The sons of al-Manṣūr[566] find you their worthiest of this,
  though what they show is different from what they hide.

Al-Amīn rewarded them all but preferred him. Then al-Amīn sent for Ismāʿīl ibn Ṣabīḥ,[567] his private secretary, and asked him, "What do you think, Ibn Ṣabīḥ?"

“I predict a blessed reign, a sound caliphate, and a propitious state of affairs! May God through His grace bring all this to pass in abundance for the Commander of Believers!”

“I don’t want you to be a preacher, I want to know what you think!”

Ismāʿīl replied, “If the Commander of the Believers would be so good as to clarify the matter to me, so that I can counsel him and advise him as well as I am able!”

“I have a mind to depose my brother ʿAbd Allāh from his governorship of Khurāsān and to appoint Mūsā, the son of the Commander of the Believers.”[568]

“God protect us, Commander of the Believers! Do not destroy a building of which al-Rashīd has laid the foundations, leveled the floor, and raised the cornerstones!”

“Al-Rashīd has been told all kinds of embellishing lies about ʿAbd Allāh. Damn you, Ibn Ṣabīḥ! ʿAbd al-Malik ibn Marwān[569] was wiser than you when he said, ‘If there are two stallions in a herd one will kill the other.’”

“If this is what you think, do not say it openly but write to him and tell him you need to see him and have him with you, so that he can assist you in the rule with which God has entrusted you over His servants and His lands. When he arrives and you have separated him from his troops you will have broken his strength and he will be in your power and be your hostage. Then you can do with him as you like.”

“Well said, Ibn Ṣabīḥ! Upon my life, that is the right way to go about it.”

So he wrote to him, saying that the burden of being caliph and governing that God had laid upon him was too heavy to bear, and asked him to come to him so that he could help and counsel him in his interests. This would be more useful to the caliph than if he stayed in Khurāsān, more beneficial to the country, more profitable, would better hold the enemy in check and be better for the protection of the state. He dispatched the letter, with al-ʿAbbās ibn Mūsā, Muḥammad ibn ʿĪsā, and Ṣāliḥ *Ṣāḥib al-Muṣallā*.[570] They traveled to Khurāsān, where they were received by Ṭāhir ibn al-Ḥusayn, who had come toward them from al-Maʾmūn, to take up the governorship of al-Rayy.[571] Together they reached al-Maʾmūn in Marw. They entered his presence and presented the letter to him. They explained that the caliph needed him and how much he expected from his proximity, to help reinforce the empire and its strength against the enemy; they were very eloquent. Al-Maʾmūn gave orders that they should be accommodated and treated as honored guests.

When night fell he sent for al-Faḍl ibn Sahl, who was his most intimate and most trusted vizier.[572] From experience he knew him to have reliable opinions and abundant prudence. He had a private talk with al-Faḍl; he showed him Muḥammad's letter and told him what the envoys had said, who had urged him to travel to his brother to assist him in his reign. Al-Faḍl said, "What he has in mind for you is not good. I think you have to refuse."

Al-Ma'mūn replied, "But how can I refuse? He has all the people and the money. And people go with whoever has the money."

"Let me sleep on it tonight. When I see you in the morning I'll give you my opinion."

"Go, with God's protection!"

Al-Faḍl ibn Sahl left and went home. Being a skilled astrologer, he spent the whole night making his calculations about the stars. In the morning he went to al-Ma'mūn and told him that he would vanquish Muḥammad and take the reign from him. On being told this, al-Ma'mūn sent for the envoys, gave them fine gifts, and asked them to present him in a favorable light to al-Amīn and to convey his apologies. In a letter to him that he gave to the envoys he wrote:

> *Caliph al-Rashīd appointed me governor of this land at a time when its enemies were raging, its defenses sapped, and its army weakened. If I am remiss or if I leave I cannot be sure that matters will not disintegrate or its enemies conquer it, which would ultimately harm the Commander of the Believers in his present situation. May the Commander of the Believers decide not to undo what Caliph al-Rashid has established.*

The envoys left with the letter. They traveled and when they reached al-Amīn they gave him the letter. Once he had read it he assembled his army commanders and said to them, "I have decided to relieve my brother ʿAbd Allāh of the governorship of Khurāsān and to let him come to me so that he can assist me. I need him. What do you think?"

The men kept silent. Then Khāzim ibn Khuzaymah[573] spoke: "Commander of the Believers, do not make your army commanders and your soldiers commit treachery, lest they betray you! Do not let them see you break a covenant, lest they break their covenant with you."

Muḥammad replied, "But the senior statesman in the dynasty, ʿAlī ibn ʿĪsā ibn Māhān, is of a different opinion.[574] He thinks that ʿAbd Allāh should be with me to help me and share the burden I am carrying."

Then he said to ʿAlī ibn ʿĪsā, "I have decided that you shall take the army to Khurāsān and govern it on behalf of Mūsā, the son of the Commander of Believers. Select those you think fit among the soldiers."

ʿAlī ibn ʿĪsā sent for the army register, which was produced, and chose sixty thousand elite fighters and horsemen. He paid them a bonus, distributed arms among them, and ordered them to march. He himself marched with the troops. Muḥammad rode with him, giving him instructions and saying, "Be generous to the army commanders there in Khurāsān. Halve the taxes of the people of Khurāsān. Don't let anybody raise a sword against you or shoot a single arrow at your army. Don't let ʿAbd Allāh stay longer than three days after your arrival and dispatch him to me."

Zubaydah[575] had also instructed ʿAlī ibn ʿĪsā, when he had come to say goodbye to her, saying, "Muḥammad may be my son, the solace of my heart, but ʿAbd Allāh also has an ample share of love in my heart. I raised him and now I am concerned for him. Do not treat him improperly, do not walk in front of him but behind him if you accompany him. If he sends for you, obey him. Do not mount your horse before he does; hold his stirrup when he mounts. Show respect and deference."

Then she gave him a silver chain, saying, "If he does not comply when you tell him to leave, put this chain on him."

Muḥammad left, having given him instructions and directions about everything he wanted. ʿAlī ibn ʿĪsā ibn Māhān marched as far as Ḥulwān,[576] where he encountered a caravan coming from al-Rayy. He asked them about Ṭāhir and they told him that he was making preparations for war. ʿAlī said, "Who's this Ṭāhir? Who is he? As soon as he hears that I have crossed the pass at Hamadhān[577] he will abandon al-Rayy."

He marched on until he had left the pass at Hamadhān behind him. There, another caravan came toward him. He asked them for news and they told him that Ṭāhir had given extra pay to his men, distributed arms among them, and had prepared for war. ʿAlī asked, "How many are they?"

They replied, "Some ten thousand men."

Then al-Ḥasan,[578] the son of ʿAlī ibn ʿĪsā, turned to his father and said, "Father, if Ṭāhir wanted to flee he would not have stayed in al-Rayy one day longer."

ʿAlī answered, "My dear boy, real men prepare to meet their peers, but Ṭāhir does strike me as the kind of man who would prepare to meet someone like me, or for whom someone like me should prepare himself."

It is said that the old men in Baghdad had said, "We have never seen an army better armed, more perfectly equipped, with more horses, or with nobler men, than the army of ʿAlī ibn ʿĪsā, the day he marched. They really were elite troops."

Ṭāhir ibn al-Ḥusayn had assembled all his commanders and consulted them. They advised him to fortify himself in al-Rayy and fight the enemy from its walls until reinforcement would come from al-Maʾmūn. He said to them, "Damn you, I know more about warfare than you. If I fortified myself I would show myself to be weak. The townspeople would incline toward him because of his strength, and they would give me more trouble than my enemy, because they fear ʿAlī ibn ʿĪsā. He may win over some of my own men, exploiting their greed. The thing to do is to let cavalry meet cavalry and infantry meet infantry, and victory will come from God."

He ordered his troops to leave the town and pitch camp at a place called al-Qalūṣah.[579] As soon as they had left, the people of al-Rayy went to the town gates and locked them. Ṭāhir said to his men, "Men, concern yourself with those in front of you and don't pay attention to those behind you. Know that your only stronghold, your only refuge, lies in your swords and lances, so make them your fortresses."

ʿAlī ibn ʿĪsā advanced toward al-Qalūṣah and the two armies stood opposite each other, ready for battle. Then they clashed. Ṭāhir's men fought well in the attack; ʿAlī ibn ʿĪsā's ranks were broken. In the mêlée ʿAlī ibn ʿĪsā shouted to his soldiers, "Men, turn back! Attack with me!"

But one of Ṭāhir's men, having ascertained ʿAlī's identity, took aim when he was within reach; he shot him with an arrow that hit him in the chest, pierced the coat of mail and penetrated his body. He fell, having lost consciousness, and died. His men were routed and Ṭāhir's troops kept killing them as they fled, until nightfall made this impossible. They took all the arms and goods in their army as spoils.

When the news reached Muḥammad he appointed ʿAbd al-Raḥmān al-Abnāwī commander of thirty thousand men of the Abnāʾ.[580] He enjoined them not to be deluded like ʿAlī ibn ʿĪsā and not to underrate the enemy. ʿAbd al-Raḥmān marched and reached Hamadhān. When Ṭāhir heard this he advanced toward him. They met, there was some fighting, but ʿAbd al-Raḥmān's men did not hold their ground. He fled and his troops followed. They entered the town of Hamadhān and fortified themselves there for a month, until their food had run out. ʿAbd al-Raḥmān al-Abnāwī asked for quarter for himself and his men, which was granted by Ṭāhir.

The town gates were opened and Ṭāhir's army entered, joining the other army. Then Ṭāhir left, marching toward the pass and pitching camp near Asadābādh.[581]

'Abd al-Raḥmān began to think, saying to himself, "How can I defend myself to the Commander of the Believers?" He mobilized his troops and at dawn marched with his men toward Ṭāhir, who was taken off guard. They killed a number of them. Some infantry of Ṭāhir's men held their ground, protecting their horsemen until they had mounted their horses and put on their armor. Then they attacked 'Abd al-Raḥmān and his troops, killing many of them. When 'Abd al-Raḥmān saw this he dismounted among his guard. They fought until 'Abd al-Raḥmān and those with him were killed.

When Muḥammad was informed of this he was at a loss. He brought out his troops and gave 'Abd Allāh al-Ḥarashī the command of five thousand men and Yaḥyā ibn 'Alī ibn 'Īsā of a similar number. The two marched until they reached Qarmīsīn.[582] When the news reached Ṭāhir he marched toward them and they fled without any fighting, returning to Ḥulwān; then they fled until they reached Baghdad. Ṭāhir stayed in Ḥulwān until he was joined by Harthamah ibn A'yan, coming from al-Ma'mūn with thirty thousand Khurāsānians. Ṭāhir set out from Ḥulwān toward Basra, while Harthamah advanced on Baghdad. Everything went wrong for Muḥammad and he was eventually killed, after everything that happened.[583] Ṭāhir went up from Basra and Harthamah advanced until they had surrounded Baghdad, laying siege to Muḥammad al-Amīn. They set up mangonels aimed at his palace, causing great distress to Muḥammad. Harthamah was prepared to do his best for al-Amīn and spare his life. Muḥammad wrote to him, asking him to look after him and to reconcile him to al-Ma'mūn; he would abdicate from the caliphate and let his brother reign instead. Harthamah wrote back as follows:

> *You should have requested this before matters came to a head. But now "the torrent has flooded the heights" and "the jewels have become too dear to the owners to be lent."*[584] *Nevertheless I will do my best to effect a reconciliation. Come to me tonight so that I can write a letter on your behalf to the Commander of the Believers*[585] *and make a binding covenant with you. I will spare no effort in doing anything that will be in your interest and may bring about a rapprochement between you and the Commander of the Believers.*

When Muḥammad heard this he asked the advice of his counsellors and viziers. They recommended him to do as he was told, as they were eager to see him spared. When night fell he embarked, together with a number of his inner circle, trusted servants, and slave girls, wanting to cross the river to meet Harthamah. But Ṭāhir got wind of the correspondence between the two and the agreement they had made. When Muḥammad approached, with his company aboard, Ṭāhir attacked and took him and those with him prisoner. He had him brought to his place, cut off his head, and sent it immediately to al-Ma'mūn.

Al-Ma'mūn advanced, entered the City of Peace,[586] and became the sole ruler of the Empire, in complete command. The death of Muḥammad al-Amīn took place on the eve of Sunday, 5 Muḥarram of the year 198;[587] he was twenty-eight years old when he was killed. He had reigned for four years and eight months. The oath of allegiance to al-Ma'mūn, ʿAbd Allāh, son of al-Rashīd, was sworn on Monday, 25 Muḥarram of the year 198. He was an astute, ambitious, proud man, the star among the Abbasids in science and philosophy. He had learned something of every field of knowledge. It was he who procured a copy of Euclid's *Geometry* from Byzantium and ordered it to be translated and divided into chapters.[588] During his caliphate he organized gatherings wherein to hold debates about religions and doctrines. His teacher in these matters was Abū l-Hudhayl Muḥammad ibn al-Hudhayl al-ʿAllāf.[589] He went to Northern Mesopotamia and Syria, where he stayed a long time; then he campaigned against the Byzantines, making many conquests and showing himself to be a brave warrior. He died near the al-Badandūn River[590] and was buried in Tarsus on Wednesday 8 Rajab of the year 218, having reigned for twenty years, five months, and thirteen days. He was thirty-nine years old.

Moral Tales and Parables: Passages from *Rasāʾil Ikhwān al-Ṣafāʾ* (*The Epistles of the Sincere Brethren*)

The Ikhwān al-Ṣafāʾ (The Pure, or Sincere, Brethren) were a society of writers and propagandists apparently associated with the Ismāʿīliyyah (a Shīʿah sect), active in the fourth/tenth century. The names of some of them are known but much else is uncertain. Their *Epistles*, a rare example of collective authorship in Arabic (unless they were all written by one of them), is a kind of popular encyclopedia, dealing with mathematics, natural science, the humanities, religion, ethics, and the occult, often in combination. It is written in a relatively easy style, often addressing the reader whom they hope to convert to their views and thereby offer salvation. These views are remarkably syncretistic and eclectic: their work is full of Aristotelian, Pythagorean, Neoplatonic, Christian, and Judaic elements; they see connections and parallels everywhere, notably between the macrocosm and microcosm (i.e. humans). They make effective use of parables and stories. In many "orthodox" Muslim circles their writings were regarded as suspect.[591]

I. The Complaint of the Beasts of Burden, from the debate between Man and Animals[592]

Then the leader of the beasts said: O King, we and our ancestors used to inhabit the earth before Adam, the father of mankind, was created. We lived in all its regions, traveled along its paths, every group of us coming and going in God's lands in search of subsistence, freely looking after its own welfare, each one of us in a place suitable for his purposes, be it steppes, sea, forest, plain, or mountain, each kind in the company of its own kind, engaged in reproduction and rearing our young, leading a good life with the food and the drink that God allotted us. We were secure in our homelands, and healthy[593] in our bodies, praising God and sanctifying Him and professing His unity day and night, neither disobeying Him nor worshiping another with Him. In this way, long epochs and times went by.

Then God, praised be He, created Adam, the father of mankind, and made him a deputy on earth.[594] His children reproduced and his descendants became numerous. They spread over the earth, across land and sea, in the lowlands and the mountains, and constricted our places and homelands. Many of us were taken captive: sheep, cows, horses, mules, and donkeys. They subjugated us and made us work for them, wearing us out with toil and drudgery, through hard labor, carrying, being ridden, being tied to yokes,[595] waterwheels, and mills, forcibly and by their greater power, with blows and humiliation and various kinds of torment, our whole lives long. Those of us who could fled to the steppes, deserts, and mountaintops. The humans prepared to pursue us using various forms of trickery, and those of us that fell into their hands they tied up with shackles and fetters or put in cages. They oppressed us with slaughter, flaying, ripping bellies open, cutting off limbs, breaking bones, tearing sinews, plucking feathers, clipping hair and wool, then with the fire of cooking and the spit and roasting and various kinds of torture the true nature of which cannot fully be described.

And on top of all this these humans are not content until they claim that they are necessarily entitled to this, that they are our overlords and we their slaves.

II. The Superiority of the Horse[596]

The Human said to the Hare, "Hold it! You have found a lot of faults with the Horse.[597] But if you knew that it is the best animal ever tamed by humans, you wouldn't speak like this."

The King said to the human, "What is all this goodness you are talking about? Tell us."

"The Horse has praiseworthy qualities, a pleasant character, a wonderful discernment; for instance its beautiful appearance, the harmony of its limbs, the purity of its color, its beautiful coat and mane, its speed, its obedience to its rider, turning wherever he wishes, being led right or left, forward or back, in pursuit or in flight. And its intelligence, sharp senses, and good manners: it will not defecate or stale as long as its rider is seated on it, it does not shake its tail when it is wet so that its rider will not be sprayed with water. It has the strength of an elephant: it carries its rider with his helmet, coat of mail, and weapons, together with saddle, harness, its own coat of mail and metal equipment totaling perhaps a thousand pounds, yet coursing at speed. It has the endurance of a donkey when its breast is being stabbed or its neck slashed in battle. In raids and pursuits it courses at speed like a wolf's attack. It walks proudly like a bull,[598] it bounds like a hare, with sudden turns like those of 'a boulder hurtled down by the torrent from above,'[599] rushing and advancing in competition, as if in a race it seeks to win."

The Hare said, "Yes, but in spite of all these praiseworthy qualities and its fine character it has a great fault that outweighs all those qualities."

"What is it? Explain it to me, said the King."

"Ignorance, a lack of understanding of reality. For it runs just as fast in flight when ridden by its owner's enemy[600] whom it has never seen, as when its runs in pursuit when ridden by its owner in whose house it was born and bred. It carries its owner's enemy in pursuit of its own master just as it carries its master in pursuit of his enemy.[601] In all its qualities it is just like a sword that has no soul, no perception, no feeling, no understanding: it cuts the neck of him who has polished it just as readily as it cuts the neck of him who wants to break, bend, or damage it. It does not know the difference between the two."

"In fact, the same is true of humans," continued the Hare. "A human will feud with his own parents, friends, or relatives, scheming against them and maltreating them, just as he would a remote enemy from whom he has experienced neither friendliness nor beneficence. The fact is that these humans drink the milk of cattle just as they drank their mothers' milk; they ride on the backs of these animals just as they rode on their fathers' shoulders when they were small. They use the wool, fleece, and hair of animals for their clothes and furniture, and in the end they slaughter, flay, disembowel, and dismember them and make them taste the fire by cooking or roasting, showing no mercy and unmindful of all the good things that the animals did for them or of all the favors and blessings they derived from them."

III. The Human Body as a House[602]

Know that this body stands in relation to this soul of ours as does a house to its inhabitant; a house that is well built, divided into rooms, its storerooms full, its roofs raised, its doors open, its curtains drawn, and equipped with everything that the owner of the house needs, such as beds, kitchenware, furniture, and other household goods, in the most perfect, the most complete and the most accomplished manner. Thus his feet, on which the body stands, are like the foundations of the house. His head, on the highest part of the torse, is like the loft. His back, behind him, is like the back of the house; his face, in front, is like the house's façade; his neck, with its length, is like the porch; the opening of his throat through which the voice moves is like the vestibule; the chest in the middle of his body is like the courtyard of the house; the cavities in his chest are like the rooms and storerooms in the house; his lungs and the coolness they provide are like the summer room; the nostrils, with the breath moving through the throat, are like the ventilation shaft;[603] his heart, with its natural heat, is like the winter room; his stomach, where the food is cooked, is like the kitchen; his liver, where the blood is produced,[604] is like the drinking room; his veins, through which the blood flows and pulsates to all the extremities of the body,[605] are like the corridors of the house; his spleen, where the blood becomes turbid,[606] is like the storeroom for furniture; his gall bladder, with the force of the yellow bile, is like the armory; his abdomen with its membranes is like the women's quarters; his bowels, containing the superfluities,[607] are like the toilet; his bladder, where the urine collects, is like the urinal; the two downward passages in his body are like the drains of the house; his bones, which support the body, are like the walls of the house; the sinews that are stretched over the limbs are like the beams and rafters on the walls; his flesh between the bones and sinews is like the mortar; his ribs are like the house's pillars; the cavities inside the bones are like boxes and drawers; the marrow in them is like precious stones and goods in those drawers; the holes at the ends of the bones are like skylights in the upper chambers of the house; his breathing is like chimney smoke; the middle of his cranium is like the portico; his eyeballs are like the reception room;[608] the membranes in them are like curtains; his mouth is like the front door; his tongue is like the doorman; his intelligence in the middle of his brain is like the king who sits in the middle of his court, in the place of honor of the house and the gathering; his internal senses[609] are like his drinking companions; his external senses are like soldiers and spies; his eyes are like sentries; his ears are like informers; his hands are like servants; his fingers are like laborers. In short, there is no organ or limb in the body that has no counterpart in the trappings of the owner of a dwelling.

IV. Why we die[610]

Know, my friend, that the body is like a ship, and the soul like a mariner. Good works are like the merchant's wares and goods. The world is like the sea, the days of one's life are like the passage, and death is like the coast one is heading for. The hereafter is like a merchant's town, Paradise is the profit, and God is like the king who rewards. If the merchant has crossed the sea and his goods are safe and sound, but he does not leave his ship, then he cannot enter his town to trade, and he will fail to reap the profit from his wares. It is just so with the soul and the body, for when one has spent the days of one's life on earth doing good works, lived in a just manner, acquired a good character, firmly upheld correct opinions, has looked at things that may be perceived with the senses and come to know them correctly, looked into the true nature of things that are grasped by the intellect and mastered them—when one has reached the end of one's life and the body has become decrepit—then the only prudent action is to depart, that is, the death of the body. For if death did not exist, the soul could not ascend to the kingdom of heaven, nor enter among the hosts of the angels, nor arrive in Paradise, and it would fail to meet God the Exalted and attain the bliss of the Hereafter, just as an unborn child fails to view the true nature of this world if it stays in the womb and does not come out. Therefore death is a wise thing, a mercy, and a blessing, since we can only arrive at our Lord after we have left this physical structure and have departed from our bodies. «Every soul shall taste death; then unto Us you shall be returned.»[611]

Know that the world is like a racecourse: the bodies are noble horses; the souls, racing toward good things, are riders; God, the Exalted, is the king who gives a bountiful prize. Just as the winning rider, having arrived at the gate of the king, cannot enter into the king's presence unless he dismounts from his horse, or else would fail to receive his prize and his robes of honor and other marks of respect, so it is with souls that race toward good things and good works, when they have spent the days of their lives on earth striving after good things, as God has said in praise of them: «[Truly they vied with one another], hastening to good works and called upon Us out of yearning and awe, and they were humble to Us.»[612] Thus, when life has come to an end, the body has become decrepit and hoary, and the soul feels uneasy staying there, having become perfect, it cannot ascend to the kingdom of heaven unless it departs from the body. For it is not appropriate for this heavy, deteriorated, corrupted body to appear in that lofty and noble place. No, it is the soul that can ascend to that place to be rewarded for the good it has done. Therefore death is a wise thing and a mercy.

Also, the world is a plantation. The wombs of women are like tillage, as God the Exalted says:[613] «Your women are a tillage for you», a drop of sperm is like seed, birth is like the sprouting of a plant, the days of youth are like growth, the days of middle age are like ripeness, and the days of old age are like withering and desiccation. After these stages there must be harvesting and cutting, namely death. Life's Path[614] and the Hereafter are like a threshing floor. Just as a threshing floor brings together crops of every kind, which are being threshed and sifted, while husks, leaves, straw, kernels and fruits are cast away and made into fodder for animals and fuel for fires, so in the Hereafter the nations of those who came first and those who come last of every religion will be gathered, and secrets will be disclosed. God will «distinguish the corrupt from the good, and place the corrupt one upon another, and so heap them up all together, and put them in Gehenna.»[615] «But God shall deliver those that were God-fearing in their security; evil shall not visit them, neither shall they sorrow.»[616]

V. The Golden Age of Islam[617]

Know that in the time of the Prophet, peace be upon him, who was sent to his people, religion and divine law both came from God, the Exalted; there could be no difference of opinion about these two things, nor any mutual hatred or enmity. The believers were all of one opinion in his time; their love for one another would be pure and unsullied. They would be peaceful, help to establish a worldly order and fight the unbelievers. They fought them, not because of enmity toward them, but in order to lead them back to the Truth, so that the Muslims would no longer have to worry about their deceit and their looting. They were content to take the poll tax from unbelievers, if they did not accept the true religion, because they would not feel secure from them if they let them be without demanding the poll tax at regular intervals. For, as the proverb has it, "Raid the Romans, or they will raid you."[618] This is why they fought the unbelievers; otherwise they had no liking for shedding blood, killing people or destroying lands. It was against their will that these things were inflicted upon their (viz. the unbelievers') bodies: it was necessary, because of what I told you, since such deeds are outwardly the deeds of wicked people without mercy or compassion.

Therefore, when the Messenger of God (God bless him and his family) wished to fight the polytheists, he sent someone to them to give notice in advance, to warn them, to explain to them the error of their ways, and to call them to the Truth that he had to offer, as God commanded in His words, «Call thou to the way of the Lord with wisdom and good admonition, and dispute with them in the better way.»[619] He also commanded him to be kind and said, «And speak words hitting the mark»[620] and "Say to them honorable words."[621] He said to Moses, when He sent him together with Aaron to Pharaoh, «Speak gently to him, that haply he may be mindful, or perchance fear.»[622] This the prophet Moses did. But when they refused and behaved arrogantly and said, “We do not like your religion,” then, if they were from among the People of Scripture, the Prophet Muḥammad would command them to pay the poll tax, after our legal provisions were applied to them and they had refrained from harming us, so that it would humble them and so that they would not harbor any illusions about vanquishing the believers.

Prose Narrative: Four Stories by al-Tanūkhī

Al-Faraj ba'd al-shiddah (*Relief after Distress* or *All's Well That Ends Well*) is a collection of stories with happy endings, compiled by Abū 'Alī al-Muḥassin ibn 'Alī al-Tanūkhī (329/940–384/994), a judge from Baghdad.

I. The Girl of al-Ramlah[623]

Like all stories told by al-Tanūkhī, this tale is presented as fact (but see Hamori, "Folklore in Tanūkhī: The Collector of Ramlah"). It is part of section eight,"On escaping from being killed," which is appropriate (see the end of the story); but one could hardly call it a story with a happy ending. Al-Ṣafadī summarizes the story in a passage where he argues that courage in women is to be condemned.[624]

Abū l-Mughīrah Muḥammad ibn Ya'qūb ibn Yūsuf, the poet from Basra,[625] said: I was told by Abū Mūsā ibn 'Abd Allāh al-Baghdādī: A friend of mine related to me:

I was on my way to al-Ramlah,[626] by myself, a town I had never visited before. I reached it after people had gone to sleep when night had fallen, so I went to the cemetery and entered one of the domes built over the graves. I laid down a leather shield I had with me and rested on it. Holding my sword close to my body, I lay down to sleep, intending to enter the town in the morning. I felt uneasy about the place and I could not sleep. When I had been awake for a while I heard[627] some movement.

I said to myself, they are robbers passing by; if I show myself I won't be safe. Perhaps there's a whole band of them. So I remained where I was and did not move. Then, very fearfully, I stuck my head out of one of the doors of the dome, and I saw an animal like a wolf,[628] moving about. It was heading toward a dome opposite me, turned and circled around it for some time, and then went inside. I had misgivings about it and I didn't much like what I saw. But I was curious to find out what it was doing.

It entered the dome, came out again after a short while, then began to look around, then entered and came quickly out again. Finally it entered, my eyes being fixed upon it, and it struck the earth of a grave in the dome with its paw, scattering it about.

Surely a grave robber, I said to myself. I watched it digging with its paw[629] and I noticed that in its paw it held an iron implement with which it was digging. I let it be until it felt safe. It kept digging a great deal for a long while. Then I took my sword and my shield and went on tiptoe and entered the dome. It noticed me and stood upright, like a human being, and advanced toward me. It moved as if to hit me with its paw so I struck the paw with my sword, severing it so that it flew into the air. It cried out, "Ah! You've killed me! God curse you!"

He ran away from me and I pursued him—it was a moonlit night—until he entered the town. I stayed behind, but without overtaking him, staying where I could see him. He went through many streets. All the while I was marking the road so as not to lose my way. Finally he arrived at a door, pushed it open and went in; I heard him lock the door. I marked the door and retraced my steps by means of the marks I hade made. I reached the dome where the grave robber had been. I searched for the hand, found it, brought it into the light of the moon and with some effort I extricated the severed hand from the iron implement, which turned out to be like a glove, in the shape of a hand, with the fingers inserted into its fingers. And behold, it was a hand adorned with henna tracings and two gold rings! So I knew it was a woman's hand. When I realized that the creature was a woman I was sad. I looked at the hand, and it was the most beautiful hand in the world, soft, tender, fleshy, and pretty. I wiped off the blood and went back to sleep in the dome I was in originally. In the morning I entered the town, looking for the marks I had made, and found the door. I asked to whom the house belonged and was told it belonged to the town judge.

A large crowd gathered at the door and a venerable old man emerged. He performed the morning prayer with the people and sat down in the prayer niche.[630] I became more and more amazed about it all. I asked one of those present, "What is the name of this judge?"

They gave his name. I sat for a long time, talking about him, and learned that he had an unmarried daughter and a wife. I was sure that the grave robber was his daughter. I addressed him and said, "There is something I should like to discuss with Your Honor, God bless you, which can only be done in private."

He stood up and went inside the mosque. When we were alone he said, "Speak."

I produced the hand and said, "Do you recognize this?"

He looked at it closely for a long time. Then he said, "Not the hand, no, but the two rings belong to a young daughter of mine. What is the story behind this?"

I told him the whole story. Then he said, "Come with me."

He took me inside his house, locked the door and ordered some food, which was served. He called for his wife, and the servant said to her, "Come out of your room."

But she replied, "Say to him, how can I come when there's a stranger with you!"

The servant left and told the judge what she had said. He said, "She must come and eat with us. This is someone in front of whom I do not feel embarrassed."

She still refused, upon which he swore he would divorce her unless she came. So she came, crying, and sat down with us. The judge said, "Have your daughter come."

She replied, "Husband, have you gone mad? What is wrong with you? You have already disgraced me, an old woman; how can you now dishonor an unmarried girl?"

But he swore he would divorce her unless she made the girl come. So she came. The father said, "Eat with us!"

I beheld a girl who was like a gold dinar, more beautiful than my eyes had ever seen before; but her complexion was very pale and she looked sickly. I knew that this was because of the loss of blood from her hand. She began to eat with her left hand[631] and her right hand remained hidden. Her father said to her, "Show your right hand."

Her mother said, "An abscess has appeared on it; it is bandaged."

But he swore that she should show it. His wife said to him, "Think of your reputation, husband, and of your daughter's! By God, (and here she swore many solemn oaths) I have never known anything wicked about this girl until last night; she came to me after midnight and woke me up. 'Mother,' she said, 'help me, or I will die!' 'What is wrong with you?', I asked, and she said, 'My hand has been cut off and I am losing blood, I will die any moment; attend to it!' And she showed me her arm with the hand cut off.[632] I struck my face in horror. 'Mother,' she said, 'don't cause a scandal for me and for yourself by crying out to my father and the neighbors, just attend to my wound!' I said, 'I don't know how to treat it!' and she said, 'Boil some oil and cauterize the stump with it.' So I did that, I cauterized it and bandaged it. I said to her, 'Now tell me what happened to you,' but she wouldn't. I said, 'By God, if you don't tell me I will reveal everything to your father.' So she said, 'Some years ago I had this idea that I should dig up graves.

I went to this servant girl and told her to buy me a goatskin with the hair still on it, and I had an iron glove made. I would open the door when it was dark, and order the girl to sleep in the hall and not lock the door. I would put on the skin and the iron glove and I would walk on all fours, so that whoever would see me, from a rooftop or wherever, would think that I was a dog. Then I would go to the cemetery, having learned who among the notables of the town had died during the day, and where he was buried. Then I would go to his grave, dig it up, and take the shrouds, putting them inside the goatskin. Then I would move in the same manner and return home while the door was still unlocked. I would go inside, lock it, take off the glove and hand it to the girl together with the shrouds I had taken. She would then hide them in a room you don't know about. I have gathered some three hundred shrouds by now, or a number close to that. I don't know what to do with them; but going out like that and doing this gave me inexplicable pleasure; only this disaster has struck me as a result! Last night I was overpowered by a man who had caught sight of me; he seemed to be guarding that grave. I stood up to hit him in the face with the iron glove, so that he would leave me alone and I could run away. But he got out his sword to strike me, I warded off the blow with my right hand and he cut it off.'"[633]

"I said to her, 'You must pretend that an abscess has appeared on your hand and behave as if you are sick; your paleness will lend credence to your words. Then, after a few days, I'll say to your father that if your hand is not amputated your whole body will be infected and you will die. He will then give permission for it to be amputated, we will pretend that we have had it cut off. This news will then spread and your reputation will be saved.' So that's what we did, after I had asked her to repent, which she did, swearing to God Almighty that she would never do anything like that again. I had made up my mind to sell the servant girl to some travelers who would take her far away from this town. And I would keep an eye on the girl, having her sleep next to me. But now you have exposed her and yourself to shame!"

The judge asked the girl, "What do you have to say?"

"My mother has spoken the truth. I swear to God that I will never do it again and I repent to God the Exalted."

Then her father said to her, "Here is this man of yours who cut off your hand."

She nearly died of shock. Then he asked me, "Young man, where are you from?"

"From Iraq."

"Why have you come here?"

"To look for a job and a livelihood."

"Well, you've found it, all fine and legal! We are well-to-do people; God has blessed us with wealth and good standing. Please do not destroy this blessing, do not expose us! I will give you this daughter of mine in marriage, I'll make you independent with my money and you can live with us in this house."

I said, "Fine!"

The food was taken away. The judge went to the mosque, where people had already gathered and were waiting for him. He gave a sermon and married us. Then he got up, returned, and made me settle in his house.

I was delighted with the girl, to such an extent that I almost died of love for her. I took her maidenhood and we spent some months together. But she had an aversion to me, even though I was friendly to her, cried for the loss of her hand and apologized to her. She made a show of accepting my apology, saying that her behavior was caused by the grief for her hand, when in fact she was growing ever more resentful.

Finally, one night when I was asleep I felt a heaviness in my dream, I perceived a weight on my chest. I woke up with a fright, and there was my wife, kneeling on my chest with her knees on my arms, securing them tightly. She held a razor in her hand and she was about to cut my throat. I wriggled, trying to free myself, but this proved impossible, and I was afraid that she would be too quick for me. So I stopped moving[634] and said to her, "Tell me one thing, then do what you want!"

"Ask!"

"Why are you doing this?"

"Did you really think that you could cut off my hand and dishonor me, that someone like you could marry me, and survive unscathed? By God, that cannot be!"

I said, "You can no longer cut my throat, but you could inflict serious injuries. You can't be sure that I won't break loose, kill you, and escape, or expose you and your actions and hand you over to the authorities. Then your first crime and your second will come to light, your father and your family will wash their hands of you, and you will be executed."

"Do what you want, but you must die. We have become completely estranged from each other."

I considered the situation. It was unlikely that I could escape from her; she would certainly wound me somewhere on my body, which could be the death of me. I said to myself, I must think of something. I said to her, "Isn't there another possibility?"

"Talk!"

"I'll divorce you right now and you'll be rid of me. Tomorrow I'll leave the town, I won't ever see you again and you won't ever see me again. Your story won't be exposed in town, and you'll be able to marry anyone you like. And when it becomes generally known that you had your hand amputated because of an abscess, your reputation will remain secure."

She said, "I won't agree unless you swear that you will not stay in this town, that you will never expose me, and unless you divorce me right now."

So I divorced her[635] and swore solemn oaths that I would leave and not shame her. She got off my chest and ran away, afraid that I would get hold of her. She threw the razor away, I don't know where, and then she came back. She began to pretend that all she had done had just been a jest and began to caress me. But I said, "Get away from me, you are now forbidden to me and I am not allowed to touch you. Tomorrow morning I'll leave."

Then she said, "Now I know that you are sincere; for, by God, if you had done otherwise you would not have escaped from my hand."

She got up and brought me a purse, saying, "Here are one hundred dinars; take them for your expenses. You must write a document divorcing me and leave in the morning."

I took the dinars and left at dawn, after having written a note for her father, explaining that I had irrevocably divorced her and that I had left, feeling too ashamed to meet him.

To this day I have never seen them again.

II. The Prisoner of War[636]

Like the preceding story, this one, the longest in al-Tanūkhī's collection, also contains some motifs common in folklore.

Ḥumayd, the Secretary of Ibrāhīm ibn al-Mahdī[637] transmitted that Ibrāhīm related to him that Makhlad al-Ṭabarī, the Secretary of al-Mahdī[638] in charge of the department of confidential correspondence, related to him:

Sālim,[639] the affiliate of Hishām ibn ʿAbd al-Malik[640] and his Secretary in charge of the chancery, informed him that one day, when he was being trained—the way young people are trained in the various departments—a letter arrived from the postmaster general of the Syrian frontier region, addressed to ʿAbd al-Malik,[641] informing him that some Byzantine cavalry had appeared to the Muslims. A detachment had hurried toward them, then returned, bringing with them a man who had been taken prisoner in the days of Muʿāwiyah ibn Abī Sufyān.[642] The writer mentioned that when the Byzantines had met the Muslims they had told them that they had not come to fight but to bring this Muslim in order to hand him over to the Muslims, as the Byzantine emperor had ordered them to do.

The postmaster mentioned that the detachment said they had asked the Muslim man about what the Byzantines had said. His answer agreed with what they had said. He said that the Byzantines had treated him well. Then they left. "I asked him," (the writer added) "how he had got away. But he said that he would tell nobody except the Commander of the Believers."

ʿAbd al-Malik ordered for the man to be brought to him, so he was sent to Damascus. When he came into ʿAbd al-Malik's presence, the caliph asked him, "Who are you?"

"Qatāt ibn Rāzīn, of the tribe of Lakhm..."

(The author of this book adds: This is how it appears in the source from which I have copied it, viz. Qatāt. But I think this is a mistake, because he is commonly known as Qabāth ibn Razīn al-Lakhmī. He transmitted hadith on the authority of ʿAlī ibn Rabāḥ al-Lakhmī, on the authority of ʿUqbah ibn ʿĀmir al-Juhanī. Unless it was someone else; God knows best.)[643]

Back to the story:

"... and I live in Fusṭāṭ in Egypt, in a place known as al-Ḥamrāʾ.[644] I was taken prisoner in the time of Muʿāwiyah, when the tyrant ruling the Byzantines was Tūmā ibn Marzūq."[645]

ʿAbd al-Malik asked him, "How did he treat you all?"

"I have never known anyone more hostile to Islam and its adherents than he. But he was mild-mannered and the Muslims were better off in his time than with others. Eventually he was succeeded by his son Liyūn,[646] who said as soon as he assumed power: 'If prisoners of war stay in the same place for a long time they get accustomed to it, no matter how bad it is. There is nothing that hurts[647] them more than being transferred from one place to another.'" He ordered for twelve arrow shafts to be brought and wrote the name of a patrician of a particular province on the end of each of them.[648] The arrows were to be drawn four times each year. The Muslims were to be transferred first to the patrician whose name came out first, who would imprison them for one month; then they would go to the second, then the third, after which the arrows would be thrown again.

Whenever we arrived at one of the patricians, he would say to us: "Praise God that He has not inflicted upon you the patrician of the Bulgars!"[649] So we would be terrified every time he was mentioned, and would thank God for not having inflicted him upon us. We remained like this for several years.[650] Then the arrows were thrown again, the first and second came out for two patricians and the third for the patrician of the Bulgars. Accordingly we spent two months in great trepidation, expecting the worst. The two months passed and we were transported to him. At his gate we saw a larger crowd than we were used to, and we saw that his henchmen[651] were more ruthless than any we had ever seen. We came into his presence and based on what we saw of his uncouthness and ruthlessness we were certain that we would perish at his hands. He called for blacksmiths and ordered for the Muslims to be shackled with a multiple of chains, compared with what others had done. The irons were clapped on the feet of one man after another, until the blacksmith reached me. I looked at the patrician's face and saw that he was looking at me in particular, more than at the others. He addressed me in Arabic and asked me my name, my lineage and where I used to live—precisely as the Commander of the Believers just asked me! I answered all his questions truthfully. Then he asked me, "What parts of your Book have you memorized?"

I told him that I knew it by heart. He said, "Recite 'The Family of 'Imrān!'"[652]

I recited fifty verses of it. He said, "You are an accomplished Qur'an reciter!"

Then he asked me if I had memorized poetry and I told him that I had committed a great deal of it to memory. He asked me to recite poetry by a number of poets. He said, "You have a good memory!"

Then he said to his second-in-command, "I like this man! Do not put chains on him."

And he continued, "It would not be just to harm his friends either. Take their chains off, all of them, give them a comfortable place to stay and don't be stingy when feeding them."

Then he called for his chef and said to him, "As long as this Arab is with me I will not have any meal unless he dines with me. So take care not to let anything enter your kitchen that Muslims are forbidden to eat, and do not put alcohol in any of your dishes."

Then he called for food to be brought. He asked me to come closer and I sat down next to him. I said to him, "Esteemed Sir,[653] I should like you to tell me to which Arab tribe you belong."

He laughed and said, "I am not an Arab, so I cannot give you an answer!"

"In spite of your fluency in Arabic?"

"If knowing a language could give someone another nationality, the one whose language he has mastered, then you would be a Byzantine, since you are as fluent in Greek as I am in Arabic. According to your logic you should be a Byzantine and I should be an Arab!"

I admitted that he was right. I stayed with him for two weeks in the pleasantest circumstances that I had known since I was born. But on the eve of the sixteenth day I realized that one half of the month had now gone by, and that the days and nights[654] would bring me ever closer to being transferred to someone else's charge and I spent the whole night worrying. His messenger came to me on the sixteenth day, inviting me to eat with the patrician. When the food was before us he saw that I was eating less than usual. He laughed and said, "I am guessing, Arab, that since half the month has now passed you are thinking that the days are bringing you closer to the time when you will be transferred to someone else, someone who will not treat you as I do, and with whom you will not enjoy the lifestyle such as the one you are enjoying here with me. As a result, you could not sleep and you are worried, and this has spoiled your appetite!"

I told him that he was right. He said, "I would not be a noble man if I did not choose the best option for a friend. God has spared you from what you fear. For on the day you arrived here I immediately asked the Emperor to assign you to me as long as you are in Byzantine territory. You will not be transferred from me and if you leave it will only be to go to your own country. I hope that God will make me the cause of that."

I was much relieved. I stayed with him until the end of the month. When the month had passed the arrows were thrown. The first, second and third came out for other patricians. My friends were transferred and I stayed behind on my own. That morning I had a meal with the patrician. It had been my custom to go to my Muslim companions after the meal; we would have friendly talks, recite the Qur'an, perform the ritual prayer together, discuss religious duties, and listen to what we told each other of what we knew.[655] That day I left the table and went to the place I would repair to when the Muslims were still around; but I found only unbelievers. I felt so depressed that I wished I were with my friends. I spent a troubled night without ever closing my eyes. The following morning I was the most dejected and most miserable of God's creatures.

The messenger came to get me at breakfast time and I went to the patrician. My worries were clearly visible on my face. I reached for the food, but he saw that I stretched my hand in a way he was not accustomed from me. He laughed and said, "I think you are depressed because you are separated from your friends!"

I told him that he was right and asked him if there was a way to bring them back under his charge. He answered, "The Emperor has had your friends transferred from my authority to someone else's for no other reason than to make them miserable by so doing. It is unthinkable that he should abandon his method of harming them just because I happen to like you. I can't do anything about this."

Then I asked him to ask the Emperor to take me away from him and join me with my companions, so that I could be wherever they were. But he said, "That can't be done either, for I will not allow you to be transferred from comfort to distress, from an honored position to humiliation, and from blessing to misery."

When he said this, my despondency was clearly visible, overwhelmed as I was by unhappiness. He said, "You really are extremely dejected!"

I told him I was, to such an extent that I would rather die than go on living, knowing that only then would I be at peace. He said, "If you are speaking the truth, well, relief is at hand!"

I asked him what proof he had. He replied, "I myself once fell into misfortunes that were even more terrible than the one you're in; but I was saved in the end."

He told me that the patriciate in his country had always been held among his forefathers, who inherited it from one another. There had been many of them, but finally only his father and his uncle remained; it was his uncle, not his father, who held the patriciate. But his father and uncle remained childless for a long time. They spent a great deal of money on doctors, for a cure that would make men fit for women. In the end the uncle turned out to be a hopeless case; he despaired of ever getting a proper erection. One of the physicians then turned his attention to treating the patrician's father, and his mother got pregnant. When the uncle learned that the mother had become pregnant, he assembled a number of pregnant women speaking different languages, among them Arabic, Greek, Frankish, Slavic, Khazarī, and other languages.[656] They gave birth in his palace. When the patrician's mother had given birth to him, the uncle ordered all these women to care for the baby, and he gave instructions that each one of them should speak to him only in their own tongue. Before he was four years old he spoke all the languages of the mothers who had nursed him.[657] Then he gave orders that his playmates and tutors should be chosen from the same nationalities as those of the women who had brought him up. They taught him to write and to read their books. He was not yet nine years old before he had learned all that. Then his uncle ordered a number of horsemen to be joined with him, to teach him to fight with a lance, to handle horses, and all things horsemen need to learn. He gave instructions that the boy should be prevented from dwelling in houses, that he should live in tents, and that he should be forbidden to eat meat unless he had hunted it with a bird of prey perched on his hand, or with a hunting dog running before him, or had killed it with his own bow and arrow.

In this way he lived until he was ten years old. Then his uncle died and his father succeeded him in the patriciate. The latter ordered him to come to him and when he saw him, and noticed his sound sense, his good manners, and his good qualities in general, he was greatly pleased with him. He allowed him to have what even kings would not allow their children. He equipped him with tents and pavilions made of brocade and joined to him a large group of horsemen. He provided all of them amply with everything they needed and sent him off, to live once more in tents, telling him to stay far from the dwellings of his father. The patrician continued, "One day, when I was fifteen years old, I went out riding, to explore a place to move to. I noticed a pond, which I estimated at a thousand cubits long and between three and four hundred cubits wide.[658] I gave orders for my tents to be pitched next to it, and I went hunting. That day God provided me with more game than I could ever hope to hunt. I entered one of the tents and ordered the cooks to prepare the food I wanted to eat. The table was set up before me. Then, the moment I watched the food being ladled out, I heard a loud noise. Before I knew what the matter was I saw the heads of my companions fall one after the other from their bodies. I moved away, took off the clothes I was wearing, and put on the clothes of one of my slaves. Then I looked left and right and saw only corpses around me. As it turned out, this was the doing of a troop of Bulgar horsemen. I was taken prisoner, just like any slave; all our belongings, tents, and everything else, were carried away and I was taken to the king of the Bulgars.

"When he saw me—he had no male child—he gave orders that I should be treated well and that I should stand by his side; he called me his son. The king had a daughter, on whom he doted. He had taught her horsemanship, how to joust with horsemen, and to race and gallop with them. In my presence he said to a number of his patricians, 'Which of you will go to the Byzantine Emperor and bring me a scribe from his country, who can teach my daughter to write?'

"I told him that his messenger could not possibly bring him anyone who could write better than me. He told me to write in his presence, I wrote, and he appreciated my handwriting. He compared it with letters that had come to him from my father, and saw that my handwriting was better than in those. Then he handed over his daughter to me and gave orders that I should teach her to write.

"I fell in love with her and she with me.

"She stayed with me until she was thirteen years old. Then, one day, she came running to me, crying. I asked her, 'Why are you crying, my lady?'

"She said, 'Leave me alone! I have good reason to cry!'

"I asked her why, and she said, 'Last night I was sitting with my father and mother. My eyes felt heavy and I lay down.[659] Then I heard my father say to my mother: "I see that your daughter's breasts are getting full, and I noticed that this Byzantine boy is rude in his speech. From now on they should no longer be together. When she sits with him tomorrow you must send someone to separate them, so that he will see her no more, nor she him."'"

The patrician added that it was customary among the Bulgars for the father to ask someone to marry his daughter, but he would only ask someone that the girl had chosen. He continued, "I said to the king's daughter, 'If your father asks you, which man would you like me to ask to marry you, say to him: I only want this Byzantine!'

"But she replied angrily, saying, 'How could I possible ask my father to marry me to a slave?!'

"I replied, 'But God did not create me a slave. I am a prince, and my father is the king of the Byzantines!'"

Here the patrician explained that the Bulgars called the Byzantine patrician who ruled the Bulgar marches[660] "king of the Byzantines."

He continued, "Then she asked me, 'Are you telling the truth?'

"I told her it was the truth. No sooner had we finished talking than the king's messenger arrived and separated us. No more than three days later the king summoned me. When I entered his presence I saw evil signs firmly set in his face. He said to me, 'You wretch, what made you lie about your lineage? I condemn to death anybody who falsely claims to be the son of someone who is not his father!'

"'I have not claimed to be anybody's son except my father's!'

"'Are you saying[661] that you are the son of the king of the Byzantines?'

"I told him I was and called upon him to investigate the matter.

"He replied, 'I need send no messenger to inquire about you in order to investigate your case. I know a few things myself with which to examine you, so as to tell your truthfulness from your lies.'

"I urged him to investigate by whatever means he liked.[662] Then he called for a horse, a saddle blanket, a saddle, and a bridle, and ordered me to take the horse. I took the horse from the groom. Then he told me to take the saddle blanket. I took it. Then he told me to put it on the horse. I did what he asked. Then he ordered me to take the saddle. I took it. He told me to fasten the girth around his belly, the crupper, and the girth around its breast, and to take the bridle and put it on the horse. I did all that. Then he told me to mount the horse. So I mounted it. He ordered me to ride forward and back, which I did. Then he told me to dismount and I dismounted. Thereupon he said, 'I testify that he is the son of the king of the Byzantines, for he has handled the horse like a king and performed all the other things just as kings do. Be my witness that I am marrying him to my daughter!'

"When they said, 'We witness!' he said, 'Do not testify!'

"When I heard him say 'Do not testify!' I feared that he would kill me. But he continued, 'I did not interrupt the witnessing because I dislike you, but we have a stipulation that we cannot violate. We cannot rule out that you may be forced to comply with it and that we have to hold you to our condition, while we have not properly informed you of it and made you aware of it, in which case we would have wronged you; or else we would have to waive the custom of our land, and thereby abandon our religion.[663] It is our custom, Byzantine, not to separate spouses if one of them dies. If the man dies before his wife we make her lie down with him on his bier and we carry them together, until we lower them into a pit which is the resting place for our dead. We provide them with food and drink[664] for three days, then let them down into the pit. When they reach the bottom we let the ropes slip down on them. It is the same when the woman dies before the man: we put her on her couch and her husband next to her. We take them to the pit together. Now if you agree to this custom, then may God bless you with your spouse, and if you do not agree we will exempt you and we will not marry you: it would not be right to break our custom.'

"My passion for her forced me to say, 'I agree to this custom.'[665]

"Then he gave orders for the girl to be made ready and to hand her over to me. He joined us in matrimony and I spent forty days with her during which we thought we were on top of the world. But then she fell ill and she fell into a coma, such that everyone who saw her thought she had passed away. She was prepared for burial in her most splendid clothes, and I was similarly prepared. We were laid on one bier. The king and his court mounted their horses and escorted us until they had brought us to the edge of the pit. They fastened ropes to the lower parts of the bier. They put food and drink for three days with us on the bier. Then they lowered us until we landed on the floor of the pit. The ropes were allowed to slip down on us. One of the ropes fell on the girl's face; the pain took her out of her coma and she woke up. When she woke up I thought the world was all mine again.[666]

"My eyes got used to the darkness and I saw in that place enough dry bread and wine to last us a long time. We began to eat together.

"Rarely did a day go by without a bier being lowered, upon it two spouses, one dead and the other alive. If the man coming down was alive, I took it upon myself to kill him, so that there would be no other man with my wife. Likewise, if the living one was a woman, my wife would take care of killing her, so that nobody but she would be with her husband. We spent more than a year in the pit in these circumstances. Then, one day, a bucket was lowered into the pit and I noticed that he who had done so was not a Bulgar; I knew that the only people coming to that spot besides the Bulgars would be Byzantines. It occurred to me that I should let the girl get out before me, so that she could escape and then tell them about me. They would then lower the bucket to me and I would come out.

"I put the daughter of the king inside the bucket with all her clothes, ornaments and jewels, the people pulled her up and the girl got out. The people turned out to be slave soldiers of my father. It did not occur to them to ask about me, and the girl was too afraid of them to say anything.[667] They had seen how my mother and my father were grieving about losing me, so they took the girl to them so that they would find some consolation in her. They were pleased with her and did find comfort in her. The girl remained afraid of them and thus caused much harm to happen.[668]

"My father had a friend who was cultured and wise and who could paint. He had painted for them a portrait of me, beautifully executed on a panel, which he placed in a room. He had said to my parents, 'Whenever you are thinking of your son and you are very sad, go to that room and look at the portrait. You will cry a lot and that will give you some consolation.' Now when the girl was staying with my parents, she saw them enter that room often, and leave it having cried. One day she followed them when they were inside and she caught sight of the picture.

When she saw it she slapped her face, pulled her hair, and tore her clothes. They asked her why she was doing this to herself and she answered, 'This is the portrait of my husband!'

"They asked her his name and the names of his father and mother, and she gave all their names.[669] They asked her, 'Where is your husband?'

"'In the pit I was rescued from.'

"My father and mother rode out with most of the people of the town, with the servants who had taken the girl out of the pit. When they arrived at the pit they lowered a bucket. I had just unsheathed the sword that had been lowered with me and put its tip at my chest, in order to lean on to it and let it come out of my back, so that I would be relieved of this world, because I was so overcome with grief. Now I jumped up and got in the bucket. They pulled me up and I saw my father, my mother, and my wife standing at the edge of the pit. They had brought horses for me to ride to my country, where my father had become king. But I did not obey them; I told them that it was better to send for the girl's father and mother, so that they could see their daughter, 'just as you are seeing me now.'[670]

"This they did. They sent a message to the girl's father, the ruler of the Bulgars, and he came, accompanied by his retinue, and saw her. A new wedding celebration was held and a peace between the Byzantines and the Bulgars was concluded, in which solemn oaths were sworn not to attack each other for thirty years. Then the people returned to their country and we returned to our homes.

"My father died and I inherited the patriciate from him; and I was blessed with a son by the daughter of the king of the Bulgars. Now, Arab, even though you are as miserable as you say you are, relief is at hand!"

The patrician had no sooner finished speaking than a messenger of the Byzantine emperor entered, summoning him. He went to see him and when he returned to me he said, "Arab, you will be free! I was with the emperor when the Arabs were mentioned. The patricians unanimously condemned them all, saying that they were neither intelligent nor civilized, and that their victory over the Byzantines was by superior numbers and fortuitous, not on account of their excellent planning. Then I told the emperor that it was not as they said, and that some Arabs were civilized, bright, and able to organize things. The emperor said to me, 'It is because you are so fond of that Arab guest of yours that you exaggerate and attribute to the Arabs virtues they do not possess!' I replied, 'If the Emperor sees fit, let him allow me to bring this Arab here, and let him join these theologians, so that he discover his merits.' Then he gave orders that I should take you to him!"

I said, "This is an awful thing you've done for me! I'm afraid that he will despise me if his companions have the better of me; and if I am victorious he will resent it!"

The patrician answered, "That is how ordinary people would react. Kings are different. I tell you that if you have the better of them you will gain the emperor's respect and you will be in a position to have him grant you a request. If, however, they vanquish you he will be pleased to see his co-religionists win. This, too, will secure your protection. The least thing he will do is grant you a request. So whether you win or lose, ask him to let you go from his lands and send you back to your country; for he will do that."

Qabāth continued:

When I entered into the emperor's presence he told me to sit close to him; he favored and honored me and said, "Debate with these patriarchs!"[671]

I told him that I could not bring myself to debate with them and that I would only debate with the Grand Patriarch, so the emperor summoned him. When he entered, I greeted him and said, "Welcome, great Master!"

Then I said to him, "Master, how are you?"

"I am well."

"Is everything all right with you?"

"As well as can be desired."

"And how is your son?"

All the patriarchs began to laugh. They said, "The patrician (meaning the one who was my friend) claimed that this was a civilized person and that he was intelligent. But he does not even know, in his ignorance, that God the Exalted has safeguarded this patriarch against having a son!"

I said, "It seems to me that you think he is above having a son."

"Certainly, by God! We think too highly of him for that; for God has exalted him above such things!"

Then I said, "Now, that is a strange thing! Is one of God's servants too lofty to have a son, whereas God Himself, the Creator of all creation, would not be above having a son?"

The patriarch snorted, startling me. Then he said, "Sire, expel this man from your land this instant, or else he will corrupt your subjects!"

The emperor called for some horsemen and had me join them. He ordered some horses of the postal service to be brought for me, to put me on them and to hand me over to whichever Muslims they might encounter in Islamic territory. This is how they came to hand me over to those border troops who received me.

Then he[672] told a story about ʿAbd al-Malik with this man that has no connection with this chapter, so I will not mention it. And God the Exalted, praised be He, knows best about its correctness.[673]

III. The Mystic and the Elephant[674]

The tale is an example of the extensive body of Arabic stories and anecdotes about mystics.

Abū Isḥāq Ibrāhīm ibn Aḥmad ibn Muḥammad the notary public known as al-Ṭabarī related to me: Jaʿfar ibn Muḥammad al-Khuldī, the Ṣūfī related to me: Ibrāhīm al-Khawwāṣ, the Ṣūfī (God rest his soul) related to me the following.[675]

I traveled by boat with a group of Sufis.[676] Our ship was wrecked; some of us survived on a raft, made from the wood of the ship. We were cast ashore on an unknown coast. Not finding anything to eat for days, we expected to die of starvation. Someone suggested, "Let's make a pledge to God, that we will give up something, so that God may have pity on us and save us from this hardship." One man said, "I'll keep the fast forever";[677] another said, "I'll perform a number of extra prayers every day," and another said, "I'll give up all worldly pleasures," until all of them had said something. But I kept silent. "You must say something, too," they said to me. But the only thing that occurred to me was, "I'll never eat elephant flesh."

"What are you saying?," they exclaimed, "and in this situation?!"[678] But I answered, "I swear by God, I did not mean to say this, but from the moment you began to make pledges to God I kept proposing many things to myself, but I could not bring myself to give them up. Nothing occurred to me that I could give up for God; but the only thing that came into my heart was what I said. There must have been a reason why it came to my lips."

After a short while someone said, "Let us explore this place, separately, and look for food. If someone finds something he must warn the others. Let's meet back at this tree."

So we went off to explore, separately. One of us came across a small elephant calf. We called to one another and having joined forces our companions caught it. Then they contrived to roast it; they sat down and ate. "Come eat with us," they said to me. But I replied, "You know that I have just given it up as a pledge to God. I cannot go back on my words. Perhaps that which came to my lips will be the death of me, for I haven't eaten for days. I won't do otherwise. God will not see me breaking my promise to Him, even if I have to die." I sat down at a distance while my companions ate.

Night fell. I sought shelter by a tree trunk and I spent the night there. My companions dispersed and went to sleep. Only a moment later an enormous elephant appeared suddenly, bellowing. The earth shook with this bellowing and its great speed; then it went for us! We said to one another, "This is the end!" They uttered the Creed,[679] they prayed for God's forgiveness and praised Him, and they cast themselves down on their faces.[680] The elephant turned to each one in turn, sniffing him from top to toe, not omitting a single spot. Then it lifted one of its legs, put it down, and crushed him. When it had ascertained that the man was dead it turned to the next and did the same to him. This went on until I was the only one left. I was sitting upright, witnessing what went on, craving God Almighty's forgiveness and praising Him.[681] The elephant turned to me and when it came near me I lay down on my back. It did the same sniffing as before with my companions, and then it repeated this two or three times, which it had not done with the others. All the while I nearly gave up the ghost from fright. Then it wrapped its trunk round me and lifted me in the air. I thought it wanted to kill me so I loudly prayed for God's forgiveness. Then it wrapped its trunk around me[682] and put me on its back. I sat up straight, making some effort to keep myself in place. The elephant set off, at times running and at other times walking, while I sometimes praised God for postponing my end, hoping to live, and at other times expected that it would throw me up and kill me. Again, I kept praying for God's forgiveness, suffering a lot of pain and fear all the while because of the elephant's fast pace.

I remained like this until dawn broke and its light spread. Then it wrapped its trunk round me. I thought, this is the end; death has come. I vigorously asked God's forgiveness. But lo and behold, it took me gently down off its back and put me on the earth. Then it went back the way it came. I could not believe my luck.

When it had disappeared from sight and I could no longer hear it, I fell to the ground prostrating myself before God, and I only lifted my head when I felt the sun. I found that I was on a road. I walked for some eight miles and arrived at a large town. I entered it. The people were amazed about me. They asked me about my story, which I told them. They maintained that the elephant had walked several days' march in a single night and they found it a curious thing that I should have escaped with my life. I stayed with them until I had recovered from the hardship I had suffered and my body was refreshed. Then I departed with some merchants, I boarded a ship, and God granted me a safe return to my country.

IV. The Caliph al-Muʿtaḍid as Detective[683]

Al-Muḥassin [al-Tanūkhī] said: A story has reached us about the Caliph al-Muʿtaḍid billāh[684] that one day one of his servants came to him and informed him that he had been standing on the bank of the Tigris, in the caliph's palace, when he saw a fisherman who had cast his net. It was heavy with something, so he pulled it in and took it out of the water. And lo, there was a leather bag inside. He thought that it contained money, so he picked it up and opened it. It turned out that there were some bricks inside, and between the bricks there was a hand painted with henna. The servant produced the bag, the hand, and the bricks. Al-Muʿtaḍid was appalled and said, "Tell the fisherman to cast his net again at the same spot, a bit higher, a bit lower, and nearby."

This was done, and another leather bag appeared, containing a foot. They kept looking but nothing else emerged. Al-Muʿtaḍid was saddened by this and said, "In this town there is somebody among us who kills a person, cuts off his[685] limbs and sinks them in the river, and I don't know about him? This is not the way to rule over a country!"

All day long he did not eat a thing. The following morning he called for one of his trusted agents, gave him the empty bag, and said to him, "Go around to everyone who makes leather bags in Baghdad, and if anyone of them recognizes this one, ask him to whom he sold it. If he then directs you to the buyer, ask him who bought it from him. But do not tell anyone about the matter."

The man went off and returned three days later. He stated that he had sought out all the tanners and bag makers until he found the one who had made it. He had asked him about it and the man told him that he had sold it to a perfume merchant in the Yaḥyā souk.[686] He had gone to the perfume merchant and had shown it to him. The man had said, "I say, how did you get hold of that bag?" The agent continued, "I said to him,[687] 'Do you recognize it, then?'

"'Yes, So-and-so, the Hāshimī[688] bought ten[689] leather bags from me three days ago. I don't know what he needed them for. This is one of them.'

"I asked him, 'And who is this So-and-so the Hāshimī?'

"'A descendant of ʿAlī ibn Rayṭah, one of the children of al-Mahdī.[690] He is called So-and-so and he is an important person.[691] But he is the most wicked and evil of people, a great corrupter of the women of decent Muslims, always eager to practice his wiles against them;[692] but there is no one in the world who would dare inform al-Muʿtaḍid of his behavior, for fear of his evil doings and because of his extremely high position in the dynasty and because of his wealth.'

"He went on telling me all kinds of ugly stories about him, while I listened. Finally he said, 'Suffice it to tell you that a few years ago he fell in love with So-and-so, the singer, a slave girl of So-and-so the singer. She was as beautiful as a minted golden dinar, like the full moon when it rises, and an exceedingly good singer. He bargained over her with her mistress, but she would not come near him. A few days ago he heard that her owner wanted to sell her to a buyer who had presented himself and was prepared to spend thousands of dinars on her. He sent the owner a message, saying, "The least you could do is to send her to me so that she can say farewell to me!" So she sent the girl to him, once he had paid up to hire[693] the girl for three days. When the three days had passed, the man abducted her and kept her hidden from her owner. Nothing more was heard of her, and he claimed that she had fled from his house. The neighbors said that he had killed her, whereas others said, "No, she is with him!" Her mistress held a funeral service for her; she went to the man's house and cried at the door, making a spectacle of herself,[694] but all to no avail.'"

When al-Muʿtaḍid heard this he prostrated himself, thanking God because the matter had now been revealed to him. He immediately sent some people to raid the Hāshimī's house and fetch the singing girl. He produced the hand and the foot, showing them to the Hāshimī, who turned pale when he saw them; he realized that he was a dead man and confessed. Al-Muʿtaḍid then gave orders that the price of the slave girl be paid to her mistress from the treasury and he sent her away. He imprisoned the Hāshimī; some say that he had him executed, others say that he died in prison.

The Isfahan Maqāmah by Badīʿ al-Zamān al-Hamadhānī[695]

حدثنا عيسى بن هشام قال :

كنت بإصفهان أعتزم المسير إلى الريّ ☆ فحللتها حلول الفي ☆ أتوقع القافلة كل لمحة ☆ وأترقب الراحلة كل صبحة ☆ فلمّا حُمّ ما توقعته ☆ نُودي للصلاة نداءً سمعته ☆ وتعيّن فرضُ الإجابة ☆ فانسللت من بين الصحابة ☆ أغتنم الجماعة أدركها ☆ وأخشى فوت القافلة أتركها ☆ لكني استعنت ببركات الصلاة ☆ على وعثاء الفلاة ☆ فصرت إلى أول الصفوف ☆ ومثلت للوقوف ☆

ḥaddathanā ʿīsa bnu hishāmin qāl:

*kuntu bi-ʾiṣfahāna ʾaʿtazimu l-masīra ʾila r-rayy * fa-ḥalaltuhā ḥulūla l-fayy * ʾatawaqqaʿu l-qāfilata kulla lamḥah * wa-ʾataraqqabu r-rāḥilata kulla ṣabḥah * fa-lammā ḥumma mā tawaqqaʿtuh * nūdiya liṣ-ṣalāti nidāʾan samiʿtuh * wa-taʿayyana farḍu l-ʾijābah * fa-nsalaltu min bayni ṣ-ṣaḥābah * ʾaghtanimu l-jamāʿata ʾudrikuhā * wa-ʾakhshā fawta l-qāfilati ʾatrukuhā * lākinnī staʿāntu bi-barakāti ṣ-ṣalāh * ʿalā waʿthāʾi l-falāh * fa-ṣirtu ʾilā ʾawwali ṣ-ṣufūf * wa-mathaltu lil-wuqūf...*

A *maqāmah* (literally, "place or occasion where one stands," sometimes translated as "assembly") is a short, usually narrative "picaresque" text in ornate rhymed prose, often with interspersed poetry, involving a fictional narrator and a fictional vagabond-like character, who reappears (in a series of individually independent *maqāmahs*) in various disguises, usually swindling or coaxing people (including the narrator) to part with their money. The term is also applied more loosely, for non-narrative didactic or moralistic pieces employing rhymed prose.[696]

ʿĪsā ibn Hishām and Abū l-Fatḥ al-Iskandarī are the two fictional personages who occur in most *maqāmahs* by al-Hamadhānī, as narrator and trickster-vagabond, respectively. Aḥmad ibn al-Ḥusayn al-Hamadhānī (358/968–398/1008), nicknamed Badīʿ al-Zamān ("Wonder of the Age") is the "inventor" of the *maqāmah*; his fame was overshadowed by later and more artful practitioners of the form such as al-Ḥarīrī (d. 516/1122). To separate the rhyming segments full stops are used in Arabic editions; this would be confusing in my English rhymed version and they have been replaced by asterisks.

ʿĪsā ibn Hishām related to us:

Once I * was in Isfahan, * though going to Rayy[697] * was my plan. * Therefore I only stayed * as briefly as the fleeting shade, * expecting the arrival of the caravan every second * and any morning to departure to be beckoned. * Now when the expected event was near, * the call to prayer I could hear: * it was a religious obligation, * so I slipped away from my friends to join the congregation, * and for the mosque I headed. * To miss the caravan was what I dreaded, * but it would be for the best * if by this prayer I would be blessed * so as to withstand * hardship in the desert land. *

I found a place in front and there * I stood for the start of the prayer. * The imam came to the prayer niche and at this site * he started to recite * and began * with the "Opening" Sura from the Holy Qur'an * according to the manner of Ḥamzah, * lengthening each "stretching" with the "glottal stop," i.e. the *hamzah*.[698] * On tenterhooks I sat, in suspension * and full of apprehension * about missing the caravan and being left in this place. * But the imam followed up the "Opening" with "The Great Case,"[699] * while I was being roasted upon the fire of patience, burning, * and grilled upon the coals of frustration, tossing and turning. * But I could only be silent and be brave, * or else speak up and then the grave! * For I knew that the uncouth people of that city * would not have any pity * in case of the prayer's truncation * before the final salutation. * So under duress * I remained in this situation of stress * until the end of the sura * while my chances of catching the caravan grew ever poorer, * and I was filled with despair * of ever getting away from there. * Then the imam bent his back for the prostration * with an uncommonly humble self-abnegation * and an unusual manner of resignation. * Then, with his head and his hands raised, * he said, "May God listen to those by whom He is praised!" * Then he stood for a while, making me suppose * he had fallen into a doze. * But he came round * and bent down, hand and forehead to the ground. * I raised my head, looking for an opportunity * to slip away with impunity, * but between the rows I found no space, * so I sat down to prostrate myself in that place, * until the imam said "God is great!" for the sitting position. * And then the son-of-a-whore[700] stood up for a complete repetition! * He recited "The Opening" and "The Clatterer"[701] with an intonation * that occupied the Last

Day's duration[702] * and exhausted the spirits of the congregation. * Now when he had finished this at last he did proceed * to pronounce the Muslim Creed, * wagging his jaws, * then uttering the final salutation turning his cheeks left and right without pause. * I said to myself, "God will get me out of here * and my deliverance is near!" * But then a man stood up and said, "Whosoever loves the Prophet's Companions and the Muslim community among those gathered here * let him for a minute lend me his ear!" *

ʿĪsā ibn Hishām said: So I stayed in my place * to save face. * The man continued, "Forsooth! * I must speak and testify naught but the truth! * I have come with glad tidings from your Prophet. But I shall not convey them until God has purged this mosque of every scoundrel who denies his prophethood."[703] *

ʿĪsā ibn Hishām said: Thus as if with ropes had he trapped me * and as if in iron chains had he clapped me. * The man said, "I saw the Prophet—God bless him and keep him—in a dream: such a sight, * like the sun beneath the clouds so bright * or like the full moon at night. * He walked, followed by the stars in the sky, * dragging the train of his robe, by angels held up high. * Then he taught me a prayer, instructing me to teach it to his people. I wrote it down on paper slips, here presented, * with perfume, musk, and saffron scented. * Anybody who wants it as a gift from me, * I'll give it to him, for free. * But for the expenses of the paper, as compensation, * you may wish to make a small donation." *

ʿĪsā ibn Hishām said: Then dirhams rained upon him in such profusion * that the man was overcome by confusion. * He left and I followed him, wondering at his skill in deceiving * and his sly way of earning a living. * I was about to ask him about himself but I refrained; * or to talk to him, but silent I remained. * I pondered about this eloquence * paired with such impudence, * such elegancy * paired with this mendicancy; * and how he caught people by stealth * and with his tricks robbed them of their wealth. * I looked and what did I see? * It was Abū l-Fatḥ al-Iskandarī! * I said, "How did you devise this trick?" He smiled and recited,

"People are asses. Lead them, one by one.
Get the better of them and spare none.
When at last you have tricked them and won
What you want, then—leave and be gone."

The Debate of Pen and Sword, by Aḥmad Ibn Burd al-Aṣghar[704]

The "literary debate" in which objects or concepts are personified and boast of their superiority is already found in Sumerian literature. In Arabic it occurs sometimes in verse but mostly in ornate prose, in a style not unlike that of the *maqāmah*, with *saj*ʿ and the inclusion of some verse.[705] The most common of several terms for the genre is *munāẓarah* (which is also used for the scholarly or religious dispute). A popular theme is the debate of pen and sword, which stand metonymically for civil administration and military rule, respectively, or civil servants and soldiers, literature and warfare, civilization and brute force, peace and war, rhetoric and physical power, words and deeds, and so on.

The first fully developed literary debate of pen and sword appears in Spain, written by Abū Ḥafṣ Aḥmad ibn Burd al-Aṣghar (d. 445/1053–54), who dedicated it to al-Muwaffaq Abū l-Jaysh Mujāhid ibn ʿAbd Allāh al-ʿĀmirī, the ruler of Denia from 400/1009 until 436/1044; the concluding part of the epistle is an illustration of eulogy in prose, with a final short poem.[706] In my translation I have not attempted to imitate the rhyme.

أما بعد حمد الله بجميع محامده وآلائه ☆ والصلاة والسلام على خاتم أنبيائه ☆ فأن التسابق من جوادَين سبقا في حلبة ☆ وقضيبين نُسقا في تربة ☆ والتحاسد من نجمَين أنارا في أفق ☆ وسهمَين صارا على نسق ☆ والتفاخر من زهرتَين تفتّحتا من كمامة ☆ وبارقتَين توضّحتا من غمامة ☆ لأحمدُ وجوه الحسد ☆ وإن كان مذموماً مع الأبد ☆

*ammā baʿda ḥamdi llāhi bi-jamīʿi maḥāmidihī wa-ālāʾih * waṣ-ṣalāti ʿalā khātami anbiyāʾih * fa-inna t-tasābuqa min jawādayni sabaqā fī ḥalbah * wa-qaḍībayni nusiqā fī turbah * wat-taḥāsuda min najmayni anārā fī ufuq * wa-sahmayni ṣārā ʿalā nasaq * wat-tafākhura min zahratayni tafattaḥatā min kimāmah * wa-*

*bāriqatayni tawaḍḍaḥatā min ghamāmah * la-aḥmadu wujūhi l-ḥasad * wa-in kāna madhmūman maʿa l-abad **

The long, stately periods of the opening make place for shorter and livelier sentences in the course of the debate. Here is the passage where the sword says, "The crunching sound of a millstone but no flour!":

جعجعة رحى لا يتبعها طِحْنٌ ☆ وجلجلة رعد لا يليها مُزْن ☆ في وجه مالك تعرف أَمَرته وجهٌ لئيم ☆ وجسم سقيم ☆ وغرب يُقلّ ☆ ودم يُطَلّ ☆ ودموع سِجام ☆ كأنهن سُخام ☆ ورأس لم يتقلقل فيه لبّ ☆ وجوف لم يتخضخض فيه قلب ☆ أوحش من جوف العَير ☆ يشهدوا عليه كثرة الجوْر ☆ بقلّة خير ☆ فهُبَّ من نومك ☆ وأفطِرْ من صومك ☆

*jaʿjaʿatu raḥan lā yatbaʿuhā ṭiḥn * wa-jaljalatu raʿdin lā yalīhā muzn * fī wajhi mālika taʿrifu amaratahū wajhun laʾīm * wa-jismun saqīm * wa-gharbun yuqill * wa-damun yuṭall * wa-dumūʿun sijām * ka-annahunna sukhām * wa-raʾsun lam yataqalqal fīhi lubb * wa-jawfun lam yatakhaḍkhaḍ fīhi qalb * awḥashu min jawf al-ʿayr * yashhadū ʿalayhi kathratu l-jawr * bi-qillati l-khayr * fa-hubba min nawmik * wa-afṭir min ṣawmik **

Having praised God for all His praiseworthy qualities and favors, and having blessed the Seal of His Prophets, we say:

The rivalry between two noble steeds in a race, or two sapling trees planted side by side in a plot of earth, or the mutual envy between two stars that shine at the horizon, or two arrows shot together, or the mutual boasting between two flowers opening from their calyces, or two flashes that light up in a cloud: these are surely the most laudable forms of envy, even if, ultimately, rivalry must be condemned. One of the two horses may be one step ahead, one of the two saplings may rise higher, one of the two arrows may penetrate further, one of the two stars may be brighter, one of the two flowers may be fresher and lusher, and one of the two flashes may be more intensely brilliant. But the one that falls short will look forward to catching up and the closeness of their positions will kindle the fire of competition, even though they are separated by the calumny of critics and the envy of antagonists.

The Pen and the Sword—which are two lamps that guide those who strive for glory toward their goal; two ladders that cause those who want to attain high ranks to join the stars; two roads that cause those who seek it to arrive at the path of nobility and that garner proud honor for those who jostle for it; two tools that cause the mouth of him who loves sublime acts to kiss their lips and that cause the hand of him who has desires to extend to them; two mediators whose intercession is never too late; and two instruments that join what cannot be separated—trailed the trains of conceit in mutual boasting and stuck up the nose of pride in mutual contestation. Each one of them claimed to have won victory as his prize and to be the first to strike fire from his flint, saying that the pearls had come from his oyster shells, that he had won the maiden for the bridal procession, that the edifice was of his making, that he had cut the sleeves to fit the mantles,[707] that the frankincense of praise was reserved for his censer, that the preacher of proud glory was restricted to his pulpit, that the cloaks of glorious deeds were woven on his loom, and that all the individual superb feats were born from his marriage. When the dispute had cast off its veil, when the argument had stretched its arm, when disdain had shrugged its sides, and when noses were raised, sniffing scornfully, they both stood up to compete in speech and vie in their qualities, each mentioning the superiority of the fruits of his orchard, boasting of a virtue that rivalled the star al-Suhā in height,[708] of a rank that he had tamed and humbled, of a supremacy as elevated as Orion's locks whom he had made his quarry, and of an eminence that he had won riding on the back of the star Capella.

The PEN said, "Ha! Allāhu akbar! You are asking for a beginning that will tie your tongue and perplex your mind, an opening that will fill your ears and constrict your reach: the best of sayings is Truth and the most praiseworthy of traits is truthfulness. The superior one is he whom God has preferred in His revealed word, he by whom He has sworn to His Messenger, saying «*Nūn*. By the Pen and what they inscribe,»[709] and «Recite: And thy Lord is the Most Generous, who taught by the Pen.»[710] Glorious He who swore, mighty the oath! Don't you see me, how I have taken a place between the eyelid and the eye of Faith, how I have moved between mankind's heart and mind? I have taken precedence from head to foot, I have led glory by its bridle."

The SWORD said, "Let us not speak about religion but rather turn to nature, not about Islam but about good qualities! I do not act secretly but openly. 'The value of every man is what he is good at.'[711] A shoulder that carries me is truly fortunate. An arm that is my pillow at night is indeed well-armed. A man who takes me as a guide is rightly guided. A man who makes me his envoy is respected. Through me he will cleave the darkness with a lamp and confront every door with a key. I am eloquent though the hero be dumb, I smile when death frowns. I am decisive without compromise, I am incisive and will not be deflected. I despise any protection against me,[712] and I rend a coat of mail as if it were a shirt!"

The PEN replied, "God protect us from decrease after increase, shame on this flaunting one's tyranny, on this perfidy[713] that blackens what honesty had whitened, that soils what brotherly affection had made pure, which reinforces occasions for temptations, and shakes the gambling arrows of seditions.[714] But truth has dawned and falsehood has stuttered. (...)[715] I judge and I am just. I testify and I am accepted. My decisions travel to the east and the west though I myself do not travel. I promise and fulfill. I am asked for protection and give it. I milk wealth from its udders, I pluck generosity from its branches. What else am I but an axis on which dynasties rotate, a noble racehorse that makes one reach the goal, the intercessor of every ruler, assisting him in achieving his ambitions, his tool for his gains, the one who is witness to his innermost thoughts before every other witness, the one who has access to his intention before everyone else?"

The SWORD said, "'O God! The young camels are galloping, even the ulcer-ridden ones!'[716] 'There's many a thunderclap without rain.' You are trying to reach out but your arm is too short! You want to get up and fly with a broken wing. A would-be Arab[717] bought for a penny! An imported immigrant, the whole world is your homeland! A naked body and dripping tears! You are barefoot and are shod by being trimmed, until your body has become a mere shadow. But kings hasten to hold me, they envy one another in possessing me, they pass me on from one generation to the next, and through me their reputation is greatly enhanced. They crown me with coral and make me shoes of gold, they wrap me in scabbards like mantles and sword straps like ostrich feathers,[718] so that I emerge as an Indian sword on a brilliant day, bright as a meadow after rain."

The PEN said, "He who listens badly will answer badly. I seek refuge with God from the kind of prattle on which you are pasturing your cattle, and from the errors with which you have opened your speech. Your contempt for the ease with which I can be found and for the lowness of my price is a defect in your nature and a deficiency in your capability. Gold, after all, is found in earth but it is the most precious metal. Fire, hidden in a flint, is one of the basic elements. Water, which is life itself, is found more abundantly than all other kinds of subsistence and the cheapest. Precious objects are rarely found except in lowly places. As for being naked, our beauty makes us dispense with trailing skirts. What is the use of a pearl before its shell has been cast away? Will palm flowers blossom brightly before the branches have been pruned? Will dawn shine before the dusk is cleared away? It is well known that men go out in the forenoon sun, whereas women must be guarded inside. If people did not polish you to remove your rust, you would quickly turn to dust."

The SWORD said, "The crunching sound of a mill-stone but no flour!" "Thunderclaps but no rain!" "From the face of the cattle one knows how it thrives!" Base face! Sickly body! Cut nib! Blood shed! Tears in streams, black as soot! Head with neither pith nor mind![719] Rump in which there beats no heart! You're emptier than a wild ass's belly.[720] Your gross injustice testifies to your scant usefulness. Wake up from your sleep, break your fast, judge with discerning eye: I have a body of water[721] and a mantle of fire. If an ignorant person were to unsheathe me I would make him fancy that I am liquid and he would flee fearing he might drown and turn away afraid that he might get burned, in a sea with flames for foam and lightning with scabbards for clouds. If I were unsheathed during an eclipse of the sun, its reappearance would not be noticed; if it happened in years of drought a camelherd would be certain of rain.[722] The traces on my finely worked blade are like tiny moles on the cheeks of pretty women. On a day of battle I drink in the chest of a hero and return like a cheek that blushes with shame, as if I had absorbed red anemones or had drunk liquid carnelian.[723]

The PEN said, "If you are a wind, you have now met a hurricane. All that is white is not fat, nor is all that is black a date! Your 'liquid' water is frozen; your 'burning' body is cold. Nobody would 'drown' in it any more than in arid plains, nobody would get 'burned' by it any more than if he fell into the false fire of the fireflies. Raise the veil of blindness from your eyes, untie the belt of stupidity from your waist, and you may be able to discern in me an ivory rod, the taper of a lamp, a silver arrow-shaft clothed with gold, a mantle of narcissus over a body of daisies, its temples daubed by the night, its side-locks moistened with musk.[724] I rise from paper pages like a rain cloud from gardens,[725] I write in folios what spring cannot write in a lush garden, with fine streaks proudly between stripes, and lines on sheets stitched together."[726]

*

Having thus debated extensively and contended at length, each one of them countering the combined forces of the other with his own, parrying blow with blow, neither of the two blades suffering a blunting and neither retreating sullenly, they both hastened to make peace, flying its flag, and they came to the watering-place of alliance.

They both agreed,[727] "It would be unbefitting if our opinions were divided and our views differed, seeing that God has brought us together in a noble and familiar place, and made us dwell in an irreproachable position: in the loftiest hand that has fulfilled our hopes, that has given in full whatever could be desired where it was needed, that knocks on every door when it finds it closed, raises every veil when it finds it lowered, restores every fortune when it finds it has stumbled, makes the well-spring flow again with every hope when it finds it has dried up: that is the hand of al-Muwaffaq Abū l-Jaysh, the master of sublime deeds, making them his slaves, worthy of noble qualities and deserving of them, who flies the banner of glory as high as the locks of the star al-Simāk,[728] who proudly looks down on the celestial spheres, who advances when heroes flinch, who laughs when Death weeps, who travels through the night to reach the highest elevation when noble men only departed just before daybreak, whose views are awake when people slumber, who with his generosity avenges the poverty of the indigent, who doubles the favors received by his abundance, who keeps his promises but not his threats, who makes the sap flow in withered ambitions, and who makes radiance rise in gloomy hopes."

"Since he has judiciously balanced the two of us,[729] between a day of war and a day of peace, exceeding the limits of conciliation with you and exceeding the limits of harshness with me, only discarding you when he has reached his aim, nor discarding me until he has achieved his desire, neither falling short in taking me to a goal that he made you reach, nor giving precedence to you in a rank where he kept me behind, the most fitting cloak we could wear, the most excellent shoes we could put on, the surest path we could follow, the purest spring from which we could drink, is a companionship that we should don proudly and willingly, an association from which we will pluck the fruits and drink the wine." (...)[730]

Then the PEN said, "In order to confirm our pact and set down our agreement, whereby we can support each other if the situation requires—for Time has its vicissitudes—we must draft an appropriate document that will represent us and keep a vigilant eye on us. For Time and its scorpions will creep between a man and those closest to him and will spread slander between two branches of the same stock."

The SWORD said, "Eloquence is your department; for me, war and the battlefield."[731]

The PEN said, "Prose is too plain for such a thing; poetry has more gravitas. It is sung by the camel driver and it is the food of all travelers that come and go. I prefer it to prose as a tribute:"

The sword is now no longer better than the pen: both are
made subject to a hero who with them achieved the heights.
If glory's fruits are plucked fresh from its branch,
the planting of the tree was only theirs.
Whenever they compete in hope and reach the goal
they share the qualities of precedence.
Time made them swallow bitter discord—Fate
is fickle and will sever bonds of kin—
At last, when foolish ignorance's eye fell fast asleep
and reason's eye woke up, they gnashed their teeth remorsefully.
Now both are held in Abū l-Jaysh's hand, which has
created clouds that always rain with boons.
Their severed bond is knotted once again,
their unity, once broken up, is now restored.
O king, whose high ambitions reach the sky,
defying all ambitions aiming high:
Had I not tried to make a novel kind of eulogy on you,
I would not have praised Pen and Sword prior to you.
'Twas but a hint, by which I have revealed a kind
of eloquence that until now was veiled.

A Visit to Heaven and Hell, by Abū l-ʿAlāʾ al-Maʿarrī [732]

The maverick Abū l-ʿAlāʾ (d. 449/1057) has already appeared as poet, above. His prose works are no less remarkable than his verse. In his *Risālat al-Ghufrān* (*The Epistle of Forgiveness*) he mockingly imagines how a contemporary of his, the philologist Ibn al-Qāriḥ, has entered (not without difficulty) Heaven. There he converses with colleagues and poets, and during an excursion to Hell he meets further poets and heretics from the past. The story satirizes not only the protagonist but apparently also some popular conceptions of the Hereafter (as well as what seems to be medieval bureaucracy). It is set in the imagined future and therefore told in the present tense in Arabic. Many of the discussions are on technical matters of linguistics and philology; some more accessible passages have been translated here. The text uses *sajʿ* occasionally, which has been imitated in the translation. At the beginning of the first passage, Ibn al-Qāriḥ is at the entrance of Paradise, on the Last Day; he is telling some fellow human how he arrived at that place.

Then the shaykh says (may God make him speak meritoriously when he says something, if his Lord will him to say something):

I'll tell you my own story. After I got up and rose from my grave and had arrived at the Plane of Resurrection ("plane" being like "plain," with a different spelling),[733] I thought of the Qur'anic verse, «To Him the angels and the Spirit ascend in a day the length of which is fifty thousand years. So be patient in a decent manner.»[734] It did seem a long time to me; I got parched and torrid (meaning "very hot, with not a puff of wind"), as your friend al-Numayrī says:[735]

The girls, in their wraps, are like ostrich eggs
exposed by drizzle and the heat of a sultry night.

I am easily desiccated (that is, "quick to thirst"), so I thought about my situation, which I found quite unbearable. There came an angel to me, the one that had recorded all the good deeds I had performed. I found that my good deeds were as few as tussocks of grass in a destitute year (a tussock being a tuft of vegetation, destitute being a drought). But my repentance at the end shone like a light, bright like a lamp for travelers at night.

When I had stood there for one or two months, fearing I would drown in my sweat, I persuaded myself that I should compose a few lines for Riḍwān, Paradise's Porter Angel. I made them on the meter and rhyme pattern of

> Stop, you two, for the memory of a beloved, and the recognition...[736]

In them I incorporated the name of Riḍwān. Then I jostled my way through the people until I stood where he could hear and see me, but I don't think he noticed what I said. I waited for a short while, perhaps ten days in earthly reckoning, and then I made some lines on the pattern of

> The gathered clans have parted. If I'd had my way,
> they wouldn't have. They severed bonds of loving union.[737]

Again I mentioned Riḍwān in it; I approached him and did as before. But he did not appear to hear: it was as if I tried to move Mount Thabīr,[738] or attempted to extract scent from cement ("cement" being a mixture of limestone and clay). Then I continued with all other metrical patterns that could accommodate "Riḍwān" until I had exhausted them. Still he did not help me and I don't think he even understood what I said. When I had tried everything without success I cried out as loud as I could, "Riḍwān, who are trusted by the Omnipotent Almighty, charged with guarding Paradise! Can't you hear me calling on you for help?"

He replied, "I heard you mention Riḍwān, but I had no idea that you meant me. What do you want, poor wretch?"

"I am a man who cannot endure to be dehydrated (that is thirsty); it is for the Reckoning that I have waited and waited. I've got my Document of Repentance, which cancels all my sins. I have made numerous poems in praise of you, mentioning you by name!"

Riḍwān asked, "Poems, what's that? This is the first time I have heard that word."

"Poems," I replied, "is the plural of 'poem,' which is speech that is metrical and, on certain conditions, sounds pleasant. If the meter is defective, either by an excess or a shortfall, one notices it. People in the temporal world used to ingratiate themselves with kings and lords by means of poems. So I made some for you, hoping you might let me enter Paradise by this gate. I think people have waited long enough now. I am only a weak, feeble person. Surely I am someone who may hope for forgiveness, and rightly so, if God the Exalted wills."

But Riḍwān said, "Do you expect me to allow you to enter without permission from the Lord of Glory, you dimwit? Forget it! Forget it! «How could they attain it from a remote place?»"[739]

So I left him and, expectantly, turned to a guard who was called Zufar. For him I made a poem, mentioning him by name, on the meter of Labīd's line:

My two daughters hope their father will live;
but don't I belong to Rabīʿah or Muḍar?[740]

I approached him and recited the poem; but it was as if I was speaking to a mute and solid rock in the end, trying to get a wild ibex to descend.[741] I made poems using the name Zufar in every possible meter and rhyme, but to no avail each time. I said, "God have mercy on you! In the past world we would seek the favor of leaders and kings with two or three lines of verse and our wishes would be fulfilled; but for you I have composed enough to fill a tome of collected poems and still you don't seem to have heard one susurrus, i.e. a whisper!"

He replied, "I have no idea what you are expostulating (i.e., talking about). I suppose all that jabbering of yours is the Qur'an of the Devil, that rebel! But the angels won't buy it! It belongs to the jinn, who taught it to Adam's children. Now what do you want?"

I explained what I wanted. He said, "By God, I can't help you in what you need; for humans I cannot intercede. What community are you from?"

"The community of Muḥammad ibn ʿAbd Allāh ibn ʿAbd al-Muṭṭalib."

"Ah, yes, the prophet of the Arabs. So that is why you have come to me with that poetry, because the accursed Devil spat it out in the lands of the Arabs, where women and children learned it. I'll give you some good advice: look for your friend and perhaps he will be able to let you have your way."

Thus I despaired of him. I worked my way through the multitude. Then I saw a man bathed in a glimmering of light, surrounded by others who shone with bright lights. I asked, "Who is that man?"

They said, "That is Ḥamzah ibn ʿAbd al-Muṭṭalib, the one who was killed by Waḥshī; those around him are those Muslims who died as martyrs at Uḥud."[742]

Inspired with false hope I said to myself: poetry will work better with them than with the Porter of Paradise, because Ḥamzah is a poet, as were his brothers and his father and his grandfather. It could well be that each and every one of his forefathers from Maʿadd ibn ʿAdnān on have composed verses. So I composed some lines after the model of Kaʿb ibn Mālik's elegy[743] on Ḥamzah, which opens with

Ṣafiyyah, get up, don't be weak!
  Let the women weep for Ḥamzah!

I approached him and called out: "Lord of martyrs, uncle of God's messenger, God bless him! Son of ʿAbd al-Muṭṭalib!"

When he turned to me I recited the verses. But he said, "Shame upon you! Must you eulogize me here, of all places? Haven't you heard this Qur'anic verse:[744] «Every man of them that day will have enough to preoccupy him»"?

"Yes, I've heard it; and I've also heard what follows: «Some faces that day will be bright, laughing and expecting delight; other faces that day will be glum, by gloom overcome: these are the unbelievers, the sinners»!"[745]

He replied, "I can't do what you ask, but I will send a nuncio (meaning a messenger) along with you to my nephew ʿAlī ibn Abī Ṭālib, who can speak to the Prophet, God bless him and give him peace, on your behalf."

[The Conversation with ʿAlī ibn Abī Ṭālib]

He sent a man with me. When he had told my story to the Commander of the Believers,[746] the latter asked, "Where is your evidence?"

He meant the document with my good deeds.[747]

[Ibn al-Qāriḥ explains that, distracted by a discussion with the tenth-century grammarian Abū ʿAlī al-Fārisī, he had lost this document. He continues:]

I went back to look for it but could not find it!

I displayed much confusion and distress. But the Commander of the Believers said, "Don't worry. Did anybody witness your repentance?"[748]

"Yes, I replied, the qadi of Aleppo and his notaries."

"What's his name?"

"ʿAbd al-Munʿim ibn ʿAbd al-Karīm, the qadi of Aleppo (may God guard it) in the days of Shibl al-Dawlah."[749]

He got a crier to stand up and call out: "ʿAbd al-Munʿim ibn ʿAbd al-Karīm, qadi of Aleppo in Shibl al-Dawlah's time! Have you any knowledge of the repentance of ʿAlī ibn Manṣūr ibn Ṭālib (ibn al-Qāriḥ), the Aleppine man of letters?"

But no one answered. I was dismayed and began to tremulate (i.e., to tremble). The man cried out a second time, and again nobody answered. I was prostrated (i.e., I fell down in a swoon). Then he cried a third time, and someone spoke up: "Yes, I have witnessed the repentance of ʿAlī ibn Manṣūr, in the nick of time![750] And a number of notaries were present at my place when he repented. I was then the qadi of Aleppo and adjacent districts. It is God whom we ask for succor!"

At that I got up and was able to breathe again. I told the Commander of the Believers (peace be upon him) what I wanted, but he turned away, saying, "You want something impossible. Follow the example of the other children of your forefather Adam!"

[The Conversation with Fāṭimah, the Prophet's Daughter]

I wanted to get to the Basin[751] but had real difficulty getting there. I drank a few gulps after which there would never be any thirst. The unbelievers also tried to reach the water, but the Angels of Hell drove them away with sticks that burned like fire, so that they retreated, with scorched faces or hands, wailing and squealing. I walked to the Chosen Progeny[752] and said, "In the past world I always wrote at the end of any book of mine: 'God bless our lord Muḥammad, the Seal of Prophets, and his excellent and good descendants,'[753] to show my respect and hoping for a favor."

They said, "What can we do for you?"

I replied, "Our lady Fāṭimah[754] (peace be upon her) entered Paradise ages ago. But from time to time she leaves it for twenty-four hours, of the reckoning of the transitory world, to greet her father who is busy testifying for God's judgment. Then she returns to her place in Paradise. Now when she appears as usual, please could you all ask her on my behalf? Perhaps she will ask her father to help me."

When the time had come for her to emerge a crier called out: "Lower your eyes, people that stand here, until Fāṭimah, the daughter of Muḥammad (God bless and preserve him) has passed!"

A large number of men and women of Abū Ṭālib's family[755] gathered, people who had never drunk wine or done evil things, and they came to meet her on her way. When she saw them she asked, "What is this crowd? Is anything the matter?"

They answered, "We are fine; we enjoy the presents from those that dwell in Paradise. But we are being kept here because of the «word that preceded»;[756] we do not want to enter Paradise precipitously, before our time. We are safe and having a good time, on account of God's word: [757] «Those who have already been given the finest thing that came from Us, they shall be kept far from it, nor shall they hear any sound of it but they shall forever be in what their souls desire, the greatest distress shall not grieve them and the angels shall receive them: this is your day, that you have been promised!»"

ʿAlī ibn al-Ḥusayn and his two sons, Muḥammad and Zayd, were among them,[758] with other pious and righteous persons. Next to Fāṭimah (peace be upon her) stood another woman, who resembled her in nobility and majesty. People asked, "Who is she?"

The answer was: "That is Khadījah,[759] daughter of Khuwaylid ibn Asad ibn ʿAbd al-ʿUzzā."

With her were some young men, riding horses of light. People asked, "Who are they?"

They were told: "They are ʿAbd Allāh, al-Qāsim, al-Ṭayyib, al-Ṭāhir, and Ibrāhīm, the sons of Muḥammad (God bless him and give him peace)."[760]

Then those whom I had asked said, "This man is one of our followers. His repentance is genuine and there can be no doubt that he will be among those in Paradise. He turns to you in supplication, God bless you, that he may be relieved from the terrors of this Place of Judgment, that he may enter Paradise and hasten to attain the triumph."

Thereupon Fāṭimah said to her brother Ibrāhīm (God bless him), "You look after this man!"

He said to me, "Hold on to my stirrup."

The horses then passed through the throng, whole nations and peoples making way for us. Where the crowd was too dense they flew up in the air, while I was holding on to the stirrup. They halted at Muḥammad (God bless him and give him peace).

[The Prophet's Intercession]

The Prophet asked, "Who is this alien? (meaning 'stranger')."

Fāṭimah replied, "This is a man for whom So-and-so and So-and-so have interceded."

She named some of the Pure Imams.[761] He said, "First one must look at his works."

He inquired about them and they were found in the Grand Register, sealed with Repentance. Then he interceded for me and I was permitted entrance. When Fāṭimah, the Resplendent (peace be upon her), returned I grabbed the stirrup of Ibrāhīm (God bless him).

[The Crossing of the Bridging Path]

Having thus left the multitudes behind me I was told, "This is the Bridging Path, now cross it![762] I noticed it was empty, not one soul on it. I braced myself to cross but I found that I could not control myself. Fāṭimah, the Resplendent (God bless her) said to a servant-girl of hers, 'Girl, help him cross!'"

The girl began to push and pull me while I was tottering to the right and the left. I said, "Girl, if you want me to arrive safely, then do with me as the poet put it in the temporary world:"

> Madam, if I'm tiring you,
> then let me ride you piggyback.

"Piggyback, what is that?"

"That is when you put your hands on someone's shoulders, who holds your hands and carries you, belly-to-back. Haven't you heard the line by al-Jaḥjalūl from Kafr Ṭāb,[763] when he says,"

> My state improved backward
> until I began to move piggybackward.[764]

She replied, "I've never heard of piggyback, or al-Jaḥjalūl, or Kafr Ṭāb before!"

She picked me up and crossed like a bolt of lightning. When I reached the other side Fāṭimah the Resplendent (peace be upon her) said, "I am giving you this girl. Take her and she will serve you in Paradise."

[Second Conversation with Riḍwān; the Entry into Paradise]

When I arrived at the gate of Paradise, Riḍwān asked, "Have you got your permit?"

"No."

"Then you can't enter."

I was desperate. I saw at the gate, just inside Paradise, a willow tree. I asked, "Can I have a leaf of that willow tree, so that I can go back to the Place of Judgment and get a permit, with it as proof?"

"I won't let anything leave Paradise without permission from the Most High, sanctified and blessed be He."

I was at my wits' end at this new blow and said, "We belong to God and to Him we shall return! If Abū l-Murajjā, the Emir,[765] had had a treasurer like you we would never have received a groat from his coffers."

(A groat is a silver coin worth fourpence). But then Ibrāhīm (God bless him) turned around! He saw me—I had stayed behind. Now he came back and he dragged me along with him and brought me into Paradise. I had spent six months, earthly reckoning, at the Place of Judgment.

> [In Paradise Ibn al-Qāriḥ meets a number of poets from the past and discusses their poetry with them.]

[The Banquet]

It occurs to the shaykh (may God buttress his fame) that he should give a banquet in Paradise, to be attended by as many poets as possible, those born in the pre-Islamic period who died as Muslims, or those born in Islam: those who consolidated the speech of the Arabs such as it is now preserved in books; in addition to some others with a measure of erudition who might be good company. He thinks it should be like a banquet of the fleeting world; after all, the Creator (sublime is His glory) is not incapable of bringing them everything needed, without effort or delay.

Thus, mills are erected at the Kawthar stream,[766] which noisily grind heavenly wheat, as superior to the wheat described by the poet of the Hudhayl tribe, who said,

May I not thrive if I regale their visitor
  on crusts and peelings while I have a store of wheat[767]

as Heaven is superior to earth. He suggests (may the Omnipotent fulfill his suggestions) that some girls with black, lustrous eyes[768] come before him, to work the handmills: one millstone is made of pearl, another of gold, others from precious stones never yet seen by dwellers in the fleeting world. When he looks at the girls he praises God for His gift and is reminded of the words of the *rajaz* poet who describes a handmill:

For guests and neighbors I've prepared
  Two girls, hard-working, who cooperate,
Without compassion, though they feed us.[769]

He smiles to them and says,

"Grind along! Sideways and contrary!"

They ask him,

"What are sideways and contrary?"

"Sideways is to the right and contrary is to the left. Haven't you heard the words of the poet:"

In the morning, having breakfast, we are fattest,
  but at dinner in the evening we are hollow-bellied.
We grind with handmills, sideways and contrary;
  and if they gave us spindles we would not tire.

They say these verses were written by a prisoner-of-war to his people.

In his mind the shaykh (may God let him live long and joyously) sees millstones being turned by animals. Before him appear all kinds of buildings, containing precious stones of Paradise. Some mills are turned by camels that graze on the paradisical thornbushes, she-camels that do not bend over their calves, and various kinds of mules, cattle, and wild asses.

When he thinks enough flour has been milled for the banquet, his servants, the youths who live forever, disperse and return with yearlings, that is kids, various kinds of edible birds such as pigeon chicks, pea chicks, fat chickens of Mercy, and pullets of Eternity. Cows, sheep, and camels are driven to be slaughtered. There rises a loud camel-groaning, a goat-whickering, a sheep-bleating, and a cock-crowing, when they see the knife. Yet, God be praised, none suffers any pain: it is in earnest but like play.[770] There is no god but God, who creates marvelously out of nothing, without having to think about it, and shapes it without having a model.

Now when the chunks of meat lie on the meat planks, as they say in the dialect of Ṭayyi'[771] instead of "blocks," he says (may God increase the efficacy of his intentions), "Let the cooks of Paradise come, all those who have worked in Aleppo through the ages!"

A large crowd comes forward. He orders them to take the food: a delicious treat from God, sublime is His might, in accordance with His word: [772] «In it is what the souls desire and the eyes delight in; you shall dwell therein forever. That is Paradise, which you have inherited as a reward for what you used to do. Therein you shall have fruits in plenty of which you may eat.» When the dishes arrive his servant boys, who are like «well-kept pearls»,[773] disperse to collect the invited guests. Not one poet from the Islamic period did they leave behind, nor any of those who straddled the pre-Islamic and the Islamic periods, nor any scholar learned in various disciplines, nor any erudite person: they fetched them all. Thus a large throng, or many people, gathered. (The word "throng" is used by a poet:[774] "Throngs flock at his doors / from distress in years of famine.")

Golden tables are erected and silver trays are put down. The dinner guests sit down. Bowls are brought; and a bowl remains with them while they eat its contents for a time as long as the lifetimes of Kuwayy and Surayy, the two "vultures" among the stars.[775] When all have eaten their fill the cupbearers come with various potations and singing girls who produce sweet-sounding intonations.

[Conversation ensues about singers and poets, poems are recited and sung.]

[Beer, Marinated Peacock, and Roast Goose]

The shaykh happens to think of beer, the kind that used to be made in the deceptive world. Instantly God, in His omnipotence, lets rivers of it flow; one draught of it is nicer and more refreshing than all the delights of the perishing world from God's creation of heaven and earth until the day that all nations are wrapped up by the Hereafter. He says to himself, "I know that God is omnipotent, but really I wanted the kind I used to see with the beer sellers in the fleeting world!"

No sooner has he said that than God gathers all beer sellers in Paradise, Iraqis, Syrians, and from other regions, preceded by the immortal youths,[776] who carry baskets to the company.

The shaykh (may God preserve him for all lettered people) asks the scholars that are present, "What are these baskets called in correct Arabic?"

They are taciturn, i.e., silent. One of them says, "They are called 'hampers', in the singular 'hamper'."

One of the others says, "And which lexicographer says that?"

The shaykh replies (may his learning never fail to reach his companions), "It is mentioned by Ibn Durustawayh."[777]

He happens to be present. Al-Khalīl[778] asks him, "Where did you find that word?"

Ibn Durustawayh answers, "In the writings of al-Naḍr ibn Shumayl,"[779]

Al-Khalīl asks, "Is that correct, Naḍr? You are a reliable source in my view."

Al-Naḍr replies, "I can't remember precisely, but I think the fellow is quoting accurately, if God wills."

At that moment there comes along, past the throng, i.e. the assembled people, a paradisical peacock, a veritable feast for the eye. Abū ʿUbaydah[780] would like to eat it marinated. Instantly it is like that, on a golden plate.[781] When he has eaten his fill the bones reassemble and become a peacock as before. They all exclaim, "Glory to Him «who revives the bones after they have decayed»! It is just as it says in the Qur'an: «When Ibrāhīm said, 'My Lord, show me how Thou revivest the dead!' He said, 'Don't you believe me, then?' 'Yes, I do,' he said, 'but just so that my heart be reassured.' 'Then,' He said, 'Take four birds and cut them up, then put a piece of them on each hill, then call them and they will come running toward you! Know that God is all-mighty and all-wise!'»"

Then the shaykh (may God delight mankind with his life) asks, "What is the mode of 'be reassured'?"

They reply, "Subjunctive, because it is dependent on the conjunction 'so that' in the sense of purpose."

The shaykh asks, “Could there be another interpretation?”

[... A grammatical digression follows.]

Then a goose comes along, big like a Bactrian camel.[782] One person wants it roasted, and thus it appears, on a table of emerald. As soon as he has had his fill, it returns, with God’s permission, to its former winged state. Another prefers it as kebab, someone else wants it spiced with sumac, yet another with milk and vinegar, and so on, while the goose turns into whatever is desired. This process repeats itself for some time.

Then Abū ʿUthmān al-Māzinī[783] says to ʿAbd al-Malik ibn Qurayb al-Aṣmaʿī,[784] “I say, Abū Saʿīd, what is the morphological pattern of *iwazzah*, ‘goose’?”

Al-Aṣmaʿī replies, “Are you insinuating something, you scorpion? You were in my class in Basra for so long when nobody paid any attention to you. The pattern of *iwazzah* is factually *ifaʿlah* (’iC1aC2C3ah) but originally *ifʿalah* (’iC1C2aC3ah).”[785]

Thereupon al-Māzinī asks, “What is your proof that the glottal stop ʾ is secondary and not an original root consonant, the pattern then being *fiʿallah* (C1iC2aC3C3ah)?” Al-Aṣmaʿī answers, “That the glottal stop is secondary is proved by the fact that people also say *wazz*.”

“But that does not prove that the glottal stop is secondary, for people say *nās* (‘people’), the original form of which is *ʾunās*, and *mīhah*, for ‘sheep pox,’ which is in fact *ʾamīha*.”

Al-Aṣmaʿī says, “Don’t you and your friends, the ‘Analogists,’[786] assert that the pattern is *ʾifʿalah* (’iC1C2aC3ah)? If they then build a noun from the root *ʾ-W-Y* (‘to seek refuge’) on the pattern of *ʾiwazzah*, they would say *ʾiyyāh*![787] And if the pattern were *fiʿallah* (C1iC2aC3C3ah), they would say *ʾiwayyah*; if it were *ʾifaʿlah* (’iC1aC2C3ah), the *ʿayn* having no vowel, they would say *ʾiyayyah*, in which the y that follows the glottal stop—which is the original glottal stop of the root *ʾ-W-Y*—has been changed into a *y* because two glottal stops coincide here, and because a short *i* precedes it, while it has itself been voweled with a short *a*. If you soften the glottal stop in *miʾzar* (‘loin-cloth, wrap’) you say *mīzar*, with a pure, long *ī*.”

Al-Māzinī says, “This is merely an arbitrary interpretation and claim of our colleagues, for it has not been established conclusively that the glottal stop in *ʾiwazzah* is secondary.”

Al-Aṣmaʿī says,

The tribe of Jurhum feathered arrows; Jurhum then
was shot by notches and by tips of their own arrows![788]

You followed them, deriving much benefit; then you came back and attacked what they said! You and they are like the ancient poet who said,

I taught him shooting, every day;
and when his arm was steady he shot me.[789]

Angrily, he gets up; the people of that session go their separate ways, having a blissful time.

[The Conversation with the Two Damsels]
Thereupon he is alone (may God's beneficence never leave him alone) with two black-eyed damsels of Paradise. Dazzled by their beauty he exclaims, "Alas, the poor Kindite, who perished![790] You remind me of his verses:"

As was your wont before her, with Umm al-Ḥuwayrith,
and her neighbor friend, Umm al-Rabāb, in Maʾsal:
When they rose the scent of musk would waft from them,
like the eastern breeze, bringing the smell of cloves.

and his verses:

Just like two oryxes, ewes from Tabālah, bending tenderly
toward their calves; or like some Hakir statues:[791]
When they rose the scent of musk would waft from them,
of perfume from a flask, and odoriferous aloe wood.

But his girlfriends are no match for you, no nobility, no treat for the eye! Sitting in your company for even one minute of earthly reckoning is better than the realm of Ākil al-Murār and his kin, or that of the Naṣrids in al-Ḥīrah, or the Jafnids, kings of Syria.[792]

He turns to the two girls, sipping their sweet saliva, and says, "Imru' al-Qays is a poor, poor soul! His bones are burning in hellfire, while here I am quoting his verse:

It seems the coolness of her teeth,
 when birds at dawn are warbling, is
infused with wine, with rain, the smell
 of lavender, the scent of aloe wood.

"or his verses:

Days when her mouth, as I roused her from her sleep,
 would smell like musk, kept in its filter overnight,
Wine the color of gazelle's blood, kept for years,
 vintage from ʿĀnah or the vineyards of Shibām."[793]

One of the girls begins to laugh uncontrollably. The shaykh asks, "Why are you laughing?"

"For joy, because of the favor that God has bestowed on me, and the forgiveness that he showed to me! Do you know who I am, ʿAlī ibn Manṣūr?"

"You are one of the black-eyed damsels whom God has created as a reward for the god-fearing. He said of you: «It is as if they are rubies and pearls.»"[794]

She says, "Yes, I am indeed, through God Almighty's kindness. But in the fleeting world I was known as Ḥamdūnah and I used to live in Iraq Gate in Aleppo, where my father worked a mill. A rag-and-bone dealer married me, but he divorced me because of my bad breath. I was one of the ugliest women in Aleppo. When I realized that I became pious and renounced this delusive world. I devoted myself to religious worship and earned a living from my spindle. This made me what you see now."

The other one says, "And do you know who I am, ʿAlī ibn Manṣūr? I am Black Tawfīq, who used to work in the House of Learning in Baghdad in the time of Abū

Manṣūr Muḥammad ibn ʿAlī al-Khāzin.[795] I used to fetch the manuscripts for the copyists."

He exclaims, "There is no god but God! You were black and now you have become more dazzlingly white than camphor, or camphire[796] if you like."

"Do you find that odd? After all, the poet says of some mortal being:

One mustard-seed of light from him, with all
black people mixed, would whiten all the blacks."[797]

[The Tree of Damsels]

At that instant an angel comes along. The shaykh asks him, "Servant of God, tell me about the damsels with black, lustrous eyes: doesn't it say in the Holy Book:[798] «We have raised them and made them virgins and loving companions for the people on the right»?"

The angel replies, "There are two kinds. One kind has been created by God in Paradise and they have never known otherwise, and there is another kind that God has transferred from the temporary world because they have done pious deeds."

The shaykh is stupefied, i.e. amazed by what he has heard. He asks, "Where are the ones that have never been in the transitory world? And how do they differ from the others?"

The angel answers, "Just follow me and you will see a wondrous example of God's omnipotence."

He follows the angel, who takes him to some gardens the true nature of which only God knows. The angel says, "Take one of these fruits and break it open. This tree is known as the tree of the black-eyed damsels."[799]

The shaykh takes a quince, or a pomegranate, or an apple, or whatever fruit God wills, and breaks it open. A girl with black, lustrous eyes whose beauty dazzles the other damsels of the Paradisical gardens emerges. She says, "Who are you, servant of God?"

He gives his name. She says, "I was promised I would meet you four thousand years before God created the world!"

At that the shaykh prostrates himself to magnify the omnipotent God and says, "Thus it says in the hadith: 'I have prepared for my believing servants things no eye has seen nor any ear has heard—let alone that I should have told them about it!'[800] ('let alone' is used in the sense of 'don't think about why')."

It occurs to him, while he is still prostrate, that the girl, though beautiful, is rather skinny. He raises his head and instantly she has a behind that rivals the hills of 'Ālij, the dunes of al-Dahnā', and the sands of Yabrīn and the Banū Sa'd.[801] Awed by the omnipotence of the Kind and Knowing God, he says, "Thou who givest rays to the shining sun, Thou who fulfillest the desires of everyone, Thou whose awe-inspiring deeds make us feel impotent, and summon to wisdom the ignorant: I ask Thee to reduce the bum of this damsel to one square mile, for Thou hast surpassed my expectations with Thy measure!"

An answer is heard: "You may choose: the shape of this girl will be as you wish."

And the desired reduction is effected.

[Between Paradise and Hell]

Then it occurs to him that he would like to see the people in Hell and how things are with them, that his gratitude for his blessings be magnified. For God says,[802] «One of them said: I had a companion who would say, "Are you really one of those who believe that if we die and have turned to dust and bones we will be judged?" He said, "Won't you look down?" So he looked down and saw him in the midst of blazing Hell. He said, "By God, you had nearly let me perish; but for my Lord's blessing I would have been one of those brought there!"»

[The Paradise of the Demons]

The shaykh mounts one of the animals of Paradise and goes forth. He sees some towns unlike the towns of Paradise, without the scintillating light; there are caves and dark, wooded valleys. He asks one of the angels, "What are they, servant of God?"

He replies, "This is the Paradise of the demons[803] who believed in Muḥammad (God bless him), those that are mentioned in the Sura of the Sand Dunes and the Sura of the Jinnees.[804] There are lots of them."

The shaykh says, "I should like to pay them a visit; I am bound to hear some wonderful stories from them!"

He turns toward them and sees an old person who is sitting at the mouth of a cave. He greets him and the other answers the greeting politely, asking, "What brings you to this place, human? You would deserve a better one; like you there is none!"

The shaykh replies, "I heard that you are the believing jinnees, so I've come to ask for some stories about the jinnees, and perhaps to hear some poems by the rebellious jinnees."[805]

The old jinnee says, "You've hit the bull's eye; you've found me like the moon in its halo in the sky, like someone who waits before pouring away the hot fat:[806] here am I! Ask whatever you like."

The shaykh asks, "What is your name, old man?"

"I am al-Khaytaʿūr, one of the sons of al-Shayṣabān.[807] We are not descended from the devil: we belong to the jinnees that lived on earth before the children of Adam (God bless him)."

[The Poetry of the Demons]

The shaykh says, "Tell me about the poems of the jinnees! Someone called al-Marzubānī has collected a fair number of them."[808]

The old man replies, "But that is all rubbish, wholly unreliable. Would humans know more about poetry than cattle know about astronomy and geodesy? They have fifteen different meters, and rarely transcend them;[809] whereas we have thousands of meters that humans have never heard of. Some naughty toddlers of ours happened to pass by some humans and spat some poetry at them, a trifle like a splinter from an arak tree of al-Naʿmān.[810] I myself composed informal *rajaz* and formal *qaṣīd* poetry an eon or two before God created Adam. I have heard that you, race of humans, are rapturous about Imruʾ al-Qays's poem, 'Stop, let us weep for the remembrance of a loved one and a dwelling place,'[811] and make your children learn it by heart at school. But if you wish I could dictate to you a thousand poems with the same meter and the same rhyme, *-lī*, a thousand such poems rhyming in *-lū*, a thousand in *-lā*, a thousand in *-lah*, a thousand in *-luh*, and a thousand in *-lih*, all composed by one of our poets, an unbeliever now burning in the depths of Hell."

The shaykh (may God make him happy continually) says, "You have got a good memory, old man!"

The jinnee replies, "We are not like you, children of Adam, overcome by forgetfulness and moistness, for you have been created from «molded mud»[812] but we have been created from «a fiery flame»"[813]

The shaykh is moved by a desire for erudition and literature to ask the old man, "Will you dictate some of these poems to me?"

"If you like, I will dictate to you loads more than camels can carry and all the pages of your world can contain."

The shaykh has a mind (may his mind ever be lofty) to take some dictation from him. But then he says to himself, "In the transitory world I was always wretched when I pursued a literary career; I never profited from it. I tried to curry the favor of leading persons but I was milking the udder of a bad milch-camel and was exerting myself with the teats of a slow cow. I'll never be a success if I give up the pleasures of Paradise in order to copy the literature of the jinn. I've got enough erudition as it is, all the more so because forgetfulness is so rife among the dwellers in Paradise that I have turned out to be one of those with the greatest erudition and the largest memory, thanks be to God!"

He asks the old man, "How should I address you respectfully?"[814]

"As Abū Hadrash. I have fathered God knows how many children, whole tribes of them, some in the burning Fire, others in Paradise."

The shaykh asks him, "Abū Hadrash, how come you are gray-haired? I thought those who dwell in Paradise would be young."[815]

"Humans have been given that privilege, but we have been denied it because we could change shape in the past world. Anyone of us could be a speckled snake if he so wished, or a sparrow if he wanted, or a pigeon. But in the Hereafter we are forbidden to change shape. We are left as we were created originally. The children of Adam have been given a beautiful appearance by way of compensation. As some human said in the world that was: we have been given make-shift (*ḥīlah*), and the jinnees have been given shape-shift (*ḥūlah*)."

[Abū Hadrash tells stories and recites poems by the jinn. Ibn al-Qāriḥ travels on and meets various speaking animals and, on the outskirts of Paradise, the poets al-Ḥuṭay'ah and al-Khansā', who wants to be as close as possible to her lamented brother Ṣakhr, now in Hell (see above, p. 12). At the very edge of Paradise, he can see Hell.]

The shaykh looks down and sees Satan[816] (God curse him!), writhing in fetters and chains, while Hell's angels have a go at him with iron cudgels. The shaykh says, "Thanks be to God, who has got the better of you, enemy of God and of His friends! How many generations of Adam's children you have destroyed, only God can count."

The devil asks, "Who is this man?"

"I am ʿAlī ibn Manṣūr ibn al-Qāriḥ, from Aleppo. I was a man of letters by profession, by which I tried to win the favor of rulers."

"A bad profession indeed! You'll live on a minimum income, hardly enough to keep your family. It's a slippery business; many like you have gone to perdition because of it. Congratulations on being saved! «So beware, and again, beware!»[817] But I'd like you to do something for me. If you do I will be much obliged."

"I cannot possibly do anything to help you, for there is a Qur'anic verse already about those in Hell; I mean the words of the Exalted,[818] «Those in Hell will call to those in Paradise, 'Pour us some water or whatever God has given you!' They will reply, 'God has forbidden these things to the unbelievers!'»"

Satan says, "I am asking you none of that. I am asking you to tell me something: wine is forbidden to you in the temporal world but permitted in the Hereafter; now, do the people in Paradise do with the immortal youths what the people of Sodom and Gomorra did?"

The shaykh exclaims, "Damn you, haven't you got enough to distract you? Haven't you heard what the Exalted says:[819] «There they will have pure spouses and they will live there forever»?"

[After a trip to Hell, where he speaks with pre-Islamic poets mainly about the philological problems of their poetry, Ibn al-Qāriḥ returns to Paradise.]

Passing through the fields of Paradise he meets the girl that had come out of the fruit. She says, "I have been waiting for you for some time. What has kept you from visiting me? Surely I have not been with you long enough yet to bore your ears with my conversation! I am entitled to preferential treatment from you like any newly wedded wife! A husband has to give her special attention, more than his other wives."

The shaykh replies, "I felt like having a chat with the people in Hell and when I had done what I wanted, I came back to you. Now follow me, between the Ambergris Hills and the Musk Dunes!"

They cross the hills of Heaven and the sands of Paradise, and she says, "Dear departed servant of God, I think you are imitating the deeds of the Kindite,[820] when he says:

Then I got up, taking her with me, as she trailed
over our tracks the train of an embroidered gown.
When we had crossed the clan's enclosure, turning to
a sandy coomb with twisting slopes,
I drew her side-locks toward me and she leaned
to me, slender her waist but plump her calves."

The sheihk replies, "God's omnipotence is truly marvellous! You have said precisely what I was thinking, too, in my heart of hearts. But how do you know about Imru' al-Qays? I thought you had grown up in a fruit, far from jinnees and humans?" She answers, "God is able to do everything."

He remembers the story of Imru' al-Qays at Dārat Juljul.[821] Instantly God, the Almighty, creates girls with black, lustrous eyes, who contend with one another in plunging into one of the rivers of Paradise, playing together. In their midst is one prettier than all the others, like Imru' al-Qays's girlfriend. They throw bitter, acid weeds to one another,[822] but they smell like the costliest perfume of Paradise. He slaughters for them his riding animal; he eats and they eat some of it, which is indescribably delicious and delectable.

[With the Rajaz Poets]

He passes by some houses that are not as lofty as the other houses in Paradise. He asks about them and is told that this is the Garden of the *Rajaz* Poets,[823] the dwelling place of al-Aghlab al-ʿIjlī, al-ʿAjjāj, Ru'bah, Abū l-Najm, Ḥumayd al-Arqaṭ, ʿUdhāfir ibn Aws, and Abū Nukhaylah,[824] and all the others who received forgiveness.[825]

[The shaykh says,] "Blessed be the Almighty Giver! The Prophetic Tradition that has come down to us has come true: 'God loves that which is lofty and dislikes that which is lowly.'[826] *Rajaz* is really a lowly sort of poetry: you people have fallen short so you have been given short measure."

Ru'bah[827] appears on the scene. The shaykh says to him, "Abū l-Jaḥḥāf! You were rather fond of unpleasant rhyme-letters. You made poetry on the letter *gh*, on *ṭ*, on *ẓ*, and other intractable consonants! And you have produced not even a single memorable saying nor a single sweet expression."

Ru'bah says angrily, "And you are saying that to me, though I am quoted by al-Khalīl and Abū ʿAmr ibn al-ʿAlāʾ![828] And, in the past world, you yourself used to flaunt your knowledge of words that those scholars have taken from me and my colleagues!"

Seeing Ru'bah's high self-regard, the shaykh (may his opponent ever be defeated) replies, "If your *rajaz* verse and that of your father were melted down you wouldn't get one single decent *qaṣīdah* out of it. I have heard that Abū Muslim[829] was talking to you and spoke of the son of a 'slattern' and you did not know the word, so that you had to ask about it in your tribe! You have received rewards from kings without deserving them; others would have been more entitled to them."

Ru'bah answers, "But surely your leader, in the past, whose views were accepted as normative,[830] used to quote my verses as evidence, making me a kind of authority!"

The shaykh, quick at repartee, says, "Being quoted is nothing to boast about.[831] For we find that they also quote any sluttish slave girl who brings brushwood to fan a fire that blazes on a cold morning when frost has shaken out its feathers and a hoary-headed man fashions firewood from his humble hut, flinging it into the flames so that he can huddle in its heat; to pick mushrooms and fungi is her most glorious day, or to follow a camel driven away. Her master is a brute who is stupid and doesn't care a hoot. And how often do grammarians quote any tiny tot, who knows of letters not a jot? Or any person of the female gender, in need of men to defend her?"

Ru'bah replies, "Have you come to my place only to quarrel with me? In that case, please be on your way! You criticize everything I say!"

The shaykh says (may God silence his opponent), "I swear that your verses are not suitable for praising those that hear them:[832] they are no better than tar with which you besmear them! You hit your patrons' ears with verses like boulders; one would rather be pleased with the scent of mandal wood when it smoulders.[833] When you pass from describing the need of a long-suffering camel to describing a galloping steed or barking hounds at full speed, then you are lost indeed!"

Ru'bah replies, "God, praised be He, has said,[834] «They hand one another cups; neither drivel is there nor recrimination.» But what you say is truly drivel; it is neither fair nor civil!"

After this lengthy exchange between him and Ru'bah, al-ʿAjjāj hears of it and approaches to separate the two. The shaykh is reminded (may God remind him of pious deeds) that those who drink old wine will reposefully recline. This is what he now chooses, but with a mind unbefuddled and a foot unstumbling.[835] And behold, he imagines the wine seeping through his relaxed limbs like ants creeping on a dune in the light of the moon. He hums the verse of Iyās ibn al-Aratt:[836]

If you, fault-finding woman, would drink wine
 till all your fingers tingled,
You would forgive me, knowing I was right
 to squander all my money.

He reclines on a silk mat, telling the damsels with their black, lustrous eyes to lift the mat and put it on one of the couches of the dwellers in Paradise. It is made of peridot, or of gold. The Creator has formed rings of gold, fixed on all its sides, that the immortal youths and the girls, who have been compared to pearls,[837] can take hold of a ring each. In this manner Ibn al-Qāriḥ is carried to the dwelling place that has been erected for him in the Eternal Abode. Whenever he passes a tree, its twigs sprinkle him with rosewater mixed with camphor, and with musk, though not from a musk rat's blood obtained, but by God the Almighty ordained. The fruits call at him from every side, as he lies on his back: "Would you like me, Abū l-Ḥasan, would you like me?"

Thus, if he wants a bunch of grapes, for instance, it is plucked from its branch by God's will and carried to his mouth by His omnipotence, while the people of Paradise shower him with various greetings: «Their final call will be: Praise be to God, Lord of all Beings!»[838] Thus he is employed, for aye and ever, blessed in length of time delectable, not to change susceptible.

Poetics: Ibn Rashīq on the Definition and Structure of Poetry[839]

Abū ʿAlī al-Ḥasan ibn Rashīq al-Qayrawānī (390/1000–456/1065 or 463/1071) was a poet active in North Africa (present-day Tunisia) and Sicily. He also wrote several works on poetry, the most famous of them being *al-ʿUmdah* (*The Support*), a kind of encyclopedia of poetry and poetics.

The Definition and Structure of Poetry

Poetry is made from four things (besides intention), viz. wording, meter, meaning, and rhyme.[840] This is the definition of poetry, since some speech is metrical and rhymed yet not poetry, because the purport and intention are lacking, such as some revealed parts of the Qur'an or the words of the Prophet (God bless him and give him peace)[841] and other such discourse to which the term poetry cannot be applied. (...)[842]

One scholar said poetry is built on four cornerstones: panegyric, invective, love poetry (*nasīb*),[843] and elegy.[844] They also said the fundaments of poetry are four: desire, fear, emotion,[845] and anger. Panegyric and gratitude go with desire, apology and asking for sympathy go with fear, yearning and delicate love poetry go with emotion, and invective, threat, and hurtful reproach go with anger.

Al-Rummānī ʿAlī ibn ʿĪsā[846] said: The regular "purposes"[847] of poetry are generally five: love poetry, panegyric, invective,[848] vaunting poetry, and description. Comparison and metaphor fall under the category of description.

ʿAbd al-Malik ibn Marwān once said to Arṭāh ibn Suhayyah, "Will you compose any poetry today?" He answered, "By God, I feel no emotion, I am not angry, I am not drinking, I desire nothing. Poetry comes only with one of these things."[849]

Abū ʿAlī al-Baṣīr[850] said,

I have praised the emir al-Fatḥ,[851] asking for his favor.
  Can a poet be asked for more when he desires something?
He has exhausted the genres of poetry, and they are many,
  but his good deeds and qualities are not yet exhausted.

Thus he made desire an aim to which nothing can be added.

ʿAbd al-Karīm[852] said: Four kinds encompass all poetry, viz. panegyric, invective, wisdom,[853] and light verse.[854] Several types branch off from each kind. Thus elegies, vaunting, and gratefulness derive from panegyric; blame, reproach, and complaining about slow fulfillment of promises derive from invective; proverbial sayings, calling for abstinence,[855] and admonitions derive from wisdom; and love poetry, hunting poetry, the description of wine and bawdy verse derive from light verse.[856]

Some people say that all poetry is one of two kinds: panegyric and invective. To panegyric belong elegy, vaunting, love poetry, and all praiseworthy descriptions connected with these such as the descriptions of remnants and traces (at abandoned campsites), and beautiful comparisons; and similarly edifying poetry[857] such as proverbial and wise sayings, admonitions, renunciation of worldly things, and contentedness. Invective is the opposite of all these. Only reproach holds an intermediate position, because it is at the edge of both kinds. Likewise incitement is neither panegyric nor invective, since you do not incite someone by saying that he is despicable or abject, or else you and he will suffer the consequences, nor do you intend to praise him with panegyric poetry, so that he will have it his way.[858]

A line of poetry is like a building:[859] its basis is natural talent,[860] its roof is the ability to transmit poetry,[861] its pillars are knowledge, its door is practice, and its inhabitant is meaning. A "house" that is uninhabited is no good. The various meters and rhyme-words are like the measures and models[862] used for buildings, or like ropes and pegs used for tents. All other things, such as poetic embellishments, are only an ornament that may be applied afterward; if they are lacking they can be dispensed with.

The qadi ʿAlī ibn ʿAbd al-ʿAzīz al-Jurjānī,[863] author of *The Mediation*, says:

> *Poetry is one of the sciences of the Arabs, in which participate natural talent, the ability to transmit poetry, and intelligence; subsequently, practice gives substance to it and gives strength to each one of its causes. He in whom these characteristics are combined will be proficient and will excel. The greater his share of them, the higher will his level of proficiency be.*

He also says:[864]

> *In this matter I do not speak out in favor of either the ancient or the modern poets, of the pre-Islamic ones or transitional ones,[865] the Bedouin Arab poets or those not wholly Arab.[866] Only I do find that the modern poet has a stronger need of memorisation and learning (poetry) by heart. If you seek to*

> *discover the reason for this you will find that it is caused by the fact that an intelligent and naturally gifted poet can only make the vocabulary of a Bedouin his own by being a transmitter of poetry. The only way to be a transmitter is by listening; and the basis of listening is memorisation.*

Diʿbil[867] says in his book:

> *He who wants to compose a panegyric should do it with desire,*[868] *he who wants to make an invective poem should do it with hatred, he who wants to make amatory poetry*[869] *should do it with yearning and passionate love, and he who wants to reproach in poetry should do so with a complaint of tardiness.*[870]

As you see, he divided poetry into these four categories. Elegy counted as panegyric for him, as I said before;[871] he substituted reproach in its place.[872]

More than one scholar has said: Poetry is that which contains proverbial sayings,[873] splendid metaphors, and apt comparisons; everything that is different from this bestows on its maker no other merit than the meter.

Isḥāq ibn Ibrāhīm al-Mawṣilī[874] said, "I asked a Bedouin, 'Who is the best poet?' He answered, 'The one who rapidly composes; when he is fast he amazes; when he speaks he makes people listen; when he praises, he raises; when he inveighs he debases.'"

An erudite man was asked, "Who is the best poet?" He replied, "The one whose poetry forces you to inveigh against your own people and to praise your enemies." He meant a poet you admire so much that you memorize poems of his which contain disgraceful material about yourself, against your liking. This is the gist[875] of Abū l-Ṭayyib (al-Mutanabbī)'s line:

And I hear in his words expressions which my ear
would enjoy even if it had contained insults of me.[876]

He took this from Abū Tammām's verse:

If your enemy does not praise you, dejectedly quoting me,
know then that I am not (properly) praising you.[877]

Al-Buḥturī followed him, too in this motif:

The caravan of my widely traveling verse will surely always
follow you, so fine that enemies will transmit it for you.[878]

ʿAbd al-Ṣamad ibn al-Muʿadhdhal[879] said: All poetry lies in three words; but not every person knows how to compose them properly. If you praise, you say "You are (*anta*)," if you inveigh, you say "You are not (*lasta*)," and if you elegize you say "You were (*kunta*)."[880]

A certain critic said, "The most difficult[881] kind of poetry is elegy, because it is made neither with desire (for a reward) nor with fear." Ibn Qutaybah said that Aḥmad ibn Yūsuf al-Kātib[882] said to Abū Yaʿqūb al-Khuraymī,[883] "You are a better poet in your panegyrical poems for Muḥammad ibn Manṣūr, the secretary of the Barmakids,[884] than in your elegies on him!" Abū Yaʿqūb replied, "At the time we composed in hope (of a reward), today we do so out of loyalty."[885] The author says, "From this prose remark al-Baṣīr stole (but God knows best!) his verse quoted before, on al-Fatḥ ibn Khāqān."[886]

Someone was asked, "What is the best poetry?" He answered, "What is given free rein and will its goal attain." Abū ʿAbd Allāh,[887] the vizier of al-Mahdī, said, "The best poetry is what is understood by the masses and what pleases the elite." I have heard a certain authority say, "Intelligent people have said, 'If eloquence consisted in longwindedness, Abū Nuwās and al-Buḥturī would not have attained it.'" Some intelligent later critic said, "The best poet is he who manages to make a good panegyrical poem or elegy on a woman."[888] Ibn al-Muʿtazz said, "A madman was asked, 'What is the best poetry?' He replied, 'That which is not veiled from the heart by anything.'"[889]

Literary Criticism: From *The Secrets of Eloquence* by ʿAbd al-Qāhir al-Jurjānī[890]

Abū Bakr ʿAbd al-Qāhir ibn ʿAbd al-Raḥmān, a Persian from Jurjān (or Gurgān, at the southeast corner of the Caspian Sea), died in 471/1078 or 474/1081. He wrote some works on Arabic grammar, but became famous with his two very influential books on literary style. *Dalāʾil al-iʿjāz* (*Proofs of the Inimitability [of the Qur'an]*) explores how syntax contributes to meaning and to stylistic excellence, not only in the Qur'an but also in artistic prose and especially in poetry. Imagery is the main subject of *Asrār al-balāghah* (*The Secrets of Eloquence*), in which he offers a perceptive and penetrating analysis of comparison, metaphor, and related tropes. The ideas proposed in these works were no less novel than their style, which is essayistic, often passionate and to some extent unordered. In the present excerpt little attempt has been made to make the translations of the poetic quotations more "literary" by means of a meter.

There is no compelling reason why literary criticism should itself have "literary" qualities (a fact all too familiar to modern readers), and many Arabic works falling in this category have the non-literary characteristics of scholarly works when they deal with matters of philology, grammar, lexicography, stylistics, rhetoric, poetics, the study of poetic motifs, plagiarism, and all the other elements that together form literary criticism. There are some exceptions, however, and when ʿAbd al-Qāhir writes about poetic language and imagery his prose style is itself of a quality that justifies inclusion here. Another reason is that it is important to get an idea of how Arabic poetry was received and discussed by discriminating critics.

It is important to realize that comparisons may acquire a certain magical power that words cannot describe and that the art of exposition fails to match in elegance and beauty. For the comparison may reach a point where it turns disinterested acquaintances into suitors, diverts the bereaved from their grief, cools the anger of alienation, reminds people of lost pleasures, bears witness to the feeling of glory, and demonstrates all the power and ability that eloquence possesses.

This is shown by the verses by Ibn al-Rūmī:[891]

The rose's[892] cheeks became ashamed because they were preferred:
 their rosy blushes testify to that.
The rosy-colored rose would not have been ashamed if he
 who falsely favored it had been less obstinate.
The narcissus is clearly to be preferred, though some will
 deny this and stray from the straight path.
Decisive in this case is that the one is the leader of
 the garden flowers, and the other drives them away.[893]
How different the two! One threatening
 to strip the world, the other full of promise.
Its glance deters the drinking friends from mischief
 and it enhances the enjoyment of wine and singing.
Seek in your mind its namesake among pretty women,
 and you'll be sure always to find one[894]
Think hard: only the rose bears its own name,
 no pretty woman is named after it.
It is the stars above that raised them both
 with rain from clouds, just like a father does.
Look at the two brothers[895]: the one
 more closely like his father is the glorious one.[896]
Where are cheeks, compared with eyes, in preciousness
 and leadership, except in false analogy?

The ordering of the artistry[897] in this passage is as follows: first, he effects the reversal of the terms of comparison,[898] as has been discussed above, in the chapter on comparison. Thus he compares the redness of the rose to the redness of blushing in shame. Then he pretends to forget this, deceiving himself into the belief that it is real shame. Then, having become assured of this in his heart, after the image has taken hold, he looks for a cause[899] for that shame and makes that cause the fact that the rose has been preferred to the narcissus and has been given a place that even it does not think it deserved. It begins to feel embarrassed and becomes fearful of the blame of critics and the taunts of mockers. It finds itself being extolled with praise that is clearly false and so exaggerated that his praise becomes, as it were, a mockery of the one meant by it instead. Then the poet, thanks to his penetrating intelligence and productive natural talent for the magic of eloquence, adds to this the concoction of arguments in favor of the narcissus, as you have seen, and how it is entitled to being preferred to the rose. In this way he achieves a beauty and excellence the like of which is hardly to be found in others.

The following verses by Abū Hilāl al-ʿAskarī are worthy of being placed alongside this piece, and of being associated with it in the subtlety of their artistry:

The violet claimed to be as lovely as his [the beloved's] downy cheek,[900]
so they tore its tongue from its throat.
They did no wrong by making an example of it,
since it had so badly overpraised itself.[901]

Recent poets have occasionally produced witty, subtle, original, and charming examples of this artistry, which cannot be commended enough and the excellence of which offers ample scope for praise. Among these is Ibn Nubātah's description of a horse:

A black one, from whom the night draws its ink
the Pleiades rising between his eyes,
Who went at night, chasing dawn, flying in its course,
folding up the spheres behind him:
When he feared it was about to escape,
he held on to it with legs and face.[902]

Even better and more accomplished in artistry is his verse from another piece:

It is as if dawn has slapped its forehead,
then it retaliated and rushed into its insides.[903]

The beginning of this piece is:

The noble steed you gave has come to us,
    its neck linking earth and sky:
Have you made us governor and sent it as a lance,
    the hairs of its mane being the lance's vane?
Proudly we ride it, with its white blaze and fetlocks,
    the water of dark nights being a drop of its water.
It is as if dawn has slapped its forehead,
    then it retaliated and rushed into its insides.
Moving at leisure, yet "Lightning" is one of its names,
    veiled, but beauty is one of its peers.
Fires would not conceal their heat
    if fires had any of its flare.[904]
Glances fix themselves on its flanks
    only when you curb some of its ardor.
A noble horse (*ṭirf*) will not show its beauties in full
    until the eye (*ṭarf*) is one of its captives.[905]

Pride of place in this type clearly goes to the following verses, by virtue of their striking and effortless originality:

Water flowing over the pebbles (...),
As if from the fast flow it is struck with madness
    and the winds have clothed it in chains.[906]

The poet was fortunate inasmuch as his road had already been paved, since the comparison of ripples woven on the surface of ponds to the rings of a coat of mail was well known. Going one step further, he turns them into chains, just as Ibn al-Muʿtazz had done:

Watercourses that were made to pour forth like chains,
    to suckle the children of sweet herbs and flowers.[907]

Then he skillfully completes the image by attributing to the water a quality that made it necessary to throw it into chains. This is easily done: violent motion and excessive quickness are characteristic of madness, just as a gentle pace and slow deliberation are among the attributes of reason.

Of this type are the verses on a sword by Ibn al-Muʿtazz, from a poem on al-Muwaffaq:[908]

A knight, sheathed in armor
  that cuts to shreds the striking sword,
(a coat of mail) like water that once flowed on him
  until it disappeared in him and froze.
In his hand he holds a sharp sword: when he brandishes it
  you would think it trembles, fearing him.[909]

He wants to devise a cause for the sword's shaking, so he makes it the trembling that overcomes it out of fear and awe inspired by the patron. It would seem that Ibn Bābak[910] had this verse in mind and relied on it when he used the motif of trembling in the following verses:

The teeth of misfortunes may test me with their bite
  and Time may weaken the strands of my strength,
Yet the sword does not shake from fear,
  nor does the lance tremble from cold.

Here, however, the poet uses another method. What he means to say is: The fact that the movements of the lance look superficially like the movements of someone who trembles does not necessarily mean that it has some defect or condition. It is as if he turned the matter round, denying that the quality of trembling in the lance had the same causes that it has in living beings. Note that Ibn al-Muʿtazz, by contrast, asserts that the movement in the sword has the same real cause as that found in living beings.

He (i.e. Ibn Bābak) repeated this (motif of) trembling in a manner altogether identical to the one I described above:

They said, His grief has weighed him down, so his back is bent!
  But I said (and doubt is certainty's foe):

The narcissus is not thin from love's longing,
nor is pining the cause of the jasmine's pallor;
The sword's trembling is not from cold,
nor the bending of the lance from its being too soft.

A verse that deserves to be a model for this type is this one by al-Buḥturī:

[The lances] blunder into necks and faces,
intoxicated with the blood they've drunk.[911]

He transforms the act of those who stab with lances into a blundering on their part, just as Ibn al-Muʿtazz had turned the moving and brandishing of a sword into a trembling. Then he seeks a cause for this blundering, just as Ibn al-Muʿtazz had sought one for the trembling. The following verse by ʿUlbah is also of this kind:[912]

It is as if the clouds held a wedding feast with the earth,
and the scattered confetti was camphor[913]

—and the verse by Abū Tammām:

It is as if the white clouds had buried under them (viz. the abandoned abodes)
a loved one: their tears did not cease flowing,[914]

so too the verse by al-Sarī in which he describes a new crescent moon:[915]

The month of joys, Shawwāl, has come to you,
and a murderer has killed the month of fasting![916]

After that, he says:

It is like a tight silver (*fiḍḍah*) shackle, broken (*fuḍḍa*)
from the fasting people's feet, who now walk proudly.

All these poets [ostensibly] deceive themselves, ignoring the comparisons, and erroneously give the illusion that what commonly serves as the basis of the comparison is present and has happened in reality, in their presence. Then, rather than restricting themselves to claiming that this has happened, they devise a cause for it and come up with something that attests to it. Thus ʿUlbah posits a wedding being celebrated by the sky and the earth, Abū Tammām gives the clouds a loved one buried in the dust, and al-Sarī pretends that those who fasted were fettered with a tight shackle which is broken in half, or bent apart so that it widens and assumes the shape of a new moon. The difference between the verse by ʿUlbah and those of the two Ṭāʾite poets[917] is that comparing snow to camphor is usual and common, used by everybody, as is turning raindrops that fall from the clouds into tears, or describing the clouds and the sky as weeping. The comparison of the sickle moon to a shackle, on the other hand, is unusual, even though its counterpart is common and the same motif is found in the same form. By this counterpart I mean the comparison of the crescent moon to a broken[918] bracelet, as mentioned before. Thus a poet says:[919]

Resembling half a bracelet
of blazing gold,

and al-Sarī himself says:

The crescent moon appeared to us like half a necklace
on the neck of a woman dressed in blue.[920]

Note, however, that this is simple and does not contain an aetiology (*taʿlīl*) that would make it necessary for the moon to be a bracelet or a necklace.

I saw that someone[921] quotes the verse by al-Sarī, "It is like a tight silver shackle," together with other verses, quoting a piece by Ibn al-Ḥajjāj:[922]

O master of the house,
both of whose guests have died,[923]
Why is it that I see the spherical loaf
is so honored and exalted with you,
Like the full moon, which we do not expect
to appear until evening?

Then he says: "He compares the bread with the full moon for two reasons: its roundness and the fact that it appears (only) in the evening." He also says, "The best comparison is that which combines two motifs, like the verses by Ibn al-Rūmī:[924]

You, who resemble the full moon in beauty
and in being unattainable:
Be generous! Fresh water
will sometimes burst from a rock."[925]

He also quotes Ibrāhīm ibn al-Mahdī:

You have shown compassion to young children like sandgrouse chicks
and to the moaning of distraught woman, like the bow of him who draws it.[926]

He continues: "Similar is the verse by al-Sarī, 'It is like a tight silver shackle'." But this does not resemble the other examples that he mentions, apart from the fact that it can be said to express both the shape of the crescent, through a broken shackle, and its color, through silver. If, however, he considers this to be the point that constitutes the verse's striking originality, then it should not be quoted together with the other verses, because not one of these other verses contains an aetiology. There is nothing more to them than the joining of one *tertium comparationis*[927] to another, such as the twanging and the curvedness of the bow, or the roundness of the full moon and its appearance in the evening. None of these motifs is the cause of the other, none of the two similarities mentioned needs to be validated by another.

A verse that is a true counterpart to al-Sarī's verse and that uses the same approach is one by Ibn al-Muʿtazz:

> He poured me wine when dawn's sword was already drawn
> and night had fled in fear.[928]

Here the poet is not content with a comparison of outward appearance and unconstrained expression, as he was in his verse:

> Until the morning appeared from behind its veil,
> like a sword blade from its sheath.[929]

or in his verse:

> When the tunic of darkness became thin
> and dawn's whiteness came like a rusty sword.[930]

Rather, he wishes to validate his claim that there was a drawn sword, and to behave as if he really did not know that it was merely a comparison, intended to convey whiteness and elongated shape. He does this by turning the darkness into a defeated enemy who feels threatened by a drawn sword and flees, fearing he will be struck with it.

So too in the following verse, where he makes the night fear dawn, though not using the same technique I am dealing with here:

> We arrived there[931] before the Dawn, who was masked
> and hiding in ambush, while Night's heart was wary of him.[932]

And here is a piece by Ibn al-Muʿtazz, one verse of which illustrates our point:

> Look at a world of Spring[933] that comes
> like a strumpet, all tarted up for the fornicators.

She comes as a visitor, like last year,
dressed up, perfumed with flowers.
When morning strips[934] to reveal its (white) camphor,
birds of all kinds speak in their languages.
The rose laughs at the narcissus's eyes that have become
inflamed, those still alive showing signs of dying.[935]

It is this last verse that I mean. That roses and other kinds of fragrant and blossoming flowers laugh when they open is a well known and common motif. In this verse the poet has given this a cause, by turning the rose, as it were, into a rational and discriminating being, gloating over the narcissus's imminent demise, the reversal of its fortune, and the signs of impending extinction. He repeats this motif of the laughing rose in the following:

The rose laughed at the gillyflower
and we were relieved from shivering from cold.

He means that summer has come and the air is warm, as one sees from what follows:

And we enjoyed a midday nap in the cool shade
and smelled the basil, with camphor.
Depart, depart, you army of pleasures,
from every garden and pond![936]

Ibn al-Rūmī blames the rose for this (viz. announcing the end of spring):

Decisive in this case is that the one is the leader of
the garden flowers, and the other drives them away.

Ibn al-Muʿtazz makes it laugh because it drives them away, just as a conquering and victorious person laughs having stripped others of their worldly powers and taken complete possession. A case where the laughter is given some kind of cause is when he says:

Love has died in me, my youth has gone,
and I have had my fill of all the pleasures I craved.
Now when, in company, I try to behave like a young lover[937]
my gray hair laughs at me with my friends.[938]

There is no doubt that the laughter is given an additional meaning that it does not have, for instance, in Diʿbil's verse:

[... a man] on whose head
the gray hair laughs, so he weeps.[939]

This addition is nothing more than the poet making the gray hair laugh like someone who is amazed to see a man attempt to do something unbefitting him and affect something for which he is not suited. Here, the form of the comparison is concealed, as I have mentioned, and supposedly forgotten. The same is the case with the following verses by Ibn al-Muʿtazz:

When they saw us in a blazing army
In bright sunlight that laughed, but without bemusement,[940]
As if gold had been poured upon the earth,
And our swords appeared from their sheaths,
So as to be a cause of their death,
While we swaggered in iron armor and the earth shook,
And sinew twanged and *nabʿ* wood clamored,[941]
They shielded themselves from fighting by fleeing.[942]

What concerns us here are the words "laughed, but without bemusement." The very denial of a cause is an indication that the laughter could have been given a cause, and that it was definitely real. After all, if you were to revert to the explicit comparison and say, "the sun's beaming looked like someone laughing," and then add “without bemusement,” it would be unacceptable. You will see this also in the following verse by a Bedouin Arab, if you were to count it among the same kind:

A coat of mail that mocks the arrowheads,
Like a snake’s slough.[943]

There is another kind of aetiology. It occurs when a certain concept or some act or other has a well-known customary or natural cause; then a poet comes along who denies this and posits another cause. An example of this is al-Mutanabbī’s verse:

He is not bent on killing his adversaries
but he takes care not to disappoint the expectant wolves.[944]

What people are familiar with is that when a man kills his adversaries he does so because he wants to destroy them and defend himself against the harm they may do, so that his domain remains safe and uncontested. As you can see, al-Mutanabbī claims that his patron has another reason for killing his enemies.

One should note that the introduction of such a pretended novel reason is possible only if it conveys a noble quality in relation to the patron, or an effective kind of blame. Thus al-Mutanabbī, in this verse, intends to describe him with a high degree of generosity and munificence, as someone dominated by his noble natural disposition; someone whose love of living up to the expectation of those who approach him and whose desire not to dash their hopes have reached such an extent that, knowing that wolves will anticipate plentiful sustenance and a time of abundance on account of the slaying of the enemies when he goes to war, he is loath to disappoint them, to frustrate their hopes by not aiding them. There is yet another kind of praise here, namely that he defeats his enemy and utterly routs them so that they will not thereafter aspire to repeat their conduct: that he will then no longer need to kill them and shed their blood; and that he is not someone who gives in to his wrath and rancor, killing wantonly, or who withholds forgiveness when he is in power, and similar praiseworthy qualities.

A striking, though somewhat tortuous example of this kind is offered by Abū Ṭālib al-Maʾmūnī’s verses, in an ode praising a vizier of Bukhara, as follows:

[He is] fond of praise, loves earning glory
and agitated, happy to give,
Only tasting slumber because he hopes to see
the apparition[945] of a petitioner at eventide.[946]

It seems he specifies the evening because petitioners and those bringing requests would arrive in his presence only early in the day, as is the custom of rulers. Therefore, since such visitors seldom come in the evening or at other times when they would not be granted an audience, he longs for them and sleeps, in the hope of seeing them appear in his dreams. But an excessive tortuousness can impair the motif one wishes to underscore: you will notice that these words can also mislead one into thinking that the poet argues that the patron is someone whose gifts are not desired by everyone, and that he does not belong to the same category as the man of whom it has been said,

Your gift is an ornament to a man if you bestow
something good on him—not every gift is an ornament.[947]

But this objection is easily rebutted and one should pay little attention to it, given that the poet is always intent on proving that his patron is generous, someone hankering after petitioners, always glad to see them; bent on denying that he is a dour miser, someone who knits his brow when he has to force himself to disburse and who has to fight his inner self to part with his money just so that he can be called a generous man, all the while loving praise and riches at the same time, someone who does not let himself be guided by what Abū Tammām intends by his verse:

East and West have never come together for a traveler,
nor glory and dirhams in the palm of a man.[948]

Such a man will hasten to listen to panegyric poems but will be slow to reward the panegyrist. Now, if it is taken for granted that this was the poet's purpose, one should banish any misgivings from one's mind.

Such misgivings as I mentioned might, however, occur in connection with al-Mutanabbī's verse:

Before he gives to petitioners he gives to the one who announces
their arrival, as if he were told about water when thirsty.[949]

But this is an aside and will, God willing, be dealt with in full elsewhere.

The verse about the apparition of the petitioner builds from verses such as

I get under the covers even though I do not feel sleepy:
perhaps a dream vision of yours will meet mine.[950]

It is not too far-fetched to see in this model, too, the invention of an unusual cause, only it is not quite as striking and out of the ordinary. After all, one may easily imagine that someone madly in love wants to see his beloved if he has not been with her for a long time; and if he wants that, he may well wish he were asleep for that particular purpose.

The following verse is to be connected with this section:

Solace departed with my departure; it is as if
I have made my sighs follow it, as an escort.[951]

Here the poet gives a striking cause for the sighs rising from his breast, ignoring the usual, well-known reason and cause for it, namely sadness and sorrow. The meaning is: solace has departed from me with my departing from you, i.e. at my departing, and together with it, and through it. Since the breast is the place of fortitude, and sighs rise there too, it is as if solace and deep sighs have lodged together there as two companions. When one departed, the other was bound to escort it, as a duty of friendship.

The following verses by Ibn al-Muʿtazz are of this type, follow the same path, and are strung on the same thread:

I punished my eye[952] with tears and sleeplessness,
since my heart was jealous of my sight, for you.
It bore this patiently, victoriously
gaining the pleasure of seeing you.[953]

The usual reason eyes are tearful and sleepless is the beloved's aloofness, or the intervention of the chaperone, and other such reasons for grief. As you can see, he has abandoned all that, claiming that the cause is as he said, the heart's jealousy of the eye on account of the beloved, preferring to be her sole beholder; and claiming that, to please his heart and obey its command, he sought to punish his eye, making it cry and robbing it of sleep. He uses the same motif of punishing the eye with tears and sleeplessness in a poem that begins:

Say to the sweetest creature in shape and figure:
 are you avoiding me in earnest or aren't you?
That is not what my desires told me;
 Alas, I see you have betrayed love!
What do you think of a lover enthralled by you,
 submissive, who cannot but be humble?
If his eye whores with another, then lash it
 with long insomnia and tears, as legal punishment.[954]

Here he has made weeping and sleeplessness a punishment for a crime that he imputes to the eye, as he did in the verse quoted before. The crime, however, takes a different form here from the crime in the other verse. Here, the eye's crime is looking at someone other than the beloved, and considering as licit what is illicit and forbidden; there, the crime is looking at the beloved himself[955] and competing with the heart in seeing it. Here, the heart's jealousy of the eye is the reason for the punishment, whereas there the jealousy exists between the beloved and some other person.

There is no doubt that the second verse falls short of the first and that the first is vastly superior. For in it he made one part of himself jealous of another, extremely wittily and subtly creating a quarrel between his eyes and his heart over the beloved. The jealousy in the second verse, on the other hand, is of the ordinary kind. Moreover, the word "whores"—even though what follows has added charm by being artfully crafted and is made more acceptable by the allusion to the Prophetic tradition "the eye whores,"[956]—is nevertheless bound to rouse some aversion.

If you want to see this motif displaying the same artfulness in its most wonderful and wittiest form, consider these verses:

She came to me, scolding me for crying—
Welcome, she and her scolding!
She said, with bashfulness in her words:
"Do you cry with the eye you see me with?"
I said, "If it approves of anyone but you,
I command tears to discipline it."[957]

With the word "discipline" the poet shows you the good discipline of the astute man who guards his diction from what is offensive and requires an apology. Still, mastery is evident in the verse by Ibn al-Muʿtazz. Not every excellence is evident at first glance: rather, it is apparent after a perusal and reflection, by thinking about the matter from beginning to end. As you know, there is no more eloquent way of showing the enormity of the crime he wishes to denounce than to mention the prescribed penalty [for fornication]; and that can only be achieved by means of the word "whores." In this way many poets without natural talent who followed the method of Abū Tammām have come to grief. This is not the place to expatiate on this subject; my purpose is now to show you some types of make-believe (*takhyīl*) and to lay down rules, as it were, which may be found helpful in the detailed exposition that follows.

Popular Science: Two Chapters from al-Damīrī's *Encyclopedia of Animals*

The term "polythematic" is often used for the Arabic *qaṣīdah*; it is equally apt for many prose works. *Ḥayāt al-ḥayawān al-kubrā* (*The Great Life of Living Beings*), an encyclopedia of animals by the Egyptian author Muḥammad ibn Mūsā al-Damīrī (742/1341–808/1405), arranged alphabetically, is a useful and often entertaining mixture of popular zoology, folklore, poetry, proverbs, lexicography, religion (especially Islamic law on food regulations: "can one eat it?"), medicine, dream interpretation, and many other topics. Among its striking elements is a potted history of the caliphs, a considerable portion of the whole, by way of digression in the section *iwazz*, "geese" (geese figure in the story of the murder of ʿAlī, the fourth caliph).

I. The Roc[958]

The roc (*rukhkh*, رخ), spelled with a final dotted *kh*,[959] is a bird found on the isles of the Chinese Sea. A single wing may be ten thousand fathoms[960] long. Al-Jāḥiẓ mentions it,[961] as does Abū Ḥāmid al-Andalusī,[962] who says:

A certain man, one of the merchants who traveled to China and stayed there for some time, arrived in the Maghreb.[963] He had with him the shaft of one of its feathers, which could contain a skinful of water.[964] He said that he was once traveling on the Chinese Sea when a storm swept them to a large island. The sailors disembarked and went to the island to get water and firewood. There they saw an enormous dome, higher than one hundred cubits, which shone brightly. Amazed, they approached it and found that it was a roc egg. They began to strike it with sticks, axes, and stones, until it split open, revealing a chick that looked like a mountain. They latched on to a feather on one of its wings and pulled, but it flapped its wing and the feather came loose in their hands, pulled out at the root. It was not yet fully formed. They killed it and carried away as much of its flesh as they could. One of them boiled a cauldronful of its meat on the island, stirring it with a piece of firewood, and they ate it. Some of the ship's party were old. The following morning their beards had turned black again, and afterward no one who had shared that meal ever grew a gray hair. They said that the stick they had used to stir the cauldron was a piece of the Tree of Youth.[965] At sunrise the roc appeared in the air, like a big cloud, carrying in its claws a stone as large as an enormous house, bigger than the ship. When it came alongside the ship it suddenly dropped the stone, but it fell into the sea, because the ship had outrun it. God, blessed and exalted, saved them through His grace and mercy.

The roc (rook) is also a chess piece.[966] Its plural is *rikhākh* or *rikhakhah*. Ibn Sīdah[967] says: Sarī al-Raffāʾ[968] said it well in his verses:

Lads among whom the flower of good manners had blossomed,
more splendid and more radiant than flowers of fragrant plants,
Who went straight for the wine, like the rook moves, and then left
while the wine made them walk like queens.[969]

Good verses by him are also the following:[970]

How dear to me, the one to whom I generously give my soul,
whereas he's stingy with his greeting and his salutation!
My demise lies hidden in his eyes,
just as death lies hidden in the sword's edge.

Dream interpretation: A roc in a dream is an indication of strange news and faraway travels. Perhaps it indicates gibberish in both correct or faulty speech. It is the same with the *ʿanqāʾ* bird. God knows best. The legal opinion (concerning the legitimacy of eating the roc) will follow under the letter *ʿAyn*.[971]

II. The Hoopoe[972]

This chapter has been chosen because it contains background stories taken from Qur'anic exegesis (*tafsīr*) on the story in Sura 27 about Solomon/Sulaymān, who in Islam is famous not merely for his wisdom but also for his control over the natural world, including the animals (whose languages he speaks) and the winds. Al-Damīri's story is one of many accounts; ultimately the content goes back to Jewish sources.

The hoopoe, *hud'hud*: a well-known, striped, and many-colored bird. Its nicknames are Abū l-Akhbār ("Father[973] of news"), Abū Thumāmah ("Father of a Blade of Grass"), Abū l-Rabīʿ ("Father of Spring"), Abū Rūḥ ("Father of Spirit"), Abū Sajjād ("The Prostrater"), and Abū ʿAbbād ("The Worshipper"). It is also called *hudāhid*, as in the verse by al-Rāʿī:[974]

> Like a hoopoe (*hudāhid*) whose wing is broken by the bowmen.

The plural is *hadāhid*, with an *a*. It is a bird that stinks by nature, because it builds its nest in dung; this is generally the case in its species. It is said that it can see water inside the earth just as people can see it inside a glass. They assert that it served as Solomon's guide to find water. That is why Solomon looked for him when he missed him.[975] The reason for the hoopoe's absence from Solomon (peace be upon him) was as follows: When Solomon had finished building the Temple in Jerusalem he intended to go to the Sacred Precinct (i.e. Mecca). He prepared himself and took his companions from among jinn, humans, demons, birds, and wild animals, until his army extended one hundred parasangs.[976] Then wind carried them. When they arrived at the Sacred Precinct he stayed there as long as God willed he should stay. Every day during his sojourn in Mecca he slaughtered five thousand she-camels, five thousand bulls, and twenty thousand sheep. To those nobles of his people who came into his presence he said, "From this place an Arab prophet will rise, who will look like this (describing him); he will be given victory over those who oppose him, and he will inspire awe over a distance of a month's travel. Persons both close and distant will be equal to him in rights. No blamer can attach any blame to him."

They said to him, "Prophet of God, which religion will he have?"

"The religion of monotheism.[977] Blessed are those who will live in his time and believe in him."

"Prophet of God, how much time is there between us and his appearance?"

"A period of one thousand years. Let those of you who witness it tell those who are absent, for he is the Lord of Prophets and the Seal of Messengers."

Solomon (peace be upon him) stayed in Mecca until he had performed the rites of pilgrimage. Then he left Mecca in the morning and went toward Yemen. He arrived in Sanaa at sunset, having covered a distance of a month's travel. He saw a beautiful country, boasting luscious greenery, and he wanted to stay there to perform the ritual prayer and have a meal. When he dismounted, the hoopoe said to himself, "Solomon is busy dismounting," so he flew up into the sky. He looked at the length and the breadth of the world, and south and north, and then he saw a garden that belonged to Bilqīs.[978] He went toward the green vegetation and alighted in it. There he found another hoopoe, a Yemenite one. Solomon's hoopoe was called Yaʿfūr.[979] The hoopoe of Yemen said to Yaʿfūr, "Where have you come from, and where are you heading?"

"I have come from Syria with my master Solomon son of David, peace be upon them both."

"Who is Solomon?"

"The king of the jinn, mankind, demons, birds, beasts, and the wind."

He told him about Solomon's majesty and how God had given him power over all things. He asked, "And who are you?"

The other hoopoe said, "I am from this country."

He described the realm of Bilqīs, saying that twelve thousand army commanders were under her authority, each of whom commanded one hundred thousand warriors. Then he asked, "Will you come with me and look at her realm?"

"I fear that Solomon will miss me at prayer time when he wants water."

The other hoopoe replied, "Your master will be pleased to hear about this queen."

So he went with the other and looked over the realm of Bilqīs. It was only in the afternoon that he returned to Solomon. Solomon had stopped at a place without water; he had asked the humans, the jinn, and the demons to find water but they could not. Then he reviewed the birds and noticed that the hoopoe was missing. He called for the vulture, who was the supervisor of the birds, and asked about the hoopoe; but the vulture had no knowledge of his whereabouts. Then Solomon (peace be upon him) became angry and said, «Assuredly I will chastise him with a terrible chastisement! ....»[980]

Then he summoned the eagle, who was the lord of the birds, and said to him, "Bring me the hoopoe right away!"

The eagle flew up into the sky and looked at the world the way a man looks at a bowl in his hand. He turned to the south and the north, and then he saw the hoopoe approaching from Yemen. The eagle swooped down on him, but the hoopoe implored him, saying, "I ask you, by Him who gave you strength and gave you power over me, have pity on me and do me no harm!"

The eagle let him go and said, “Damn you, may your mother be childless! The prophet of God has sworn to chastise you or to slaughter you.”

“Cannot a prophet of God make an exception?”

“Yes, he can. He said, «... or he bring me a clear authority.»”

“Then I am saved!”

The hoopoe and the eagle flew back together until they came to Solomon (peace be upon him). When the hoopoe approached him he drooped his tail and his wings, humbly dragging them on the earth. Solomon took his head and drew it toward him.[981] The hoopoe said, “Prophet of God, think of how you stood before God Almighty!”[982]

Solomon shuddered. He forgave him; then he asked him the reason for his absence. The hoopoe told about the realm of Bilqīs. Parts of her story have already been told under the letters *D* and *ʿAyn*, in the sections on “worms” (*dūd*) and “demon” (*ʿifrīt*).

Al-Zamakhsharī says:[983]

(...) As for God’s words «Assuredly I will chastise him», He chastised him in a manner such as he could bear, so that all others of his kind would be admonished thereby.[984] It is said that Solomon punished the bird by plucking its feathers and tail, to stand him in the sun in this bald condition, unprotected from ants and vermin of the earth. This is the best attested version. It is also said that he was covered in pitch and stood in the sun, or that he was thrown on an ant heap to be eaten by them, or put into a cage, or separated from his friends, or made to live in the company of his adversaries—someone said “in the narrowest of prisons, in the company of his adversaries”—or detained with none of his own kind, or made to serve his equals, or made to wed an elderly bird. If you were to ask, “Why was he allowed to punish the hoopoe?” then I would answer, “It is possible for God to allow him that, just as He allowed the slaughtering of animals and birds as food or for other useful purposes.”

Al-Qazwīnī[985] relates that the hoopoe said to Solomon (peace be upon him), “I would like to receive you as a guest.”

Solomon replied, “Me on my own?”

“No, you and your army, on (such-and-such)[986] an island on such-and-such a day.”

Solomon (peace be upon him) and his troops arrived. The hoopoe flew up and caught a locust. He strangled it, cast it into the sea, and said, “Eat, prophet of God! Those who miss out on the meat can have the marrow.”

Solomon and his troops laughed about this for a whole year. About this the following lines were made:

When Solomon came to the hoopoe, the day he reviewed all his troops,
She[987] gave him a locust she'd caught in her beak.
She recited (or seemed, in this state, to recite):
“Any gift is commensurate with him who gives.
But if to a human were given as much as he's worth,
then to you would be given the world and all it contains.”

ʿIkrimah[988] said, Solomon refrained from slaughtering the hoopoe because a hoopoe is good to his parents, bringing them food and feeding them when they are old.

Al-Jāḥiẓ says,[989] “The hoopoe is loyal, keeps his promise, and is affectionate: if his partner is absent he will not eat or drink or seek food or anything else, and he will not stop crying out until she has returned. If something happens to her and he loses her, he will not mate with any female after her ever again and he will cry for her as long as he lives. He will never eat his fill after she has gone. Rather, he will have what barely keeps him alive; only when he is on the brink of death will he take a little.”

In *The Complete Book*[990] and al-Bayhaqī's *The Branches of Belief*[991] it says that Nāfiʿ ibn al-Azraq[992] asked Ibn ʿAbbās (God be pleased with them both), “Why was Solomon, with all the power God had bestowed on him, concerned with the hoopoe, small as he is?”

Ibn ʿAbbās replied (as was said before), “He needed water and the earth was like glass to the hoopoe.”

Ibn al-Azraq said to Ibn ʿAbbās, “Wait, how could he see water beneath the earth and not see a snare covered by a mere finger of earth?”

Ibn ʿAbbās replied, “When the Divine Decree comes the eye is blinded.”

About this people quote the epigram by Abū ʿUmar the Ascetic:[993]

If God wills something for a man.
though he be clever, insightful,

Resourceful, thinking how he might avert
what God's decree might have in store for him,
God covers both his ears and sense and plucks
him from his mind as if he were a hair.
Then, having carried out His judgment He
restores his sense: a lesson to be learned.

Nāfiʿ ibn al-Azraq was the leader of a Khārijite sect called (after him) the Azraqites. They declared ʿAlī ibn Abī Ṭālib (God be pleased with him) to be an unbeliever when he consented to the Arbitration, whereas before the Arbitration they considered him to be the Just Imam.[994] They also declared the two arbiters, Abū Mūsā and ʿAmr, to be unbelievers. They are of the view that children may be killed[995] and they do not apply the prescribed punishment for those who falsely accuse married men of adultery, though they apply it to those who falsely accuse married women; and they hold opinions along similar lines.

Abū l-Shīṣ said, describing the hoopoe:[996]

Do not entrust a secret, mine or yours,
to anyone, nor to the folds of paper,
Nor to a bird I will portray here and describe:
it always pecks and pokes[997] the earth;
One with black claws, cocked locks,
with yellow lids, in beauty steeped.

The "claws" are its nails, the "locks" its feathers,[998] and its "lids" its eyelids.

Abū l-Ḥasan ʿAlī ibn al-Ḥusayn ibn ʿAlī ibn Abī l-Ṭayyib, the author of *The Palace's Statue*—which is a sequel to *The Solitary Pearl of the Time*—, who was killed in 467/1075, said,[999]

Don't find it strange, dear ʿAzzah, if a high-born man
lies low whereas a lowly born man rises:
Hawks' heads are bare of ornament,
a crown adorns the hoopoe's head.

It is said that when the mother of the imam, *Ḥāfiẓ*[1000] Abū Qilābah ʿAbd al-Malik ibn Muḥammad al-Raqāshī[1001] was pregnant with him, she dreamed that she gave birth to a hoopoe. They told her that if hers was a true dream she would give birth to a boy who would pray a lot; and so she did, for when he grew up he would perform four hundred *rakʿah*s every day.[1002] He transmitted from memory sixty thousand Prophetic traditions. He died in the year 276, God have mercy on him.

The legal judgement: According to the most correct opinion, one is forbidden to eat it because the Prophet (God bless him and give him peace) forbade it since it stinks and feeds on worms. Others say that eating it is permissible, because it is said on the authority of al-Shāfiʿī[1003] that compensation for it is obligatory.[1004]

Idiomatic expressions: One says "prostrating oneself like a hoopoe," referring to someone accused of being a willing catamite;[1005] and they say "being sharp-sighted like a hoopoe," because it can see water in the earth, as was said before.

Special properties: If a house is fumigated by burning one of its feathers this will repel insects. If its eye is carried by a forgetful person he will remember what he has forgotten; the same if its heart is roasted and eaten together with rue. (...)[1006]

Dream interpretation: In a dream a hoopoe stands for a rich man who is praised in a bad way, on account of his stench. Whoever dreams of a hoopoe will gain power and wealth. If a hoopoe speaks to him he will receive something good[1007] from the ruler, because of God's word, «I have come from Sheba to thee with a sure tiding.»[1008] Ibn Sīrīn[1009] said, If one dreams of a hoopoe one will be visited by a traveler. It is said that the hoopoe stands for a man who is an accountant, a clever fellow, who informs the ruler about affairs, because the hoopoe informed Solomon (peace be upon him) truthfully about Bilqīs. Dreaming of it may denote protection for someone who is afraid. Ibn al-Muqrī[1010] said that dreaming of it means the destruction of an inhabited house, or anything inhabited, on the basis of its name: *hud'hud*.[1011] It may also mean a truthful person, or proximity to rulers, or a spy, or a learned, very argumentative man. It can stand for being saved from hardships and punishment. It may also denote knowledge of God and of the religion and the ritual prayer that He ordained. If a thirsty person dreams of it he will be guided toward water. God knows best.

A Section from an *Adab* Encyclopedia: The Chapter on Stinginess from *The Precious and Refined in Every Genre and Kind* by al-Ibshīhī[1012]

Al-Mustaṭraf fī kull fann mustaẓraf, by the Egyptian author Bahāʾ al-Dīn Muḥammad ibn Aḥmad al-Ibshīhī (sometimes called al-Abshīhī, 790/1388–ca. 850/1446), is a popular example of a genre that flourished since the ninth century, when Ibn Qutaybah (d. 276/889) provided a model with his *ʿUyūn al-akhbār*. *Al-Mustaṭraf* is one of many thematically arranged anthologies with sayings, anecdotes, stories, and poetic quotations on a wide range of topics, religious and secular, serious and jesting, mostly dealing with the humanities and ethics but also including popular science, all designed to entertain, inform, and edify: in short, *adab*. For almost all anecdotes and verses earlier sources can be found, which are listed here only exceptionally. A major source for anecdotes on misers, one also used by al-Ibshīhī, is the entertaining work *al-Bukhalāʾ* by al-Jāḥiẓ (d. 255/868–69).[1013] This chapter, the thirty-fourth of eighty-four chapters, is intended to illustrate several genres—the anecdote (*nādirah*), the satirical epigram (*hijāʾ*), the sentential or gnomic epigram (*ḥikmah*), and of course the genre of "*adab* anthology" itself. It is preceded by the chapter on its opposite, generosity, and is followed by a chapter on food and table manners, a logical sequence in view of the role of food in matters relating to stinginess and generosity.[1014]

Chapter 34: On stinginess, avarice, and misers and their stories.
God the Exalted says,[1015] «... such as are niggardly, and bid other men to be niggardly, and themselves conceal the bounty that God has given them...» God's messenger—God bless him and give him peace—said: "Beware of stinginess, for stinginess has destroyed those that lived before you." He also is reported to have said, "Miserliness combines all the bad qualities of the heart; it is the rein by which one is led to all that is evil." Umm al-Banīn,[1016] the sister of ʿUmar ibn ʿAbd al-ʿAzīz—God be pleased with them—said, "If miserliness were a shirt I would not put it on; if it were a road I would not walk on it!"

It is said that there were four Arab misers: al-Ḥuṭay'ah, Ḥumayd al-Arqaṭ, Abū l-Aswad al-Du'alī, and Khālid ibn Ṣafwān. Someone passed al-Ḥuṭay'ah[1017] who was standing at the door of his house, holding a stick. "I am a guest," the man said. Al-Ḥuṭay'ah pointed at the stick and said, "I have prepared this for the heels of guests!" As for Ḥumayd al-Arqaṭ,[1018] he made lampoons on guests, using gross language. Once some guests stayed with him; he gave them dates and then lampooned them, claiming they had eaten them stones and all.[1019] Abū l-Aswad al-Du'alī[1020] gave a beggar a date as alms; the man said to him, "May God give you a similar share in Paradise." He would say, "If we gave the poor what they wanted of our possessions, we would be worse off than they." Whenever Khālid ibn Ṣafwān[1021] came in possession of a dirham he would say to it: "You wander with your mates: how much longer would you roam and fly? I shall confine you for a long time!" Then he would throw it into a box and lock it. People said to him, "Why don't you spend more? Your wealth is so vast!" He replied, "Eternity is vaster still."

Someone recited:

Suppose I gathered wealth and stored it all, and then
'twas time to die: could I buy yet more life with it?
A miser, if he stores his money, will inherit naught
but misery succeeded by a heavy burden.

Jaḥẓah[1022] asked permission to visit a stingy friend of his. When he was told that the friend was feverish, he said, "You must eat in his presence, so that he will sweat it out." Sahl ibn Hārūn[1023] wrote an epistle in praise of stinginess and dedicated it to al-Ḥasan ibn Sahl, who wrote on the back: "We have made your reward in accordance with what you recommend in it."

Ibn Abī Fanan[1024] said:

Leave me, woman, let me spend my money, for I love
that virtue that is best of all.
Most worthy to be blamed: a poet blaming men
for being miserly, when he is miserly himself.

'Umar ibn Yazīd al-Asadī,[1025] who was very stingy, fell ill with colic. The doctor gave him an enema with lots of oil. When the loosened contents of his belly ended up in the bowl he said to his servant, "Strain the oil that has come out and use it as lamp oil."

Al-Manṣūr[1026] was very stingy. Once on the way to the Hajj, Muslim, the camel driver passed him, singing the words of the poet:

A light shines bright between his brows,
Adorned by modesty and goodness,
His musk is mixed with camphor;
And when he dines, all screens are raised.

Al-Manṣūr was so enraptured that he kicked the ceremonial litter[1027] with his foot. "Rabīʿ,"[1028] he said, "Give the man half a dirham!" Muslim said, "Half a dirham, Commander of the Believers? I have sung camel driver's songs for Hishām[1029] and he gave me thirty thousand dirhams!" The caliph replied, "You have taken thirty thousand dirhams from the money of the Muslims?! Rabīʿ, appoint someone to get this money back from him!" Rabīʿ related, "I moved back and forth between the two, negotiating the matter. In the end Muslim pledged to sing camel driver's songs for free, both going and returning."

Abū l-ʿAtāhiyah and Marwān ibn Abī Ḥafṣah were both proverbially stingy.[1030] Marwān said, "I have never been as pleased as when al-Mahdī[1031] gave me a hundred thousand dirhams and I weighed them and I found I had one extra dirham so I bought some meat with it!" Once he bought meat for one dirham. When he had put it in the cooking pot he was invited by a friend. So he took the meat back to the butcher, [getting the dirham back] less two *dānaq*s.[1032] The butcher then advertised the meat, crying, "This is the meat of Marwān!" One day he passed a Bedouin woman, who received him as a guest. He said to her, "If the caliph gives me a hundred thousand dirhams I'll give you one dirham." But the caliph gave him seventy thousand dirhams; so he gave the woman four *dānaq*s.

Among those said to be stingy are the people of Marw.[1033] One of their customs, it is said, is that when they travel together each one buys a piece of meat which he puts on a piece of string. They cook all the meat together in the cooking pot while each holds the end of his piece of string. When the meat is cooked each one pulls his string and eats his own meat; they divide the stock.[1034]

A miser was asked, "What is a brave man?" He replied, "He who hears the molars of other people working on his food without his gallbladder bursting."

Someone was asked, "Would Muḥammad ibn Yaḥyā[1035] not give you a robe?" "By God," he answered, "if he had a house full of needles and Jacob came to him with all the prophets as intercessors and the angels as guarantors, to borrow one needle to mend the shirt of Joseph that 'was torn from behind',[1036] he would not lend it to him. So how could he give me a robe?" Someone put this in verse:

Suppose your house were stuffed with needles, and
your courtyard far too small for them,
And Joseph came and asked if he could borrow one
to mend his shirt, you would say no.

Al-Mutanabbī[1037] was very stingy. A man composed an ode in praise of him. Al-Mutanabbī asked, "How much had you hoped to get for your eulogy?" "Ten dinars." "By God," the poet responded, "if you used the rainbow[1038] to card all the cotton of the earth onto the faces of the angels I still wouldn't give you a *dānaq*."

Di'bil[1039] said: We were at Sahl ibn Hārūn's home and stayed until we[1040] almost died of hunger. He said to his servant, "Bring us food!" and he brought a bowl with a chicken on top of a little bit of *tharīd*.[1041] He looked at the chicken and saw it didn't have a head. "Where is the head?" he asked the servant, "I threw it away." "By God," said Sahl, "I wouldn't want anyone to throw away the feet, let alone the head! Damn you, don't you know that the head is the chief of all the parts of the body? The cock crows with it and no one would want him if he didn't crow. On it is the comb, which people consider to be a blessing. In it are the eyes, which are proverbial,[1042] which is why one speaks of 'a wine limpid as a cock's eye.' Its brains are a wonderful remedy for kidney trouble. And you will never find bones that are more tender to the teeth than its bones. Let us suppose you thought I wouldn't eat it, didn't it occur to you that someone here with me might want to? Now, go to where you have thrown it, find it, and bring it here." The servant said, "By God, I don't know where I threw it." "I know where," said Sahl, "You have 'thrown' it into your belly, God forgive you!"

It is said that some people are stingy with food but generous with money and vice versa. Someone said about Abū Dulaf,[1043]

Abū Dulaf spends a million
but defends a loaf with the sword.
Yes, there's smoke[1044] in Abū Dulaf's kitchen
but swords are drawn defending it.

A man from Marw suffered from pain in the chest caused by coughing. They prescribed *sawīq*[1045] with almonds, but he thought this too expensive and decided that to bear the pain was easier for him than paying for the medicine. After suffering for days he was visited by a friend, who prescribed drinking an infusion of bran. "It will clear the chest," he said. So the man got some bran, boiled it, and drank the infusion. His chest cleared and he realized it was a fortifying protection. When lunch was served he gave orders that the food be taken away until dinnertime. "Boil some bran for our family," he said to his wife, "I've found it gives good protection and clears the chest." "With this bran," she said, "God has given you both medicine and food. God be praised for this blessing!"

Khāqān ibn Ṣubayḥ[1046] said: One evening I visited a man from Khurāsān. He brought us an oil lamp with an extremely thin wick to which he had attached a piece of wood on a thread. "Why have you tied that little stick to it?" I asked. He said, "This stick has soaked up oil. If it gets lost we'll need another, but then we will only find a thirsty stick that will soak up the oil, I fear."[1047] I was still expressing my amazement at this, saying "God preserve us!" when an old man from Marw arrived. He looked at the stick and said to my host, "Man, you have fled from one evil only to fall into something worse. Don't you know that the wind and the sun make all liquids evaporate? They will dry up this stick of yours. Why don't you use an iron needle? Iron is smoother and does not absorb oil. Besides, some cotton thread from the wick may adhere to your stick, and this will impair it." The man from Khurāsān said, "May God guide you and bless us with your beneficial advice! Really, I have been most wasteful."

Al-Haytham ibn ʿAdī[1048] said: Abū Ḥafṣah,[1049] the poet, was visited by a man from al-Yamāmah.[1050] He left him alone in his house and fled, fearing that he would have to give him a meal that evening. The guest went outside, bought what he needed, and returned. Then he wrote to the poet:

You who have left your house,
  fleeing in fear, distressed:
Your guest has bought some bread:
  come back, be your guest's guest!

A miser bought a house and moved in. A beggar stopped at the door. The miser said to him, "May God help you!" A second beggar came and he said the same. A third one arrived and he said the same thing again. Then he turned to his daughter and said, "What a lot of beggars, in this place!" "Father," she replied, "as long as you stick to what you said to them, why should you care whether they are many or few?"

The most vile and miserly of them all was Ḥumayd al-Arqaṭ, who was nicknamed "Lampooner of Guests." In one poem of his he composed this verse about one of his guests, describing how he ate:

Between the first mouthful
  the man swallows down, and
the second that follows
  there is but the length of one nail.

Likewise he says,

His hands dispatch, his throat sends down
  toward the stomach, what his fingers grasp.

A Bedouin was eating dates with Abū l-Aswad al-Du'alī. He ate rather a lot. When Abū l-Aswad stretched out his hand to take a date the Bedouin reached it first; the date fell on the dusty earth but Abū l-Aswad took it up and said, "I won't let the Devil eat it." The Bedouin commented, "No, by God, nor Gabriel or Michael: if they came down from Heaven he would not leave it for them."

A Bedouin said to someone who had come to stay with him: "You have come to a wadi that rain has not filled, * and to a man who is not thrilled; * so stay and nothing you'll get, * or depart with regret * (*nazalta bi-wādin ghayr mamṭūr * wa-rajul bika ghayr masrūr * fa-aqim bi-ʿadam * aw irḥal bi-nadam* *)."

Al-Ḥamdūnī said:[1051]

I saw Abū l-Zurārah one day, when he said to his porter,
  while holding a sword in his hand,
"If the table is laid and a person appears,
  I'll cut off your head. And that's that!"
He replied, "Except for your father, for he is a nasty
  old man, and words will not stop him."
Thereupon he recited a verse, out of spite,
  that can't be considered correct:
"My father and both of his sons are to me
  just as dogs, when my dinner is served.

Tell me plainly (he said), you son of a dog,
  is my bread to be seized and impounded unjustly?
When the food is brought to the table
  I don't owe a thing to my parents, not I!
There isn't an uglier sight on the earth
  than a table with bread on it, thronged with a crowd."

Contrast this with the following:

A miser thinks that generosity is shame;
  a real man thinks that avarice is shame:
If he is rich but friends do not expect to benefit,
  may he expect an early death!

Someone else said:

She told me: be stingy! I said, stop it, please!
  This cannot be done for as long as I live.
I see people befriending a liberal man
  but a niggardly man has no friend in the world.

It is said: If you ask something from a base person, then ask for it quickly and don't let him think about it; for the longer he thinks about it the more he will keep aloof. Rib'ī al-Hamdānī[1052] said:

I have amassed all sorts of wealth by every means,
  but only from the hands of noble folk.
I hope that when I die I will have led my life
  without being indebted to ignoble men.

Al-Jāḥiẓ quotes Abū l-Shamaqmaq:[1053]

Who taught you this,
  never to give a thing away?
Perhaps you met a slave
  of a slave of Ḥātim of Ṭayy?[1054]

Verses by poets on misers and their food:
Among the best satirical verses said about them is this verse by Jarīr:[1055]

When food is hinted at with an "ahem!" the Taghlibite
scratches his arse and mumbles platitudes.

He also said,[1056]

When they are eating, they speak softly, and
secure the bolts on door and gate.
When guests make their dog bark they tell
their mother, "Quick, piss on the fire";
But she is stingy and withholds her piss;
she only urinates for them in dribs and drabs.
Bread is as precious to them as is Indian ambergris,
while wheat comes cheap at fifty bushels per dinar.

Contrast this with what another poet said:[1057]

A light shines bright between his brows;
Whenever he dines, all screens are raised.

Someone else said about a miser:

A miser served us with flat loaves of bread
as thin as dirham coins.
So light if someone at the table breathed,
they'd fly up through the room.

Another said:

You can see them: mute, for fear of guests,
performing prayer without the call of the muezzin.

Another, about a miser who spent the night with him:

We spent the night as if we held a wake
for a deceased one, in his grave deposited,
While talking all the while about our grief,
exhorting one another to be firm.

Another said:

Such neighbors we have never seen before:
they celebrate a feast, or break their fast,
They light a fire and make a lot of smoke,
but what the fire is cooking we won't know.

Another expressed it well:

His oaths are sincere if he swears with alacrity,
"No, by my bread!"—then you know it's the truth.
But if you have evil designs against him, spoil his bread!
For to him it is placed 'twixt his flesh and his blood.
I would greatly admire him if he were as jealous
of his wives as he is of his loaves.

Another:

All noble, generous people have gone, none are left;
only rogues and poltroons remain,
Those who never forgive,[1058] those who never give,
and the smell of whose food is never smelled.

Another:[1059]

You two, my friends of Kaʿb,[1060] please help your brother
in his plight: a noble man will help.
And don't be niggardly like Ibn Qazʿah: he,
for fear of being asked for favors, always worries.
Whenever you visit him with a request he bars his door:
you'll never catch the man unless you ambush him.

Another:

Two days he has: a day of bounty and a day
  when sword is drawn from sheath:
His bounty is bestowed on whores,[1061]
  his sword is wielded against dogs.

Another:

I gave Nabhān this ode, my purest thoughts, to be his bride,
  I gave her pride of place within this book.
He kissed her tenfold, loved her dearly. When I told
  him what her dowry was, she was divorced, tenfold.[1062]

Another:

If he were to cross the sea with its waves
  on a dark and icy night,
While holding a handful of mustard seed,
  not a single seed would he drop.[1063]

Another:

O you who stay and sit at home,
  completely useless and unable:
Your guests have all been starved to death;
  recite the Sura of the Table.[1064]

Another:

Your gifts are protected by thorns,
  your bread as remote as the Pleiades.
If you dreamed of a guest in your sleep
  you'd banish your sleep till you die.

Another:

Don't be surprised at the bread that it slipped from his hand:
On occasion an unlucky star will bring rain to the land.[1065]

Ibn Abī Ḥāzim:[1066]

They said to me, "Suppose you praised a noble man!"
I said, "Where do I find a noble man?
I've searched for fully fifty years—a man
of such experience is all you need—
but one can count on nobody for one good day,
and nobody gives freely to the poor."

Among the leading misers was Muḥammad ibn al-Jahm.[1067] It was he who said, "I wish there were ten jurists, ten orators, ten poets, and ten men of letters who would agree to cooperate in blaming me and raise their voices[1068] to scold me, so that this would become generally known and nobody would expect anything from me or bother me with a request." One day his friends said to him, "We are concerned that we may outstay our welcome when we sit with you. Why don't you give us a sign by which we would know the moment you are bored with our company!" He replied, "The sign is that I say, 'Boy, get my lunch!'"

'Umar ibn Maymūn said, "I was walking in a street in Kufa when I saw a man who was quarreling with a neighbor. I asked, 'What is the matter?' One of the two said, 'A friend of mine came to visit me and he wanted to eat sheep's head. So I bought one and we made a meal of it. I took the skull and put it outside the door of my house, to show off. Then this man came and took it and put it on his own doorstep, to make people think he had bought the head!'"

A miser said to his sons, "Buy me some meat." They bought it and he told them to cook it. When it was ready he ate it all, leaving nothing but the bone, as the boys watched him. Then he said, "I'll only give this bone to the one among you who can give me a good description of how he's going to eat it." The oldest son said, "Daddy, I'll suck and slurp out the marrow, without leaving lunch for an ant!" "You're not going to get it," said the father. The middle one said, "Daddy, I'll chew it and lick it so that nobody will know if it will last me one year or two!" "You won't get it either," said the father. Then the youngest said, "Daddy, I'll suck it and I'll pound it and then swallow the powder!" "It's yours," said the father, "Take it and may God increase you in knowledge and prudence."

A Bedouin stopped at Abū l-Aswad al-Duʾalī's when he was eating. He greeted him and Abū l-Aswad returned the greeting, turning to his meal again without inviting the man to join him. The Bedouin said, "I passed your family." "Yes, that must have been on your way here." "And your wife was pregnant." "She was when I last saw her." "She has given birth!" "Well, that was bound to happen, wasn't it?" "She has been delivered of two boys!" "Just like her mother!" "One of them died!" "Well, she would not have been strong enough to feed two." "And then the other died!" "Well, he wouldn't survive after his brother's death." "And the mother died, too!" "From grief for her two boys." "I say, what nice food you have!" "That's why I'm eating it alone; by God, you'll taste nothing of it, you Bedouin!"

A Bedouin had been appointed governor of a district by al-Ḥajjāj.[1069] He went there and stayed a long time. One day a Bedouin from his own tribe arrived. He gave food to the man, who was hungry. He asked him about his family, saying, "How is my son ʿUmayr?" The man replied, "As well as one could wish: he has filled the earth and the tribe with men and women." "And how is his mother, Umm ʿUmayr?" "She is fine too." "And how is the house?" "Thriving, full of people." "And our dog Īqāʿ?"[1070] "He has filled the tribe with his barking." "And how is my camel Zurayq?" "You'd be pleased if you saw him." Then the host turned to his servant and said, "Take the food away!" He took it away, while the Bedouin was still hungry. Then the host turned to his guest and said, "All right, Blessed-be-your-forelock, now tell me again what I asked you about." "Ask away!" "So how is my dog Īqāʿ?" "He's dead." "What did he die of?" "He choked on one of the bones of your camel Zurayq and died." "So my camel Zurayq is dead?" "Yes." "And what did he die of?" "Of having to carry a lot of water to the grave of Umm ʿUmayr." "So Umm ʿUmayr is dead?" "Yes." "And what did she die of?" "Of crying a lot for ʿUmayr." "So ʿUmayr is dead?" "Yes." "And what did he die of?" "The house collapsed on top of him." "So the house has collapsed?" "Yes." Then he took a stick and started beating the man, who fled.

It is related that someone said, "I was traveling and lost my way. I saw a tent in the desert so I went to it. There was a Bedouin woman inside. When she saw me she asked, 'Who might you be?' 'A guest,' I said. 'Welcome, you are my guest! Do stay!' she said. So I did. She brought me food, which I ate, and water, which I drank. While I was thus engaged her husband arrived. He said, 'Who is this?' and she replied, 'A guest.' 'He's not welcome here, what have we to do with guests!' When I heard these words I got on my camel immediately and went on my way. The following morning I saw a tent in the desert. I turned toward it and found a Bedouin woman inside. When she saw me she asked, 'Who might you be?' 'A guest,' I said. 'You're not welcome here; what have we got to do with guests!' While she was addressing me thus her husband arrived. When he saw me he asked, 'Who's he?' She said, 'A guest.' The man said, 'Welcome, you are my guest!' He brought me some nice food, which I ate, and water, which I drank. I thought of my experience of the day before and I smiled. 'Why are you smiling?', the man asked. So I told him the story of what had happened to me with the other Bedouin woman and her husband, and what I had heard them say. Then he said, 'Don't be surprised: that woman is my sister and her husband is my wife's brother. Every individual is influenced by the nature of his family.'"[1071]

There are many stories of such people and those like them, and the reports and anecdotes about them are widely known. But what I have quoted should suffice. I ask God, the Exalted, to give me success and guidance; He can do whatever He wills and He can grant prayers. There is no strength and no power except through God the Lofty, the Mighty. May God bless and give peace to our lord Muḥammad, his family, and his companions.

A Fairytale: The Tale of the Forty Girls[1072]

This tale (*Ḥadīth al-arbaʿīn al-jāriyah*) is taken from an anonymous manuscript dating from the thirteenth or fourteenth century, featuring "Wonderful Tales and Strange Stories" that are akin to those in the *Thousand and One Nights*. The story, about a prince who plays Goldilocks to forty girls, eating from their plates and sleeping in their beds (though not alone), is not known from other sources, although its various motifs are well known in Middle Eastern and European folktales. The tale (which I confess I find rather silly and which suffers from a surfeit of girls) resembles several stories of the *Thousand and One Nights*: in "The Third Qalandar's Tale" (embedded in the story of "The Porter and the Three Ladies") a man lives in a castle belonging to an Amazon community, opens a forbidden door, and is carried off by a flying horse (trans. Lyons, I:101–5); in "The Man Who Never Laughed During the Rest of His Days" (part of the cycle "The Craft and Malice of Women") a man also marries an Amazon-like girl and opens a forbidden door (trans. Lyons, II:575); and the same is found in the story of "Hasan of Basra" (trans. Lyons, III:161–69).[1073] The language of the story often deviates from standard grammar (such as using masculine plural forms where feminine forms are required, or plural instead of dual forms) and the style is simple, with only occasionally a florid passage in *sajʿ* (imitated in the translation in most cases).

The Tale of the Forty Girls and What Happened to Them with the King; with a Happy Ending.

It is told—but God knows best, He who is the greatest and loftiest, the mightiest and most bountiful, the kindest and most merciful—that in times of yore there was a mighty king of Persia who reigned over a huge realm. He had three sons and he lived a life of opulence until he was eighty years old. Then, one day, he thought about his kingdom and who would succeed him after his death.[1074] He called for his eldest son, who was called Bahrām, and said to him, "Know that last night I dreamed that I was riding a black horse. I was carrying a sword in its scabbard and I was wearing a black turban and a robe of black brocade. I was riding in an empty desert, without water or pasture. Eventually I reached a turbulent river.[1075] Being terrified of that desert I flung myself, just as I was, into that sea, on my horse, crossed it, and reached the other side. How do you think, my son, one should interpret this dream?"

He replied, "Father, the horse is might, the sword is power, the black color is the many years you will live, and the river is life—more than a hundred years in lasting rule and might that is here to stay."

The king was glad with his son's interpretation of the dream. He said, "My dear boy, rejoice and be of good cheer! For you will be my successor and inherit my kingdom after my death."

When the eldest son left the presence of his father the king called for the middle son and said to him, "My son, I dreamed . . ."

And he told him exactly what he had told his brother about what he had seen in his dream. The son answered, "Father, you will rule over a mighty kingdom and you will increase in power, from this country of yours as far as the Sea of Darknesses.[1076] Perhaps you will advance into the Darknesses one day's march or more, since you plunged into that black river with your horse."

The king was pleased and said, "Dear son, you will be my partner in my kingdom and the inheritor of my riches."

The son left and the king called for his youngest son, saying to him, "My son, I dreamed ..."

And he told him what had told his brothers. At that the son's face grew pale and he said, "Sire, I seek refuge with God from this dream, for the black color means great trouble. Perhaps another king will oppose you, whom you cannot repel. Perhaps it will be one of your sons! It could be me!"

The storyteller continues: When the king heard this he became very angry and said, "Woe unto you! You belittle my power and underestimate me, and you dare to talk to me like this!"

He gave orders that he should be beheaded; but his viziers and courtiers gathered and asked him to spare him. He consented and said, "I grant your request on condition that you take him to an empty desert and cast him there, leaving him to die of hunger and thirst."

The storyteller continues: They did as the king had commanded. When they were in the middle of that wasteland they set him down[1077] and started to head back. The vizier handed him a jug of water and a little food, which he placed in his robe. He said to him, “My son, this food will suffice for three days. After that, may God the Exalted save you!”

He bade him farewell and left, returning with his servants. The boy kept walking in that land without knowing where he was going, the first day, the second, and the third. On the fourth day his food ran out. His heart was beating fast with fear of dying and he soon found himself at the point of death, his strength had gone and sandstorms were blowing over him. He wept and raised his head toward the sky, calling out, “O Thou Who art near with relief, who savest the drowned from the deep!”

He looked right and left, hoping to find someone who might help and support him; and there appeared a shape in the distance. He went toward it, nearly giving up the ghost, but going steadily until the sun had reached the zenith. He was parched with extreme thirst and was at his wits’ end. Then he discerned the shape: it was a high-walled castle, with a broad court, rising high in the air. It reminded him of his father’s castle and his city, of his close friends and his brothers, of how he was separated from them, of his loneliness; tears streamed down his cheeks. He went toward the castle and found a mighty iron-plated gate, inlaid with gold and silver. Draperies in the hall showed pictures of singing birds.[1078] The gate was open. The boy entered, expecting certain death. He went from hall to hall, in which straw mats were spread, and where felt was nailed to the walls. He arrived at a door that was beautifully inlaid and panelled. Divans stood in opposite rows, copper vessels and jugs stood on the floor, everything was very elegant. In the palace were forty apartments, each apartment containing a bed, on each bed beautiful bed clothes of various colors. The doors of these apartments faced each other; one could go from the first to all the other apartments through doors inside. They were decorated with gold and beautiful paints. The apartments contained various kinds of mattresses and cushions, fit for daughters of great kings. In the middle of the entrance hall stood a table made of red gold, on which lay forty plates of white silver, with a circle of forty loaves of white bread.

The boy could not restrain himself and approached the food. He ate one bite from each plate. When he had eaten enough he withdrew. He looked for water and discovered, next to the entrance hall, a room designated for drinking. In it were forty royal seats embroidered with gold, with a wonderfully attractive seat at the place of honor. Before each seat was a golden tray with a crystal bottle, containing wine more fragrant than musk. On one side were herbs and greens, on the other fruit, and in the middle were flowers, aromatic plants, censers with aloe, and perfume continuously emitting its fragrance.

The boy looked from the windows, after he had drunk a mouthful from each bottle. Looking down he saw below the windows a large valley and a broad meadow. In front of the meadow was an orchard that had of every fruit-bearing tree a pair * the trees rising high into the air. * All kinds of fruits and flowers that trees could bear * were to be found there. * Birds in the treetops sang many an expressive and suggestive air. *

The storyteller continues: The boy looked up; light-headed because of the wine * and feeling fine. * He felt completely at ease.[1079] When the sun was sinking he heard the sound of horses' hooves. He looked out of a window and saw forty armed horsemen approaching, holding their weapons steady, * for war and battle ready. * A knight rode in front; his brocaded clothes were red, * and he wore a green turban on his head. * A black horse with white blaze carried him on his back, * like a crow deep black. * When they arrived at the gate of the castle they dismounted and took the horses into a stable next to the castle and tied them to their mangers.

The storyteller continues: When the boy saw them he hid in a corner inside the castle. When they entered the hall they took off their armor and riding clothes, and Behold! They were women, more beautiful than the black-eyed damsels of Paradise. They went to the dining room, while the boy was looking at them from where they could not see him. He was dazzled by their beauty and charm and by their clothes and had no idea who they were. When they were seated at the table each one of them saw that a bit had been broken from her loaf of bread and that there was a speck of food on it.[1080] They found this strange and each looked at the loaf of the others. Then they said to the one who sat on the raised seat, and who had been riding the black horse, "Mistress, what are these traces that we have never seen before today? Is it jinn or human who has been so bold?"

She answered, "Be patient, be not over-hasty. I will look into the matter. He who did it is bound to return."

They ate until they had their fill. Then they washed their hands, with the boy still watching them. They moved to the drinking chamber, their bodies swaying like boughs full of grace, * each with a beautiful face, * as the poet says,[1081]

"Slim-waisted girls who kill with charming glances:
they stab us with wide eyes as if with lances.

Beauty has made their eyes as black as coal,
as if made up with kohl, not needing kohl.
Advancing in the clothes of beauty clad,
they have bereft me of what sense I had.
They struggle when they step, they hardly budge,
as if they move their feet through mud or sludge."

The storyteller continues: Then they drank cup after cup * keeping their spirits up * with stories to tell and poems to recite * and thus passed the night * and then appeared morning's light. * Then they stood up and each one of them put on a new dress and each a spear grasped * and a sharp iron sword to her belt clasped. * They mounted their horses and went out through the castle gate.

Their mistress was a mighty sorceress. She made that food, that wine, those fruits, and herbs, with her excellent magic. She went out with her companions but then said to them, "You must go out today as usual, but I have decided to hide so that I can find out about that person who broke into our castle and violated our privacy."[1082]

She returned to a hiding place near the castle. The boy patiently remained where he was until the sun had risen into the sky. Then he left his place and walked toward the table. He stretched forth his hand and took some food. He was about to put it into his mouth when the girl appeared and approached him. When he saw her his limbs began to tremble; he was so shocked and terrified that the food fell from his hand. But when she looked at him and saw how handsome he was and how terrified he was, she came closer and smiled at him. She sat down next to him and began to talk to him in a friendly manner. In due course he told her about his plight and she embraced him and kissed him.

"My darling," she said, "are you human or jinn?"

"I'm human, a royal prince. But Fate has betrayed me and separated me from my family and friends."

"How did that happen and what has brought you here?"

He told her his story with his father, explaining everything that had happened to him. When she had heard his words and when she had seen what a beautiful and well-bred youth he was, love for him took hold of her heart. She said to him, "Don't worry, cheer up! For I have fallen in love with you. I will keep your secret from all my cousins and friends."

She ate some of the food with him. Then she took him to the drinking chamber and he drank some pure wine with her. Then she offered herself to him, and he jumped on her and took her maidenhood; she was a virgin. They kept at it until evening and the time for the other girls to return approached. She told him to hide in the same place that he had been the previous day. The girls arrived and entered the castle. They took off their battle dress, changed into women's dresses, and sat at the table. Their leader looked at the food and saw that it had been touched. She asked the girl who had hidden herself, to find out about the person who had touched their food the previous day, "Well, sister, who has spoiled our food?"

"I have no idea."

"You're lying!"

But she kept her secret and told nobody. They ate until they had eaten enough, washed their hands and moved to the drinking chamber, as was their habit, where they stayed until morning. Then the leader ordered another girl to stay behind in the castle to see who was spoiling their food and to tell her. They mounted their horses and left. The girl hid in a place that nobody knew about.[1082] When the boy knew they had gone he left his place and looked for the dining room. He went to the table, sat down, and stretched out his hand in order to eat. But then the girl appeared. She was impressed by his beauty and his fine and perfect appearance. When he saw her he was afraid of her, he was terrified, in shock, and at his wits' end. But she said, "My darling, don't be afraid! Tell me who you are and why you have come here!"

He felt more at ease and his fright abated when he heard her speak these sweet words and when he saw her beauty and charm. He told her his story and what had happened to him and his father. She sat next to him and said, "You'll be fine."

She ate some food with him. Then they moved to the drinking chamber and she drank wine with him. When they were in good spirits she offered herself to him and he complied; she turned out to be a virgin, a maiden as God had created her. Love for the boy had taken hold of her heart and pervaded her inner being. They had a time of great pleasure and rapture until the end of the day. Then the other girls arrived and the boy hid in his hiding place as before. The girls entered, took off their battle dress and changed into women's clothes. They sat down at the table. Their leader looked at the food and saw that it had been touched. She asked the girl who had stayed behind about the food and why it had been touched. The girl replied, "Mistress, I have seen nothing and nobody but me has eaten the food."

The storyteller continues: Their mistress left a different girl behind each day, until the boy had had them all; all had become fond of him. Time passed until it was clear that they all had become pregnant, but each had kept it a secret from the others.

The *narrator* continues: But the matter had not remained hidden from their mistress. On the forty-first day she ordered them to ride out as usual but she herself stayed behind in the castle, saying to herself, "By God, nobody will clear up this matter but me!"

She hid in a place that nobody knew about. When the boy knew that the place was empty he came out, as usual, heading for the table and sitting down. When the sorceress noticed him and saw his beauty and fine appearance she trembled all over from love and she could not contain herself but came out toward him. She threw herself upon him. When the boy saw her his limbs trembled too, the food fell from his hand, and he was overcome and dazzled by her beauty and charm. She noticed his feelings. She sat down next to him, was nice to him and said, "My darling, you're going to be all right, for I am the leader of these girls. I am yours and at your disposal."

They sat at the table and ate, while she fed him, taking food from her hand to his mouth, until they had eaten their fill. They washed their hands and returned to the drinking chamber. She drank and poured him wine until he became quite inebriated.

"My darling," she said, "tell me your story and everything about yourself, and how you got to this place."

He told her his story in full, from beginning to end. He told her about his father's dream and how he was angry with him, how he had given orders to put him down in an empty desert, how he had nearly died, how he arrived at the castle, what had happened with the girls and what he had done with them. When she had taken in what he said she said to him, "You'll be all right. These girls belong to me and I give them to you as a present from me. I noticed they were pregnant.[1084] Perhaps you will have sons by them and God the Exalted will come to your help and you will be happy. But I am a more fitting partner for you than the other girls; from today I am taking you as my lover and special friend, so do not go near any of my girls, for I am yours now and at your disposal. If you have an affair with any of the others I'll have you imprisoned and punished severely, clasped in iron fetters!"

"I hear and obey!"

Then they drank more wine while the sorceress kept kissing him. She recited these verses:[1085]

I did not expect him, this sweet-natured guest;
    my life for this guest who's my solace, my rest!
He looks like the sun or a moon that has set
    on a branch, in his prettiness dressed.
May God never separate us till we are
    in our shrouds and our tombs laid to rest.

She clasped him to her breast and offered herself to him. He took her maidenhood and found her to be a virgin maid, not deflowered by a husband or touched by a human being. This pleased him and he loved her very much, and she loved him many times as much. They had a most delightful time until the girls returned from the hunt. They took off the clothes they were wearing and put on women's clothes. They greeted their mistress, sat down at the table, and ate. Then she turned to them and said, "Come on, you must tell me what happened to you!"

They turned pale, for they realized that she too had seen the young man. There was no point in denying it, so they told her what had happened, saying, "Mistress, we didn't dare tell you what happened to us, for none of us knew about the others. We are at you disposal, do with us as you like."

"You should know that I have now taken him as my special friend and none of you may come near him from now on. Take care of yourselves until you give birth."

The storyteller continues: The boy remained there, living a most pleasant life with the girl for a long time. She was also pregnant by him and she loved him greatly. One day she said to him, "Darling, I want to go away and leave you for one day. If you feel depressed, open these storerooms and have a good look at what they contain, except this storeroom: be careful not to come near it and do not open it!"

"I hear and obey!"

She handed him the keys of the storerooms, mounted her horse and set off with the other girls. The boy stayed behind, alone. He began to think about his situation and felt depressed. He stood up and went to the storerooms and began to open them, one after another, and amused himself looking at all the wealth and treasures they contained, the precious stones, rubies, weapons, suits of armor, and other goods such as no king on earth possessed. He kept doing this until he arrived at the last remaining storeroom, which was the one she had forbidden him to open. His inner whisperings made him say to himself, "If this room did not contain the most precious thing she possesses she would not have forbidden me to look."

He went to the door and looked through a crack. He saw a horse as beautiful as any horse could be. The horse called out to him in clear speech, "Boy, open the door for me and untie the hobble on my foot so that I can carry you to a nice country, a great kingdom! You will love that better than being on your own, alone with that cursed, wicked, sly sorceress."

The boy was amazed to hear these words. He opened the door, untied the horse's hobble, and saddled and harnessed it. When he was about to mount it, he saw the girl coming toward him! She had felt in her heart that this might happen. When he saw her his trembling legs were shaking him * and all his resolve was forsaking him. * The horse said to him, "Do not fear, mount me, for she cannot overtake you now."

At that, the boy mounted the horse and it flew away with him, up in the air, as the girl screamed, "Damn you, you've done it now, you bastard!"

The horse answered, "Yes, he has done it! God has freed me through him!"

Then the horse took him over the earth, crossing deserts, wastelands, flat plains, and rugged terrain, while the girl followed behind in pursuit. In the end she was unable to overtake them and the boy was far ahead of her. The horse kept going until it reached an enormous city, impossible to describe, and said, "Dismount, boy!"

The boy dismounted. Night had fallen. The horse then said, "Don't be afraid. Sit down so that I can talk to you: I shall tell you my story."

The boy sat down and said, "Tell me about yourself and tell me your story."

"Know that I am the sister of the one you lived with, the mistress of those girls. We have another sister who lives in this city; she is the most beautiful and the loveliest of all God's creatures. I and the sister with whom you lived learned sorcery until we were skilled in that art. She fled from our father with those girls and they lived all by themselves in that castle. After she had left I learned some more sorcery and then I joined her and stayed with her. One day I rebuked her for her behavior; she became furious and she cast a spell on me, changing me into a horse and detaining me in that room, as you have seen. I stayed there for thirteen months until God sent you to me and freed me at your hands. I swear that I will be devoted to you and carry you through any desert and wilderness. You should know that my younger sister has a large castle beyond a wide river, and that she has slave girls who serve her. My father has put a river between her and the people; whoever crosses it may marry her. Many princes have sought to win her but they could not cross the river because it flows so fast and its waves are so powerful. Tomorrow morning you must mount me and enter the city. Go to the king's castle, enter his presence if he permits it and ask for my sister's hand in marriage. If he says to you, 'Do you know the condition, of crossing the river?,' say to him, 'I do.' Then, when you stand on the river bank you will cross it and possess that peerless princess, that matchless beauty, and also this city and what lies around it."

The boy was much pleased to hear all this and thanked her[1086] profusely. As soon as he perceived that morning had broken he mounted the horse and set off, full of joy and happy anticipation. When he entered the city the people were bewildered by his beauty and charm. He passed through many streets until he stood at the gate of the king's castle, with the people around him staring at the beauty and perfection with which God had clothed him. He greeted the royal doormen and asked leave to enter. They gave permission and he entered. He saw a huge castle with a wide courtyard, of a grandeur such as only God could command. When he stood before the king he greeted him in a fitting, polite, and eloquent manner. The king told him to sit, having returned the greeting and having been favorably impressed with his appearance. He addressed him in a friendly manner and asked him what he wanted. The boy replied, "Sire, I have come to you with a desire and a request; * may it be your behest * that I will not fail the test! *"

When the king heard what he had to say he asked him, "My son, have you heard about the condition of crossing the river?"

"Yes, Sire, I have, and I wish to be your son-in-law. If I succeed it will be through my good fortune, if I perish I shall be following the example of those before me."

"My son, you are undertaking a grave task, with terrors that will whiten the hair of a child."

"There is no might or power except through God, the Exalted and Almighty."

"My son, spend the night here and decide what you want to do in the morning!"

The young man complied. He spent a very pleasant night with the king. In the morning the king ordered the soldiers to mount, which they did in a trice. The king mounted and the young man mounted that horse of his. The people rode out with the boy in front, until they arrived at a large river. The king and all his soldiers halted; they were sorry for that handsome and charming youth who was about to perish. The boy looked at the river, seeing how big it was, and at the castle on the other side. He turned pale and felt perplexed, saying to himself these words that have never failed those who said them: "There is no might or power except through God, the Exalted and Almighty." Then he said farewell to the king, shouted to his horse, which sped forth with him like a well-aimed arrow. It plunged into that river as the king and everyone else watched. The horse cleft through the waves and crossed that river that was like a sea, bringing him to the other side. Then he returned and stood before the king. When the king saw this he rejoiced, gave him a robe of honor, and proclaimed to the leading persons in his kingdom: "Whoever loves me shall honor him!"

Thereupon they overwhelmed him with many robes of honor. Then the king returned to his castle with the boy at his side. The king summoned the judge and the witnesses and married the boy to his daughter, sending him to her in a boat, and arranging a great wedding feast. The girl was led to the boy and when he was alone with her he saw that she was more radiant than the sun and more beautiful than the moon. He fell in love with her and she fell in love with him even more. Then she asked him about himself and he told her everything that had happened to him with his father, how he had come to the castle, and what had happened with her elder sister. Then he related the story of her middle sister, the horse that had carried him to her. She was amazed at that; she stood up and went toward her, and it was her sister, in the shape of a horse! She came near and said, "Are you my sister Shāhzanān?"[1087]

"Yes, Badr al-Zamān! Your sister is the grief of the kings of Khurasan. She did this to me, put a spell on me and turned me into what you see. But God, the Mighty and Glorious One, granted me this young man."

At that she kissed her sister between her eyes and asked her to revert to her normal shape. But she replied, "By God, I cannot do that, for I have given myself to this young man and I have resigned myself to my lot. I have decided you should have him, for he is suitable for someone like you, and you for someone like him."

Her sister thanked her and honored her greatly.

The storyteller continues: The young man stayed with the princess for five years. Then her father, King Bahrām, became seriously ill and was on the verge of death.[1088] He called for the young man and bequeathed to him his kingdom upon his death. He died a few days later and went to meet his Lord. The young man ascended his throne and reigned over all his lands and vassals, with benevolence and beneficence. The girl bore him three sons. He taught them everything that princes need to know: writing, shooting with bow and arrow, horseriding, and polo.

One day he was riding his horse toward the racecourse. His sons were around him, with their handsome faces and twig-like figures, and surrounded by slaves like stars, dressed in clothes of many colors, when a dust cloud arose that obscured the horizons. The young man said to those around him, "Do you know what that dust cloud is?"

"By your grace, no, master."

The storyteller continues: The horse he was riding spoke to him and said, "Master, you should know that it is my elder sister and her girls. She is coming to you with everything she possesses, now that she has found out that you have come to reign over this large kingdom. She is carrying all the gold, silver, and precious stones she had in her castle, and is bringing it to you. Know that each of the girls who were pregnant by you has given birth to a male child more handsome than the moon. All are riding noble Arab horses. My sister has given birth to a boy who surpasses the sun in beauty and charm; he is the leader of the forty boys."

When the young man heard this he dismounted, thanked God the Exalted, and mounted again. He went on, his three sons around him and his soldiers and warriors following behind. When they were near the others he saw what the horse had described and rejoiced even more, thanking God and praising Him. When the girls saw him they all dismounted and came toward him. The princess approached him and kissed him; he welcomed her warmly and was very glad to see her. She said to him, "Greet your sons! I have brought them up and taught them everything that kings need to know. You have been unfaithful to me, but I have been faithful and I have brought you myself and all I possess."

Thereupon he fell down, prostrating himself to God, and asked Him to reward her. She said to her son and his brothers, "This is your father, and these three boys are your brothers. Go to him and serve him, for God has united you with him."

His forty sons surrounded him and he returned to the city, with a host of sons and spouses around him. People were amazed at this wonderful story and these strange events. When he was back in his castle he let the eldest princess dwell in a fine castle next to his own. He arranged for a regular emolument to be paid to her, sufficient for her and her girls, adding estates and villages such as no tongue could describe—all this because he was afraid of her sorcery and the evil she might do to the middle sister. But she was aware of his intention and said to him one day, "I should like to meet my sister."

He replied, "I will not have it, for I fear for her because of your sorcery and wiles."

"But I repent here before you of my practice of sorcery and give it up for ever. I have moved from that castle only because I have repented to God, the Mighty and Glorious."

When he heard her words he felt at ease and made her promise God the Exalted that she would never again practice sorcery. Then he brought her and her sister together; each sister was pleased to see the other. The princess never again meddled with the practice of magic. But the horse remained as it was; its sisters would come to her and ask her to revert to her former shape, but she would refuse.

The storyteller continues: One day the prince was thinking of his father and what he had done to him, having him thrown in that desert. Then he prayed to God the Exalted, asking Him to reunite him with his father so that he could see him and see what God had bestowed upon him: a kingdom, wealth, and children; and God answered his prayer. One day he was riding his horse; she knew what he had wished for in his prayer to God, and she said, "Master, would you like me to bring you and your father together so that he can see what you have achieved, gaining a kingdom, wealth, and sons?"

"How can this be accomplished?"

"Be of good cheer and do not worry, for I have remained as I am for this reason alone: I shall make your wish come true."

"I should like my father to see what God the Exalted has given me."

"It will be a pleasure."

Then she spoke some words he did not understand, and there appeared before him a huge demon, black as the night, called Qudāḥ. She said to him, "Qudāḥ, you know what this young man has done for me. He wants to see his father and to show him that God the Exalted has given him a kingdom, wealth, and sons."

"Ask him how he wishes to see him, either well or ill."

"On his royal throne, as a mighty ruler."

"Ask him if he wishes to go to his father or for his father to come to him."

"He wants to go to his father with all his soldiers, his horsemen, and his sons."

"When would you like it to be?"

"Tomorrow night."

"I hear and obey."

Then he left her. He gathered his helpers and fellows from among the rebel jinn[1089] and said to them, "Know that the princess has asked me to fulfill a wish for her, and she is entitled to expect it from me. I want you all to come tomorrow night, each one of you carrying one or two horsemen from the prince's army. As soon as it is morning his whole army will have arrived at the gate of his father's city, with tents pitched and lances planted."

"We hear and obey."

The horse told the prince to command his soldiers to come forward with their armor, their weapons, and all their traveling equipment; this he did. The following evening all had come forward as he had ordered. The prince decked out his sons in fine clothes and let them mount noble Arab horses. He took with him hoards of money, treasures, and equipment. Not one of his soldiers left without a complete set of armor and provisions. All this took a whole day. When night was falling the demon came in the midst of all his fellows and troops. God sent a sleep over everybody and when they were asleep the demons began to pick up the soldiers, each with his armor and horse, and put them down at the gate of the castle of the young man's father, while they were sleeping and unaware. Having set them down at the city gate, they pitched their tents and pavilions. When morning broke the king saw those soldiers. He was perplexed and bewildered, all the more so since the prince had given orders for the drums to be beaten and the trumpets to be blown. The standards were raised and the clamor rose.

The king was greatly confused by what he saw. He sent a messenger to find out what the matter was, after he had closed the city gates. The messenger was the king's vizier, who had taken the young man to that empty wasteland. When he arrived at the prince's pavilion he asked permission to enter, which was given. He entered and greeted politely and eloquently; the prince returned the greeting and then asked him, "You are So-and-So the vizier, who took me into that empty desert and gave me water and food, though my father wanted me to die. My Lord had mercy on me and saved me, giving me this kingdom, wealth, and sons. God be praised! I have not come to fight him, but in order to show him what God the Exalted has given me."

The storyteller continues: When the vizier heard this he fell down and prostrated himself to God, amazed by the turn the young man's fortunes had taken. The prince said, "I am happy and content with what God the Exalted has given me. Go back to him and let him know this; reassure him about himself and his kingdom."

The vizier returned to the king and informed him of this. The king was very glad and went out to receive him; he rejoiced and embraced him, kissing and blessing him. He said, "My son! Tell me about yourself!"

He told him everything that had happened to him. Then he said, "Father, I possess a kingdom and a country such as no eye has seen and no ear has heard about. But I will stay here in order to indulge my longing to see you and my brothers. In a few days' time I will depart for my country."

He called for his brothers, greeting them and welcoming them. He gave each of them a town and a large estate. Then he returned to his horse and said to it, "Mistress, the wish is fulfilled. Now I would like you to return to your former shape so that I can be favored with your service!"

"Master, would that please you?"

"Indeed, may God reward you!"

At that she disappeared for a moment and returned in a shape that put the sun's beauty to shame. When he saw her he was enthralled. That very instant he called for the judge and the witnesses and the marriage contract was drawn.[1090] Dinars were scattered all round, a wedding feast was held, the like of which had never been heard of in any country. When she was led to him he discovered that she was a virgin maid, still with the seal that her Lord had given her, which pleased him greatly. He loved her more than anyone and gave her a fine castle, one of the castles of her sisters. Then he resolved to return to his country. He bade his father farewell, who said to him, "My son, I wish you would not leave me, so that you can bury me and rule after me among your brothers."

"Father, that is the interpretation of your dream; my Lord has made it come true."

The king died and went to meet his Lord. The prince's brothers were always grateful for the boons he had bestowed on them. Thus his good fortune helped him to achieve his desires. He lived a most pleasant, enjoyable, opulent, and carefree life ever afterward, until death came to him.

Erotica: The Young Girl and the Dough Kneader, from al-Tīfāshī's *The Old Man's Rejuvenation*[1091]

The Egyptian writer al-Tīfāshī (580/1184–651/1253) is famous for his work on mineralogy and precious stones, *Azhār al-afkār fī jawāhir al-aḥjār*, and infamous for his erotological work *Rujūʿ al-shaykh ilā ṣibāh fī l-quwwah ʿalā l-bāh* (*The Old Man's Rejuvenation in His Powers of Copulation*). Most of it is concerned with aphrodisiaca: endless lists of recipes and recommendations to enhance one's sexual prowess and both sexes' enjoyment of sex, and descriptions of sexual techniques, without any literary elements. However, the author also includes a chapter with stories. They are obviously meant to entertain, but their purpose is practical, not literary: like the recipes, their function is to stimulate sexual appetite. There are no feeble excuses of literary pretensions here: the author merely wants to titillate. Indeed, the sixteenth-century physician Dāwūd al-Anṭākī recommends, in a discussion of sexual stimulants, "reading poems and stories such as are found in *The Intelligent Man's Direction* and *The Old Man's Rejuvenation in His Powers of Copulation*..."[1092] Ten monologues by women, apparently prostitutes of a superior kind, are embedded in a frame story in which a vizier intends to demonstrate that women's sexual appetites are inexhaustible and exceed those of men (the choice of accomplished prostitutes no doubt prejudiced the outcome). The last and longest of these ten tales is translated here. By comparison with other tales in the book it is only moderately pornographic. The text should not be regarded as an early ego-document about a woman's experience, as it was doubtless written by a man. The translation to some extent imitates the traditional Arabic layout in manuscripts and early printed texts (and the edition used here), without punctuation and capital letters (apart from the pronoun I). This is also intended to simulate the girl's breathless monologue; but it is a far cry from Molly Bloom. The male in the story would be imprisoned as a pedophile today, but at least the sex is described as consensual.

The tenth girl came forward and said:

I've been a prostitute from my early days the fact is my father was a baker and we had a servant in the bakery who kneaded the dough he had a big body like an elephant but good-looking I was ten years old at the time I knew nothing of fucking I didn't know about the pleasures of sex I used to go into the bakery and leave with that dough kneader because I liked him for his sweet looks and whenever I left I saw him following me with his eyes and moaning heavily which made me love him even more but I didn't know what he wanted because in those days I had not yet reached puberty and had no knowledge of the joys of intercourse almost everyday he would make a piece of pastry for me with real butter bake it and give it to me to eat and I liked him more every day because I saw that he grew ever more affectionate toward me and was nice to me and welcomed me when I visited the bakery when the others weren't there so I followed him in the bakery wherever he went and I would joke with him and ride on his back and he would tolerate everything I did now one day he came into the room where the fuel was stored and he saw that I was alone with him for all the other servants in the bakery were absent then he came toward me and took me gently with both his hands and pressed me to his breast and began to kiss my cheeks and my neck and I did the same to him because I loved him so and he was so dear to my heart I thought he only did it because he loved me so much then we left the storeroom and I went home while he stayed in the bakery as usual and afterwards whenever he found the bakery empty of people he'd do the same as before pressing me to him embracing me kissing me sucking my lips until my cheeks and lips were almost bleeding I thought all that was merely because he loved me so much and I was glad of it and I made it a point of being alone with him because I loved him too then one day he got hold of me in an empty part in the bakery that my father had furnished for himself to have a rest in the afternoon while the servants were busy at work in the bakery then he pressed me to his breast passionately and lovingly and kissed my cheeks and my neck more than usual then he took my tongue in his mouth sucking it I wasn't familiar with that and I didn't like it I wanted to free my tongue but I couldn't for he was sucking so strongly then he moved his hand to my hips and began to touch my belly and my waist while I was wondering what he was doing and I thought what on earth does he want with that but then his hand went down to the outside of my cunt[1093] he began to rub it and touch it energetically it made me feel pain in my whole body so I said tell me what you want since you're doing something you've never done before today and you've hurt me with that biting and pinching he said what I want is for you to take off your trousers I said why would you want that and what's the use he said you'll see and then he took off my trousers and I didn't resist and he took off his trousers partly and held me to his breast like before and pressed his belly on mine and it so happened that his penis hit the opening of my womb so he felt an enormous pleasure it showed on his face and then he took his penis in his hand and began to put spittle on it then he rubbed it fervently between my nether lips all the while I was baffled by him and his doings and I was amazed by what he did but because I noticed that he enjoyed it I let him and I kept watching until he'd finished after a short while I found that a hot liquid had come from him on my womb and my thighs I thought he'd urinated and I found it distasteful and moved away from him and I scolded him for what he'd done what's that you've done I said you're pissing on me and my clothes what should I say when my mother and my family see it then when he saw my state he came towards me and said my love that stuff won't harm you he produced a handkerchief that he had with him and he wiped my clothes and thighs all the while saying nice things to me so I was all right with him because I felt such love and affection for him he said this is the only thing I want from you so don't deny it to me so I went back to him and said nevermind do what you like if that gives you pleasure then I left him and went home after I'd inspected my clothes so that no traces remained visible and I kept coming to the bakery regularly as usual every day nobody saw anything wrong in that and as soon as we were alone he would take me and do to me as before and I didn't mind him doing it in fact I complied with his wishes because I loved him so much when this had gone on between us for a long time for years[1094] and I had grown up I'd almost reached puberty I came to feel a great pleasure in it I'd look forward to being alone with him even more than I used to and I'd say to him at the time satisfy me and do it a lot to me because I find it so nice he was pleased when I said that and he practiced all manners of fucking on me very strange kinds indeed while I enjoyed it more every time[1095] and then at last I became a woman and came to know the pleasures of sex but then my parents said I couldn't go to the bakery or the markets any more but I began to feel an unbearable longing for him and for what he used to do to me I would dream of him every night doing his usual thing to me in the bakery then I'd get up longing even more for him and for his doings and my lust made me want to take frightful risks but I restrained myself and bore it patiently waiting for an opportunity finally one day my mother had gone to a wedding taking with her all the others in the house so I found myself left on my own to prepare the meal for my father and my brothers now as fate would have it that young man the dough kneader needed flour so he came to the house that day to get some flour he knocked on the door I opened it and when I bumped into him and recognized him I couldn't restrain myself I grabbed him by his collar dragged him inside locked the door I said to him why all this time I have been waiting for you and when he saw the state I was in he said I'm scared your father and your brothers will come in unexpectedly and see me with you then what will we say to them I said[1096] let them come come what may and then I took him inside to my own room this is my room I said and nobody will enter it then I took off my clothes until I was completely naked I went to him and embraced him I kissed his cheek and neck and he did the same to me but he was dazed feeling uneasy afraid while my heart was in turmoil with lust and passion and longing for him but he was slow unlike his usual manner what's wrong with you today I said are you stupid or what you're not moving at all he said I'm really scared someone will find us out I said don't be afraid relax my brothers are busy at work they'll only come home in the evening and my father is also busy buying and selling he can't leave the bakery he's got nothing to do here so relax don't be scared and take this opportunity then he revived because of my words and turned to me holding me by my waist carrying me to a bed opposite the door he lay down on it he pressed me tenderly to his breast gently lovingly he took my tongue into his mouth sucking it forcefully it as usual then I undid his trousers and sat on his chest I put his head under my belly and every vein in my whole body throbbed with a desire to fuck I got up and uncovered his penis and pulled it out it was stretched and hard like a stick I started kissing and sucking it[1097] saying sweet things to him gently flirting with him then he drew near to me no longer turning away from me he grabbed my hips lifting them then dragging me forcefully down on the floor sitting astride my chest he held me under him and began to suck my lips one suck after another while I added to his excitement and roused his lust with words that would have moved a rock if it had heard them then when lust had taken complete hold of his body and had wholly dislodged his reason and he had forgotten all fear and terror and the veil of shame had been lifted he pressed me to him so hard that to this day I've never forgotten it I felt as if all my limbs had become detached so strong was my longing he had bared his penis it was like a pillar so thick and hard he began to rub it vigorously between my nether lips almost making them bleed he bent down over me kissing me while I lay under him melting like hot lead because of the passion that had overcome my body I said to him when I had this strong lustful feeling and a desire to fuck and all this painful love damn you why don't you fuck like normal people and extinguish my burning fire and yours too you've already given me enough pain in my nether lips by your doing you've set fire to my body with the heat of my lust so why this hanging back from doing your business and mine come stuff it into my belly let me hear its noise inside my womb perhaps my heart will be cured of its misery then he huffed and puffed in all his grossness and said damn you what can I do you're a virgin I can't put it into you well that's a strange thing I said can't virgins be fucked oh yes they can he said but I'm afraid of the consequences so I said don't be afraid don't be so timid be brave man here's our chance we don't always get such an opportunity please please let go of your fears and fuck me until I am satisfied and let my family do whatever they like I can't go on without it now that the time is right and the place is empty so get on with it and fuck me as much as I need this being apart has killed me when he heard all this from me he got on to his feet in a stupor because of the lust that had overcome his body now there was in the place we were yet another room and he carried me there I had a bare wooden bench without cushions and because he was anxious that I might be hurt because I was naked he didn't want to put me down on it so he put one of his knees on the bench and left the other on the floor then he made me sit on his knee making my back rest against a pillow and my legs around his waist he put one of his hands under my thighs and the other behind my back then he made the tip of his penis disappear in my womb just a bit and he took my tongue into his mouth sucking it the way he liked for a short while then he turned to me and said take care and don't scream then he gave it one big push and no sooner was I aware of this than it seemed to be inside my very heart then he began to make love to me vigorously without interruption while I let him hear my gasps and tender words such as he'd never heard before in his life so he became even more enamored of me his lust increased and he fucked me thoroughly he was in fact well acquainted with the art so he went on until he came inside me three times in one session having satisfied me with his fucking and thrusting then he withdrew it and I got up from under him while I was covered with blood but my lust had been so strong that I hadn't felt any pain when my maidenhood was taken well from that day onward I was a whore I only like big pricks I'll fall in love with any nice civilized man[1098] making the appointment with him or he with me.

*

When the son of the vizier heard this he was amazed at the strength of the lustful feelings of women. He learned that women have a stronger libido than men. He gave orders that each of the ten girls be given a robe of honor and one hundred dinars. They all drank wine and had a merry time until the evening and then the girls went home. Every now and then they would visit him again, right up until his death.

Two Burlesque Stories from *Brains Confounded* by al-Shirbīnī

Al-Shirbīnī, who completed his *Hazz al-quḥūf* in 1097/1686, is the author of a remarkable work, entitled (in the recent editor's translation) *Brains Confounded by the Ode of Abū Shādūf Expounded* (elsewhere I have myself rendered the somewhat ambiguous words *Hazz al-quḥūf* as *The Nodding Noddles, or Jolting the Yokels*).[1099] It describes the Egyptian fellahin in an endless array of anecdotes, stories and poems, mocking them as brutish and stupid yokels (but at the same time exposing their pitiful circumstances to such an extent that one modern Arab scholar has interpreted the book as a *J'accuse* directed at the Ottoman rulers). The first half of the book is a general description of the peasants; the second half is written as a mock commentary on a poem in colloquial Arabic supposedly written by a peasant called Abū Shādūf, which satirizes traditional philological scholarship as well as the fellahin.

I. The Peasant and the Scholar[1100]

The following story, written in simple prose with the peasant speaking Egyptian dialect, has been chosen because it is another version of the burlesque ending of al-Tanūkhī's tale "The Prisoner of War," translated above (see p. 230). The story exists in many versions in other cultures; for a version involving a pope and a rabbi, see Cray, "The Rabbi Trickster," 342–43.

Our shaykh told us that some years ago a Persian came to Cairo (may God protect it) where he met its vizier. He told him he was a Persian scholar and that nobody rivalled him in knowledge. He so impressed the vizier and others with his words that the vizier took a shine to the man, whom he held in high esteem. The vizier asked him, "Are you able to engage in a debate with the ulema of the Azhar Mosque?"

"Certainly. I shall ask them a question in your presence, and if they give the right answer I will be at their command; if not, I can boast that I am better than they are."

The vizier sent for the Azhar ulema (may God support them and make them the imams of the Muslims until the Day of Judgment). Once they had arrived and the place had filled up with people, he explained the matter to them. They said, “Let that Persian ask whatever he likes.”

The Persian stood before them and began to ask questions using gestures without any words being uttered. The ulema said, “Vizier, gestures are used only with the deaf and dumb. We don't know what he is saying.”

But the vizier told them that they had to reply to his question; he insisted on this because he liked the Persian very much. So they said to him, “Give us three days respite, so that we can consult the other shaykhs.”

The vizier granted this. The ulema (may God preserve them) left him and said to one another, “How shall we rebut this Persian and send him back to his country in defeat?”

One of them said, “I think we should look for some yokel or bumpkin from the countryside who knows neither sky from earth nor length from breadth. Let's make him our shaykh and dress him like one of the ulema. We'll walk behind him and go with him to the vizier and say to him, ‘This is our shaykh and he will answer the Persian.’ We'll treat the Persian the way he deserves to be treated; we'll set the dog on the swine.”

He and a number of others went to search for someone of that description. They found a country bumpkin, tall, with a broad neck, thick legs, a large beard, wearing a high bonnet on his head, and a woolen cloak that reached to his knees. He was sitting in a shop, eating boiled eggs; he had one egg left when they entered. Seeing them come in he thought they wanted to take his egg from him, so he took it and put it into his bonnet, on the inside. He wanted to make a run for it but they grabbed hold of him. He said, “I'm under your protection, O poets!”

They said, “Don't be scared, fellah, you have nothing to be afraid of.”

“I'm scared that you'll take me to my master and that he'll cut off my head! I've never before been to Cairo in my life before this year. I was hungry and had only four eggs left. I boiled them[1101] and ate three; one is left. I got scared when I saw you and put it inside my bonnet. I owe money to the authorities; I'm in arrears for two piastres!”

“All we want is to do you a favor. If you cooperate with us we'll give you the two piastres, we'll give you a meal and make you happy.”

“Well, if you've got a well to be dug or a wall to be torn down, or earth to be carried or dung, I'll do it in one hour flat! Or if you've got a fight, then give me a cudgel and I'll give them a beating: even if there's a thousand of them, I'll floor them all."

"That is not what we are after. We only want to make you out as our shaykh and present you to a foreigner, a Persian. He will ask you a question and you will answer him and have the better of him. But this Persian will speak in gestures, so you must speak to him the way he speaks to you."

"Take me to the pimp! And if you want me to beat him up I'll punch him in the face and kill him, even if it's in the presence of the sultan or the vizier. I've killed often, and stolen too, when I've had to pay money to the sultan. I'll give that Persian a right drubbing!"

So they took him with them, dressed him up like a jurist, and placed a round turban on top of his bonnet. He put the egg inside his breast pocket and they said to him, "Leave it here until you get back!"

But he replied, "Upon your life, I won't leave it behind 'cause it's the egg of my hen, the first she laid. I'm going to eat it when I get hungry."

So they told him he could keep it on him. They accompanied him to the vizier's, just as they were, and found the Persian sitting before him. The vizier stood up and received them with all honor. They said, "This is our shaykh; he will answer the Persian's questions."

The Persian was sitting down with his legs crossed, the polite way, like a student; the fellah sat down too, but with his legs stretched, and not caring about the formality of the gathering, as if he were in a cattle pen. When the Persian saw this he was greatly impressed; he said to himself, "If this man isn't one of the great ulema he would not show his contempt for the gathering by stretching out his legs in the presence of the vizier!"

Then the Persian asked his questions by means of gestures, demanding an answer. He raised one finger. The fellah put up two fingers. The Persian raised his hand toward the sky. The fellah put one of his hands on the floor. Then the Persian produced a box from his pocket, opened it, took out a small chick, and threw it toward the fellah. The fellah remembered the egg in his bonnet;[1102] he removed it and threw it to the Persian. Thereupon the Persian shook his head and expressed his amazement. He said to the vizier and the other ulema, "He has answered the questions I have put to him. I swear I shall become one of his pupils and followers!"

The vizier then honored the fellah and the ulema, who were victorious. Once they had left they asked the fellah, "We have understood neither the true nature of the questions nor that of the answers. Explain them to us!"

The fellah said, "What a shame! You're jurists but you can't answer people's questions! When I sat opposite him I looked at his face and saw that he had the eyes of a traitor; they were red. He was angry and he gestured to me with his finger, saying 'Careful, or else I'll poke out your eye with this finger of mine!' So I also gestured to him and I said, 'If you poke out my eye with your finger, I'll poke out both your eyes with these two fingers of mine!' and I raised them in his face. Then he lifted his hand toward the roof, telling me, 'If you don't obey I'll crucify you on the roof!' So I put my hand on the floor, telling him, 'If you try to do to me what you're saying I'll wipe the floor with you and beat the demons out of your body!' Now when he saw that I was having the better of him and getting the upper hand, he got out a small chick, showing me that he eats chicken every day and always has fine food and drink. So I produced the boiled egg and showed him that I had a fine meal too, with my boiled egg. That's how I defeated him and answered his questions."

When they heard the fellah's words and understood what he had meant they got up and went to the Persian. They sat with him and asked him about the answers. He said, "All my life I have been questioning scholars and disputing with them like this. But that shaykh of yours is the only one who has understood my questions."

"Tell us about you questions and their true nature!"

"Well, I raised my finger for him, indicating that God is One. Then he raised two fingers for me, indicating that there is no second to God. Then I raised my hand, indicating that God 'has raised up heaven without pillars.'[1103] Then he put his hand on the earth, meaning 'and He spread out the earth on water that had become solid.'[1104] Then I took out the chick for him to see, indicating that «He brings forth the living from the dead.»[1105] And he got out his egg, meaning «and He brings forth the dead from the living.»[1106] Thus he comprehensively answered all my questions. I have never met a more learned person."[1107]

They realized that the fellah had meant one thing and the Persian another, as the poet said:

She went east and I[1108] went west: and O how far
the eastward and the westward bound!

II. The Peasants in the Hammam[1109]

This burlesque story should be compared with the refined and florid description of a visit to the bath by al-Ḥaymī al-Kawkabānī that follows it.

It happened that three country bumpkins wanted to go to town. They traveled until they were close. The oldest, the clever one, said, "Cairo is all Turkish mamluks and soldiers who cut off heads and we're just peasants. If we don't act like them and jabber in Turkish like they do, they'll cut off our heads."

His friends said to him, "Abū Daʿmūm, we don't know Turkish or anything!"

"I learned Turkish ages ago when I sat knee-to-knee with the overseer and the Christian."[1110]

His friends said to him, "Teach us Turkish, then!"

"When we arrive in the town we'll go to the hammam which they say is paradise on earth.[1111] We'll have a bath there and wash our skins. They say there's a deep hole in which they piss and shit. After we've come out of that paradise on earth and we've stood up and wrapped ourselves in our cloaks and are done, I'll say to you, '*Qardāsh* Muḥammad,'[1112] and you say 'Here I am and *hāh nawār*,'[1113] then I'll say, 'Have you got *bīr munqār*?',[1114] meaning 'a *jadīd*;'[1115] then you say '*Yoq yoq*,' meaning 'We've got nothing.' Then the bath superintendent will be afraid of us and he'll say to himself, 'Those are foreign mamluks who will cut off our heads,' and they'll let us go without paying. People will fear us and we'll be like emirs in Cairo. The news about us will spread in the village that we have become emirs and jabber in Turkish and the shaykhs of the village will be afraid of us and they'll stop telling us what to do once and for all."

His friends said, "That's a good proposition, Abū Daʿmūm."

So they set off for Cairo. They asked for the hammam and were shown where it was. They went inside, took off their woolen robes and threw off their cloaks and many layers of clothing until they were naked, just as they would do in ponds and wells. The bath attendant said to them, "Cover yourselves!"

They wanted to grab their mantles to cover themselves, but the servants in the bath threw them some old towels, rejects of the hammam. Reluctantly, they tied these round their private parts, but their genitals remained mostly uncovered, their pricks hanging down. They entered the bath like water buffalo bulls, or billy goats, and went right inside the hammam, where they washed off the dirt and soot. They plunged into the basins like bulls or kids. They came out again, making the floor shake, looking like bulls and cows. They put on their woolen robes and wrapped themselves in those many layers, put their cudgels on their shoulders and wanted to leave without further ado. But the superintendent of the hammam shouted to them, “Hey you pimps, you’ve got to pay, you blackguards!”

The eldest of them turned round and said to his friends, “*Qardāsh* Muḥammad!”

They answered, “Here we are, and *hāh nawār*!”

“Have you got *bīr minqār*?” (meaning a *jadīd* coin).

“*Yoq yoq*!” (meaning, we haven’t got anything).

The bath superintendent said, “You oafs, when did you learn this broken Turkish, and turn yourselves into grandees and emirs? What’s all this shitty Turkish! I swear by God, none of you pimps leaves until he’s paid the fee and extra; else take off your mantles as a security!”

He ordered his servants to pummel and beat them and take their mantles from them. They left and arranged for the money by borrowing it from the people of their village, then retrieved their mantles, and went on their way.

Lyrical Prose: A Visit to the Bath, by al-Ḥaymī al-Kawkabānī[1116]

The Yemenite author al-Ḥaymī (d. ca. 1151/1738) modeled his collection *ʿIṭr nasīm al-ṣabā* (*The Perfume of the Zephyr's Gentle Breeze*) on *Nasīm al-ṣabā* (*The Zephyr's Gentle Breeze*) by Ibn Ḥabīb al-Ḥalabī (d. 779/1377). Both works consist of lyrical "sketches" in rhymed, poetic, "euphuistic" prose, with a slight narrative element, interspersed with verse quotations, always without attribution; the authors say in their introductions (*Nasīm*, p. 35, *ʿIṭr* p. 19) that the prose is theirs, the verse by others (I have not been able to identify all the poets). Though akin to the *maqāmāt* of al-Hamadhānī and al-Ḥārīrī, they are obviously different and not called *maqāmāt* by the authors. They are told by the author's persona. Al-Ḥaymī also wrote a treatise on the bath, called *Ḥadāʾiq al-nammām fī l-kalām ʿalā mā yataʿallaq bil-ḥammām*, ed. ʿAbd Allāh Muḥammad al-Ḥibshī (Beirut, 1986), in which he deals with its religious, legal, medical, and literary aspects. The literary side of the hammam has rather little to do with having a good wash, as is also borne out by the following text. There is a large amount of word play, often wholly untranslatable, some of it explained in the notes. I have again imitated the rhymed prose. The text was chosen because it offers a nice contrast with the preceding story on the Egyptian peasants; and the end of the present text, with its allusions to Paradise, can be compared with the end of the excerpt from Abū l-ʿAlāʾ al-Maʿarrī's *Epistle of Forgiveness* (above, p. 276).

كنت في زُمرة من الأصحاب ☆ وجماعة من لطفاء الأتراب ☆ نتراود في الكلام ☆ وندير كأس المحاورة في دخول الحمّام ☆ فقال من نعتمد عليه ☆ ونلقي مقاليد الرأي إليه ☆ المبادرة إلى الدخول مقصودة ☆ وإزالة الدرن محمودة ☆ وهذا وقت خال عن الشاغل ☆ وأوان ليس بيننا وبين اغتنام اللذّة فيه حائل ☆ والحمام نعمة لا يقوم ببعضها شكر الشاكر ☆ والمريد لحصر مدحه غير قادر ☆ فقلنا ويشهد بذلك قول سيد الأنام ☆ نِعمَ البيت الحمام ☆

*kuntu fī zumratin mina l-ʾaṣḥāb * wa-jamāʿatin min luṭafāʾi l-ʾatrāb * natarāwadu fī l-kalām * wa-nudīru kaʾsa l-muḥāwarati fī dukhūli l-ḥammām * fa-qāla man naʿtamidu ʿalayh * wa-nulqī maqālīda r-raʾyi ʾilayh * ʾal-mubādaratu ʾilā d-dukhūli maqṣūdah * wa-ʾizālatu d-darani maḥmūdah * wa-hādhā waqtun khālin ʿani sh-shāghil * wa-ʾawānun laysa baynanā wa-bayna ghtināmi l-ladhdhati fīhi ḥāʾil * wal-ḥammāmu niʿmatun lā yaqūmu bi-baʿḍihā shukru sh-shākir * wal-murīdu li-ḥaṣri madḥihī ghayru qādir * fa-qulnā wa-yashhadu bi-dhālika qawlu sayyidi l-ʾanām * niʿma l-baytu l-ḥammām **

Chapter 20: The Bath

Once, together with a number of good and gentle friends, * we were talking about various odds and ends, * passing along the cup of conversation on its circular path * and discussing a visit to the bath. * Someone on whom we always relied * and whom we would often let decide, * said, "Such a visit is good for one's health, * as it is laudable to get rid of one's filth. * This is a time of leisure, * when nothing can stand in the way of taking this opportunity for taking this pleasure. * The bath is a blessing by which we are blessed: * sufficient thankfulness for it can never be expressed, * and whoever wants to sing all its praises will never rest." *

We said, "This is attested by the lord of the human race,[1117] * when he said, 'A bath: what a good place!'" *

So we got up and went, anticipating the pleasures it offers, * looking to empty joy's treasures from its coffers, * longing for it as we long for flowers * that yearn for the water of rivers and clouds' showers; * its blazing heat was not our desire, * since each had enough of his own passion's fire. *

I did not seek in the hammam the heat that's burning:
Why should I? In my chest there burn the fires of yearning.
My flood of tears was not enough, for all its seeping:
I came so that from all my limbs I would be weeping.[1118]

On its wide door we knocked, * and by a servant, at our behest, it was unlocked. * We had a good long look at him, * examining his every limb: * he was like a lion cub or the fawn of a gazelle, * casting on the beholder his spell. * His mouth and lips * were purer than rain when it drips, * his face was fairer * than that of the "Turban-wearer."[1119] * He would put to shame the desert's white antelope; * his reply to those wanting to be his lovers would a thousand times be "Nope." * His forehead shone like a lamp, bright; * clear and brilliant was its light; * his side-lock curled like a scorpion's tail that hovers, * ready to sting, above the hearts of his tormented lovers, * or curled like the letter *C* for whose sake the *C* of my Cover * was changed into an *L* and I became his Lover,[1120] * my heart for him aching, * for him all others forsaking; * not like the *C* of Conjunction; *[1121] or else he would not have made me endure humiliating torment with no compunction. *

With *C*-shaped curls he drowns my heart in misery:
I had not thought that one could drown in such a *C*.[1122]

Those who love to browse * on his pitch-black eyebrows * are robbed of sleep, unable to drowse; * sober men are of their senses bereft, * by the wounds in every limb that the arrows of his brow-bow left. *

But for the *Nūn*-curve of his brow—by *Qāf* I swear—
my P-A-T-I-E-N-C- and E would still be there. [1123]

His lashes have corrected * the manners and morals of those by love for him affected; * with his eyes they have set, * to ensnare the lovers, a net. * By his eyes, languid, broken, * many an eyelid has been woken; * when his eyes with languor break * many a heart will ache * and its lifeblood in all their feebleness forcefully they take. * His eyes' darts * were aimed at men's hearts; * the eyes a cutting sword each: * a wondrous figure of speech:[1124] *

His eyelids hide his eyes just as a sword sits in its sheath.
His languid looks are swords: they're sharp and keen beneath.[1125]

His cheeks were soft and lush, * fresh, and with a bright red blush; * in them two opposites seemed to conspire: * moisture and fire. * Hearts were scorched within their rib cages by the glow of each cheek; * seeing their redness all colors seem weak. * The rose and the anemone borrow their hue * from the charm of his cheeks' dew.[1126] * On one there was a mole * that bewitched the observer's soul, * which we began to admire * as a piece of ambergris upon fire. *

Bilāl the Black stands on the surface of this cheek:
he's looking at the dawn that from his forehead shines.[1127]

Like licit magic[1128] his words did sound; * his face was with the crown of glory crowned. * Slimmer than a toothbrush was his waist all round. * I uttered moaning sighs * and thus betrayed to my enemies my love of his eyes. * Thus I found myself possessed and full of folly,* and overcome by melancholy. * My share of happiness lies in his figure, tall like a Khaṭṭī lance; * that he would keep his promise is my last chance! *

When we had given him the sweet fragrance of our salutation * and had made his branch-like body bend to us by the Zephyr of our brilliant conversation, * he took us by the hand as a guide * and welcomed us inside. * We walked on and we undressed * in a room with the vestments of all kinds of joy blessed, * a place filled with all our wishes, * overflowing with everything souls find delicious. * The room was vaulted * and its splendor could not be faulted. * Violets blossoming up between daffodils and lilies from its smooth plaster could be seen;[1129] * the ox-eye of its gold boasted to its sleeve-like leaves of green. * The basin had dresses of every hue: * ruby red, diamond white, jet black, emerald green, and turquoise blue. * The gardens of its carpets were embroidered and with twisting bands ornamented * and with gazelle's musk scented. * We had a short afternoon nap there * and cast off the heavy loads of care. * Then we stripped ourselves of dirt * and did the heavy burden of sorrows desert. *

How much the bath resembles death! To think
of this, it every thinking man enjoins.
Stripped of our wealth and of our clothes we are;
All that is left: a cloth to cover our loins.[1130]

From room to room we roamed * and found each one to be domed. * We enjoyed a large share of the hammam's charms * and it received us with open arms. * It scattered on us its pearly sweat as a sign of respect * and said: "My rising breaths will have on you a wholesome and cooling effect." * It poured on us precious tears that would make Ubullah's canal of little worth,[1131] * and for which the Milky Way's stream would abandon the crescent moons that face it and descend to earth.[1132] * Its echo spoke to us: * "Welcome, people so noble and illustrious!" * It endowed on us the dinars of delight from its lockets * and all its pockets; * it arrayed tables with every dish * that for genial company one could wish; * it circulated the cups full of the wine of pleasure; * and it clothed us in the brocade of relaxing leisure. *

Our bath: so full of fire and water
    that it seemed
we could not possibly be more
    highly esteamed.[1133]

Thus the dirt of bodies and minds was eliminated * and every heart felt elated. * Adorned with the pearls of sweat that dripped, * into our bathrobes we slipped, * and into the henna our hands and feet were dipped.[1134] * The lovely bath gazelle we pinched * and thus our love-thirst was quenched. * From his rosy cheeks he shed the dew of his tears, anguished, * and thereby, it seemed, the fire that burned in our breasts was extinguished. * The silver of his swaying body so tenderly built, * seemed, dyed with henna, as if it were gilt. *

If, in the bath, you saw the henna
on his limbs, his body glowing,
He would entice you with his figure:
solid water and gold flowing.[1135]

He kept flirting with us with his eyes, while he poured * water on us like the tears of those by whom he is adored. *

Our bath gazelle brings water
and pours it on us till it drips.
"A cool, soft drink?" he asked;
"O yes," I said, "from your sweet lips."[1136]

When we had used his services completely * and had thanked him for his favors done so neatly, * we entered a place that was a joy to see,[1137] * a garden for any pleasant company, * one of the earthly paradises, * that with its ornaments entices * like a robe of honor stretching to the horizons * for its fortunate denizens; * pleasures' stopping place, * for all things fine and subtle a gathering-space. * Its flowers were ready to be plucked, its branches in green robes * and with yellow rings on their earlobes. *

Polished smooth is the earth's breast; its perfume
swirling up to praise the showering stars.[1138]

There, brooks streamed forth from wells * and lions were overcome by gazelles.[1139] * Doves were cooing, * waterbasins ever flowing, * the pleasant breeze blew lovingly, * the wine cups' mouths were filled, bubblingly, * the river's applause could be heard * while the treetop hovered over the water like a bird. * Tears of the morning clouds were shed by every narcissus's eye, * while its stars were rising toward a leafy sky.*

The nightingale sings eloquently in
the treetop, while the blackbird merely stammers.

There, among all flowers, the rose is my prize * and the wine-pourer is a girl who has fled from the heavenly damsels of dark eyes. * The anemones are glowing embers where fire still lingers, * and the trees wear signet rings of ruby and carnelian on their fingers. *

The dew has sprinkled water on the treetops' clothes,
seeing the blazing[1140] braziers of its blossom in its skirts.

The violets gave us their turquoises, * we kissed the blood-red cheeks of the roses, * we gathered the well-strung pearls of the chamomile, * and in the willows the wilful breeze came to rest a while. *

The branch, blown in the breeze, is bewildered,
burdened with unbearable yearning.

The soft down of the sweet basil crept on the cheek of the river; * the quicksilver cup of the dew was full and aquiver. * The earrings of the ox-eye throbbed * as if they were lovers' hearts of their senses robbed. * Well-rooted felt every tree, * stretching its branches with glee, * while the right hand of the north wind did not fail * to weave on the water's surface a coat of mail. *

But if the breeze disturbs the water, let it go:
the coat of mail may sink in it.

So we passed from bliss to bliss, * thanking Him who graciously poured over us all of this. * We let our eyes dwell * on every spring and well, * and looked at these branches so various * and blessings multifarious. * We took from the fruits, from us by no means hidden, * of many kinds, "unfailing, unforbidden."[1141] *

The branches' hands reached us their fruits,
out of their leafy sleeves.[1142]

Notes

1 Source: *Dīwān* ed. Charles Lyall (Cambridge: E.J.W. Gibb Memorial Trust, 1931), 23–26 (translation pp. 25–26), ed. Tawfīq Asʿad (Kuwait: Wizārat al-Iʿlām, 1989), 98–100. See Jacobi, "The Origins of the Qasida Form," in Sperl and Shackle (eds.), *Qasida Poetry in Islamic Asia and Africa*, vol. I:21–34 (analysis) and vol. II:64–67 (text and translation), 415 (brief commentary and notes). The following translation owes something to those of Jacobi and Lyall. A sprinkling of alliteration has been added, to compensate for meter and rhyme.

2 A girl's name, very common in early Arabic; it rhymes with "sinned".

3 Name of a place; location unknown.

4 Textiles from Yemen are usually described as striped.

5 *Ṭarab* is "strong emotion, transport," sometimes of joy, often of grief, and at times a mixture of both, e.g. when remembering past joys.

6 Jacobi: "Yet sometimes I soothe;" but in early Arabic *qad* + imperfect often refers to the past, which is obviously better here.

7 The sweetness of the beloved's saliva (even upon waking up) is a very frequent motif in Arabic love poetry, somewhat difficult to render into English; cf. also the poems of ʿUmar ibn Abī Rabīʿah (line 11, p. 32), al-ʿAbbās ibn al-Aḥnaf (line 10, p. 45), and—in a reversed simile—Ibn al-Fāriḍ (line 34, p. 81).

8 Source: *al-Mufaḍḍaliyyāt* (an anthology compiled by al-Mufaḍḍal, d. ca. 163/780), ed. Lyall, vol. I:762–86; ed. Shākir & Hārūn, 390–96 (omitting a few lines that do not appear in all redactions); among other versions, see e.g. al-Akhfash al-Aṣghar, *al-Ikhtiyārayn*, 647–56 and al-Aʿlam al-Shantamarī, *Sharḥ Dīwān ʿAlqamah ibn ʿAbadah*, 17–39. There is some variation in the order of the lines. Earlier translations and studies include: Lyall, *The Mufaḍḍalīyāt: Vol. II: Translation and Notes*, 327–33 (imitating the Arabic meter in English); Stetkevych, "Pre-Islamic Panegyric," 1–58 (on ʿAlqamah and his poem see pp. 2–20); Montgomery, *The Vagaries of the Qaṣīdah*, Ch. 1: "ʿAlqamah's Petition for the Release of his Brother Sha's" (pp. 10–51). Some echoes of these three renderings may be heard in mine.

9 On the *nasīb*, see e.g. Stetkevych, *The Zephyrs of Najd: The Poetics of Nostalgia in the Classical Arabic Nasīb*; Jacobi, entry "Nasīb" in *EI2*, VIII:978–83.

10 As is very common, the poet addresses himself, changing to the first person (and reverting momentarily to the second person in line 7).

11 Rabīʿah is her clan; Tharmadā', its location uncertain, is apparently far away. Several ancient commentators suggest this could mean that the "well" is a grave: she will never come back and will die in Tharmadā'.

12 Montgomery has "diseases [caused by] women," which is a possible reading. Al-Shantamarī glosses it as "women's characters."

13 This is a common, formulaic transition device from *nasīb* to the description of the camel and the desert journey, which in a panegyric poem often leads to the patron (who is here, somewhat unusually, mentioned already in the next line, even though the eulogy proper starts only in line 22).

14 Montgomery takes the *ridāf* to be the "saddlebags at her rear," perhaps because in the poem the poet travels alone.

15 *Ṣabīb* is said to be a tree used for dyeing, or possibly "spilled water," "spilled blood," or "the juice of *ʿandam* (tarragon)." This line, not in Lyall's edition, is placed by some after line 21.

16 The comparison of the poet's camel with an oryx or (as in Dhū l-Rummah's poem below) with an onager (wild ass) is very common. Such comparisons regularly take the form of an inserted narrative episode in which the camel is temporarily forgotten; here it is a mere one line and a half.

17 Unlike the early commentators, Stetkevych and Montgomery make the oryx shelter among the trees, rather than the hunters. It is true that oryxes are often said to shelter in *arṭā* trees, but the syntax suggests that, here, the poet thought fit to vary.

18 "Nearing brought me near" is my rendering of *qarrabatnī ... qarūbū* (where the word *qarūb* is unusual—al-Shantamarī says Qarūb is the camel's name). The odd apostrophe from third to second person is, like line 12, another "false" transition to the eulogy.

19 A traditional address to the Lakhmid kings in pre-Islamic times.

20 *Al-Farqadān* are two stars in Ursa Minor, not far from the Pole Star.

21 There are several versions and interpretations of the names mentioned in connection with the battle. The rider on the black horse is al-Ḥārith; the king left dead at the battlefield is al-Mundhir.

22 Swords were often given proper names.

23 Ghassān is the clan of al-Ḥārith and his dynasty; the other names are different tribes or clans.

24 Apparently an image of thunder. The commentators, probably wrongly, see a reference to the calf of the camel killed by Thamūd, the people to whom the pre-Islamic prophet Ṣāliḥ

preached in vain (Q A'rāf 7:77, Hūd 11:65, Isrā' 17:59, Shu'arā' 26:157, Shams 91:14). See also Jamil, "Playing for Time: Maysir Gambling in Early Arabic Poetry," 75–77.

25 Source: *al-Mufaḍḍaliyyāt*, ed. Shākir & Hārūn, 287–92; annotated English prose translation by Lyall, *The Mufaḍḍalīyāt*, II:228–32.

26 Tribes gather at pasturage during springtime; they separate in summer, ending affairs between lovers.

27 This and the other places are located in eastern Arabia.

28 *Bukht*, here meaning a cross between the Arabian one-humped and the Asian two-humped camel.

29 Reading *raqman* instead of *'ukhrā* (as in the version of the anthology *Muntahā l-ṭalab*).

30 *Thaqqabna*: it is said that the poet got his nickname, "the Piercer," from this verse.

31 The "pledge" may stand for the lover's heart according to the commentator.

32 The feathering of arrows may be a metaphor for the composition of the poem. Lyall wonders if the third person singular pronoun refers to all of the women or only one; I have opted for the latter, connecting *bihā* (contra Lyall's *lahā*) with *bi-talhiyatin*: singing her praises distracts the poet to some extent from his love-pains.

33 The poet addresses himself.

34 This image recurs in several ancient passages. Lyall (pp. 107–98), discarding "demonic" interpretations, prefers a natural one, based upon the antipathy between nomad and sedentary animals. See also Montgomery, "The Cat and the Camel."

35 An allusion to the exertions of the camel, making her lose weight. The repetition of the rhyme-word (*al-waḍīn*, "the girth," cf. line 21) at such short distance is considered a defect.

36 She marks the earth with five callosities (four legs and chest).

37 Apparently alluding to her long neck and generally slim body.

38 Lovers of camel anatomy are referred to the Arab commentators and Lyall for the interpretation of this perplexing verse. It appears that the camel has grown fat, whereas before, more in keeping with poetic convention, she was lean.

39 An early tenth-century critic, Ibn Ṭabāṭabā, finds it silly and unrealistic thus to put words into the camel's mouth (*'Iyār al-shi'r*, p. 200, though he likes lines 1–4 and 42–45). But such verses are not uncommon.

40 An unusual image; as Lyall says, the gaunt frame of the camel is compared to a doorkeeper's hovel near the gate of a great mansion. The word used for "doorman," here the plural *darābinah*, is borrowed from Persian *darbān*.

41 Some think the king of al-Ḥīrah, ʿAmr ibn Hind, is meant. Lyall, following al-Aṣmaʿī (d. ca. 216/831), thinks the poet's tone is too familiar and disrespectful for this to be plausible; the Arab editors disagree.

42 Source: *Dīwān*, ed. ʿAwaḍayn, 212–24; ed. Abū Suwaylim, 290–303.

43 Arabic often uses a singular, as here, where a dual is clearly intended.

44 See the note on the poem "O doves of al-Liwā,", p. 27. It is one of the several expressions meaning "forever".

45 Clans of the tribe of Sulaym; al-Khansāʾ and her brothers belonged to the Khufāf tribe.

46 A difficult line; reading *ẓirrihā* (suggested by the commentary) instead of *ẓahrihā*.

47 The meaning of this verse is unclear.

48 Presumably they gave birth during the campaign and had to leave them; for the same motif see *Dīwān* (ed. ʿAwaḍayn), 45.

49 There is some confusion among the commentators about the precise identity of these two; they seem to belong to the tribe of Murrah, who were involved in the death of Muʿāwiyah, rather than his brother Ṣakhr.

50 The meaning of *al-jarjāris* is obscure.

51 Source: *Naqāʾiḍ Jarīr wal-Akhṭal*, pp. 134–39; I have also used the different redaction in al-Akhṭāl, *Dīwān*, 166–69. Unlike the reply by Jarīr this poem does not open with a *nasīb* but comes straight to the point.

52 The poet is speaking about horses (standing metonymically for the tribes themselves). Tamīm is Jarīr's tribe.

53 Kulayb ibn Yarbūʿ is Jarīr's clan within the Tamīm tribe.

54 Muʿriḍ is a relative of Jarīr's mother; Muʿayd and al-Khaṭafā are his maternal and paternal grandfathers.

55 A line often admired by the critics since much satire is packed in it. At night weary travelers may make barking noises hoping to hear real dogs respond and thus find shelter and hospitality. Jarīr's people extinguish their fire to make it more difficult for them to be found; they have no respect for their mothers; their fires are small (since they can be extinguished by an old woman's urine). In the following line (not in the source text but taken from another redaction) the mother herself is said to be stingy too. See also p.312, in al-Ibshīhī's text.

56 At the battle of Dhū Qār (probably between AD 604 and 611) the tribe of Bakr ibn Wāʾil (descending from Maʿadd, a legendary ancestor of the "North Arabs") defeated their opponents (including Jarīr's tribe Tamīm), who were aided by Persian Sassanid troops.

57 Kisrā: the Arabicized form of Persian Khusraw (Chosroes in Greek), generally used in Arabic for any Sasanid emperor.

58 Shuraḥbīl ibn al-Ḥārith, of the tribe of Kindah, was killed at Kulāb, one of the famous pre-Islamic tribal battles.

59 Various clans.

60 Abū Ḥanash ʿUṣm (or ʿUṣum) ibn al-Nuʿmān belonged to Taghlib Wāʾil, al-Akhṭal's tribe. Al-Ward (meaning "reddish-bay") is the name of his horse.

61 Lahāzim: a confederation of clans within Bakr ibn Wāʾil.

62 Jarīr is often called "son of *al-marāghah*" by his opponents, a word explained as a she-ass that rolls in the dust willing to be mated with. Here he is also called "pregnant," an allusion to an incident often gleefully remembered by Jarīr's enemies: a few men of his tribe had unwittingly drunk milk maliciously mixed with human sperm.

63 Source: *Naqāʾiḍ Jarīr wal-Akhṭal*, pp. 140–46; see also the different redaction in Jarīr, *Dīwān*, 233–39.

64 A very common motif in *nasīb*: the absent beloved appears as a vision, dream, or fantasy *(khayāl)*.

65 Compare line 19 of al-Akhṭal's poem.

66 Dhū l-Bayḍ is said to be a tract in the long and narrow dune desert called al-Dahnāʾ that stretches from northwest to southeast in the Arabian Peninsula; Duwwār is said to be a well in the territory of the Banū Usayyid, a clan of Tamīm.

67 The hide of a slaughtered calf is stuffed and set up as a dummy to stimulate the mother's milk production.

68 Invoking the rain is a very common form of blessing. The Bedouins had a kind of popular meteorology based on the stars; some stars and constellations were associated with rain. See also below, Dhū l-Rummah's poem line 2.

69 Taghlib is Jarīr's tribe.

70 Compare the opening of al-Akhṭal's poem.

71 Khindif is a large tribal confederation that includes Tamīm.

72 Murr is the father of Tamīm, eponymous ancestor of Jarīr's tribe; Khuzaymah is the ancestor of various other tribes.

73 Quraysh is the Prophet's tribe; the Helpers (al-Anṣār) are those Medinans who supported him after the Hijra.

74 Qays ibn ʿAylān is a very large tribal confederation, often mentioned by Jarīr, opponents of Taghlib, al-Akhṭal's tribe; they had great political significance in the Umayyad period. The "fire stick" is a stick that produces fire by means of friction.

75 The appropriation is figurative, for Tamīm does not belong to Qays. But Muḍar (see the next verse), in the genealogy the grandfather of Qays, is also an ancestor of Tamīm (as well as of Quraysh). For the history of the poet's tribes, see e.g. M. Lecker's entries "Taghlib

b. Wā'il" and "Tamīm b. Murr" in *EI2*, X (Leiden: Brill, 2000): 89–93 and 72–76, respectively.

76 Another reference to al-Akhṭal's poem (see line 4).

77 See al-Akhṭal's poem, lines 10–11.

78 See al-Akhṭal's poem, line 17. The men are identified as Jaz' ibn Sa'd ibn 'Adī ibn Zayd and Qa'nab ibn 'Iṣmah ibn Qays ibn 'Āṣim.

79 Bisṭām ibn Qays, of the tribe of Shaybān (Bakr ibn Wā'il) was taken captive at the pre-Islamic battle of al-Ghabīṭ; Ḥajjār ibn Abjar belonged to the tribe of 'Ijl.

80 The clans of Badr ibn 'Amr and Manẓūr ibn Sayyār belonged to the tribe of Fazārah.

81 'Āmir ibn al-Ṭufayl (d. ca. 10/632), of the tribe of 'Āmir ibn Ṣa'ṣa'ah, famous hero and poet, opponent of the Prophet; Ḥārith ibn Ẓālim, legendary hero of the tribe of Murrah. "Ḥāri" is a hypocoristic (shortened form used when addressing someone called Ḥārith or al-Ḥārith).

82 Zuhayr ibn Jadhīmah, hero and head of the 'Abs tribe.

83 Identified as either Ḥuṣayn ibn Ḍamḍam or Ḥuṣayn ibn Ḥumām, both of Murrah.

84 Shamkh: a clan of the tribe of Fazārah.

85 The word *khuzr* means "having narrow eyes" but is obviously meant as an allusion to a pig (*khinzīr*): the tribe of Taghlib were still largely Christian (and therefore pork eaters), as was al-Akhṭal.

86 See al-Akhṭal's poem, lines 1–2. Taghlib, very powerful in pre-Islamic times, had little impact on early Islamic history because they lived in Iraq, relatively far from the political centers of the time (Medina, Damascus), and because they long remained Christian.

87 The Khābūr is a tributary of the Euphrates, in northern Mesopotamia.

88 In other words, al-Akhṭal's father is a swine; compare al-Akhṭal's poem, line 22.

89 In poetry, wine is often compared to blood. The line refers to a judgment by al-Akhṭal in which he pronounced al-Farazdaq to be a better poet than Jarīr. Jarīr suggests that al-Akhṭal was influenced by his mother; in fact, Bishr ibn Marwān, the governor of Iraq, had put pressure on al-Akhṭal, who had at first preferred Jarīr. See Abbott, *Studies in Arabic Literary Papyri, III: Language and Literature*, p. 110.

90 Source: Dhū l-Rummah, *Dīwān*, ed. Abū Ṣāliḥ, 1189–226 (66 lines), ed. Macartney, 77–92 (62 lines).

91 See above, Jarīr's poem, line 10. Al-Thurayyā, the Pleiades, was especially associated with rain.

92 Sells reverses the word order ("Tears, yes"), which does not show the interruptive syntax of the original. Lines 3–4 are an instance of enjambment, which is usually avoided.

93 This verse is not found in all versions, and is omitted by Sells. It sounds rather like a variation of the following line. The word translated as "heart" is *kabid*, literally "liver", the seat of passions.

94 Note that the poet addresses himself here, after having used the first person singular. This is not because of metrical necessity: he could have said *fu'ādiya* "my heart" instead of *fu'ādika*. Such changes are very common in poetry.

95 Sells's "right flank turned to the camel mounts" suggests that the gazelle is coming from the left, but it is the other way round (though the ancient explanations are sometimes confusing and seem to suggest the opposite). What matters is that the root *S-N-Ḥ* stands for a good omen; compare below, line 30.

96 Mushrif, in the dune desert called al-Dahnā' (see above, note 66), is mentioned several times by Dhū l-Rummah.

97 The line describes the smoothness, softness, and straightness of her arms and legs by comparing them to twigs of a plant that dictionaries give as *Asclepias gigantea* and others as "calotrope" (*Calotropis procera*, a plant used in securing and fortifying dunes, and which at least explains the second hemistich). The word for "wristlet" is *ʿāj*, which also means "ivory". One commentator says that they are made of ivory; another specifies that they are made "of the backbones of a sea animal."

98 In Arabic poetry buttocks are erotic, not normally (as often in western literature) associated with obscenity and jocularity; see Bauer, *Liebe und Liebesdichtung in der arabischen Welt*, p. 309 n. 111. It poses a problem for the translator.

99 "Where her tears flow down" is a poetic way of saying "cheeks," more or less as Early English uses *kennings* (e.g. *hron-rād*, "whale's riding place" means the sea). This does not imply that she is crying: that is the lover's task. "Loosely" implies, as a commentator explains, that she has a slender belly.

100 A way of saying that she has a long neck, a sign of beauty.

101 These verses describe her teeth, white as chamomile flowers, cool and fresh as dew: a standard topos in Arabic love poetry. Twigs of the thorny *arāk* tree serve as toothbrushes; it is suggested that her sweet breath lends its fragrance to the twig.

102 This line is not found in Abū Ṣāliḥ's edition.

103 Dhū l-Rummah took this motif from Tamīm's poem line 9: "Suppose Dahmá' would speak to a deaf-mute, he would speak loud, almost, and clear."

104 The rhyme-word *burraḥū* (cognate with the rhyme-word of the preceding line *mubarriḥū* "painful") means "coming from the left," an evil omen (cf. line 15).

105 Crows traditionally announce, and therefore symbolize, lovers' separation.

106 The "rod of parting" is proverbial. The "changing" of Mayyah's plans may be her own doing, but the wording allows the possibility that others have decided for her, which is probably what happened (see line 35). It turns out (in the next line) that she is married.

107 The poet very often uses the shortened form Mayy instead of Mayyah (twice in this line, and in lines 1, 11, 14, 34 twice, 37, 40, 66a), usually for metrical reasons. I have done the same in two places. One supposes that the husband is saddened by the arrival of male rivals who have traveled from afar.

108 The bull is an oryx. Aṭlāl is the poet's camel, or his horse, according to different commentators. That his camel is called Ṣaydaḥ in line 51 seems to confirm that lines 41–42 do not really belong to the poem.

109 The locusts are said to hop as if unable to stand still on the hot earth.

110 *Ṣaydaḥ* ("Shouter"), among countless camels described in poetry, is one of the few known by name. She appears four times in Dhū l-Rummah's verse.

111 A woman who marries outside her own clan has no friends or relatives to tell her how she looks and would often have to use her mirror, which she keeps in good shape.

112 The more or less extended comparison of a camel to a wild ass or onager is very common in early Arabic poetry. On the onager passage see Bauer, *Altarabische Dichtkunst*. Bauer discusses 83 passages in detail, 14 of them by Dhū l-Rummah, including the present one (II: 442–43).

113 Lances are often said to be "from Khaṭṭ," said to be a place name near Bahrain. See also below, al-Buḥturī's poem, line 14, al-Mutanabbī's poem, line 11, and al-Ḥaymī's text, below, pp. 345ff..

114 A slightly perplexing image for "standing motionless," which builds on a similar comparison by an older poet, al-Shammākh, who died in the middle of the seventh century: "[The female onagers] stand still as if birds are perched upon their heads [not wanting to disturb them]." The image has persisted and is found in twentieth-century Arabic.

115 The line takes up the description of the she-camel again.

116 On this line, see my introduction to the poem.

117 Sources: al-Iṣfahānī, *Aghānī*, V:233–34, anonymous, sung by Ibrāhīm al-Mawṣilī; ibid., XII:47 attributed to "a Bedouin," sung by Muḥammad ibn al-Ḥārith ibn Buskhunnar.

118 For two stories from the same work see below, "Lives of the Poets" (pp. 123f.) and "Bedouin Romance" (pp. 127ff.).

119 Source: Majnūn Laylā, *Dīwān*, 44–45.

120 Compare, from the poem in the same meter and rhyme by Bashshār ibn Burd, *Dīwān*, I:272: "I drew her likeness and sat down, complaining / to her about what I have encountered, lamenting, // Speaking to a vague form of her in the dust / like someone who seeks

protection from torment, // As if I complained to her about / my sorrows, whereas my complaint is to the dust." It is unclear why Magda Al-Nowaihi considers this to be an elegy on his wife rather than a love-plaint; see Al-Nowaihi, "Elegy and the Confrontation of Death in Arabic Poetry," pp. 13–14.

121 The Arabic for "possessed" is *majnūn* (from the same root as *jinn* "jinnees, demons").

122 Source: *Dīwān*, I:27; cf. al-Iṣfahānī, *Aghānī*, I:103–4.

123 The Station (*al-Maqām*) is the place where Abraham/Ibrāhīm prayed to God (cf. Q Baqarah 2:125); identified as a spot near the Kaaba in Mecca. The Stone is the black stone (said to be a meteorite) encased in the Kaaba.

124 The girls are circumambulating the Kaaba as part of their pilgrimage rituals.

125 The verb *ghamaza* can mean "winking, signaling" but also "touching" (which would not be wholly impossible in the crowd of pilgrims); I have opted for the less daring translation.

126 "Stoning the Devil" with a number of pebbles is another part of the pilgrimage ritual. Instead of the edition's *shakl*, I read *shikl* ("coquetry, flirtation").

127 Source: Ibn Abī Ṭāhir Ṭayfūr, *Balāghāt al-nisāʾ* (ed. Beirut, 1987), 330–31, (ed. Cairo, 1908), 200.

128 Reading *damʿuhā* instead of the unmetrical *damuhā* their "blood."

129 Three syllables are lacking; they could be, for instance, *wa-ḥubbī* or *gharāmī.*

130 Both editions have *al-Ḥājī*, which does not scan; the emendation *al-Ḥājibī* is a guess, inspired by two anonymous lines (*ṭawīl*, rhyme *-rū*) in Ibn Dāwūd al-Iṣbahānī, *al-Zahrah*, 418.

131 The word *ẓill* can be "shadow" as well as "shade"; both senses are possible here, the former stressing close inseparability and the latter protection (as in the following line).

132 Unable to make sense of *yḥṣrū* I have added a dot and derived it from the verb *khaṣira* "to suffer from cold (in the hands, feet)."

133 Source: Bashshār ibn Burd, *Dīwān*, I:389–91; cf. Beeston, *Selections from the poetry of Baššār*, 11–12 (Arabic), 50–52 (translation); the translation was published again, with some minor changes, in a chapter by Gregor Schoeler on Bashshār and other poets, in *ABL*, 279–80. For a (shortened) German translation, see Schoeler, "Ein Wendepunkt in der Geschichte der arabischen Literatur," 296–97. For an earlier version of the present translation see van Gelder, "An Experiment with Beeston, Labīd and Baššār."

134 If Bashshār claims Caesar as his ancestor it is not necessarily because he literally claims Roman as well as Persian descent: mentioning Caesar (Qayṣar) and Chosroes (Kisrā) together is a topos.

135 This line is followed by an obviously corrupt line, which (like Beeston) I have not translated.

136 As the editor of the *Dīwān* and Beeston remark, this may be a poetic license since Aleppo has only one river.

137 The editor and Beeston point out that the Abbasid armies never got as far as Tangier.

138 This line is followed by an obscure line, omitted by Beeston and me; it seems to congratulate Abū l-Faḍl, identifiable as al-ʿAbbās, eponymous ancestor of the Abbasids and kinsman of the Prophet.

139 Source: Abū Nuwās, *Dīwān*, vol. IV:15. For a German translation, see Wagner, *Abū Nuwās*, 50–51; for a study of this poem, see Schoeler, "Arabistische Literaturwissenschaft und Textkritik," 329–31.

140 For an introduction to Abū Nuwās, see Kennedy, *Abu Nuwas: A Genius of Poetry*.

141 Source: Abū Nuwās, *Dīwān*, IV:178–80.

142 See Abū Nuwās, *Dīwān*, IV:141–42, also al-Thaʿālibī, *Thimār al-qulūb*, 553–54, both ascribing the passage to al-Jāḥiẓ, who may not have been an Arab but usually took up the cause of the Arabs. On the subject of homoerotic poetry see e.g. Wright and Rowson (eds), *Homoeroticism in Classical Arabic Literature*; Bauer, *Liebe und Liebesdichtung*; and El-Rouayheb, *Before Homosexuality in the Arab-Islamic World, 1500–1800*.

143 This kind of enjambment, with a relative pronoun at the end of a line, is rare and generally disapproved.

144 Source: *Dīwān*, III:106–7. For other poetic English renderings of this epigram, see e.g. Tuety, *Classical Arabic Poetry*, 201, and Colville, *Poems of Wine and Revelry: The khamriyyat of Abu Nuwas*, 42.

145 On the genre and Abū Nuwās's role, see e.g. Kennedy, *The Wine Song in Classical Arabic Poetry*.

146 Source: *Dīwān*, III:126–29. In the edition by al-Ghazālī, p. 28, lines 2–3, 6–7, 11, 14 have been expurgated. For another translation, see Colville, *Poems of Wine and Revelry*, 53–54.

147 Reading *hujr* instead of the *Dīwān*'s *hajr* ("separation, forsaking").

148 The commentator of the *Dīwān* adds: "He means their stomachs are empty."

149 Source: *Dīwān*, II:73–74.

150 See e.g. van Gelder, "Waspish Verses: Abū Nuwās's Lampoons on Zunbūr Ibn Abī Ḥammād." On the genre and its mixed reception, see also van Gelder, *The Bad and the Ugly: Attitudes Towards Invective Poetry (Hijāʾ) in Classical Arabic Literature*.

151 Source: al-ʿAbbās ibn al-Aḥnaf, *Dīwān* (ed. Beirut), 72–73.

152 *Dīwān*, 180 (*basīṭ*, rhyming in *-āsī*). For the motif, see also the poem by Umm Khālid, pp. 33ff..

153 *Miswāk* is usually translated as "toothpick," but it is a toothbrush rather than a toothpick; see also p. 23 and note 101, above.

154 On ʿUlayyah, see Gordon, "The Place of Competition: The Careers of ʿArīb al-Ma'mūniyyah and ʿUlayyah bint al-Mahdī, Sisters in Song;" al-Samarai, *Die Macht der Darstellung. Gender, sozialer Status, historische Re-Präsentation: zwei Frauenbiographien aus der frühen Abbasidenzeit*; Caswell, *The Slave Girls of Baghdad*, 96–123.

155 She would only drink date wine or sing when she was having her period; see al-Ṣūlī, *al-Awrāq (Ashʿār awlād al-khulafā')*, 55; al-Iṣfahānī, *Aghānī*, X:163. Menstruation exempts a woman from performing the ritual prayer.

156 Sources: al-Iṣfahānī, *Aghānī*, X:165, al-Ṣūlī, *al-Awrāq (Ashʿār awlād al-khulafā')*, 71.

157 A technical flaw: the correct form *yunshara* does not fit the meter.

158 Source: al-Ṣūlī, *al-Awrāq (Ashʿār awlād al-khulafā')*, 74.

159 Arabic *ḥalfā'*, also known as alfa or esparto grass; cf. the collection of proverbs by al-Maydānī (d. 518/1123), *Majmaʿ al-amthāl*, I:449: "quicker than fire in halfa grass."

160 Literally "I would remain between the door and the house," i.e. in a state of uncertainty.

161 Source: al-Ṣūlī, *al-Awrāq (Ashʿār awlād al-khulafā')*, 65.

162 Source: Abū l-ʿAtāhiyah, *Dīwān*, 341–42. There is a German prose translation by Oskar Reşer (Rescher), *Der Dîwân des Abû 'l-ʿAtâhija, Teil I: Die zuhdijjât*, 219.

163 The editor (following the Beirut edition, 1886, p. 238) assumes that the rhyme ends in *-ām*, making the meter one syllable shorter. But since all thirteen rhyme-words can be read with the ending *-āmū* it is better to take this as the intended rhyme.

164 Source: Ibn al-Rūmī, *Dīwān*, 1029. For a translation with analysis, see Schoeler, "Ibn ar-Rūmī's Gedicht über die Dichtung und seine Gedankenlyrik," and its English version: "On Ibn al-Rūmī's Reflective Poetry: His Poem about Poetry". Following Schoeler (and supported by another redaction), I have decided to reverse the order of lines 7 and 8.

165 On Ibn al-Rūmī, see Gruendler, *Medieval Arabic Praise Poetry: Ibn al-Rūmī and the Patron's Redemption*, and McKinney, *The Case of Rhyme versus Reason: Ibn al-Rūmī and his Poetics in Context.*

166 The pre-Islamic convention of addressing two companions survived for centuries.

167 Source: Ibn al-Rūmī, *Dīwān*, 1653–58.

168 He should not be confused with the earlier Abū ʿAbd al-Raḥmān ʿAbd al-Malik ibn Ṣāliḥ al-Hāshimi, who died in 199/814.

169 See Ullmann, *Der Neger in der Bildersprache der arabischen Dichter*, 168–174.

170 Al-Ablaq was the name of the legendary castle, near Taymā' in northwestern Arabia, belonging to the pre-Islamic Jewish-Arab poet and hero al-Samaw'al ibn ʿĀdiyā', a paragon of loyalty. It was said to be built of red and white stone.

171 "Buying praise" is of course meant as a metaphor: praise is earned by his great generosity (but in reality it happens that praise is bought literally, of course; the irony will not have been lost on Ibn al-Rūmī and his contemporaries). That ʿAbd al-Malik ibn Ṣāliḥ was not quite as generous as the poet would have wished becomes clear toward the end of the poem (lines 73–74) in three other complaining poems on him (see the *Dīwān*, 1595–97, 2317–18).

172 The verse is not wholly clear but I believe *al-riyaq* should be emended to *al-ribaq*.

173 The meaning seems to be that he protects his reputation by giving money away.

174 Literally, *kal-saṭr... lā l-laḥaq* seems to mean approximately "like a (proper) line (in a letter), not like a postscript."

175 The story of Exod. 14 was known to the Muslims (see e.g. Q Baqarah 2:49–50, Anfāl 8:54).

176 I am not wholly certain of the correctness of the translation. The word *muṭrib* suggests that it is about singing.

177 The English pun is supposed to represent a more intricate Arabic one: "well-being" is *salāmah*, "peace" is *silm* and (the second time) *salām*; as the following verse mentions, the singer's nickname or teknonym (*kunyah*) is Abū Sulaymān, from the same root *S-L-M*.

178 The legendary people of ʿĀd are often mentioned in the Qur'an; they flourished in Arabia soon after the time of Noah and perished after rejecting their prophet Hūd. They were supposed to be very large, cf. Q Aʿrāf 7:69 (trans. A. J. Arberry): «He appointed you as successors after the people of Noah, and increased you in stature broadly»; i.e. between sixty and one hundred cubits tall, according to various authorities (see al-Thaʿlabī, *Qiṣaṣ al-anbiyā'*, 53).

179 I do not know what is meant by this strange line. If the "thing" is the wineglass, as the following lines make clear, perhaps the fly will be overcome by the powerful smell, or else, it will crash into the invisible glass.

180 The glass, nearly invisible, seems to be the (forbidden) wine it contains (but then "its drinkers" would be a strange image).

181 *Ghāliyah* and *sukk* are well-known, expensive compound perfumes (*ghāliyah* means "expensive").

182 This rather difficult, artful verse contains paronomasia (*ḥubb* "love" and *ḥabbat al-qulūb* "the kernel of hearts") and hints at the expression *suwaydā' al-qalb*, "heart of hearts", literally "the little black thing of the heart."

183 The *Dīwān* has the euphemism *han* ("little thing"); other old sources (al-Ḥuṣrī, *Zahr*, 276, al-Tujībī, *al-Mukhtār min shiʿr Bashshār*, 243) have the straightforward "two-letter word" "*ḥir*".

184 The text has wrongly *kharr* instead of *khazz*.

185 Al-Ḥuṣrī says (*Zahr*, p. 274) that the poet was asked to provide a full description; he recalls (pp. 276–77) the verses ascribed to the pre-Islamic poet al-Nābighah al-Dhubyānī, who in an ode for the king of al-Ḥīrah had described imagined sex with the king's wife al-Mutajarridah, and consequently got into trouble (see e.g. Ibn Qutaybah, *al-Shiʿr wal-shuʿarāʾ*, p. 166).

186 The last three words render the Arabic *bahaq*, the same rhyme-word as in line 44 (where I translated it as "albino-pale"). It may indicate a skin disease. Lines 69–70 look out of place and are better inserted, it seems, after line 64.

187 I do not quite understand this verse. The "robe of honor," as is clear from what follows, is not "blackness" but the poem itself, continuing line 65. Apparently those jealous of the patron for being given this ode will waste away from spite.

188 The idiom is derived from milking camels: *fīqah* is the amount of milk that accumulates between two milkings. The poet seems to imply that he has been "milking" the patron in vain with his odes.

189 Iskāf lies some 45 miles southeast of Baghdad on the River Nahrawān, a tributary of the Tigris. "The Monastery" (al-Dayr) is probably Dayr al-ʿĀqūl, a few miles south of Iskāf.

190 Source: al-Buḥturī, *Dīwān*, IV:2087–92. For partial prose translations and an analysis of the nature description, see Schoeler, *Arabische Naturdichtung*, 154–61, also Meisami, *Structure and Meaning in Medieval Arabic and Persian Poetry*, 366–68.

191 The word *khayāl* has many meanings, including "apparition, shadow, imagination, fantasy." Here it refers above all to the very common motif in *nasīb* of the nightly apparition of the beloved to the lover, be he dreaming, daydreaming, or hallucinating (see Jarīr's poem above and ʿAbd al-Qāhir's discussion below, pp. 17, 281).

192 Happy days are short, bad days seem long, but in youth this is no great matter, says the poet.

193 The extremely common motif of "tears of blood" is a hyperbole for having bloodshot eyes.

194 He uses the old, pre-Islamic formula *inʿamū ṣabāḥan.*

195 The word *fatā* literally means "young man," but in a panegyric context it has strong heroic connotations, making "young man" too tame. In Ibn al-Rūmī's *qaṣīdah* above, line 5, I have translated it as "valiant man."

196 Literally, "the nights"; cf. below, line 12 of al-Mutanabbī's poem.

197 Nizār and Yaʿrub are the legendary ancestors of the North and South Arabs, respectively.

198 It is customary to compare a generous person with a "*baḥr*", mostly translated as "sea," although the word is also used for any big river, which, in view of the connotations of fertility, may be more appropriate.

199 "Ill," of course, for his enemies. In this line the poet apostrophizes the patron, changing to the second person, a common feature of eulogies. The Arabic term for this, *iltifāt*, literally means "turning," and one imagines that the poet actually turned toward his patron when reciting.

200 The second hemistich (*ta'akhkhara min mas'ātihim mā taqaddamā*) is not wholly clear to me.

201 Said to be mountains overlooking Tabūk, in northwestern Arabia (Yāqūt, *Muʿjam al-buldān*), or, more vaguely "the name of a mountain in the desert" (Ibn Manẓūr, *Lisān al-ʿarab*, s.v. *Sh-R-Y*).

202 *Naw-rūz*, Persian for New Year's Day, coincided with the vernal equinox (although at other times it was equated with the summer solstice).

203 Interpreting *mā*, like Schoeler, as an interrogative. One could also, like Meisami, take *mā* as a negative ("It does not imprison the wine... nor forbid the strings...").

204 Meisami interprets sun, moons, and stars as the hierarchy of patron, boon-companions, and servants, which seems possible, although it is more likely that the stars are the wine-cups (mentioned in the following verse), a very common simile in Bacchic poetry.

205 Source: *Dīwān*, with commentary by al-Wāḥidī, ed. F. Dieterici [= Dietrich], 548–56. Text and another English translation in Arberry, *Arabic Poetry: A Primer for Students*, 84–91. See the studies by Latham, "Towards a Better Understanding of al-Mutanabbī's Poem on the Battle of al-Ḥadath;" Hamori, "The Siege of al-Ḥadath;" idem, *The Composition of Mutanabbī's Panegyrics to Sayf al-Dawla*, passim; idem, "al-Mutanabbī," in *ABL*, 308–10.

206 An introduction to al-Mutanabbī is Larkin, *Al-Mutanabbi: Voice of the ʿAbbasid Poetic Ideal.*

207 *Nusūr* are vultures, sometimes wrongly rendered as "eagles." This and the next line offer a variation on the old motif of scavenging birds and other carrion-eaters rejoicing when a battle results in much carnage; cf. also line 30. "Offering oneself as someone's ransom" is a common way of expressing respect and devotion.

208 Al-Ḥadath, a fortress on the frontier with the Byzantine Empire, is said to have been called "Red" either because of its red soil (Yāqūt, *Muʿjam al-buldān*) or because of the Byzantine blood shed there. The two "wine-pourers" are the clouds and the bodies of the slain. The word *sāqī*, used here, is often used for the cup-bearer, the person serving (red) wine.

209 See the passage above by Dhū l-Rummah. With this verse the poet turns from third to second person singular. Also see note 113 re: Khaṭṭī lances.

210 *Al-layālī*, "the nights," often has connotations of fate and destiny.

211 The "preventing prefixes" (*jawāzim*) are the particles governing the jussive, viz. *lā* ("don't... !"), *li-* ("let him... !") and *lam* ("he didn't...").

212 These "Russians" (*Rūs*) were in fact the Varangian Guard; the Varangians were originally Scandinavians ("Vikings") who had settled in Rusland.

213 The enemy army is compared to a bird; "coverts" (*khawāfī*) are the feathers covering the quill-bases of wings and tail.

214 Spears are often said to be "Rudaynī," allegedly after a legendary woman called Rudaynah skilled in making spears. Fighting with spears is "despised" as being less heroic than fighting at close quarters with swords. The honorific name Sayf al-Dawlah means "Sword of the Dynasty" (cf. line 44).

215 Wordplay on *fatḥ*, which means "opening" as well as "victory."

216 A nearby hill (literally, "the little hunchback").

217 The poet uses a foreign word (*dumustuq*), the Byzantine title of the enemy commander, whose "neck blames his face" because it would rather retreat.

218 In poetry good swords are often said to be from Mashraf, after an obscure location (see the various explanations in Yāqūt, *Muʿjam al-buldān*, s.v. "Mashārif").

219 Being glad to give is normally a characteristic of a generous person; but the Domesticus is glad to give everything to save his life.

220 The Arabs are traditionally divided into the "South Arabs," descended from Qaḥṭān, and the "North Arabs," descended from ʿAdnān. Rabīʿah (to whom Sayf al-Dawlah belonged) and Muḍar are the two main branches of the North Arabs.

221 The verses of a poem are very often likened to pearls that are strung (*naẓm* means "stringing" as well as "versifying").

222 Sayf al-Dawlah had given the poet some horses.

223 Source: Ibn Khafājah, *Dīwān*, 24. For a prose translation and analysis of this epigram, see al-Nowaihi, *The Poetry of Ibn Khafājah: A Literary Analysis*, 113–14.

224 Instead of *qaṭrin jāmidin* a variant has *quṭrin ʿāṭilin* "an unadorned country" (cf. Al-Nowaihi).

225 Source: *Dīwān*, 11.

226 Translator's license: the original has *qurṣan* ("a disk").

227 The light, shining through the filled glasses, seems to dye the hands.

228 Sources: Ibn Bishrī, *ʿUddat al-jalīs*, 187–88; Ibn al-Khaṭīb, *Jaysh al-tawshīḥ*, 26–28; Monroe, *Hispano-Arabic Poetry*, 248–51 (with translation); Stern, *Hispano-Arabic Strophic Poetry*, 161–65 (with translation).

229 The transcription given below is Monroe's but it is rejected by others; cf. Jones, *Romance Kharjas in Andalusian Muwaššaḥ Poetry*, 76–84, Zwartjes, *Love Songs from al-Andalus: History, Structure and Meaning of the Kharja*, 239.

230 Uttered by pilgrims during the Hajj at various stages.

231 Used for the ritual "stoning of the devil" during the Hajj.

232 Translation uncertain; Monroe has "Joy after him may choose whom it wills," Stern has "yet after him other company counts for naught".

233 The *kharjah* or final strophe is usually in the form of a quotation, spoken or sung, often (but not here) by a woman. Monroe reads the last three obscure lines as as *mw l-ḥabīb ʾnfrmw dhy mw ʾmr | kʾn dhʾy shnʾr | ynqys ʾm byn kshʾd mw lghʾr,* tentatively to be read as *meu l-ḥabīb enfermo de meu amar | que no ha d'estar?| non ves a mibe que s'ha de no llegar.* They are translated by him as "My beloved is sick for love of me. How can he not be so? Do you not see that he is not allowed near me?" In the translation, French has been chosen, as being the reader's most likely second language (compare Paul McCartney's "Michelle").

234 Sources: Ibn Sanāʾ al-Mulk, *Dār al-ṭirāz,* ed. al-Rikābī, ed. 1949, pp. 56–58, ed. 1977, pp. 76–78; Ibn al-Khaṭīb, *Jaysh al-tawshīḥ,* pp. 273–74. Another English translation in Compton, *Andalusian Lyrical Poetry and Old Spanish Love Songs*, pp. 21–23.

235 The sartorial title is inspired by the term *muwashshaḥah,* which is derived from *wishāḥ*, "sash", on account of the fixed rhyme that recurs like patterned embroidery on clothing.

236 See ed. 1977, p. 76, note.

237 A reference (one of thousands in Arabic homoerotic verse) to the incipient beard of the boy, harbinger of the end of the affair.

238 Earlier poets said the skin of the beloved was so tender that it could be hurt by mere glances; the present poet imagines that the boy's cheek could bleed (or blush) from mere imagination.

239 A dark lock of hair (the snake) hangs over the red cheek (*ʿandam*, brazilwood, is a reddish wood used for dyeing).

240 It seems that the (white) Nabataeans and the Zanj (East African Blacks, not Ethiopians as Compton has it, pp. 22 and 68–69) stand for the bright face and the black hair, respectively; compare a verse by ʿAbd al-Muḥsin al-Ṣūrī (d. 419/1028) quoted in al-Thaʿālibī, *Yatīmat al-dahr*, I:308: "You, on whose cheek there are two armies of Negroes and Byzantines".

241 A reference to Moses/Mūsā, see Q Qaṣaṣ 28:29ff..

242 Camphor is pure white. The boy has a slim waist and a big behind, in accordance with the beauty standards of Arabic erotic verse, whether on girls or boys.

243 That is, "with my own life," although oddly the next line seems to suggest that he is prepared to give his father's life as a ransom, and therefore I am tempted to read *wa-ʾin yattam* as *wa-ʾin tayyam* "though he makes (me) a slave of love." The concept of "ransoming someone with one's own or one's father's life" is very common way in Arabic to express love and devotion. The earlier line "How dear to me" is literally "With my father('s life I would ransom)."

244 One could read either *ʾamālahā n-nahd* "the breasts make her sway" or *ʾa-mā lahā n-nahd* "Ah, what breasts she has!" The twig (body) is clothed in leaves (mantle) and flowers with roses (cheeks).

245 This erotic motif has a long history; see e.g. Jarīr, *Dīwān*, p. 844, who mentions "the knocking of anklets against bracelet" in a rape scene, or Abū Nuwās, who makes a girl say "Gently, you're hurting me and you've joined my anklet to my earring" (*Dīwān*, II:61, V:383).

246 Source: Carra de Vaux, *La Ḳaçîdah d'Avicenne sur l'âme* (with French prose translation); for other versions with differences in wording or verse order, see e.g. Ibn Abī Uṣaybiʿah, *ʿUyūn al-anbāʾ fī ṭabaqāt al-aṭibbāʾ*, ed. A. Müller, II:10–11; Ibn Khallikān, *Wafayāt al-aʿyān*, II:160–61; al-ʿĀmilī, *al-Kashkūl*, 415–16. For earlier verse translations into English, see Browne, *A Literary History of Persia*, II:110–11, and Arberry, *Avicenna on Theology*, 77–78.

247 Quoted by Ibn Qayyim al-Jawziyyah, *Rawḍat al-muḥibbīn*, 140.

248 The word *ʿārif* "one who knows" often refers to mystics; Ibn Sīnā, though not really a mystic himself, was certainly closer to mysticism than many other philosophers.

249 The letters in the original of lines 6–7 are *H* (*hubūṭ*), *M* (*markaz*), and *Th* (*thaqīl*), respectively. One wonders if there is more to it: like many of his contemporaries, Ibn Sīnā practiced esoteric letter symbolism. Is it relevant that *H* and *M* are associated with fire and *Th* (of *thaqīl*, "heavy") with earth? The commentators are silent on this point. Browne sees a "downward curve" in the letters *H* and *M* and sees a pun in the name of the letter *Th* (*thāʾ* "defect") but I cannot follow him here. Dhāt al-Ajraʿ sounds like a typical desert toponym ("The Sandy Tract") but is not mentioned as a real place by the lexicographers; the commentary used by Carra de Vaux believes that it refers to the physical world (hence his negative rendering "*sur une terre desséchée*"). Syntactically, however, it is perhaps better connected with "her Station," in which case it should have a positive connotation (a very similar place-name, al-Jarʿāʾ, has such a connotation in the mystical poem by Ibn al-Fāriḍ translated below, line 36).

250 Source: Abū l-ʿAlāʾ al-Maʿarrī, *al-Luzūmiyyāt*, II:147. For earlier translations, see Nicholson, *Studies in Islamic Poetry*, 186, and (for a much freer version) Wightman and al-Udhari, *Birds Through a Ceiling of Alabaster*, 103.

251 Source: *al-Luzūmiyyāt*, II:431; compare Nicholson, *Studies*, 186.

252 Source: *al-Luzūmiyyāt*, II:330.

253 Source: *al-Luzūmiyyāt*, I:246–47; a rhyming translation in Nicholson, *Studies*, 85.

254 See below, note 533.

255 Source: *al-Luzūmiyyāt*, II:208. A rhymed translation of four of its six verses in Nicholson, *Studies*, 167.

256 This line begins with *qāla* "he said"; it is not clear who is speaking.

257 The Arabic has *al-ḥanīfah*, a synonym of *al-ḥanīfiyyah* or *al-dīn al-ḥanīf*, usually referring to Islam; Nicholson translates it as "Moslems."

258 I was tempted, for reasons of prosody, to translate *dīn* as "faith"; but I decided to resist the fashionable trend of replacing "religion" with "faith," as if the two were synonymous. The Arabic for "faith" would be *īmān*.

259 Source: *Dīwān*, ed. Scattolin, 162–65; ed. Beirut, 1962, 145–47; a translation with useful commentary by Arberry, *The Mystical Poems of Ibn al-Fāriḍ*, 27–34; another, less reliable translation by Wheeler M. Thackston, Jr. in Lichtenstadter, *Introduction to Classical Arabic Literature*, 312–14. For a good translation together with the commentary by the important mystic ʿAbd al-Ghanī al-Nābulusī (d. 1143/1731), see Th. Emil Homerin, "'On the Battleground:' Al-Nābulusī's Encounters with a Poem by Ibn al-Fāriḍ." See also, by the same author: *ʿUmar Ibn al-Fāriḍ: Sufi Verse, Saintly Life* and *From Arab Poet to Muslim Saint: Ibn al-Fāriḍ, His Verse, and His Shrine*.

260 The lover is fatally struck by the glance of the beloved; neither the slain nor the slayer is guilty.

261 In this poem many words for "love" and "passion" are used (*hawā, gharām, jawā, wajd, ḥubb, maḥabbah*); it is difficult to translate them all differently and "love" has to do heavy duty.

262 Wasting away, the lover has become invisible. In a mystical sense this stands for the *fanāʾ* or "annihilation" of the mystic's self.

263 The slanderer (cf. line 39), like the reproacher (cf. lines 20–21, 27) and the spy or chaperone, is one of the stock personages in love poetry.

264 The "lovers" are the mystics.

265 "Those who know" (*al-ʿārifūn*) is a common term for the mystics. The verse puns on *ʿārif* ("knower"), *muʿtarif* ("confessing") and, implicitly, *ʿarf* ("scent").

266 The perfect balance of the two hemistichs is paralleled in the sounds: *wa-ʾin nawā sāʾiran yā muhjatī rtaḥilī / wa-ʾin naʾā zāʾiran yā muqlatī btahijī*.

267 The two adjectives, *barr* and *raḥīm* (*raʾūf* in the Beirut edition) are often applied to God.

268 He tells his critics not to meddle with the lovers/mystics. The word *ḥayy* ("tribe, quarter") could also mean "living" (an epithet of God).

269 In love poetry the bright teeth of the beloved when smiling are often compared to lightning; the word *falaj* means "gap (between the teeth)," "parting (between the lips)," as well as "dawn".

270 *munʿaraj al-jarʿāʾ*: a reference to lovers' meeting places mentioned in Bedouin poetry, introducing a passage with allusions to the Prophet and the early Muslims.

271 At Badr, near Medina, the early Muslims led by the Prophet defeated their Meccan opponents in AD 624. The word *badr* also means "full moon". There is a hadith in which the Prophet says, "Do whatever you want, for you will deserve Paradise," or "... for I have forgiven you" (al-Bukhārī, *al-Ṣaḥīḥ, Kitāb Faḍāʾil aṣḥāb al-nabī, bāb Qiṣṣat ghazwat Badr*).

272 *fa-khlaʿ mā ʿalayka*: Arberry sees an allusion to line 24 (*khalaʿtu ʿidhārī* "I've thrown off all restraint"), but there is a clear reference to Q Ṭā Hā 20:12, where God says to Mūsā/Moses at the burning bush: *fa-khlaʿ naʿlayka* "take off your shoes!". Whether the feet or the whole body is meant, the stripping is metaphorical: the mystic must strip himself from the physical world, from his belongings, from his self. Compare the end of the mystical *zajal* by al-Shushtarī, below.

273 That is, as the commentators suggest, in God's presence.

274 Sources: al-Shushtarī, *Dīwān* ed. al-Nashshār, 293–95, F. Corriente, *Poesía estrófica (Cejeles y/o muwaššaḥāt) atribuida al místico Granadino aš-Šuštarī* (siglo XIII d. C.), 132–33 (with a Spanish translation, p. 287). My transliteration is eclectic, between al-Nashshār's more classicizing vocalization and Corriente's system, which is presumably closer to the Andalusian dialect. Unlike Corriente I have indicated prosodical length and omitted stress indications.

275 *Maʿ al-huwayy*: Corriente translates "*con el viento,*" taking *huwayy* as the diminutive of classical Arabic *hawāʾ* "wind." It seems to me that it could equally be derived from *hawā* "passion, whim, arbitrary opinion" and I have translated accordingly, as if both meanings are meant.

276 Corriente: "*en nuestro lugar*"; but *ḥayy* is rather "tribe" (meaning the mystics); cf. above, Ibn al-Fāriḍ's poem, line 22.

277 For nakedness as a metaphor, compare the conclusion of Ibn al-Fāriḍ's poem, above. Ghaylān is Dhū l-Rummah, the Umayyad poet (see above, pp. 21ff., for his poem for his beloved Mayy or Mayyah). This line also concludes two other poems by al-Shushtarī (nos. 89 and 94). I am not aware of the two having walked around naked; but there may be an allusion to the anecdote told in al-Iṣfahānī, *al-Aghānī*, XVIII:28: Dhū l-Rummah, piqued when Mayyah finds him ugly, says (in verse, possibly spurious) that she may look superficially pretty but "hides shame beneath her clothes." Thereupon she lifts her clothes and shows him how wrong he was; they are reconciled.

278 Jayyusi, "Arabic Poetry in the Post-Classical Age," in *PCP*, p. 56.

279 Personal communication.

280 Source: Ibn Nubātah al-Miṣrī, *Dīwān*, 516–17.

281 The poet expresses the not uncommon paradoxical motif of saying, in verse, that he has forsaken verse. I do not understand the last word of this verse (*bil-maʿāyinī/muʿayinī*) and my translation is based on the possibility that it is an error for *bil-mafātinī.* A Bodleian manuscript of the *Dīwān* (MS Marsh 273:38v–39r) has *fa-lā bil-muʿānī wa-lā bil-muʿāyinī,* which is not clear to me either. I thank Adam Talib for this and other references to manuscript copies of the *Dīwān.*

282 In Q Taghābun 64:9 ("Sura of Mutual Fraud") the "Day of Gathering" (*yawm al-jamʿ*, another phrase for the Day of Judgment, or of Resurrection, *yawn al-ḥashr,* as in the poem) is said to be a Day of Mutual Fraud (*yawm al-taghābun*). The term is disputed but said by some to mean that the believers will "cheat" the unbelievers of their dwellings and possessions.

283 MS Marsh 273 has "stepping" (*khaṭw*) instead of "figure" (*qadd*).

284 "The Path to Paradise" is *al-Ṣirāṭ,* the "path" or bridge across Hell that on the Day of Judgment may be crossed by the believers on their way to Heaven. The Scales are for the weighing of deeds.

285 Source: Ibn Nubātah al-Miṣrī, *Dīwān*, 73–74.

286 Using the ancient "two companions convention," the poet is in fact addressing his two eyes.

287 I have replaced the Arabic grammatical word-play (*ʿaṭf* "conjunction" or "sympathy, inclination," *nidāʾ* "vocative" or "call," and *naʿt* "attribute, adjective" or "description") with an English equivalent; a more literal version would be "A young woman: I once had her tender sympathy, but the only thing left to me now is calling her and describing her."

288 I have adopted the version of MS Marsh 273: *ʿalā samʿi l-mutayyami,* in preference to the edition's *ʿalā ṣamti l-mutayyamī,* which does not make sense.

289 Source: Ibn Iyās, *Badāʾiʿ al-zuhūr*, I, ii:648–50, also in al-Jammāl, *al-Adab al-ʿāmmī fī Miṣr fī l-ʿaṣr al-mamlūkī,* 124–25, where the poem is attributed to Nāṣir al-Dīn al-Ghayṭī (d. first half of ninth/fifteenth century). Both editions obscure or ignore the meter on several occasions.

290 Haim Blanc argued that this pronunciation was an eighteenth-century innovation, but there are indications that it is older. See Humphrey Davies's introduction to his edition of al-Shirbīnī, *Hazz al-quḥūf*, p. xxxv.

291 *bagmūn*; see Aḥmad Taymūr, *Muʿjam Taymūr al-kabīr,* II:113 (where it is voweled *bagamūn*, which does not scan in line 8).

292 The appearance of a comet in that month, referred to in lines 38–42, is mentioned in al-Suyūṭī, *Ḥusn al-muḥāḍarah,* II:308: "In Rajab of the year [804] a star as large as the Pleiades appeared. It had a clearly visible tail and it rose and set; its light was very bright so

that it could be seen in the light of the moon and even in day-time, in the beginning of the month of Shaʿbān." For a similar accident in the twelfth century, in which an elephant fell off a bridge, see Ibn al-Athīr, *al-Kāmil*, X:469–70. He mentions that some people recited Q Fīl 105: «Have you not seen what your Lord did to the people of the elephant?»

293 The river harbor of Cairo (which at that time lay at some distance from the Nile).

294 *shyw'* is unclear (perhaps read *shwy'* "a little bit"?). I have adopted the reading *shāshū* given in al-Jammāl, *al-Adab al-ʿāmmī fī Miṣr*.

295 In a *zajal* a poet often mentions himself at the end, as a kind of signature.

296 This is not meant to suggest that Arabic meters are derived from Greek, as some western scholars thought in the nineteenth century. The standard work on *rajaz* poetry is Ullmann, *Untersuchungen zur Rağazpoesie*.

297 On some of these poets, see al-Maʿarrī's text, below, pp. 255ff..

298 Source: al-Iṣfahānī, *Aghānī*, XII:338, a variant e.g. in Ibn Hishām, *al-Sīrah al-nabawiyyah*, II:68; cf. the translation by Guillaume in Ibn Ishaq, *The Life of Muhammad*, 374.

299 The meaning of "the daughters of Ṭāriq" is unclear. According to one opinion (al-Iṣfahānī, *al-Aghānī*, XII:338–39), by Ṭāriq the Pleiades are meant (cf. Q Ṭāriq 86, "The Night-Star," taken to refer to the Pleiades), here a metaphor for a lofty and noble lineage. The absence of the definite article in the poem makes this somewhat doubtful, however. Another opinion is that the verses are by a certain Hind bint Bayāḍah ibn Rabāḥ ibn Ṭāriq al-Iyādī: see Ibn Manẓūr, *Lisān al-ʿArab*, s.v. *Ṭ-R-Q*; al-Baṭalyawsī, *al-Iqtiḍāb*, III:76–78. Lines 5, 3, 6–7 (in that order) are also found in the account of a pre-Islamic tribal battle, see Abū ʿUbaydah, *Naqāʾiḍ Jarīr wal-Farazdaq*, 641; al-Iṣfahānī, *al-Aghānī*, XXIV:95 (ascribed to a daughter of the poet al-Find al-Zimmānī).

300 Source: al-Iṣfahānī, *al-Aghānī*, IV:36. The above four couplets are a selection of a selection: Abū l-Faraj quotes twenty-three couplets of a very long poem. See Abū l-ʿAtāhiyah, *Dīwān*, 444–65, where the poem, called *Dhāt al-amthāl* ("The One with the Proverbs") has 280 couplets and twenty triplets. That the order of the lines hardly matters is clear from Abū l-Faraj's selection; the four couplets translated here are nos. 122, 37, 21, and 30–31 in the *Dīwān*.

301 Source: Ibn Mālik, *Alfiyyah*, 3–4.

302 Source: Ibn Abī Uṣaybiʿah (d. 668/1270), *ʿUyūn al anbāʾ fī ṭabaqāt al-aṭibbāʾ*, ed. Müller, II:149–51; ed. Nizār Riḍā, 620–23. The following translation, with more annotation and a study of Abū l-Ḥakam, was published (badly, and un-proofed) in van Gelder, "The Joking Doctor."

303 Both editions have *qāfiz*; read *qāquz*, which is a poetic license for *qāquzz* or *qāqūz* (see al-Zabīdī, *Tāj al-ʿarūs*, see s.v. *Q-Q-Z*).

304 *qashqil lahum*: the translation is a guess.

305 The Arabic has "rose water" (*māʾ al-ward*); "julep" is derived from the Persian for "rose water," *gul āb*.

306 *abū tallūr*: the translation is a guess.

307 This couplet is not found in Nizār Riḍā's edition.

308 The "Balance" probably has eschatological connotations here. *Ṣāḥib al-daʿwah* ("Host") is a pun: *daʿwah* means "invitation" as well as "religious propaganda" for an imam. *Ṣāḥib al-daʿwah* is therefore a near synonym of *ṣāḥib al-zamān*, which is the more common synonym of *ṣāhib al-waqt* ("Lord of Time," here "Latter-Day prophets" of line 77).

309 The expression *ṣaqʿ al-jurb* is not clear to me.

310 Source: al-ʿĀmilī, *al-Kashkūl*, 77–83. The present translation comprises some two-thirds of a poem of 164 *rajaz* couplets in paired rhyme; for shortened versions, see al-Ghuzūlī, *Maṭāliʿ al-budūr*, I:147–50, and al-Nawājī, *Ḥalbat al-kumayt*, 42–45, 337 (where the title of the poem is given as *ʿUmdat al-ḥurafāʾ wa-qudwat al-ẓurafāʾ*, approximately "The Support of Friends and the Model of the Refined"). I have also used a manuscript at the Bodleian Library in Oxford (MS Pococke 440, fols. 91v–96r) that contains the poem. I have occasionally preferred those readings (indicated as MB, ḤK, and Bod., respectively). A small portion of the present translation has been published in van Gelder, "Arabic Didactic Verse."

311 Reading with MB, ḤK, and Bod. *maṭbūʿah* instead of *muṭīʿah*.

312 Instead of *ʾasluk* (sic) *maʿa l-jamāʿah / fī ṭuruqi l-khalāʿah*, Bod. has *ʾusalliku l-jamāʿah / fī ṭuruqi l-khalāʿah* ("I make people walk the ways of depravity"). Alternatively, one could read imperatives here (*ʾusluk*) and the next line (*ʾajidda*), cf. Wagner, "Verse über Abū Nuwās," 345.

313 Reading *taḥbis*, with ḤK, rather than *tashḥadh* (MB, Bod.) or *tahjur* (Kashkūl).

314 al-Qāḍiyah: see Q Ḥāqqah 69:27.

315 *dabb* or *dabīb*, literally "creeping," stands for homosexual rape of sleeping boys, a common topic in poems and anecdotes.

316 Reading *ruʾī*, with ḤK, instead of *ruzī*.

317 Reading *jāzawhu*, with ḤK, MB, and Bod., instead of *jāwizhu*.

318 I have assumed that *laṭāʿah* (or *liṭāʿah*) is to be connected with *talaṭṭaʿa ʿalā*, translated in Dozy, *Supplément aux dictionnaires arabes*, II, 539 as "*naqueter, attendre servilement à la porte de quelqu'un.*"

319 The rare expression *lā tuṣaqqiʿ dhaqnaka* ("do not whiten/cool your beard") is also found in Ibn Taghrī Birdī, *al-Nujūm al-zāhirah*, IX:76, in a context suggesting the sense "don't be stupid"; the same story in Ibn Shākir al-Kutubī, *Fawāt al-Wafayāt*, II:378 (with *tusaqqiʿ*,

with *sīn* instead of *ṣād*). See also *Alf laylah wa-laylah*, II:287: *yā sāqiʿ al-dhaqn mā asqaʿ dhaqnak*, translated by Lyons, *The Arabian Nights: Tales of 1001 Nights*, II:204 as "Whitebeard, what a fool you were!"

320 Instead of *ṭīzan* (*Kashkūl*) or *ṭarzan* (Bod.) I prefer to read *ṭanzan*; an alternative is *ṭurran* ("all of them"), as in MB.

321 Six couplets, partly unintelligible to me, have been omitted.

322 Instead of *waṣiyyatu l-ʿawwāmī* (*Kashkūl*) I read *fa-ʿuṣbatu l-ʿawāmmī* (MB, ḤK, Bod.).

323 *wa-mussa naḥrahū wa-qudd*; a less violent version is found in ḤK and Bod.: *wa-sus'hu wa-tmaskhar wa-qud*, "and manage him, make jokes, and be a procurer," which better fits the following couplet.

324 I do not understand what looks like *wa-wṣī* (for *wa-ʾawṣī*?) and *wa-fid* (for *wa-ʾafid*?).

325 Following *Kashkūl* (*lā tuhazzir*) instead of MB (*lā tuʿazziz*), ḤK (*lā tugharrir*, or *tugharrar*), or Bod. (*lā tuʿazzir*).

326 *qilāʿ*; or perhaps read, with Bod., the less unlikely *tilāʿ* ("hills").

327 The Maghrib. Instead of *al-ghurrabī* (*Kashkūl*) I prefer reading *al-ʿurbī* (Bod.).

328 While eating lizards is generally considered permissible in Islam (even though Bedouins and those of Arab descent are often mocked for it, see p. 35), the jurists differ of opinion about eating hedgehogs. The Ḥanafites, to whom Ibn Makānis belonged, did not allow it.

329 Fifty-one couplets have been omitted, in which the poet waxes lyrical (a night with a girl, an extended description of the new moon, etc.)

330 Source: al-Iṣfahānī, *Aghānī*, XXI:171; al-Sukkarī, *Sharḥ ashʿār al-Hudhaliyyīn*, 846 (reading and translation somewhat uncertain).

331 Or perhaps "urging a band of followers"; cf. Wagner, *Grundzüge der klassischen arabischen Dichtung*, I:116: "*mit (deinen) Gefolgsleuten.*"

332 Source: al-Iṣfahānī, *al-Aghānī*, XV:247 (one of many different versions quoted in the sources; cf. e.g. al-Jāḥiẓ, *al-Bayān wal-tabyīn*, I: 308–9; Abū Ḥātim al-Sijistānī, *al-Muʿammarūn*, 77; al-Masʿūdī, *Murūj al-dhahab*, I:76–77; Ibn ʿAbd Rabbih, *al-ʿIqd al-farīd*, IV:128).

333 Source: al-Iṣfahānī, *Aghānī*, IX:84; cf. R. Blachère, *Histoire de la littérature arabe*, II:192–93.

334 Source: al-Bāqillānī, *Iʿjāz al-Qurʾān*, 157; cf. e.g. al-Jāḥiẓ, *al-Ḥayawān*, V:530; al-Ṭabarī, *Tārīkh*, I:1934, 1975.

335 The tribe of the Prophet Muḥammad.

336 Source: al-Ṭabarī, *Tārīkh*, I:1934; al-Bāqillānī, *Iʿjāz al-Qurʾān*, 157. Compare this with, for example, the beginning of Q ʿĀdiyāt 100: «*wal-ʿādiyāti ḍabḥā * fal-mūriyāti qadḥā * fal-mughīrāti ṣubḥā * fa-atharna bihī naqʿā * fa-wasaṭna bihī jamʿā * ʾinna l-ʾinsāna li-rabbihī la-kanūd * wa-ʾinnahū ʿalā dhālika la-shahīd * …*», in Arberry's translation: «By the snort-

ing chargers, * by the strikers of fire, * by the dawn-raiders * blazing a trail of dust, * cleaving there with a host! * Surely Man is ungrateful to his Lord, * and surely he is a witness against that!»

337 Source: al-Jāḥiẓ, *al-Bayān wal-tabyīn*, I:286.

338 See Ibn Hishām, *al-Sīrah al-nabawiyyah*, I:71–73, translated by A. Guillaume in Ibn Ishaq, *The Life of Muhammad*, 699–701; Abū Ḥanīfah al-Dīnawarī, *al-Akhbār al-ṭiwāl*, 50–51; al-Ṭabarī, *Tārīkh*, I:827–30, trans. C.E. Bosworth, in *The History of al-Ṭabarī*, V:31–37; al-Masʿūdī, *Murūj al-dhahab*, II: 402–4, French translation, II:543–44; al-Maqdisī, *al-Bad' wal-ta'rīkh*, III:157–58 (French translation, III:161–62); Ibn al-Faqīh, *Mukhtaṣar kitāb al-buldān*, 130–31; al-Iṣfahānī, *al-Aghānī*, II:140–44 (trans. J.C. Bürgel, *Tausendundeine Welt*, 368–69); al-Thaʿālibī, *Ghurar akhbār mulūk al-Furs*, 489–94 (with French translation); Ibn Ḥamdūn, *al-Tadhkirah*, III:32–33; al-Dimashqī, *Nukhbat al-dahr*, 38; [pseudo-] Ibn Qayyim al-Jawziyyah, *Akhbār al-nisā'*, 76–77 (German translation by Dieter Bellmann in Ibn Qayyim al-Ǧauziyya, *Über die Frauen*, 208–9); Yāqūt, *Muʿjam al-buldān*, II:268–69 (s.v. al-Ḥaḍr); al-Qazwīnī, *Āthār al-bilād*, 355–56; al-Nuwayrī, *Nihāyat al-arab*, I:381; al-Ibshīhī, *al-Mustaṭraf*, I:210; Ibn Khallikān, *Wafayāt al-aʿyān*, V:165–66 (trans. De Slane, III:318–20); Ibn al-Shajarī, *Amālī*, I:98–100. A Persian version is found in al-Firdawsī's *Shāh-nāmah* (Ferdowsi, *Shahnameh: The Persian Book of Kings* , trans. Dick Davis, 578–82). Although the story is set in the pre-Islamic period, the versions offered here cannot be said to belong to pre-Islamic literature. Like pre-Islamic poetry, they were collected and written down in Islamic times, but whereas poetry, we can assume, was transmitted fairly faithfully on the whole, the wording and content of prose stories varied wildly, as the present versions attest. Studies: Christensen, "La princesse sur la feuille de myrte et la princesse sur le pois" (on the relationship with the European versions, where the myrtle leaf has become a pea, and the ending less gruesome); Zakeri, "Arabic Reports on the Fall of Hatra to the Sasanids: History or Legend?"; Ch. Pellat, "al-Ḥaḍr" in *EI2*.

339 Al-Bayhaqī, *al-Maḥāsin wal-masāwi'* (ed. Beirut, 1970), 564 (= ed. Friedrich Schwally, 604–5). This is a relatively simple version, from the section "Masāwi' al-banāt" ("Bad daughters"), taken from a work devoted to "Good and Bad Sides of Things." In the Beirut edition it forms the whole section, since a preceding bawdy anecdote has been expurgated.

340 Al-Ḍayzan ibn Muʿāwiyah, ruler of al-Ḥaḍr (ancient Hatra, approximately 90 km SSW of Mosul). The story is normally told about Hatra, not al-Ḥīrah. In al-Dīnawarī the unnamed city is said to be (unlike Hatra) on the Euphrates, near al-Raqqah.

341 Sābūr (the Arabic form of Shāpūr) II, son of Hurmuz (Hormizd), Sasanid ruler (r. AD 309–79), nicknamed Dhū l-Aktāf ("Shoulderman") because he had the shoulders

of captives pierced or dislocated (as he does in this story in al-Dīnawarī's version). See *EI2*, s.v. "Shāpūr." In the version of Ibn Qutaybah the king is called Ardashīr, in al-Akhfash the conqueror is a general of Sābūr called Sharwīn.

342 She is called Mulaykah (or Malīkah) in al-Dīnawarī; al-Firdawsī calls her Mālikah (and her father, Ṭā'ir, with a strange corruption of Sāṭirūn). In most sources (e.g. al-Mas'ūdī, Abū l-Faraj al-Iṣfahānī, Ibn al-Faqīh, al-Maqdisī) she is called al-Naḍīrah ("blooming, fresh"). In al-Akhfash (see below) the unnamed girl is said to be the wife as well as the daughter of the king of al-Ḥaḍr (who is here, as in Ibn Hishām, called Sāṭirūn, which may originally have been a title). Perhaps the name al-Naḍīrah is taken from a line quoted anonymously in al-Iṣfahānī, *Aghānī*, II:144, Ibn Khallikān, *Wafayāt*, V:165: *Aqfara l-Ḥaḍru min Naḍīrata fa- / l-Mirbā'u minhā fa-jānibu l-Tharthārī*, which sounds like a line of *nasīb*.

343 In some versions (*Aghānī*, Ibn al-Faqīh, al-Nuwayrī, al-Ibshīhī) the girl is taken outside the town because she is menstruating ("They used to do that with their women").

344 The words *arsalat ilayhi* leave it undecided whether she sent a letter or a person; the latter is unlikely in the circumstances. In some sources (e.g. Ibn Qutaybah) she sends the note by means of shooting an arrow (*nushshābah*).

345 In some versions (al-Ṭabarī, Ibn al-Faqīh, al-Qazwīnī, al-Nuwayrī, al-Ibshīhī) the town is conquered by magic: "Take the menstrual blood of a blue-eyed woman and write (a charm) with it on a piece of paper; fasten it to the neck of a turtle-dove and let it loose. If the bird settles on the citadel it will crumble with everyone inside" (Ibn al-Faqīh).

346 Literally, "moist."

347 Bone marrow, not the vegetable; it may also refer to brains. Instead of *mukhkh*, al-Mas'ūdī has *muḥḥ* (egg yolk); al-Tha'ālibī has both.

348 *Darmak*, mentioned in the hadith (e.g. on Paradise: *wa-turbatuhā al-darmak*). The words *wa-huwa l-ḥuwwārā* are probably an insertion by a narrator or copyist. In other versions the girl is fed on "honey, cream, and marrow" (Ibn Qutaybah) or "cream, marrow, bees' honey, and purest wine" (*Aghānī*), etc.

349 *Ṭabarzad*, from Persian *tabar-zad* "rock-salt, white sugar" (lit., struck with a hatchet, axe, etc.); thus *sukkar ṭabarzad* refers to a sugar loaf. See D. Waines, "sukkar" in *EI2*, IX:804b.

350 One MS of Ibn Khallikān adds at this point: "The proof of this that in the desert near al-Tharthār there is a place known as al-Warik ('the hip'), another called al-Katif ('the shoulder'), and another known as al-A'ḍā' ('the limbs'). These are the places where her limbs were found and which were then called after the limb found in it." In al-Ibshīhī, where the story is part of the section on betrayal, the author also condemns Sābūr, for he adds at the end: "*qaṭa'ahu llāhu mā aghdarahū.*" Ibn Hishām, *al-Sīrah al-nabawiyyah*, I:73 (trans. A. Guillaume Ibn Ishaq, *The Life of Muhammad*, 700–701) quotes six lines attributed to 'Adī

ibn Zayd referring to the story (in Guillaume's translation: "Fate descended on al-Ḥaḍr from above, / A grievous disaster. / A spoilt darling did not protect her father / When her watchmen gave up hope because of her treachery / When she made his evening cup of unmixed wine / (For wine destroys the mind of the drinker). / She betrayed her people for a night of love, / Thinking that the prince would marry her. / But the bride's lot was that at the light of dawn / Her locks ran red with blood. / Al-Ḥaḍr was destroyed and given up to plunder. / The clothes-racks of her chamber did not escape the fire." (Four lines in al-Masʿūdī, *Murūj*, II:404 and Yāqūt, *Muʿjam al-buldān*, s.v. al-Ḥaḍr, three lines in al-Maqdisī, *Bad'*, III:158). The verses come at the end of a poem of twenty-two lines by ʿAdī ibn Zayd; see Cheikho (Shaykhū), *Shuʿarā' al-Naṣrāniyyah*, II:457–59.

351 Ibn Qutaybah, *ʿUyūn al-akhbār*, IV:119–20 (in the chapter on women, section on women's bad qualities). Taken from an important literary anthology, sometimes called "*adab* encyclopedia," by an author who was an authority on Islamic religion as well as a philologist and a literary scholar.

352 Probably the work elsewhere called *Siyar mulūk al-ʿAjam*, a royal chronicle (*Khudāynāmah*) of the Sassanids, translated from the Pahlavi into Arabic by Ibn al-Muqaffaʿ; parts of it survive.

353 Ardashīr I, founder of the Sasanid Empire, first half of third century AD.

354 *Al-Sawād*, lit. "the black (lands)," the fertile region between the Euphrates and the Tigris.

355 *Mulūk al-Ṭawā'if*, lit. "the kings of the territorial divisions," the Arabic term used for the successors of Alexander the Great in Iran during the Parthian and Arsacid period.

356 Al-Akhfash al-Aṣghar, *Kitāb al-ikhtiyārayn*, 710–11: a rather different, myrtle-leafless version, in the course of the commentary on a poem by the pre-Islamic poet ʿAdī ibn Zayd, in which al-Ḥaḍr is mentioned.

357 Northern Mesopotamia, the region between the Tigris and the Euphrates.

358 A custom often associated with the pre-Islamic Zoroastrian Persians; see the text by al-Tawḥīdī in this volume, below, pp. 195ff..

359 The name is unknown, the reading uncertain, and its function in the story unclear.

360 It lies, in fact, close to the river al-Tharthār, much closer to the Tigris (approximately 50 km) than to the Euphrates (about 140 km). Al-Furāt may be a scribal corruption of al-Tharthār. The following details about the military operation are rather obscure. In some versions (e.g. al-Maqdisī) the town is subdued by having its water supply cut off at the girl's direction.

361 The sense is not quite clear.

362 Source: Muḥammad ibn Ḥabīb (d. 245/860), *Asmāʾ al-mughtālīn min al-ashrāf fī l-jāhiliyyah wal-islām wa-asmāʾ man qutila min al-shuʿarāʾ* (*The Names of Noblemen and Poets Murdered in Pre-Islamic and Islamic Times*), 124–25.

363 A fuller genealogy is given e.g. in al-Kalbī, *Ğamharat an-nasab / Das genealogische Werk des Hišām ibn Muḥammad al-Kalbī*, ed. Werner Caskel, Tables 275, 274, 176: Yalammaqah (Bilqīs) bt. Ilīsharaḥ ibn Dhī Jadan ibn Ilīsharaḥ ibn al-Ḥārith ibn Qays ibn Ṣayfī ibn Sabaʾ (al-Aṣghar, "the younger") ibn Kaʿb ibn Zayd ibn Sahl, ultimately going back to Ḥimyar ibn Sabaʾ (the Biblical Sheba) ibn Qaḥṭān (ancestor of the "South Arabs"). For a different genealogy, see e.g. Ibn Qutaybah, *al-Maʿārif*, 628. The name Bilqīs, by which the Queen of Sheba is known in Arabic lore, has been connected with the Greek *pallakis* (παλλακίς), "concubine."

364 ʿImlīq ibn Lāwadh ibn Iram ibn Sam (Shem) ibn Nūḥ (Noah), king of Ṭasm: another legendary tyrant; for the story, see al-Iṣfahānī, *Aghānī*, X:164–67.

365 For the story of the hoopoe, the Queen of Sheba, and Sulaymān/Solomon, see below, "The Hoopoe," from al-Damīrī's encyclopedia.

366 Source: *Murūj al-dhahab* (*Meadows of Gold*), by Abū l-Ḥasan ʿAlī ibn al-Ḥusayn al-Masʿūdī (ca. 282/896–345/956). The two sections chosen here are taken from the edition by Charles Pellat, I:249–51 and II:27–29. There is a French translation by the 19th-century editors, Barbier de Meynard and Pavet de Courteille, revised by Ch. Pellat, see I:188–89, (origin of wine), II:265–67 (story of Cleopatra).

367 For another version, with many differences, see al-Nawājī (d. 859/1455), *Ḥalbat al-kumayt*, 11–12.

368 The precise vocalizations and the identities of these two persons, said to be kings of the pre-Islamic Syrians, are uncertain.

369 In al-Nawājī's version seven old men are brought, who suffer from various ailments; they all benefit from the drink.

370 Q Hūd 11:44.

371 *Ḥikmah*, "wisdom," includes philosophy and science. In Ibn al-Nadīm, *al-Fihrist*, 354, a *Book of Queen Cleopatra* (*Kitāb Qalūbaṭrah al-malikah*) is mentioned among "the titles of books written by the sages" in a chapter on alchemy.

372 The passage is obviously confused.

373 See *Murūj al-dhahab*, II:34–35.

374 The word is not found in the dictionaries. *Fitr* is "the distance between the tips of the outstretched thumb and index finger," *shibr* "the distance between the tips of the outstretched thumb and little finger"; here the terms seem to refer to circumference or thickness of the snake rather than its length.

375 A strange, roundabout way of saying "he dies."

376 Source: Abū l-Faraj al-Iṣfahānī (d. ca. 363/973), *al-Aghānī*, XXI:340–43; for parallels see Ibn Qutaybah, *al-Shiʿr wal-shuʿarāʾ*, 122–24; al-Anbārī, *Sharḥ al-qaṣāʾid al-ṭiwāl*, 13–15; Ibn ʿAbd Rabbih, *al-ʿIqd al-farīd* (Cairo, 1948–53), VI:395–96; al-Zawzanī, *Sharḥ al-Muʿallaqāt*, 3; al-Tibrīzī, *Sharḥ al-qaṣāʾid al-ʿashr*, 8–9; ʿAbd al-Qādir al-Baghdādī, *Khizānat al-adab*, III:456–59; Imruʾ al-Qays, *Dīwān*, 10.

377 Correctly al-Raʾlān, see al-Anbārī, *Sharḥ*, 13; al-Baghdādī, *Khizānah*, III:456.

378 A *rāwī* is a transmitter or reciter of poetry; in the early period famous poets often had their personal *rāwī*.

379 *Dārah* "house, court, upland, tribe, circle," *juljul* "bells attached to the neck of beasts of burden." Dārat Juljul is mentioned in Imruʾ al-Qays's poem: "O yes, so many splendid days you had with them [viz. the girls], / One day at Dārat Juljul in particular!" For different ideas about the precise location, see e.g. Yāqūt, *Muʿjam al-buldān*, s.v.

380 Al-Baghdādī, *Khizānah*: Fāṭimah, who was nicknamed ʿUnayzah ("Little She-Goat"); she is mentioned in the *Muʿallaqah*.

381 Source: Abū l-Faraj al-Iṣfahānī, *al-Aghānī*, IX:180–220. For parallel versions, all dependent on *al-Aghānī*, see e.g. al-Tanūkhī, *al-Faraj baʿd al-shiddah*, IV:383–92 (he only mentions the happy ending, not the sad one); al-Anṭākī, *Tazyīn al-aswāq*, I:130–49; Mughulṭāy, *al-Wāḍiḥ al-mubīn*, 312–26. On the story, see Kilpatrick, "*Aḫbār manẓūma*: The Romance of Qays and Lubnā in the *Aġānī*"; Sakkal, "Passage du récit des amours de Qays et Lubnā à travers les genres littéraires arabes médiévaux"; Skarżyńska-Bocheńska, "Qays et Lubnā: Victoire de l'amour sur l'autorité du père et de la tribu."

382 A reference to the failed attack on Mecca by Abrahah, the year the Prophet was born. Al-Mughammas is a place near Mecca.

383 The precise meaning of *bi-janbi l-mashʿar* is not clear.

384 He means that his uncle, now that he is rich, should give them some camels.

385 Compare the different version quoted below, on p. 191 of the *Aghānī* text.

386 Ibn Abī ʿAtīq, the great-grandson of Abū Bakr, was a friend of many poets and singers, who appears in many stories and anecdotes as a kind of wit.

387 i.e., Why didn't you let us come to you?

388 The second caliph.

389 A variant of this saying with its supportive chain of transmitters has been omitted.

390 The period during which a woman may not remarry after becoming a widow or being divorced; in Lubnā's case this would have been three menstrual periods. See *EI2* s.v. "ʿidda."

391 See *al-Aghānī*, II:89–90.

392 Some short poems or part of poems are marked with "*ṣawt*" (literally, "voice"), indicating that they were set to music. The author usually tells which singers and musicians did so, with some technical information about the musical modes and rhythms. In the chapter on Qays twenty-three such song texts are specified; the technical information has been omitted on some occasions in the following, and no notes are given on the various singers and composers, many of them famous.

393 Reading Qurayṣ, with Ibn al-Nadīm, *Fihrist*, ed. Flügel, 156; ed. Ṭawīl, 251, instead of Qurayḍ in the edition.

394 A poetic license, one supposes, for saying that his heart has left his ribs.

395 When a camel calf was slaughtered its stuffed skin was presented to its mother, to stimulate milk production; cf. above, Jarīr's poem, line 7.

396 These lines are sometimes ascribed to Jamīl or to Majnūn Laylā; see al-Ṣūlī, *al-Awrāq: Ashʿār awlād al-khulafāʾ*, 115; al-Ḥuṣrī, *al-Maṣūn fī sirr al-hawā al-maknūn*, 99–100, idem; *Zahr al-ādāb*, 218; Ibn Ḥamdūn, *Tadhkirah*, VI:69; Majnūn Laylā, *Dīwān*, 211. Such uncertainties about attributions are especially common here, because Majnūn's name is also Qays.

397 *Yaghshayna l-ʿaṣiyya* (*al-Aghānī*) is not clear to me; I have followed the reading *al-ʿiṣiyya*, as in *Dīwān al-ʿUdhriyyīn*, 409, where it is glossed as *al-qaṣab*. Other versions (al-Ḥuṣrī, *Zahr*, *Maṣūn*) have *yakhshayna* ("they fear").

398 Sind is the region around the lower Indus river, now in Pakistan. Zubdah means "Butter-lump."

399 Compare the different version quoted above, p. 181 of the *Aghānī* text.

400 In eastern Arabia.

401 This belief is listed as one of the peculiar habits and beliefs of the Bedouin Arabs by the poet and critic Ibn Ṭabāṭabā (d. 322/934) in his *ʿIyār al-shiʿr*, 57, with several verses on the motif. A case could be made for the belief: thinking of one's beloved would make the heart beat faster and revive the flow of blood in the affected limb. When someone recommended the same remedy to ʿAbd Allāh ibn ʿUmar (son of the second caliph), he cried out the Prophet's name to good effect (told in Ibn Manẓūr's dictionary *Lisān al-ʿArab*, s.v. *Kh-D-R*).

402 These lines are sometimes attributed to Majnūn Laylā, see his *Dīwān*, 81; or to Jamīl (al-Masʿūdī, *Murūj al-dhahab*, IV, 243; Ibn Dāwūd, *Zahrah*, 54).

403 cf. Q Qadr 97:3. The Night of Power, *laylat al-qadr*, also rendered as Night of the (Divine) Decree, is a night toward the end of Ramadan. This verse (with *ḥusnan* "in beauty" instead of *lubnā*) also occurs in a poem by Jamīl (*Aghānī*, VIII:151).

404 ʿUrwah ibn Ḥizām, who died of love for his cousin ʿAfrāʾ, and ʿAmr ibn ʿAjlān, doing the same for Hind, are two other famous unhappy lovers.

405 The text differs very slightly from the previous quotation of these lines.

406 There is some ambiguity: "her" could also refer to *al-dunyā* ("this world").

407 Literally, "transmission" (*riwāyah*), which probably refers to his knowledge of a lot of poetry and tribal lore.

408 The Anṣār or "Supporters" were those Medinans who supported the prophet Muḥammad and the cause of Islam after the Hijra.

409 First caliph of the Umayyads, r. 41/661–60/680, residing in Damascus.

410 Kinsman of Muʿāwiyah and his governor in Medina in 41/661–48/668 and 54/674–57/677; later briefly caliph (64/684–65/685).

411 Preferring the variant given in the note (*fa-qalbī l-yawma man bānā*) to *fa-hāja l-qalba man bānā* ("the one who has gone stirred my heart").

412 A member of the Umayyad clan, d. 59/679; governor of Kufa and Medina.

413 d. 184/800; his grandson al-Zubayr ibn Bakkār (d. 256/870) was a historian and littérateur.

414 Died 252/866.

415 A place a few miles from Mecca that plays a part in the pilgrimage.

416 *Iṣfarrat* would normally be "it grows pale, or yellow," but "red" seems to fit the context better.

417 Meaning not wholly clear. *Al-malā* ("the open country") could also be a place-name, see Yāqūt, *Muʿjam al-buldān*, V, 188–89. This hemistich, with *kunta ʾaqdarā* instead of *ʾanta ʾaqdarū*, is also found in a poem by ʿUrwah ibn al-Ward (*Aghānī*, III:81).

418 *Fa-lid-dunyā buṭūnun wa-ʾaẓhurū*, literally "for the world has bellies/low places and backs/heights"; my interpretation is somewhat uncertain.

419 Al-Gharīḍ (d. 98/716), Maʿbad (d. ca. 125/743), Mālik (d. ca. 136/754): famous singers and musicians.

420 Perhaps meaning "I never tire of hearing the stories about you."

421 Muʿāwiyah's son, who reigned after him (60/680–64/683).

422 Al-Ghābah ("the Forest"): According to Yāqūt's topographical dictionary (*Muʿjam al-buldān*) this is the name of a mail-post on the way from Damascus to Medina; al-Madhād is a place in Medina.

423 After this, one line of unclear sense has been omitted.

424 Grammarian from Baghdad, d. 291/904.

425 For a prayer one has to be ritually clean; normally a "minor ablution" is sufficient, but in some cases (e.g. after sexual intercourse) a "major ablution" (e.g. in a hammam) is required.

426 The lines beginning "Has Lubnā left," quoted above (p. 213 of the Arabic text), belong to the same poem. For a longer version (52 lines), see al-Qālī, *Amālī*, ii, 314–17. The present fragment consists of lines 11, 29, 15, 16, 24, 9, 7, 49, 17, 39, 38, 40, 51, 50, 25, 26, 28, 27, 45, 30, 31, 13, and 12 of al-Qālī's version, and the fragment on p. 213 corresponds with lines 33, 38, 35–47, 41, and 42; all of which goes to show how little the order of the individual lines matters in this genre.

427 Again, *kabid* "liver" has been translated as "heart."

428 A poet of mostly love poetry, who lived in the first half of the second/eighth century (his dates are very uncertain).

429 This would have been a fitting end to the story. It is something of a disappointment to see that according to modern scholars Qays lived to the age of sixty or even seventy-five, far too old for the traditional hopeless lover; see T. Seidensticker in *EAL*, 635, and Sezgin in *Geschichte des Arabischen Schrifttums*, II:411. The following alternative ending is also wholly inappropriate for the classical romantic tale and may have been made up by someone who did not like unhappy endings or, more probably, someone who liked to mock the traditional tear-jerking model. The same Ibn Abī ʿAtīq also seems to make fun of the sad story of ʿUrwah and ʿAfrāʾ (al-Iṣfahanī, *Aghānī*, XXIV:162).

430 Presumably al-Ḥasan.

431 Source: Ibn al-Muqaffaʿ (ca. 102/720–ca. 139/756), *Kalīlah wa-Dimnah* (*Kalilah and Dimnah*), 71–72. For a medieval European version, see Jacobus de Voragine, *The Golden Legend*, trans. W. G. Ryan, II:360 (story of Barlaam and Josaphat = *Bilawhar wa-Būdāsaf/Yūdāsaf*), which goes back ultimately to the story of Gautama Buddha (Būdāsaf = Bodhisattva); it contains the present story as "Elephant and the Man in Chasm" (see *EI2*, s.v. "Bilawhar wa-Yūdāsaf").

432 The speaker, in this autobiographical introduction to *Kalīlah wa-Dimnah*, is the physician and sage Burzōya (Burzōe, Burzōy, Barzawayh), who addresses Buzurjmihr ibn al-Bakhtakān, the vizier of king Anūsharwān. Burzōya made a Pahlavi translation of the Sanskrit *Pañcatantra* in the sixth century, which was in turn translated into Arabic by Ibn al-Muqaffaʿ.

433 In the Persian versions it is apparently a camel, see e.g. the illustrations in Bernard O'Kane, *Early Persian Painting*: Kalila wa Dimna *Manuscripts of the Late Fourteenth Century*, 58–68, 102–3, figs. 13–19, pl. 7–8; in European versions it is a unicorn.

434 I have chosen to translate the Arabic perfect tense with a kind of present tense ("has escaped... he looks...") to suggest the timelessness of the parable.

435 Reading *ʿalā shafāhā* "on its brink, verge, edge" instead of *ʿalā samāʾihā*.

436 Arabic *tinnīn*: cf. the *tannīn* or *tannīm* of the Hebrew bible, translated in the Authorized Version as "dragon" (e.g. Ps. 148:7), "serpent" (see e.g. Isa. 27:1), or "whale" (Gen. 1:21). It is a mythological monster, in cosmogony said to be responsible for eclipses of sun and moon; also the Arabic name for the constellation Draco.

437 viz. blood, yellow bile, black bile, and phlegm.

438 The interpretation omits to explain what the elephant stands for (apparently Fate; compare the story by al-Tanūkhī, "The Mystic and the Elephant", below).

439 Source: Ibn al-Muqaffaʿ, *al-Adab al-kabīr*, ed. Muḥammad Kurd ʿAlī, in *Rasāʾil al-bulaghāʾ* (Cairo, 1954), 40–41 and 42–54. For a French and a German translation of the work, see Tardy, "Traduction d'*al-Adab al-kabīr* d'Ibn al-Muqaffaʿ"; Rescher, "Das Kitâb ʿel-adab el-kebîr' des Ibn el-Moqaffaʿ."

440 *Adab*, which has several meanings, including "polished manners, good behavior, rules of conduct, erudition..."

441 *Laṭāʾif al-umūr* could mean "subtle things" but the context requires something less positive.

442 Reading *min al-ʿajab* instead of the edition's *min al-ʿujb*.

443 The meaning of *baʿda l-taraffuʿ* is not clear to me.

444 Reading the version given in the editor's note.

445 I have hesitated between reading *malik* ("king, ruler, prince"), as in the edition, and *mulk* ("reign"). The text reads better when one opts for *malik* (except perhaps the last sentence of the section).

446 The meanings of *hawā* include "passionate love, inclination, arbitrary view, whim, heretical opinion."

447 I am not certain of the meaning of *jazaw bi-ghayr nayl* ("who reward without obtaining") and have translated as if the text had *jaraw bi-ghayr nayl*.

448 The original seems to have "in suspecting his scrutiny with the eye of misgiving and his heart with the eye of hatred" which is rather convoluted and unclear, while *maqt* ("hate") seems too strong here. My translation is somewhat uncertain.

449 *Laṭāʾif al-umūr*, translated above (p. 41 of the Arabic text) as "insignificant matters"; the present sentence directly contradicts what is said there and may be a later addition.

450 Source: al-Jāḥiẓ, *al-Ḥayawān* (*Living Beings*), III:298–409 (selections).

451 The word *ummī*, originally probably "belonging to the nations without scripture (Gentiles, Goyim)" is traditionally interpreted as "illiterate" or "unlettered," which stresses the miraculous nature of Muḥammad's prophethood.

452 This seemingly contradicts the idea (often expressed in the Qur'an) that all creation is subservient to mankind.

453 He uses two words, *namlah* and *dharrah*; the latter is usually said to be a small ant. It may also mean "speck of dust, mote" and in modern Arabic is used for "atom."

454 In Arabic such expressions usually have the form of a comparative ("more ... than a ..."); I have used the form that is more common in English.

455 Presumably because the herd as a whole is endangered or already diseased.

456 From an ode on Caliph Yazīd ibn Muʿāwiyah, see al-Akhṭal, *Dīwān*, 141.

457 Poet and leading member of Asad, his tribe; a contemporary of the Prophet.

458 I have adopted the reading of Ibn Ḥamdūn, *Tadhkirah*, V:42 and VII:208: *ihdāʾ l-ḍaghāʾini baynahum*, instead of *ihdāʾ al-qaṣāʾidi baynanā*, which seems to make less sense. See also al-Akhfash al-Aṣghar, *Ikhtiyārayn*, 169 (*ihdāʾu l-hawājiri baynanā*).

459 This is not found in the authoritative collections. Al-Jāḥiẓ quotes the hadith on p. 392: "ʿAnbasah told us: Ḥanẓalah al-Sadūsī told us: Anas ibn Mālik informed us: The messenger of God (God bless and preserve him) said: 'The life of a fly lasts forty days; and flies are in hell.'"

460 Often ascribed to Abū l-Shamaqmaq (d. ca. 180/796) but also to Abū Nuwās (*Dīwān*, ed. Wagner, I:20).

461 ʿAbd Allāh ibn Hammām al-Salūlī (d. ca. 99/717), cf. *Ḥayawān*, VI:76. The allusions are not clear and Ibn Muḍārib is not known to me, nor Ibn Muqarrab, the variant found in al-Thaʿālibī, *Thimār al-qulūb*, 504.

462 Senior official, Muʿtazilite, wit and philosopher in the time of al-Maʾmūn (see G. Lecomte, "Muḥammad ibn al-D̲jahm," *EI2*).

463 In present-day Mozambique.

464 A broth made of cereals.

465 A town in of southern Iraq, approximately midway between Basra and Baghdad (*Wāsiṭ* means "middle").

466 The word *juʿal* (pl. *jiʿlān*) has been translated as "dung beetle" and *khunfusāʾ* (pl. *khanāfis*) as "black beetle."

467 *Al-dūdah al-ḥamrāʾ*: identification unknown, since *dūdah* can mean maggot, worm, or caterpillar.

468 Died 228/842–43. He (or his son Sawwār, see *Ḥayawān*, II:187) may be the one who donated a large library to Basra (see *EI2* II:127a, VI:197b, VIII:416b). For another English translation of this passage, see Pellat, *The Life and Works of Jāḥiẓ*, translated by D. M. Hawke, 154–55 (incorporated in Robert Irwin, *Night and Horses and the Desert*, 90–91); for a French translation, see Souami, *Le cadi et la mouche: anthologie du Livre des animaux*, 309–10.

469 A traditional Bedouin way of sitting.

470 A way of saying that he did not use the toilet during the day.

471 Q Ḥajj 22:73. For a related anecdote, see *al-Sharīf al-Murtaḍā Amālī*, II:105: "It is related that one of the Abbasid caliphs—I think it was al-Rashīd—ascended the pulpit in order to preach the sermon, when a fly landed on his face. He chased it away but it returned, so that he became inhibited and was unable to continue. He said, 'I seek refuge with God, the Hearing One, the Knowing One: «O men, a similitude is struck; so listen to it. Those upon whom you call, apart from God, shall never create a fly even though they banded together for it. And if a fly should rob them of anything, they would never rescue it from him. Feeble indeed are the seeker and the sought!»' Then he descended. People admired him for this."

472 In Basra.

473 *Ṭaylasān*, a kind of cowl or headshawl often worn by religious scholars, lawyers, or cadis.

474 An otherwise unknown person.

475 On this topic see Kruk, "A Frothy Bubble: Spontaneous Generation in the Medieval Islamic Tradition."

476 Dhū l-Rummah, *Dīwān* (Abū Ṣāliḥ), 1121; (Macartney), 313; see also al-Jāḥiẓ, *al-Ḥayawān*, V:404. However, the word *farāsh*, normally "moths" or "butterflies," is here to be interpreted as "scant remains of water," according to the commentaries in the *Dīwān* and Ibn Manẓūr, *Lisān al-ʿArab*, s.v. *F-R-Sh* (quoting this verse). This explanation is also incorporated, between square brackets, in the present text, but has been omitted by me since it is obviously a later addition and not by al-Jāḥiẓ.

477 Thaqīf: a tribe settled in al-Ṭāʾif, southeast of Mecca. *Nabīdh* is wine made from fruit other than grapes (and allowed by some Muslim scholars).

478 Minor poet and friend of al-Jāḥiẓ.

479 Naṣībīn, ancient Nisibis/Nasibis, modern Turkish Nusaybin, in northern Mesopotamia. The alleged profusion of its scorpions is said to date from the siege by the pre-Islamic Persian king Anūsharwān, who pelted the town with scorpions brought from southern Iraq (Yāqūt, *Muʿjam al-buldān*, s.v. Naṣībīn).

480 Attributed to al-Farazdaq in other sources; see e.g. Ibn Manẓūr, *Lisān al-ʿarab*, s.v. *W-N-M*; not found in the *Dīwān* (so that one cannot decide between "on it" and "on him").

481 A place near Basra, named thus ("little ruin") because of the ruins of a Sassanid castle found there.

482 I prefer to read the variant given in the note: *wa-mā aẓunnuka*; reading *wa-mā ẓanantuhū* means that the narrator is speaking rather than the bargeman; but then one could have expected *fa-mā* instead of *wa-mā*.

483 Al-Jāḥiẓ often mentions these "mosque people"; see e.g. Montgomery, "Al-Jāḥiẓ and the Masjidites of Basra."

484 Aristotle.

485 See Aristotle, *Part of Animals*, 648a 20.

486 Not identified.

487 Q Ḥijr 15:22.

488 Umayyad caliph, r. 65/685–86/705.

489 Minor Bedouin poet who settled in Basra, noted for his lampoons.

490 Identification uncertain. Abū Ḥuzābah joined the rebellion of Abd al-Raḥmān ibn Muḥammad Ibn al-Ashʿath (80/699–82/701) and was probably killed during it (al-Iṣfahānī, *Aghānī*, XXII:260),

491 Not identified.

492 Q Ḥajj 22:73.

493 Q Māʾidah 5:110, in the story of Jesus (a wholly human being according to Muslims) who is said to have created a bird, with God's permission.

494 Q Muʾminūn 23:14. The plural seems to imply that God is not the only creator.

495 Zuhayr (pre-Islamic), in an ode in praise of Harim ibn Sinān; see Ahlwardt, *The Divans of the Six Ancient Arabic Poets*, 82.

496 See above, note 459.

497 Abū Isḥāq Ibrāhim ibn Sayyār al-Naẓẓām (d. between 220/835 and 230/845), leading Muʿtazilite theologian.

498 Muʿtazilites, contemporaries of al-Jāḥiẓ.

499 *Al-ʿuṣm* (pl. of *aʿṣam*), "with white markings": not clear; often denoting ibexes, but also used for a kind of crow (see Ibn Manẓūr, *Lisān al-ʿArab*, s.v. *ʿ-Ṣ-M*), which seems more likely here.

500 Source: Abū Ḥayyān al-Tawḥīdī (ca. 315/927–after 400/1010), *al-Imtāʿ wal-muʾānasah*, I:70–82, 86–87, 89–96 (*The Seventh Night*). For another, shortened, translation of the beginning of this text, see Lewis, *Race and Slavery in the Middle East*, 143–45; for a summary see Bergé, "Mérites respectifs des nations".

501 See C. E. Bosworth, entry "Shuʿūbiyya" in *EAL*, 717; S. Enderwitz, entry "Shuʿūbiyya" in *EI2*, IX:513–16; H. T. Norris, "*Shuʿūbiyyah* in Arabic Literature," in *ABL*, 31–47.

502 In what follows "Arabs" mostly refers to the pre-Islamic and early Islamic Bedouin Arabs. The word *al-ʿAjam* is ambiguous, as is clear from what follows: either non-Arabs in general, or (very often) specifically the Persians.

503 ʿAbd Allāh ibn al-Muqaffaʿ (executed ca. 139/756), one of the founders of Arabic literary prose, translator of works from Pahlavi into Arabic (including the famous collection of

animal fables *Kalīlah wa-Dimnah*) and author of epistles on various topics, including *al-Yatīmah* on *adab* and practical wisdom; see above.

504 Arab orator and narrator of stories, d. after 162/778; the text has wrongly "Shabbah." A version of the following story involving Ibn al-Muqaffaʿ is also found in the large anthology *al-ʿIqd al-farīd* by Ibn ʿAbd Rabbih (d. 328/940), III:324–25.

505 Famous camel market near Basra, an important meeting place of town with desert. "Standing," as the following shows, means sitting on their animals (presumably mules).

506 Unidentified; the version in Ibn ʿAbd Rabbih, *ʿIqd*, III: 324 has "Nayrūz," equally unknown.

507 Q Wāqiʿah 56:29, in a description of Paradise.

508 cf. Q Ṭā Hā 20:53 and Zukhruf 43:10.

509 *Al-Zanj* specifically refers to the inhabitants of East Africa. Ibn ʿAbd Rabbih's version, instead of al-Zanj, has "the Blacks" (*al-Sūdān*), called "the worst of God's creation" by Ibn al-Muqaffaʿ; in addition, one finds the Khazars (a powerful nomadic nation in early Islamic times, in southern Russia and the Caucasus); they are called "pasturing cattle."

510 The terms used are *rabīʿī, ṣayfī, qayẓī* (from *qayẓ*, "intense heat," rather than *kharīf*, "autumn"), and *shitāwī*.

511 An ancient and popular form of Arab meteorology that associated some stars and constellations with rain; see above, Jarīr's poem, line 10 and Dhū l-Rummah's poem, line 2.

512 Daylam is a mountainous region in northern Iran, the home of the Būyid dynasty that ruled the central Arab lands in al-Tawḥīdī's time.

513 This seems to contradict the earlier statement that they were only good at building and geometry; but the Byzantines (*al-Rūm*) are here obviously equated with the ancient Greeks (usually *al-Yūnān*).

514 Sassanid ruler from AD 531 to 579; Kisrā is the Arabicized form of Persian Khusraw (Chosroes in Greek).

515 Tribal leader and poet who converted to Islam in 8/629.

516 ʿAbd al-Muṭṭalib ibn Hāshim was the paternal grandfather of the Prophet Muḥammad and of ʿAlī (the fourth caliph), and the father of al-ʿAbbās (eponymous ancestor of the Abbasids).

517 See above, al-Mutanabbī's poem, line 27, p. 63.

518 From Khwārazm, ancient Chorasmia, the region south of the Aral Sea.

519 Al-Tawḥīdī refers to the avoidance in Arabic of consonant clusters and of adjacent consonants with similar places of articulations (e.g. no roots such as *S-Sh-Z* or *Ḥ-ʾ-Kh*).

520 Reading *faṣlan* rather than *faḍlan*. In the preceding there are a few textual difficulties and a few phrases have been omitted here.

521 Several viziers of the Samanids (who were Persian proto-"nationalists") were called al-Jayhānī, one of whom wrote a book called *al-Masālik wal-mamālik* (not preserved). For the problems of identification, see Ch. Pellat, "al-Djayhānī" in *EI2*, Supplement.

522 Arabic *yarbūʿ*, a small rodent.

523 Reading, with the errata, *yataghāwarūn*.

524 This list of foreign titles would require extensive annotation, here omitted (the same with the following locations in Arabia). It is strange to see the term *faghfūr* applied to Khurasan, as it normally refers to the Chinese emperor; see *EI2* s.v. "faghfūr." Askanān stands for the Arsacids (the Parthian dynasty reigning after Alexander); Ardawān may be equated with the Artabans mentioned by the Greeks.

525 *Al-jāhiliyyah al-ūlā wal-thāniyah*: either the period from Adam to Noah and from Christ to Muḥammad, respectively, or the pre-Islamic period and the sinfulness in Islamic times (cf. the commentaries on Q Aḥzāb 33:33).

526 Q Āl ʿImrān 3:26, Arberry's translation.

527 Here al-Tawḥīdī goes on to describe the civilization of the allegedly uncivilized Bedouin Arabs. Through their annual markets, held all over the Peninsula, they could import foreign goods from various countries. The early Islamic conquests made them acquire many regions and riches, without losing their original virtues.

528 Famous work on astronomy by Ptolemy (second century AD), translated into Arabic first from Syriac ca. 800 and later in the ninth century from the original Greek.

529 One might think that this Abū Ḥāmid was present at the session with the vizier; but this is ruled out since he died in 362/973. He is often quoted by al-Tawḥīdī. An ardent partisan of the Arab cause, he may have been a Persian himself; at least he spoke with a strong Khurasanian accent. The following passage is quoted and discussed in van Gelder, *Close Relationships*, 39–51. Close-kin incest is mentioned as meritorious in ancient Zoroastrian texts, even though it is not certain that it was widely practiced.

530 Reading *maʿīf* instead of *ḍaʿīf*.

531 Or Zarathustra (Arabic: Zarādusht).

532 e.g. Jews and Christians.

533 An old syncretistic group of "astrolators" in Ḥarrān (Carrhae), tolerated though pagan, and barely surviving at the time of the debate; see T. Fahd, entry "Ṣābiʾa" in *EI2*.

534 Some words supplied to make the text coherent.

535 A saying meaning "they went from bad to worse."

536 *Ghayrah* is the mixture of appropriate sexual jealousy and sense of honor that men are supposed to have with regard to their female kin.

537 A short passage is omitted in which it is argued that the revolutionary religious movement led by Mazdak was crushed by a strong Sassanid ruler in AD 528 or 529, whereas Zoroaster found a weak king, willing to elevate and support him.

538 I am not certain of the meaning of *farāghuhum* here; the context seems to suggest "being (temporarily) free from lust."

539 Burying infant girls, forbidden in Islam, was practiced by some pre-Islamic tribes. See Leemhuis, entry "wa'd al-banāt" in *EI2*.

540 The expression occurs in Q A'rāf 7:128 and several other Qur'anic passages.

541 The editors, unable to identify him, suggest reading al-Anṭākī, and think 'Alī ibn Aḥmad al-Anṭākī could be meant, who died in Baghdad in 376/986–87. However, a certain Abū l-Ḥasan ibn Ka'b al-Anṣārī is quoted several times by al-Tawḥīdī as one of his contemporaries and described as a Mu'tazilite *adīb* and theologian.

542 The Prophet Muḥammad.

543 The line is attributed in other sources to the pre-Islamic 'Abd al-'Āṣ ibn Tha'labah al-Tanūkhī or to the more famous poet al-Nābighah al-Dhubyānī.

544 Apparently believing that incest through the maternal line is less harmful (see also the following poem).

545 Literally perhaps "that ripple like waves" (*tamūju*), therefore "are crooked."

546 I am not sure if *khālid* is used here as a personal name, or if it is relevant that of two famous members of Asad, called "the two Khālids" (al-Khālidān), one, Khālid ibn Naḍlah, was nicknamed al-Mahzūl ("the Skinny"). I have not found any succession of generations called Khālid, so perhaps *khālid* means "vigorous old man" here.

547 Reading *shibr* "span" instead of *sirr*.

548 The argument is unclear.

549 cf. Q Āl 'Imrān 3:128, Anfāl 8:51, Ḥajj 22:10, Fuṣṣilat 41:46, Qāf 50:29.

550 Source: Abū Ḥanīfah al-Dīnawarī (d. 282/895 or later), *al-Akhbār al-ṭiwāl*, 383–85, 388–96. For al-Ṭabarī's lengthy account of the same episode, see his *Tārīkh al-rusul wal-mulūk*, III:i: English translation in *The History of al-Ṭabarī. vol. XXXI: The War Between Brothers*, translated by Michael Fishbein. Many details, anecdotes, and poems are also given by al-Mas'ūdī; see the English translation of selected passages in Mas'udi, *The Meadows of Gold: The Abbasids*, translated by Paul Lunde & Caroline Stone, 80–85, 132–221.

551 174/790–91.

552 See *EI2*, Supplement s.v. (C.E. Bosworth); he owed his rise from humble origins to his being brother to the eventual mother of the caliph Hārūn al-Rashīd.

553 Grammarian, d. 189/805 or later. Variants of this passage are found in several later sources, such as al-Mas'ūdī, *Murūj al-dhahab*; al-Bayhaqī, *al-Maḥāsin wal-masāwī*; al-Marzubānī,

Nūr al-qabas; Ibn Ḥamdūn, *al-Tadhkirah*; al-Zamakhsharī, *Rabīʿ al-abrār*; Yāqūt, *Muʿjam al-udabāʾ*; al-Damīrī, *Ḥayāt al-ḥayawān*; and al-Ibshīhī, *al-Mustaṭraf.*

554 Also known as Zubaydah ("Butter Lump"), her proper name being Amat al-ʿAzīz, grandchild of al-Manṣūr; b. 145/763, married al-Rashīd 165/781–82. Her only child was Muḥammad, later al-Amīn, born 170/787, six months after ʿAbd Allāh, later al-Maʾmūn, son of a Persian concubine; she died in 210/831.

555 For another version of Zubaydah's dream see al-Masʿūdī, *Murūj*, IV:261–62, trans. Lunde and Stone, 253–54. There, three women appear in her dream on the night al-Amīn is conceived; the speeches of the first two are wholly different in wording but substantially the same as in *al-Akhbār al-ṭiwāl*; the third is also similar in wording. Two similar dreams follow.

556 cf. al-Masʿūdī, *Murūj al-dhahab*, IV:210–12 (trans. Lunde and Stone, 80–81), where al-Kisāʾī is named instead of al-Aṣmaʿī; it is a more flowery and elaborated version, which is found (shortened) also in Ibn Ḥamdūn, *Tadhkirah*, IX: 291–92; al-Zamakhsharī, *Rabīʿ al-abrār*, III:553–55. Another version, set in the year 182/798 and also mentioning al-Kisāʾī, but without the sad ending, is in al-Marzubānī, *Nūr al-qabas*, 284; Yāqūt, *Muʿjam al-udabāʾ*, XIII:172–73; al-Ibshīhī, *Mustaṭraf*, II:11.

557 *Awṣiyāʾ*: see *EI2* s.v. "waṣī" (E. Kohlberg); in Shīʿite Islam, the legatee, successor, or inheritor of the Prophet, specifically ʿAlī and the imams.

558 The seventh imam of the Twelver Shiʿites, Mūsā al-Kāẓim (ibn Jaʿfar al-Ṣādiq ibn Muḥammad al-Bāqir ibn ʿAlī Zayn al-ʿĀbidin ibn al-Ḥusayn ibn ʿAlī), 128/745–183/799 (other dates are also given).

559 This rather Shīʿite passage is also found, without Mūsā being mentioned, in al-Masʿūdī, but not in other versions such as al-Ḥamdūnī, al-Zamakhsharī, or al-Marzubānī.

560 Vizier of al-Rashīd and al-Amīn; 138/757–ca. 207/823.

561 Marw or Merv, town in Khurāsān (now called Mary, in Turkmenistan).

562 Black clothes are not necessarily a sign of mourning, since it was the official color of the Abbasid dynasty.

563 Better known as Abū Nuwās, who became al-Amīn's boon companion and shared his love of wine and boys.

564 See Abū Nuwās *Dīwān*, I:134–36, 11 lines; it is a somewhat daring combination of wine-song and eulogy (but the famous "Mantle Ode" by Kaʿb ibn Zuhayr, recited to the Prophet, also mentions wine in the opening section, as does a poem by Ḥassān ibn Thābit, "the Prophet's poet," see his *Dīwān*, 71–73).

565 The cup is adorned with jewels.

566 That is, the leading members of the dynasty, descendants of al-Manṣūr, who reigned from 136/754 to 158/775.

567 The name is sometimes voweled as Ṣubayḥ.

568 That is, his own son, a young child at the time. Given the honorific name of al-Nāṭiq bil-ḥaqq ("Speaker of Truth"), he is described as unable to speak, stupid, and needing a nurse night and day (al-Masʿūdī, *Murūj al-dhahab*, IV:271).

569 The Umayyad caliph who reigned 65/685–86/705.

570 Leading members of the dynasty and the court; the title of the last-mentioned, "Keeper of the Prayer Mat," refers to the official responsible for the personal prayer rug of the ruler (Ṣāliḥ's son, ʿAlī, held the same office later).

571 Near present-day Tehran. Ṭāhir, probably of Persian origin, trusted general of al-Maʾmūn, was to become the founder of the virtually autonomous dynasty of governors in Khurāsān, called the Ṭāhirids.

572 Of Iranian origin, he had been al-Maʾmūn's tutor. He was assassinated in 202/818 (some said al-Maʾmūn was behind it).

573 In al-Ṭabarī (*Tārīkh*, III:i, 809) and al-Masʿūdī (*Murūj al-dhahab*, IV, 263) there are two speakers, called ʿAbd Allāh ibn Khāzim and Khuzaymah ibn Khāzim.

574 He had been governor of Khurāsān under Hārūn al-Rashīd.

575 Al-Amīn's mother (see above, note 555).

576 A town, approximately 120 miles northeast of Baghdad, near the entrance of the pass through the Zagros mountains.

577 A town, about 170 miles from al-Rayy.

578 In al-Ṭabarī he is called al-Ḥusayn.

579 An Arabicized spelling of what appears in al-Ṭabarī as "Kalwāṣ."

580 The Abnāʾ (short for Abnāʾ al-Dawlah, "Sons of the Dynasty") were the descendants of the Khurāsānian troops who had helped the Abbasids come to power, some sixty years before, and who enjoyed a privileged status in Baghdad.

581 Approximately thirty-five miles west of Hamadhān.

582 In Persian called Kirmān-Shāh, about a hundred miles southwest of Hamadhān.

583 The lengthy and bloody siege of Baghdad, here summarized in a few laconic sentences, is described in graphic detail in other sources such as al-Ṭabarī's *Tārīkh* and al-Masʿūdī's *Murūj al-dhahab*.

584 Two proverbs, the first a very common one meaning that things have come to a head or have gone too far; the latter is a hemistich from an anonymous poem, see e.g. Abū Hilāl al-ʿAskarī, *Jamharat al-amthāl*, I:444–45. Ignace Kratchkovsky's "correction" of the rhyme

word *yuʿārā* to *yuʿāra* (in his *Préface, variants et index* to the edition, Leiden: Brill, 1912, 81) is therefore inappropriate.

585 He is referring of course to al-Maʾmūn, using this title slightly prematurely.

586 Madīnat al-Salām, the official name of Baghdad. Al-Maʾmūn's entrance into Baghdad did not take place, in fact, until 104/819, six years after al-Amīn's death. He became the "sole ruler" only after quashing the movement that installed his uncle Ibrāhīm ibn al-Mahdī (gifted singer, composer, poet, and chef) as caliph in 201/817.

587 5 September 813. The entries "al-Amīn" and "al-Maʾmūn" in *EI2* (I:437b, VI:334) both have "24–25 September 813," based on a version, as found in al-Ṭabarī, that has *li-khamsin baqīna* instead of *li-khamsin khalawna*.

588 Al-Maʾmūn played an important role in the translation movement from Greek into Arabic; but Euclid had already been translated in the second/eighth century, during al-Manṣūr's reign; see e.g. Gutas, *Greek Thought, Arabic Culture*, 30, 32, 52.

589 Leading Muʿtazilite theologian, d. 226/841 or later.

590 Said to be at a distance of one day's march from Tarsus, near the border with the Byzantine Empire. Yāqūt, *Muʿjam al-buldān*, s.v. vowels it as Badhandūn; but Budandūn might be better, since the name is "translated" as "stretch your legs!" (al-Masʿūdī, *Murūj al-dhahab*, IV:342), which suggests something like "*podon-don*" in Greek (al-Maʾmūn took it as an omen presaging his death).

591 For a recent introduction, see de Callataÿ, *Ikhwan al-Safa: A Brotherhood of Idealists at the Fringe of Orthodox Islam*.

592 For an English translation and critical Arabic text of this lengthy debate, see *Epistles of the Brethren of Purity: The Case of the Animals versus Man Before the King of the Jinn. An Arabic Critical Edition and English Translation of Epistle* 22, edited and translated by Lenn E. Goodman and Richard McGregor. For the following passage, see 106–7 (English), 45–47 (Arabic). See also the slightly different text of Ikhwān al-Ṣafāʾ, *Rasāʾil*, II:208.

593 Reading *muʿāfayn* with the Beirut text instead of *muʿāwinīn*.

594 A reference to Q Baqarah 2:30, Ṣād 38:26, Anʿām 6:165, etc.

595 *faddān* or *fadān*, pl. *afdina*, *fadādīn* or *fudun* "pair of bulls or oxen for ploughing, yoke of oxen."

596 Goodman & McGregor, 122–23 (English), 61–63 (Arabic); cf. Ikhwān al-Ṣafāʾ, *Rasāʾil*, II:220–21.

597 The hare has criticized horses for ignorantly letting themselves be used to hunt hares as well as gazelles, wild asses, and other animals.

598 Reading, with Goodman & McGregor, *thawr* instead of *sinnawr* ("cat") as in the Beirut text.

599 A hemistich from the horse description in the *Muʿallaqah* by Imruʾ al-Qays.

600 Reading *taḥta ʿaduwwi ṣāḥibihī*, instead of Goodman and McGregor's *taḥta ṣāḥibihī* or *taḥta ʿadwi ṣāḥibihī* of the Beirut text.

601 Reading, with the Beirut text, *fī ṭalabi ʿaduwwihī* instead of *fī tilka l-ʿudwah* (Goodman and McGregor).

602 Ikhwān al-Ṣafāʾ, *Rasāʾil*, II:383–84.

603 Lit. "wind catcher" in Persian; also called *malqaf*; see e.g. Rosenthal, "Poetry and Architecture: the *bādhanj*."

604 cf. M. Rodinson, *EI2*, IV:327–33 s.v. "kabid" (esp. 330).

605 The mention of pulse (*nabḍ*) suggests that not only veins but arteries (*shiryān*, pl. *sharāyīn*) too are meant. Another word for "vein" is *warīd*, pl. *awridah*.

606 See e.g. al-Qazwīnī, *ʿAjāʾib al-makhlūqāt* (ed. Cairo, 1970), 221; it is said to be connected with the liver which extracts the black bile, and with the stomach, where it stimulates appetite.

607 Reading *thufl* ("dregs, residues, sediment") instead of *thiqal*.

608 *Bayt al-ʿarḍ*; translation uncertain.

609 The internal senses, or spiritual faculties, include imagination, thought, and memory.

610 Ikhwān al-Ṣafāʾ, *Rasāʾil*, III:44–45.

611 Q ʿAnkabūt 29:57, Arberry's translation.

612 Q Anbiyāʾ 21:90, Arberry's translation.

613 Q Baqarah 2:223, Arberry's translation.

614 See above, p. 86 and note 613.

615 Q Anfāl 8:37, Arberry's translation.

616 Q Zumar 39:61, Arberry's translation.

617 Ikhwān al-Ṣafāʾ, *Rasāʾil*, III:162.

618 Literally, "If they are not raided, the Rūm (Byzantines) will raid." The proverb has not been found in the standard collections.

619 Q Naḥl 16:125, Arberry's translation.

620 Q Aḥzāb 33:70, Arberry's translation.

621 *(Wa-)qul lahum qawlan maʿrūfan* echoes Q Nisāʾ 4:5 and 8: *qūlū lahum qawlan maʿrūfan*.

622 Q Ṭā Hā 20:44, Arberry's translation.

623 Source: al-Tanūkhī, *al-Faraj baʿd al-shiddah*, III:378–85; cf. al-Tanūkhī, *Nishwār al-muḥāḍarah*, III:236–43. For an earlier English translation by D. S. Margoliouth, see [al-Tanūkhī], *The Table-Talk of a Mesopotamian Judge*, 230–35; for a German translation by Arnold Hottinger see at-Tanūkhī, *Ende Gut, Alles Gut: Das Buch der Erleichterung nach der Bedrängnis* (Zurich: Manesse, 1979), 194–203.

624 Al-Ṣafadī, *al-Ghayth al-musajjam*, I:413.

625 A few verses of this obscure poet are quoted in *Nishwār al-muḥāḍarah*, III:243, where he is described as having a "long (impudent) tongue," i.e. a poet of lampoons and eulogies.

626 Important town in Palestine.

627 *Ḥiss* is sensory perception in general, but very often refers specifically to hearing.

628 *Nishwār*: "like a bear" (*dubb*, possibly a misreading of *dhiʾb*).

629 It is difficult to decide where to switch from "it" and "paw" to "he" and "hand" (identical in the Arabic). "grave robber" seems to imply a human, but when the narrator says "like a human being," he is apparently still thinking of an animal.

630 They have entered a mosque, which has not been mentioned before.

631 Contrary to Muslim table manners.

632 Literally, "she showed her hand, cut off."

633 Amputation of the right hand for theft, even when the amputation is the result of an accident, is somehow fitting; cf. Abū Dāwūd, *Sunan, kitāb al-Ḥudūd* (32) 19 = IV:367 on *qaṭʿ al-nabbāsh*. It could be argued, however, that it is not a proper theft since the deceased is not a legal person: this would be a case of *shubhah* ("semblance; occasion for doubt"), which would prevent the *ḥadd* or "fixed punishment" for theft in Islamic law.

634 Reading *sakantu*, with *Nishwār*, rather than *sakattu* "I was silent."

635 Divorce occurs when the man repeats three times (to make it irrevocable) the formula "I divorce you" or something of the same purport; the document produced afterward merely serves as visible proof.

636 Source: al-Tanūkhī, *al-Faraj baʿd al-shiddah*, II:191–205 (cf. ed. Cairo, 1955, 144–53, which is bad but has some variants mentioned in the notes). For a French translation (very lightly annotated) and study, see Canard, "Les aventures d'un prisonnier arabe et d'un patrice byzantin à l'époque des guerres bulgaro-byzantines"; for a German translation without annotation see Arnold Hottinger (at-Tanūkhī, *Ende Gut, Alles Gut*, 101–19).

637 Son of the Caliph al-Mahdī (162/779–224/839); see above, note 636. The scribe Ḥumayd is not known, nor is Makhlad al-Ṭabarī.

638 Abbasid caliph who reigned 158/775–169/785. As Canard remarks (p. 63), there is a large gap between the time of al-Mahdī and that of Sālim.

639 On him see J. D. Latham in *ALUP*, 155–64.

640 Umayyad caliph, r. 105/724–125/743.

641 Umayyad caliph, r. 65/685–86/705.

642 First Umayyad caliph, r. 41/661–60/680.

643 On the *muḥaddith* Abū Hāshim Qabāth ibn Razīn ibn Ḥumayd ibn Ṣāliḥ ibn Aṣram al-Lakhmī al-Miṣrī (d. 156/773), see e.g. Ibn Ḥajar, *Tahdhīb al-Tahdhīb*, VIII:343–44. The

name is also vocalized as Qubāth (s.v. al-Suyūṭī, *Ḥusn al-muḥāḍarah*, I:277). Ibn Ḥajar (d. 852/1449) has read al-Tanūkhī's story and is understandably puzzled by the chronology: "I saw in *al-Faraj baʿd al-shiddah* by Abū ʿAlī al-Tanūkhī a story about this Qabāth, who was taken prisoner by the Byzantines during the reign of ʿAbd al-Malik ibn Marwān. This would mean that he lived a very long time, because there is some seventy years between ʿAbd al-Malik's death and his. To this should be added some twenty years, putting his birth around the year 66, or even earlier, for the story tells that he was taken prisoner during Muʿāwiyah's caliphate, in which case he would have lived more than a hundred years. Perhaps Muʿāwiyah (II) ibn Yazīd ibn Muʿāwiyah is meant..."

644 Fusṭāṭ, now also known as "Old Cairo."

645 Obviously a corruption. The emperors during Muʿāwiyah's reign were Constans II (641–68) and Constantine IV Pogonatos (668–85). The edition of Cairo 1955 has "Warqāʾ ibn Mūriqah" (or Mawriqah), which is possibly a corruption of Heraklios, son of Maurikios (Maurikios reigned 582–602). Al-Masʿūdī (*Murūj al-dhahab*, II:53–54) mentions "Mūriq ibn Hiraql." For more details, see Canard, "Les aventures," 64–66.

646 Leontius reigned 695–98; but possibly Leon III (717–41) is meant.

647 *Ankaʾ* is a mistake for *ankā*. The Cairo edition has *ankar*, which is also possible ("more disagreeable").

648 Shaking arrow shafts from a quiver to draw lots was also practiced by the pre-Islamic Arabs in the "game" called *maysir*, which may have inspired this description. *Biṭrīq*, or "patrician," here means local governor or military commander. The geographer Ibn Khurradādhbih (d. ca. 300/911) mentions that there are twelve such commanders, six in Constantinople and six in the provinces. See *EI2* s.v. "Biṭrīḳ" (Irfan Kawar), where it is mentioned that the term is sometimes confused with "patriarch" (normally *baṭrak*, also *baṭriyark*); toward the end of this story one finds precisely this.

649 The word Burjān sometimes refers to the Burgundians but often, like here, to the Bulgars (who are also called al-Bulghār), who were around in the Balkan (as in this story) and in the Volga area.

650 Canard comments that this is no doubt a mistake for "some months." But of course it is not at all impossible that the name of the dreaded patrician did not come up for some years.

651 The word *zabāniyah* is taken from Q ʿAlaq 96:18, where it is traditionally interpreted as the angels who take sinners to Hell: "Hell's Angels."

652 The third and second-longest sura, called after ʿImrān (Amram in the Old Testament), the father of Mūsā/Moses.

653 The Arabic literally has the common expression "May my soul be ransom for you, and (I'll give) my father for you!"

654 The Arabic has "the nights"; since one counts nights rather than days. Moreover, "*al-layālī*" has connotations of inexorable Fate.

655 *ʿIlm* could be "science, scholarship" or simply "knowledge." In this context it could refer to knowledge of Islamic "Prophetic Tradition" in particular (cf. Canard: *traditions prophétiques*).

656 *Ifranjī* could be any west-European language, but Frankish or proto-French is the most likely here. The Cairo edition adds "Kurdish." The Khazars were a Turkic people in Southern Russia.

657 In Islam, nursing (implying breastfeeding) creates a bond of kinship, with consequences for the regulations concerning incest.

658 The significance of these details is not clear; presumably the exactness adds to the verisimilitude of the tale.

659 One could translate "I fell asleep"; but the verb *nāma* can also mean "to lie down" (cf. below, where *nawwama* must mean "to make s.o. lie down").

660 *Ḥadd* is the equivalent of the Roman *limes*, border area. As Canard says (p. 68), there was no "province of the Bulgars" in the Byzantine Empire (it would have been the province of Thrace).

661 The Cairo edition has "My daughter says you are..."

662 As Gabrieli ("Il valore letterario e storico del *Faraĝ baʿda š-šiddah* di Tanūḫī") and Canard also noticed ("Les aventures," 71–72), the story contains elements also found in Sindbad's fourth voyage. For the motif of knowledge of horses and horses' gear as a means to attract the attention of a king and being married to his daughter, see *The Arabian Nights: Tales of 1001 Nights*, trans. Malcolm C. Lyons, II: 483.

663 Reading *millatinā* with the Cairo edition, instead of *sunnatinā*, which would be a pointless repetition.

664 *Sharāb* "drink" is often "wine," and later wine (*khamr*) is in fact mentioned.

665 For the motif of being buried alive with a deceased spouse, see again Sindbad's fourth voyage in *The Thousand and One Nights* (trans. Lyons, II:485–89). Unlike our hero, Sindbad is not warned about the custom before the marriage, and his wife is really dead. However, his behavior in the pit is just as callous as that of the couple. For the parallels with folklore, see also Chauvin, *Bibliographie des oeuvres arabes ou relatifs aux arabes*, VII:19, and cf. VII:74, VI:165.

666 That they did not think of shouting to the people above, either at this stage or later when other couples are lowered, is one of the several improbable moments in the story.

667 Another unlikely reaction, which makes one doubt the girl's devotion.

668 Even if the unintelligible *al-hibyah* is read as *al-haybah*, the sentence is not very clear. The Cairo edition has "their affection (*ulfatuhumā*) for the girl remained and a good thing was the result."

669 If she knew their names she must have realized that the couple were her parents-in-law: all the more reason to query her earlier behavior.

670 A sudden shift from reported to direct speech.

671 As was already apparent when the Emperor spoke of "theologians" (*mutakallimūn*), there is a confusion here between "patricians" and "patriarchs," both *baṭāriqah*, pl. of *biṭrīq* (see above, note 648). For this episode, compare the story of the similar dispute of al-Tanūkhī's contempory al-Qāḍī al-Bāqillānī (d. 403/1013) in Constantinople with a Metropolitan (*muṭrān*), told in al-Qāḍī ʿIyāḍ, *Tartīb al-madārik* (quoted in the introduction of al-Bāqillānī, *Iʿjāz al-Qur'ān*, 32–33). For a farcical version of the same, involving a simpleton who unwittingly defeats a Christian theologian, see Ibn ʿĀṣim al-Gharnāṭī, *Ḥadā'iq al-azhār*, 183–84. In another variant the theologian is an Azharite Muslim; see al-Shirbīnī, *Hazz al-quḥūf*, ed. Humphrey Davies, 70–75, trans. Humphrey Davies, 48–49; this text has also been translated below, p. 339.

672 Presumably Sālim, the *mawlā* of Hisham (see the beginning of the story).

673 This final sentence, not found in all manuscripts, may be a copyist's way of expressing some doubt about the truth of the whole story.

674 Source: al-Tanūkhī, *al-Faraj baʿd al-shiddah*, IV:129–32 (in the rather defective edition of Cairo, 1955, it is found pp. 288–89), from the chapter on escaping from dangerous animals; cf. al-Tanūkhī, *Nishwār al-muḥāḍarah*, III:195–97. See also the translation by D. S. Margoliouth (*The Table-Talk of a Mesopotamian Judge*, 212–14); for a German translation, see Arnold Hottinger, at-Tanūkhī, *Ende Gut, Alles Gut*, 223–26. For a study of this text and many parallels (including some in Persian, and some involving a different protagonist) see van Gelder, "To Eat or Not to Eat Elephant: A Travelling Story in Arabic and Persian Literature."

675 The transmitters are mentioned in other sources. Ibrāhīm al-Khawwāṣ ("maker of palm-leaf baskets"), the protagonist and narrator of the story, was born in Samarra in Iraq and died in Rayy (near present-day Tehran) in 291/903. Many wonderful events about him are told in the sources; see e.g. Gramlich, *Die Wunder der Freunde Gottes*, 119–20, 157–58, 326–27, 366–67, 368, 407.

676 Many Sufis were great travelers. The company in this story ends up, apparently, in India.

677 As a kind of perpetual Ramadan.

678 They think he is joking; the oath is all the more strange because according to most specialists in Islamic law, eating elephant flesh is forbidden (because elephants have tusks and are aggressive).

679 I.e. they said "I testify that there is no god but God and that Muḥammad is His messenger."

680 In an illustration to this story (in the version of the great Persian mystic Rūmī) one sees the contrast between the companions, who lie prostrate (as if turning their back to God) and the protagonist, who reclines on his back; see e.g. *EI2*, s.v. "Fīl," or (in color) in Lewis (ed.), *The World of Islam: Faith, People, Culture*, p. [136].

681 Ibrāhīm is not gloating: it is a Muslim custom to praise God also for misfortunes.

682 Instead of this clumsy repetition the *Nishwār* version has "it did not remove its trunk from me."

683 Source: al-Tanūkhī (d. 384/994), *Nishwār al-muḥāḍarah*, VII:71–73; the editor has taken the text from Ibn al-Jawzī, *al-Adhkiyā'* (*Clever People*), 64–66. See Malti-Douglas, "The Classical Arabic Detective," 59–66.

684 He reigned from 279/892 to 289/902. The sources describe him as astute and energetic, though given to cruelty (al-Mas'ūdī, *Murūj al-dhahab*, V:138, 155 gives examples of his ingenuity in devising barbaric forms of execution). For more stories involving al-Mu'taḍid as "detective," see Malti-Douglas's article.

685 The masculine is used in a general, impersonal sense (of course the caliph knows that the hennaed hand belonged to a female).

686 See the editor's note and see e.g. Yāqūt, *Mu'jam al-buldān*, s.v.; it is called after Yaḥyā ibn Khālid al-Barmakī, famous vizier under Hārūn al-Rashīd.

687 Such sudden transitions from third to first person, from reported speech to direct speech, are common in medieval Arabic narratives.

688 That is, a member of the ruling dynasty, the 'Abbāsids.

689 The number may be without significance (but one could think of bags for each of two hands, two feet, two arms, two legs, a rump, and a head).

690 Rayṭah (d. 170/786–87), a daughter of al-Saffāḥ, the first 'Abbāsid caliph, married al-Mahdī, the third caliph.

691 Malti-Douglas interprets *'aẓīm* as "a huge man," which seems less likely here.

692 One wonders if one should read *makāyidihinna*, with the feminine possessive pronoun, for *makāyidihim*, since "wiles" are regularly ascribed, in a misogynist vein, to women. Perhaps, therefore, translate "eager to benefit from the women's wiles."

693 Malti-Douglas's interpretation seems correct; read perhaps *ajrahā* instead of *jidhrahā* (*Nishwār*) or *ḥadharahā* (*Adhkiyā'*), neither of which makes sense.

694 Literally, "she blackened her face," but probably to be taken in a figurative sense (cf. Malti-Douglas: "and, in fact, made a disgrace of herself").

695 Source: Badīʿ al-Zamān al-Hamadhānī, *al-Maqāmāt,* with commentary by Muḥammad ʿAbduh, 51–54, ed. Constantinople, 1298/1880–81, 17–18; cf. the translation (unrhymed) by W.J. Prendergast, *The Maqámát of Badíʿ al-Zamán al-Hamadhání* (London, 1915), 55–58. There are rhymed translations of this *maqāmah,* imitating the *sajʿ* in the original, in German and Dutch, and an unrhymed one in French: Gernot Rotter, *Vernunft ist nichts als Narretei,* 58–61; Geert Jan van Gelder, "Isfahaan, of Het gebed zonder end," in Vrolijk (ed.), *De taal der engelen,* 437–38; Régis Blachère & Pierre Masnou, *Al-Hamaḏānī: Choix de Maqāmāt (Séances),* 73–77; René Khawam, *Le Livre des Vagabonds,* 59–62.

696 On the *maqāmah,* see Hämeen-Anttila, *Maqama: A History of a Genre.*

697 On the site of contemporary Tehran.

698 In Qur'an recitation the sequence *-āʾ-* is pronounced much longer than a normal long vowel. Ḥamzah (d. 156/772), an authority on the text and recitation of the Qur'an, was especially known for this lengthening.

699 Q Wāqiʿah 56.

700 This expression is not found in ʿAbduh's edition (made for teaching purposes).

701 Q Qāriʿah 101.

702 According to the Qur'an it will last fifty thousand years (Q Maʿārij 70:4), or perhaps only a thousand years (Q Sajdah 32:5).

703 There are no rhymes in this part of his speech.

704 The Arabic text is taken from the large anthology of Andalusian poetry and prose by Ibn Bassām al-Shantarīnī (d. 542/1147), *al-Dhakhīrah fī maḥāsin ahl al-jazīrah,* Pt. I, vol. 2 (Cairo, 1942), 435–41, where it was inserted by a later copyist; see also the edition by Iḥsān ʿAbbās (Beirut, 1979), I, 1:523–28. For a Spanish translation, see Fernando de la Granja, "Dos epístolas de Aḥmad Ibn Burd al-Aṣgar," 399–406, also published in his *Maqāmas y risālas andaluzas,* 3–53.

705 On the genre, see e.g. Wagner, "Die arabische Rangstreitdichtung" and Reinink and Vanstiphout (eds.), *Dispute Poems and Dialogues in the Ancient and Mediaeval Near East.*

706 On this and some later, more elaborate texts on the same theme, see van Gelder, "The Conceit of Pen and Sword: On an Arabic Literary Debate"; on the background see also Gully, "The Sword and the Pen in the Pre-Modern Arabic Heritage."

707 Perhaps this is the sense of *anna l-mulāʾ min taʿḍīdih* (cf. Ibn Manẓūr, *Lisān al-ʿArab* s.v. *ʿ-Ḍ-D*: *thawb muʿaḍḍad: mukhaṭṭaṭ ʿalā shakl al-ʿaḍud*).

708 Al-Suhā is a dim star in Ursa Minor, the highest constellation in the sky; Capella (al-ʿAyyūq), mentioned below, is a bright star in Auriga, near the zenith in winter.

709 Q Qalam 68:1, Arberry's translation. *Nūn* is the Arabic letter *N*, one of the letters or letter combinations that open a number of suras; their meaning is unknown. The Pen may be God's primeval pen that has recorded everything that will happen; "they" are either the angels recording human deeds, or humans endowed with the divine gift of writing.

710 Q ʿAlaq 96:4, Arberry's translation; thought to be part of the first revealed section of the Qur'an.

711 A common saying, attributed to ʿAlī ibn Abī Ṭālib.

712 I cannot make sense of *uzrī bil-wafā'* (both editions) and prefer to read *uzrī bil-wiqā'*.

713 Adopting the suggestion of the ʿAbbās edition (*al-khiyānah*) for the lacuna in the manuscripts.

714 *Tuwakkidu asbāba l-fitan wa-taḍribu qidāḥ al-fitan*: I have assumed the author uses *fitan* in two different senses; the arrow shafts I have taken to allude to the pre-Islamic "game" of *maysir* (see above, note 648).

715 A short sentence, marred by a lacuna, is unclear and has been omitted.

716 A proverb, to say that the pen is claiming things that are beyond him.

717 Possibly alluding to the fact that the true Bedouin Arabs did not write. Interestingly, the Arabic for "pen" (*qalam*) is derived from Greek κάλαμος, while "sword" (*sayf*) may also be Greek, from ξίφος.

718 *Khamā'il* can also mean "luxuriant foliage"; neither seems very appropriate (the choice of the word is inspired by *ḥamā'il* "sword straps").

719 The word *lubb* means both.

720 A reference to a verse found in some versions of Imru' al-Qays's *Muʿallaqah*: "A wadi (empty) like the belly of a wild ass," see his *Dīwān*, 372, a phrase also found in another poem by him, p. 92, where various explanations are given.

721 The lustre and the wavy appearance of the sword's blade.

722 He would think the "lightning" of the sword promises rain.

723 Granja translates *al-ʿaqīq* as if it were a place name in the Hijaz ("hubiera bebido agua de al-ʿAqīq"). I prefer to think that the red stone carnelian is meant.

724 Musk is black.

725 The pen's effect on the pages is like that of a rain cloud on vegetation.

726 Apparently sartorial imagery (embroidery, etc.) is used for writing. The sense of the last word (*musarrad*) is not clear to me. Probably a play on words is involved: *musahham* ("with stripes") could also be "made into arrows" and *musarrad* "made into coats of mail" (cf. Granja's translation, 40–41).

727 In fact only the sword speaks at this stage, as is apparent after a few sentences.

728 Either Arcturus or Spica Virginis, symbols of loftiness and high ambitions.

729 For once, no empty praise, because al-Muwaffaq not only had a warlike spirit, conquering Sardinia from the Christians in 1014–15, he was also a patron of literature and scholarship.

730 I have omitted one line of text neither the syntax nor the sense of which is quite clear to me.

731 *Wa-ḥarban wal-maydān* (ed. Cairo), *wa-jaryan wal-maydān* (ed. Beirut); neither is clear and I have added the words "for me."

732 Source: Abū l-ʿAlāʾ al-Maʿarrī, *Risālat al-Ghufrān* (*The Epistle of Forgiveness*), ed. ʿĀʾishah ʿAbd al-Raḥmān "Bint al-Shāṭiʾ" (Cairo, 1993), 248–54, 256–62, 268–72, 280–81, 283–93, 309, 372–79. For an earlier English partial translation and summary by R.A. Nicholson, see *Journal of the Royal Asiatic Society* 1900, 634–720; 1902, 75–101, 337–62, 813–47; and see the translation (based on a much shortened and simplified edition) by G. Brackenbury, 74–80, 81–87, 91–92, 98–107, 124–25, 154–59. The present translation and annotation have been made in collaboration with Gregor Schoeler; a full translation is to appear in the Library of Arabic Literature.

733 The shaykh (or rather the author) has an irritating habit of using unusual words and explaining them himself; it has been imitated in the translation.

734 Q Maʿārij 70:4–5. For eloquent descriptions of the arid plain where the waiting humans, naked and barefoot, crowding together, are tormented by heat and thirst, see e.g. al-Ghazālī (d. 505/1111), *Iḥyāʾ ʿulūm al-dīn*, iv, 512–15: "the place of assembling and its people," "the sweating," "the length of the Day of Resurrection", all of it supported with relevant quotations from Qurʾan and hadith.

735 He is ʿUbayd ibn al-Ḥuṣayn al-Numayrī, nicknamed al-Rāʿī, "the Camelherd" (d. ca. 96/714).

736 The beginning of a *qaṣīdah* by the pre-Islamic poet Imruʾ al-Qays, not his famous *Muʿallaqah* but another, with a near-identical opening line. The rhyme is *-ānī*, which accommodates the name Riḍwān in the genitive.

737 The opening of a poem by the famous poet Jarīr (d. 111/729), rhyming in *-ānā*, which suits the name Riḍwān in the accusative.

738 A mountain near Mecca.

739 Q Sabaʾ 34:52.

740 Labīd was a famous pre-Islamic poet who converted to Islam. Rabīʿah and Muḍar are two ancient ancestors of the Arabs, giving their names to large tribal confederations. Labīd's father was also called Rabīʿah.

741 A common image for something impossible.

742 Ḥamzah, the Prophet's uncle, was killed in 3/625 at the battle against the Meccans at Uḥud, not far from Medina. Waḥshī ("Savage") was an Abyssinian slave fighting with the Meccans, who were victorious; it was only a temporary setback for the Muslims.

743 Kaʿb ibn Mālik, like Ḥassān ibn Thābit, was one of the poets who supported Islam; he converted before the Hijra and died ca. 50/670. For this and other elegies on Ḥamzah, see Guillaume's translation of Ibn Isḥāq's *al-Sīrah al-nabawiyyah, The Life of the Prophet*, 420 (with several other elegies made after the battle, pp. 404–26).

744 Q ʿAbasa 80:37, on the Day of Judgment.

745 Q ʿAbasa 80:38–42.

746 Customary phrase for addressing or speaking of caliphs, in particular ʿAlī.

747 cf. e.g. Q Ḥāqqah 69:18–23, «On that day you will be exposed, not one secret of yours will be concealed. Then as for him who is given his writ in his right hand, he will say, "Here it is, read my writ! I thought that I should meet my reckoning." He will be in a pleasing life, in a lofty Garden, its clusters within reach».

748 In Islamic law written documents are considered valid and legally binding only when two or more witnesses can testify to their validity.

749 Nāṣir ibn Ṣāliḥ Shibl al-Dawlah, Mirdāsid ruler of Aleppo, 420/1029–429/1038, at the time al-Maʿarrī wrote his *Epistle of Forgiveness*. Abū Yaʿlā ʿAbd al-Munʿim ibn ʿAbd al-Karīm ibn Aḥmad, known as al-Qāḍī al-Aswad ("the black judge") lived in Aleppo in the author's time.

750 Some Islamic scholars are of the view that repentance shortly before one's death will not save one from Hell.

751 The place where the believers will meet the Prophet on the Day of Judgment; see e.g. A. J. Wensinck, entry "Ḥawḍ" in *EI2*, III:286.

752 The Prophet's descendants.

753 This is a customary formula written by copyists at the end of a manuscript.

754 The Prophet's daughter and ʿAlī's wife, the mother of al-Ḥasan and al-Ḥusayn, through whom all descendants of the Prophet trace their descent.

755 Abū Ṭālib, who died in AD 619, was the Prophet's paternal uncle and the father of ʿAlī. He looked after Muḥammad when he became an orphan in early childhood and protected him when Muḥammad's preaching evoked opposition and persecution, even though he himself did not convert to Islam.

756 see e.g. Q Yūnus 10:19, Hūd 11:110, Fuṣṣilat 41:45: «but for a word that preceded from your Lord» (to postpone Judgment).

757 Q Anbiyāʾ 21:101–103; "it" refers to hell.

758 Al-Ḥusayn, the principal martyr of Shiʿite Islam (he died in 61/680 at Karbala), is one of the sons of ʿAlī and Fāṭimah; his two sons are, like him, Shīʿite imams.

759 The first wife of Muḥammad, who was her third husband; mother of Fāṭimah. She died in AD 619, having been the Prophet's first supporter.

760 They all died young, without issue.

761 The word "imam" has several meanings; here it refers to ʿAlī and his male descendants mentioned before.

762 The path (*al-Ṣirāṭ*, from Latin *strata*, via Greek and Syriac) that bridges Hell toward Paradise is not mentioned in the Qur'an but found in the hadith. It can only be crossed by the believers.

763 Kafr Ṭāb is a town between Maʿarrat al-Nuʿmān and Aleppo. Al-Jaḥjalūl (if it is a real person at all) has not been identified.

764 The sense is rather obscure. The words *ilā l-warā* are (possibly intentionally) ambiguous: "toward people" and "backward" (as a poetic license for *ilā l-warāʾ*).

765 Apparently a benefactor of the shaykh or the author; perhaps he is Sālim ibn ʿAlī ibn Muḥammad al-amīr Abū l-Murajjā al-Ḥamawī, mentioned in Ibn al-ʿAdīm's *Bughyat al-ṭalab*.

766 Al-Kawthar ("Abundance") is a river in Paradise.

767 The verse is by the pre-Islamic Hudhalī poet al-Mutanakhkhil.

768 *Al-ḥūr al-ʿīn*: the paradisial damsels or "houris" (see Q Dukhān 44:54, Ṭūr 52:20, Wāqiʿah 56:22).

769 The two merciless "girls" are the two grinding millstones.

770 Abū l-ʿAlāʾ, exceptionally in Islam, was a vegan who preached abstinence from meat, fish, eggs, milk, and honey, in order not to harm animals.

771 An important Arab tribe.

772 Q Zukhruf 43:71–73.

773 Q Ṭūr 52:24.

774 Kaʿb ibn Mālik, a contemporary of the Prophet, in a boasting poem (the original has "our shelters" instead of "his doors").

775 Translation uncertain and meaning unclear. A vulture (*nasr*) is proverbial in Arabic for its longevity. Kuwayy and Surayy are unidentified. The former is called "one of the rain stars" in the dictionary *Lisān al-ʿArab*, but this is not confirmed by other sources. *Nasr* is also the name of two stars: *al-nasr al-ṭāʾir* (Altair, or alpha *Aquilae*,) and *al-nasr al-wāqiʿ* (alpha *Lyrae*). Perhaps these two stars are called Kuwayy and Surayy, and here used for longevity because they are both "vultures."

776 See Q Wāqiʿah 56:17 and Insān 76:19.

777 Grammarian and lexicographer, d. 347/958.

778 al-Khalīl ibn Aḥmad was one of the earliest and greatest Arab grammarians, teacher of Sībawayh, compiler of the first Arabic lexicon, the first work on Arabic metrics, and a treatise on music; his death is given as 160/776, 170/786, or 175/791.

779 Expert in grammar and lexicography, d. ca. 204/820.

780 Famous philologist, specialist in ancient Arabic language, lore, and poetry (d. 210/825).

781 Compare hadiths quoted by al-Ghazālī, *Iḥyā' 'ulūm al-dīn*, IV:540: "Ibn Mas'ūd said: the messenger of God, God bless and preserve him, said: Truly, you will merely look at a bird in Paradise and desire it, and it will fall before you, roasted." "Ḥudhayfah said, The messenger of God, God bless and preserve him, said: There are birds in Paradise like Bactrian camels. Abū Bakr, may God be pleased with him, asked: Are they nice, messenger of God? He answered, Nicer than they are those who eat them, and you, Abū Bakr, will be among those who eat them!" The following Qur'anic quotations are Q Yā Sīn 36:78 and Baqarah 2:260.

782 The Central Asian, "Bactrian" camel has two humps and is bigger than the Arabian, one-humped camel.

783 Philologist from Basra (d. 246/861 or some years later).

784 Famous philologist and specialist in ancient Arabic language, lore, and poetry (d. ca. 216/831).

785 Morphological patterns in Arabic are expressed by means of the "dummy" root *F-'-L* (of the verb *fa'ala* "to do"); prosodists do the same for metrical feet (e.g. *fa'ūlun* is short-long-long). Here the three root consonants are given, alternatively, as C1, C2, C3. The pattern of *iwazzah* is discussed e.g. by Ibn Jinnī (d. 392/1002), *al-Khaṣā'iṣ*, III:6–7.

786 The grammatical "school" of Basra (to which al-Māzinī belongs) traditionally accords a greater role to analogy in formulating grammatical rules than the rival "school" of Kufa, which is more tolerant of irregularities sanctioned by actual usage.

787 'iC1C2aC3ah would give **'i'wayah*; Arabic phonotactic rules would automatically change *'i'* into *'iy*, the sequence *yw* into *yy*, and *aya* into *ā*, giving *'iyyāh*.

788 A verse from a famous poem by al-Afwah al-Awdī (a pre-Islamic poet, d. ca. AD 570); the authenticity of the poem is dubious (see al-Jāḥiẓ, *Ḥayawān*, VI:275, 280). Jurhum was an ancient Arabian tribe that according to traditional lore reigned in Mecca before the Prophet's tribe Quraysh.

789 A verse often quoted as a proverb, attributed to several poets (Ma'n ibn Aws, Mālik ibn Fahm al-Azdī, or 'Aqīl ibn 'Ullafah), on being shot by one's own son.

790 The great poet Imru' al-Qays (first half of sixth century); see above, p. 123. The first quotation is from his *Muʿallaqah*; the poet (addressing himself) reminisces about his amorous adventures.

791 Tabālah is said to be a place in Yemen. Hakir (or Hakr), according to the sources, is a place, or a palace, or a monastery; it is located in Yemen, or forty miles south of Medina, or a Roman name...; in other words, nobody knows.

792 Three pre-Islamic Arab dynasties, in Central Arabia, Iraq, and Syria, respectively. Ākil al-Murār was an ancestor of Imru' al-Qays.

793 ʿĀnah: a place on the Euphrates in Northern Mesopotamia; Shibām: in Yemen. Both places are associated with wine production.

794 Q Raḥmān 55:58.

795 Librarian of the Dār al-ʿIlm (House of Learning), d. 418/1027. Abū l-ʿAlā' knew him during his sojourn in Baghdad and addressed an ode to him.

796 The shaykh uses two Arabic forms of the word, the usual *kāfūr* and the rare *qāfūr*.

797 By al-Ḥusayn ibn Muṭayr (d. ca. 179/786), on the Abbasid caliph al-Mahdī.

798 Q Wāqiʿah 56:35–38.

799 The English word "houri," now no longer well known, goes back, via Persian and French, to Arabic *ḥūr* (plural of *ḥawrā'*), the word used in the Qur'an and here for the "black-eyed damsels" in Paradise.

800 Compare I Corinthians. 2:9 (which is not about damsels).

801 Heavy posteriors are part of the ideal beauty in classical Arabic love poetry, whether on women or boys; the standard poetic simile is that of the sand hill or dune. The location of ʿĀlij is controversial; al-Dahnā' is a very long (some 1000 km) strip of sand desert in Arabia, connecting the Nafūd in the northwest with the "Empty Quarter." Yabrīn is located in central or eastern Arabia.

802 Q Ṣāffāt 37:51–57.

803 *ʿAfārīt*, plural of *ʿifrīt* ("afreet, afrit"), a demon of the more malicious kind; the general word for demons is *jinn* (singular *jinnī*, "jinnee, djinnee, genie").

804 See Q Aḥqāf 46:29–32 and Jinn 72:1–16, respectively.

805 The *maradah* (sg. *mārid*), a particularly evil kind of jinn, who rebelled with Satan against God.

806 All editions have *lā kal-ḥāqin min al-ihālah*; the negative particle *lā* is problematical, because without it the idiom refers to a person with skill and experience: "someone who retains the melted fat (waiting with pouring it until it cools down, so as not to burn the vessel)," see the identical explanations in Abū ʿUbayd al-Bakrī, *Faṣl al-maqāl*, 298; al-ʿAskarī,

Jamharat al-amthāl, II:135; al-Maydānī, *Majmaʿ al-amthāl*, I:76. Apparently, the word *lā* is a mistake, perhaps a misreading of *anā* "I am," on the part of the author or a scribe.

807 Thus, instead of "al-Khaythaʿūr" as found in the MSS. *Khaytaʿūr* is an unusual word for "mirage" or "fata morgana"; *shayṣabān* is said to mean "male ant" or perhaps "termite mound."

808 Muḥammad ibn ʿImrān al-Marzubānī (d. 384/993) wrote a (lost) book on the poetry of the jinn, said to have contained over one hundred folios. Several of his other works about poetry have been preserved.

809 This refers, of course, to Arabic. Al-Khalīl ibn Aḥmad was the first to describe and systematize the meters (some of which are hardly ever found but were constructed for the sake of his system).

810 A wadi in the Hijaz between Mecca and al-Ṭāʾif. Twigs of the *arāk* tree were used as toothbrushes or toothpicks.

811 The first half of the opening line of the *Muʿallaqah* by Imruʾ al-Qays, probably the most famous verse in Arabic.

812 Q Ḥijr 15:26, 28, 33.

813 Q Raḥmān 55:15.

814 He asks for the *kunyah*, a name beginning with Abū/Umm ("father/mother of"), usually followed by the name of the eldest son.

815 It is said in the hadith (see e.g. al-Zamakhsharī, *Kashshāf*, on Q Wāqiʿah 56:37) that everyone in Paradise will always be thirty-three years old.

816 In English, "Satan" is the devil's name; Arabic reverses this, for al-Shayṭān ("the Satan," or the devil) is the more general designation, whereas his name (used here) is Iblīs (derived from Greek *diabolos* and cognate with "devil").

817 Q Qiyāmah 75:35; the interpretation of the verse is uncertain. It could also mean "nearer to you and nearer."

818 Q Aʿrāf 7:50.

819 Q Baqarah 2:25.

820 Imruʾ al-Qays; the lines are from his *Muʿallaqah*.

821 In the story connected with the poem the poet sees some girls, including his beloved ʿUnayzah, bathing in a pool; he takes away their clothes and returns them only after they have let him admire their charms. Then he slaughters his camel and regales them on the meat.

822 In the *Muʿallaqah* the girls throw chunks of raw meat to one another, after the poet has slaughtered his camel. The rare word *tharmad*, a bitter herb, may have been chosen because the verb *tharmada* means "to undercook meat."

823 The simplest poetic meter, deemed inferior to the other meters; see above, pp. 93ff..

824 All of them *rajaz* poets from the first/seventh and second/eighth centuries.

825 There is a short lacuna in the text; the following words between square brackets must be supplied.

826 This saying of the Prophet is found in the hadith.

827 Ru'bah (d. 145/762), with his father al-ʿAjjāj, is among the most famous *rajaz* poets; on account of their extremely rich diction they are quoted very often by lexicographers. Al-ʿAjjāj was the first to use *rajaz* for longer poems and odes.

828 Abū ʿAmr (d. ca. 159/776), philologist from Basra, was one of the earliest scholars who systematically collected early poetry; also a famous Qur'an reciter.

829 The propagandist and organizer of the revolution that brought the Abbasids to power in 132/749–50; his former employers had him murdered in 136/754.

830 The "leader" could be al-Khalīl, father of Arabic lexicography and a founder of Arabic grammar; or else Sībawayh (d. ca. 177/793), author of the famous first grammar, simply called *Kitāb Sībawayh*, in which Ru'bah is often quoted.

831 In the following purple passage the shaykh employs rhymed prose and again displays his fondness of obscure words, not imitated here.

832 The shaykh apparently condemns the use of the lowly meter for the lofty genre of eulogy and for the *qaṣīdah* form (in which praise of the patron is often preceded by a camel description).

833 *Mandal* or *mandalī* is a kind of wood from India, used as incense; Mandal is said to be a place in India (perhaps Mandal in Rajasthan).

834 Q Ṭūr 52:23.

835 cf. Q Wāqiʿah 56:18–19, in a description of Paradise: «a cup from a spring; their brows will not be throbbing, to them no befuddling».

836 A poet quoted in Abū Tammām's anthology *al-Ḥamāsah*; dates unknown.

837 Q Wāqiʿah 56:23.

838 Q Yūnus 10:10.

839 Source: Ibn Rashīq, *al-ʿUmdah*, ed. Muḥammad Muḥyī l-Dīn ʿAbd al-Ḥamīd (Beirut, 1972), I:119–23 (ed. Cairo, 1907, I:77–80).

840 *Lafẓ, wazn, maʿnā, qāfiyah*, respectively; *maʿnā* also means "motif, conceit, idea."

841 Metrical speech made unintentionally does not count as poetry. Thus those short Qur'anic passages that may be scanned according to one of the recognized poetic meters are not to be called "poetry" (since this would contradict one of the main tenets concerning the Qur'an); it is the same with the words of the Prophet, who was not a poet (cf. Q Yā Sīn

36:78). Kahf 18:29 is in *ṭawīl* meter: *fa-man shāʾa fa-l-yuʾmin wa-man shāʾa fa-l-yakfur*; Aḥqāf 46:25 is *basīṭ*: *fa-aṣbaḥū lā yurā illā masākinuhum*, etc.

842 A passage with a linguistic digression on the word *muttazin* "having a meter" has been omitted.

843 *Nasīb* seems to be broader than "amatory introduction of a *qaṣīdah*" here and to include *ghazal*, *taghazzul*, or *tashbīb*. See *al-ʿUmdah, II*, 117 for the author's view on these terms.

844 Compare al-Usaydī quoted in Ibn Sallām, *Ṭabaqāt fuḥūl al-shuʿarāʾ*, 319–20, mentioning *fakhr* (vaunting), *madīḥ* (panegyric), *nasīb* (amatory), and *hijāʾ* (invective).

845 *Ṭarab* is strong emotion, either joy or rapture or grief, induced especially by passion and music.

846 A grammarian, rhetorician and Muʿtazilite theologian, who died 384/994 at a great age.

847 *Gharaḍ* is often used in the sense of "poetic theme" or "mode."

848 Or vituperative verse, lampoon, satire.

849 See also Ibn Qutaybah, *al-Shiʿr wal-shuʿarāʾ*, 80; ʿAbd al-Malik was an Umayyad caliph (r. 65/685–86/705), Arṭah ibn Suhayyah was a poet who died ca. 86/705.

850 Al-Faḍl ibn Jaʿfar, poet and *kātib* ("secretary, civil servant") of Persian descent, lived in Kufa, Baghdad, and Samarra; d. after 252/866.

851 Al-Fatḥ ibn Khāqān, close associate of Caliph al-Mutawakkil; murdered together with the latter in 247/861.

852 Al-Nahshalī al-Qayrawānī, a teacher of Ibn Rashīq. The following is also found, with a few changes, in Ibn Wahb (fourth/tenth century), *al-Burhān fī wujūh al-bayān*, 135.

853 Or gnomic verse.

854 *Lahw*: entertainment, amusement.

855 *Tazhīd*, often called *zuhd* (renunciation of worldly things, asceticism, abstinence, abstemiousness).

856 Both editions have *al-makhmūr* ("inebriated"), which is odd and has here been emended to *al-mujūn*, as in *al-Burhān*.

857 Literally, "beautification of morals," *taḥsīn al-akhlāq*.

858 Translation not wholly certain.

859 *Bayt* means "tent," "house," "room," or "line of verse"; some technical terms related to meter are connected with tents (e.g. *watid*, "tent peg," or the stable combination of a short and a long syllable in a metrical foot; *sabab* "tent rope," for variable parts of a foot). Here, the simile implies a house rather than a tent.

860 On the discussion of *ṭabʿ* "nature, natural talent" versus *ṣanʿah* "craftmanship, artfulness" in poets and their poetry, see e.g. Ajami, *The Neckveins of Winter: The Controversy over*

Natural and Artificial Poetry in Medieval Arabic criticism, and see *al-ʿUmdah*, I:129–34 (*Fī l-maṭbūʿ wal-maṣnūʿ*).

861 *Riwāyah* literally means "transmission," which would suggest that the line itself should be transmitted and gain currency. In fact the intended meaning is that in order to be a good poet one should have memorized and be able to transmit a great quantity of good poetry of earlier poets. This is often stressed (cf. below, the quotation of al-Qāḍī al-Jurjānī).

862 Or patterns (*amthilah*).

863 Literary critic and poet (d. 382/1001). His *al-Wasāṭah bayn al-Mutanabbī wa-khuṣūmihi* (*The Mediation Between al-Mutanabbī and his Opponents*) is an important work of literary criticism. The following quotation is found on p. 15.

864 The words follow immediately on the previous quotation, pp. 15–16.

865 The *mukhaḍramūn* (sg. *mukhaḍram*), who straddle the pre-Islamic and the Islamic periods.

866 *Muwallad* has several meanings, including "born among Arabs but not of Arab blood, half-breed, post-classical." See *EI2* s.v. "Muwallad."

867 Diʿbil ibn ʿAlī al-Khuzāʿī (d. 246/860), poet and author of a book on poets, *Ṭabaqāt al-shuʿarāʾ*, fragments of which have survived.

868 Desiring a reward or a favor.

869 *Tashbīb*, a near-synonym of *ghazal*.

870 That is, tardiness in fulfilling promises (a common topic in poetry addressed to a patron or a beloved).

871 Probably referring to the anonymously cited opinion that some critics classify elegy as part of panegyric. It may well be better to read *ka-anna l-rithāʾ ʿindahu ...* "It seems that elegy, in his opinion ... ."

872 The division *madḥ - hijāʾ - nasīb - rithāʾ* (cf. p. 277) is here replaced by *madḥ - hijāʾ - tashbīb (=nasīb) - ʿitāb*.

873 *Al-mathal al-sāʾir*. A *mathal* is at the same time a parable or *exemplum* in the form of a proverb.

874 Musician, composer, courtier, and poet, d. 235/850.

875 I do not understand "*[dhawb] qawl Abī l-Ṭayyib*"; the word *dhawb* is not found in the edition of 1907, where the word *awwalan* is added after *al-Ṭayyib*.

876 *Dīwān* (ed. Dietrich), p. 131, in a poem praising al-Ḥusayn ibn Isḥāq al-Tanūkhī.

877 Literally, "about you." *Dīwān*, II:77.

878 *Dīwān*, I:22.

879 Poet from Basra known especially for his invective, d. ca. 240/854.

880 The same is ascribed to the minor ninth-century poet ʿAmr ibn Naṣr al-Qiṣāfī in Ibn al-Jarrāḥ, *al-Waraqah*, 9.

881 Reading *aṣʿab* with the edition of 1907 rather than *aṣghar* which does not make sense.

882 First half of third/ninth century; from a family of high officials (*kuttāb*, sg. *kātib*, "secretary"), several of whom made poetry (Sezgin, *Geschichte*, II:604–5).

883 Minor poet of non-Arab origin, d. 214/829. Sezgin, *Geschichte*, II: 550–51.

884 Muḥammad ibn Manṣūr ibn Ziyād in Ibn Qutaybah, *Shiʿr*, 79; see e.g. al-Jahshiyārī, *al-Wuzarāʾ wal-kuttāb*, 190, 193, 224, 241–42, 266–68. The Barmakids were a renowned family of high officials and viziers in early Abbasid times; their "dynasty" fell spectacularly in 187/803 during the reign of Hārūn al-Rashīd.

885 See Ibn Qutaybah, *al-Shiʿr wal-shuʿarāʾ*, 79 and 854; Ibn ʿAbd Rabbih, *al-ʿIqd al-farīd*, V:327.

886 See above, note 851.

887 Abū ʿAbd Allāh Yaʿqūb ibn Dāwūd, a *mawlā*, d. 186/802. See *EI2*, I:103.

888 On this, see e.g. *ʿUmdah*, II:154–57.

889 Cf. Ibn al-Muʿtazz, *al-Badīʿ*, 14.

890 The translation is based on Hellmut Ritter's edition of the work (İstanbul, 1954, 245–96). For another English translation of the first part of the extract (pp. 245–62), see Vicente Cantarino (*Arabic Poetics in the Golden Age*, 158–75). The whole work has been translated into German by Ritter (*Die Geheimnisse der Wortkunst des ʿAbdalqāhir al-Curcānī*, Wiesbaden, 1959), from whose interpretation and annotation I have benefited (see *Geheimnisse*, 306–46). For a longer section including this one, with fuller annotation, see van Gelder and Hammond, eds. and trans., *Takhyīl: The Imaginary in Classical Arabic Poetics*, 29–69. The present version has been revised.

891 Ibn al-Rūmī (d. 283/896), going against common opinion, repeatedly lampooned the rose and preferred the narcissus. ʿAbd al-Qāhir quotes lines 1, 2, 6, 3–4, 9–14 of a poem of 14 lines, Ibn al-Rūmī, *Dīwān*, II, 643–44 (with some variants), cf. also Schoeler, *Arabische Naturdichtung*, 204ff.; Heinrichs, "Rose versus Narcissus: Observations on an Arabic Literary Debate," 184–85; and McKinney, *The Case of Rhyme versus Reason*, 218–22.

892 Strictly speaking *ward* is a collective that should be translated as "roses." In English, however, the personification only works if the singular is chosen. Another problem for the translator is the choice of pronoun: Arabic has no neuter and the masculine word *ward* is referred to as "he," but in English one has to choose between "he" and "it." The former would enhance the personification, but one runs into trouble with lines 7–8, on women called after flowers.

893 The poet refers to the fact that the rose blooms in early summer, thus heralding the end of spring.

894 Arabic differs from English: Narjis ("narcissus") is a common name for girls, unlike Ward ("rose").

895 Both *narjis* and *ward* are grammatically masculine.

896 The narcissus is often compared to a star or to an eye (see the next line), whereas the rose is routinely compared to a cheek (or *vice versa*).

897 The following paragraph is also translated by Meisami, *Structure and Meaning*, 328–29, and Abu Deeb, *al-Jurjānī's Theory of Poetic Imagery*, 158. With "ordering" (*tartīb*), the author refers not so much to the order of the lines and motifs as to the stages of the poetic process leading to the initial conceit on which the piece is based.

898 *Ṭarafā l-tashbīh*, "the two ends, or extremities, of the comparison," correspond to the *primum* and *secundum comparationis* in traditional Western rhetoric. The corresponding Arabic terms are *al-mushabbah* and *al-mushabbah bihi*.

899 *ʿIllah*, which could also be rendered as "reason" or "pretext."

900 The word for "cheek," *ʿidhār*, also implies the down on the cheeks of adolescent boys, hence the dark violet rather than the rose. For the common motif of the "downy cheek" in homoerotic Arabic poetry, see e.g. Bauer, *Liebe und Liebesdichtung*, 255–80.

901 Abū Hilāl al-ʿAskarī, a literary critic and poet who died after 400/1010; see his *Dīwān*, 224, and id., *Dīwān al-maʿānī*, I:249, II:24.

902 Ibn Nubātah al-Saʿdī, a poet who died in 405/1015. The black horse has a white blaze, compared first to the Pleiades, then to dawn, and white fetlocks, also compared to dawn. In Ritter's translation of the last line it is the dawn that fears being overtaken, and clings to the horse's feet and face; but *fawt* means the opposite of "being overtaken," and syntactically too the horse is the more likely subject of *khāfa* ("it feared").

903 cf. al-ʿAskarī, *Dīwān al-maʿānī*, II:110, and, al-ʿAskarī, *al-Ṣināʿatayn*, 258.

904 As Ritter remarks, this is possibly an allusion to the Muʿtalizite debate on the concept of "latency," such as that of fire in wood or firestick; see *EI2* s.v. "kumūn" (J. van Ess).

905 By Ibn Nubātah al-Saʿdī, in al-Thaʿālibī, *Yatīmah*, II: 391–92.

906 Poet unidentified by Ritter. The missing part of the first line has been added by Muḥammad ʿAbduh in his edition of *Asrār al-balāghah*: "like frightened adders seeking refuge," even though *taṭlubu mawʾila* does not form a proper rhyme with *salāsila* (it could perhaps be emended to *tabghī mawāʾila*). The poet is in fact Abū Saʿīd al-Rustamī and the first line should be completed with "like golden sheets smelted into brooklets" (al-Thaʿālibī, *Yatīmah*, III:206).

907 Ibn al-Muʿtazz, *Dīwān*, ed. Sharīf, I:478.

908 Abū Aḥmad al-Muwaffaq (d. 278/891), son of the Caliph al-Mutawakkil and virtual ruler of the caliphate as regent since 261/875.

909 Ibn al-Muʿtazz, *Dīwān*, I:472 (where it is said to be from a poem on the Caliph al-Muktafī rather than his grandfather al-Muwaffaq) and II:174; ed. Lewin, IV:82–83.

910 ʿAbd al-Ṣamad ibn Manṣūr Ibn Bābak (d. 410/1019).

911 *Dīwān*, I:18.

912 See Ritter's notes in *Asrār*, 267 n. 338 and *Geheimnisse*, 312 n. 338 on the possible identity of this poet. In some sources the line is attributed to al-Ṣāḥib ibn ʿAbbād (al-Thaʿālibī, *Yatīmah*, III: 276).

913 The "confetti" (or fruit, scattered at a wedding) white like "camphor" is snow.

914 Abū Tammām, *Dīwān*, IV:580.

915 The following two lines (with a third intervening) in al-Thaʿālibī, *Yatīmah*, II:178.

916 An Islamic month begins with the appearance of a new moon. Ramadan and Shawwal are the ninth and tenth months. Arabic has three different words for moon: full moon, crescent moon, and moon in general (*badr*, *hilāl*, and *qamar*, respectively).

917 This, as Ritter remarks, is confusing, since with "the two Ṭā'ite (poets)" normally Abū Tammām and al-Buḥturī are meant, but ʿAbd al-Qāhir is not referring to these two but to Abū Tammām and "ʿUlbah"/Abū Saʿīd al-Rustamī.

918 The text has *munfaṣim*. Since, according to the lexicographers (see e.g. al-ʿAskarī, *al-Furūq al-lughawiyyah*, 123) the difference between *faṣama* and *qaṣama* is that the break is invisible in the former and visible in the latter, perhaps one ought to read *munqaṣim* to make the comparison with the crescent moon more plausible.

919 By Abū Bakr Muḥammad ibn Yaḥyā al-Ṣūlī (d. ca. 335/946), courtier, man of letters, poet, and a great chess player. The verse is quoted in al-Marzubānī, *Muʿjam al-shuʿarā'*, 421.

920 Al-Thaʿālibī, *Yatīmah*, II:178.

921 Unidentified.

922 Al-Thaʿālibī, *Yatīmah*, III:77.

923 Of hunger and thirst, as the following line in *al-Yatīmah* (not quoted by ʿAbd al-Qāhir) makes clear. The guests are plural there, not dual as here.

924 *Dīwān*, V:1910.

925 A reference to Q Baqarah 2:74 («For there are stones from which rivers come gushing») and Aʿrāf 7:160 (Moses striking the rock). The first line illustrates the combination of two comparisons.

926 The bow provides a double comparison: the twanging sound of the string is the woman's moaning, the bow's curve is her bent posture. See al-Ṭabarī, *Tārīkh*, III: 1076; al-Ṣūlī, *Awrāq (Ashʿār awlād al-khulafā')*, 19; al-Iṣfahānī, *Aghānī*, X:117.

927 *Shabah* or *wajh al-shabah* is the common factor that links the two terms of a comparison.

928 *Dīwān*, ed. Sharīf, I:455.

929 *Dīwān*, ed. Lewin, IV:10.

930 *Dīwān*, ed. Lewin, III:43.

931 Quṭrabbul, a place famous for its wine, not far from Baghdad.

932 *Dīwān*, ed. Lewin, III:47.

933 The word *rabīʿ* is customarily translated as "spring," originally referring to the season in which the earth is covered with vegetation after rainfall. Ritter's *spätsommer* ("late summer") is based on the opening line of the poem (not quoted here), which refers to lengthening nights, and on the last line quoted here.

934 Ritter emends *taʿarrā l-ṣubḥu min* to *tafarrā l-ṣubḥu ʿan*, with little difference in meaning. The emendation is possible but unnecessary; the "nudity" implied in *taʿarrā* rather fits the context.

935 *Dīwān*, ed. Lewin, III:24.

936 *Dīwān*, ed. Lewin, III:64; ed. Sharif, II:264. Summer pleasures should be enjoyed indoors, as the epigram's concluding line (not quoted here) makes clear.

937 Abu Deeb (*Al-Jurjānī's Theory of Poetic Imagery*, 159) translates the words *idhā aradtu taṣābiyan*, even more wordily than I, as "If I ever want to approach a young girl, like a young person does." But neither the verb nor the verse refers to a girl.

938 *Dīwān*, ed. Lewin, IV:186.

939 Diʿbil (d. 246/860), *Dīwān*, 249.

940 Meaning, as the following commentary explains, "without cause." The word *ʿajab* usually means "amazement" or "admiration."

941 Sinew (or more literally "artery," *sharyān*): bowstring; *nabʿ*: a kind of wood used for makings bows.

942 *Dīwān*, ed. Sharīf, I:229–30.

943 Anonymous in Ibn Abī ʿAwn, *Tashbīhāt*, 149; Ibn Qutaybah, *al-Maʿānī*, 673; Ibn Manẓūr, *Lisān al-ʿarab* s.v. *H-L-L*. ʿAbd al-Qāhir adds that the word *hilāl*, normally "crescent moon," here means "snake shedding its skin."

944 *Dīwān*, 223.

945 The poet gives a sensual twist to the patron's love of munificence, for the "apparition" or phantom (*ṭayf*) is an allusion to the extremely common motif in love poetry in which the lover at night sees the image of his beloved, either in a dream, in a hallucination, or simply in his imagination. This apparition is often called *ṭayf al-khayāl*. *Khayāl* means both "imagination" and "imagined apparition." The verbal noun derived from it, *takhyīl*, is used by ʿAbd al-Qāhir and before him by writers of Greco-Arabic poetics for something that

has variously been rendered as "making someone imagine," "evoking images," "creative imagination," "imaginative creation," "imaginative representation," "make-believe," and "phantasmagoria."

946 Al-Thaʿālibī, *Yatīmah*, IV:170. The addressee is Abū Naṣr Aḥmad ibn Abī Zayd, vizier of Nūḥ ibn Manṣūr.

947 By Umayyah ibn Abī l-Ṣalt (a contemporary of the prophet Muḥammad), praising ʿAbd Allāh ibn Judʿān, see al-Iṣfahānī, *Aghānī*, VII:328; al-ʿAskarī, *Dīwān al-maʿānī*, I:46; idem, *Ṣināʿatayn*, p. 48, etc.

948 *Dīwān*, III:178.

949 *Dīwān*, 274.

950 Qays ibn al-Mulawwaḥ, known as Majnūn Laylā, *Dīwān*, 233.

951 al-Mutanabbī, *Dīwān*, 59.

952 Arabic often uses the singular "eye" where one would expect a dual. Normally, a plural would be called for in English, but for the sake of "humanization" a singular is to be preferred.

953 *Dīwān*, ed. Sharīf, I:363–64.

954 *Dīwān*, ed. Sharīf, II:243. See also ed. Lewin, III:41–42. The last line alludes to the lashing as punishment of illicit sexual intercourse in Islamic law. The English pun on "eye" and "lash" is fortuitous.

955 The beloved is described in the poem as a slender, rosy-cheeked cupbearer, masculine grammatically and probably biologically.

956 There are several variants. Aḥmad Ibn Ḥanbal's large Hadith collection entitled *al-Musnad* contains the Prophetic tradition "eyes can whore, and their whoring is looking"; both Ibn Ḥanbal and al-Tirmidhī have "every eye whores."

957 By Ibn al-Muʿtazz, see his *Dīwān*, ed. Sharīf, I: 324.

958 Source: al-Damīrī, *Ḥayāt al-ḥayawān al-kubrā* (Cairo, n.d., I:368 (= ed. Cairo, 1970, I:524). The mythical bird called *rukhkh* (roc) is found in other Arabic sources; cf. Abū Ḥāmid al-Gharnāṭī, *Tuḥfat al-albāb*, ed. Ferrand, 108–9; ed. al-ʿArabī, 131–32. It also appears in *The Thousand and One Nights*, see "ʿAbd al-Raḥmān al-Maghribī's Story of the Rukhkh," (*The Arabian Nights: Tales of 1001 Nights*, trans. Malcolm C. Lyons, II:222–23; Marzolph & van Leeuwen, *The Arabian Nights Encyclopedia*, II:694), and see Sindbad's second voyage (*The Arabian Nights*, trans. Lyons, II:465–66). For stories on giant birds see also *Travels of Sir John Mandeville*, 167 (griffon in Bactria); Marco Polo, (gryphon bird in Madagascar called *rukh*, with feathers twelve paces long); and the story of St. Brendan's ship being attacked by a griffon. Reports may concern the now extinct "elephant bird," *Aepyornis maximus*, of Madagascar, see Vernet, "Rujj = Aepyornis maximus" and Dawkins, *The Ancestor's Tale*, 286–88. It was a heavy-set bird, "a kind of feathered tank with a big

head and neck," three meters tall. Its eggs were up to a meter in circumference, but unlike the roc it could not fly. It may have lived on Madagascar "perhaps until as late as the seventeenth century, although more probably around AD 1000." On the *rukhkh* and the connections with chess see Kruk, "Of rukhs and rooks, camels and castles."

959 In lexicography one does not take chances with the hazards that could befall the dots that distinguish different consonants; al-Damīrī makes clear the word is spelled with خ *kh* (*khā'*), which has a dot on top, unlike ح (*ḥā'*). The *j* (ج) has one dot underneath, but being called *jīm* cannot cause confusion here.

960 One *bā'* is the span of the outstretched arms, equivalent to a fathom.

961 Not found in his extant works.

962 Al-Gharnāṭī (d. 565/1169–70), traveler and collector of *'ajā'ib* ("mirabilia"), author of *Tuḥfat al-albāb*.

963 The author of *Tuḥfah* adds: "Returning to his country, the Maghreb, with great wealth."

964 *Tuḥfah* adds: "People marveled at this. The man was known as 'Abd al-Raḥīm the Chinaman. He would relate marvellous things." (cf. the story of 'Abd al-Raḥmān al-Maghribī in *The Thousand and One Nights*). On giant feathers, see also al-Rāmhurmuzī, *'Ajā'ib al-Hind/Livre des merveilles de l'Inde*, 61–62 (Freeman-Grenville's translation, p. 37, has "nine buckets of water," misreading *tasa'u* as *tis'*). See *'Ajā'ib al-Hind*, p. 36 on a giant bird in Sufālā (present-day Mozambique) that seizes animals, and p. 178 on (the same) bird that kills an elephant, with a feather holding two buckets. Richard Burton, in a note to his translation of the *Arabian Nights* (*The Book of the Thousand Nights and a Night*, IV:84): according to someone not a feather shaft but the frond of the palm *Raphia vinifera*, which has the largest leaf in the vegetable kingdom.

965 Read, with *Tuḥfah*, *al-shabāb* ("youth") instead of *al-nushshāb* ("arrows").

966 The *rukhkh* of chess (rook in Modern English) has apparently nothing to do with the mythical monster bird but seems to be a corruption of an Indian word *ratha* or *rat'h*, Bengali *rot'h*, "chariot". Perhaps the intermediate form was Pahlavi *rakhw* (F. Rosenthal, entry "shaṭrandj" in *EI2*). Yet it seems likely that the bird *rukhkh* played its part in the corruption of the original word.

967 Died 458/1066, author of the thesaurus *al-Mukhaṣṣaṣ* and the dictionary *al-Muḥkam*.

968 Poet, d. ca. 363/972.

969 Read *farāzīn* instead of *barādhīn* ("nags, packhorses"). The poem (al-Sarī al-Raffā', *Dīwān*, II:734) is often quoted. The translation is (necessarily) rather misleading, for the poet says that the men are unable to walk straight: the *firzān*'s movement (diagonal, one step at a time) on the chessboard is far more restricted than today's queen; moreover, the *firzān* was a "counsellor" rather than a "queen."

970 Al-Sarī al-Raffāʾ, *Dīwān*, II:686. The verses have nothing to do with the present subject.

971 Apparently referring to the entry *ʿanqāʾ*, II:162–64, where, however, nothing is said on the legal matter. The *ʿanqāʾ* is a fabulous bird not unlike the phoenix.

972 Source: al-Damīrī, *Ḥayāt al-ḥayawān al-kubrā* (Cairo, n.d., II:378–81.)

973 In Arabic, "father of" (*abū*) is often used in the sense of "the one with."

974 ʿUbayd ibn Ḥusayn al-Numayrī (d. ca. 96/714), often called al-Rāʿī ("the camelherd").

975 A reference to Q Naml 27:20 (Arberry's translation): «And he (Sulaymān/Solomon) reviewed the birds; then he said, "How is it with me, that I do not see the hoopoe? Or is he among the absent? Assuredly I will chastise him with a terrible chastisement, or I will slaughter him, or he bring me a clear authority."» The following story of Solomon and the hoopoe is nearly identical with the version in al-Thaʿlabī (d. 427/1035), *Qiṣaṣ al-anbiyāʾ* (*The stories of the Prophets*), 276–78; for an English translation see al-Thaʿlabī, *ʿArāʾis al-majālis fī qiṣaṣ al-anbiyāʾ, or "Lives of the Prophets"*, trans. and annot. by William M. Brinner, 519–24 (where the continuation of the story of Solomon and the Queen of Sheba may be read). For another version see al-Ṭabarī, *Taʾrīkh*, I:576–78, trans. William M. Brinner in *The History of al-Ṭabarī*, III:157–58.

976 One *farsakh* ("parasang," from Persian) is about six kilometers.

977 *Al-ḥanīfiyyah*, usually meaning the "pure," "natural" religion as illustrated by Abraham/Ibrāhīm and some other individuals before Islam.

978 The name of the Queen of Sheba in the Islamic tradition. One should compare the Islamic story with that of the Old Testament (1 Kings 10; 2 Chron. 9:). For the story of how she became queen, see above.

979 Other sources add that the Yemenite hoopoe's name was ʿUfayr; both names are derived from a root denoting the color of dust.

980 Q Naml 27:21; the completion of the verse follows below.

981 He is about to slaughter him.

982 This may refer to Solomon's period of disgrace told briefly in Q Ṣād 38:31–34; cf. *EI2*, s.v. "Sulaymān b. Dāwūd" (J. Walker and P. Fenton).

983 Al-Zamakhsharī (d. 538/1144), philologist (author of a famous book on grammar) and theologian, author of an important commentary on the Qurʾan, *al-Kashshāf* (*The Uncoverer*), much esteemed but somewhat tainted, according to mainstream Islam, by its Muʿtazilite ("rationalist") tendencies. The following passage begins with an almost verbatim repetition of the preceding, which has here been omitted. Both the omitted and quoted parts differ somewhat from the text of al-Zamakhsharī's *al-Kashshāf*, II:195 (at Q Naml 27:21).

984 Apparently some thought that it is not fitting that God should be represented as going back on His oath (as in the previous version).

985 Zakariyyā ibn Muḥammad al-Qazwīnī (d. 682/1283), author of a very popular cosmographical encyclopedia, *ʿAjāʾib al-makhlūqāt* (*Wonders of Created Beings*), see ed. Wüstenfeld, I:426.

986 The parenthesis is taken from the edition of al-Qazwīnī's *ʿAjāʾib*.

987 In the poem the hoopoe has changed sex.

988 Probably the famous transmitter of early Qur'anic exegesis (d. ca. 105/723).

989 I have not found the following in al-Jāḥiẓ's book on animals, *al-Ḥayawān*, or other works of his. It is also quoted by al-Nuwayrī, *Nihāyat al-arab*, X:247.

990 *Al-Kāmil*, a famous book by al-Mubarrad (d. 285/898); see ed. W. Wright (Leipzig, 1874–92), 568–69.

991 The author of this work (*Shuʿab al-īmān*) has not been identified. The exchange is also given by al-Jāḥiẓ, *al-Ḥayawān*, III: 512–13 (where Ibn ʿAbbās's answer has a proper rhyme: *idhā jāʾa l-qadar ʿamiya l-baṣar*, where al-Damīrī has *qaḍāʾ* instead of *qadar*).

992 As al-Damīrī says below, he was one of the early leaders of the Khārijites, d. 65/685. ʿAbd Allāh ibn al-ʿAbbās (d. 68/687), son of the Prophet's cousin al-ʿAbbās, is considered to be the earliest exegete of the Qur'an.

993 Abū ʿUmar al-Zāhid Muḥammad ibn ʿAbd al-Wāḥid, also known as Ghulām Thaʿlab (d. 345/957).

994 When the conflict between the fourth caliph, ʿAlī, and Muʿāwiyah, the governor of Syria, had reached deadlock after the battle of Ṣiffīn (37/657), ʿAlī consented to arbitration (by Abū Mūsā l-Ashʿarī and ʿAmr ibn al-ʿĀṣ), which ultimately led to Muʿāwiyah becoming the founder of the Umayyad dynasty. ʿAlī's decision turned some of his fervent followers into fanatic opponents, called Khārijites ("Those who seceded, rebelled"), who developed into a politico-religious sect.

995 In war.

996 The verses by Abū l-Shīṣ (d. ca. 196/812) are found in al-Jāḥiẓ, *al-Ḥayawān*, III:518–19 and Ibn Qutaybah, *ʿUyūn al-akhbār*, I:41–42.

997 Reading *tadsīs*, as in al-Jāḥiẓ, instead of *tadrīs* (al-Damīrī) or *taʾsīs* (Ibn Qutaybah). The hoopoe is singled out, it seems, not only because it "pecks" for hidden matters but also because it served as Solomon's spy.

998 Rather, its crest.

999 He is known as al-Bākharzī; his anthology of contemporary poets *Dumyat al-qaṣr* (*The Palace's Statue*) is a kind of continuation of *Yatīmat al-dahr* (*The Solitary Pearl of the Time*) by al-Thaʿālibī (d. 429/1038). The verses are found in *Dumyat al-qaṣr*, I:651.

1000 *Ḥāfiẓ*: someone who knows the Qur'an by heart.

1001 Died 276/889; the anecdote about his mother's pregnancy is found in al-Khaṭīb al-Baghdādī, *Tārīkh Baghdād*, X:426.

1002 A normal ritual prayer (*ṣalāt*), to be performed five times a day, consists of between two and four *rak'ahs*, each *rak'ah* consisting of a cycle of movements and utterances. The hoopoe's pecking of the earth is likened to such movements.

1003 One of the leading authorities on Islamic law, eponym of the Shāfi'ī legal school; d. 204/820.

1004 That is, if one is responsible for the death or loss of a hoopoe belonging to someone else.

1005 See also al-Maydānī, *Majma' al-amthāl*, I:449 (but the following expression is not found in this work).

1006 The remainder of the long section on special properties, which takes up around one fifth of the entry on the hoopoe, has been omitted.

1007 All editions consulted have *khayr*, as has the parallel passage in 'Abd al-Ghanī al-Nābulusī's dictionary of dream interpretation, *Ta'ṭīr al-anām fī tafsīr al-aḥlām*, II:320. Nevertheless, I think the original reading may have been *khabar* ("news"), in view of what follows.

1008 Q Naml 27:22 (trans. Arberry).

1009 Died 110/728, considered the father of oneiromancy in Islam. A very popular, much later work on the subject is ascribed to him; but the present statement is not found in the entry on the hoopoe in [Ibn Sīrīn], *Muntakhab al-kalām fī tafsīr al-aḥlām*, ed. together with al-Nābulusī's *Ta'ṭīr al-anām*, I:149.

1010 Not identified; possibly Ismā'īl ibn Abī Bakr ibn al-Muqrī (d. 837/1433), but I do not know about a work on dream interpretation by him.

1011 The verb *hadda*, imperf. *yahuddu*, means "to break, pull down (a building)."

1012 Source: al-Ibshīhī, *al-Mustaṭraf fī kull fann mustaẓraf*, I:171–76. There is a French translation of *al-Mustaṭraf* (almost devoid of annotation): Śihâb-ad-Dîn Âḥmad al-Âbśîhî, *Al-Mostaṭraf: recueil de morceaux choisis*, trans. par G. Rat (Paris, 1899), see pp. 533–47 for the present text.

1013 See the translations by R. B. Serjeant (*The Book of Misers*, Reading, 1997) and J. Colville (*Avarice and the Avaricious*, London, 1999).

1014 On *al-Mustaṭraf*, see Marzolph, "Medieval Knowledge in Modern Reading: A Fifteenth-Century Arabic Encyclopaedia of *omni re scibili*".

1015 Q Nisā' 4:37, translation by Arberry. The verse begins «Surely God loves not the proud and boastful...».

1016 Umm al-Banīn bint 'Abd al-'Azīz was the sister of 'Umar ibn 'Abd al-'Azīz, the "good" Umayyad caliph, who reigned 99/717–101/720.

1017 Poet (d. after 40/661), known especially for his satire.

1018 Poet of the Umayyad period.

1019 The poem is found in Ibn Qutaybah, *'Uyūn al-akhbār*, III:343.

1020 Minor poet, said to be the first to have written on Arabic grammar; d. ca. 69/688.

1021 From Basra, famous for his eloquence; d. 135/752.

1022 The text has Ḥanẓalah, a mistake for Jaḥẓah (d. 324/936), a minor poet and wit who is mentioned in other sources in connection with this anecdote.

1023 High official and man of letters (d. 215/830); the epistle is quoted in al-Jāḥiẓ's book on misers, *al-Bukhalā'* (see the translation by Serjeant, 8–14). Al-Ḥasan ibn Sahl was another high official (d. 235/850).

1024 Minor poet from Baghdad, d. between 260/874 and 270/883.

1025 A commandant of the police in the Umayyad period. The story is taken from al-Jāḥiẓ's *Misers*, see Serjeant's translation, 131.

1026 Abbasid caliph, r. 136/754–158/775.

1027 The ceremonial camel-borne litter sent by the caliph to Mecca with the Hajj caravan.

1028 The vizier Rabī' ibn Yūnus.

1029 Umayyad caliph, r. 105/724–125/743.

1030 Two poets, d. 210/825 and 182/797, respectively.

1031 Abbasid caliph, r. 158/775–169/785.

1032 A *dānaq* is one-sixth of a dirham.

1033 Marw or Merv, town in Khurāsān (now Mary, in Turkmenistan). The Khurāsānians (and the Persians in general) have a reputation for stinginess in Arabic sources.

1034 For a fuller version, see al-Jāḥiẓ, *Misers*, 19 (with more anecdotes on the Mervians).

1035 Son of the vizier Yaḥyā ibn Khālid al-Barmakī, described as a miser in al-Jāḥiẓ, *Misers*, 60.

1036 By Potiphar's wife who tried to seduce him; cf. Q Yūsuf 12:25–28.

1037 The poet (see above).

1038 To card cotton a bow-like instrument is used.

1039 Poet, d. 246/860.

1040 Reading *namūtu* instead of *yamūtu* "he died."

1041 A popular dish, a kind of broth containing bread.

1042 For their brightness and limpidity.

1043 Abū Dulaf al-'Ijlī, general under the Caliphs al-Ma'mūn and al-Mu'taṣim, famous for his largesse and patronage of poets, d. 226/840.

1044 The text has *qinnār* "butcher's hook," which does not scan; read *quṭār* as in Ibn Qutaybah, *'Uyūn al-akhbār*, III:247.

1045 A sweet made of barley and other ingredients.

1046 Thus instead of Ṣubḥ; the story is taken from al-Jāḥiẓ, *Misers*, 16.

1047 The version in al-Jāḥiẓ makes it clear that the stick is used to raise the wick when necessary.

1048 Scholar, especially of Arab genealogy and lore, with anti-Arab tendencies, d. ca. 207/822. This story is found in Ibn ʿAbd Rabbih, *al-ʿIqd al-farīd*, VI:185.

1049 A mistake for Marwān ibn Abī Ḥafṣah.

1050 In eastern Arabia.

1051 Possibly the anthologist of that name (d. 562/1166), but there are other candidates.

1052 Not identified.

1053 Minor poet, d. ca. 180/796.

1054 Ḥātim of the tribe of Ṭayy (or Ṭayyiʾ), pre-Islamic poet and proverbial for his generosity. The epigram is found in al-Thaʿālibī, *Thimār al-qulūb*, 97, who also says he is quoting al-Jāḥiẓ; but it is not found in his *Misers* or any other work of his.

1055 Major poet of the Umayyad period, d. ca. 111/729. Here he attacks the tribe of Taghlib.

1056 The verses are not by Jarīr; the second, oft-quoted verse is by his contemporary and rival al-Akhṭal (d. ca. 92/710), see his poem above, p. 15, line 6. Lines 1 and 3–4 of the present epigram may be later additions (with the "urban" line 1 jarring with the Bedouin nature of lines 2–4).

1057 The verse has been quoted before.

1058 Reading *yuqīlu* (with *al-ʿIqd al-farīd*, VI:190) instead of *yqbl*.

1059 Bashshār ibn Burd (d. 167/783); see above, p. 34. The lines are often quoted as an instance of *istiṭrād*, an invective "side-stab." The only known thing about ʿUbayd Allāh Ibn Qazʿah is that he was the brother of a minor Muʿtazilite theologian.

1060 A tribe.

1061 Other versions have "on the Christians": *al-ʿIqd al-farīd*, VI: 193; Ibn Ḥamdūn, *al-Tadhkirah*, IV:78 (where the poet is named as Abū l-ʿAwādhil, lampooning al-Ḥasan ibn Sahl, who had dogs killed during an epidemic).

1062 A triple divorce (expressed in one utterance) would be sufficient to make it irrevocable.

1063 Compare the different, less bizarre version in al-Jāḥiẓ, *Misers*, 194.

1064 The fifth sura of the Qurʾan, so called after the reference to the table sent down, with food and all, from heaven to ʿĪsā/Jesus.

1065 In traditional Arab meteorology rains are governed by certain stars and constellations.

1066 Read (Muḥammad) ibn Ḥāzim (al-Bāhilī): a poet specializing in satire, contemporary of al-Maʾmūn (r. 198/813–218/833); see e.g. al-Iṣfahānī, *al-Aghānī*, XIV:103.

1067 Contemporary of Caliph al-Maʾmūn; sometimes given the *nisbah* al-Barmakī, probably because of his association with that illustrious family.

1068 Reading *istahallū* with Ibn ʿAbd Rabbih, *al-ʿIqd al-farīd*, VI:177, instead of *istasʾhalū*.

1069 Governor under the Umayyads, famous for his power, ability, and cruelty, d. 75/714.

1070 The name could be translated as "Attack" or "Rhythm".

1071 A somewhat different version of this story, where it is told by al-Haytham ibn ʿAdī as having happened to his father, is found in al-Marzubānī, *Nūr al-qabas*, 292–93, (Ibn) al-Qifṭī, *Inbāh al-ruwāh*, III:365–67, and Ibn Khallikān, *Wafayāt al-aʿyān*, VI:107–8, trans. de Slane, III:635–36.

1072 Source: *Kitāb al-ḥikāyāt al-ʿajībah wal-akhbār al-gharībah / Das Buch der wunderbaren Erzählungen und seltsamen Geschichten*, ed. Hans Wehr (Wiesbaden, 1956), 105–21. There are two German translations: Otto Spies, "Das Märchen von den vierzig Mädchen," reprinted in Marzolph (ed.), *Das Buch der wunderbaren Geschichten*, 143–62, and Max Weisweiler, *Arabische Märchen*, I: 69–89.

1073 See Marzolph and van Leeuwen, *The Arabian Nights Encyclopedia*, I: 207–8, 285–86, 340–41.

1074 In the Islamic world, precedence in matters of succession does not follow primogeniture as a matter of course as it traditionally does in the Western world.

1075 Spies translates "Meer" (sea). The word *baḥr* is ambiguous and often means "big river," which seems more likely here since the king reaches the other side (but subsequently the reference to *baḥr al-ẓulumāt* makes one doubt again).

1076 Both a mythical sea (the one reached by Alexander the Great on his quest for eternal life) and the equivalent of the Atlantic Ocean.

1077 The erratum on p. 511 changes *waḍaʿūh* "they put him down" into *waddaʿūh* "they said farewell to him"; but I have opted for the former.

1078 Spies thinks either real birds in cages or artificial birds are meant; I believe the birds may be depicted as if singing; I have not adopted Wehr's suggestion (errata, p. 511) of reading *ṣāfirāt* ("whistling") instead of *ṣifāt*.

1079 Literally, "he carried the matter on his finger."

1080 Perhaps the bread was dipped in the sauce or broth of the main course, not mentioned earlier.

1081 According to Ibn al-Muʿtazz, *Ṭabaqāt al-shuʿarāʾ*, 383, the poet is Mānī l-Muwaswis ("Mānī the Maniac"), also called Mānī l-Majnūn ("Mad Mānī," d. 245/859); in Abū Tammām, *al-Waḥshiyyāt*, 198, they are ascribed to Ṣāliḥ ibn ʿAbd al-Quddūs (d. second half of second/eighth century).

1082 Later, it turns out that it is not the leader herself who stays behind but one of her companions; the narrator has obviously made a mistake.

1083 A pious reader of the manuscript has added here in the margin, "except God."

1084 One assumes the sorceress's mastery of magic enabled her to notice this after a mere forty days.

1085 Poet unidentified; the second hemistich of the second line (*ʾaw qamaran rākibin ʿalā ghuṣunī*) is very close to Abū Tammām's hemistich *yā qamaran mūfiyan ʿalā ghuṣunī*

(*Dīwān*, IV:281). The word *sakan*, in the first line, does not mean "Bewohner" (inhabitant), *pace* Spies.

1086 The horse/girl is now referred to as a female; hereafter its/her linguistic gender oscillates between masculine (here rendered as neuter) and feminine.

1087 The name (Persian) means "Queen of Women"; Badr al-Zamān (Arabic) translates as "Full Moon of the Age."

1088 That the young man's older brother is also called Bahrām (see the beginning) is clumsy from a storytelling perspective (as is perhaps the fact that the name of the boy himself is never mentioned). Bahrām is the Persian name of the planet Mars and a common name of pre-Islamic Persian kings and heroes.

1089 The demon himself is an *ʿifrīt* (once common in English as "afreet"), a particularly powerful and usually dangerous kind of *jinnī*; the "rebel" jinn are *maradah*, sg. *mārid*, likewise a generally bad but powerful kind of demon.

1090 A copyist has added in the margin: "It is not permis[sible] in the religion of Islam to marry two sisters (...) perhaps [the story took place] in pre-Islamic times." He is right about the rule (see Q Nisāʾ 4:23).

1091 Source: Shihāb al-Dīn Abū l-ʿAbbās Aḥmad ibn Yūsuf al-Tīfāshī, *Rujūʿ al-shaykh ilā ṣibāh fī l-quwwah ʿalā l-bāh* (Cairo, 1309/1891–92 H), 77–79. The edition wrongly attributes the work to Aḥmad ibn Sulaymān Kamāl Bāshā.

1092 Dāwūd al-Anṭākī, *al-Tadhkirah*, 384. *The Intelligent Man's Direction* (*Irshād al-labīb*) is a work by Ibn Ghāzī al-Miknāsī (d. 919/1513). Al-Anṭākī also suggests reading two works by the polymath al-Suyūṭī (d. 911/1505), conversing with women, wearing thin clothes, smelling perfumes, and watching copulating animals.

1093 This is the only occurrence in the story of the "vulgar" word *ḥir*; elsewhere the author uses the somewhat inaccurate *raḥim*, "womb" instead. For the male counterpart, likewise, he prefers the "decent" term *dhakar*, using the vulgar version only once, toward the end. He has apparently no objection to the vulgar word for copulation.

1094 The text has, surely wrongly, *ayyāman* "days."

1095 From the subsequent descriptions it becomes clear, however, that penetration and full sexual intercourse has not yet taken place.

1096 The text has mistakenly *qālat* ("she said").

1097 Or "him"? The syntax is ambiguous. Oral sex in Arabic literature is rare but not absent.

1098 Emending *wal-ʿishq al-ẓarīf* to *wa-aʿshaqu l-ẓarīf*.

1099 *The Nodding Noddles, or Jolting the Yokels: A Composition for Marginal Voices* by al-Shirbīnī (fl. 1687).

1100 Source: Yūsuf al-Shirbīnī, *Hazz al-quḥūf bi-sharḥ Qaṣīd Abī Shādūf*, Vol. I: Arabic text, ed. and introduced by Humphrey Davies, 70–75; cf. ed. Cairo, 1308/1890–91 H, 34–35, and ed. Muḥammad Qindīl al-Baqlī, Cairo, [1963], 61–65. My translations of this and the following story were made before the appearance of the splendid full translation of *Hazz al-quḥūf* by Humphrey Davies (vol. 2: *Yūsuf al-Shirbīnī's Brains Confounded by the Ode of Abū Shādūf Expounded*, see 74–78). For an earlier English translation, somewhat freer than mine, see Howarth and Shukrallah, *Images from the Arab World*, 21–23.

1101 As Davies remarks, the text in fact has "I roasted."

1102 Apparently he has taken it out of his breast pocket.

1103 A near quotation of Q Raʿd 13:2 (which has the plural *al-samawāt* "the heavens").

1104 This is not Qur'anic.

1105 e.g. Q Anʿām 6:95, 31.

1106 Q Yūnus 10:31.

1107 In a version given by Ibn ʿĀṣim al-Gharnāṭī (d. 829/1427), *Ḥadā'iq al-azāhir*, 183–84, the disputants are the Byzantine emperor and a Muslim; the more earthly interpretation of the gestures is given, rhetorically perhaps more effectively, after the theological one. Instead of a chick, the Christian produces an olive, to point at God's marvellous creation. This is countered by the Muslim's egg, which the Christian acknowledges to be even more marvellous. The Muslim interprets the exchange as "I can only give you one olive" and "poor chap, I'm better off than you because I've got an egg left."

1108 Davies's edition has *ṣirta* "you went," which may be correct. I have nevertheless preferred reading *ṣirtu*, as being more in line with traditional love poetry.

1109 Source: al-Shirbīnī (fl. 1097/1686), *Hazz al-quḥūf*, ed. Humphrey Davies, 41–43 (and see his translation, 48–49); cf. ed. Būlāq, 1308/1890–91 H, 20–21 and the bowdlerized version in ed. Cairo [1963], 43–45.

1110 "The Christian" (*al-Naṣrānī*), apparently an administrator charged with collecting the taxes or rent, is mentioned several times (e.g. pp. 257, 258, 261, 275) together with the overseer (*mushidd, multazim*).

1111 ʿAbd Allāh ibn ʿUmar, the pious son of the second caliph, said (disapprovingly), "the hammam is a bit of paradise that (people) have produced (*al-ḥammām min al-naʿīm alladhī aḥdathūh*," quoted in al-Ghazālī, *Iḥyā' ʿulūm al-dīn*, I:140). ʿAbd Allāh used to blindfold himself when entering the hammam, so as not to be tempted by the nudity there (ibid., I:139). See also below, note 1117.

1112 "Brother (*kardeş*) Muḥammad."

1113 "Right, what's the matter?" (*hah, ne var?*).

1114 *bir munqār/minqār* "one *minqār*," see Dozy, *Supplément aux dictionnaires arabes*, "Coin de petite taille se rapprochant de la forme de la cheville."

1115 A copper coin (see Dozy, *Supplément*).

1116 Source: Shihāb al-Dīn Aḥmad ibn Muḥammad al-Ḥaymī al-Kawkabānī (1073/1663–ca. 1151/1738), *ʿIṭr nasīm al-ṣabā*, ed. Aḥmad ibn Aḥmad al-Muṭāʿ, 124–31.

1117 The prophet Muḥammad. He (or someone else) is also reported as having said the opposite: "A bath: what a bad place!": see e.g. ʿAbd al-Raʾūf al-Munāwī, *al-Nuzhah al-shahiyyah*, 25. The attitudes of religious scholars toward the hammam are very ambivalent: it is a reminder of hell and of heaven alike.

1118 By Ṣadr al-Dīn Ibn al-Wakīl; see al-Ḥaymī, *Ḥadāʾiq*, 100; al-Ghuzūlī, *Maṭāliʿ al-budūr*, II:10. The same motif of water (or sweat) standing for tears is used in an epigram by Shams al-Dīn ibn Samandiyār (?) al-Dhahabī: "I did not visit the hammam to seek relief; / I've wept all tears away and down the drain. / But here my whole body can weep from grief, / as if a tear duct was its every vein." (See al-Ḥaymī, *Ḥadāʾiq*, 101; al-Ghuzūlī, *Maṭāliʿ*, II:106).

1119 Saʿīd ibn al-ʿĀṣ ibn Abī Uḥayḥah ibn al-ʿĀṣ ibn Umayyah, nicknamed Dhū l-Tāj or (as here) Dhū l-ʿImāmah, a contemporary of the Prophet.

1120 A somewhat tortuous conceit, literally "like the letter *wāw*, for whose sake the letter *rāʾ* of my *ṣabr* ('self-control, patience, endurance') was elided, leaving me a *ṣabb* (passionate lover)". Such conceits, based on letters or grammatical terminology, were very common.

1121 Literally, "not like the letter *wāw* (i.e. the particle *wa-*, 'and') which is the conjunction of lovers."

1122 Replacing an untranslatable pun with another; literally, "With the letter *N* of his curls he drags (*yajurr*) my heart to woe / I did not imagine that the letter *N* is one of the particles (like *K* [*ka-* 'like'], *B* [*bi-* 'with'], *L* [*li-* 'for']) that go with a genitive (*jarr*, literally 'dragging')."

1123 Another untranslatable line. *Qāf* is the letter *Q*; it is a letter that opens a Qur'anic sura (Q Qāf 50), as is *Nūn*, the letter *N* (Qalam 68). Twenty-nine of the Qur'an's 114 suras include such mysterious letters. A reversed *nūn* somewhat resembles an eyebrow with an eye under it. The word *ṣabr* (see above) is spelled out as *ṣād*, *bāʾ*, *rāʾ*. The poet is Burhān al-Dīn al-Qīrāṭī (d. 781/1379), see al-Nawājī, *Taʾhīl al-gharīb*, 75.

1124 With a pun on a technical term: *istiʿārah mujarradah* "'unprepared' metaphor" or "bared borrowing."

1125 The original puns on the two meanings of *ajfān*: "eyelids" and "scabbards" or "sheaths".

1126 Another untranslatable pun involving a technical term (*istiʿārah murashshaḥah* "'prepared' metaphor" or "borrowing sprinkled with water").

1127 The poet is Ḥusām al-Dīn al-Ḥājirī (d. 622/1225), see al-Nawājī, *Ta'hīl al-gharīb*, 437. Bilāl ibn Rabāḥ, a slave of Ethiopian descent and one of the earliest converts to Islam became the first muezzin because of his powerful voice. The breaking of dawn (i.e. the boy's bright face) will give him his cue.

1128 A common description of eloquence.

1129 A reference, no doubt, to the skylights with glass of different colors often found in hammams.

1130 The poet is Ibn al-Wardī (d. 749/1349); see al-Ḥaymī, *Ḥadā'iq*, 49–50.

1131 Ubullah was the harbor town of Basra, connected by a canal to the Tigris. The canal of Ubullah is often mentioned (with the Ghūṭah around Damascus, the Valley of Bawwān and other places) as one of the "paradises on earth."

1132 The sense is not wholly clear.

1133 A groanworthy pun to replace an untranslatable and intricate play on words, of the type called *tawriyah* (double entendre) in the second line, in Arabic *qad nazalnā bihā ʿalā bni maʿīnin / wa-rawaynā ʿanhu ṣaḥīḥi l-bukhārī*. At least four puns are involved: (1) *bukhār* "steam" and al-Bukhārī, the compiler of the most authoritative collection of Prophetic Traditions, (2) *maʿīn* "spring, source of water" and Yaḥyā ibn Maʿīn, a specialist in hadith (d. 233/847), (3) *ṣaḥīḥ* "sound, healthy" and *al-Ṣaḥīḥ*, the title of al-Bukhārī's work, (4) *rawīnā* "we had our fill, were irrigated" and *rawaynā* "we transmitted (a hadith)." The poet is the Andalusian Ibn Baqī (d. 540/1145–46), according to al-Ḥaymī, *Ḥadā'iq*, 49.

1134 Henna was not only used for dying hair and decorating hands, but was supposed to have medicinal properties; see e.g. Ibn al-Jawzī, *al-Ṭibb al-nabawī*, 89–90, Dāwūd al-Anṭākī, *Tadhkirah*, 130.

1135 The poet is Mujīr al-Dīn Muḥammad ibn Tamīm al-Dimashqī (d. 684/1285); see al-Ḥaymī, *Ḥadā'iq*, 105, 117; al-Ṣafadī, *al-Ghayth al-musajjam*, I:121.

1136 Literally, "from your sweet saliva". The poet is Ṣārim al-Dīn Ibrāhīm ibn Ṣāliḥ al-Hindī (d. 1101/1689–90): see al-Ḥaymī, *Ḥadā'iq*, 65.

1137 Here the company apparently has left the hammam for a garden, a typical *locus amoenus*.

1138 The poet is Sharaf al-Dīn (Rājiḥ ibn Ismāʿīl) al-Ḥillī (d. 627/1230), see al-Nawājī, *Ta'hīl al-gharīb*, 82. For the "showering stars" see above, Dhū l-Rummah's poem, line 2.

1139 That is, adult men became smitten with the love of a boy or a girl.

1140 The text has *nafaḥat* ("being fragrant"), which is a possible reading; in view of the context I have preferred to read *lafaḥat*.

1141 Q Wāqiʿah 56:33.

1142 Another untranslatable pun: *akmām* means "sleeves" (going with "hands") and "calyces" or "perianths" (going with "fruits").

Chronology

Dates	Authors in the Anthology	Dynasties and Rulers	Other Persons and Events of Note
AD 400		Sasanid Empire,	
	earliest known poetry	Eastern Roman Empire	
AD 500	‘Abīd ibn al-Abraṣ	Ghassānids, Lakhmids	
	‘Alqamah	(Arab vassal kingdoms)	
	Imru’ al-Qays		ca. AD 570 birth of Prophet Muḥammad
	al-Muthaqqib		
AD 600	al-Khansā’		AD 610–632 revelation of the Qur’an
	Ḥassān ibn Thābit		1/622 Hijrah from Mecca to Medina
		10/632–40/661 the four “Rightly Guided” caliphs	10/632 death of Muḥammad
			early conquests
	‘Urwah ibn Ḥizām		19/640 Kufa and Basra founded
			20/642 fall of Sasanid Empire
		40/661–60/680 Mu‘āwiyah, first caliph of the Umayyad Dynasty	36/656–40/661 first Civil War
	Qays ibn Dharīḥ		
			61/680 martyrdom of al-Ḥusayn, son of ‘Ali (Shī‘ite Imam)
		65/685–86/705 ‘Abd al-Malik, Umayyad caliph	
	‘Umar ibn Abī Rabī‘ah		
	al-Akhṭal		
	al-Farazdaq		
	Jarīr		
80/700	Dhū l-Rummah		92/711 conquest of Spain
		132/750 fall of Umayyad Dynasty, founding of Abbasid Dynasty	114/732 Battle of Tours
	Ibn al-Muqaffa‘		
			146/763 founding of Baghdad
		136/754–158/775 al-Manṣūr, Abbasid caliph	al-Khalīl ibn Aḥmad (grammarian)
	Bashshār ibn Burd		
		138/755–422/1031 Umayyad Dynasty in Spain	Sībawayh (grammarian)

Dates	Authors in the Anthology	Dynasties and Rulers	Other Persons and Events of Note
183/800	al-ʿAbbās ibn al-Aḥnaf	170/786–193/809 Hārūn al-Rashīd, Abbasid caliph	193/809–198/813 civil war between brothers al-Amīn and al-Maʾmūn for the caliphate
	Abū Nuwās		
	Abū l-ʿAtāhiyah	198/813–218/833 al-Maʾmūn, Abbasid caliph	
	Abū Tammām		
	al-Jāḥiẓ	193/809–296/909 Aghlabids in North Africa and Sicily	Jābir (Geber, alchemist)
	Ibn Qutaybah		221/836–276/889 Samarra is made caliphal residence
	al-Dīnawarī		
	Ibn al-Rūmī		Aḥmad ibn Ḥanbal (jurist)
	al-Buḥturī		al-Kindī (philosopher)
286/900		296/909 founding of Fāṭimid Dynasty in North Africa	al-Ṭabarī (historian, exegete)
	al-Masʿūdī		Abū Bakr al-Rāzī (Rhazes, physician, philosopher, alchemist)
	al-Mutanabbī		
	Abū l-Faraj al-Iṣfahānī	300/912–350/961 ʿAbd al-Raḥmān III, Spanish Umayyad Emir and Caliph	
	Ikhwān al-Ṣafāʾ		al-Fārābī (philosopher)
	al-Tanūkhī		
	al-Tawḥīdī	358/969 Fāṭimids conquer Egypt	358/969 founding of Cairo
		334/945–447/1055 Būyid occupation of Baghdad	
390/1000	al-Hamadhānī		
		422/1031 end of Umayyad Dynasty in Spain; "Petty Kingdoms"	
	Ibn Sīnā (Avicenna)		
		447/1055 Seljuqs occupy Baghdad	
	Abū l-ʿAlāʾ al-Maʿarrī		463/1071 Seljuq victory over Byzantines at Manzikert
		454/1062–542/1147 Almoravids in North Africa and Spain	
	Ibn Rashīq		
	ʿAbd al-Qāhir al-Jurjānī		492/1099 Jerusalem taken by Crusaders
493/1100	al-Ḥarīrī		al-Ghazālī (theologian, Sufi)
	al-Aʿmā al-Tuṭīlī	525/1130–668/1269 Almohads in North Africa and Spain	
	Ibn Khafājah		
		566/1171 Ṣalāḥ al-Dīn (Saladin) ends Fāṭimid Dynasty; founds Ayyūbid Dynasty	83/1187 Ṣalāḥ al-Dīn defeats Crusaders
			Ibn Rushd (Averroes, philosopher)

Dates	Authors in the Anthology	Dynasties and Rulers	Other Persons and Events of Note
596/1200	Ibn al-Fāriḍ		
	al-Tīfāshī	648/1250–922/1517 Mamluks in Egypt and Syria	Ibn al-ʿArabī (Sufi, philosopher)
	al-Shushtarī		
		656/1258 Abbasid Caliphate succumbs to the Mongol invasions	658/1260 Mamluk victory over Mongols at ʿAyn Jālūt
699/1300	Ibn Nubātah al-Miṣrī		
	Ibn Makānis		
	al-Damīrī		Ibn Khaldūn (historian)
802/1400	al-Ibshīhī		
			897/1492 Spanish conquest of Granada, fall of Naṣrid Dynasty
			al-Suyūṭī (polymath)
905/1500		922/1517 Ottoman occupation of Egypt	
		941/1534 Ottomans conquer Baghdad	
1008/1600	al-Shirbīnī		
1111/1700	al-Ḥaymī al-Kawkabānī		
			1213/1798 Napoleon conquers Egypt
1214/1800		1219/1805–1264/1848 Muḥammad ʿAlī in Egypt	
1317/1900			

Glossary of Names and Terms

adab good manners, erudition, rules of conduct, belles-lettres.
ʿajab amazement.
ʿajāʾib sg. *ʿajībah* mirabilia, wonders.
ʿāmmiyyah vernacular.
ʿarūḍ prosody.
badīʿ novel, original, figures of speech.
baḥr pl. *buḥūr* meter, lit. sea, big river.
balāghah eloquence.
bayt pl. *abyāt* line of verse.
dīwān pl. *dawāwīn* collected poetry.
fakhr self-praise, vaunting.
fiqh jurisprudence.
fuṣḥā pure, standard Arabic.
gharaḍ pl. *aghrāḍ* purpose, theme.
ghazal love poetry.
ghazal muʾannath love poetry on women.
ghazal mudhakkar love poetry on men.
ghuṣn pl. *aghṣān* strophe, lit. branch.
ḥadīth tradition, esp. about the Prophet.
hijāʾ invective, lampoon, satire.
ʿifrīt pl. *ʿafārīt* demon.
ʿilm al-ʿarūḍ the science of prosody.
inshāʾ composition, letter-writing, epistolography.
istiʿārah metaphor.
istiṭrād digression; satirical aside.
ʿitāb reproach.
jinn sg. *jinnī* demons, spirits.
kāhin pl. *kuhhān* soothsayer, diviner.
kalām speech; speculative theology.
kātib pl. *kuttāb* secretary, civil servant, lit. writer.
khamriyyah pl. *khamriyyāt* Bacchic poem.

kharjah lit. exit; last segment of a *muwashshaḥah.*

khayāl apparition, shadow, imagination.

khayāl al-ẓill shadow play.

khuṭbah pl. *khuṭab* oration, speech, sermon.

kitāb pl. *kutub* book.

kunyah teknonym, name beginning with Abū or Umm.

lafẓ pl. *alfāẓ* word, wording, expression.

lahw amusement, entertainment.

laqab pl. *alqāb* nickname, agnomen, honorific.

madīḥ panegyric, eulogy.

maʿnā pl. *maʿānī* meaning, sense, motif.

maqāmah pl. *maqāmāt* maqamah.

marthiyah pl. *marāthī* elegy, lament.

mathal pl. *amthāl* proverb, common saying, parable.

maṭlaʿ opening stanza.

maysir pre-Islamic form of gambling.

muḥdath pl. *muḥdathūn* "modern" [poet/poetry].

mukhaḍram pl. *mukhaḍramūn* [poet] straddling [the pre-Islamic and Islamic eras].

munāẓarah pl. *munāẓarāt* debate.

mushabbah *primum comparationis.*

muwallad pl. *muwalladūn* non-classical [poet].

muwashshaḥah pl. *muwashshaḥāt* a kind of strophic poem.

naqīḍah pl. *naqāʾiḍ* polemical poem, in reply to another poem .

nasab genealogy, lineage.

nasīb amatory or lyrical introdution.

nathr prose.

naẓm versification, poetry.

qāfiyah pl. *qawāfī* rhyme, rhyme-word.

qarīḍ poetry, excluding rajaz and other non-classical forms.

qaṣīdah pl. *qaṣāʾid* qasida, ode, longer poem.

qiṣaṣ al-anbiyāʾ Tales of the Prophets.

raḥīl journey.

rajaz name of a simple poetic meter.

rāwī pl. *ruwāh* transmitter or reciter of poetry.

risālah pl. *rasāʾil* letter, epistle.

rithāʾ elegy, lament.

riwāyah transmission.
rubāʿiyyah quatrain.
sabab element of metrical analysis.
sajʿ rhyming prose.
ṣanʿah artfulness.
ṣawt voice; song text.
shāʿir pl. *shuʿarāʾ* poet.
shiʿr poetry.
simṭ pl. *asmāṭ* strophe.
sīrah pl. *siyar* conduct, biography; epic, romance.
ṭabʿ natural talent.
tafsīr [Qur'anic] exegesis.
takhyīl make-believe.
ṭarab strong emotion, rapture, transport.
tashbīb amatory verse.
tashbīh pl. *tashbīhāt* comparison, simile.
urjūzah pl. *arājīz* poem in rajaz meter.
wajh al-shabah *tertium comparationis*.
waṣf pl. *awṣāf* description, ekphrasis.
waṣf al-nāqah description of one's she-camel.
watid element of metrical analysis.
wazn pl. *awzān* meter, lit. weight.
zajal pl. *azjāl* zajal, strophic poem in vernacular Arabic.
zuhd asceticism, renunciation.
zuhdiyyah pl. *zuhdiyyāt* ascetic, renunciant poem.

Bibliography

The Arabic article in its various forms (al-, Al-, El-) has been ignored in the alphabetical order.

ʿAbbās ibn al-Aḥnaf, al-. *Dīwān*. Beirut: Dār Ṣādir, 1965.

Abbott, Nabia. *Studies in Arabic Literary Papyri, III: Language and Literature*. Chicago: University of Chicago Press, 1972.

ʿAbīd ibn al-Abraṣ. *Dīwān*, edited by Charles Lyall. Cambridge: E. J. W. Gibb Memorial Trust, 1931.

———. *Dīwān*, edited by Tawfīq Asʿad. Kuwait: Wizārat al-Iʿlām, 1989.

Abū l-ʿAtāhiyah. *Dīwān*, edited by Shukrī Fayṣal. Damascus: Dār al-Mallāḥ, 1965.

Abū Dāwūd. *Al-Sunan*, edited by ʿIzzat ʿUbayd al-Daʿʿās and ʿĀdil al-Sayyid. 5 vols. Beirut: Dār Ibn Ḥazm, 1997.

Abu Deeb, Kamal. *Al-Jurjānī's Theory of Poetic Imagery*. Warminster, Wilts.: Aris and Phillips, 1979.

Abu-Haidar, Jareer. "*Qifā nabki*: The Dual Form of Address in Arabic Poetry in a New Light." *Journal of Arabic Literature*, 19 (1988): 40–48.

Abū Ḥātim al-Sijistānī. *Al-Muʿammarūn*, edited by Ignaz Goldziher, in *Abhandlungen zur arabischen Philologie, 2 Theil*. Leiden: Brill, 1899.

Abū Nuwās. *Dīwān*, edited by Aḥmad ʿAbd al-Majīd al-Ghazālī. Cairo, 1953, reprinted Beirut: Dār al-Kātib al-ʿArabī, 1984.

———. *Dīwān*. Vol. I, edited by Ewald Wagner. Cairo - Wiesbaden: Franz Steiner; 2nd rev. ed. Beirut and Berlin: Das Arabische Buch, 2001.

———. *Dīwān*. Vol. II, edited by Ewald Wagner. Wiesbaden: Franz Steiner, 1972.

———. *Dīwān*. Vol. III, edited by Ewald Wagner. Wiesbaden: Franz Steiner, 1988.

———. *Dīwān*. Vol. IV, edited by Gregor Schoeler. Wiesbaden: Franz Steiner, 1982.

Abū Tammām. *Dīwān*, edited by Muḥammad ʿAzzām. 4 vols. Cairo: Dār al-Maʿārif, 1976.

———. *Al-Waḥshiyyāt, wa-huwa al-Ḥamāsah al-ṣughrā*, edited by ʿAbd al-ʿAzīz al-Maymanī al-Rājakūtī and Maḥmūd Muḥammad Shākir. Cairo: Dār al-Maʿārif, 1987.

Abū ʿUbaydah. *Naqāʾiḍ Jarīr wal-Farazdaq*, edited by Anthony Ashley Bevan. 3 vols. Leiden: E. J. Brill, 1905–12.

Ahlwardt, Wilhelm, ed. *The Divans of the Six Ancient Arabic Poets*. London: 1870, reprinted Osnabrück: Biblio Verlag, 1972.

Ajami, Mansour. *The Neckveins of Winter: The Controversy Over Natural and Artificial Poetry in Medieval Arabic Criticism*. Leiden: Brill, 1984.

Akhfash, al-Aṣghar al-. *Al-Ikhtiyārayn*, edited by Fakhr al-Dīn Qabāwah. Damascus: Majmaʿ al-Lughah al-ʿArabiyyah, 1974.

Akhṭal, al-. *Dīwān al-Akhṭal*, edited by Mahdī Muḥammad Nāṣir al-Dīn. Beirut: Dār al-Kutub al-ʿIlmiyyah, 1994.

Aʿlam al-Shantamarī, al-. *Sharḥ Dīwān ʿAlqamah ibn ʿAbadah*. Algiers: Jules Carbonel, 1925.

Alf laylah wa-laylah. 4 vols. Cairo: Maktabat Ṣubayḥ, n.d.

Allen, Roger. *The Arabic Literary Heritage: The Development of its Genres and Criticism*. Cambridge: Cambridge University Press, 1998.

———. *An Introduction to Arabic Literature*. Cambridge: Cambridge University Press, 2000.

———, and D. S. Richards, eds. *Arabic Literature in the Post-Classical Period*. Cambridge History of Arabic Literature. Cambridge: Cambridge University Press, 2006.

ʿĀmilī, Bahāʾ al-Dīn al-. *Al-Kashkūl*. Beirut: Dār al-Kitāb al-Lubnānī, 1983.

Anbārī, Abū Bakr Muḥammad ibn al-Qāsim al-. *Sharḥ al-qaṣāʾid al-ṭiwāl*, edited by ʿAbd al-Salām Muḥammad Hārūn. Cairo: Dār al-Maʿārif, 1969.

Anṭākī, Dāwūd al-. *Tazyīn al-aswāq*, edited by Muḥammad Altūnjī. 2 vols. Beirut: ʿĀlam al-Kutub, 1993.

———. *Tadhkirat Dāwūd al-Anṭākī al-musammā Tadhkirat ulī l-albāb wal-jāmiʿ lil-ʿajab al-ʿujāb*, edited by Aḥmad Shams al-Dīn. Beirut: Dār al-Kutub al-ʿIlmiyyah, 2000.

The Arabian Nights. Translated by Husain Haddawy. Based on the text of the fourteenth-century Syrian manuscript edited by Muhsin Mahdi. New York: W. W. Norton, 1990.

The Arabian Nights, 2: Sindbad and Other Popular Stories. Translated by Husain Haddawy. New York: W. W. Norton, 1995.

The Arabian Nights: Tales of 1001 Nights. Translated by Malcolm C. Lyons. 3 vols. London: Penguin, 2008.

Arberry, A. J. *Avicenna on Theology*. London: Murray, 1951.

———. *The Mystical Poems of Ibn al-Fāriḍ*. Dublin: Emery Walker, 1956.

———. *The Koran Interpreted*. London: Oxford University Press, 1964.

———. *Arabic Poetry: A Primer for Students*. Cambridge: Cambridge University Press, 1965.

———. *Poems of al-Mutanabbī: A Selection with Introduction, Translations and Notes*. Cambridge: Cambridge University Press, 1967.

Ashtiany, Julia et al., eds. *ʿAbbasid Belles Lettres*. Cambridge History of Arabic Literature. Cambridge: Cambridge University Press, 1990.

ʿAskarī, Abū Hilāl al-. *Dīwān al-maʿānī*. 2 vols. Cairo: Maktabat al-Qudsī, 1352/1932–33.

———. *Al-Furūq al-lughawiyyah*, edited by Ḥusām al-Dīn al-Qudsī. Cairo: Maktabat al-Qudsī, 1353/1934–35.

———. *Kitāb al-Ṣināʿatayn al-kitābah wal-shiʿr*, edited by ʿAlī Muḥammad al-Bajāwī. Cairo: ʿĪsā al-Bābī al-Ḥalabī, 1971.

———. *Dīwān*, edited by Jūrj Qanāziʿ. Damascus: Majmaʿ al-Lughah al-ʿArabiyyah, 1979.

———. *Jamharat al-amthāl*, edited by Aḥmad ʿAbd al-Salām. 2 vols. Beirut: Dār al-Kutub al-ʿIlmiyyah, 1988.

Baghdādī, ʿAbd al-Qādir al-. *Khizānat al-adab*, edited by ʿAbd al-Salām Muḥammad Hārūn. 13 vols. Cairo: Dār al-Kātib al-ʿArabī/Maktabat al-Khānjī, 1967–86.

Baghdādī, al-Khaṭīb al-. *Tārīkh Baghdād*. 14 vols. Cairo: Maktabat al-Khānjī, 1931.

Bākharzī, Abū l-Ḥasan ʿAlī ibn al-Ḥasan al-. *Dumyat al-qaṣr wa-ʿuṣrat ahl al-ʿaṣr*, edited by Muḥammad al-Tūnjī. 3 vols. Beirut: Dār al-Jīl, 1993.

Bāqillānī, Abū Bakr Muḥammad ibn al-Ṭayyib al-. *Iʿjāz al-Qurʾān*, edited by al-Sayyid Aḥmad Ṣaqr. Cairo: Dār al-Maʿārif, 1963.

Bashshār ibn Burd. *Dīwān*, edited by Muḥammad al-Ṭāhir ibn ʿĀshūr. 4 vols. Algiers and Tunis: al-Sharikah al-Waṭaniyyah/al-Sharikah al-Tūnisiyyah, 1976.

Baṭalyawsī, al-. *Al-Iqtiḍāb fī sharḥ Adab al-kātib*, edited by Muṣṭafā al-Saqqā and Ḥāmid ʿAbd al-Ḥamīd. 3 vols. Cairo: al-Hayʾah al-Miṣriyyah al-ʿĀmmah, 1981–83.

Bauer, Thomas. *Altarabische Dichtkunst: Eine Untersuchung ihrer Struktur und Entwicklung am Beispiel der Onagerepisode*. 2 vols. Wiesbaden: Harrassowitz, 1992.

———. *Liebe und Liebesdichtung in der arabischen Welt des 9. und 10. Jahrhunderts: Eine literatur- und mentalitätsgeschichtliche Studie des arabischen Ġazal*. Wiesbaden: Harrassowitz, 1998.

Bayhaqī, Ibrāhīm ibn Muḥammad al-. *Al-Maḥāsin wal-masāwiʾ*, edited by Friedrich Schwally. Giessen: J. Ricker, 1902.

———. *Al-Maḥāsin wal-masāwiʾ*. Beirut: Dār Ṣādir, 1970.

Beeston, A. F. L. *Selections from the poetry of Baššār, edited with translation and commentary and an introductory sketch of Arabic poetic structures*. Cambridge: Cambridge University Press, 1977.

——— et al., eds. *Arabic Literature to the End of the Umayyad Period*. Cambridge History of Arabic Literature.Cambridge: Cambridge University Press, 1983 .

Bergé, Marc. "Mérites respectifs des nations selon le *Kitāb al-Imtāʿ wal-muʾānasa* d'Abū Ḥayyān al-Tawḥīdī (m. en 414/1023)." *Arabica*, 19 (1972): 165–76.

Blachère, Régis. *Histoire de la littérature arabe*. 3 vols. Paris: Maisonneuve, 1952–66.

The Book of the Thousand Nights and a Night, translated by R. F. Burton. 12 vols. London: H. S. Nichols, 1897.

The Brethren of Purity. *The Case of the Animals*. *See* Ikhwān al-Ṣafaʾ.

Browne, Edward G. *A Literary History of Persia*. 4 vols. Cambridge: Cambridge University Press, 1951–53 (1st ed. 1902).

Buḥturī, al-. *Dīwān al-Buḥturī*, edited by Ḥasan Kāmil al-Ṣayrafī. 5 vols. Cairo: Dār al-Maʿārif, 1972–78.

Bürgel, J. C. *Tausendundeine Welt: Klassische arabische Literatur vom Koran bis zu Ibn Chaldûn, ausgewählt und übersetzt*. München: C. H. Beck, 2007.

Cachia, Pierre. *The Arch Rhetorician, or The Schemer's Skimmer: A Handbook of Late Arabic badīʿ drawn from ʿAbd al-Ghanī an-Nābulsī's Nafaḥāt al-Azhār ʿalā Nasamāt al-Asḥār*, summarized and systematized by Pierre Cachia. Wiesbaden: Harrassowitz, 1998.

———. *Arabic Literature: An Overview*. London: RoutledgeCurzon, 2002.

Callataÿ, Godefroi de. *Ikhwan al-Safa: A Brotherhood of Idealists at the Fringe of Orthodox Islam*. Oxford: Oneworld, 2005.

Canard, Marius. "Les aventures d'un prisonnier arabe et d'un patrice byzantin à l'époque des guerres bulgaro-byzantines." *Dumbarton Oaks Papers*, 9–10 (Cambridge, Mass., 1956), 49–72, reprinted in Marius Canard, *Byzance et les musulmans du Proche Orient*. London: Variorum, 1973.

Cantarino, Vicente. *Arabic Poetics in the Golden Age: Selection of Texts Accompanied by a Preliminary Study*. Leiden: Brill, 1975.

Carra de Vaux. "La Ḳaçîdah d'Avicenne sur l'âme." *Journal Asiatique*, Neuvième Série, 14 (1899): 157–73.

Caswell, Fuad Matthew. *The Slave Girls of Baghdad: The Qiyān in the Early Abbasid Era*. London: I. B. Tauris, 2011.

Chauvin, Victor. *Bibliographie des oeuvres arabes ou relatifs aux arabes*. 12 vols. Liège: no publ., 1892–1909.

Cheikho, L. *Shuʿarā' al-Naṣrāniyyah*. 2 vols. Beirut: Maṭbaʿat al-Ābā' al-Mursalīn al-Yasūʿiyyīn, 1890.

Christensen, A. "La princesse sur la feuille de myrte et la princesse sur le pois." *Acta Orientalia*, 14 (1936): 241–57.

Colville, Jim. *Poems of Wine and Revelry: The khamriyyat of Abu Nuwas*. London: Kegan Paul, 2005.

Compton, Linda Fish. *Andalusian Lyrical Poetry and Old Spanish Love Songs: The Muwashshaḥ and its Kharja*. New York: New York University Press, 1976.

Corriente, F. *Poesía estrófica (Cejeles y/o muwaššaḥāt) atribuida al místico Granadino aš-Šuštarī (siglo XIII d. C.)*. Madrid: Consejo Superior de Investigaciones Científicas, 1988.

Cray, Ed. "The Rabbi Trickster." *The Journal of American Folklore*, no. 306 (1964): 331–45.

Damīrī, Kamāl al-Dīn Muḥammad ibn Mūsā al-. *Ḥayāt al-ḥayawān al-kubrā*. 2 vols. Cairo: al-Maktabah al-Tijāriyyah al-Kubrā, n.d.

———. *Ḥayāt al-ḥayawān al-kubrā*. 2 vols. Cairo: Muṣṭafā al-Bābī al-Ḥalabī, 1970.

Dawkins, Richard. *The Ancestor's Tale*. London: Phoenix, 2005.

Dhū l-Rummah. *Dīwān*, edited by C. H. H. Macartney. Cambridge: Cambridge University Press, 1919.

———. *Dīwān Dhī l-Rummah*, edited by ʿAbd al-Quddūs Abū Ṣāliḥ. 3 vols. Beirut: Mu'assasat al-Īmān, 1982.

Diʿbil ibn ʿAlī al-Khuzāʿī. *Dīwān*, edited by ʿAbd al-Ṣāhib ʿImrān al-Dujaylī. Beirut: Dār al-Kitāb al-Lubnānī, 1972.

Dimashqī, Shams al-Dīn Muḥammad ibn Abī Ṭālib al-. *Nukhbat al-dahr*, edited by A. F. Mehren. St. Petersburg: Académie Impériale des Sciences, 1866.

Dīnawarī, Abū Ḥanīfah al-. *Al-Akhbār al-ṭiwāl*, edited by V. Guirgass. Leiden: Brill, 1888.

Dīwān al-ʿUdhriyyīn, edited by Yūsuf ʿĪd. Beirut: Dār al-Jīl, 1992.

Dozy, R. *Supplément aux dictionnaires arabes*. 2 vols. Leiden: Brill, 1927.

EAL see Meisami and Starkey, eds.

EI2 = *The Encyclopaedia of Islam*, New [= Second] Edition. 11 vols. with Supplement vol. and Index vol. Leiden: Brill, 1960–2009.

Frolov, Dmitry. *Classical Arabic Verse: History and Theory of ʿArūḍ*. Leiden: Brill, 2000.

Gabrieli, Francesco. "Il valore letterario e storico del Faraĝ baʿda ś-śiddah di Tanūḫī." *Rivista degli Studi Orientali* 19 (1941): 16–44.

Gharnāṭī, Abū Ḥāmid al-. *Tuḥfat al-albāb*, edited by Gabriel Ferrand. Paris: Imprimerie Nationale, 1925.

———. *Tuḥfat al-albāb*, edited by Ismāʿīl al-ʿArabī. Casablanca: Dār al-Āfāq al-Jadīdah, 1993.

Ghazālī, Abū Ḥāmid al-. *Iḥyāʾ ʿulūm al-dīn*. 5 vols. Cairo: Maktabat al-Mashhad al-Ḥusaynī, n.d.

Ghuzūlī, ʿAlāʾ al-Dīn ʿAlī ibn ʿAbd Allāh al-. *Maṭāliʿ al-budūr fī manāzil al-surūr*. Cairo: Maṭbaʿat al-Waṭan, 1299–1300/1881–83.

Gordon, Matthew S. "The Place of Competition: The Careers of ʿArīb al-Maʾmūniyyah and ʿUlayyah bint al-Mahdī, Sisters in Song." In *ʿAbbasid Studies: Occasional Papers of the School of ʿAbbasid Studies*, Cambridge, 6–10 July, 2002, edited by James E. Montgomery, 61–81. Leuven: Peeters, 2004.

Gramlich, R. *Die Wunder der Freunde Gottes. Theologien und Erscheinungsformen des islamischen Heiligenwunders*. Wiesbaden: Franz Steiner, 1987.

Granja, Fernando de la. "Dos epístolas de Aḥmad Ibn Burd al-Aṣgar." *Al-Andalus* 25 (1960): 383–418.

———. *Maqāmas y risālas andaluzas: Traducciones y estudios*. Madrid: Instituto Hispano-Árabe de Cultura, 1976.

Gruendler, Beatrice. *Medieval Arabic Praise Poetry: Ibn al-Rūmī and the Patron's Redemption*. London: RoutledgeCurzon, 2003.

Gully, Adrian. "The Sword and the Pen in the Pre-Modern Arabic Heritage: A Literary Representation of an Important Historical Relationship." In Sebastian Günther, ed., *Ideas, Images, and Methods of Portrayal: Insights into Classical Arabic Literature and Islam.* Leiden: Brill, 2005, 403–30.

Gutas, Dimitri. *Greek Thought, Arabic Culture: The Graeco-Arabic Translation Movement in Baghdad and Early 'Abbāsid Society (2nd–4th/8th–10th centuries).* London: Routledge, 1998.

Hamadhānī, Badī' al-Zamān al-. *Al-Maqāmāt.* Constantinople: Maṭba'at al-Jawā'ib, 1298/1880–81.

[———] Al-Hamaḏānī. *Choix de Maqāmāt (Séances), traduites de l'arabe, avec une étude sur le genre, par Régis Blachère & Pierre Masnou.* Paris: C. Klincksieck, 1957.

[———]. *The Maqámát of Badí' al-Zamán al-Hamadhání, translated from the Arabic, with an introduction and notes historical and grammatical by W. J. Prendergast.* London: Curzon, 1973 (1st ed. London, 1915).

———. *Al-Maqāmāt,* edition and commentary by Muḥammad 'Abduh. Beirut: Dār al-Mashriq, 1973 (1st ed. 1889).

[———]. Al-Hamadhânî. *Vernunft ist nichts als Narretei. Die Maqâmen, aus dem Arabischen vollständig übertragen und bearbeitet von Gernot Rotter.* Tübingen: Erdmann, 1982.

[———]. Badî' al-Zamâne al-Hamadhânî. *Le livre des vagabonds: Séances d'un beau parleur impénitent,* translated by René R. Khawam. Paris: Phébus, 2009.

Hämeen-Anttila, Jaakko. *Maqama: A History of a Genre.* Wiesbaden: Harrassowitz, 2002.

Hamori, Andras. "The Siege of al-Ḥadath." In *Studia Arabica et Islamica: Festschrift for Iḥsān 'Abbās,* edited by Wadād al-Qāḍī, 195–208. Beirut: American University of Beirut, 1981.

———. "Folklore in Tanūkhī: The Collector of Ramlah." *Studia Islamica,* 71 (1990): 65–75.

———. *The Composition of Mutanabbī's Panegyrics to Sayf al-Dawla.* Leiden: Brill, 1992.

Ḥassān ibn Thābit. *Dīwān,* edited by Sayyid Ḥanafī Ḥasanayn. Cairo: Dār al-Ma'ārif, 1983.

Ḥaymī al-Kawkabānī, Shihāb al-Dīn Aḥmad ibn Muḥammad al-. *'Iṭr nasīm al-ṣabā,* edited by Aḥmad ibn Aḥmad al-Muṭā'. Beirut: Dār Āzāl, 1985.

———. *Ḥadā'iq al-nammām fī l-kalām 'alā mā yata'allaq bil-ḥammām,* edited by 'Abd Allāh Muḥammad al-Ḥibshī. Beirut: Manshūrāt al-Madīnah, 1986 [on title page wrongly "al-Ḥaysamī" instead of al-Ḥaymī].

Heinrichs, Wolfhart. "Rose versus Narcissus: Observations on an Arabic Literary Debate." In *Dispute Poems and Dialogues in the Ancient and Mediaeval Near East: Forms and Types of Literary Debates in Semitic and Related Literatures,* edited by G. J. Reinink and H. L. J. Vanstiphout, 179–98 . Leuven: Peeters, 1991.

Holes, Clive. *Modern Arabic: Structure, Functions, and Variations.* Rev. ed. Washington, DC: Georgetown University Press, 2004.

Homerin, Th. Emil. *From Arab Poet to Muslim Saint: Ibn al-Fāriḍ: His Verse, and His Shrine.* Columbia, SC: University of South Carolina Press, 1994.

———. *'Umar Ibn al-Fāriḍ: Sufi Verse, Saintly Life.* New York: Paulist Press, 2001.

———. "'On the Battleground': Al-Nābulusī's Encounters with a Poem by Ibn al-Fāriḍ." *Journal of Arabic Literature,* 38 (2007): 352–410; also published in *Arabic Literary Thresholds: Sites of Rhetorical Turn in Contemporary Scholarship,* edited by Muhsin al-Musawi. Leiden: Brill, 2009, 143–206.

Howarth, Herbert, and Ibrahim Shukrallah. *Images from the Arab World.* London: The Pilot Press, 1944.

Ḥuṣrī, Abū Isḥāq Ibrāhīm ibn 'Alī al-. *Zahr al-ādāb wa-thamar al-albāb,* edited by Zakī Mubārak and Muḥammad Muḥyī l-Dīn 'Abd al-Ḥamīd. 4 vols. in 2, Beirut: Dār al-Jīl, 1972.

———. *Al-Maṣūn fī sirr al-hawā al-maknūn,* edited by al-Nabawī 'Abd al-Wāḥid Sha'lān. Cairo: Dār al-'Arab, 1989.

Ibn 'Abd Rabbih. *Al-'Iqd al-farīd.* 7 vols. Cairo, 1948–53, repr. Beirut: Dār al-Kitāb al-'Arabī, 1983.

Ibn Abī 'Awn. *Tashbīhāt,* edited by M. 'Abd al-Mu'īd Khān. London: Luzac, 1950.

Ibn Abī Ṭāhir Ṭayfūr, Aḥmad. *Balāghāt al-nisā'.* Cairo: Maṭba'at Madrasat Wālidat 'Abbās al-Awwal, 1908.

———. *Balāghāt al-nisā'.* Beirut: Dār al-Ḥadāthah, 1987.

Ibn Abī Uṣaybi'ah. *'Uyūn al-anbā' fī ṭabaqāt al-aṭibbā',* edited by Nizār Riḍā. Beirut: Dār Maktabat al-Ḥayāh, n.d.

———. *'Uyūn al-anbā' fī ṭabaqāt al-aṭibbā',* edited by A. Müller. Cairo–Königsberg: al-Maṭba'ah al-Wahbiyyah, 1882–84.

Ibn 'Āṣim al-Gharnāṭī. *Ḥadā'iq al-azāhir,* edited by Abū Hammām 'Abd al-Laṭīf 'Abd al-Ḥalīm. Sidon–Beirut, al-Maktabah al-'Aṣriyyah, 1992.

Ibn al-Athīr, 'Izz al-Dīn. *Al-Kāmil fī l-tārīkh,* edited by C. J. Tornberg. 12 vols. Beirut: Dār Ṣādir, 1965–67.

Ibn Bassām al-Shantarīnī. *Al-Dhakhīrah fī maḥāsin ahl al-jazīrah,* Part I, vol. 2. Cairo: Lajnat al-Ta'līf, 1942.

———. *Al-Dhakhīrah fī maḥāsin ahl al-jazīrah,* edited by Iḥsān 'Abbās. 8 vols. Beirut: Dār al-Thaqāfah, 1978–79.

Ibn Bishrī, 'Alī. *'Uddat al-jalīs,* edited by Alan Jones. Cambridge: E. J. W. Gibb Memorial Trust, 1992.

Ibn Dāwūd al-Iṣbahānī, Abū Bakr Muḥammad. *Al-Zahrah,* edited by Ibrāhīm al-Sāmarrā'ī. Al-Zarqā', Jordan: Maktabat al-Manār, 1985.

Ibn Durayd, Abū Bakr Muḥammad. *Jamharat al-lughah*, edited by Ramzī Munīr Baʿlabakkī. 3 vols. Beirut: Dār al-ʿIlm lil-Malāyīn, 1987.

Ibn al-Faqīh, Abū Bakr Aḥmad ibn Muḥammad. *Mukhtaṣar Kitāb al-buldān*, edited by M. J. de Goeje. Leiden: Brill, 1885.

Ibn al-Fāriḍ, ʿUmar. *Dīwān*. Beirut: Dār Ṣādir, 1962.

———. *Dīwān*, edited by Giuseppe Scattolin. Cairo: IFAO, 2004.

Ibn Ḥabīb, Muḥammad. "Asmāʾ al-mughtālīn min al-ashrāf fī l-jāhiliyyah wal-islām wa-asmāʾ man qutila min al-shuʿarāʾ", edited by ʿAbd al-Salām Hārūn. In ʿAbd al-Salām Hārūn, *Nawādir al-makhṭūṭāt*. Cairo: Muṣṭafā al-Bābī al-Ḥalabī, 1973, II: 105–278.

Ibn Ḥajar. *Tahdhīb al-Tahdhīb*. Hyderabad: Dāʾirat al-Maʿārif al-ʿUthmāniyyah, H 1325–27/1907–10.

Ibn Ḥamdūn, Muḥammad ibn al-Ḥasan. *al-Tadhkirah al-Ḥamdūniyyah*, edited by Iḥsān ʿAbbās and Bakr ʿAbbās. 10 vols. Beirut: Dār Ṣādir, 1996.

Ibn Hishām. *Al-Sīrah al-nabawiyyah*, edited by Muṣṭafā al-Saqqā, Ibrāhīm al-Abyārī and ʿAbd al-Ḥafīẓ Shalabī. 2 vols. Cairo: Muṣṭafā al-Bābī al-Ḥalabī, 1955.

Ibn Ishaq. *The Life of Muhammad: A Translation of Ishāq's [sic] Sīrat Rasūl Allāh*, translated by Alfred Guillaume. Oxford: Oxford University Press, 1955.

Ibn Iyās. *Badāʾiʿ al-zuhūr fī waqāʾiʿ al-duhūr*, edited by Muḥammad Muṣṭafā. Vol. I, ii. Cairo–Wiesbaden: Franz Steiner, 1974.

Ibn al-Jarrāḥ, Abū ʿAbd Allāh ibn Dāwūd. *Al-Waraqah*, edited by ʿAbd al-Wahhāb ʿAzzām and ʿAbd al-Sattār Aḥmad Farrāj. Cairo: Dār al-Maʿārif, n.d.

Ibn al-Jawzī. *Al-Ṭibb al-nabawī*, edited by Shuʿayb al-Arnaʾūṭ and ʿAbd al-Qādir al-Arnaʾūṭ. Beirut: Muʾassasat al-Risālah, 1985.

———. *Al-Adhkiyāʾ*, edited by Muḥammad ʿAbd al-Raḥmān ʿAwaḍ. Beirut: Dār al-Kitāb al-ʿArabī, 1986.

Ibn Khafājah. *Dīwān*. Beirut: Dār Ṣādir, n.d.

Ibn Khallikān. *Biographical Dictionary*, translated by Mac Guckin de Slane. 4 vols. Paris: Oriental Translation Fund of Great Britain and Ireland, 1842–71.

———. *Wafayāt al-aʿyān wa-anbāʾ abnāʾ al-zamān*, edited by Iḥsān ʿAbbās. 8 vols. Beirut: Dār al-Thaqāfah, 1968–72.

Ibn al-Khaṭīb, Lisān al-Dīn. *Jaysh al-tawshīḥ*, edited by Alan Jones. Cambridge: E. J. W. Gibb Memorial Trust, 1997.

Ibn Mālik, Jamāl al-Dīn Muḥammad ibn ʿAbd Allāh. *Alfiyyat Ibn Mālik*, edited by Mūsā ibn Muḥammad al-Dāghistānī. Cairo: Maktabat al-Ādāb, 1984.

Ibn Manẓūr. *Lisān al-ʿarab*. 20 vols. Cairo: al-Dār al-Miṣriyyah lil-Taʾlīf wal-Tarjamah, n.d. (repr. of ed. Būlāq, H 1300/1882–1308/1891).

Ibn Maymūn, Abū Ghālib Muḥammad ibn al-Mubārak. *Muntahā l-ṭalab min ash'ār al-'Arab*, facsimile edition. Frankfurt am Main: Institute for the History of Arabic-Islamic Science, 1986–93.

Ibn al-Muqaffa'. "Al-Adab al-kabīr." In *Rasā'il al-bulaghā'*, edited by Muḥammad Kurd 'Alī. 4th ed., Cairo, H 1374/1954, 39–106.

Ibn al-Muqaffa', 'Abd Allāh. *Kalīlah wa-Dimnah*. Beirut: Dār Ṣādir, 1984.

Ibn al-Mu'tazz, 'Abd Allāh. *Al-Badī'*, edited by Ignatius Kratchkovsky. London: Luzac, 1935.

———. *Dīwān*, edited by Bernhard Lewin, 2 vols. (III and IV). İstanbul: Maṭba'at al-Ma'ārif, 1945–50.

———. *Ṭabaqāt al-shu'arā'*, edited by 'Abd al-Sattār Aḥmad Farrāj. Cairo: Dār al-Ma'ārif, 1968.

———. *Dīwān*, edited by Muḥammad Badī' Sharīf. 2 vols. Cairo: Dār al-Ma'ārif, 1977–78.

[Ibn] al-Nadīm. *Al-Fihrist*, edited by G. Flügel. 2 vols. Leipzig: F. C. W. Vogel, 1871–72.

———. *al-Fihrist*, edited by Yūsuf 'Alī Ṭawīl. Beirut: Dār al-Kutub al-'Ilmiyyah, 2002.

Ibn Nubātah al-Miṣrī. *Dīwān*. Cairo: Maṭba'at al-Tamaddun, 1905.

Ibn Qayyim al-Ǧauziyya. *Über die Frauen*, translated by Dieter Bellmann. München: C. H. Beck, 1986.

Ibn Qayyim al-Jawziyyah. *Rawḍat al-muḥibbīn*. Beirut: Dār al-Kutub al-'Ilmiyyah, n.d.

[pseudo-]———. *Akhbār al-nisā'*. Cairo: Maṭba'at al-Taqaddum, 1319/1901–02.

[Ibn] al-Qifṭī, Jamāl al-Dīn Abū l-Ḥasan 'Alī ibn Yūsuf. *Inbāh al-ruwāh 'alā anbā' al-nuḥāh*, edited by Muḥammad Abū l-Faḍl Ibrāhīm. 4 vols. Cairo: Dār al-Fikr al-'Arabī, 1986.

Ibn Qutaybah. *'Uyūn al-akhbār*. 4 vols. Cairo: Dār al-Kutub, 1925–30.

———. *Kitāb al-Ma'ānī l-kabīr*. Hyderabad: Dā'irat al-Ma'ārif al-'Uthmāniyyah, 1949.

———. *Al-Shi'r wal-shu'arā'*, edited by Aḥmad Muḥammad Shākir. Cairo: Dār al-Ma'ārif, 1966–67.

———. *Al-Ma'ārif*, edited by Tharwat 'Ukāshah. Cairo: Dār al-Ma'ārif, 1981.

Ibn Rashīq, Abū 'Alī al-Ḥasan. *Al-'Umdah fī maḥāsin al-shi'r wa-ādābihi wa-naqdih*, edited by Muḥammad Badr al-Dīn al-Na'sānī al-Ḥalabī. 2 vols. Cairo: Maṭba'at al-Sa'ādah, 1907.

———. *Al-'Umdah fī maḥāsin al-shi'r wa-ādābihi wa-naqdih*, edited by Muḥammad Muḥyī l-Dīn 'Abd al-Ḥamīd. 2 vols. repr. Beirut: Dār al-Jīl, 1972.

Ibn al-Rūmī. *Dīwān*, edited by Ḥusayn Naṣṣār. 6 vols. Cairo: al-Hay'ah al-Miṣriyyah al-'Āmmah, 1973–81.

Ibn Sallām al-Jumaḥī. *Ṭabaqāt fuḥūl al-shu'arā'*, edited by Maḥmūd Muḥammad Shākir. Cairo: Dār al-Ma'ārif, 1952.

Ibn Sanā' al-Mulk. *Dār al-ṭirāz*, edited by Jawdat al-Rikābī. Damascus: no publ., 1949, and Damascus: Dār al-Fikr, 1977.

Ibn al-Shajarī. *Ḥamāsat Ibn al-Shajarī.* Hyderabad: Dā'irat al-Ma'ārif al-'Uthmāniyyah, H 1345/1926–27.

———. *Al-Amālī.* Hyderabad: Dā'irat al-Ma'ārif al-'Uthmāniyyah, H 1349/1930–31.

Ibn Shākir al-Kutubī. *Fawāt al-Wafayāt*, edited by Iḥsān 'Abbās. 5 vols. Beirut: Dār Ṣādir, 1973–74.

Ibn Ṭabāṭabā. *'Iyār al-shi'r*, edited by 'Abd al-'Azīz ibn Nāṣir al-Māni'. Riyadh: Dār al-'Ulūm, 1985.

Ibn Taghrī Birdī. *Al-Nujūm al-zāhirah*, Vol. IX. Cairo: Dār al-Kutub, 1942.

Ibn Wahb, Abū l-Ḥusayn Isḥāq ibn Ibrāhīm. *Al-Burhān fī wujūh al-bayān*, edited by Ḥifnī Muḥammad Sharaf. Cairo: Maktabat al-Shabāb, 1969.

[Ibshīhī, al-] Śihâb-ad-Dîn Âḥmad al-Âbśîhî. *Al-Mostaṭraf: recueil de morceaux choisis, trans. par* G. Rat. Paris: E. Leroux, 1899.

———. *Al-Mustaṭraf fī kull fann mustaẓraf.* 2 vols. Cairo: Muṣṭafā al-Bābī al-Ḥalabī, 1952.

[Ikhwān al-Ṣafā'] The Brethren of Purity. *The Case of the Animals versus Man Before the King of the Jinn: An Arabic critical edition and English translation of Epistle 22*, edited and translated by Lenn E. Goodman and Richard McGregor. Oxford: Oxford University Press, 2009.

Ikhwān al-Ṣafā'. *Rasā'il Ikhwān al-Ṣafā'.* 4 vols. Beirut: Dār Ṣādir, 1957.

Imru' al-Qays. *Dīwān*, edited by Muḥammad Abū l-Faḍl Ibrāhīm. Cairo: Dār al-Ma'ārif, 1969.

Irwin, Robert. *Night and Horses and the Desert: An Anthology of Classical Arabic Literature.* London: Penguin, 1999; reprinted as *The Penguin Anthology of Classical Arabic Literature.* London: Penguin, 2006.

Iṣfahānī, Abū l-Faraj al-. *Al-Aghānī.* 24 vols. Cairo: Dār al-Kutub–al-Hay'ah al-Miṣriyyah al-'Āmmah, 1927–74.

Jacobi R[enate]. "Nasīb," in *EI2*, VIII:978–83.

Jacobus de Voragine. *The Golden Legend: Readings on the Saints*, trans. William Granger Ryan. 2 vols. Princeton, NJ: Princeton University Press.

Jāḥiẓ, al-. *Al-Bukhalā'*, edited by Ṭāhā al-Ḥājirī. Cairo: Dār al-Ma'ārif, n.d.

———. *Al-Ḥayawān*, edited by 'Abd al-Salām Muḥammad Hārūn. 8 vols. Cairo: Muṣṭafā al-Bābī al-Ḥalabī, 1965–69.

———. *Al-Bayān wal-tabyīn*, edited by 'Abd al-Salām Muḥammad Hārūn. 4 vols. Cairo: Maktabat al-Khānjī, 1968.

———. *The Book of Misers (al-Bukhalā')*, translated by R. B. Serjeant. Reading, U.K.: Garnet, 1997.

———. *Avarice and the Avaricious*, translated by Jim Colville. London: Kegan Paul, 1999.

Jahshiyārī, al-. *Al-Wuzarā' wal-kuttāb*, edited by Muṣṭafā al-Saqqā et al. Cairo: Maktabat Muṣṭafā l-Bābī al-Ḥalabī, 1980.

Jamil, Nadia. "Playing for Time: Maysir Gambling in Early Arabic Poetry." In R. G. Hoyland and Ph. F. Kennedy, eds., *Islamic Reflections, Arabic Musings: Studies in Honour of Professor Alan Jones*. Oxford: E. J. W. Gibb Memorial Trust, 2004.

Jammāl, Aḥmad Ṣādiq al-. *Al-Adab al-ʿāmmī fī Miṣr fī l-ʿaṣr al-mamlūkī*. Cairo: al-Dār al-Qawmiyyah, 1966.

Jarīr. *Dīwān Jarīr*, edited by Nuʿmān Muḥammad Amīn Ṭāhā. 2 vols. Cairo: Dār al-Maʿārif, 1986.

Jones, Alan. *Romance Kharjas in Andalusian Muwaššaḥ Poetry*. London: Ithaca Press, 1988.

———. *Early Arabic Poetry, I: Marāthī and Ṣuʿlūk Poems, II: Select Odes, Edition, Translation and Commentary*. Reading, U.K.: Ithaca Press, 1992, 1996.

Jurjānī, al-Qāḍī ʿAlī ibn ʿAbd al-ʿAzīz al-. *Al-Wasāṭah bayn al-Mutanabbī wa-khuṣūmih*, edited by Muḥammad Abū l-Faḍl Ibrāhīm and ʿAlī Muḥammad al-Bijāwī. Cairo: Dār Iḥyāʾ al-Kutub al-ʿArabiyyah, n.d.

Jurjānī, ʿAbd al-Qāhir al-. *Asrār al-balāgha*, edited by Hellmut Ritter. İstanbul: Wizārat al-Maʿārif, 1954.

[———]. *Die Geheimnisse der Wortkunst (Asrār al-balāġa) des ʿAbdalqāhir al-Curcānī*, aus dem Arab. Translated by Hellmut Ritter. Wiesbaden: Franz Steiner, 1959.

Kalbī, al-. *Ǧamharat an-nasab / Das genealogische Werk des Hišām ibn Muḥammad al-Kalbī*, edited by Werner Caskel. 2 vols. Leiden: Brill, 1966.

Kennedy, Philip F. *The Wine Song in Classical Arabic Poetry: Abū Nuwās and the Literary Tradition*. Oxford: Oxford University Press, 1997.

———. *Abu Nuwas: A Genius of Poetry*. Oxford: Oneworld, 2005.

Khan, Ruqayya Yasmine "Substitution and Sacrifice in the Classical Love Story of al-Muraqqish al-Akbar." *History of Religions*, 39:1 (1999): 50–64.

Khansāʾ, al-. *Dīwān*, edited by Ibrāhīm ʿAwaḍayn. Cairo: Maṭbaʿat al-Saʿādah, 1986.

———. *Dīwān*, edited by Anwar Abū Suwaylim. Amman: Dār ʿAmmār, 1988.

Kilpatrick, Hilary. "*Aḫbār manẓūma*: The Romance of Qays and Lubnā in the *Aġānī*." In W. Heinrichs and G. Schoeler, eds., *Festschrift Ewald Wagner zum 65. Geburtstag, Band 2: Studien zur arabischen Dichtung*. Beirut–Stuttgart: Franz Steiner, 1994, 330–61.

———. *Making the Great Book of Songs: Compilation and the Author's Craft in Abū l-Faraj al-Iṣbahānī's Kitāb al-Aghānī*. London: RoutledgeCurzon, 2003.

Kruk, Remke. "A Frothy Bubble: Spontaneous Generation in the Medieval Islamic Tradition." *Journal of Semitic Studies*, 35:2 (1990): 265–82.

———. "Of Rukhs and Rooks, Camels and Castles." *Oriens*, 36 (2001): 288–98.

Larkin, Margaret. *Al-Mutanabbi: Voice of the ʿAbbasid Poetic Ideal*. Oxford: Oneworld, 2008.

Latham, J. Derek. "Toward a Better Understanding of al-Mutanabbī's Poem on the Battle of al-Ḥadath." *Journal of Arabic Literature*, 10 (1979): 1–22.

Lewis, Bernard, ed. *The World of Islam: Faith, People, Culture*. London: Thames and Hudson, 1976.

———. *Race and Slavery in the Middle East*. New York and Oxford: Oxford University Press, 1990.

Lichtenstadter, Ilse. *Introduction to Classical Arabic Literature*. New York: Twayne, 1974.

Lowry, Joseph E., and Devin J. Stewart, eds. *Essays in Arabic Literary Biography, 1350–1850*. Mîzân: Studien zur Literatur in der islamischen Welt, Bd. 17: Essays in Arabic Literary Biography, 2. Wiesbaden: Harrassowitz, 2009.

Lyall, Ch. J. *see al-Mufaḍḍaliyyāt*.

Lyons, M. C. "The Two Companions Convention." In *Islamic Philosophy and the Classical Tradition (Festschrift Richard Walzer)*, edited by S. M. Stern, Albert Hourani and Vivian Brown. Columbia, SC: University of South Carolina Press, 1972, 225–34.

Lyons, Malcolm C., trans. *The Arabian Nights: Tales of 1001 Nights*. 3 vols. London: Penguin, 2008.

[Maʿarrī, Abū l-ʿAlāʾ al-] Nicholson, Reynold A. "The Risālatu 'l-Ghufrān by Abū 'l-ʿAlā' al-Maʿarrī." *Journal of the Royal Asiatic Society* (1900): 637–720; (1902): 75–101, 337–62, 813–47.

———. *Al-Luzūmiyyāt*, edited by Amīn ʿAbd al-ʿAzīz al-Khānjī. 2 vols. Cairo: Maktabat al-Khānjī, [1924].

[———]. Abul Ala' Al Maʿarri. *Risalat ul Ghufran: A Divine Comedy*, trans. from the Arabic by G. Brackenbury. Cairo: Al-Maaref, n.d. [preface dated 1943].

———. *Risālat al-Ghufrān*, edited by ʿĀʾisha ʿAbd al-Raḥmān "Bint al-Shāṭiʾ." 9th ed. Cairo: Dār al-Maʿārif, 1993.

Majnūn Laylā. *Dīwān*, edited by ʿAdnān Zakī Darwīsh. Beirut: Dār Ṣadir, 1994.

Malti-Douglas, Fedwa. "The Classical Arabic Detective." *Arabica*, 35 (1988): 59–91.

[Mandeville]. *Travels of Sir John Mandeville*, translated by C. W. R. D. Moseley. London: Penguin, 1983.

Maqdisī, al-Muṭahhir ibn Ṭāhir al-. *Al-Bad' wal-ta'rīkh*, edited by Clément Huart. 6 vols. Paris: Ernest Leroux, 1899–1919.

Marzolph, Ulrich. "Medieval Knowledge in Modern Reading: A Fifteenth-Century Arabic Encyclopaedia of *omni re scibili*." In *Pre-Modern Encyclopaedic Texts: Proceedings of the Second COMERS Congress, Groningen, 1–4 July 1996*, edited by Peter Binkley. Leiden: Brill, 1997, 407–19.

———, ed. *Das Buch der wunderbaren Geschichten. Erzählungen aus der Welt von Tausendundeine Nacht*. Munich: C. H. Beck, 1999.

———, and Richard van Leeuwen. *The Arabian Nights Encyclopedia*. Santa Barbara, CA: ABC-Clio, 2004.

Marzubānī, Muḥammad ibn ʿImrān, al-. *Muʿjam al-shuʿarāʾ*, edited by ʿAbd al-Sattār Farrāj. Cairo: Dār Iḥyāʾ al-Kutub al-ʿArabiyya, 1960.

———. *Nūr al-qabas, al-mukhtaṣar min al-Muqtabas fī akhbār al-nuḥāh wal-udabāʾ wal-shuʿarāʾ wal-ʿulamāʾ, ikhtiṣār Abī l-Maḥāsin Yūsuf ibn Maḥmūd al-Yaghmūrī / Die Gelehrtenbiographien*, edited by Rudolf Sellheim. Wiesbaden: Franz Steiner, 1964.

Masʿūdī, al-. *Les prairies d'or*, translated by Barbier de Meynard and Pavet de Courteille, revised by Charles Pellat. 5 vols. Paris: Société Asiatique, 1962–97.

———. *Murūj al-dhahab*, edited by Barbier de Meynard and revised by Pavet de Courteille , rev. by C. Pellat. 7 vols. Beirut: al-Jāmiʿah al-Lubnāniyyah, 1966–79.

[Masʿūdi, al-] Masʿudi. *The Meadows of Gold: The Abbasids*, translated by Paul Lunde and Caroline Stone. London: Kegan Paul International, 1989.

Maydānī, Abū l-Faḍl Aḥmad ibn Muḥammad al-. *Majmaʿ al-amthāl*, edited by Naʿīm Ḥusayn Zarzūr. 2 vols. Beirut: Dār al-Kutub al-ʿIlmiyyah, 1988.

McKinney, Robert C. *The Case of Rhyme versus Reason: Ibn al-Rūmī and his Poetics in Context.* Leiden: Brill, 2004.

Meisami, Julie Scott. *Medieval Persian Court Poetry*. Princeton, NJ: Princeton University Press, 1987.

———. *Structure and Meaning in Medieval Arabic and Persian Poetry: Orient Pearls*. London: RoutledgeCurzon, 2003.

———, and Paul Starkey, eds. *Encyclopedia of Arabic Literature*. 2 vols. London: Routledge, 1998.

Menocal, María Rosa, Raymond P. Scheindlin and Michael Sells, eds. *The Literature of Al-Andalus*. Cambridge History of Arabic Literature Cambridge: Cambridge University Press, 2000.

Monroe, James T. *Hispano-Arabic Poetry: A Student Anthology*. Berkeley, California: University of California Press, 1974.

Montgomery, James E. "Al-Jāḥiẓ and the Masjidites of Basra." *Journal of Arabic Literature*, 24 (1993): 236–45.

———. "The Cat and the Camel: A Literary Motif." In Mustansir Mir, ed., *Literary Heritage of Classical Islam: Arabic and Islamic Studies in Honor of James A. Bellamy*. Princeton: The Darwin Press, 1993, 137–45.

———. *The Vagaries of the Qaṣīdah: The Tradition and Practice of Early Arabic Poetry*. Cambridge: E. J. W. Gibb Memorial Trust, 1997.

Mubarrad, al-. *Al-Kāmil*, edited by W. Wright. 2 vols. Leipzig: Brockhaus, 1874–92.

Mufaḍḍaliyyāt, al- edited by Aḥmad Muḥammad Shākir and ʿAbd al-Salām Muḥammad Hārūn. Cairo: Dār al-Maʿārif, n.d.

[*Mufaḍḍaliyyāt, al-*] *The Mufaḍḍalīyat: An Anthology of Ancient Arabian Odes compiled by al-Mufaḍḍal*, ed by Charles James Lyall, vol. I: Arabic Text. Oxford: Clarendon Press, 1921, Vol. II: Translation and Notes.Oxford: Clarendon Press, 1918.

Mughulṭāy. *Al-Wāḍiḥ al-mubīn fī dhikr man ustushhida min al-muḥibbīn*. Beirut: al-Intishār al-ʿArabī, 1997.

Mumayiz, Ibrahim. *Arabesques: Selections of Biography and Poetry from Classical Arabic Literature*. Antwerp–Apeldoorn: Garant, 2006.

Munāwī, ʿAbd al-Raʾūf al-. *Al-Nuzhah al-shahiyyah fī aḥkām al-ḥammām al-sharʿiyyah wal-ṭibbiyyah*, edited by ʿAbd al-Ḥamīd Ṣāliḥ Ḥamdān. Beirut: al-Dār al-Miṣriyyah al-Lubnāniyyah, 1987.

Murtaḍā, ʿAlī ibn al-Ḥusayn al-Sharīf al-. *Al-Amālī (Ghurar al-fawāʾid wa-durar al-qalāʾid)*, edited by Muḥammad Abū l-Faḍl Ibrāhīm. 2 vols. Cairo: ʿĪsā al-Bābī al-Ḥalabī, 1954.

Mutanabbī, al-. *Dīwān*, edited by F. Dieterici [= Dietrich]. Berlin: Mittler, 1861.

Nābulusī, ʿAbd al-Ghanī al-. *Taʿṭīr al-anām fī tafsīr al-aḥlām*. 2 vols. Cairo: ʿĪsā al-Bābī al-Ḥalabī, n.d.

Naqāʾiḍ Jarīr wal-Akhṭal, edited by Anṭūn Ṣāliḥānī (A. Salhani). Beirut: Dār al-Mashriq, 1922.

Nawājī, Shams al-Dīn Muḥammad ibn Ḥasan al-. *Ḥalbat al-kumayt*. Cairo: al-Maktabah al-ʿĀlamiyyah, 1938.

———. *Taʾhīl al-gharīb*, edited by Aḥmad Muḥammad ʿAṭā. Cairo: Maktabat al-Ādāb, 2004.

Nicholson, Reynold A. *Translations of Eastern Poetry and Prose*. Cambridge, 1922, reprinted with introd. by C. E. Bosworth, London: Curzon, 1987.

Nicholson, Reynold Alleyne. *Studies in Islamic Poetry*. Cambridge: Cambridge University Press, 1924.

Nowaihi, Magda M. al-. *The Poetry of Ibn Khafājah: A Literary Analysis*. Leiden: Brill, 1993.

Nowaihi, Magda Al-. "Elegy and the Confrontation of Death in Arabic Poetry." In Marlé Hammond and Dana Sajdi, eds., *Transforming Loss into Beauty: Essays on Arabic Literature in Honor of Magda Al-Nowaihi*. Cairo: AUC Press, 2008, 3–20.

Nuwayrī, al-. *Nihāyat al-arab fī funūn al-adab*. Cairo: Dār al-Kutub, 1923–.

O'Kane, Bernard. *Early Persian Painting: Kalila and Dimna Manuscripts of the Late Fourteenth Century*. London: I. B. Tauris, 2003.

Pellat, Charles. *The Life and Works of Jāḥiẓ: Translations of Selected Texts*, translated by D. M. Hawke. London: Routledge and Kegan Paul, 1969.

Qālī, Abū ʿAlī al-. *Al-Amālī*. 2 vols. Cairo: Dār al-Kutub al-Miṣriyyah, 1926.

———. *Dhayl al-Amālī (al-Nawādir)*. Cairo: Dār al-Kutub al-Miṣriyyah, 1926.

Qazwīnī, Zakariyyā ibn Muḥammad al-. *ʿAjāʾib al-makhlūqāt wa-gharāʾib al-mawjūdāt*, edited by F. Wüstenfeld. Göttingen: Verlag der Dieterichschen Buchhandlung, 1848–49.

———. *ʿAjāʾib al-makhlūqāt wa-gharāʾib al-mawjūdāt*. Cairo: Muṣṭafā al-Bābī al-Ḥalabī, 1970.

———. *Āthār al-bilād*. Beirut: Dār Bayrūt, 1979.

Qifṭī, Jamāl al-Dīn ʿAlī ibn Yūsuf al-. *Inbāh al-ruwāh*, edited by Muḥammad Abū l-Faḍl Ibrāhīm. 4 vols. Beirut, 1986.

Rāmhurmuzī, Buzurg ibn Shahriyār al-. *ʿAjāʾib al-Hind/Livre des merveilles de l'Inde*, edited by P. A. van der Lith, translated by L. Marcel Devic. Leiden: Brill, 1883–86.

[———]. Buzurg ibn Shahriyar of Ramhormuz. *The Book of the Wonders of India: Mainland, Sea and Islands*, edited and translated by G. S. P. Freeman-Grenville. London: East-West Publications, 1981.

Reinink, G. J. and H. L. J. Vanstiphout, eds. *Dispute Poems and Dialogues in the Ancient and Mediaeval Near East: Forms and Types of Literary Debates in Semitic and Related Literatures*. Leuven: Peeters, 1991.

Rescher, Oskar. "Das Kitâb 'el-adab el-kebîr' des Ibn el-Moqaffaʿ." *Mitteilungen des Seminars für Orientalische Sprachen*, 20 (1917): 35–82.

Reşer [Rescher], O. *Der Dîwân des Abû 'l-ʿAtâhija, Teil I: Die zuhdijjât*. Stuttgart: no publ., 1928.

Rosenthal, Franz. "Poetry and Architecture: the *bādhanj*." *Journal of Arabic Literature*, 8 (1977): 1–19.

———. "The Stranger in Medieval Islam." *Arabica*, 44 (1997): 35–75.

Rouayheb, Khaled El-. *Before Homosexuality in the Arab-Islamic World, 1500–1800*. Chicago: University of Chicago Press, 2005.

Ṣafadī, Khalīl ibn Aybak al-. *Al-Ghayth al-musajjam fī sharḥ Lāmiyyat al-ʿajam*. 2 vols. Beirut: Dār al-Kutub al-ʿIlmiyyah, 1975.

Sakkal, Aya. "Passage du récit des amours de Qays et Lubnā à travers les genres littéraires arabes médiévaux." In F. Bauden, A. Chraïbi, and A. Ghersetti, eds., *Le Répertoire narratif arabe médiéval: transmission et ouverture*, Genève: Droz, 2008, 107–20.

Samarai, Nicola Lauré al-. *Die Macht der Darstellung. Gender, sozialer Status, historische Re-Präsentation: zwei Frauenbiographien aus der frühen Abbasidenzeit*. Wiesbaden: Reichert, 2001.

Sarī al-Raffāʾ, al-. *Dīwān*, edited by Ḥabīb Ḥusayn al-Ḥasanī. 2 vols. Baghdad: Dār al-Rashīd, 1981.

Sarrāj, Abū Muḥammad Jaʿfar ibn Aḥmad al-. *Maṣāriʿ al-ʿushshāq*. 2 vols. Beirut: Dār Ṣādir, n.d.

Schoeler, Gregor. *Arabische Naturdichtung. Die Zahrīyāt, Rabīʿīyāt und Rauḍīyāt von ihren Anfängen bis Aṣ-Ṣanaubarī. Eine Gattungs-, Motiv- und Stilgeschichtliche Untersuchung*. Beirut–Wiesbaden: Franz Steiner: 1974.

———. "Arabistische Literaturwissenschaft und Textkritik." *Der Islam*, 55 (1978): 327–39.

———. "Ein Wendepunkt in der Geschichte der arabischen Literatur." *Saeculum*, 35 (1984): 293–305.

———. "Ibn ar-Rūmī's Gedicht über die Dichting und seine Gedankenlyrik." In W. Heinrichs and G. Schoeler, eds., *Festschrift Ewald Wagner zum 65. Geburtstag, Band 2: Studien zur arabischen Dichtung*. Beirut–Stuttgart: Franz Steiner, 1994, 318–36.

———. "On Ibn al-Rūmī's Reflective Poetry: His Poem about Poetry." *Journal of Arabic Literature* 27, no. 1 (1996): 22–36.

Sells, Michael A, trans. and introd. *Desert Tracings: Six Classic Arabian Odes by 'Alqama, Shánfara, Labíd, 'Antara, Al-A'sha, and Dhu al-Rúmma*. Middletown, Connecticut: Wesleyan University Press, 1989.

Sezgin, Fuat. *Geschichte des arabischen Schrifttums. Band II: Poesie bis ca. 430 H.* Leiden: Brill, 1975.

Shaykhū *see* Cheikho.

Shirbīnī, Yūsuf al-. *Hazz al-quḥūf fī-sharḥ Qaṣīd Abī Shādūf*. Cairo: al-Maktabah al-Maḥmūdiyyah, 1308/1890–91.

———. *Hazz al-quḥūf fī-sharḥ Qaṣīd Abī Shādūf*, edited by Muḥammad Qindīl al-Baqlī. Cairo: Dār al-Nahḍah al-'Arabiyyah [1963 (date of preface)].

———. *Hazz al-quḥūf fī-sharḥ Qaṣīd Abī Shādūf / Yūsuf al-Shirbīnī's Brains Confounded by the Ode of Abū Shādūf Expounded*, edited and translated by Humphrey Davies. Vol. I: Arabic Text, Leuven: Peeters, 2005, vol. II: English translation, introduction and notes, Leuven: Peeters, 2007.

Shushtarī, al- *see also* Corriente.

Shushtarī, al-. *Dīwān Abī l-Ḥasan al-Shushtarī*, edited by 'Alī Sāmī al-Nashshār. Alexandria: Munsha'at al-Ma'ārif, 1960.

Skarżyńska-Bocheńska, Krystyna. "Qays et Lubnā: Victoire de l'amour sur l'autorité du père et de la tribu." In B. Michalak-Pikulska and A. Pikulski, eds., *Authority, Privacy, and Public Order in Islam. Proceedings of the 22nd Congress of l'Union Européenne des Arabisants et Islamisants*. Leuven: Peeters, 2006, 133–45.

Souami, Lakhdar. *Le cadi et la mouche: anthologie du Livre des animaux*. Paris: Sindbad, 1988.

Sperl, Stefan, and Christopher Shackle, eds. *Qasida Poetry in Islamic Asia and Africa*. 2 vols. Leiden: Brill, 1996.

Spies, Otto. "Das Märchen von den vierzig Mädchen." *Fabula*, 4 (1961): 1–19; repr. in Marzolph, ed., *Das Buch der wunderbaren Geschichten*, 143–62. Munich: C. H. Beck, 1999.

Stern, Samuel M. *Hispano-Arabic Strophic Poetry*, Studies selected and edited by L. P. Harvey. Oxford: Oxford University Press, 1974.

Stetkevych, Jaroslav. *The Zephyrs of Najd: The Poetics of Nostalgia in the Classical Arabic Nasīb.* Chicago: University of Chicago Press, 1993.

Stetkevych, Suzanne Pinckney. *Abū Tammām and the Poetics of the ʿAbbāsid Age*. Leiden: Brill, 1991.

———. *The Mute Immortals Speak: Pre-Islamic Poetry and the Poetics of Ritual.* Ithaca and London: Cornell University Press, 1993.

———. "Pre-Islamic Panegyric and the Poetics of Redemption: *Mufaḍḍalīyah* 119 of *ʿAlqamah* and *Bānat Suʿād* of Kaʿb ibn Zuhayr." In *Reorientations / Arabic and Persian Poetry*, edited by S. P. Stetkevych. Bloomington: Indiana University Press, 1994, 1–57.

———. *The Poetics of Islamic Legitimacy: Myth, Gender, and Ceremony in the Classical Arabic Ode*. Bloomington, Indiana: Indiana University Press, 2002.

———. *The Mantle Odes: Arabic Praise Poems to the Prophet Muḥammad*. Bloomington, Indiana: Indiana University Press, 2010.

Stoetzer, W. F. G. J. *Theory and Practice in Arabic Metrics*. Leiden: Brill, 1989.

Sukkarī, al-. *Sharḥ ashʿār al-Hudhaliyyīn, ṣanʿat Abī Saʿīd al-Sukkarī*, edited by ʿAbd al-Sattār Aḥmad Farrāj and Maḥmūd Muḥammad Shākir. 4 vols. Cairo: Maktabat Dār al-ʿUrūbah, 1965.

Ṣūlī, Abū Bakr al-. *Al-Awrāq (Ashʿār awlād al-khulafāʾ)*, edited by J. Heyworth Dunne. London: Luzac, 1936.

Suyūṭī, al-. *Ḥusn al-muḥāḍarah fī tārīkh Miṣr wal-Qāhirah*, edited by Muḥammad Abū l-Faḍl Ibrāhīm. 2 vols. Cairo: ʿĪsā al-Bābī al-Ḥalabī, 1968–69.

Ṭabarī, al-. *Tārīkh al-rusul wal-mulūk*, edited by M. J. de Goeje et al. 3 vols. Leiden: Brill, 1879–1901.

———. *The History of al-Ṭabarī, vol. III: The Children of Israel*, translated by William M. Brinner. Albany, NY: State University of New York Press, 1991.

———. *The History of al-Ṭabarī, vol. XXXI: The War Between Brothers*, translated by Michael Fishbein. Albany, NY: State University of New York Press, 1992.

———. *The History of al-Ṭabarī, vol. V: The Sāsānids, the Byzantines, the Lakhmids and Yemen*, trans. and annot. by C. E. Bosworth. Albany, NY: State University of New York Press, 1999.

[Tanūkhī, al-Muḥassin al-] at-Tanūkhī. *The Table-Talk of a Mesopotamian Judge*, translated from the original Arabic (*Nishwār al-muḥāḍarah*) by D. S. Margoliouth. London: Royal Asiatic Society, 1922.

———. *Al-Faraj baʿd al-shiddah*. Cairo: Maktabat al-Khānjī, 1955.

———. *Nishwār al-muḥāḍarah*, edited by ʿAbbūd al-Shāljī. 8 vols. Beirut: Dār Ṣādir, 1972.

———. *Al-Faraj baʿd al-shiddah*, edited by ʿAbbūd al-Shāljī. 5 vols. Beirut: Dār Ṣādir, 1978.

[———]. at-Tanūkhī. *Ende Gut, Alles Gut: Das Buch der Erleichterung nach der Bedrängnis*, translated by Arnold Hottinger. Zürich: Manesse, 1979.

Tardy, Jean. "*Traduction d'al-Adab al-kabīr d'Ibn al-Muqaffaʿ*". *Annales Islamologiques*, 27 (1993): 181–223.

Tawḥīdī, Abū Ḥayyān al-. *Al-Imtāʿ wal-muʾānasah*, edited by Aḥmad Amīn and Aḥmad al-Zayn. 3 vols. Cairo: Lajnat al-Taʾlīf, 1939–53.

Taymūr, Aḥmad. *Muʿjam Taymūr al-kabīr*, edited by Ḥusayn Naṣṣār, vol II. Cairo: al-Hayʾah al-Miṣriyyah al-ʿĀmmah, 1978.

Thaʿālibī, al-. *Qiṣaṣ al-anbiyāʾ (ʿArūs al-majālis)*. Beirut: Dār al-Maʿrifah, n.d.

———. *Ghurar akhbār mulūk al-Furs wa-siyarihim / Histoire des rois des Perses*, edited and translated by H. Zotenberg. Paris: Imprimerie Nationale, 1900.

———. *Yatīmat al-dahr*, edited by Muḥammad Muḥyī l-Dīn ʿAbd al-Ḥamīd. 4 vols. Cairo: Maktabat al-Ḥusayn al-Tijāriyyah, 1947.

———. *Thimār al-qulūb*, edited by Muḥammad Abū l-Faḍl Ibrāhīm. Cairo: Dār al-Maʿārif, 1985.

———. *ʿArāʾis al-majālis fī qiṣaṣ al-anbiyāʾ, or "Lives of the Prophets"*, translated and annotated by William M. Brinner. Leiden: Brill, 2002.

Tibrīzī, al-. *Sharḥ al-qaṣāʾid al-ʿashr*, edited by Charles James Lyall. Calcutta, 1894, repr. Ridgewood, NJ: Gregg Press, 1965.

[Tīfāshī, Shihāb al-Dīn Abū l-ʿAbbās Aḥmad ibn Yūsuf al-] Aḥmad ibn Sulaymān Kamāl Bāshā (attrib.). *Rujūʿ al-shaykh ilā ṣibāh fī l-quwwah ʿalā l-bāh*. Cairo: al-Maṭbaʿah al-Kubrā al-Amīriyyah, 1309/1891–92.

Tuetey, C. G. *Classical Arabic Poetry: 162 Poems from Imrulkais to Maʿarri. Translated with an introduction*. London: Routledge and Kegan Paul, 1985.

Tujībī, Abū Ṭāhir Ismāʿīl ibn Aḥmad al-. *Al-Mukhtār min shiʿr Bashshār*, edited by Muḥammad Badr al-Dīn al-ʿAlawī. Cairo: Lajnat al-Taʾlīf, n.d.

Ullmann, Manfred. *Untersuchungen zur Rağazpoesie: Ein Beitrag zur arabischen Sprach- und Literaturwissenschaft*. Wiesbaden: Harrassowitz, 1966.

———. *Der Neger in der Bildersprache der arabischen Dichter*. Wiesbaden: Harrassowitz, 1998.

ʿUmar ibn Abī Rabīʿah. *Dīwān*, edited by Paul Schwarz. 4 vols. Leipzig: Dieterich, 1901–09.

Usama ibn Munqidh. *The Book of Contemplation*, translated by Paul M. Cobb. London: Penguin, 2008.

van Gelder, G. J. H. *Beyond the Line: Classical Arabic Literary Critics on the Coherence and Unity of the Poem*. Leiden: Brill, 1982.

van Gelder, Geert Jan. "The Conceit of Pen and Sword: On an Arabic Literary Debate." *Journal of Semitic Studies* 32 (1987): 329–60.

———. *The Bad and the Ugly: Attitudes Towards Invective Poetry (Hijāʾ) in Classical Arabic Literature*. Leiden: Brill, 1988.

———. "The Joking Doctor: Abū l-Ḥakam ʿUbayd Allāh Ibn al-Muẓaffar (d. 549/1155)." In *Actas XVI Congreso UEAI, Salamanca*, edited by Concepción Vázquez de Benito and Miguel Ángel Manzano Rodríguez. Salamanca: Agencia Española de Cooperación Internacional / Consejo Superior de Investigaciones Científicas, 1995, 217–28.

———. "Arabic Didactic Verse." In *Centres of Learning: Learning and Location in Pre-Modern Europe and the Near East*, edited by Jan Willem Drijvers and Alasdair A. Macdonald, 103-117. Leiden: Brill, 1995.

———. "Waspish Verses: Abū Nuwās's Lampoons on Zunbūr Ibn Abī Ḥammād." *Annali di Ca' Foscari* (Venezia), 35 no. 3 (1996): 447–55.

———. *Een Arabische tuin: klassieke Arabische poëzie*. Amsterdam: Bulaaq, 2000.

———. "The Nodding Noddles, or Jolting the Yokels: A Composition for Marginal Voices by al-Shirbīnī (fl. 1687)." In *Marginal Voices in Literature and Society*, edited by Robin Ostle. Aix-en-Provence: Maison Méditerranéenne des Sciences de l'Homme, 2000, 49–67.

———. "To Eat or Not to Eat Elephant: A Travelling Story in Arabic and Persian Literature." *Bulletin of the School of Oriental and African Studies*, 66 no. 3 (2003): 419–30.

———. *Close Relationships: Incest and Inbreeding in Classical Arabic Literature*. London: I. B. Tauris, 2005.

———. "An Experiment with Beeston, Labīd and Baššār: On Translating Classical Arabic Verse," *Proceedings of the Seminar for Arabian Studies*, 36 (2006): 7–15.

——— and Marlé Hammond, eds. and trans. *Takhyīl: The Imaginary in Classical Arabic Poetics*. [Cambridge:] E. J. W. Gibb Memorial Trust, 2008.

Vernet, J. "*Rujj = Aepyornis maximus*." *Tamuda*, 1 (1953): 102–5.

Versteegh, Kees. *The Arabic Language*. Edinburgh: Edinburgh University Press, 1997.

Vrolijk, Arnoud, ed. *De taal der engelen: 1250 jaar klassiek Arabisch proza*. Amsterdam: Contact, 2002.

Wagner, Ewald. "Die arabische Rangstreitdichtung und ihre Einordnung in die allgemeine Literaturgeschichte." *Akademie der Wissenschaften und der Literatur in Mainz, Abhandlungen der geistes- und sozialwissenschaftlichen Klasse*, 8 (1962), 435–76.

———. *Abū Nuwās: Eine Studie zur arabischen Literatur der frühen ʿAbbāsidenzeit*. Wiesbaden: Franz Steiner, 1965.

———. *Grundzüge der klassischen arabischen Dichtung*. 2 vols. Darmstadt: Wissenschaftliche Buchgesellschaft, 1987–88.

———. "Verse über Abū Nuwās." In *Orientalistiche Studien zu Sprache und Literatur. Festgabe zum 65. Geburtststag von Werner Diem*, edited by Ulrich Marzolph. Wiesbaden: Harrassowitz, 2011, 343–56.

Wehr, Hans, ed. *Kitāb al-ḥikāyāt al-ʿajībah wal-akhbār al-gharībah / Das Buch der wunderbaren Erzählungen und seltsamen Geschichten*. Damascus–Wiesbaden: al-Maṭbaʿah al-Hāshimiyyah–Franz Steiner, 1956.

Weisweiler, Max. *Arabesken der Liebe: früharabische Geschichten von Liebe und Frauen*. Leiden: Brill, 1954.

———. *Arabische Märchen*, 2 vols. Düsseldorf/Köln: E. Diedrichs, 1965–66.

Wightman, G. B. H., and A. Y. al-Udhari. *Birds Through a Ceiling of Alabaster: Three Abbasid Poets. Arab poetry of the Abbasid Period*, translated with an introduction. Harmondsworth: Penguin, 1975.

Wright Jr., J. W., and Everett K. Rowson, eds. *Homoeroticism in Classical Arabic Literature*. New York: Columbia University Press, 1997.

Yāqūt. *Muʿjam al-udabāʾ*, edited by Aḥmad Farīd Rifāʿī. 20 vols. Cairo 1936–38, repr. Beirut: Iḥyāʾ al-Turāth al-ʿArabī, n.d.

———. *Muʿjam al-buldān*. 7 vols. Beirut: Dār Ṣādir, 1995.

Young, M. J. L., J. D. Latham and R. B. Serjeant, eds. *Religion, Learning and Science in the ʿAbbasid Period*. Cambridge History of Arabic Literature. Cambridge: Cambridge University Press, 1990.

Zabīdī, Murtaḍā al-. *Tāj al-ʿarūs*, edited by ʿAbd al-Sattār Farrāj. 40 vols. Kuwait: Maṭbaʿat Ḥukūmat al-Kuwayt, 1965–2001.

Zakeri, Mohsen. "Arabic Reports on the Fall of Hatra to the Sasanids: History or Legend?" In *Story-Telling in the Framework of Non-Fictional Arabic Literature*, edited by Stefan Leder. Wiesbaden: Harrassowitz, 1998, 158–67.

Zawzanī, Abū ʿAbd Allāh al-Ḥusayn ibn Aḥmad al-. *Sharḥ al-Muʿallaqāt*. Cairo: al-Maktabah al-Tijāriyyah al-Kubrā, 1967.

Zwartjes, Otto. *Love Songs from al-Andalus: History, Structure and Meaning of the Kharja*. Leiden: Brill, 1997.

Further Reading

Reference works

Meisami, Julie Scott and Paul Starkey, ed. *Encyclopedia of Arabic Literature*. London: Routledge, 1998.

Contains entries on poets, writers, genres, forms, and many other topics. The following are particularly relevant: ʿAbbāsids; *adab*; ancients and moderns; anthologies, medieval; artistic prose; didactic literature; encyclopedias, medieval; epigram; fables; *fakhr*; fiction, medieval; genres, poetic; *ghazal*; *hazl*; *hijāʾ*; *ḥikma*; historical literature; humour; Jāhiliyya; *khamriyya*; literary criticism, medieval; *madīḥ*, *madḥ*; Mamlūks; *maqāma*; Mirrors for Princes; *muḥdathūn*, "the moderns"; *mujūn*; *muwashshaḥ*; oral composition; Persian literature, relations with Arabic; poetry vs. prose; popular literature; prose, non-fiction, medieval; prosody (*ʿarūḍ*); *qaṣīda*; *qiṭʿa*; *rajaz*; religious poetry; rhetoric and poetics; rhetorical figures; *rithāʾ*; *sajʿ*; satire, medieval; *Shuʿūbiyya*; Spain; story-telling; Ṣūfī literature, poetry; Ṣūfī literature, prose; theatre and drama, medieval; travel literature; Umayyads; *waṣf*; *zajal*; *zuhdiyya*.

The Encyclopaedia of Islam, New [= second] Edition. Leiden: Brill, 1960–2009. A third edition began to appear in 2007 in print and online.

Many relevant entries as in the preceding title, often more detailed. Note the divergent transliteration used: *dj* for *j* and *ḳ* for *q* (the third edition has abandoned this).

Encyclopædia Iranica. London and New York: Routledge & Kegan Paul, 1982–, also online.

In progress; with many relevant entries because the numerous Arabic poets and writers of Persian descent are incorporated. One should be aware of the transliteration system, with "Ebn" for Ibn (and *o* for *u*, *i* for *ī*, *u* for *ū*, *ż* for *ḍ*, etc.).

Cooperson, Michael and Shawkat M. Toorawa, ed. *Arabic Literary Culture, 500–925*. Dictionary of Literary Biography, vol. 311. Detroit: Thomson Gale, 2005.

Contains chapters on the following poets and authors included in this anthology: Abū al-ʿAtāhiyah, Abū Nuwās, Bashshār ibn Burd, al-Buḥturī, Dhū al-Rummah, Ibn al-Muqaffaʿ, al-Jāḥiẓ, Jarīr, al-Khansāʾ, ʿUmar ibn Abī Rabīʿah.

Lowry, Joseph E. and Devin J. Stewart, ed. *Essays in Arabic Literary Biography, 1350–1850*. Wiesbaden: Harrassowitz, 2009, pp. 251–62. (Mîzân: Studien zur Literatur in der islamischen Welt, Bd. 17: Essays in Arabic Literary Biography, 2).

Contains chapters on Jamāl al-Dīn Ibn Nubātah and al-Shirbīnī, represented in this anthology.

The Cambridge History of Arabic Literature.

A series of six multi-authored volumes, five of which deal with the pre-modern period. The contributions are of varying quality. The volumes are:

Beeston, A. F. L., T. M. Johnstone, R. B. Serjeant, and G. R. Smith, ed. *Arabic Literature to the End of the Umayyad Period*. Cambridge: Cambridge University Press, 1983.

Ashtiany, Julia, T. M. Johnstone, J. D. Latham, and R. B. Serjeant, ed. *ʿAbbasid Belles Lettres*. Cambridge: Cambridge University Press, 1990.

Young, M. J. L., J. D. Latham, and R. B. Serjeant, ed. *Religion, Learning and Science in the ʿAbbasid Period*. Cambridge: Cambridge University Press, 1990.

Menocal, María Rosa, Raymond P. Scheindlin, and Michael Sells, ed. *The Literature of Al-Andalus*. Cambridge: Cambridge University Press, 2000.

Allen, Roger and D. S. Richards, ed. *Arabic Literature in the Post-Classical Period*. Cambridge: Cambridge University Press, 2006.

Two recent single-volume surveys of Arabic literature in all its periods

Allen, Roger. *The Arabic Literary Heritage: The Development of its Genres and Criticism.* Cambridge: Cambridge University Press, 1998; a shortened version appeared as *An Introduction to Arabic Literature*, Cambridge, 2000.

Cachia, Pierre. *Arabic Literature: An Overview.* London: RoutledgeCurzon, 2002.

Other anthologies with English translations

General:

Nicholson, Reynold A. *Translations of Eastern Poetry and Prose.* Cambridge: The University Press, 1922, reprinted with introduction by C. E. Bosworth. London: Curzon, 1987.

Literary translations from classical Arabic and Persian prose and poetry.

Howarth, Herbert and Ibrahim Shukrallah. *Images from the Arab World.* London: The Pilot Press, 1944.

Prose and poetry (verse translations), in no apparent order; mostly classical with some modern authors; no annotation.

Irwin, Robert. *Nights and Horses and the Desert: An Anthology of Classical Arabic Literature.* London: Penguin, 1999. Reprinted as *The Penguin Anthology of Classical Arabic Literature*, London: Penguin, 2006.

A good selection of translations by many different translators, all previously published (but with diacritical signs expurgated), with the compiler's commentary and linking passages, printed in a larger font size than the texts themselves, a priority which the present anthology reverses.

Poetry:

Arberry, A. J. *Arabic Poetry: A Primer for Students.* Cambridge: Cambridge University Press, 1965.

Contains the Arabic texts of poems for the pre-Islamic period to the early 20th century with facing prose translations, with some annotation.

Arberry, A. J. *Poems of al-Mutanabbī: A Selection with Introduction, Translations and Notes*. Cambridge: Cambridge University Press, 1967.

Arabic texts with facing prose translations and some annotation.

Jones, Alan. *Early Arabic Poetry, I: Marāthī and Ṣuʿlūk Poems, II: Select Odes, Edition, Translation and Commentary*, 2 vols. Reading, U.K.: Ithaca Press, 1992, 1996. Reprinted in one volume as *Early Arabic Poetry: Select Poems*, 2011.

Very instructive volumes with Arabic texts, scholarly translations in prose and detailed philological commentary. The poems in vol. I are elegies and odes by the *ṣaʿālīk* ("brigand poets") including the famous *Lāmiyyat al-ʿarab*; vol. II contains *qaṣīdahs*, including the celebrated *Muʿallaqāt* poems by Imru' al-Qays, Labīd, and ʿAbīd ibn al-Abraṣ. All poems date from the pre-Islamic or very early Islamic period.

Lyall, Charles James. *The Mufaḍḍalīyat: An Anthology of Ancient Arabian Odes compiled by al-Mufaḍḍal, Vol. II: Translation and Notes*. Oxford: Clarendon Press, 1918.

Richly annotated translations (mostly in prose) of an important early anthology of pre-Islamic and early Islamic poems, with useful thematic index.

Beeston, A. F. L. *Selections from the Poetry of Baššār, edited with translation and commentary and an introductory sketch of Arabic poetic structures*. Cambridge: Cambridge University Press, 1977.

Arabic texts and annotated prose translations.

Sells, Michael A., translator and introduction. *Desert Tracings: Six Classic Arabian Odes by ʿAlqama, Shánfara, Labíd, ʿAntara, Al-Aʿsha, and Dhu al-Rúmma*. Middletown, Connecticut: Wesleyan University Press, 1989.

Reliable and readable poetic translations of longer poems from the pre-Islamic and early Islamic periods, with short introduction and analysis of each poem.

Tuetey, C. G. *Classical Arabic Poetry: 162 poems from Imrulkais to Maʿarri. Translated with an introduction*. London: Routledge and Kegan Paul, 1985.

Good verse translations. Cherry-picking: almost all items are short fragments of longer poems; the use of obscure editions makes it difficult to consult the original texts.

Wightman, G. B. H. and A. Y. al-Udhari. *Birds Through a Ceiling of Alabaster: Three Abbasid Poets. Arab Poetry of the Abbasid Period Translated with an Introduction.* Harmondsworth: Penguin, 1975.

Epigrams, mostly very short, by al-ʿAbbās ibn al-Aḥnaf, Ibn al-Muʿtazz, and Abū l-ʿAlāʾ al-Maʿarrī, in very free, "modernizing" verse translations, lacking references to sources.

Monroe, James T. *Hispano-Arabic Poetry: A Student Anthology.* Berkeley, California: University of California Press, 1974.

Arabic texts of poems from Arab Spain, with facing prose translations; annotated.

Mumayiz, Ibrahim. *Arabesques: Selections of Biography and Poetry from Classical Arabic Literature.* Antwerp–Apeldoorn: Garant, 2006.

Contains rhymed translations of fragments from poems by two pre-Islamic poets (Imruʾ al-Qays and ʿAntarah) and two Abbasid poets (al-Mutanabbī and al-Maʿarrī), without references to sources. Suffers badly from archaizing tendencies and what could be called poetic apostrophitis ("invis'ble," "succ'lent," "lim'ted," "s'long as," "No oth'r calam'ty," etc.).

Index

About the NYU Abu Dhabi Institute

The Library of Arabic Literature is supported by a grant from The NYU Abu Dhabi Institute, a major hub of intellectual and creative activity and advanced research. The Institute hosts academic conferences, workshops, lectures, film series, performances, and other public programs directed both to audiences within the UAE and to the worldwide academic and research community. It is a center of the scholarly community for Abu Dhabi, bringing together faculty and researchers from institutions of higher learning throughout the region.

NYU Abu Dhabi, through the NYU Abu Dhabi Institute, is a world-class center of cutting-edge research, scholarship, and cultural activity. The Institute creates singular opportunities for leading researchers from across the arts, humanities, social sciences, sciences, engineering, and the professions to carry out creative scholarship and conduct research on issues of major disciplinary, multidisciplinary, and global significance.

About the Typefaces

The Arabic body text is set in DecoType Naskh, designed by Thomas Milo and Mirjam Somers, based on an analysis of five centuries of Ottoman manuscript practice. The exceptionally legible result is the first and only typeface in a style that fully implements the principles of script grammar (*qawāʿid al-khaṭṭ*).

The Arabic footnote text is set in DecoType Emiri, drawn by Mirjam Somers, based on the metal typeface in the naskh style that was cut for the 1924 Cairo edition of the Qur'an.

Both Arabic typefaces in this series are controlled by a dedicated font layout engine. ACE, the Arabic Calligraphic Engine, invented by Peter Somers, Thomas Milo, and Mirjam Somers of DecoType, first operational in 1985, pioneered the principle followed by later smart font layout technologies such as OpenType, which is used for all other typefaces in this series.

The Arabic text was set with WinSoft Tasmeem, a sophisticated user interface for DecoType ACE inside Adobe InDesign. Tasmeem was conceived and created by Thomas Milo (DecoType) and Pascal Rubini (WinSoft) in 2005.

The English text is set in Adobe Text, a new and versatile text typeface family designed by Robert Slimbach for Western (Latin, Greek, Cyrillic) typesetting. Its workhorse qualities make it perfect for a wide variety of applications, especially for longer passages of text where legibility and economy are important. Adobe Text bridges the gap between calligraphic Renaissance types of the 15th and 16th centuries and high-contrast Modern styles of the 18th century, taking many of its design cues from early post-Renaissance Baroque transitional types cut by designers such as Christoffel van Dijck, Nicolaus Kis, and William Caslon. While grounded in classical form, Adobe Text is also a statement of contemporary utilitarian design, well suited to a wide variety of print and on-screen applications.

About the Translator

Geert Jan van Gelder was Laudian Professor of Arabic at the University of Oxford from 1998 to 2012. He has published widely on classical Arabic literature in Dutch and English, particularly on the history of poetics and criticism and on literary themes as diverse as food, the hammam, and incest. His books include *Beyond the Line: Classical Arabic Literary Critics on the Coherence and Unity of the Poem* and *Of Dishes and Discourse: Classical Arabic Literary Representations of Food.*